Presidents and the American Presidency

Presidents and the American Presidency

LORI COX HAN
Chapman University

DIANE J. HEITH
St. John's University

New York Oxford
OXFORD UNIVERSITY PRESS

Oxford University Press is a department of the University of Oxford. It furthers the University's objective of excellence in research, scholarship, and education by publishing worldwide.

Oxford New York
Auckland Cape Town Dar es Salaam Hong Kong Karachi
Kuala Lumpur Madrid Melbourne Mexico City Nairobi
New Delhi Shanghai Taipei Toronto

With offices in
Argentina Austria Brazil Chile Czech Republic France Greece
Guatemala Hungary Italy Japan Poland Portugal Singapore
South Korea Switzerland Thailand Turkey Ukraine Vietnam

Published in the United States of America by
Oxford University Press
198 Madison Avenue, New York, NY 10016

For titles covered by Section 112 of the US Higher Education Opportunity Act, please visit www.oup.com/us/he for the latest information about pricing and alternate formats.

Library of Congress Cataloging-in-Publication Data
Han, Lori Cox.
Presidents and the American presidency/Lori Cox Han, Diane J. Heith.
p. cm.
Includes bibliographical references and index.
ISBN 978-0-19-538516-8
1. Presidents—United States—History. 2. Political leadership—United States—History. I. Heith, Diane J. II. Title.
E176.1.H265 2012
352.23'60973—dc23 2012034281

Printing number: 9 8 7 6 5 4 3 2 1
Printed in the United States of America
on acid-free paper

To the memory of our advisors and mentors on the American presidency,
William W. Lammers, University of Southern California
and
Elmer E. Cornwell, Jr., Brown University

BRIEF CONTENTS

CONTENTS

PREFACE

Perhaps the most common debate among presidency scholars centers on the question of how best to study both the presidency as a political institution and the men who have held the office. In developing this textbook, we wanted to provide a comprehensive text that combined both approaches by including contemporary issues surrounding presidents as individual leaders as well as the institutional perspectives and evolution of the office. Our goal was to focus on the "real" presidency; that is, to provide a unique perspective and analysis that explains exactly what a president does on a day-to-day basis and how the governing and institutional environment in which he finds himself affects that daily outcome. We also wanted to incorporate what we consider to be an under-utilized resource on the presidency for undergraduate students, which are the millions of archival documents available at presidential libraries. We have each conducted extensive research at presidential libraries across the country (to date, all of the libraries from FDR through Clinton), and know firsthand the significance and richness of the many memos, letters, and oral histories available to scholars and journalists alike. These documents add a personal knowledge and perspective of what actually happened behind the scenes in the White House and help to explain the strategic and decision-making processes of presidents during the past century. As a result, we believe that these documents add an important pedagogical tool for an instructor's use at the undergraduate level.

We have also incorporated our own experiences in teaching the presidency over the years into the presentation of the topics throughout the text. Both of us are faculty members at universities (Chapman University and St. John's University, respectively) that value classroom instruction as much as faculty scholarship. The presidency is, for both of us, not only our major field of expertise but also a favorite course that we each teach regularly. We have learned over the years what works when attempting to engage students beyond a cursory and fleeting knowledge of the material in an attempt to prepare for an exam. We share a pedagogical approach to teaching the presidency that provides students with a deeper understanding of the presidency as an institution and its importance within the constitutional framework of the American government. Specifically, we consider the leadership qualities of the men who have held the office and why that matters for their ultimate success or failure; and, from a broader perspective, why is it important to develop critical thinking and analytical skills when studying American government. The former two issues serve to pique many students' interest in the subject, while the latter helps students to become more informed citizens.

The plan of the book is straightforward; we cover all of the important topics necessary to gain a comprehensive understanding of the topic within a semester/quarter-long course on presidents and the presidency. Chapter 1 provides an introductory discussion on the historical context, theories and methodologies, and sources that are all part of the study of presidents and the presidency. Chapter 2 analyzes the presidency within the framework of the U.S. Constitution and how the various interpretations of presidential powers since the founding era have shaped the office and the decisions made by its occupants. Chapters 3, 4, and 5 consider the public connection of presidents and the presidency to the American electorate—presidential campaigns and elections, presidential communication strategies, the president's relationship with the news media, and public opinion. Chapters 6, 7, and 8 consider the institutional aspects of the office in how presidents interact and manage their relationships with Congress, the federal courts, and the executive branch. Finally, Chapters 9 and 10 cover the important topics of presidential domestic and foreign policymaking and the role that presidents play in the development and implementation of policy outcomes.

Along the way, we also incorporate numerous archival documents to highlight key issues; some show the seriousness and gravity of the decisions that presidents face while in office; others provide an interesting and sometimes light-hearted view of the real governing process in the White House and how partisan concerns can also play a role. In each chapter, we also provide two features: "Then and Now" and "In Their Own Words." "Then and Now" takes a specific issue and compares a more historical approach to a more contemporary approach to analyze how presidents have dealt with certain challenges while in office. For example, "Then and Now" in Chapter 2 considers the political implications of the presidential power to pardon. "In Their Own Words" highlights one archival document that helps to illustrate a specific topic of each chapter. For example, in Chapter 10, which deals with presidents and foreign policy, we highlight a letter from General Lauris Norstad to President John F. Kennedy about the global political implications following the Cuban Missile Crisis. Throughout each chapter, we also have an icon indicating additional archival documents, audio recordings, video clips and Web links, which can be found on the *Presidents and the American Presidency* website. We also provide a "Suggested Readings" list of some of the most important works (both historical and contemporary) on the presidency, as well as an additional list of Web resources for students in each chapter.

ACKNOWLEDGMENTS

We have many people to thank for their contributions to this book. First, we are truly grateful for the guidance and patience of our editor at Oxford University Press, Jennifer Carpenter, who provided encouragement, guidance, and deadlines when needed. Maegan Sherlock also provided much help throughout the editorial process. We are indebted to the many reviewers who took time out of their busy schedules to give helpful feedback on individual chapters as well as the manuscript as a whole:

David M. Barrett
Villanova University

Peter J. Bergerson
Florida Gulf Coast University

Curtis R. Berry
Shippensburg University

Meenekshi Bose
Hofstra University

James Cox
California State University–Sacramento

Jonathan Day
Western Illinois University

Casey Dominguez
University of San Diego

Matthew Eshbaugh-Soha
University of North Texas

Victoria A. Farrar-Myers
The University of Texas at Arlington

John Robert Greene
Cazenovia College

Jan C. Hardt
University of Central Oklahoma

Lionel Ingram
University of New Hampshire

Gibbs Knotts
Western Carolina University

Magen Knuth
American University

Glen Krutz
The University of Oklahoma

William M. Leiter
California State University–Long Beach

Rhonda Longworth
Eastern Michigan University

Joshua Meddaugh
University of Pittsburgh at Bradford

Andrew O'Geen
Stony Brook University

John David Rausch, Jr.
West Texas A&M University

Geoffrey C. Rogal
Northern Illinois University

Margaret E. Scranton
University of Arkansas at Little Rock

Andrew H. Sidman
John Jay College of Criminal Justice

Barry L. Tadlock
Ohio University

Adam L. Warber
Clemson University

Dana Ward
Pitzer College

Alissa Warters
Francis Marion University

Timothy Werner
University of Wisconsin–Madison

Your insight, critiques, and expertise were truly appreciated. In addition, the many archivists at presidential libraries that have assisted our research over the years deserve our thanks and appreciation as well. We are also grateful for the many colleagues we have had the pleasure to work with over the years who share our passion for studying the presidency. Our involvement in the Presidency Research Group (now called Presidents and Executive Politics) has enriched our professional lives on many levels. We also consider ourselves blessed to have studied with some of the best researchers of the American presidency, who helped to set us on our own paths as presidency scholars. At the undergraduate level, we took courses with Larry Berman at UC Davis and Theodore Lowi at Cornell University, respectively. And, it is to our graduate advisors, Bill Lammers at USC and Elmer Cornwell at Brown University, respectively, that we dedicate this book.

Lori Cox Han would also like to thank her husband, Tom Han, and children, Taylor and Davis, for their continued support, inspiration, and unconditional love. In addition, several friends and colleagues at Chapman University deserve special recognition, including Ann Gordon, David Shafie, Chuck Hughes, Drew Moshier, Nadia Arriaga, and Erika Gonzalez, who all make Chapman a better place to work.

Diane Heith would also like to thank her husband, Stephen Kline, and her son Owen, for their love and support. Rosalyn and Elliott Heith also provided much needed support and assistance, which were essential components for finishing a project like this one. At St. John's, Patricia Bittner is the glue that holds everything together, and she deserves much gratitude for all her help.

Finally, the many students over the years who have taken Dr. Han's and Dr. Heith's respective presidency courses at Chapman, Austin College, and St. John's (and even the very first courses at UCLA and Brown) deserve thanks for their contributions to this final product.

TABLES AND FIGURES

CHAPTER 1

Introduction: Studying Presidents and the Presidency

At 9:45 a.m. on Wednesday, April 27, 2011, President Barack Obama entered the White House press room to make a seemingly routine statement to members of the press. While presidents for decades have made similar announcements on any number of issues to White House reporters, this particular announcement was like nothing that Americans had ever witnessed before. The purpose of Obama's statement was not to announce a personnel change to his staff, a judicial nomination, or a policy initiative. Instead, Obama announced the release of his "long form" birth certificate from the state of Hawaii. The release of the much-discussed birth certificate was an attempt by the Obama administration to finally put to rest the rumors, first begun during the 2008 presidential campaign, that Obama had not been born in the United States (a constitutional requirement to hold the office of president). The so-called "birther" movement, with much help from the press, had continued to demand proof that Obama was a bonafide citizen of the United States and that he had not been born in Kenya, the homeland of his father. The short-form birth certificate from Hawaii (which earned its statehood in 1959, two years prior to Obama's birth in Honolulu), released during Obama's presidential campaign, had not satisfied the small group of conspiracy theorists, headed by then-potential Republican presidential candidate Donald Trump, who were convinced that Obama had something to hide.

In the much-heralded release of the long-form birth certificate (as the story had dominated the news for several days), Obama summed up his frustration over such a political distraction:

> Now, normally I would not comment on something like this, because obviously there's a lot of stuff swirling in the press on any given day and I've got other things to do. But two weeks ago, when the Republican House had put forward a budget that will have huge consequences potentially to the country, and when I gave a speech about my budget and how I felt that we needed to invest in education and infrastructure and making sure that we had a strong safety net for our seniors even as we were closing the deficit, during that entire week the dominant news story wasn't about these huge, monumental choices that we're going to have to make as a nation. It was about my birth certificate. And that was true on most of the news outlets that were represented here.... We're going to have to make a series of very difficult decisions about how we invest in our future but also get a hold of our deficit and our debt.... But we're not going to be able to do it if we are distracted. We're not going to be able to do it if we spend time vilifying each other. We're not going to be able to do it if we just make stuff up and pretend that facts are not facts. We're not going to be able to solve our problems if we get distracted by sideshows and carnival barkers. I know that there's going to be a segment of people for which, no matter what we put out, this issue will not be put to rest. But I'm speaking to the vast majority of the American people, as well as to the press. We do not have time for this kind of silliness. We've got better stuff to do. I've got better stuff to do. We've got big problems to solve. And I'm confident we can solve them, but we're going to have to focus on them—not on this.[1]

All of the excitement in the press over the birth certificate story ended up being just the start of what would become several eventful days of Obama's presidency; his schedule for the next five days would certainly highlight the complexity of the job of the modern presidency, as well as the various skills needed by a president to succeed in the position. For example, after the announcement to the White House press corps about his birth certificate, Obama and his wife, Michelle, traveled to Chicago to tape an episode of the Oprah Winfrey Show (the first time a sitting president and first lady had made an appearance during Oprah's twenty-five-year run as the leading voice of daytime television) before ending the day in New York at a Democratic Party fundraiser 🖱. The following day, Obama held meetings with his national security team over the ongoing situation in Libya, met with Hispanic leaders from across the nation about immigration reform, and also met and held a joint press conference with Panamanian President Ricardo Martinelli. On Friday, the First Family traveled to Alabama for the President and First Lady to meet with local officials and to survey the damage from the devastating tornadoes that had occurred earlier that week. Then, the Obamas traveled to Cape Canaveral, Florida, to view the launch of the Space Shuttle Endeavor, and President Obama ended his day with a commencement address at Miami Dade College before returning to the White House. On Saturday evening, Obama appeared at the White House Correspondents' Association Dinner, an annual event where presidents (and a guest comedian) roast Washington reporters 🖱🖱. While at the Correspondents' Dinner, Obama and his advisors knew that a major story was potentially unfolding halfway around the world; the next evening, on Sunday, May 1st, Obama would announce

---

🖱 Watch the President and the First Lady on Oprah.

🖱🖱 Watch Presidents perform at the Correspondents' Dinner.

to the world that Osama bin Laden had been killed in Pakistan by a special operations team of U.S. Navy Seals.

While the killing of bin Laden, the Al Qaeda leader who planned and orchestrated the 9/11 terrorist attacks, was certainly an extraordinary event for the Obama administration, the remaining presidential activities during those few days exemplify the complexities of the contemporary presidency. The president must serve as both the head of state and head of government; his public and political activities, as well as those as commander in chief of the armed forces, represent only a few of the many responsibilities that go along with the job title "President of the United States." On any given day, a president may order military actions, oversee and direct major policy initiatives implemented by the executive branch of the government, hold a press conference or give interviews to members of the press, hold a state dinner at the White House for a visiting dignitary, veto a congressional bill, nominate a federal judge or ambassador, or make a political appearance on behalf of other members of his party or for his own reelection. While members of Congress may have opportunities to develop policy expertise by serving on or chairing particular committees, and while Supreme Court justices are experts of U.S. constitutional law, the president must be all things to all Americans—politically, constitutionally, and symbolically. As such, presidents and their staffs must be able to multitask while juggling the variety of demands placed upon the nation's chief executive. As Obama himself stated in his first interview after the killing of bin Laden with *60 Minutes*, "The presidency requires you to do more than one thing at a time."[2]

The American presidency is a unique political position, from the institutional nature of the job as well as from the many ways that an individual president can shape the office itself. This book considers both American presidents and the presidency; that is, those who have held the position and the institutional structure of the office within the executive branch of government. We examine the strengths and weaknesses of the presidency as a political institution, as well as the strengths and weaknesses of some of our recent presidents and their leadership skills. However, we seek to examine the "real" presidency; that is, not just the theoretical analysis of the institution or assessments of the men who have served as president, but the actual day-to-day responsibilities and challenges that go with the job. To showcase the "real" aspects of the presidency, as well as the differences between individual and institutional perspectives on decision making, we incorporate archival documents from multiple administrations to reveal the inner workings of the White House. The documents and oral histories at presidential libraries and other archives around the country represent a virtual treasure trove of detailed analysis and stories of what actually happened, not only publicly but behind the scenes, in each presidential administration. It is through inter- and intra-office memos among the president and his closest advisors that governing strategies are developed and policy decisions are made, and it is through oral histories of administration officials that candid assessments are made regarding the successes and failures of each presidency. We rely on these documents to allow a president and/or members of his administration, through their own words, to animate the discussions in each chapter from the perspective of political actors who were actually present to understand and appreciate the depth and breadth of presidential power and leadership in the twenty-first century.

HISTORICAL CONTEXT

The President of the United States is easily the most recognizable political figure to any American citizen, and globally is seen as one of, if not the, most powerful leaders in the world. As a political institution, the American presidency has long been a fascinating case study of the powers and intricacies of the office, as it defies comparison to anything before or since. To date, a total of forty-four men have held the office of the presidency, and while these individuals have served their country with varying degrees of success, the presidency as an institution remains a focal point of political power both nationally and internationally. Yet, only minor changes related to the presidency have been adopted in the U.S. Constitution since its ratification in 1789. The essential characteristics of the American presidency are as recognizable today as they were more than two hundred years ago. However, the presidency of the eighteenth century outlined by the framers seems weak compared to the powers that have emerged with the office throughout the twentieth and into the twenty-first centuries. The American presidency is one of the most resilient political institutions ever developed, enduring numerous wars (not the least of which was the Civil War from 1861 to 1865), scandals (such as Watergate that led to Richard Nixon's resignation from office in 1974), economic turbulence (such as the Great Depression following the stock market crash in 1929), and even assassinations (four presidents have been killed by an assassin's bullet, including Abraham Lincoln in 1865, James Garfield in 1881, William McKinley in 1901, and John F. Kennedy in 1963). Still, the powers of the office, along with the governing strategies of each individual president, have varied at different times due to different circumstances (political and otherwise). In general, and based on the work of presidential scholar Louis W. Koenig, the history of the presidency can be divided into three principal eras: the traditional presidency, the modern presidency, and the postmodern/contemporary presidency.[3]

The Traditional Presidency

This era includes presidents from the late eighteenth century until the turn of the twentieth century, and with a few notable exceptions, most of these men were not particularly memorable. During this era, the presidency was not the grand political prize that it is considered today, and many early politicians did not aspire to hold the office. The presidency offered modest prestige, narrow authority, and meager resources; in fact, governors of prominent states, such as New York, Massachusetts, and Virginia, wielded more political power and prestige than the president. Although presidents during the early years of the republic were honored and respected for their public service and political contributions prior to 1789, they occupied an office that was unassuming and limited with respect to national defense and foreign policy. This is what the framers of the Constitution had intended, which left presidents for the most part as passive participants in the policymaking process. As a result, throughout the nineteenth century, most presidents merely carried out the laws passed by Congress, which assumed the role of the dominant policymaking branch.

The four most memorable administrations during the traditional era include the more notable presidencies of George Washington (1789–1797), Thomas Jefferson (1801–1809), Andrew Jackson (1829–1837), and Abraham Lincoln (1861–1865),

Abraham Lincoln is often considered the greatest U.S. president due to his leadership during the Civil War.

all of whom are "towering exceptions" during an era when presidential powers remained modest and limited.[4] Washington, as the first to hold the office, set many precedents and shaped the model of presidential leadership for generations to come. For example, Washington began the tradition of presidents serving only two terms (this would not be broken until Franklin Roosevelt ran for a third term in 1940; the Twenty-Second Amendment now limits the president to two terms). Jefferson, as the author of the Declaration of Independence and one of the most prominent among the founding fathers, is remembered for articulating his beliefs in republicanism and a limited national government. Yet, he pushed the constitutional boundaries of presidential powers with his purchase of the Louisiana Territory in 1803 and his decision to use military force against the Barbary Pirates in 1801 (he did not consult Congress on either decision). Jackson became the first "common man" to hold the presidency, and rose to power as both grass roots politics and political parties became prominent electoral fixtures as voting rights were expanded beyond land-owning elites. Lincoln, considered by some scholars and many Americans as the greatest president, held the nation together during the Civil War, and issued the Emancipation Proclamation in 1863, by executive order, to end slavery 🖱. Yet, Lincoln is also known for expanding presidential powers by relying on extraconstitutional and/or unconstitutional measures in doing so (including the suspension of habeas corpus, among other actions).

🖱 View Lincoln's Executive Order.

The Modern Presidency

The expansion of presidential powers, particularly in regards to shaping the national agenda, waging wars, and connecting with the American public, would not become a regular and expected feature of the presidency until the twentieth century. The development of the modern presidency, including the powers of the office and the large bureaucracy of the executive branch, reshaped the more humble office created by the framers. Of the three branches of government, the executive branch has moved farthest from its origins and least resembles the intent of its framers. According to Koenig, Theodore Roosevelt (1901–1909) and Woodrow Wilson (1921–1929) were the modern presidency's "architects, as asserters of bold undertakings in domestic and foreign affairs, as gifted mobilizers of public opinion, as inducers of congressional concurrence."[5] Then, with the election of Franklin D. Roosevelt in 1932, a new political era began that included a dramatic expansion of the federal government in both size and power. Roosevelt's presidency (1933–1945) brought with it several important changes that solidified the modern presidency: enhanced presidential staff resources, a greater presidential role in policymaking, a stronger relationship with the mass public, and a greater presence in the realm of international relationships. Roosevelt's presidency yielded new understandings of the modern presidency, focusing on increased expectations for presidential action and the increased capacity to pursue presidential leadership.[6]

FDR's New Deal, as well as America's involvement in World War II, began what would be an era of expansive growth in domestic and foreign powers of both the presidency and the executive branch of government. During this time, the presidency eclipsed Congress and even political parties as the "leading instrument of popular rule."[7] Harry Truman (1945–1953) and Dwight Eisenhower (1953–1961) would also preside over the continued growth and influence of the presidency as the lead role in domestic and international affairs, due in part to the growth of the U.S. economy and the continuing Cold War. Similarly, the public aspects of the office, along with the public's expectation for strong presidential leadership, continued to expand, particularly with the presidency of John F. Kennedy (1961–1963) and his administration's successful use of television. This era is also marked by the strength and dominance of the United States as a global and economic superpower, which allowed presidents to pursue extensive policy agendas both at home (such as the Great Society and the War on Poverty during the 1960s) and abroad (containing the spread of communism as part of America's Cold War strategy). Yet, the failure of U.S. containment policy during the protracted Vietnam War would call into question the powers of the modern presidency; both Lyndon Johnson (1963–1969) and Richard Nixon (1969–1974) would be labeled "imperial" presidents for their actions in Vietnam and for Nixon's involvement in and eventual resignation due to the Watergate scandal.[8] The success generated by Roosevelt's extraconstitutional tools no longer appeared attainable.

The Postmodern/Contemporary Presidency

Following the Vietnam War and Watergate, the powers of the modern presidency, according to some scholars, had been diminished due to the fact that the resources necessary for a president to wield power "fall well short of the tasks he is expected to perform and the challenges to be faced."[9] By the 1980s, presidents were no longer able to pursue big domestic political agendas; divided government became more common (with the White House controlled by one political party and at least one house of Congress controlled by the other), and with a spiraling national debt and increasing budget deficits, the president had much less room to shape the domestic agenda through the creation of new and expansive federal programs like those during the New Deal and Great Society. Instead, Ronald Reagan's (1981–1989) electoral success and popularity with the American public was based in part on his promise to reduce the size of the federal government. In addition, with the end of the Cold War by the end of the 1980s, presidents had lost power in the international arena. Cooperation in what George H. W. Bush (1989–1993) called "the new world order" became more important than protecting the United States from the spread of communism and the imminent threat of a nuclear war with the Soviet Union. Yet, George W. Bush did reassert power with military actions in both Afghanistan and Iraq based upon the belief that the United States must preempt and prevent potential threats to national security (known as the Bush Doctrine).

Other trends have contributed to the contemporary presidency, including the way in which Americans select their presidents; the political skills necessary for a candidate to succeed on the campaign trail are different from those needed to handle the complex domestic, economic, and global demands of the job of president.[10] The challenges faced by Bill Clinton (1993–2001), George W. Bush (2001–2009), and Barack Obama (2009–present) represent both the increased powers and diminished capacities of governing that have evolved in recent decades. In the post-9/11 era, the War on Terror may have helped to expand presidential powers in some areas, yet the Bush and Obama Administrations have also faced trying economic circumstances that severely limit presidential powers over the policymaking agenda. In addition, presidents must now contend with a political environment dominated by hyperpartisanship and fueled by unyielding yet fragmented news media coverage. While the president today may still be the "focal point of public life," the reality is that "presidents are seldom in command and usually must negotiate with others to achieve their goals."[11]

THEORIES AND METHODOLOGIES

While presidential studies itself is considered a subfield within the discipline of political science, specific areas within presidential studies have also emerged in recent years as part of the growing literature on both presidents and the presidency. One way to categorize different theories or methodologies associated with the study of the presidency is to simply ask whether the approach is "president centered" (meaning, the focus of study is on various aspects of the individual holding office at a particular time) or "presidency centered" (meaning, the focus of study is on the institutional aspects of the office and/or the executive branch). More specifically, the president-centered approach can include exploring the informal power structure within the White House and its impact on presidential leadership, exploring the behaviors of presidents through a psychoanalytic approach, or analyzing a president's leadership style through the public aspects of the office, to name just a few areas of study. The presidency-centered approach can include studies focusing on the formal powers of the executive office, presidential–congressional relations, or the executive branch as a political institution. In the presidency-centered approach, scholars focus their attention in an effort to better understand (and sometimes predict the actions of) the president, his staff, and other relevant political actors within the executive branch. In addition, interdisciplinary research on the presidency has merged the growing literature in political science with that of psychology, history, communication, economics, and sociology, among others. As a result, both the quality and the quantity of research devoted to the presidency continue to grow and evolve.

Classics in Presidential Studies

The first study of the presidency as a social and political institution is considered to be the 1825 publication of *The Presidency of the United States* by Augustus B. Woodward, whose work included five categories of study: the man; public politics; Washington politics; executive politics; and didactic reviews (attempts to synthesize the other categories and draw lessons from the presidency).[12] During the twentieth century, as the discipline of political science expanded, so too did the study of the presidency. During the 1940s and 1950s, prominent works on the presidency focused mostly on the constitutional powers of the office and other interpretive works that provided descriptive analysis of the White House and its occupants. For example, Edward S. Corwin, in his classic *The President: Office and Powers* (first published in 1940), analyzed the framers' intent regarding presidential powers as an "invitation to struggle" between the presidency and Congress, particularly regarding matters of foreign policy. Perhaps the most quoted line of Corwin's work suggests that the powers of the presidency can be defined by the man who holds the office: "Taken by and large, the history of the presidency is a history of aggrandizement, but the story is a highly discontinuous one.... That is to say, what the presidency is at any particular moment depends in important measure on who is President...."[13] Similarly, Clinton Rossiter's *The American Presidency*, first published in 1956, explores the evolution of presidential powers and the president's many roles as chief of state, chief executive, commander in chief, and chief diplomat, among others. Through his interpretive and historical analysis, Rossiter concluded: "The President is not one kind of official during one part of the day, another kind during another part—administrator in the morning, legislator at lunch, king in the afternoon, commander before dinner, and politician at odd moments that come his weary way. He is all these things all the time, and any one of his functions feeds upon and into all the others."[14]

In 1960, one of the most quoted books of all time on the presidency was published—*Presidential Power* by Richard Neustadt. A former advisor to President Harry Truman, Neustadt was one of the first political scientists to recognize that personality, character, and political skill are important in the development of presidential leadership. According to Neustadt, real power is found in the president's ability to bargain and persuade. Neustadt defined power as personal influence on governmental action, which is separate from the formal powers outlined by the Constitution. He argued that there is great weakness in the presidency, mainly present in the gap between public expectations and the actual capabilities for leadership. Neustadt sought to better understand "personal power and its politics: what it is, how to get it, how to keep it, how to use it." In reality, Neustadt had a fairly pessimistic view of the presidency, in that the president must stand alone and rely on his own political skills to get things done. Others within the system have competing agendas, and only the president himself can wield influence to achieve his goals. As such, the theme of Neustadt's work is actually presidential weakness, since the president needs more than his formal constitutional powers to achieve policy results. The president shares powers, so he must bargain with others within government out of need. Despite his formal powers, which are not that broad, real presidential power is the power to persuade, so, in effect, the president is a clerk and has five constituencies: executive officials who need guidance, Congress who needs an outside agenda, partisans who need a record to run on in the next election, citizens who need a symbol to complain to or seek aid from, and foreign countries where U.S. policies play a role. In the end, a successful president is one who knows how to harness his power and use it wisely, especially when juggling the responsibilities from these five constituencies. A fine balance must be struck between a man who is hungry enough to seek power, yet not so hungry as to abuse it. FDR represented presidential leadership at its finest in Neustadt's view.[15]

Newer Methodologies Evolve

Political scientists would not significantly expand methodological perspectives in the subfield for another two decades. The shift to bring the subfield more in line with the disciplinary rigor of political science got its start in 1977 when political scientist Hugh Heclo published a report on the state of research devoted to the presidency. Heclo concluded that while the topic itself was "probably already overwritten," there existed "immense gaps and deficiencies" stemming from a lack of empirical research and too much attention paid to topics such as presidential power, personalities, and decision making during a crisis.[16] At the time, many studies were devoted to the more recent presidencies of Eisenhower, Kennedy, Johnson, and Nixon, along with more contemporary political topics such as the Cold War, the Cuban Missile Crisis, the Vietnam War, and Watergate. As a result, Heclo argued that the field of presidential studies needed more reliance on primary documents, a better understanding of how the presidency works day-to-day (in order to help it perform better), and a broader, more interdisciplinary approach.[17] Despite several "well-intentioned publications" on the presidency, Heclo concluded: "... [C]onsidering the amount of such writing in relation to the base of original empirical research behind it, the field is as shallow as it is luxuriant. To a great extent, presidential studies have coasted on the reputations of a few rightfully respected classics on the Presidency and on secondary literature and anecdotes produced by former participants. We still have remarkably little substantiated information on how the modern office of the President actually works."[18]

By the early 1980s, presidency scholars began reassessing the trends of their research, and, as a result, many began to bemoan the state of their "underdeveloped subfield."[19] Along with the classics on presidential power and personalities, presidential research up until that point also tended to focus on a "political-actor perspective" that centered on the question of determining "how presidents differed in their decisions." This president-centered approach to research often relied on descriptive analyses or anecdotal comparisons between presidents, and suffered from what many scholars referred to as the infamous "n = 1" syndrome, meaning that presidents provided rather small data sets from which to conduct studies befitting the methodologically rigorous standards of social science research practices.[20]

In 1983 presidential scholars George C. Edwards III and Stephen J. Wayne published *Studying the Presidency*, in which the authors argued that more "theoretically sophisticated and empirically relevant" work was necessary to expand the presidency literature to keep pace with the "phenomenal growth of the presidency: the expansion of its powers, the enlargement of its staff, the evolution of its processes."[21] Problems in studying the presidency had traditionally stemmed from the general unavailability of data, the lack of measurable (particularly quantitative) indicators, and the absence of theory, all of which "impede the collection and analysis of data, thereby discouraging empirical research." Specific problems included the fact that operational and institutional aspects of the presidency were usually shrouded in secrecy, presidential documents can remain closed for years if not decades, primary source material is not always readily available, interviews with administration officials can be biased and incomplete, and high-profile journalists are more likely to gain access than most scholars. Given that, little about the presidency had lent itself to quantitative and comparative study, other than public opinion, voting studies, and legislative scorecards.[22] The authors also suggested that fellow presidency scholars should develop newer methodologies more in line with scientific approaches found within social science generally and political science specifically, including legal perspectives (sources and uses of presidential powers); institutional perspectives (analysis of the workings of government); roles and responsibilities (understanding presidential actions within the institutional setting); structure and process (how the president and the presidency function, operate, and interact with other political actors and institutions); political perspectives (power orientation and decision making); and psychological perspectives (analyzing the personalities of individual presidents).[23]

The President-Centered Approach

By the late 1980s and early 1990s, a robust discussion had emerged among presidency scholars on how to develop a rigorous and systematic approach more in line with the traditions of political science to study both the president and the presidency. Many scholars have maintained an emphasis on presidential leadership and its importance in understanding the role of the president in both policymaking and governing, yet at the same time have begun to change the direction of research by relying on a broader theoretical perspective and including extensive data for comparative analysis. Many still rely on Neustadt's *Presidential Power* for at least a starting point in their research, while also recognizing the limitations that an individual president can face in effecting political change.[24] "Leadership," particularly in the political context, has a variety of definitions and is considered a malleable term, but in general it is defined as a process involving influence that occurs in groups and includes attention to goals; attention is also paid to the individual traits of the leader, his or her behavior, patterns of interacting, and relationships with others.[25] While no clear standard has yet to emerge, many scholars have provided useful insights as to what makes a president successful as a leader, as well as which presidents have failed and why. As Bert Rockman states, the study of presidential leadership is both fascinating and complex in that presidents may vary in temperaments, but all are confronted with similar pressures while in office—"it is the manipulable factor in a sea of largely nonmanipulable forces."[26]

One of the most widely recognized theories of leadership would be the work of James MacGregor Burns, who introduced the idea of transformational leadership in the late 1970s.[27] For Burns, leadership is more than just the act of wielding power; it involves the relationship between leaders and followers. Burns states that transactional leadership refers to what most leaders are able to accomplish—the day-to-day exchanges between leaders and followers that have come to be expected. Transformational leadership, on the other hand, provides more than just a simple change in the political process. A transformational leader provides broader changes to the entire political system that raises the level of motivation and morality in both the leader and the follower. As Burns states, "transforming leaders define public values that embrace the supreme and enduring principles of a people."[28] Similarly, Bruce Miroff defines five presidents as "icons of democracy" (John Adams, Abraham Lincoln, Theodore Roosevelt, FDR, and John F. Kennedy) as American leaders who fostered the American democratic ideal.[29] Miroff argues that successful democratic leaders respect their followers, are committed to the notion of self-government, and nurture the possibilities of civic engagement through a public dialogue, and that true political leadership must come from an honest dialogue between citizens and their leader.[30]

While many studies of presidential leadership can still be traced back to Neustadt's view that modern presidential power equates the ability to bargain and persuade,[31] other important works have redefined, modified, and/or expanded the notion of presidential leadership to encompass various views of presidents and the presidency, including the president as a transformational leader as well as the state of the postmodern/contemporary presidency.[32] Other topics contributing to the growing literature on presidential leadership consider changes in the political environment,[33] the institutionalization of and leadership within the executive branch,[34] policymaking and the president's relationship with Congress,[35] and the public presidency and changes in White House communication strategies.[36]

Seeking to better understand the effect of a president's personality on his administration's successes and failures, along with the notion of "presidential greatness," represents another line of inquiry among those presidency scholars interested in the president-centered approach. Americans expect their presidents to be the epitome of political leadership, and several presidents come to mind when thinking about presidential greatness, including George Washington, Thomas Jefferson, Abraham Lincoln, Theodore Roosevelt, FDR, and Ronald Reagan.[37] However, while some presidents have moments of great leadership, few have been great leaders. According to Thomas E. Cronin and Michael A. Genovese, three important aspects of presidential leadership must be understood: political time (that is, different types of leadership are necessary for different circumstances); political vision (a strong presidential vision can energize the nation and achieve political power); and political skill (personality can make a difference in presidential leadership, and under certain circumstances the right individual can make a difference, but not all presidents can succeed in a given situation).[38]

Leadership style and presidential personality can also be determining factors in the success or failure of a president's tenure in office. According to Fred Greenstein, the presidential "difference," that is, determining the effect that a president can have on the many facets of his administration and of the presidency itself, can be best understood by considering the following factors: public communication skills, organizational capacity, political skill, policy vision, cognitive style, and emotional intelligence.[39] James David Barber's work on presidential character is best known for its categorization based on psychology and personality types: levels of activity as either active or passive, and affect (or feelings) toward activity as either positive or negative, which point to a president's deeper layers of personality and how that will determine his success or failure while in office.[40] While other presidency scholars have criticized Barber's approach as being too narrow to offer a consistent analysis across presidencies, given that reducing "personality to a handful of types ignores the complexity of human motivation," the fact that the first edition of Barber's work was published during the Nixon administration gave the work high prominence, as Richard Nixon provided a fascinating case study of presidential leadership through a psychological/political lens.[41]

Public leadership—that is, the art and skill of communication on the public stage—has gained increasing significance in terms of understanding the more general notion of presidential leadership. The importance of public leadership to effective governance is perhaps most pronounced when viewing that of a president. In its political context, public leadership can be defined simply as the ability of a public official to use the public component of a political office to accomplish a specific task, goal, or agenda item. As such, the end result of public leadership can be something as specific and tangible as the passage of a new law or the start of a government initiative, or something as broad based and intangible as rhetoric that motivates, inspires, or comforts the masses. However, at either extreme, public leadership skills matter and play a large role in allowing a public official to accomplish his or her political goals.[42]

As such, the public presidency and presidential communications have also emerged as important fields of inquiry. According to Jeffrey Tulis, the founders were quite suspicious of a popular leader and/or demagogue in the office of the presidency, since such a person might rely on tyrannical means of governing.[43] However, the presidency experienced a fundamental transformation by becoming a "rhetorical presidency" during the early part of the twentieth century, causing an institutional dilemma. By fulfilling popular functions and serving the nation through mass appeal, the presidency has now greatly deviated from the original constitutional intentions of the framers, removing the buffer between citizens and their representatives that the framers established.[44] Roderick Hart also argues that the rhetorical presidency is a twentieth-century creation and a constitutional aberration. The president is not merely a popular leader vested with unconstitutional powers, but also uses rhetoric as a "tool of barter rather than a means of informing or challenging a citizenry."[45]

According to Samuel Kernell, presidents of the modern era have utilized public support by "going public," a style of presidential leadership where the president sells his programs directly to the American people. Going public is contradictory to some views of democratic theory, but is now practiced by presidents as a result of a weakened party system, split-ticket voting, divided government, increased power of interest groups, and the growth of mass communication systems.[46]

More recent scholarship has expanded on and even questioned Kernell's theory of "going public." George C. Edwards III argues that presidents are not always successful in changing public opinion on certain issues by simply giving a major speech or engaging in other public activities.[47] And, according to Jeffrey Cohen, the polarization of political parties and the growth and fragmentation of media sources have forced presidents to develop innovative public strategies to target key constituencies, which is a dramatic shift from the more simplified view of going public to a national constituency as first argued by Kernell in the 1980s.[48]

The Presidency-Centered Approach

On the other end of the methodological spectrum are those scholars who support the institutional approach to studying the presidency, arguing that it is the institution itself that shapes both presidential behavior and political outcomes. According to this view, the presidency became greatly institutionalized and politicized during the twentieth century, leaving the president out of the loop, so to speak, and mostly irrelevant as an individual in much of the decision-making processes. As a result, scholarly endeavors should not waste time on understanding the role of presidential leadership, but should instead rely on a rational choice model of presidential theory building.[49] For example, Terry Moe provides such an institutional approach, explaining that presidents have considerable resources and strategies at their disposal to meet expectations for leadership. The ambiguity of the Constitution in relation to presidential power offers presidents important structural advantages over Congress and other political actors. Congress, for example, cannot match the resources of the executive branch in terms of expertise, experience, and information. The president can also act unilaterally in some instances, and therefore act more swiftly and decisively, than Congress. To avoid the need for bargaining, presidents can make sure that appointees within the executive branch are loyal to him (similar to political patronage), and can also centralize decision making within the White House to increase his own power (policy decisions and implementation, such as through executive orders).[50]

A modified approach known as "new institutionalism" suggests the need to look beyond institutions to also include an analysis of the ideas and people that influence those institutions.[51] In his book *The Politics Presidents Make*, Stephen Skowronek provides a theory of "political time" by offering a cyclical explanation of presidential power, dependent on the political time during which a president serves. When a president takes office, the political environment that he encounters is due in part to the actions of his predecessors as well as recent national and world events. Therefore, the president's circumstances, or the "political time" in which he finds himself in office, will determine how much authority he has to achieve political change. According to Skowronek, there are four distinct phases of political time: reconstruction, articulation, disjunction, and preemption. Each phase depends on the status of the ruling political order and the president's relationship to that ruling political order. Four presidents who are considered our greatest were reconstruction presidents—Thomas Jefferson, Andrew Jackson, Abraham Lincoln, and FDR—opponents of the vulnerable ruling political order. Each was elected to office as a result of sweeping political change; that is, their respective elections represented a major political defeat to the opposing political party. Articulation describes a resilient ruling order of which the president is an ally. Lyndon Johnson's election in 1964 is a good example, as the Democratic Party held a strong majority in the Congress when Johnson was elected in his own right, following his succession to office in 1963 upon Kennedy's assassination. Disjunction represents a vulnerable ruling order of which the president is an ally. For example, both Republican Herbert Hoover and Democrat Jimmy Carter were elected at a time when their parties controlled Congress, yet each became a one-term president as the policies of their parties became unpopular with voters. Finally, preemption represents a president who is an opponent of a resilient ruling order. Richard Nixon provides a good example, as he was elected in 1968 despite Democrats maintaining a strong majority in Congress.[52]

Other works have also offered important methodologies and/or theories about studying the presidency as an institution. Louis Fisher has written extensively on the legal and constitutional aspects of the presidency, including presidential war powers and the separation of powers between the president and Congress. For example, in his book *The Politics of Shared Power: Congress and the Executive*, Fisher analyzes the practical implications of this constitutional relationship: "Very few operations of Congress and the presidency are genuinely independent and autonomous. For the most part, an initiative by one branch sets in motion a series of compensatory actions by the other branch—sometimes of a cooperative nature, sometimes antagonistic." Fisher argues that the presidency as an institution, and the powers that belong to individual presidents, are best understood by recognizing that both the presidency and Congress operate within a political environment that also consists of the judiciary, the bureaucracy, independent regulatory commissions, political parties, state and local governments, interest groups, and other nations, since the Constitution "anticipates a government of powers that are largely shared but sometimes exclusive." The practical result of this institutional relationship simply means that a president's power to achieve results can depend on many factors, including cooperation and/or resistance from Congress, the Courts, or other political institutions with whom the president and the executive branch must share power.[53]

Finally, Lyn Ragsdale's research relies on three dimensions to describe the parameters of the presidency as an institution: organization, behavior, and structure. She recognizes that presidents can make marginal changes to the organization of the presidency, but the office is not reinvented with each new occupant in the White House. Also, presidents tend to behave in similar ways, since they are faced with a similar political and institutional environments. Her view moves beyond the institutional approach to include structural elements, which "describe the most typical features of a single institution." It is through rigorous data analysis across several presidencies that explanations can be found to define the president's role within the institution of the presidency; ultimately, "the institution of the presidency shapes presidents as much as presidents, during their short tenures, shape the institution."[54]

SOURCES

A variety of sources exist for those studying the American presidency, whether undergraduate students or senior academic scholars. Primary sources, which include original documents from a particular administration (such as memos written by members of the Kennedy White House during the Cuban Missile Crisis), the transcript of a presidential speech (such as Barack Obama's State of the Union Address in 2011), or collections of writings from a particular president (such as the writings and correspondence of Thomas Jefferson), can be found at various libraries (including presidential libraries) as well as numerous online data bases. Secondary sources, which would include oral histories of various administration officials, interviews of presidents and administration officials by the news media, or various studies published by academic scholars of the presidency, to name just a few, are also readily available. The presidency, and the men who have held the office, remains one of the most studied features of American government. As such, the public's interest in the topic has in part encouraged the availability of information and numerous sources for novice and professional observers alike. Two of the most important sources of information on the presidency include the presidential library system, which is under the auspices of the National Archives and Records Administration (NARA), and the *Public Papers of the Presidents of the United States*, published by the federal government.

Presidential Libraries

While access to presidential documents is only one source of information out of many available when studying a particular president and his administration, the memos, notes (sometimes handwritten), and other documents from those who worked in the administration provide a unique perspective into the decision making and thought processes of some of the most powerful figures in American government. Perhaps one of the best examples is Fred Greenstein's work on the Eisenhower presidency. As Greenstein writes in the introduction to his now-classic book, *The Hidden-Hand Presidency: Eisenhower as Leader*, he thought a visit to the Eisenhower Library in Abilene, Kansas, would confirm the widely held view that Eisenhower was a "pliable puppet of his aides" who was "lacking in political skill and motivation" and merely a "figurehead chief executive." Instead, while going through numerous files, Greenstein discovered a much different president:

> I had barely begun examining the recently opened files of Eisenhower's personal secretary, Ann Whitman, which contained Eisenhower's most confidential correspondence, his private diary, notes on his meetings and telephone conversations, and even transcripts of secret recordings of his one-to-one meetings with other high officials, when I experienced a shock of nonrecognition. The Eisenhower revealed in Mrs. Whitman's files could scarcely have been less like the Eisenhower who spawned the pre-Beltway Washington joke that, while it would be terrible if Eisenhower died and Vice-President Nixon became president, it would be worse if White House Chief of Staff Sherman Adams died and *Eisenhower* became president. The Eisenhower of Mrs. Whitman's files *was* president—he, not Sherman Adams, and not Secretary of State John Foster Dulles, was the engine force of the Eisenhower presidency. To my surprise, the Whitman papers and other records of the copiously documented Eisenhower presidency were laden with evidence of an alert, politically astute Eisenhower who engaged in the traditional kinds of persuasion and bargaining which are the standard activities of other presidents but which were believed to have been abjured by the amiable Ike. To my greater wonder, the records also testified to a

> nonstandard mode of presidential leadership on Eisenhower's part, one in which the president characteristically worked his will by indirection, concealing those of his maneuvers that belied his apolitical exterior.[55]

Greenstein's work on the Eisenhower presidency, as well as countless other projects which stem from research at presidential libraries, serves as a reminder that much insight can be gained by examining the memos, correspondence, diaries, phone and visitor logs, and numerous other documents available to the public at presidential libraries.

According to NARA, presidential libraries are repositories for the papers, records and historical materials of the presidents as they work to ensure that these irreplaceable items are preserved and made available for the widest possible use by researchers. The goal of presidential libraries is to "promote understanding of the presidency and the American experience" as well as to "preserve and provide access to historical materials, support research, and create interactive programs and exhibits that educate and inspire."[56] The working papers for each administration since Herbert Hoover are available in presidential libraries. The Library of Congress houses the papers for most administrations prior to Hoover. NARA's Office of Presidential Libraries administers a nationwide network of thirteen presidential libraries, while six other libraries not overseen by NARA also exist (see Table 1.1). Presidential libraries are not normal libraries, as they are instead archives and museums that house the documents and artifacts of a president and his administration. Yet, they are nonetheless open to the public; millions of visitors pass through presidential museums each year, while researchers and journalists can access documents from each administration to aid in their work. Although numerous political speeches, panels, debates, or conferences may be held at each presidential library, often with events supported by the president's individual foundation (which is a private aspect of each library to help promote the legacy of each president as well as to provide financial support for educational programs), the library archives themselves are managed by NARA archivists, which ensures open access with no political or ideological affiliation.

The presidential library system first began with Franklin Roosevelt in 1939, who wanted to preserve the papers and other materials from his time in office. Prior to the precedent set by Roosevelt, papers were often dispersed to family members, administration officials, and many were even destroyed. Following Roosevelt's lead, Harry Truman also decided that he wanted a library to house his presidential papers. Toward the end of Truman's term in 1952, the White House stated publicly the President's intentions regarding his papers: "By tradition, going back to the earliest days of our Nation, papers of every President are regarded as his personal property. However it is the intention of President Truman to donate his papers to the government after the completion of a suitable library to be built from private funds."[57] Then, in 1955, Congress passed the Presidential Libraries Act, which established a system of libraries that were to be built through private funds and then turned over to the federal government to maintain and oversee the facilities once completed and that

View NARA's website.

Table 1.1 Presidential Libraries

PRESIDENTIAL LIBRARY/MUSEUM	LOCATION	OPERATED BY
John Quincy Adams	Stone Library, Adams National Historical Park, Quincy, Massachusetts	National Parks Service
Abraham Lincoln	Springfield, Illinois	State of Illinois
Rutherford B. Hayes	Fremont, Ohio	Ohio Historical Society and Hayes Presidential Center, Inc.
William McKinley	Canton, Ohio	Stark County Historical Society
Woodrow Wilson	Staunton, Virginia	Woodrow Wilson Presidential Library Foundation
Calvin Coolidge	Northampton, Massachusetts	State of Massachusetts
Herbert Hoover	West Branch, Iowa	NARA
Franklin D. Roosevelt	Hyde Park, New York	NARA
Harry S. Truman	Independence, Missouri	NARA
Dwight D. Eisenhower	Abilene, Kansas	NARA
John F. Kennedy	Boston, Massachusetts	NARA
Lyndon Baines Johnson	University of Texas Campus, Austin, Texas	NARA and the University of Texas
Richard M. Nixon	Yorba Linda, California	NARA
Gerald R. Ford (Library)	University of Michigan Campus, Ann Arbor, Michigan	NARA
Gerald R. Ford (Museum)	Grand Rapids, Michigan	NARA
Jimmy Carter	Atlanta, Georgia	NARA
Ronald Reagan	Simi Valley, California	NARA
George H. W. Bush	Texas A&M University Campus, College Station, Texas	NARA
William J. Clinton	Little Rock, Arkansas	NARA
George W. Bush	Southern Methodist University Campus, Dallas, Texas	NARA (will open in 2013)

would be open to the public. Since that time, when a president leaves office, NARA establishes a Presidential Project until the new presidential library is built and transferred to the federal government.

Subsequent laws have also been passed that have changed the governing structure of presidential libraries. In 1978, Congress passed the Presidential Records Act (PRA), which established that presidential records documenting the constitutional, statutory, and ceremonial duties of the president are the property of the United States Government. Previously, a view existed that dated back to the George Washington administration that the papers and records created by the president and/or his staff while in office remained the personal property of the president. While the first presidential libraries built acknowledged this fact, NARA had great success in persuading presidents to donate their historical materials to be housed in a NARA-run presidential library. However, Richard Nixon's resignation from office in 1974 brought with it numerous lawsuits over ownership of his presidential papers, which

Harry Truman at the construction site of his presidential library in Independence, Missouri, April 21, 1956.

in part encouraged Congress to change the law. In 1974, Congress also passed the Presidential Recordings and Materials Preservation Act, placing Nixon's papers in federal custody to prevent their destruction.[58]

Another provision of the PRA, signed into law by Jimmy Carter, stipulated that each presidential library established after Carter's would be governed by the Freedom of Information Act (FOIA), a law passed in 1966 to ensure public access to government documents of a non-classified nature. Currently, the Reagan, Bush, and Clinton libraries operate under the rules of FOIA (as will the future Bush and Obama libraries), which means that a researcher must submit a FOIA request to gain access to any documents not already opened and processed by NARA archivists. The Presidential Libraries Act of 1986 also made changes to the presidential library system by requiring private endowments from donors to be linked to the size of the actual facility. NARA then uses the endowment to offset a portion of the maintenance costs for each library. It is important to note that the process of building a presidential library and providing public access to presidential documents can take several decades, from the initial site selection, funding and construction of the facility, and especially the review and processing of documents by archivists (to fully open most collections in a presidential library can take twenty to thirty years or more).

In 2001, a controversy erupted over the release of documents at the Ronald Reagan Library; under the PRA, documents are released twelve years after a president leaves office. The George W. Bush administration sought to delay the release of the Reagan documents, and on November 1, 2001, Bush issued Executive Order

13233, which limited access to records of former presidents that reflected "military, diplomatic, or national security secrets, Presidential communications, legal advice, legal work, or the deliberative processes of the President and the President's advisers...." In effect, this provided executive privilege to the family members of former presidents to decide which documents to withhold. Executive privilege, or the government's right to maintain the secrecy of certain documents, is traditionally only given to the president himself and other executive branch officials to keep certain information confidential so as not to interfere with the administration's ability to govern (particularly in regards to national security). The Executive Order also gave the current White House the right to review any documents prior to their release, and to withhold any documents they believed should be kept classified.

Numerous groups, including the Society of American Archivists, the American Library Association, the American Political Science Association (with strong support from the Presidency Research Group, the subsection of APSA devoted to the study of the presidency[59]), and numerous historical organizations, vehemently protested the Executive Order. A statement by the Society of American Archivists proclaimed: "The archival and public information implications aspects of this order are profound, being contrary to established archival principles and standards, being inconsistent with existing statutory law, and, most important, being at odds with the principles of open access to information upon which our country is founded."[60] Lawsuits were filed, and various members of Congress sought to take action to get around the Executive Order. Even former President Gerald Ford weighed in on the controversy, stating: "I firmly believe that after X period of time, presidential papers, except for the most highly sensitive documents involving our national security, should be made available to the public, and the sooner the better."[61] Executive Order 13233 stayed in effect through the rest of George W. Bush's time in office, which meant that it also covered the records to be released in January 2005 from his father's library. On January 21, 2009, during his first full day in office, Barack Obama kept one of his campaign promises by revoking the Executive Order and issuing Executive Order 13489, which returned to the NARA archivists, and not the White House or former family members of presidents, the ability to release documents in a timely manner. (For more detailed information about conducting research at presidential libraries, see Appendix A).

Public Papers

Started in 1957, the *Public Papers of the Presidents of the United States* series is the official annual compilation of presidential papers. It provides a comprehensive public source of data on the American presidency. As it now spans numerous administrations, this resource has aided those presidency scholars interested in a more institutional approach to studying the office as it allows researchers to employ a comparative methodological approach to understanding the institution of the American presidency. The National Historical Publications Commission originally suggested this endeavor since no uniform compilation of presidential messages and papers existed. The *Public Papers* is now the annual version of the

View Executive Order 13233 and 13489.

Weekly Compilation of Presidential Documents, which began publication in 1965. As of January 2009, the *Weekly Compilation* has been replaced by the *Daily Compilation of Presidential Documents;* both, along with the *Public Papers*, are available online at GPO Access. Between 1965 and 1976, only selected press releases from the *Weekly Compilation* were contained in the *Public Papers*. Beginning in 1977, all material appearing in the *Weekly/Daily Compilation* was incorporated into the *Public Papers*.

Both the *Public Papers* and the *Weekly/Daily Compilation* are published by the Office of the Federal Register, National Archives and Records Service, and are printed by the Government Printing Office. Administrations included in the series of *Public Papers* include those of Herbert Hoover, Harry Truman, Dwight Eisenhower, John F. Kennedy, Lyndon Johnson, Richard Nixon, Gerald Ford, Jimmy Carter, Ronald Reagan, George H. W. Bush, Bill Clinton, George W. Bush, and Barack Obama. The papers of Franklin D. Roosevelt were published privately prior to the creation of the official *Public Papers* series. Other privately published series of presidential papers by scholarly presses include: *The Papers of James Madison*, published by the University of Chicago Press; *The Papers of Woodrow Wilson* by Princeton University Press; and *The Papers of Dwight David Eisenhower* by the Johns Hopkins University Press. Other series of presidential papers include *The Adams–Jefferson Letters: The Complete Correspondence Between Thomas Jefferson and Abigail and John Adams*, published by the University of North Carolina Press; and *The Writings of George Washington From the Original Manuscript Sources, 1745–1799*, published by the George Washington Bicentennial Commission.

At present, the GPO publishes volumes of the *Public Papers* approximately twice a year, and each volume covers approximately a six-month period. The papers and speeches of the President of the United States that were issued by the Office of the Press Secretary during the specified time period are included in each volume of the *Public Papers*. These include: press releases, presidential proclamations, executive orders, addresses, remarks, letters, messages, telegrams, memorandums to federal agencies, communications to Congress, bill-signing statements, transcripts from presidential press conferences, and communiqués to foreign heads of state. The *Papers* present the material in chronological order, and the dates shown in the headings are the dates of the documents or events. Remarks are checked against a tape recording, and any signed documents are checked against the original, to ensure accuracy. The appendixes in each volume of the *Public Papers* is extensive and includes listings of: a digest of the President's daily schedule and meetings and other items issued by the White House Press Secretary; the President's nominations submitted to the Senate; a checklist of materials released by the Office of the Press Secretary that are not printed full-text in the book; and a table of Proclamations, Executive Orders, and other presidential documents released by the Office of the Press Secretary and published in the Federal Register. Each volume also includes a foreword signed by the President, several photographs chosen from White House Photo Office files, a subject and name index, and a document categories list.

View the entire collection of the Public Papers.

Federal Depository Libraries contain hard copies of the *Public Papers*. With more than 1,200 locations throughout the United States and its territories, these libraries, which can include city, county, state, or university libraries, were first established in 1813 as a means to safeguard the public's right to know by collecting, organizing, maintaining, preserving, and assisting users with information from the Federal Government through no-fee access. Electronic versions of the *Public Papers* can be found at the GPO Access website as well as individual presidential library websites. In addition, The American Presidency Project (americanpresidency.org), established in 1999 by presidency scholars John Woolley and Gerhard Peters at the University of California, Santa Barbara, is an extensive online archive containing more than 90,000 documents related to the study of the presidency. The archive includes data consolidated, coded, and organized into a single searchable database for: the *Messages and Papers of the Presidents: Washington through Taft* (1789–1913); the *Public Papers*; the *Weekly Compilation*; the *Daily Compilation*; as well as numerous other documents related to party platforms, candidates' remarks, statements of administration policy, documents released by the Office of the Press Secretary, and various election databases. Finally, with its creation during the Clinton administration, the official White House web page (www.whitehouse.gov) has also evolved as an extensive data base for presidential speeches and other public remarks, as well as the president's daily schedule and other information about the work of the current administration.

CONCLUSION

Studying the modern presidency, whether from an institutional perspective or by looking at the individuals who have held the office, can be both a fascinating and yet complex task. Clearly, much has changed about the presidency since the early days of George Washington, Thomas Jefferson, and Andrew Jackson. By the twentieth century, as America gained prominence as an economic global leader, and as military and diplomatic relationships grew more complex with the Cold War and its aftermath, the presidencies of Franklin Roosevelt, Ronald Reagan, and Bill Clinton appeared quite different from those of their early predecessors. Yet, it is instructive to remember that while the circumstances in which a president must govern can change drastically, little has changed about the office vis-à-vis the powers and limitations found within the U.S. Constitution. As we have seen in this discussion, scholars relying on a variety of methodological and/or theoretical perspectives have made many notable contributions to the presidency literature. In addition, the debate among presidency scholars now has the depth and breadth that was missing several decades ago, and healthy disagreements exist on not only what questions should be asked, but how they should be answered.

Throughout the chapters that follow, we will explore the many aspects of American presidents and the presidency. Examining the strengths and weaknesses of the presidency as a political institution, as well as the strengths and weaknesses of some of our recent presidents and their leadership skills, we provide a thorough examination that considers both a "president-centered" and an "institutional-based" approach to studying the presidency. In doing so, we provide an effective approach for students of the presidency to understand the complexity of the office, the differences that can occur from the individuals who hold the office, and the uniqueness of perhaps the most fascinating political office ever created. More importantly, relying on key documents from various presidential libraries will animate various discussions about White House decision making on any number of topics, which in turn will more accurately describe the "real" presidency as an institution as well as the actual day-to-day responsibilities of the president.

BUILDING A PRESIDENTIAL LIBRARY

THEN . . .

During his second term of office, Franklin Roosevelt began to consider what to do with the numerous documents and other materials from his time in office. Knowing that many previous presidential papers had been lost, destroyed, sold for profit, or ruined in storage, Roosevelt sought to provide a public repository for future study based on the work of his presidency. Roosevelt sought the advice of Waldo G. Leland, an American historian and archivist, and other notable historians who formed an executive committee to oversee the project (of which Leland served as chair from 1938–1941).[62] In accepting the position, Leland wrote in a letter to Roosevelt in December 1938: "I shall consider it as an honor and a privilege to be of service in carrying out your plans for the permanent housing of your records and related historical material. The plan is one which appeals to me very strongly and which will, I am confident, be of great importance for the advancement of historical studies in this country."[63] In 1939, Roosevelt donated his personal and presidential papers to the federal government; he also pledged a part of his Hyde Park, New York, estate as the site of the eventual library and museum. In doing so, Roosevelt asked the National Archives to take custody of his papers and other historical materials and to oversee his library.

Leland would serve as a strong public advocate for the library project for several years. At a dinner with Roosevelt and other historians serving on the library project's advisory and executive committees, Leland articulated the importance of preserving FDR's papers:

> The proposal by the President to present to the nation his papers, archives, books and other collections, to be housed in a special building on a part of his Hyde Park estate, also to be donated by him, has naturally aroused a great deal of interest among scholars. One cannot fail to be impressed by the magnitude and importance of so generous a gift. Most scholars would argue without difficulty that the quarter of a century through which the United States is passing, from the close of the War into the decade of the 'forties, is one of the most significant periods of American history. It is a period in which great changes that have long been in preparation are manifesting themselves; it is a period in which the ideas of the people of the United States have been subjected to the most penetrating tests, and there are few citizens who will emerge from this quarter-century with the same ideas, opinions, and points of view that they held at its beginning.

> Consequently, the proposal of the President to establish, under public control, exercised by the National Archives, at which is undoubtedly the key collection for the study of this most recent period, is particularly welcome to all students of American history. If, as seems likely, the President's collections should attract other related collections, such as the papers of members of his administration, there would soon be accumulated a body of material such as does not exist anywhere else, and the Franklin D. Roosevelt Library would become one of the chief centers of research in contemporary history in the United States.[64]

At the same dinner, Roosevelt himself recalled that while a student at Harvard, he had served as the librarian of the Hasty Pudding Club and had sought advice from an aged book-dealer on Cornhill: "One of the first things that old man Chase said to me was 'Never destroy anything.' Well, that has been thrown in my teeth by all the members of my family almost every week that has passed since that time. I have destroyed practically nothing. As a result, we have a mine for which future historians will curse me as well as praise me. It is a mine which will need to have the dross sifted from the gold. I would like to do it, but the historians tell me I am not capable of doing it.... It is a very conglomerate, hit-or-miss, all-over-the-place collection on every man, animal, subject of material.... But, after all, I believe it is going to form an interesting record of this particular quarter of a century... to which we belong."[65]

The FDR Library would set several important precedents as the presidential library system developed and expanded during the next several decades. For example, in 1939, a committee was formed to raise private funds to initiate the project and construction of the building prior to the library being turned over to the federal government and NARA for oversight and maintenance. In addition, numerous FDR administration officials would donate their papers to the library, as has become the norm. While the FDR papers would not open to researchers until 1950, as early as 1943, FDR himself began to give instructions to the director of his library about what should and should not be opened to researchers:

> Before any of my personal or confidential files are transferred to the Library at Hyde Park, I wish to go through them and select those which are never to be made public; those which should be sealed for a prescribed period of time before they are made public; and those which are strictly family matters, to be retained by my family.... With respect to the file known as "Famous People's File," the same procedure should be followed. Those which are official letters may be turned over to the Library, but those which are in effect personal such as, for example, the longhand letters between the King of England and myself, or between Cardinal [Archbishop of Chicago George] Mundelein and myself, are to be retained by me or my Estate and should never be made public.... With respect to the file called "Family Letters," in the main they are to be retained by me or my Estate.... In all of the papers which are to be turned over to the Library from my personal files or from non-personal, official files, there will be some which should not be published until a lapse of a certain length of time and which, in the

> meantime, should be put under seal. This is for the reason that they may refer to people who are still alive in a way which would be embarrassing to them. . . . I should judge that the average length of time of sealing should be from ten to fifteen years, but there may be some which should be sealed for as many as fifty years.[66]

. . . AND NOW

Unlike FDR, not every former president has acreage and/or an estate to donate for the location of his presidential library and museum. Some presidential libraries have been built on or near the actual site of the president's birthplace (such as the Hoover Library in West Branch, Iowa, or the Nixon Library in Yorba Linda, California), or what is to be considered the president's hometown (such as the Truman Library in Independence, Missouri, the Eisenhower Library in Abilene, Kansas, the Kennedy Library in Boston, Massachusetts, and the Clinton Library in Little Rock, Arkansas). Other libraries have been built on university campuses (such as the Johnson Library at the University of Texas at Austin, the Ford Library at the University of Michigan, and the George H. W. Bush Library at Texas A&M University). Still other libraries, such as the Carter Library in Atlanta and the Reagan Library in Simi Valley, California, were built in areas that had regional significance to each president. And, in recent years, competition for securing a presidential library has at times been fierce.

When the George W. Bush Library opens in 2013, on the Southern Methodist University Campus in a suburb of Dallas, the state of Texas will be able to boast more presidential libraries than any other state 🖱. And, all three will be housed on major university campuses. The first, the Lyndon Johnson Library on the campus of the University of Texas at Austin, was first dedicated in 1971 with former President Johnson and then-current president, Richard Nixon, in attendance. While LBJ had not attended UT Austin (he was a graduate of Southwest Texas State Teachers' College, now Texas State University–San Marcos), he had been born and raised in the Texas hill country just outside of Austin. At the dedication ceremony, Johnson stated: "We are all partners in this hopeful undertaking. The people of Texas built this library. The National Archives will manage the Library. The documents I have saved since the 1930s are being given, along with the documents of many others who served with me. Those documents contain millions and millions of words. But the two that best express my philosophy are the words, 'Man can.' I wish President Truman, the father of the Presidential Library System, could be here. He said he didn't want his library to be a tribute to him. He wanted it to serve as a real center for learning about our government. We are doing that here."[67]

As early as one month after George H. W. Bush took office in January 1989, lobbying of the president and his administration began over where the eventual Bush presidential library would be located. Texas A&M University, located in the

---

🖱 View information about the George W. Bush Library.

central-Texas town of College Station, was in the running from the very beginning. In a brief letter to Perry Adkisson, Chancellor of the Texas A&M University System, Bush wrote in February 1989: "Just a quick note to say I appreciate your interest. Though I can say I'd like the Presidential papers to land in Texas, it will be some time before options are pursued. Send the proposal... but, again, no rush."[68] By October 1989, other sites had already made initial bids for the library, including the University of Houston,[69] Rice University in Houston, Texas Tech University in Lubbock, Yale University (Bush's alma mater), and private groups in Kennebunkport, Maine (where the Bush family had a vacation home) and Houston.[70] By then, not even a year into the Bush presidency, the president seemed to be leaning toward Texas A&M. However, Jim Cicconi, Bush's deputy chief of staff (and the eventual vice president of the George Bush Presidential Library Foundation), advised members of the administration to not let their initial preferences be made public, and vetoed the idea of a presidential meeting with Texas A&M's designated library architect:

> A meeting with the President would "jump the gun." ... While well aware of the President's inclination toward locating the library at A&M, the Houston crowd still wants the chance to be heard, and have their proposal considered by the President. This includes many long-time friends of the President who are partial to Houston.... If they feel they never had a chance, and that the whole process was an "inside deal" ... there would no doubt be hard feelings despite our best efforts. A meeting with an architect, more than anyone else, makes it look like the deal has been cut. This will undoubtedly leak into the Texas papers, and will appear as if the Archives process is a sham.... I also worry about the perception of reviewing architectural plans for a library before our first year is over. We set up the Archives process to help the President keep this decision away from the Oval Office for a while, and to insulate the President from the type of personal lobbying he has had to undergo. This meeting would bring it right back onto his desk.[71]

On May 3, 1991, Bush informed Texas A&M that they had been chosen for the site of his presidential library. Among the factors Bush cited were the University's commitment to integrate the library into the academic activities of the University; the planned public service school and Center for Presidential Studies; the "ample space for future facilities, impressive setting, and easy access for visitors" found on the campus; and the University's commitment to "provide or secure all funds necessary to construct the library and related University facilities, and to establish separately an operational and program endowment [to] ensure not only that the financial requirements of the Presidential Libraries Act are met fully, but also that the library's ongoing programs will be vigorous and of high academic quality."[72]

The George W. Bush Presidential Library, located on the Southern Methodist University campus and scheduled for completion in 2013, also faced tough competition from other universities and locations, including Baylor University in Waco (officials began lobbying Bush even before he took the oath of office in

Dedication of the George Bush Presidential Library and Museum (*left to right*: Ladybird Johnson, Jimmy and Rosalynn Carter, George and Barbara Bush, Bill and Hillary Clinton, Gerald and Betty Ford, Nancy Reagan), November 6, 1997.

2001), Texas Tech University in Lubbock, the University of Texas system, the Texas A&M system, the University of Dallas, Midland College, and the City of Arlington. Speculation grew by 2007 that SMU (of which First Lady Laura Bush was an alumna) would be the selected location, which also drew protests from some SMU faculty who claimed that the university had bypassed faculty governance in the decision-making process to compete for the library (some faculty members were also opposed to Bush administration policies and did not want SMU forever linked with his presidency).[73] A Methodist group also opposed the library's location at SMU, claiming that it was inappropriate to link Bush's presidency to a university bearing the Methodist name.[74] Nonetheless, the Bush White House announced in 2008 that SMU would house the future presidential library. As to where the future Barack Obama Presidential Library will be built, the University of Chicago (where Obama once taught at the law school) and the state of Hawaii (where Obama was born) are already reportedly making early bids to secure the project. However, like their immediate predecessors in the George W. Bush White House, Obama advisors have stated that a first term is much too early to discuss plans for a presidential library (Bush officials did not officially discuss plans for a library until 2005).[75] Given the fact that Obama claims both Hawaii and Illinois as home states, Hawaii has more than one island from which to choose, Illinois has several large university campuses, and that Obama is a graduate of both Columbia University and Harvard University School of Law, it still remains anyone's guess where Obama's presidential papers will be housed.

SUGGESTED READINGS

Corwin, Edward S. 1940. *The President: Office and Powers*. New York: New York University Press.

Edwards, George C. III, John H. Kessel, and Bert A. Rockman, eds. 1993. *Researching the Presidency: Vital Questions, New Approaches*. Pittsburgh: University of Pittsburgh Press.

Edwards, George C., III, and Stephen J. Wayne, eds. 1983. *Studying the Presidency*. Knoxville: University of Tennessee Press.

Greenstein, Fred I. 1994. *The Hidden-Hand Presidency: Eisenhower as Leader*. Baltimore: Johns Hopkins University Press.

Greenstein, Fred I. 2009. *The Presidential Difference: Leadership Style from FDR to Barack Obama*, 3rd ed. Princeton: Princeton University Press.

Heclo, Hugh. 1977. *Studying the Presidency: A Report to the Ford Foundation*. New York: Ford Foundation Press.

Koenig, Louis W. 1996. *The Chief Executive*, 6th ed. New York: Harcourt Brace.

Neustadt, Richard. 1960. *Presidential Power: The Politics of Leadership*. New York: Wiley.

Ragsdale, Lyn. 2009. *Vital Statistics on the Presidency: George Washington to George W. Bush*, 3rd ed. Washington, DC: CQ Press.

Rossiter, Clinton. 1956. *The American Presidency*. New York: Harcourt, Brace.

Skowronek, Stephen. 1993. *The Politics Presidents Make: Leadership from John Adams to George Bush*. Cambridge: Belknap/Harvard Press.

ON THE WEB

http://www.whitehouse.gov. The official White House web page, which includes a comprehensive archive of all presidential speeches, information about the President's daily schedule, and historical information related to the presidency as well as past presidents.

http://www.gpoaccess.gov/wcomp/index.html. Published each Monday by the Office of the Federal Register and the National Archives and Records Administration, the Daily Compilation of Presidential Documents is the official publication of presidential statements, messages, remarks, and other materials released by the White House Press Secretary.

http://www.presidency.ucsb.edu/. The American Presidency Project contains the *Public Papers of the Presidents* as well as numerous data sets about presidential public activities.

IN THEIR OWN WORDS

LEADERSHIP

Presidents, like presidency scholars, have long been interested in the notion of "leadership." The following unsigned memorandum from 1928, an attempt to define leadership, is among the personal papers of Franklin Roosevelt at the FDR Presidential Library:

MEMORANDUM

There is no magic in Democracy that does away with the need of leadership.

The danger in our Democracy lies in our tendency to select leaders who are similar to the rank and file of us, whereas the hope of Democracy seems to lie in our selecting leaders who are superior to the rank and file of us.

Should we hunt for leaders who will lead us, or for leaders who will follow us?

Should we look for leaders who will always think like us, or for leaders who will sometimes think for us?

Should we elect men to office because they promise to vote for certain measures, or because we can trust their minds and their morals to guide them alright on measures in general once all the facts are before them?

Shall leaders be human substitutes for their constituents or phonograph records of the fluctuating moods of their constituents?

No man of authentic greatness of mind and character will purchase political position at the price of adjourning his own intelligence and becoming the errand boy of either Main Street or of Wall Street.

We have today side by side an old political order fashioned by a pastoral civilization and a new social order fashioned by a technical civilization. The two are maladjusted. Their creative inter-relation is one of the big tasks ahead of American leadership.[76]

CHAPTER 2

Presidents and the Constitution

While it is still much too early to accurately assess George W. Bush's place in American political history, one of the most notable and enduring debates will center on Bush's expansion of presidential powers related to national security and the War on Terror. Following the terrorist attacks of 9/11, the Bush administration claimed broad presidential powers under Bush's role as commander in chief, not only in the capture, imprisonment, and interrogation tactics used against suspected terrorists but also in the U.S. invasion of Afghanistan in December 2001 and Iraq in March 2003. While Bush's supporters championed his interpretation of broad constitutional powers during a time of crisis, his political opponents railed against the president for his abuse and misinterpretation of presidential powers as outlined in Article II of the Constitution. Upon Barack Obama's election in 2008, many of Obama's supporters believed, falsely as it turned out, that the renewed "imperial presidency" of the Bush years would fade quickly. However, the Obama administration has not been without controversy in this regard, as Obama has also been challenged, at least politically, over his use of military intervention as commander in chief.

In February 2011, Obama committed U.S. troops to Libya as part of an international coalition to oust Col. Muammar Gaddafi from power. Gaddafi had begun a campaign to put down civil unrest and protests in Libya, which included killing thousands of innocent civilians. Long considered a pariah state by most other nations due to its state-sponsored terrorist activities, Libya had been under U.N. sanctions since 1993; prior to that, Ronald Reagan had ordered military air strikes against Libya in 1986 in response to a terrorist bombing of a Berlin nightclub where Americans had been killed. Given the long history of animosity toward Gaddafi's regime, Obama's decision to aid the international military effort to remove Gaddafi from power was not surprising. By March 2011, as the international coalition continued to fight Gaddafi's troops in support of those protesting his government, Obama sent a letter to Congress informing members about the military action in compliance with the War Powers Resolution:

> [Gaddafi's] illegitimate use of force not only is causing the deaths of substantial numbers of civilians among his own people, but also is forcing many others to flee to neighboring countries, thereby destabilizing the peace and security of the region. Left unaddressed, the growing instability in Libya could ignite wider instability in the Middle East, with dangerous consequences to the national security interests of the United States.... The United States has not deployed ground forces into Libya. United States forces are conducting a limited and well-defined mission in support of international efforts to protect civilians and prevent a humanitarian disaster.... I have directed these actions, which are in the national security and foreign policy interests of the United States, pursuant to my constitutional authority to conduct U.S. foreign relations and as Commander in Chief and Chief Executive. I am providing this report as part of my efforts to keep the Congress fully informed, consistent with the War Powers Resolution.[1]

A few days later, Obama addressed the nation about the importance of the mission in Libya:

> ...the United States and the world faced a choice. Gaddafi declared he would show "no mercy" to his own people. He compared them to rats, and threatened to go door to door to inflict punishment. In the past, we have seen him hang civilians in the streets, and kill over a thousand people in a single day.... We knew that if we waited one more day, Benghazi, a city nearly the size of Charlotte, could suffer a massacre that would have reverberated across the region and stained the conscience of the world. It was not in our national interest to let that happen. I refused to let that happen. And so nine days ago, after consulting the bipartisan leadership of Congress, I authorized military action to stop the killing and enforce U.N. Security Council Resolution 1973.... Moreover, we've accomplished these objectives consistent with the pledge that I made to the American people at the outset of our military operations. I said that America's role would be limited; that we would not put ground troops into Libya; that we would focus our unique capabilities on the front end of the operation and that we would transfer responsibility to our allies and partners. Tonight, we are fulfilling that pledge.[2]

While many Americans supported the idea of removing Gaddafi from power, Obama faced criticism from both sides of the political aisle; liberals worried that the United States would engage in yet another war in the Middle East (with troops still in both Afghanistan and Iraq), and conservatives complained that Obama was acting beyond his constitutional powers by committing U.S. troops (though many of those same conservatives did not complain about Bush's actions just a few years earlier). Republicans on Capitol Hill began to talk about violations of the War Powers Resolution, and in response Obama sent another letter to Congress in June 2011 stating that the War Powers Resolution did not apply after all to his actions regarding Libya since American military involvement fell short of "full-blown hostilities," asserting that "U.S. operations do not involve sustained fighting or active exchanges of fire with hostile forces, nor do they involve U.S. ground troops."[3] Whether Obama correctly asserted his powers as commander in chief, and whether he was right to claim that the War Powers Resolution did not apply, is still open to political and constitutional interpretation.

While the framers of the Constitution may have provided a rather sparse list of specific presidential powers, perhaps the most notable of those is the president's role as commander in chief of the military. Specific yet mostly undefined, this presidential power has been one of the most debated constitutional issues in recent decades. While the constitution specifically grants Congress the power to declare war in Article I, Section 8, of the more than ten conflicts in which the United States has participated since 1945, not one was sanctioned by a congressional declaration of war. In other words, despite the fact that the United States has fought many wars since the end of World War II, the last time Congress invoked its constitutional authority to declare war was in 1941. All subsequent wars have been started by America's presidents. As members of Congress became more concerned with reelection than making tough decisions over which they could lose votes, they willingly relinquished the legislature's power to declare war. America's commanders in chief, for their part, gladly seized a power not granted to them by the Constitution, thereby enhancing their ability to pursue foreign-policy objectives without political impediments.

This constitutional predicament over war powers escalated with congressional passage of the War Powers Resolution. Passed in 1973 over Richard Nixon's veto, it requires America's commanders in chief to consult with Congress prior to the introduction of troops into any military theater, but it simultaneously recognizes a presidential power to respond to exigent circumstances without notification when such notification would compromise the integrity or effectiveness of military action. The net effect of this concession was an acknowledgment in all but word of a presidential power to declare war through a statutory loophole that to many seems patently unconstitutional. Over the next three decades, Presidents Carter, Reagan, Clinton, Obama, and both Bushes availed themselves of this loophole to begin or augment American military operations all over the globe and secure a presidential power to declare war.

As both the George W. Bush and Barack Obama presidencies have recently shown, the Constitution is not always clear regarding presidential powers. After more than two centuries of constitutional development, the dominant tendency of American constitutional history has been to concentrate power in the executive branch. From a constitutional standpoint, it is clear that the presidency is now far more powerful than the framers could have intended or expected. Presidents have tended to seize power to cope with crises while in office, and there has been a long history of aggrandizement. There have been distinct periods when the presidency was considered weaker than it is today, and other times that the power and prestige of the office has been damaged. However, while largely institutionalized, the presidency is still dependent on the performance and character of its occupant. Particularly regarding foreign policy matters, institutional demands as commander in chief along with public demands regarding the president's role as head of state have often led presidents to stretch constitutional boundaries. Understanding how the framers

Read the original War Powers Resolution.

viewed executive power and how that led to the design of the presidency at the Constitutional Convention, along with how certain presidents have shaped the constitutional parameters of the office beyond the framers' intentions, helps to explain the contemporary role of presidential powers as part of the current governing process.

THE FRAMERS' PLAN AND THE CONSTITUTIONAL CONVENTION

The creation of a head of state at least as powerful as the British king who would also act as the head of government contradicted several decades of colonial history and, to many, ignored the purposes of the American Revolution. Americans had traditionally resisted a centralized executive with authority over state (previously colonial) governments, so the appearance of a comparatively assertive presidency in 1787 was rather ironic. Indeed, the Confederation government of the 1780s lacked a national executive altogether, reflecting the founding fathers' skepticism toward the consolidation of executive authority. The colonies had benefited from a long line of largely powerless and ineffective governors and a correspondingly permissive relationship with the crown during the eighteenth century, so Americans had become accustomed to ostensibly powerless chief executives. After the English revolution of 1688, real political power lay with Parliament, so British monarchs exerted decreasing control over territories in North America, where residents eventually regarded freedom from executive interference as a constitutional precedent. Following independence, political experiments at the state level only confirmed the American preference for weak central government, so all signs pointed toward the opposite of what eventually happened with the design of the American presidency in 1787.

Inherited Practices and Ideas

In the late eighteenth century, when the framers of the Constitution created the presidency, non-hereditary civilian heads of state were anything but common. The world's leading powers, as well as its lesser nation states and principalities, almost uniformly opted for hereditary monarchs or emperors of one sort or another, while others nonetheless employed some variation of authoritarian, non-representative rule. The idea that a non-hereditary elected official should preside over government was certainly unique for its time, even among some of the West's most progressive regimes, yet from a historical perspective it was hardly unprecedented. As early as the sixth-century B.C., if not before, archons chosen by lot acted as Athenian chief executives and fulfilled many of the responsibilities currently associated with presidential rule.[4] Likewise, consuls assumed some of the same duties in the Roman republic, particularly before the demise of republican rule and the emergence of imperial governance.[5] And, centuries later, during the Renaissance, several Italian city-states appointed non-hereditary princes as their chief executives.[6] Even in England, a bastion of monarchical governance, a non-hereditary commonwealth was briefly established after the execution of Charles I in 1649.[7] Finally, in the American colonies themselves, colonial governors exercised many of the executive functions that the presidency would later assume at the federal level.

Despite some historical examples of non-hereditary, even republican, rule, these were never more than isolated cases and did not constitute a tradition from which the framers could choose a relevant precedent. Although the framers embraced continuity and incremental change rather than revolution and radical transformation, the presidency was in many ways radical, if not transformative. The framers' overall constitutional design arose from innovation and adaptation, and not invention and disruption, as they borrowed, inherited, and assimilated relevant aspects of British political culture. Affirming familiar political ideals as the foundations of republican rule, they nevertheless chose something quite unfamiliar for the executive branch of the American government.

Be that as it may, the presidency does exhibit evident ties to its British heritage and also prominent strains of contemporary European political thought. As students of European history and Western political philosophy, the framers combined English commonwealth ideology with classical and Renaissance ideas about leadership into a distinctly American conception of executive authority. In addition to their experiences with colonial governance, the most significant influence over the framers was their English heritage. By the eighteenth century, Great Britain was a constitutional monarchy with a unique respect for political liberty and the rights of citizens. Although it was not progressive by today's standards, it far surpassed its European rivals, most which practiced some form of non-representative authoritarian rule.[8]

Aside from English political tradition, classical concepts about republican government shaped American political thought during the revolutionary period. The framers of the Constitution regularly consulted the writings of prominent Greek and Roman philosophers and also relied on historical accounts of the rise and demise of ancient regimes. Among others, men such as James Madison and Alexander Hamilton were greatly impressed by classical philosophy and the many political insights it offered. In addition, the histories of the Athenian and Roman republics were prominent reminders of the potential and promise of human governance. Ironically, classical ideals, which exerted such a powerful influence over American political thought, had only a marginal impact on English politics, but their contribution to the development of an American political tradition is undeniable.[9]

Classical ideas about republics (a form of government in which rulers are elected by the ruled and based on the principle of representative government), governance, civic responsibility, and the allocation of power fascinated the framers, as did ancient attempts at democratic rule. They were convinced that an understanding of the rise and subsequent fall of the Roman republic held the key to managing the birth and death of republican government. Many of them viewed the late Roman republic (before the onset of decay in the early first-century B.C.) as the best historical example of effective and legitimate republican governance, so they consciously modeled the American republic on Roman institutions, ideas, and political practices. On the other hand, the collapse of republican governance in the first century B.C. taught the framers compelling lessons about the accumulation of power within a single institution and the threats posed by an unchecked executive, even a non-hereditary one. The demise of the Roman republic and its replacement by an imperial regime demonstrated both the promise and vulnerability of republican governance. To those contemplating the complexion of the emerging American presidency, Roman history illustrated the need not only to separate civilian from military leadership but also to make the military accountable to civilian rule. Last, the history of the Roman consulship showed that executive power must be strictly confined to specific duties and responsibilities and that, as a result, republican executives should not be given general power or authority.

The Framers' World

During the late-seventeenth and eighteenth centuries, the Enlightenment transformed Europe's intellectual terrain and, by extension, the political consciousness of the American colonies. Rejecting the divine right of kings as a medieval fiction, Enlightenment thinkers doubted the ideological assumptions upon which early-modern ideas of executive authority had been predicated. In so doing, they redefined classical republicanism and simultaneously planted the seeds of what would eventually become the West's dominant political creed—liberalism.[10] In the framers' world, republicanism and liberalism were the cornerstones of political ideology and contemporary practices, and they formed the intellectual foundation for the evolution of constitutional politics. Accordingly, American founding fathers believed that some people are better equipped to rule, while others are naturally suited for non-political responsibilities. Thus, government should reflect and leverage inherent social hierarchies and should optimize the intrinsic capabilities of its citizens. Although the framers of the Constitution reconciled popular rule with such political elitism, their constitutional intentions were predominantly republican and essentially conservative.

Republicanism may have been more relevant to the American political system designed by the framers, so it dominated early in the nation's history, but liberalism eventually prevailed. By the twentieth century, the American political system had become thoroughly liberal, despite the framers' original intentions. Throughout its history, liberalism has upheld four basic principles of government, which are also the key features of modern American politics: individual rights; government by consent; limited government; and legal and constitutional neutrality toward citizens and the impartial protection of individuals and their rights.[11] More than any other aspects of liberalism, individual rights and limited government influenced the framers' plans for an American presidency. The need to protect individuals, their property, and their natural liberties was inextricably linked to the related need to limit the size of government, and especially the scope of executive authority. The framers believed that the best way to secure the rights and liberties of the American people was by preventing the accumulation of too much power by any one branch of the government, and they were convinced that an unchecked executive could pose an immediate threat to republican governance. As apparent victims of royal abuses during the 1760s and 1770s, Americans were intimately familiar with potentially tyrannical executive authority and power, so the framers intentionally restricted executive authority in the United States. Given their experiences, they concluded that a non-hereditary civilian executive would be considerably less likely to exceed his authority than a hereditary monarch or a military leader. Thus, the Constitution provides for a civilian chief executive accountable to the very people whose rights he must protect.[12]

As crown and Parliament reasserted their rightful, but dormant and largely ignored, constitutional authority over the colonies during the several years prior to the American Revolution, colonial anxieties and paranoia about executive tyranny gradually grew. By 1775, many colonial leaders had become convinced of an imperial conspiracy to deprive colonists of their rights and property through executive usurpations of power and authority, and they did whatever possible to discredit the actions of the imperial government in London. The resulting friction between colonies and mother country intensified into a constitutional debate of monumental proportions, as increasing numbers of British Americans dedicated themselves to what they perceived as a struggle against tyranny. The seemingly unconstitutional seizure of power by the British executive triggered a reaction that no one could have foreseen.[13]

The exaggerated claims of imperial tyranny in the Declaration of Independence notwithstanding, American colonists suffered more from neglect than abuse by the British crown. Consequently, their views of executive authority were a reflection less of royal and Parliamentary corruption than a relatively weak and decentralized imperial executive whose authority over military defense was unchallenged but whose power over internal matters was consistently contested. More than seventy years of de facto autonomous internal governance established a significant precedent whose impact on the political events of the 1760s and 1770s as well as initial experiments in republican government during the 1780s was undeniable. Constitutionally speaking, this precedent supported the related conviction that executive authority does not legitimately extend beyond certain aspects of foreign policy and international commerce and that the authority to regulate internal affairs had devolved to state governments. All in all, the history of imperial governance in British North America fostered a colonial tradition of weak executive rule, which formed a lasting impression on the men who created a new American presidency in 1787.

The Confederation Executive

The onset of war in 1775 did not fundamentally alter the equation, so, after independence, state governors were no more effective than the colonial governors they had replaced. At the national level, the Continental Congress became the reluctant successor to the British crown, assuming a role as the political center of the former empire and makeshift head of state. However, since it lacked formal constitutional authority over the recently independent states, political leaders from across the continent pushed for the creation of a wartime government that could legitimately handle the required tasks. Not surprisingly, diplomatic and military priorities were paramount, so little thought was given to long-term constitutional concerns. Created as an answer to those priorities, the new government operated under the Articles of Confederation, which many have considered the first American constitution. The Articles of Confederation were adopted in 1778, though they were not ratified until 1781, when the revolutionary war was all but over.

Handicapped from the beginning by a lack of constitutional foresight and political efficacy, the Confederation government had to beg, borrow, and steal in order to meet military necessities and political realities. In its dual role as lawmaker and executive, the Confederation Congress had formidable expectations, but it never became either. A legislature with symbolic powers and doubtful authority, it was restricted to an advisory capacity and was continually unable to enact prospective legislation. Adding insult to injury, the Confederation government did not even have the power to enforce the few laws it enacted. As commander in chief, it was deprived of the resources and institutional legitimacy it required for strategic and operational management, and it could not implement its decisions without prolonged bargaining and haggling. This government had no formal executive branch, so any exercise of executive power was more a function of occasional concession or peculiar circumstance than institutional authority. Real authority lay with the states, and compromise with the central government was difficult at best. The states were clearly more powerful than the central government, and they could, and usually did, undermine the central government's efforts to act decisively.[14]

By 1787, the lack of a constitutional executive with the necessary authority to succeed the crown as head of state made the Confederation government unworkable. The futility of repairing a nonexistent Confederation executive seemed obvious, as did the folly of a unified American government without a head of state. The need for an effective and legitimate executive was not the only reason, or even the primary reason, for the emergence of the Constitution, as several other factors also contributed to the decision to abandon the Confederation government. Nonetheless, had the need for a formal and active executive not existed, the outcome could have been very different. Legislative paralysis could have been addressed through reform at the state level, at least in some respects, as could the legal and jurisdictional questions that hampered the proper interpretation and enforcement of the law. Most likely, state-based or regional remedies would only have exacerbated the situation, perhaps rendering permanent union useless or impossible, but some mechanisms to confront legislative and judicial problems, at least temporarily, were available at state and local levels. However, unlike the legislative and judicial deficiencies plaguing the Confederation government, the absence of a central executive could not be addressed by state and local governments in any practical or theoretical manner.

Aside from its inability to enforce laws and coordinate national defense, the Confederation government could not adequately handle foreign affairs. Without a unified or duly authorized head of state, the Confederation government could not manage relationships with foreign regimes, nor could it settle the numerous diplomatic issues that confronted it after the war. In addition, it was powerless to regulate or facilitate international trade and interstate commerce, which simply compounded existing economic difficulties. In matters of international trade, the former colonies rarely coordinated or aligned their commercial policies, so they subjected foreign ventures and governments to overlapping and contradictory agreements that undermined continental economic efficiency and overall viability. Lack of cooperation among the states and consistent economic policies made the former colonies unattractive prospects for international trade, which further undermined the stature and credibility of the Confederation government. As such, badly needed financial assistance was slow in coming and ultimately inadequate to alleviate the strain of accumulated foreign debts 🖰.[15]

The framers of the Constitution therefore committed themselves to a presidency with sufficient authority to enforce the country's laws, insure national security, direct foreign policy, and promote international commerce. These were powers that had eluded the Confederation government, and they represented the most deficient aspects of executive authority under the Articles of Confederation. At the same

---

🖰 View the Articles of Confederation on the Library of Congress website time, the framers, heedful of their experience with the British crown and the lessons of history, assiduously avoided granting the new presidency too much power. Like the rest of the government of which it would be a part, the American presidency would have limited authority, sufficient to redress the executive deficiencies of the Confederation yet not so powerful to pose a threat to the republic or its political institutions. In addition, the constitutional and political crises of the 1780s strengthened the framers' traditional inclination to dilute and filter popular sovereignty in a way that precludes democratic excesses. Their devotion to popular sovereignty never entailed tolerance of unrestrained democracy or the unfiltered exercise of the popular will, so they shrewdly insulated the presidency from base priorities and selfish interests.

Federalism

Needless to say, federalism (the sharing of political powers between the national and state governments) was not a political panacea, but it has served the American presidency comparatively well over the past 220 years or so. It has enabled governors and state legislatures to promote state-specific priorities more effectively, such as law enforcement, emergency services, community development, and education, to name a few, and it has preserved a kind of political adaptability not possible in more centralized regimes. At the same time, federalism has allowed American presidents to focus on the issues, like national defense, foreign policy, and international commerce, that the Confederation government had been so powerless to confront. Of course, during the last one hundred years, executive powers and the scope of federal authority generally have expanded beyond the framers' intentions, but federalism has remained the defining feature of American governance nonetheless. The American presidency has acquired partial or complete authority over tax and monetary policy, health care, education, energy, workplace issues, welfare, communications, and countless other aspects of modern life in the United States, and the growth of federal power has frequently come at the expense of local and regional governance, yet the states still control an overwhelming majority of governmental duties and responsibilities.

The absence of historical or contemporary models on which to base a federal presidency was not the only challenge facing the framers. Some of the delegates to the Constitutional Convention, as well as a number of those to state ratification conventions, the most prominent of whom was Alexander Hamilton, worried that a two-tier system of politics would promote unhealthy competition and jealousy between state and federal governments and would, thus, undermine federal executive authority and credibility, if not also legitimacy. Even manifestly presidential responsibilities such as national defense and federal law enforcement could overlap with competing gubernatorial powers, especially since any federal defense and security regime would heavily depend on the deployment and cooperation of state-based militias. Also, skeptics were concerned that federalism would impede rather than facilitate the formulation and implementation of national economic policies by ceding too much power over economic and financial issues to state governments, thereby decreasing the effectiveness of the presidency over an area that represented one of the most glaring deficiencies of the outgoing Confederation government. Hamilton and his intellectual brethren may have preferred a unitary national government free

Painting by Howard Chandler Christie of George Washington presiding over the second Constitutional Convention, in 1787.

of jurisdictional ambiguities, but federalism prevailed, and the presidency created by the framers actually alleviated most of Hamilton's anxieties. Indeed, as one of the principal authors of the *Federalist* papers, Hamilton became a staunch supporter of the Constitution and the American presidency.[16]

General vs. Limited Authority

Nothing was more critical to the development of an American presidency than the distinction between general and limited executive authority, which arose from contemporary interpretations of sovereignty. On a broader level, no general concept is more important for a proper understanding of executive authority than sovereignty itself.[17] Indeed, it lies at the heart of the framers' conceptions of republican government and political power, so it is the intellectual cornerstone of the presidency itself. Sovereignty (which means the supreme authority or power over a particular territory) revolves around crucial questions regarding the nature of rule, most significantly those that examine the right to rule. This was a principal concern for the framers, not least because, through the Constitution, they hoped to identify and delimit the scope of legitimate political authority and to define the determinants of governance in an American republic. In that regard, the relationship between sovereignty and the presidency was a primary focus of constitutional inquiry, as was the viability of prevailing theories of sovereignty. Their ultimate objective was the elucidation and maintenance of the apparently clear boundary separating general and limited authority and the establishment of a limited federal government, but the centrality of sovereignty as an ideological and constitutional context was always

View the *Federalist Papers* on the Library of Congress website.

evident.[18] Like their contemporaries in other countries, they were aware that sovereignty held the key to the utilization of executive power.

For approximately two millennia, executive power was a function of the natural sovereignty of kings and their inherent right to rule, and the equation of sovereignty with absolute authority seemed indisputable. Philosophers, monarchs, and clergy all agreed that the right to govern is the sole province of a unified and omnipotent executive and that the sovereignty of the executive could not be divided, delegated, or diluted. Eventually, those ideas about the indivisibility of sovereignty and absolute power succumbed to more progressive interpretations of rule, but the fundamental link between sovereignty and authority remained. Even the Enlightenment, which questioned inherited explanations of sovereignty, never doubted the natural relationship between sovereignty and authority. And, to this very day, long after liberal-democratic governments throughout the world have rejected the concept of indivisible sovereignty, the connection between sovereignty and executive authority is still intact.[19]

Over the almost two centuries between the English settlement of Virginia and the creation of an American republic in 1787, the principle of representative, accountable executive rule based on consent and limited authority, which was linked to broader theories of popular sovereignty, became one of the foundation stones of American politics.[20] In 1787, despite wishing to replace the feckless Confederation executive by a more vigorous and powerful continental executive, most Americans still supported limitations on executive authority. They had not forgotten the alleged abuses of power by the British crown and Parliament during the years prior to independence, and they knew of too many historical examples of unchecked executive authority to accept any form of general authority. In short, prevailing eighteenth-century American practices and theories could not be reconciled with claims of general executive authority. During the early decades of the eighteenth century, ideas of specific governmental powers and limited governmental authority, though unfamiliar or irrelevant to most contemporary societies, made an indispensable contribution to colonial political thought and cemented an American bias against general authority. Such ideas ultimately formed the basis of a liberal-democratic society dedicated to limited government, individual rights and liberties, and rule by consent, and they provided the constitutional logic for a presidency whose authority would be inherently confined to positively identified powers.[21]

The concept of specific powers, or limited authority, was an American political innovation born of unique experience and historical circumstance. Partly an incarnation of colonial restrictions on royal power and gubernatorial authority and mostly a reaction to Parliamentary excesses of the 1760s and 1770s, to say nothing of Parliamentary sovereignty, the idea of limited executive authority reassured the framers, who wished to prevent future tyrannies by creating an American presidency with specific, not general, powers. Without a doubt, general executive authority would have offered American presidents greater adaptability and institutional agility, but the last thing the framers of the Constitution wanted to encourage, even with someone as trusted as George Washington (who most assumed would be the first president), was political adventurism or constitutional experimentation within the presidency. The creation of a new government unleashed tremendous political changes, but, most of all, the Constitution represented stability, certitude, and tradition. According to the framers, only limited authority could preserve those qualities. The historical record is unusually compelling and comparatively unambiguous in that regard.[22]

Therefore, presidential powers derive from a limited, not general, grant of authority by the people of the United States. Admittedly, interpretation of the framers' intent is complicated by what they assumed but did not explicitly state, particularly because most of today's Americans are not familiar with the framers' intellectual context. So, the current lack of familiarity with eighteenth-century constitutional ideologies, even among legal scholars, obscures the political principles that should still animate the implementation of relevant constitutional directives and often prevents the elucidation of the framers' intent. The situation has not been helped by the wording of Article II of the Constitution, which can appear confusing and even contradictory, but anyone familiar with the framers' world should nonetheless be aware of their opposition to general executive authority. Clearly, neither the Constitution nor its related contemporary literature can be reconciled with open-ended executive power; those documents illustrate that the framers created a presidency with limited authority comprising only specific powers that correspond to the fulfillment of nothing more than essential, or core, duties.[23] The framers perceived those duties as the only legitimate areas of executive authority, since they reflected the few political tasks Americans were incapable of fulfilling without a federal executive. Through limited executive authority, they intended to address the basic deficiencies of power that plagued the Confederation government—nothing more. From the perspective of executive responsibilities, those deficiencies included: the inability to protect and preserve individual rights and political liberty; the inability to enforce federal laws; the lack of national-defense capabilities; the inability to manage foreign affairs; and the inability to facilitate interstate or international commerce.[24]

As a direct response to those deficiencies of governance, the framers of the Constitution established the presidency: to secure and enforce the rights and political liberty of its citizens; to enforce federal laws; to provide a system of national defense; to conduct and manage foreign relations; and to coordinate interstate commerce and international trade. The Constitution granted the presidency only as much authority as was required to redress the aforementioned deficiencies, and the framers painstakingly avoided any implications to the contrary, the ambiguities in Article II notwithstanding. Above all, the presidential authority granted by the Constitution was a logical manifestation of contemporary political thought. The powers outlined in the preceding paragraph accurately reflected prevailing American conceptions of legitimate executive authority during the previous few decades, and, as such, they contained no surprises. On the other hand, a grant of general authority would have been truly surprising and unexpected.

Overall, the framers created a narrowly defined government that would discourage the accumulation of too much power in any single institution and, therefore, would minimize the potential for corruption and tyranny. Given their past and also the history of executive governance in the West, they took deliberate precautions to prevent the abuse of power and authority not only by the president but also other key players in the new American government. In addition to making the president head of government and not just head of state, those precautions included a number of constitutional impediments to the concentration of power, like the separation of powers, checks and balances, the limited scope of federal responsibility, and the establishment of constitutional qualifications and conditions for political service. Perhaps the most significant of those conditions for a government in the late eighteenth century, especially since it contradicted contemporary trends, was the subordination of military to civilian leadership. The founding generation of Americans believed that, in order to minimize the potential for tyranny and corruption, the military must be categorically accountable to, and separate from, both the voters and their civilian presidents. History was (and still is) replete with examples of military oppression and abuse of power, and the framers wanted to insure that the military would never be used against the American people.[25]

Another important precaution that reinforced the principle of limited executive authority was the designation of specific terms of office. The Constitution defines a four-year presidential term, so service cannot be extended indefinitely by power-hungry autocrats or demagogues, while political tradition quickly placed further constraints on presidential office-holding through the habit of serving no more than two terms (a tradition initiated by George Washington). Even prior to the ratification of the Twenty-Second Amendment in 1951, which limited presidents to two terms, no American president except Franklin Roosevelt ever held office for longer than two terms (FDR died just months into his fourth term in 1945). In addition, passage of the Twenty-Fifth Amendment in 1967 dealt with succession to the presidency, and provided procedures for filling a vice-presidential vacancy as well as responding to a presidential disability.[26] The credibility and legitimacy of the presidency have depended, at least in part, on the periodic and voluntary surrender of political authority to the citizens who actually possess it, which has distinguished the American system of politics from the majority of others. A president's willingness to surrender authority according to constitutional criteria and political custom and his implicit assurance that both his service and authority are inherently limited are key aspects of a system whose focus is the prevention of tyranny and political corruption.

Separation of Powers/Checks and Balances

Of the emerging liberal criteria for legitimate rule, the one that exerted a primary influence over the framers of the Constitution was limited government. Through their English political heritage, they had already developed a dedicated respect for individual rights and political liberty, but the idea of limited government was something relatively new, historically speaking. Moreover, dominant contemporary British political ideologies, devoted as they were to a justification of Parliamentary sovereignty, had long before shed any allegiance to Lockean notions of limited government. American colonists, however, imbibed heavy doses of Lockean liberalism and were especially struck by Locke's contention that legitimate government exists only to fulfill the few duties and responsibilities citizens cannot address as individuals. Furthermore, unlike their British compatriots in the mother country, residents of the colonies were convinced that the Glorious Revolution of 1688–89 enshrined the Lockean concept of limited government as a keystone of English constitutionalism, so their eventual veneration of limited government had both a theoretical and a historical foundation.[27]

Not surprisingly, the Constitution is a blueprint for limited government with specific, positive allocations of authority and power that cannot exceed designated boundaries, and one of the most conspicuous structural examples of limited government is the separation of powers. The notion that the three rudimentary functions of government—legislation, law enforcement, and dispute resolution—must be separate and mostly independent had existed in various guises for several generations before Baron de Montesquieu, the French philosopher and historian customarily credited with its discovery, addressed it in his magnum opus *The Spirit of the Laws*. Montesquieu reworked it into a form that would eventually be useful and relevant to the framers of the Constitution, but his assertion that the basic functions of government should be divided and separate was hardly new.[28] Actually, the founding fathers' experiences with Parliament and the crown during the decades prior to revolution more aptly demonstrated the dangers of combining those functions in one institution than any philosophical treatise, and the separation of powers was simply a logical progression of constitutional design. Along with checks and balances, it became a central element of American constitutionalism, and it has enabled the federal government not only to confront the complexities and vulnerabilities of modern governance more effectively and efficiently but also to operate with greater legitimacy and trust.

The framers created three separate and mostly independent branches of government whose duties and responsibilities, though overlapping in some aspects, are nonetheless distinct. The need to divide the basic functions of government and keep them from interfering with one another was driven by the rabid fear of tyranny and corruption, so the Constitution established institutional boundaries that would prevent the consolidation of too much power and authority within a single branch of government. Obviously, despite the clearly delineated division of labor and constitutionally mandated allocation of limited authority to each branch, viable governance presupposes coordination and collaboration among three branches working in concert, since the failure of any one branch would precipitate the failure of the entire regime. So, separation of powers was as much a matter of political efficiency through specialization of authority as it was a means of avoiding the emergence of tyrannical potentialities, which leveraged and, thus, optimized each branch's specific political expertise. Apart from other concerns, the framers worried that conflating naturally distinct constitutional roles within single institutions would eventually produce paralytic inefficiency and inefficacy; their government could become a jack of all trades but a master of none, thereby undermining its ability to respond to evolving circumstances.[29]

Although the framers sought political balance through the distribution of authority among three branches, they also knew that political realities would inevitably favor one of them more than the others. This may not necessarily be the case today, especially due to the unforeseen and unprecedented expansion of executive power and authority over the past seventy years, but Congress was initially the most influential, if not powerful, institution within the U.S. government—which the framers had predicted. Common sense, recent history, and their constitutional design all pointed to the emergence of a federal legislature that was the center of political activity in the newly established republic. The federal judiciary, as Alexander Hamilton observed, had the authority neither to implement nor to enforce its rulings, so its power would derive almost wholly from moral credibility, and the presidency was inherently circumscribed by necessity and tradition. Congress, on the other hand, was left to address the overwhelming majority of the duties and responsibilities of governance, as Article I, Section 8 of the Constitution demonstrably substantiates.

In light of the federal legislature's political and constitutional prominence, the framers redoubled their efforts, through the separation of powers and the allocation of crucial powers to the executive, to counteract the accumulation of potentially tyrannical power within Congress. The British Parliament had aptly illustrated the danger and imprudence of permitting a single institution to enact, enforce (through cabinet ministers), and interpret (through the House of Lords) legislation, so the framers of the Constitution curbed congressional supremacy through countervailing grants of authority to the presidency, though the creation of an independent judiciary was also an indispensable measure in that regard. Making the president both head of state and head of government was one example, as was his designation as commander in chief of U.S. military forces. In addition, providing the presidency with the authority to enforce laws was a key element of an emerging American tradition of rule of law that rested, among other things, on due process and equality before the law. Finally, presidential authority over foreign policy and diplomacy greatly decreased foreign access to the American legislative process and the related collusion between foreign and selfish domestic interests. In all, the presidency, though confined and heavily circumscribed by today's standards, was, aside from its primary purposes, a bulwark against legislative tyranny.[30]

With respect to the executive branch, separation of powers was a two-way street, so its limitations of power and authority addressed not only potential legislative tyranny but also possible presidential abuses of power. Pursuantly, separation of powers meant that, aside from obvious policy responsibilities and a constitutionally designated role at the end of the lawmaking process, unlike heads of government in parliamentary systems, presidents were unable to participate actively as legislators, or super-legislators. As crucial as it was for the framers to deprive Congress of the authority to enforce its own laws, it was just as important for them to prevent the nation's chief law-enforcement officials from shaping legislation to suit executive priorities and interests. The framers did not wish to promote the intra-institutional mixture of lawmaking and enforcement authority, regardless of whether it occurred in the legislative or executive branch. In addition, separation of powers entailed the dilution of presidential authority through the existence of an independent judiciary, which deprived the executive branch of potentially coercive powers over the nation's courts. This may not reflect a relevant political vulnerability today, at least not for the world's liberal democracies, but, prior to the creation of an American republic in 1787, history had been replete with examples of executive coercion, if not outright control, of courts, judges, and the law in general.

Through the separation of powers and related constitutional obstacles to the unauthorized use of political power, the framers insured that no single individual or political party within the executive branch would become more powerful than the presidency itself. Aside from the separation of powers, the most significant of these obstacles has been the system of checks and balances. As a logical and necessary complement to the separation of powers, this system relies on the mutual oversight authority among branches to maintain political accountability and institutional legitimacy. The framers never envisioned separation of powers, which was a critical aspect of their constitutional design, as an unqualified guarantee of institutional independence, for they recognized the dangers posed by unchecked independence and political isolation. Separation of powers was, and still is, a double-edged sword whose effectiveness against tyranny could also be harnessed to promote tyranny by facilitating the kind of institutional insularity that vitiates political accountability. Therefore, its implementation depended on the concomitant provision of a system of inter-branch accountability that would prevent complete institutional independence, and the framers' intent in this regard was absolutely clear. They established a network of mutual constitutional relationships to limit institutional insularity through cross-institutional supervision and collaboration, thereby affirming that, while both separation of powers and checks and balances were necessary, neither alone was sufficient.[31]

Historically, interactions between Congress and the presidency have been the most common examples of checks and balances, so the judiciary has not been as susceptible to institutional interference and oversight as the other two, but this is exactly what the framers intended. They assumed that the greatest internal threats to the republic could arise through the abuse of executive or legislative authority, and they conceptualized checks and balances accordingly. Moreover, although they granted the president specific authority over legislative procedures to undermine potential congressional monopolies of legislative power, the framers were evidently more worried about curbing executive power and insuring that presidential authority would remain inherently limited. As such, the Constitution empowered Congress to supervise executive action in key areas, such as treaty-making, war-making, presidential appointments, the complexion and existence of executive departments, and presidential conduct as it relates to impeachable offenses.

Rule by Elites and the Electoral College

Every four years, tens of millions of Americans go to the polls to elect a president, confident that their vote, and not the perfunctory affirmation of the Electoral College, will ultimately determine the nation's presidents. As a matter of constitutional procedure, the popular vote is converted into an electoral vote, which controls election outcomes, but the electoral vote is a function of the popular will. Presidential elections come and go, but this arcane system, based on an institution with which most Americans are utterly unfamiliar, remains. The Electoral College may be a constitutional relic that serves no obvious purpose, yet it is a conspicuous reminder of a time when the popular vote did not determine presidential elections—in fact, of a time when the popular vote was altogether irrelevant. The Electoral College was the linchpin in an electoral system that valued social hierarchy and political elitism, and, according to its creators, it was a necessary precursor for effective executive governance. The founding generation of Americans depended on it to legitimize an elective presidency and stabilize a society that had emerged from more than a dozen years of political chaos. Regardless of its current function, the Electoral College played an active and indispensable part in the selection of America's chief executives during the early republic, and it addressed an essential political need.

In modern America, electors have been reduced to mere puppets, fulfilling a ceremonial function that confirms the obvious. Their "votes" reflect and follow popular mandates within the individual states, and they have no discretion or authority to depart from prefigured results. Each state's electoral vote is assigned to the candidate that wins the popular vote, so the electors' votes are redundant. In the late-eighteenth and early-nineteenth centuries, however, the electors' votes were the only ones that mattered. The Electoral College decided presidential elections, and the general public accepted those decisions. Like today, the number of electors each state appointed was equal to the sum of its senators and allotted representatives, but, unlike today, electors had full discretion and authority to choose the candidates they, not the public, preferred. So, unsurprisingly, as the newly established American republic awaited the outcome of the first presidential election in early 1789, members of the Electoral College met (in their respective states) to elect George Washington.[32] With no primaries, political parties, or formal nominees, to say nothing of a popular vote, the first presidential election was no less legitimate than its more democratic counterpart today.

Having little say in the selection of electors and, therefore, the president himself, the public was not directly involved in the first several presidential elections, which is exactly what the framers of the Constitution intended.[33] Prior to 1828, America's chief executives owed their jobs to a cloistered, if not secretive, system designed to maintain leadership by political elites and minimize democratic influence. Acting in an ex officio capacity, congressmen named candidates with little or no input from ordinary Americans and submitted official lists of nominees to the Electoral College, which actually elected the country's presidents. For a generation, the popular will, though politically relevant in other ways, was largely irrelevant during presidential elections. Backed by tradition and a deferential citizenry, America's "natural aristocracy," as Jefferson referred to the nation's elite class, continued to dominate the presidency through the 1824 election.[34]

Wishing to insure constitutional stability and political legitimacy, the framers limited the scope of popular sovereignty (the idea that the people hold power, and that the government is subjected to the will of the people) through the Electoral College and thereby hoped to blunt the impact of political ignorance and democratic excess on the political process. As contradictory as it may sound, especially for a government based on popular sovereignty, the Electoral College was established as a counterweight to democracy. The framers may have supported popular rule (according to its contemporary conception), but they made a clear distinction between popular sovereignty and democracy. Contrary to American lore and prevailing academic misconceptions, the framers never intended to extend political rights to everyone, nor did they equate popular sovereignty with sociopolitical egalitarianism. To them, popular sovereignty did not entail rule by ordinary citizens, direct public participation in politics, or a society of equals, and it certainly did not mean everyone should enjoy the privileges of citizenship. According to the founding generation of political leaders, popular sovereignty implied rule by propertied white men, which did not include unqualified white males, women, minorities, or slaves. As such, popular sovereignty involved the separation of governance from unfiltered public opinion and the existence of an intermediate mechanism or body through which such opinion could be filtered and refined.[35]

Despite the framers' intentions to preserve the Electoral College as the guardian of presidential elections and maintain political control by elites, changing political circumstances ultimately produced significant deviations. The duties and responsibilities of the presidency invariably evolved due to social, economic, and diplomatic changes, and the process by which its occupants were chosen evolved accordingly. Starting with the election of Andrew Jackson in 1828, America's presidents gradually became more representative of the public at large, not least because the public has played an increasingly significant role in American politics and the selection of the nation's chief executives.[36] These days, Americans take the right to participate, if not their actual participation, for granted, as they do their ability to shape presidential politics. General elections determine the electoral vote, and ordinary citizens, not just political elites, have become presidents, so the public is cognizant of its indispensable role in the presidential-election process. Presidents are no longer the hand-picked representatives of a natural aristocracy, as they embody the cultural diversity of a nation with 300 million people from all walks of life and all backgrounds. Indeed, most of America's modern presidents have been ordinary men whose rise would have been prevented by the very hierarchies that characterized the first generation of American politics.

POWERS OF THE OFFICE

During the last 220 years, the American presidency has evolved beyond the intentions of the men who designed it. The executive branch and the authority it possesses have far outstripped their deliberately restrained expectations, so today's presidency often appears to share little or nothing with the modest and unassuming prototype of the founding era. Wars, economic progress, and tremendous social transformations have reshaped the function and purpose of the presidency, and related constitutional reinterpretations have enlarged the scope of legitimate executive activity. Of these changes, perhaps none has been as visible or as significant as the steady expansion of presidential authority. An ostensibly necessary, if not justifiable, response to the economic and diplomatic realities of an industrialized world, the contemporary presidency is an administrative bastion equipped with numerous cabinet departments, regulatory agencies, and advisors that run one of the most formidable bureaucracies on earth. Not surprisingly, the executive branch of the U.S. government has traveled farther from its roots than the two other branches (though the legislature is not far behind), and its constitutional link to the framers' intent has been weakened as a result.

The twenty-first-century presidency may not be the institution it once was, and it may not be the institution the framers envisioned, but the founding-era original is still relevant. The presidency's founding-era history and the framers' intentions are not just historical curiosities but, despite the constitutional innovations that have transformed the executive branch, they continue to shape constitutional interpretation and political practices. In one way or another, arguments about the viability of originalism aside, framers' intent has been the key to legitimate constitutional development, so a proper understanding of the executive branch and its constitutional authority depends on the preservation of the link between historical foundations, both practical and theoretical, and current political manifestations of executive authority. Even among critics of originalism, constitutional interpretation invariably invokes framers' intent in some fashion, as only framers' intent can reveal the authors' purposes behind relevant constitutional provisions. Without public awareness of those purposes, the Constitution may become irrelevant and meaningless and constitutional interpretation wholly illegitimate and groundless.

Particularly today, awareness of constitutional purposes can illuminate ongoing debates about the legitimate scope of presidential authority. During the George W. Bush presidency, those debates centered on his administration's sweeping claims of executive authority and privilege with respect to the prosecution of the so-called War on Terror and related constitutional justifications based on framers' intent. More recently, many have questioned President Barrack Obama's expansive use and acquisition of economic powers to substantiate market interventions and implement controversial health-care measures, which have been subject to increasing constitutional scrutiny in terms of their relationship to legitimate constitutional purposes. Unfortunately, in both cases, people on all sides of the issues have relied on framers' intent and historical precedent more as political expedients for rhetorical swordplay than veritable constitutional foundations, but the significance of framers' intent and historical precedent as constitutional anchors was apparent all the same. Such episodes, however cynical, have only confirmed the importance of the intended meaning and purposes of the constitutional provisions that define the presidency.

The Vesting Clause

Since the 1960s, but particularly over the last dozen years, the most pointed controversies regarding the scope of executive authority have, in one way or another, focused on the vesting clause in Article II. It stipulates, in a somewhat general manner, that the "executive power shall be vested" in the President of the United States but lacks the specificity that characterizes the definition of congressional authority in Article I, Section 8, for instance. The constitutional allocation of authority to Congress clearly refers to individual "legislative powers [t]herein granted," whereas Article II has no similar qualifying language. As a result, the purpose, meaning and relevance of the vesting clause, though unambiguous to the framers of the Constitution, have become obscured by latter-day interpreters. Of course, most of that confusion is a function of the present generation's comparative ignorance of the framers' political ethos and their actual constitutional intentions, but the absence of immediate specificity in the text has definitely contributed to current interpretive problems.[37]

Someone with only a passing interest in the Constitution will notice that congressional authority is limited to the specific powers enumerated in, or implied by, Article I, Section 8 of the text, but, unfortunately, even experts are frequently unable to determine the powers granted to the presidency through the vesting clause in Article II. Consequently, but regrettably, advocates of the modern presidency and its unabated accumulation of power over the last several decades, have taken advantage of the seeming ambiguity in the vesting clause to rationalize an ever-increasing scope of executive authority. Presidential apologists from both political parties have argued, wrongly as it were, that the terseness of the vesting clause reflects the framers' preference for general executive authority. More to the point, they have relied on general-authority criteria to acquire wide-ranging discretionary powers within the national-security, foreign-policy, and, to a lesser though significant extent, law-enforcement arenas. Law professor and former George W. Bush Justice Department attorney John Yoo has been one of the most infamous and visible exponents of such efforts, particularly because his defense of morally questionable interrogation tactics attracted vociferous declamations, but he is only one of many Republicans and Democrats who have worked hard to create constitutional loopholes in the vesting clause where none actually exist.[38] However, despite ongoing attempts to legitimize the imperial presidency through an ahistorical and inaccurate reading of the vesting clause by exploiting the framers' rhetorical ambiguities, framers' intent in this regard is actually quite coherent and instructive. Above all, the framers of the Constitution were neither careless nor naïve, and they never would have left the interpretation of such a critical part of the document to chance. They considered a presidency with general, or open-ended, authority as anathema to stable and legitimate governance, so a Constitution that granted general authority to the president would have been a monumental blunder and a glaring ideological inconsistency. Their experiences with the British crown during the 1770s and their awareness of European history, not to mention their dedication to emerging liberal principles, precluded the outcome embraced by today's defenders of general executive authority. As already indicated, the authors of the Constitution deliberately limited the institutional authority of any single branch of government, and their rabid fear of tyranny was a primary impetus for their constitutional innovations. Thus, without a doubt, interpreting the vesting clause of Article II as an endorsement of open-ended presidential authority is untenable. Simply put, the history of the founding era does not support assertions of general presidential authority.[39]

Admittedly, Article II itself provides few clues to the intent of the vesting clause, but, on the other hand, contemporary political literature certainly does, and it exposes assumptions about natural limits on executive power that cannot be reconciled with theories of general authority. From today's perspective, not least in light of current debates about the scope of presidential authority, the framers could be faulted for not articulating those assumptions in supporting constitutional documents or defining the "executive power" explicitly in Article II. Nevertheless, they were convinced that presidential authority was inherently limited regardless of the lack of constitutional specificity in the vesting clause, and, given the prevailing political mindset and contemporary conceptions of political authority, no one would have viewed the vesting clause as a grant of general executive authority. The founding generation could not have imagined a time, such as the twentieth and twenty-first centuries, when executive authority would be construed as anything but inherently limited or legitimate governance would not be equated with natural limits on the exercise of political power, so elaboration of the vesting clause appeared unnecessary. In the end, blaming the framers of the Constitution for omitting explanations of the obvious seems silly at best. For better or worse, they believed the vesting clause required no qualifications or restrictions and was, thus, legally sufficient.

Still, despite the ostensible plain-meaning of the vesting clause, the second and third sections of Article II identify certain presidential powers, which, like the Bill of Rights, produced a legal redundancy. The framers' underlying assumptions about executive authority made such identification unnecessary and, unfortunately, may have compromised both rhetorical and theoretical consistency, which has only exacerbated recent misinterpretation and doctrinal confusion. More than anything else, this inconsistency eventually invited misuse of the vesting clause and the corresponding expansion of executive powers based on theories of general authority. Unable or unwilling to anticipate the potential consequences of this constitutional redundancy, the framers acknowledged key aspects of the presidency, such as the powers identified in later sections, in order to address specific anxieties and necessities among founding-era Americans. For various reasons related to contemporary political circumstances and recent constitutional history under the imperial regime, some provisions seemed too important to exclude, even if the Constitution would have been legally sufficient without them.

The enumerated powers in Article II reflect the president's pivotal duties and responsibilities, at least as the founding generation envisioned them. Ultimately, the inclusion of enumerated powers alongside the implied powers of the vesting clause, many of which overlap, may undermine the theoretical efficiency and conceptual simplicity the framers endeavored to achieve in the Constitution, but, in another sense, it can only help. The framers prioritized certain aspects of the presidency above others, and they revealed their intentions through this textual redundancy, which, if anything, confirms their allegiance to limited executive authority. Not surprisingly, the powers identified in the latter sections of Article II epitomize a presidency confined largely to its national-security authority, which shows that the framers conceptualized the president mostly as head of state and commander in chief. Aside from the authority to enforce federal laws and make executive and judicial appointments subject to congressional approval, Article II of the Constitution focuses on foreign policy and national defense.

War Powers and Diplomatic Authority

Unlike today, the presidency was not a coveted political prize for founding-era public servants, not least because the head of state and commander in chief of the early American republic had very few responsibilities—and it seems safe to assume that is how the framers hoped things would remain. In an age that delegitimized professional politics and political ambition, public servants, who represented the country's social elites, had little incentive to pursue a position whose risks and uncertainties outweighed its meager status and benefits. The presidency was, at best, a humble institution, especially compared to its counterparts throughout the Western world, with narrow authority, scarce resources, and, until the political reforms of the 1820s and 1830s, restricted access. Without a doubt, governors in politically prominent states, such as New York, Massachusetts, and Virginia, had more power and prestige than the nation's presidents, and the states' resources and support staffs dwarfed the minimal capabilities of the federal executive branch. In the international arena, foreign diplomats and heads of state, though frequently impressed by the men who occupied the office, had little respect or admiration for the early American presidency itself. Adding insult to injury, most foreign observers expected this relatively unsophisticated republic in the North American wilderness to fail within a generation.[40]

The framers did not court such unflattering, if not disparaging, views of the American presidency, but its low prestige was partly a function of its design. They certainly did not intend to invite criticism or skepticism of the American presidency, but they definitely intended to make it as modest and unobtrusive as it was often perceived. Other factors, too, contributed to the ongoing restriction of executive authority in the early republic, the most prominent of which was a traditional aversion to standing armies and, by extension, the development of permanent continental military capabilities. Despite the obvious significance of the president's role as commander in chief and the fact that national-defense authority seems indispensable, for most of the nation's history both that role and its authority have been inherently restricted by Americans' unwillingness to tolerate the presence of professional armed forces at home or abroad. Opposed to professional armies since at least the late seventeenth century, but especially as a result of British deployments after 1763, Americans remained dedicated to founding-era attitudes regarding the size and utilization of federal forces, which endured almost without interruption until the second third of the twentieth century.[41]

As a result of a minimal national-security footprint, and also limited resources and responsibilities in other areas, the early executive branch was considerably smaller than the norm, to say nothing of what it has become in the last century. In addition to the President and Vice President, it included the Departments of War, State, and Treasury, several military regiments, and a few executive support personnel. The reduced military presence was particularly striking, even in an age when armed forces were much smaller than they are today. Whereas most armed forces in the West numbered in the tens of thousands, the early U.S. military was confined to no more than a few thousand.[42] The size of the Continental Army and Navy had grown substantially during the revolution, but it decreased drastically during the 1780s, leaving the defense of the continent to state militias, which is a pattern that would repeat itself until World War I. For most of the first 150 years, wartime increases in military strength were followed by peacetime reductions to the status-quo ante. However, even during wartime, particularly prior to World War I, state militias (now called national guards) constituted the bulk of America's national-defense capabilities, with the federal military responsible for strategic planning, integration of forces, and battlefield command. Obviously, federal troops had sole jurisdiction over federal lands, such as the District of Columbia and western territories, but national defense, in peacetime or otherwise, would have been impossible without state militias.

Small standing armies also made sense for Americans because, unlike today, the federal budget was meager, as was the federal government's ability to raise revenue. That fact in itself inherently reduced available and potential military resources, so the early republic could not have afforded a substantial peacetime deployment even if political support had existed. In the final analysis, Americans were averse not only to standing armies but also to public spending in general, especially federal spending, which conspired to suppress federal military expansion for a long time.[43] Needless to say, Americans' reliance on state militias did not diminish during this period, as their faith in these all-volunteer amateur armies held strong. Reassured by the deployment of civilian forces on an ad hoc basis, and increasingly devoted to popular sovereignty and political democratization, Americans considered militia service patriotic, honorable, and expedient. Militia members were laymen who accepted temporary service as required by their communities, and, coming from the very farms, villages, and towns they were protecting, these amateur soldiers were perceived as trustworthy and reliable by their fellow residents. Most importantly, because citizen-soldiers were not professional military men, dedication to their trades and ties to local communities would ensure a return to civilian life and thereby minimize the possibility of the abuse of power.[44]

Founding-era Americans were also strong advocates of neutrality, which, like the aversion to standing armies, became an almost permanent feature of national political culture, at least until the Cold War. Opposed to any type of international adventurism or foreign entanglements, Americans believed that, even if the political will for interventionism were to arise, the nation's restricted military capacities would ultimately undermine both the incentive and possibility for such action. The framers of the Constitution were particularly adamant about avoiding the foreign-policy mistakes that continually embroiled major European powers in geopolitical quagmires, and they hoped to prevent the country's presidents from encouraging, promoting, or participating in international situations that could destabilize the republic.[45] As anachronistic as such sentiments may be these days, the founding generation was profoundly skeptical of international alliances and strongly isolationist, with a marked distaste for global geopolitics in general. With recent memories of British imperial politics and diplomatic brinkmanship among leading European powers, Americans embraced neutrality as a national priority. Convinced that international commitments would only drain vital domestic resources and eventually cause internal problems, they expected their presidents to promote both neutrality and global isolationism, which is why the Constitution allocated checks-and-balances authority to the Senate over treaties and appointments through its advise-and-consent powers and to both chambers of Congress through the power to declare war and make required appropriations.

Law-Enforcement Authority

Article II, Section 3 of the Constitution instructs the president to "take care that the laws [of the United States] be faithfully executed," but the provision is buried deep within a list of ancillary powers identified by the framers. In fact, at the risk of overstating the point, the text and its supporting documents depict the president's law-enforcement authority almost as an afterthought, bereft of the constitutional and practical significance present-day Americans associate with it. Yet, the relative insignificance of the president's role as chief law-enforcement officer accurately reflects the framers' intentions and expectations. To an extent, they wanted to deprive the presidency of anything remotely resembling the by-then lapsed prerogative powers and privileges of the British crown, since, as previously indicated, the prevention of executive tyranny was a priority. As such, the textual construction clearly implies that law-enforcement authority would be neither extensive nor primary. Nevertheless, the relative insignificance of law-enforcement authority was more a function of historical realities and federal governance than anything else, even the admittedly pervasive fear of tyranny.

Over the last century, the executive branch has acquired extensive law-enforcement capabilities, and agencies like the Federal Bureau of Investigation, Drug Enforcement Administration, U.S. Secret Service, and a host of others dominate national law-enforcement efforts. Such an expansive presence reflects both the ever-growing demand for federal law-enforcement throughout the United States and the unprecedentedly wide-ranging scope of federal law-enforcement duties and responsibilities. However, that simply was not the case in the eighteenth and the first two-thirds of the nineteenth century on either front. First of all, the demand did not exist because policing, criminal law, and law enforcement were only emerging as veritable concerns, and, from a national perspective, comparatively few federal laws required actual enforcement resources.[46] Unlike today, the federal government was not a center of national political activity, and the overwhelming bulk of the nation's political business transpired at the state and local levels. Second, for political reasons already discussed and also due to contemporary socioeconomic realities, the federal government's duties and responsibilities were inherently limited, so the presidency's law-enforcement capabilities and resources were minimal.

As to the first point, much of the modern presidency's law-enforcement effort concentrates on federal crimes and misdemeanors, but criminal law was fundamentally different during the first several generations of the republic. At the end of the eighteenth century, local policing and law enforcement was in its infancy, and most communities were only beginning to address specific criminal law-enforcement needs, insofar as those needs were recognizable or relevant. Criminal law itself, i.e., the set of doctrines, statutes, and ordinances regulating the actions of individuals against society, was emerging slowly and fitfully, responding rather haphazardly and incoherently at times to quickly changing socioeconomic circumstance.[47] By the end of the nineteenth century, formalized but locally organized systems of community- and state-based criminal law enforcement, which included policing and incarceration, appeared across the continent, supplemented by federal law enforcement in western territories. Nonetheless, aside from minimal responsibilities and resources in federal territories, federal law enforcement efforts paled in comparison to those at the local level.[48] State-based law enforcement, whether criminal or otherwise, was the norm in the United States for at least the first one hundred years of its existence.

The framers did not envision the expansion of federal law-enforcement capacities beyond rudimentary levels, because they could not imagine a juncture at which law enforcement would become a principal objective of the federal government. Moreover, in the early republic, the evolution of American criminal and civil law was mostly a state-based phenomenon with little federal coordination or guidance, aside from a small group of doctrinal developments within federal common law during the latter part of the nineteenth century. Consequently, the allocation of anything more than minimal resources to federal law enforcement would have been unwarranted and wasteful. Indeed, the workhorse of modern federal law-enforcement activity, the Department of Justice, was absent from the executive branch until 1870, leaving the Attorney General, initially provided with only a clerk and a small staff, to cover federal law-enforcement responsibilities. Congress supplemented the Attorney General's office with roughly a dozen federal marshals, whose number rose as a result of steady territorial expansions westward, but their duties were often confined to the facilitation of court proceedings and enforcement of judicial rulings. Contrary to popular lore, as captured in typical epics about Wyatt Earp, Bat Masterson, and the like, the marshals service was poorly trained, understaffed, frequently mismanaged, resolutely unglamorous, and largely without the authority possessed by country sheriffs or even for-hire private law-enforcement organizations.[49]

Aside from supervision of federal territories and enforcement of judicial rulings, the most important federal law-enforcement responsibility was the prevention and prosecution of treasonous acts. Despite the prominence of certain high-profile treason cases during the last seventy years or so, especially those dealing with espionage and the revelation of national-security secrets, treason no longer poses a substantial threat to the stability or survival of the republic—for obvious reasons. However, at the end of the eighteenth century, contemporary geopolitical circumstances and the history of the West both confirmed the potential for treasonous activities sufficiently extensive to destabilize, if not topple, even the oldest regimes. The newly established American republic seemed particularly susceptible, at least according to contemporaries, to plots against the government, not least due to the federal government's limited physical resources and capabilities and the relative instability and turmoil of the two decades prior to 1787. It may be redolent of paranoia to twenty-first century ears, but the framers perceived treason as a real and, perhaps, imminent problem that necessitated corresponding vigilance within the presidency.[50] Still, as the prosecution of arguably the two most famous convicted traitors in U.S. history, Julius and Ethel Rosenberg, cogently illustrated in the early 1950s, this is a significant aspect of the executive branch's law-enforcement authority.[51]

In addition to the power to interdict and prosecute treasonous activity, albeit almost entirely unrelated, the president's pardon power was a crucial, though controversial, part of his executive authority, and still is today. Because the crown had abused its pardon privileges to protect royalist stalwarts and other political allies, many Americans were worried that any sort of presidential pardon authority, especially the power to grant general pardons, could become a naked political expedient and, thus, an instrument of executive corruption. In addition, because crimes in Great Britain were violations against the monarch, as a matter of law and constitutional principle, pardon privileges were an inherent and natural part of royal authority. However, according to American law and the very logic of republican governance, crimes were violations against the people, which apparently militated against a presidential pardon power and for congressional authority over pardons. Be that as it may, even opponents of presidential authority over pardons acknowledged the political risks and procedural inefficiencies associated with granting such authority to the legislature. Furthermore, as Alexander Hamilton forcefully argued, especially in *Federalist* 74, whose main focus was pardons for treasonous acts, the pardon power would be a necessary and uniquely effective tool for political reconciliation and even the de-escalation of insurrections and rebellions.[52] Hamilton's claims were more than aptly substantiated by events before, during, and after the Civil War.

Sadly, over the years, the pardon power has become what many of its original detractors had feared. It has occasionally been used as the framers had intended, as exemplified by President Gerald Ford's pardon of Richard Nixon to facilitate national reconciliation following the Watergate scandal or Jimmy Carter's amnesty for Vietnam-era draft evaders. Nonetheless, the pardon power has become a political tool with which outgoing presidential administrations either reward key individuals and their political supporters for personal loyalty, financial contributions, and simple partisanship or indemnify themselves from potentially damaging legal and political scrutiny regarding specific presidential acts. Eleventh-hour pardons have become a standard of sorts, with presidents, aware that accountability and even popularity are largely irrelevant concerns during the dying hours of an outgoing administration, hurriedly issuing dozens of reprieves, commutations, and other orders for executive clemency immediately prior to leaving office. President Bill Clinton's pardon of fugitive financier Marc Rich may have been one of the more visible instances of political remuneration through executive clemency, but Clinton was no different in this regard from either his recent predecessors or his successors.[53]

While the president may be the chief law enforcement officer of the federal government, presidents are not themselves immune from or above the law. As such, the framers provided for the removal of the chief executive if such a circumstance should arise; the ultimate constitutional sanction against abuse by the president is impeachment and removal from office. The Constitution defines impeachment at the federal level and limits impeachment to "The President, Vice President, and all civil officers of the United States" who may only be impeached and removed for "treason, bribery, or other high crimes and misdemeanors." While the constitutional provision of "high crimes and misdemeanors" does not have a specific definition, a common law tradition exists that suggests that any personal misconduct is an impeachable offense. Others have suggested that Congress alone may decide for itself what constitutes an impeachable offense. Only two presidents to date have been impeached—Andrew Johnson in 1868 and Bill Clinton in 1998—but both were acquitted by the Senate and remained in office.[54] Whether or not a president can be impeached for strictly political reasons, as opposed to criminal actions that are indictable, is a constitutional issue that has yet to be resolved.

Legislative Authority

The framers strictly limited the president's constitutional roles as head of government, which are confined to the approval or rejection of congressional legislation, the assessment and presentation of relevant policy issues through the State of the Union message, the recommendation of potential legislation, and, in certain circumstances, the adjournment of Congress. Compared to the legislative authority of contemporary British prime ministers, the president's authority was modest at best. The framers of the Constitution did not grant American presidents an active role in anything but the final stage of the legislative process, and they did not envision the power to approve or reject legislation as a grant of legislative authority but a check on Congressional authority itself and a constitutional filter that would promote the legitimacy of prospective federal laws.[55]

Without a doubt, the framers did not want an American prime minister, and they expected the president to devote most of his attention to national security, diplomacy, rudimentary economic coordination, and law enforcement. Yet, Article II, Section 3 of the Constitution suggests that the president is also a policymaker, if not the policymaker in chief. His responsibility to keep Congress apprised of administration objectives and to evaluate the nation's political course through the State of the Union message and his authority to present necessary legislation to Congress reveal his inherent role as policymaker. This means that, although the framers certainly did not intend to create an American prime minister, they did anticipate more than passive presidential involvement in the legislative process through, if nothing else, the formulation and coordination of relevant domestic policies and the enactment of laws that do not conflict with those policies. From a modern perspective, and the framers never would have articulated it in this way, they expected the president to have a policy agenda that would provide a political rationale and derivative strategies for prospective legislation.[56]

The framers' apparent expectations regarding presidential policymaking notwithstanding, they lived in a political world that was markedly different from anything today. Therefore, it is imperative to place those expectations in the proper context and remember that the framers of the Constitution envisioned policymaking, and the president's role in it, as something much simpler, considerably less politicized, and substantially more insular than it eventually became. In today's media-driven political environment, the president, his vast support staff, interest groups, and even the public are all active players in the policymaking and legislative processes. The president himself, especially someone as proactive, for instance, as Lyndon Johnson, Bill Clinton, or George W. Bush, has become not only a policymaker in chief but also the legislator in chief, which is definitely not what the framers intended. The Bush administration became known for shepherding targeted legislation through Congress much like a prime-ministerial cabinet and even ignoring established legislative protocols whose purpose was to minimize presidential interference in the legislative process. Though Bill Clinton and, especially, Lyndon Johnson seemed less imperious and dismissive of entrenched traditions, they were no less forceful, but their innate political skill, which Bush lacked, enabled them to persuade opponents and overcome political obstacles with unique efficacy.[57]

In the late eighteenth century, on the other hand, the politicization of the legislative and policymaking processes of the kind that characterizes modern governance would have been unthinkable to all but the most corrupt individuals. Indeed, the American republic was born into a world that delegitimized political parties and rejected professional politics, and the framers no doubt anticipated that presidents would always be part of a largely non-partisan elitist minority that preserved lawmaking and policymaking as collaborative and deliberative, not competitive and polemical, processes. Despite the fact that some scholars have referred to the Federalists and Jeffersonian Republicans of the early republic as the first political parties, they were really nothing of the sort, lacking the organization, professionalization, funding, and long-term ideological identification that define political parties.[58] So, the president's role as policymaker, or chief policymaker, was more that of a moderator in a closed debate among intellectual elites than a political competitor advocating his own, or his party's, political priorities.

Appointment and Removal Power

Ask most Americans, or even scholars, to identify the most important aspect of presidential authority, and they will rarely name his appointment and removal powers. A majority will probably point to his role as commander in chief, while some will emphasize his law-enforcement duties, and still others will look to his policymaking and legislative responsibilities, but only a few will consider anything beyond the customary responses. Yet, for over 175 years, the president's power to appoint judges, executive officials, and military officers has been one of his most potent tools for shaping the long-term political landscape in the United States. Through their appointment and removal powers, presidents have been able to influence both contemporary policies and future political developments, thereby securing legacies that have occasionally far outstripped any accomplishments from their actual tenures in office. Despite the numerous constitutional, political, and sociocultural changes that separate twenty-first-century America from the founding-era republic and the many related disparities between the framers' intent and current practices, this has been one of the few constants throughout much of American history.

The framers were acutely aware of the significance associated with the constitutional power to appoint judges and subordinate executive officials, such as department heads.[59] Even before the advent of the spoils system, or political patronage, during the Jacksonian era and its proliferation thereafter, Americans recognized the political and constitutional impact of such authority, which is why this topic caused ongoing debates among the delegates to the Constitutional Convention in 1787.[60] Historically, the appointment power had resided with the crown, but, as Parliamentary authority increased during the eighteenth century, most of it was appropriated by the legislature. To the dismay of colonial Americans, Parliament used its authority to appoint ministers, judges, and various administrative officials as nothing more than an overtly political instrument to build partisan coalitions and defeat opposing policies, largely ignoring the long-term political manifestations or constitutional consequences of its decisions.[61] In British North America, interestingly enough, colonial legislatures pressured and manipulated their governors and upper legislative chambers into concessions that suited colonial ambitions and political objectives, so colonial practices in this regard ultimately differed little from those in the mother country, despite the apparent hypocrisy of such a situation.[62]

Political experimentation at the state level following independence only confirmed that the appointment power was no safer in the hands of potentially demagogic legislatures catering to base interests than it had been with the erstwhile imperial executive. So, by 1787, the centralizing faction of American political elites, who pushed for a relatively strong national government, was committed to returning all appointment powers to the executive. A substantial contingent of Southerners, supported by some small-state delegates, remained skeptical of plenary executive authority in this area and pushed for congressional control of appointments and even a few more radical, democratically oriented options. The eventual compromise, which emerged in the final days of the Convention, produced the by-now familiar power-sharing scenario whereby the president retained the proposed appointment authority with senatorial advice-and-consent powers as part of the upper legislative chamber's checks-and-balances authority. This was not a perfect solution, but even the Anti-Federalists, who had been traditional opponents of centralization and an active presidency, realized that it was far more efficient than placing such a politically charged task in the hands of several dozen legislators.[63]

The removal power was another matter. Obviously, Congress had the power to impeach and remove corrupt judges and other public officials, including the president, but what about the rest? Federal judges would serve based on good behavior, so their removal by the president, or others, for non-impeachable factors such as policy differences or ideological incompatibilities was a non-issue. However, that still left a sizable number of executive appointees who would ostensibly serve at the pleasure of the party or parties to whom they were ultimately accountable. Who would have the authority to dismiss them? These days, Americans take it for granted that the president has the authority to remove most executive appointees, some regulatory personnel excepted, with or without cause, since this seems to be an intrinsic and logical extension of his authority to appoint them. Founding-era Americans were not so sure. Many delegates to the Constitutional Convention believed that congressional advice-and-consent powers implied corresponding privileges to participate in the dismissal of presidential appointees. Others argued that, in order to avoid the politicization of the policymaking process and, thus, deny the president any incentives to silence criticism and compel compliance through dismissal, the legislature or a special commission of sorts should have complete authority over removals.[64]

In the end, separation-of-powers criteria trumped worries about the politicization of presidential appointments, and founding-era critics of presidential appointment-authority realized that moving the power to dismiss executive personnel outside the executive branch would violate the separation-of-powers doctrine. Nevertheless, because presidential authority to dismiss, not to reappoint, or otherwise remove executive officials is not explicitly granted in Article II, states' rights advocates and other opponents of implied presidential powers continued to question the president's ability to do so for quite some time. The issue was finally settled by the 1926 Supreme Court case *Myers v. United States*, in which the justices interpreted the power to dismiss executive personnel as a logical element of presidential appointment-authority and a necessary part of his constitutional duty to execute the laws of the United States. As clarified by the high court in subsequent rulings, that power is not absolute, however, and does not categorically extend to certain regulatory appointments, whose dismissal standards are neither as lenient nor as deferential to presidential authority.[65]

Unfortunately for the framers, as was the case with presidential pardon-authority, the appointment and removal powers have become quite politicized, and many of the founding generation's fears regarding the use of such powers for the promotion of partisan priorities were, as it turned out, eminently justifiable. But, despite the ongoing use of presidential appointments to reward partisan loyalty and encourage political compliance, comprehensive bureaucratic reforms during the first third of the twentieth century enhanced, if not secured, the long-term legitimacy of the process. The high-water mark of political patronage through executive appointments, and the consequent corruption it fostered, came during the middle and late decades of the nineteenth century, as incoming administrations almost summarily replaced outgoing administrations' appointees with their own loyalists, even in the most minor and insignificant posts. Professional incompetence and lack of experience should have been obstacles to appointment, especially for key positions, but the spoils system ushered in by the Jackson and Van Buren administrations of the 1830s set a dangerous precedent that elevated party loyalty above professionalism and competence.[66] By the last quarter of the nineteenth century, repeated malfeasance, inefficiency, and inequity finally motivated Congress to act, and, over the following several decades, it spearheaded a series of civil-service reforms that enshrined merit as the key criterion for bureaucratic appointments and promotions.[67] The process is far from ideal today, but it is far more transparent, equitable, and legitimate than it was in the heyday of political patronage during the second half of the nineteenth century.

Executive Privilege and Immunity

As the Constitution does not explicitly refer to executive privilege or immunity in Article II or elsewhere, their constitutional and legal viability has been questionable, as has their scope. Therefore, constitutional interpretation of executive privilege (the right of the president to withhold documents from Congress or the courts) has been problematic for generations, a situation that has been exacerbated by the paucity of founding-era documents regarding the topic.[68] The fact that neither the Constitution nor its supporting material contains much information about executive privilege only confirms the intended modesty of the office, not least since contemporary documents suggest that the duties and responsibilities of the presidency would be sufficiently confined to obviate habitual reliance on executive privilege. In addition, as discussed earlier in the chapter, the framers expected America's presidents to remain part of a relatively narrow stratum of sociopolitical elites who rejected professional politics and organized partisanship, which supposedly would have minimized the presidency's exposure to the political liabilities that immunity and discretion are necessary to prevent.

As incredible as it may be to twenty-first century readers, the framers simply could not foresee the politicization of governance that has occurred in the United States, nor could they envision a time when the president's duties and responsibilities would be so extensive and even so imperial that executive privilege would be more than an isolated concern. However, Article I, Section 6 of the Constitution does identify specific immunities granted to members of Congress to protect them in the fulfillment of their legislative duties, so the omission of similar provisions in Article II could not have been mere oversight or coincidence. To critics of the modern presidency, this has been further proof of the comparative insignificance of executive privilege for the framers, whereas, to its advocates, it has been evidence of the framers' presumption of privilege, executive included. As it turns out, both camps are correct, but the interpretive dilemmas and debates regarding executive privilege have continued unabated. Over the years, especially since the 1970s, the Supreme Court has offered some guidance through rulings that have conditionally denied the existence of both absolute immunity and categorical discretion.[69] Most notably, the Supreme Court ruled in *U.S. v. Nixon* (1974) that executive privilege does exist, but that no one, not even the President of the United States, is completely above the law and the president cannot use executive privilege as an excuse to withhold evidence that is "demonstrably relevant in a criminal trial." The Supreme Court has also recognized broad presidential immunity against civil suits involving claims stemming from their official actions, in *Nixon v. Fitzgerald* (1982). But in *Clinton v. Jones* (1997), the Supreme Court held that presidential immunity does not extend to suits involving the president's private conduct, and allowed the sexual harassment lawsuit brought against Clinton by former Arkansas state employee Paula Jones to go forward prior to the end of Clinton's term.

EXPANSION OF PRESIDENTIAL POWERS

History has shown an expansion of presidential powers beyond what the framers originally intended for both the president as an individual political actor and the presidency as a political institution. The powers of the presidency have been expanded tremendously by certain presidents while in office, which usually coincided with times of crisis. Several presidents shaped the office in which they served by adopting broad interpretations of their responsibilities, and many expansions of power have occurred when presidents claimed "the silences of the Constitution." However, presidents themselves have viewed their own powers in office very differently, depending on the state of the economy and world affairs. Presidential personalities can also determine much about how presidential power is exercised. For example, Franklin Roosevelt was faced with a severe economic crisis when he first took office, and as a result, exercised many presidential powers. His legacy, and the constitutionality of many of his actions, is still being debated. Yet, FDR's years in the White House reflect an undeniable transformation of presidential powers, and he is one of several presidents who changed the nature of the office forever.

Theories of Presidential Power

The first several men to hold the office of the presidency set important early precedents regarding presidential powers. Many historians argue that one of the motivating factors for the framers in how they designed the office of the president at the Constitutional Convention was due to the widely shared view among them that George Washington would serve as the nation's first chief executive. As such, the framers placed much trust in Washington to shape the office for future occupants. Indeed, Washington did set an important, albeit informal, precedent of only serving two terms. He also expanded the powers of the office by setting the precedent that department heads should support the president's policies, going beyond the Constitution's suggestion to receive written opinions on policy matters. Washington also set a precedent for presidents, not Congress, to determine which foreign ambassadors to receive or which foreign countries would be granted diplomatic recognition. Similarly, Thomas Jefferson played an important role in the early development of presidential powers. Jefferson often responded to political, rather than legal, considerations, such as the Louisiana Purchase in 1803, considered controversial at the time since the Constitution did not grant specific powers to the president to acquire new territory. Jefferson was also the first president to govern through leadership of what would be considered an early iteration of a political party, and dominated the affairs of Congress through the Democratic-Republican caucus. Jefferson never had to veto legislation, because no bill he seriously opposed ever reached his desk for consideration.

Since that time, the actions of subsequent presidents have led to the development of numerous theories in an attempt to explain the constitutional role of presidential power within the American governing process. Notable among those include the prerogative, the stewardship, and the literalist theories. The prerogative theory of the presidency is most often attributed to Abraham Lincoln, who stretched the emergency powers of the office more than any other president due to the Civil War. Lincoln unilaterally authorized a number of decisions, and then called Congress back into session to make them legitimate: He called up the militia and volunteers, blockaded southern ports, expanded the army and navy beyond statute limitations, closed the mails to treasonous correspondence, arrested persons suspected of disloyalty, and suspended the writ of habeas corpus. Lincoln justified his actions as both commander in chief and through the "vesting" and "take care" clauses of the Constitution (that the laws be faithfully executed):

> I have never understood that the presidency conferred upon me an unrestricted right to act. . . . I did understand, however, that my oath to preserve the Constitution to the best of my ability imposed upon me the duty of preserving, by every indispensable means, that government—that nation, of which the Constitution was the organic law. . . . I felt that measures otherwise unconstitutional might become lawful by becoming indispensable to the preservation of the Constitution through the preservation of the nation.[70]

Theodore Roosevelt argued for the stewardship doctrine, which supports expanding the role and powers of the president, as long as it is done in the interest of the public and is not unconstitutional. At the turn of the twentieth century, Roosevelt ushered in the era of the rhetorical president, and as such, believed that he was the steward of the people. Accordingly, he effectively used the bully pulpit to link the president with the people. Similarly to Lincoln, he found broad powers within the vesting and take-care clauses, and saw the president as an agent of social and economic reform. He called his domestic program the "Square Deal," which focused on three main issues: conservation of natural resources, control of corporations, and consumer protection. Roosevelt also greatly enhanced the role of the president as a statesman in the international arena. During his presidency, he initiated the building of the Panama Canal, expanded the size and scope of the U.S. Navy, and intervened militarily in several nations (most notably in Latin America). The latter, which began to move the United States away from its traditional isolationist posture, is known as "Roosevelt's Corollary" to the Monroe Doctrine. The Monroe Doctrine, first introduced in 1823 by President James Monroe, stated that the United States would view further efforts by European countries to colonize land in the Americas as an act of aggression. Roosevelt expanded that view to justify U.S. power to act as an international police force and proclaimed the Americas independent of European control. In 1913, Roosevelt wrote in his autobiography: "I declined to adopt the view that what was imperatively necessary for the nation could not be done by the President unless he could find some specific authorization for it. My belief was that it was not only his right but his duty to do anything that the needs of the nation demanded unless such action was forbidden by the Constitution or by the laws."[71]

William Howard Taft, Roosevelt's immediate successor, argued for the opposite in terms of presidential power. A supporter of a literalist approach to the presidency, also known as the Whig theory, Taft believed that the president should only have those powers as specifically outlined in the Constitution: "The true view of the Executive functions is, as I conceive it, that the President can exercise no power which cannot be fairly and reasonably traced to some specific grant of power or justly implied and included within such express grant as proper and necessary to its exercise. Such specific grant must be either in the Federal Constitution or in an act of Congress passed in pursuance thereof. There is no undefined residuum of power which he can exercise because it seems to be in the public interest."[72] Taft's view of the presidency and its powers, more in line with James Madison's strict interpretation of the powers of the office, left him in a weaker position vis-à-vis Congress and his attempts to continue Roosevelt's policy agenda. Taft's deference to Congress, his move away from the public connection that Roosevelt had developed, and his perceived ineffective leadership due to his inability to wield the available powers of the presidency as Roosevelt had, contributed to Taft's failure to win reelection in 1912.[73] Of course, Roosevelt's entrance in that year's presidential election as a third-party candidate, challenging his former friend and political ally, also helped to open the door to Woodrow Wilson's election.

Wilson, a political scientist and former president of Princeton University, held views of presidential power similar to those of Roosevelt; both were more closely aligned with Alexander Hamilton's view of a strong, energetic presidency. Wilson sought to exercise fully the powers of the office, and while Roosevelt had sought to link the presidency directly to the people by removing the influence of political parties, Wilson instead wanted to make the president a strong party leader. While acknowledging that the president is "uniquely positioned to lead public opinion and his party," Wilson believed that "a talented and energetic executive would encourage thoughtful debates and institutions that protect the nation from an unhealthy aggrandizement of executive power."[74]

The Constitutionality of Expanded Presidential Powers

Between 1860 and 1920, the executive branch experienced significant changes, which were ultimately at odds with the framers' conception of it. Presidents Lincoln, Roosevelt, and Wilson led the charge toward a more modern presidency capable of accommodating greater authority and expanded resources. Nevertheless, despite some potentially dangerous precedents that affected the future evolution of the presidency, these changes did not yet represent an irreversible breach of constitutional principles or the framers' vision of republican government. During the late 1940s and into the early 1950s, such a breach started to appear so that, by the 1970s, the American presidency had transcended many of the boundaries of legitimate authority defined by the men who authored the Constitution. In particular, the presidencies of Lyndon Johnson and Richard Nixon have been labeled as "imperial" presidencies, due mostly to the actions of each regarding the use of military force in Vietnam (and in Nixon's case surrounding Southeast Asian countries as well) in an attempt to stop the spread of communism. According to presidential historian Arthur Schlesinger, Jr. in his classic work *The Imperial Presidency*, the use of presidential powers was out of control and had exceeded its constitutional limits during the Johnson and Nixon years.[75]

How did the system of checks and balances fail so miserably to prevent, or at least to overturn, these constitutional transgressions? Why have the American people tolerated the aggressive acquisition of power by America's commanders in chief and the abdication of congressional responsibility and oversight with respect to national defense? These questions have no easy answers. They arise from the same dilemma that resulted in questionable constitutional increases of congressional authority over social and economic issues during the last seventy years. Just as Congress acquired powers that went beyond any of those granted to it by the framers to confront the social and economic crises unleashed by industrialization (particularly FDR's actions during the Great Depression of the 1930s), the presidency amassed sufficient authority to address the military and diplomatic crises unleashed by the Cold War. In both cases, exigent circumstances required action and not political debate about constitutional amendments, so Americans and their political officials turned a blind eye to what they perceived as the necessary costs of political compromise. The most serious of these costs was what some would argue to be an unconstitutional expansion of governmental authority that equipped federal officials with powers that would have been unthinkable just a century before.

As convincing as such an explanation may be, it only tells half of the story. Because the framers of the Constitution were aware of the public's susceptibility to lapses of judgment and they worried that even majority decisions could be illegitimate, they took precautions against exactly these kinds of situations. They made sure that, even in the unlikely event that all of the regular constitutional checks and balances did not work properly, a remedy of last resort would compensate for their mistakes. That remedy was the federal judiciary, specifically the Supreme Court of the United States. As the institution charged with the interpretation of federal laws and actions that impacted the Constitution and determining the meaning of pertinent constitutional principles, the Supreme Court was established to address constitutional violations and maintain the integrity of the nation's foundational laws. Although some doubts existed during the early republic about the finality of the Court's broader theories, the founding generation had no doubts about the Court's ability to decide the constitutionality of particular acts or the finality of its opinions regarding specific cases.

Domestic Issues

In general, the Supreme Court has been willing to allow expansion of executive power over constitutional objections. Two cases, however, show the Court's willingness to define the issue of inherent powers when dealing with domestic issues. In *Youngstown Sheet & Tube Company v. Sawyer* (1952), the Court struck down Harry Truman's seizure of the nation's steel mills, rejecting Truman's argument for inherent executive power stemming from the situation of the domestic economy and the Korean War effort. The Court recognized an inherent executive power transcending particular enumerations in Article II but nevertheless found Truman's action to be impermissible since Congress had already considered and rejected legislation permitting such an executive order. This case was a reminder that the stewardship theory is neither entirely self-derived nor without limitation, and that the president's actions within the domestic sphere are subject to judicial scrutiny. Similarly, in *New York Times Company v. United States* (1971), the Court declared no threat to national security due to the publication of the Pentagon Papers. Richard Nixon had sent his Attorney General John Mitchell into federal district court to seek an injunction against the *New York Times* for its series of stories on the Pentagon Papers, a leaked classified document detailing the history of U.S. involvement in Vietnam. The ruling was a victory for advocates of freedom of the press, and a rebuke to Nixon over his claim of national security.

Foreign Policy

As political scientist Aaron Wildavsky famously argued, there are "two presidencies"—one dealing with domestic policy, and the other dealing with foreign policy. Wildavsky's "Dual Presidency Theory," which he articulated to explain the presidency during the first two decades of the Cold War, suggests that presidents prefer to focus on foreign over domestic policy because they have more constitutional and statutory authority and can act more quickly and decisively without much congressional interference. While the theory is not as accurate today, as Congress has become more involved in the development of foreign policy, Wildavsky's observation is nonetheless instructive when considering the expansion of presidential powers in the foreign policy arena.[76]

As early as 1936, the Supreme Court gave its approval on presidential primacy in the realm of foreign relations in *United States v. Curtiss-Wright Export Corporation.* In 1934, Congress had adopted a joint resolution authorizing the president to prohibit U.S. companies from selling munitions to the warring nations of Paraguay and Bolivia. Congress also provided for criminal penalties for those violating presidential prohibitions. Curtiss-Wright brought suit, claiming that Congress had unconstitutionally delegated its lawmaking powers to the president. Despite the fact that the Court had ruled against delegation of legislative power in domestic issues in *Schechter Poultry Corporation v. United States* (1935) a year earlier, the Court said that the delegation of power was constitutional when dealing with foreign affairs. The Court referred to the president as the "sole organ of the federal government in the field of international relations." This is based on the belief, first articulated by John Marshall when he was a member of the House of Representatives in 1799 (Marshall would become Chief Justice of the United States in 1801), that presidents should have independence when acting in the area of foreign policy. This is also similar to what is referred to as the unitary executive theory, which holds that the president controls the entire executive branch based on the vesting clause in Article II.[77]

Since that time, the Court has often deferred to, and recognized, congressional acquiescence to grant the president broad powers in the foreign policy arena. Presidents have authority to make treaties with foreign nations with the advice and consent of the Senate. The broad scope of this power was endorsed by the Supreme Court in *Missouri v. Holland* (1920), which involved a treaty between the United States and Great Britain involving migratory birds from Canada. The Court rejected the claim made by Missouri that Congress did not have the authority to pass regulations against the killing of such birds stemming from the treaty. Presidents also use executive agreements as an alternative to treaties, or use them to implement treaty provisions. Unlike treaties, executive agreements do not require the concurrence of the Senate. Valid executive agreements are legally equivalent to treaties, but presidents often use them to bypass Congress. Most involve minor matters of international concern, such as specification of the details of postal relations or the use of radio airwaves. The president can also terminate a treaty without Senate approval, as determined by the Court in *Goldwater v. Carter* (1979), which dealt with the termination of a defense treaty with Taiwan.[78]

War Powers

The president is the commander in chief, yet Congress has the power to declare war. The commander in chief may need to "repel sudden attacks," but must share power in this regard with the Congress to protect against the possible abuse of presidential power in waging war. Presidential power to act in a national emergency and to commit military forces to combat situations has a long heritage. In *Ex parte Merryman* (1861), Chief Justice Roger Taney declared Lincoln's suspension of habeas corpus to be unconstitutional on the grounds that only Congress has the power to suspend the writ "when in Cases of Rebellion or Invasion the public Safety may require it." In *The Prize Cases* (1863), the Court acknowledged the necessity of deferring to the president's decisions in times of crisis. With the absence of a formal declaration of war from the Congress, Lincoln in 1863 ordered the capture of vessels by the Union navy during the blockage of Southern ports. Under the existing law at the time, the vessels would become the property of the Union only with a formal declaration of war. But the Court found the seizures to be legal, stating that "the President is not only authorized, but bound to resist force. He does not initiate the war, but is bound to accept the challenge without waiting for any special legislative authority." Additionally, Justice Robert Grier noted that the "President was bound to meet [the Civil War] in the shape it presented itself, without waiting for the Congress to baptize it with a name."[79]

As discussed earlier, as a result of Vietnam, Congress passed the War Powers Resolution in 1973, which places limits on the duration of troop commitments and requires the president to make a full report to Congress when sending troops into combat. Yet, the resolution did not prevent Ronald Reagan from using military force in various places, including Lebanon, Libya, and Grenada. He complied by notifying Congress, but congressional disapproval would have been meaningless since the hostilities lasted only a few days. George H. W. Bush sought a congressional resolution in support of the Persian Gulf War, but Congress had failed to "start the clock" during the massive build-up of troops during Operation Desert Shield. Similar issues have arisen during the Clinton, George W. Bush, and Obama administrations, but to date, the War Powers Resolution seems of little constitutional consequence in limiting presidential power in this regard.

Another difficult constitutional question involves the extent of presidential power in the domestic sphere during wartime, especially as it relates to the rights of American citizens. The Court has given mixed answers to this question. For example, in *Ex Parte Milligan* (1866), the Court declared that Lincoln's orders for the trial of civilians by military courts were unconstitutional. Yet, in one of its more infamous rulings in *Korematsu v. U.S.* (1944), the Court declared constitutional the internment of Japanese Americans by the FDR administration during World War II. In 1988, Ronald Reagan signed legislation providing reparations to those same Japanese-American families.

These types of issues would again come before the Supreme Court following the 9/11 terrorist attacks and the subsequent application of presidential authority by the George W. Bush administration. The Bush White House argued that as a war-time president, Bush had greatly expanded constitutional authorities to combat terrorism and protect national security. He and his advisors relied on the unitary executive theory regarding many of their actions. For example, Bush claimed that he had

George W. Bush signs the Patriot Act into law on October 26, 2001.

the authority to indefinitely detain foreign nationals as well as U.S. citizens determined to be "enemy combatants" at Guantanamo Bay. However, the Supreme Court did not always concur with Bush's interpretation of presidential powers. In *Rasul v. Bush* (2004), the Court rejected the claim that federal courts lacked jurisdiction over foreign nationals held in Cuba and affirmed the right of these individuals to seek judicial review of the basis for their detention. In *Hamdi v. Rumsfeld* (2004), the Court ruled that the president has a right to detain U.S. citizens as enemy combatants, but that citizens have a right to consult with an attorney and to contest the basis for their detention before an independent tribunal. The right to hold an enemy combatant indefinitely was not granted under the Authorization for Use of Military Force passed by Congress to fight terrorism after 9/11. In *Hamdan v. Rumsfeld* (2006), the Court ruled that military commissions set up by the Bush administration lack "the power to proceed because its structures and procedures violate both the Uniform Code of Military Justice and the four Geneva Conventions signed in 1949." And in *Boumediene v. Bush* (2008), the Court ruled that foreign terrorist suspects held at Guantanamo Bay have constitutional rights to challenge their detention in United States courts.[80]

CONCLUSION

As we can see as recently as President Obama's decision to commit military resources to the international effort to rid Libya of Gaddafi, when considering presidential powers, the framers' intent versus contemporary practices can often present an interesting paradox. While the Constitution has changed little regarding the presidency since 1787, the framers would probably not recognize the office due not only to the size of the executive branch but also the scope of presidential powers. Yet, one can argue that modern presidents have, for the most part, governed within the parameters of the Constitution since the framers left many areas of authority vague and up to interpretation. How presidents and their advisors have interpreted the Constitution, particularly in the areas of the vesting clause and the president's role as commander in chief, is often the most significant determinant of how a president approaches his duties while in office. While some presidents have taken a strict view of the Constitution, and have not read any extra powers within the vagueness of the language of Article II, most, if not all, presidents since FDR have taken a more permissive view of the powers of the office. Those who bemoan the expansion of the executive branch and the size of the accompanying bureaucracy, as well as the willingness of so many presidents to commit U.S. military forces without a congressional declaration of war, would argue that the actions of presidents throughout the twentieth century and into the twenty-first are a constitutional aberration. Others, perhaps more realistically, recognize that the dramatic social and economic changes since World War II, not to mention national security and defense issues, require a strong presidency to react swiftly to changing world events. Regardless of one's viewpoint, there is no denying that the individuals who have held the office of the presidency have played just as important of a role in shaping presidential powers as have the changes to the institution itself.

In recent years, both the Bush and Obama administrations have not shown any interest in reversing course regarding an expansive view of presidential powers. If anything, both presidents have reignited the debate over the president's role as commander in chief (many considered the Bush years to be a reemergence of the imperial presidency) and over executive branch authority regarding domestic policies (the passage of Obama's health-care reform drew numerous lawsuits over its constitutionality, but it was ultimately upheld as constitutional by the Supreme Court in 2012). The eventual capture and killing of Gaddafi by Libyan rebels in October 2011, while celebrated by most as a victory both for the Libyan people and the global community, did little to resolve the debate over Obama's commitment of U.S. military resources to the international coalition without the approval of Congress. The remaining questions seem to be, did Obama violate the War Powers resolution, and, in the day-to-day process of governing, does it really matter if the ends justify the means?

Of course, these debates are not without partisan motivations, as many of the arguments depend on whether or not the president is "doing the right thing" (from those in the president's party) or is engaging in an unconstitutional "power grab" (from those in the opposing party). The Supreme Court, more so than Congress, has remained at least somewhat responsive in its role to check the powers of the president, while Congress has abdicated much of its responsibility (especially regarding war powers). Since precedent can play such an important role in the actions of those in power within the American system of government, it seems unlikely that a course correction regarding the expansion of presidential powers will occur anytime soon. The institutional expansion of the powers of the presidency, as well as the individuals who serve as president, will undoubtedly continue to challenge the framers' intent as well as responses from both Congress and the Supreme Court over the constitutionality of presidential actions.

PRESIDENTIAL PARDONS

THEN...

While much of Article II of the Constitution may seem open ended and vague regarding presidential powers, the framers did provide a handful of specific and enumerated powers. One of those is the power to pardon. Article II, Section 2 states that the president "... shall have Power to grant Reprieves and Pardons for Offences against the United States, except in Cases of Impeachment." There is a distinction between a reprieve and a pardon; the former reduces the severity of a punishment, while the latter removes both the punishment and the guilt of the crime. Accepting a pardon, however, is the equivalent of an admission of guilt, even though it removes the legal possibility for punishment. Normally, the modern-day process of seeking a presidential pardon begins with an application to the Department of Justice; those attorneys in the Department of Justice who handle such matters consult with other attorneys and judges in seeking recommendations. The FBI also conducts a check on the person applying for the pardon. Department of Justice attorneys then provide a list of those it recommends for a pardon to the White House Counsel; the president ultimately decides for whom to grant a pardon.

Presidents have often used the pardon power to forgive politically motivated actions. For example, George Washington granted pardons to leaders of the Whiskey Rebellion, and Andrew Johnson pardoned Confederate soldiers after the Civil War. Similar pardons were granted during the twentieth century, as Harry Truman pardoned violators of Selective Service laws during World War II and Jimmy Carter pardoned those who fled the country to avoid the

Gerald Ford signs his pardon of Richard Nixon on September 8, 1974.

draft during the Vietnam War. Perhaps the most famous, or infamous depending on one's viewpoint, pardon of all time came on September 8, 1974, when President Gerald Ford pardoned former President Richard Nixon for any and all crimes that he may have committed against the United States in relation to the Watergate scandal. Nixon, who accepted the pardon, was considered an unindicted co-conspirator in the break-in and subsequent cover-up of the burglary of the Democratic National Headquarters at the Watergate complex in Washington, D.C., in July 1972. More than two years later, Nixon resigned from office on August 9, 1974, rather than face impeachment by the House of Representatives.

Ford, who only consulted a handful of advisors within the administration prior to granting the pardon, surprised the nation with his decision. In a statement to the American people, Ford argued that the decision was in the best interests of the nation in an attempt to move past the damage to the nation's psyche from the Watergate scandal:

> [I have] searched my own conscience with special diligence to determine the right thing for me to do with respect to my predecessor in this place, Richard Nixon, and his loyal wife and family. Theirs is an American tragedy in which we all have played a part. It could go on and on and on, or someone must write the end to it. I have concluded that only I can do that, and if I can, I must. There are no historic or legal precedents to which I can turn in this matter, none that precisely fit the circumstances of a private citizen who has resigned the Presidency of the United States. But it is common knowledge that serious allegations and accusations hang like a sword over our former President's head, threatening his health as he tries to reshape his life, a great part of which was spent in the service of this country and by the mandate of its people. After years of bitter controversy and divisive national debate, I have been advised, and I am compelled to conclude that many months and perhaps more years will have to pass before Richard Nixon could obtain a fair trial by jury in any jurisdiction of the United States under governing decisions of the Supreme Court.... The facts, as I see them, are that a former President of the United States, instead of enjoying equal treatment with any other citizen accused of violating the law, would be cruelly and excessively penalized either in preserving the presumption of his innocence or in obtaining a speedy determination of his guilt in order to repay a legal debt to society. During this long period of delay and potential litigation, ugly passions would again be aroused. And our people would again be polarized in their opinions.... But it is not the ultimate fate of Richard Nixon that most concerns me, though surely it deeply troubles every decent and every compassionate person. My concern is the immediate future of this great country. In this, I dare not depend upon my personal sympathy as a longtime friend of the former President, nor my professional judgment as a lawyer, and I do not. As President, my primary concern must always be the greatest good of all the people of the United States whose servant I am.... My conscience tells me clearly and

> certainly that I cannot prolong the bad dreams that continue to reopen a chapter that is closed. My conscience tells me that only I, as President, have the constitutional power to firmly shut and seal this book. My conscience tells me it is my duty, not merely to proclaim domestic tranquility but to use every means that I have to insure it. I do believe that the buck stops here, that I cannot rely upon public opinion polls to tell me what is right.... Finally, I feel that Richard Nixon and his loved ones have suffered enough and will continue to suffer, no matter what I do, no matter what we, as a great and good nation, can do together to make his goal of peace come true.

Following Ford's announcement, his approval ratings plummeted and talk immediately began about whether or not Ford had cut a deal with Nixon over the pardon; some suggested that Ford had promised to pardon Nixon once he became president following Nixon's resignation from office. Until his death in 2006, Ford vehemently denied that any deal had been made, always claiming that he believed he had done the right thing for the nation in an attempt to heal the political wounds of Watergate. Regardless, the shock of the Ford pardon caused a stir even among his closest advisors. Ford's first press secretary and long-time friend Jerald terHorst resigned in protest over the Nixon pardon. Ford also appeared before Congress on October 17, 1974, to give sworn testimony about the pardon and testified that there had been no deal made over the pardon (he was the first president to testify before Congress since Lincoln 🖱). While most scholars agree that the Nixon pardon cost Ford the 1976 presidential election, no one will ever know for sure if that was foremost in voters' minds when electing Jimmy Carter. However, right or wrong, Ford's decision to grant the pardon remains an enduring symbol of his presidential legacy.

. . . AND NOW

While no other pardon has caused as much of a political stir since Ford's pardon of Nixon, more recent presidential pardons have been controversial nonetheless. On Christmas Eve in 1992, just weeks before he was to leave office, President George H. W. Bush pardoned six Reagan administration officials, including Secretary of Defense Caspar W. Weinberger, for their involvement in the Iran-Contra scandal. Weinberger and others had been indicted, plead guilty or already convicted of crimes connected to Iran-Contra. The pardons, which cancelled the upcoming trial for Weinberger, ended any further investigation into the matter. Critics of the pardon suggested that Bush was protecting himself as well; Independent Counsel Lawrence Walsh had been investigating Bush's involvement in Iran-Contra and had learned that Bush had withheld diaries from investigators that would have contradicted his public statements that he had not been "in the loop" as vice president over the Iran Contra affair.

🖱 Watch President Ford testify before Congress.

Whereas Bush chose to grant the Iran-Contra pardons on Christmas Eve, with the news appearing at a time when most Americans would not be paying much attention to politics, Bill Clinton followed a presidential tradition of granting pardons on his last day in office. The most controversial was what many termed his "eleventh-hour" pardons of fugitive financier Marc Rich and his business partner Pincus Green, both of whom had been indicted for tax evasion and illegal oil trading with Iran. In the "Petition for Pardon" received by the Clinton Department of Justice, the attorneys representing both Rich and Green argued:

> Mr. Rich and Mr. Green are internationally recognized businessmen and philanthropists who have contributed over $200,000,000 to charity in the past twenty years, and who have donated countless hours to humanitarian causes around the world.... [They] seek a pardon even though they have never been convicted of a criminal offense in the United States or any other country. However, they and two of their companies were wrongfully indicted nearly twenty years ago, primarily on tax and energy charges stemming from their participation in oil transactions under then-existing Department of Energy oil regulations and controls. Those controls, deemed to be unworkable, incomprehensible and counterproductive, were abolished by President Reagan in one of his first official acts in January, 1981, and now are seen as a relic of the era of excessive economic regulation of the oil industry. [They] have complete defenses to the indictment. While the indictment makes many accusations, the prosecution admits that tax-related charges were the cores of the case. Yet two of the country's leading tax professors have analyzed the tax treatment of the transactions at issue, and concluded that they were correctly reported. Nevertheless, Mr. Rich and Mr. Green remain under indictment and in effective exile from the United States. This is so even though their companies have resolved all charges, and all others who engaged in similar transactions were pursued civilly, or not at all. This petition for a pardon on behalf of Mr. Rich and Mr. Green seeks to put an end to that exile by resolving an otherwise intractable situation between Mr. Rich, Mr. Green and the United States government, and by righting an injustice that has persisted for nearly two decades. [They] are now in their late sixties. They have not traveled to the United States in over seventeen years. Without a Presidential Pardon, there is little if any chance that this matter will be resolved. The current situation is the unfortunate result of unfair and unwarranted treatment of two men against whom no criminal charges should have been brought. A Presidential Pardon will promote the interests of justice, will rectify a wrong, and will finally put this matter to rest.[81]

Clinton handed out a total of 140 pardons and several commutations on his last day in office (Nixon holds the record for most pardons in one day with 204 on December 12, 1972), including one to his half-brother Roger Clinton for drug-related charges a decade earlier, and one to Susan MacDougal who served eighteen months in prison for her refusal to testify against Clinton in the

Whitewater investigation. Yet, it was the Rich pardon that drew public outrage from both Democrats and Republicans when it was learned that Rich's ex-wife, Denise Rich, had raised and donated more than $1 million to the Democratic Party and also provided the Clintons with $10,000 for their legal defense fund and $7,300 worth of furniture and other gifts. As a result, congressional investigations were launched, and the pardons were also investigated by federal prosecutors (who eventually found no wrongdoing on Clinton's part in granting any pardons).

For George W. Bush, the pardon that became the most high-profile at the end of his eight years in office is one that never actually occurred. Much speculation arose over whether Bush would pardon I. Lewis "Scooter" Libby, former chief of staff to Vice President Dick Cheney. Libby had been convicted in federal court for obstruction of justice, perjury, and making false statements in connection to the investigation of the leak of the covert identity of CIA officer Valerie Plame. Plame's husband, former ambassador Joseph Wilson, had written an op-ed piece in the *New York Times* in 2002 that contradicted Bush administration claims that Saddam Hussein had weapons of mass destruction; Libby's leak of Plame's identity was seen as political payback. Following the conviction, Libby was sentenced to thirty months in federal prison with a $250,000 fine and two years' probation. On July 2, 2007, Bush commuted Libby's jail sentence, but left the fines and probation terms intact. Commutations are rarely issued, but Bush explained his "Grant of Executive Clemency" by stating:

> Mr. Libby was sentenced to thirty months of prison, two years of probation, and a $250,000 fine. In making the sentencing decision, the district court rejected the advice of the probation office, which recommended a lesser sentence and the consideration of factors that could have led to a sentence of home confinement or probation. I respect the jury's verdict. But I have concluded that the prison sentence given to Mr. Libby is excessive. Therefore, I am commuting the portion of Mr. Libby's sentence that required him to spend thirty months in prison. My decision to commute his prison sentence leaves in place a harsh punishment for Mr. Libby. The reputation he gained through his years of public service and professional work in the legal community is forever damaged. His wife and young children have also suffered immensely. He will remain on probation. The significant fines imposed by the judge will remain in effect. The consequences of his felony conviction on his former life as a lawyer, public servant, and private citizen will be long-lasting.

Despite heavy lobbying by Cheney, Bush declined to grant Libby a full pardon prior to leaving office. Cheney later stated publicly his disappointment over Bush's decision, and the lack of a pardon for Libby reportedly caused a rift between Bush and Cheney in their post–White House years.

SUGGESTED READINGS

Adler, David Gray, and Michael A. Genovese, eds. 2002. *The Presidency and the Law: The Clinton Legacy*. Lawrence: University Press of Kansas.

Bailyn, Bernard. 1967. *The Ideological Origins of the American Revolution.* Cambridge: Harvard University Press.

Corwin, Edward S. 1940. *The President: Office and Powers.* New York: New York University Press.

Fisher, Louis. 2007. *Constitutional Conflicts Between Congress and the President.* Lawrence: University Press of Kansas.

Fisher, Louis. 2004. *Presidential War Power,* 2nd ed. Lawrence: University Press of Kansas.

Genovese, Michael A., and Lori Cox Han, eds. 2006. *The Presidency and the Challenge of Democracy.* New York: Palgrave Macmillan.

McDonald, Forrest. 1985. *Novus Ordo Seclorum: The Intellectual Origins of the Constitution.* Lawrence: University Press of Kansas.

Milkis, Sidney M., and Michael Nelson. 2011. *The American Presidency: Origins and Development, 1776–2011,* 6th ed. Washington, DC: CQ Press.

Reid, John Phillip. 1993. *Constitutional History of the American Revolution: The Authority of Law.* Madison: University of Wisconsin Press.

Rossiter, Clinton. 1956. *The American Presidency.* New York: Harcourt, Brace.

Rozell, Mark. 2000. *Executive Privilege: The Dilemma of Secrecy and Democratic Accountability.* Lawrence: University Press of Kansas.

Wood, Gordon S. 1969. *Creation of the American Republic, 1776–1787.* New York: W. W. Norton.

ON THE WEB

http://www.law.cornell.edu/constitution. Home page of the Legal Information Institute at the Cornell University Law School. The site provides a database for the U.S. Constitution, Supreme Court rulings, and other legal issues. The stated goal of the site is to "promote open access to law, worldwide."

http://www.oyez.org. The Oyez Project at the Chicago-Kent College of Law provides an online multimedia archive of the United States Supreme Court.

IN THEIR OWN WORDS

THE WAR POWERS RESOLUTION

While the constitutionality of the War Powers Resolution has never been determined by the Supreme Court, presidents are nonetheless mindful of its provisions, as presidents do not want a constitutional showdown with Congress when initiating military action. As a result, preparing a strong case vis-à-vis the War Powers Resolution is often part of the strategic calculation, as this memo from White House Counsel C. Boyden Gray to President George H. W. Bush shows as the White House prepared for war in the Persian Gulf in the summer of 1990:

> I believe it probable that you will be asked about application of the War Powers Resolution (WPR) to the Persian Gulf crisis in your meeting tomorrow with congressional leaders. I have prepared this background paper and the attached contingency talking points for your use in connection with the meeting.

BACKGROUND

The WPR contains two basic provisions: (1) a requirement that Congress be notified within 48 hours of significant new deployments of U.S. combat forces into foreign countries, and (2) a 60-day clock that is triggered when such deployments are into hostilities or situations where hostilities are imminent.

When the 60-day clock is triggered, the President must withdraw the forces within 60 days unless Congress has declared war or passed a joint resolution authorizing continued use of the forces.

We do not dispute the constitutionality of the WPR's congressional notification requirement, but every Administration since the WPR was adopted over President Nixon's veto has considered the 60-day clock an unconstitutional infringement of the President's authority as Commander-in-Chief.

Consistent with the congressional notification requirement, you reported the Persian Gulf deployment to Congress on August 9. Your report stated that you were acting "consistent with" rather than "pursuant to" the WPR. The formulation, first used by President Carter in reporting the Desert One operation and continued by the Reagan and Bush Administrations, emphasizes the Executive branch's position that portions of the WPR are unconstitutional.

You further stated in the August 9 report "I do not believe involvement in hostilities is imminent; to the contrary, it is my belief that this deployment will facilitate a peaceful resolution of the crisis."

This sentence had the effect, in our view, of making clear that the 60-day clock had not been triggered, because the clock begins to run only when hostilities are imminent.

Some members of Congress believe that the 60-day clock has been triggered. They note that, under the WPR, the clock begins to run either when the President reports that hostilities are imminent, or when he was required to report that hostilities were imminent but failed to do so.

In other words, the basis of their position is that you were wrong in asserting in the August 9 report that hostilities were not imminent.

Chairmen [Claiborne] Pell has already written you proposing that we negotiate with the Senate Foreign Relations Committee the text of a joint resolution authorizing the deployment.

Chairman [Dante] Fascell reportedly has instructed the House Foreign Affairs Committee staff to begin drafting a similar resolution that would authorize the deployment for 15 months.

There is a precedent for such a resolution. In 1983, Congress passed a joint resolution granting authorization under the WPR for U.S. participation in the Multinational Force in Lebanon—subject to an 18 month limitation—notwithstanding that President Reagan had never reported to Congress that involvement in hostilities was imminent.

President Reagan signed the resolution into law, but issued a signing statement that, while thanking Congress for its support, noted his disagreement with the limitations contained in the resolution and with Congress' premise that the 60-day clock had been triggered by the outbreak of hostilities.

Chairmen Pell and Fascell seem eager to negotiate a similar resolution with us concerning the Persian Gulf. Such a resolution is legally unnecessary, but would have the political advantage of wedding Congress to our policy.

The disadvantage of negotiating such a resolution is that Congress, in its eagerness to prevent "another Viet Nam," may attempt to constrain the size, scope, and duration of the deployment, just as it did in the Lebanon resolution.

I recommend that you tell the congressional leadership you are prepared to work with them, but will not accept a resolution that constrains your freedom of action.[82]

CHAPTER 3

The Presidential Selection Process

When it comes to recent presidential campaigns, Senator John McCain (R-AZ) has certainly been a prominent figure. In 2000, McCain won seven primary contests, including New Hampshire, but would eventually lose the Republican nomination to then-Texas Governor George W. Bush. In late 2007, McCain trailed in both public opinion polling and fundraising behind other Republican presidential contenders, including former New York Mayor Rudy Giuliani, and former governors Mitt Romney of Massachusetts and Mike Huckabee of Arkansas. However, McCain made a strong comeback to again win the New Hampshire primary, one of thirty-one primary and caucus wins in early 2008 that would secure him the Republican nomination. Despite losing the presidency later that fall to Barack Obama, McCain would also make history with his selection of Alaska Governor Sarah Palin as his running mate—the first woman ever nominated to the Republican Party ticket.

Yet, McCain's greatest contribution to presidential campaigns may have come in the area of campaign finance reform. For years, McCain had bucked his own party's stance on the issue and crossed party lines to work with then-fellow Senator Russ Feingold (D-WI) in an effort to pass major legislation reforming America's system of campaign finance at the federal level. Their legislative efforts had paid off in 2002 when President Bush (who was not a big fan of reforming a system that had allowed him to break numerous fundraising records in 2000) signed the "Bipartisan Campaign Reform Act" into law. The so-called McCain–Feingold reforms, which took effect following the 2002 midterm congressional elections, banned soft money (unlimited donations) to political parties. Since corporations and labor unions had long been banned from giving money directly to candidates, and wealthy individuals had been limited to a contribution of $1,000 per candidate per campaign cycle, unlimited donations to political parties had, in effect, provided the essential loophole for influential groups and individuals to affect the outcome of a campaign.

As a result, all those soft money contributors had to find a new way to give money to the candidates of their choice. Enter interest groups, as well as 527s—a tax-exempt group organized under Section 527 of the Internal Revenue Code to raise money for political activities. Many 527s are run by interest groups to raise unlimited soft money, which is then spent on mobilizing voters and certain types of issue advocacy, but not for efforts that expressly advocate the election or defeat of a federal candidate (at least in theory). As it turned out, during the 2004 presidential elections the candidates, parties, and interest groups raised and spent the then-record-breaking amount of just under a billion dollars; the election was widely considered the most expensive, and the most negative, that Americans had ever witnessed. That is, until 2008, when a wide-open field for both Democrats and Republicans helped to push the spending total for all presidential campaigns to nearly $2 billion, doubling the amount spent just four years earlier. Barack Obama alone spent $741 million, became the first major-party nominee to reject federal funding for the general election, and ended up spending more than Bush and Democratic nominee John Kerry combined in 2004.

With money as one of its prominent features, there is perhaps no bigger spectacle in American politics than electing a president. A process for which the framers developed the Electoral College as a means to insulate electing a president from the American public, today's presidential campaigns and elections have become a multi-billion-dollar proposition to strategically market candidates to voters while under the never-ending scrutiny of the news media. American presidential campaigns are now candidate-centered, media- and money-driven, seemingly never-ending affairs that highlight all of the political players that take part—the candidates, their spouses, and/or family members; campaign managers, strategists, fundraisers, spokespeople, and volunteers; party officials at the national, state, and local levels; interest groups; pollsters; and political reporters and pundits in every known medium. And let's not forget the voters, who must attempt to pay attention during a campaign cycle that keeps getting longer and process the information that bombards them all in an attempt to decide which candidate will receive their vote. This is no longer the simple process that the framers envisioned, one in which a small gathering of political elites would caucus and cast votes to select the president.

How, then, does this complex and chaotic process of presidential elections continue to yield a result every four years that leads to the peaceful transition of leadership without revolution? Americans nominate and then elect presidential candidates through various stages of the campaign process, including the so-called "invisible" primary, voting in primaries and caucuses, the national party conventions, and then the general election. The process of campaigning for president has a dramatic effect on not only the election outcome but on setting the stage for the president's future governing prospects. In the end, who chooses to run for president, and who succeeds in winning the election, greatly effects not only the day-to-day governing of the nation but the institution of the presidency as well.

THE NOMINATING PROCESS IN HISTORICAL PERSPECTIVE

The rules of the presidential selection process laid out in the Constitution highlight the framers' preoccupations and predispositions. The framers believed in political elitism and contended that property ownership was evidence of the responsibility necessary to participate in political affairs. During the Constitutional Convention, the framers considered including a property qualification for the presidency. Most states required candidates for governorships to own property. The convention even adopted a motion that judges, legislators, and the executive must own property, but ultimately they rejected it, as they could not agree on an appropriate level to set the qualification.[1] Consequently, the Constitution states only that a candidate for the presidency must be a natural-born citizen, at least thirty-five years of age, and have lived in the United States for fourteen years. There was, however, a glaring omission in the focus and execution of presidential selection: Who runs for the presidency, and how are candidates chosen?

There is no method for nominating elected officials in the Constitution, as the framers did not provide for nomination procedures for elected officials because of their shared belief in an available pool of appropriate candidates. A simple ranking of the field would be sufficient in an environment that did not include firm partisan divisions. In the presence of partisan divisions and the establishment of political parties, the concept of a consensus-created pool of appropriate candidates withered. The two-party system emerged as political elites divided over ideology while recognizing that opportunities to advance that ideology improved with organization outside of government. Capturing offices in order to shape government outcomes became the driving force behind the evolution of political parties.

Between 1800 and 1824, as the party system quickly traveled from embryonic gatherings of like-minded individuals to fully formed organizations, presidential selection was rooted in the caucus. In use prior to the adoption of the Constitution, the caucus was an informal meeting of political leaders held to decide questions concerning candidates, strategies, and policies. The essence of the caucus idea, when applied to nominations, was that by sifting, sorting, and weeding out candidates before the election, leaders could assemble substantial support behind a single candidate and decrease the possibility that the votes "... will be split among several candidates."[2] The caucus system remained effective while the framers dominated the political class. Time and increased democratization eroded what was known as "King Caucus" as the scope of political participation widened.

What is now considered to have been Thomas Jefferson's "party" was the dominant political force after the implosion of the Federalists; it was the only thing closely resembling a political party between 1816 and 1824 fielding a presidential candidate. The absence of a second party did not mean ideological consensus, despite the nicknaming of the time, the "Era of Good Feeling." Political battles arose about leadership, particularly the choice for the presidential nomination. The tension produced by the lack of inclusiveness in the nominations process came to a head in the presidential election of 1824. Jefferson's Democratic-Republican Party dissolved as disparate factions within nominated four distinct candidates: John Quincy Adams, Andrew Jackson, William Crawford, and Henry Clay. Jackson received the most

Electoral College votes, but not enough for a majority, so the election fell to the House of Representatives. The Twelfth Amendment (ratified in 1804) only allows for the top three vote-getters to be considered, so the race then fell to Jackson, Adams, and Crawford. However, Henry Clay was Speaker of the House and as such exercised enormous influence on the outcome. Adams won the election, and Clay became his Secretary of State. The "corrupt bargain," as it became known, effectively dismantled the Democratic-Republican Party as it dissolved into the Whigs (who supported Adams and Clay) and the Democrats (who supported Jackson). Adams may have won the election, but Jackson won the era; by 1828, he won the presidency and his party controlled Congress.

Disgust with the outcome and the machinations of the 1824 election ushered in change to the nominating process. By 1836, both the Whigs and the Democrats used a national convention that featured state delegates (chosen by state conventions of local party leaders) to nominate their respective presidential candidates. As a result, a party's presidential nominee was connected to a widely dispersed party organization. The power of that political network as a connection to the electorate slowly became a source of power for the president, beginning as early as Andrew Jackson's linking of the presidency to the people during his two terms in office (1829–1837).

National party conventions controlled the presidential nomination process for well over one hundred years. Although the convention process enabled participation by a larger group of people who were not all of the same financial status or the same region, it was not an open process. First, only party members participated. Second, between 1850 and 1950 there was an incredible consolidation of power under party bosses. The classic picture of presidential nominations consisted of men behind closed doors in smoke-filled rooms determining the outcome, regardless of how many rank-and-file party members filled the convention hall as delegates. Power, not rules, determined the outcome, and the hold over presidential nominations by party leaders made the convention process frustratingly undemocratic for individuals who were not part of the political "in" crowd.

To counter the weight and import of the party leadership, progressive reformers introduced the primary as a means to influence the choice of the presidential nominee. During the late 1800s and early 1900s, known as the Progressive Era, voters chose sides, not candidates. Individuals voted along party lines, and split ticket voting was impossible until the adoption of the Australian ballot (allowing for choice in secret) in the late 1890s by the majority of states. Reformers revolted against the iron control of local and state party leaders making backroom deals with cronies.[3] As a result, the primary system was gradually adopted by some states while other states employed a caucus method for party rank-and-file members to select candidates. These choices by the regular membership of the party influenced the choices of the state delegates to the national convention. Each party determined for itself how influential the choices of the regular membership would be. The creation of the primary system by progressive reformers intended to undermine the power of a narrow group of party leaders. However, party leaders were reluctant to cede all control over who runs under the banner of their party.

The last major reforms to the nominating system came in 1972, following the tumultuous Democratic National Convention in 1968 that included rioting in the streets of Chicago in protest of, among other things, the Vietnam War and the selection of Vice President Hubert Humphrey as the presidential nominee. Humphrey received the nomination even though he had not competed in any Democratic primary or caucus; following the assassination of Senator Robert Kennedy in June 1968, no clear frontrunner remained for the Democrats leading into their convention. Kennedy, who had just won the California primary, led the delegate count, but did not yet have enough delegates to secure the nomination over fellow senator and anti-war candidate Eugene McCarthy. Party bosses, in effect, selected Humphrey as the nominee, ignoring the number of delegates that McCarthy had won in the primary process. Following the convention, the McGovern–Fraser Commission was formed to enact changes to the nominating process. The commission recommended a more open and democratic process for the selection of delegates, which would result in more rank-and-file party members, as opposed to party bosses, having a say in the selection of the nominee. By 1972, both Democrats and Republicans began to hold primary elections in many more states, which left party bosses with less power over the nomination process. The system in place today reveals how party insiders attempt to retain control of the nominations process while permitting a broader array of voices to participate.

THE PRE-NOMINATION PERIOD

The adoption of the primary process and the use of caucuses in some states represent efforts to broaden participation in the selection of nominees for the two major parties. The creation of what in practice amounts to a series of mini-elections summed together to produce the requisite delegate count at the national party convention changed the incentives and behavior for candidates, party elites, and voters. For example, in 2008, there were sixty-two different state primary races between January 3rd and June 3rd. In some states, like South Carolina and Wyoming, the Democrats and Republicans did not hold their primaries on the same day. Other states, like Louisiana, have Democratic primaries and Republican caucuses. Consequently, candidates for the nomination from either party need to make critical strategic decisions regarding the allocation of resources. Beginning with what is referred to as the pre-nomination period or the "invisible primary," and concluding with the national party's nominating conventions, the process of selecting major party candidates to vie for the presidency in the general election is dominated by money, media, and momentum and represents the American political version of "survival of the fittest."

Deciding to Run

Of course, all of that is preceded by the decision by candidates to run in the first place. Who decides to run, and perhaps more importantly, who is qualified to run? Technically speaking, the constitutional requirements for president are minimal (as stated previously). However, many other unofficial requirements exist to be considered a viable candidate, and those can include prior political experience, name recognition, party support, adequate funding and fundraising abilities, strong appeal to the party base (particularly during the primaries), appeal to independent or swing voters (particularly during the general election), and strong leadership and communication skills. Throughout American history, with 2008 and 2012 being prominent exceptions, other factors such as religion, race, and gender have made the pool of viable candidates for both president and vice president almost exclusively Protestant, white, and male. The health and age of the candidate, as well as family ties and personal relationships (including marital status and fidelity), are also important characteristics for potential presidential candidates.[4] The character, personality, and style of candidates matter greatly, especially as news reporting during presidential campaigns has become increasingly cynical, sensationalized, and hypercritical, leading to an increased focus on the "cult of personality" during presidential campaigns.[5] While issues and partisan loyalty still matter, American presidential campaigns have increasingly become "candidate-centered" contests in recent decades.[6]

Every campaign cycle, a short list of potential presidential candidates emerges, put together in part by the news media through speculation based on the behavior and travel patterns of notable politicians (for example, who is traveling to Iowa and/or New Hampshire, or speaking at high-profile party events). This so-called "on-deck circle" of potential candidates consists of roughly thirty to forty individuals usually made up of prominent members of Congress, governors (past and present) of larger states, former or current vice presidents, and former presidential and vice-presidential candidates.[7] The Washington insider-versus-outsider phenomenon has also emerged; four of the last six presidents elected were previous state governors. The image of "master politician" with political experience and a substantive policy record, once necessary to run for the presidency, has given way to the image of the Washington outsider, which requires strong speaking skills, an emphasis on anti-Washington rhetoric, and broad public appeal outside of Washington. This strategy proved successful for previous governors Jimmy Carter, Ronald Reagan, Bill Clinton, and George W. Bush, and even helped Barack Obama, who had only been in the U.S. Senate for four years prior to his election as president.[8] All of these "unofficial" requirements for the presidency have also contributed to the dearth of women presidential candidates, since so few women have held the appropriate leadership positions within government that allow them access to the "on-deck" circle.[9] In addition, research has suggested that a critical gender difference exists in the candidate emergence phase due to a substantial winnowing process that yields a smaller ratio of women candidates; women are often less likely to receive encouragement and support from party officials at this crucial stage, and women themselves have been less interested in running for public office—and when they do run, they choose lower-level offices instead.[10]

The Invisible Primary

First dubbed the "invisible primary" by journalist Arthur Hadley in 1976, the prenomination period is between the end of a presidential election and prior to the first primary of the next, when presidential candidates are vetted and when one candidate can emerge as the frontrunner to secure the nomination.[11] Two things seem to matter more than anything else during the invisible primary—money and media—particularly as the invisible primary has grown increasingly longer in recent years with the frontloading of primaries (which means states have moved up their primary election dates in an attempt to have greater influence over the selection of the nominee). Candidates now announce their intentions to run earlier than ever before, sometimes well over a year prior to the Iowa Caucus (which, on January 3, 2008, was the earliest any nominating contest had ever been held; the 2012 Iowa Caucus was also held on January 3). During this long pre-primary phase of the electoral calendar, candidates attempt to raise large sums of money, hire campaign staffs, shape their ideological and partisan messages, attempt to gain visibility among party elites (and gain high-profile endorsements), and hope to be "taken seriously" by the news media.[12]

As a result, this "primary before the primary" is the early contest to raise both money and support among party elites and potential voters. In recent years, the amount of money a candidate can raise to have on hand for the start of the primary season has become a preliminary mechanism to winnow the field of candidates. The 2008 presidential campaign provides an excellent example of both the never-ending campaign cycle as well as the dramatic rise in campaign fundraising and spending. What used to be a roughly ten-month process from start to finish, the 2008 campaign lasted nearly two years, with most candidates declaring their intentions to run in the early months of 2007. In addition, the increasingly front-loaded primary process, which saw the earliest nominating contests ever held (both the Iowa caucus and New Hampshire primary were held in early January 2008), along with an issue-intensive campaign, historic candidacies for both Democrats and Republicans, and the intense 24/7 coverage by the news media, American voters experienced the longest, most expensive, and perhaps most dramatic presidential election ever.[13] The 2012 campaign would not last quite as long; Republican contenders for their party's nomination waited until late spring 2011 to begin campaigning and fundraising in earnest, while President Obama had no challengers for the Democratic nomination. In addition, while Mitt Romney would not earn the necessary number of delegates to clinch the Republican nomination until late May 2012, he became the presumptive nominee weeks earlier when contenders Rick Santorum and Newt Gingrich exited the race.

A two-tiered campaign often emerges during the pre-primary period; that is, a few candidates are considered viable early on, while others never break through to that top tier of serious contenders (and, as a result, do not receive a tremendous amount of attention from the media or donors). How is this hierarchy determined? While there is not a specific formula, voters normally take their cues as to which candidate is viable and which is not from news media coverage, so the sheer number of mentions in news stories that a candidate receives can be important. It is during the invisible primary when the often relentless "horse race" coverage of the campaign begins, when "reporters feel obliged to tell us which candidates are leading or trailing well over a year before any primary election votes are cast."[14] In recent campaigns, the news media have not focused much on the effects of front-loading primaries and caucuses (such as the increased reliance on millions of dollars to even remain competitive before any votes are cast), even though they contributed to the trend since it was "saturation coverage of New Hampshire and Iowa, starting in the early seventies, after all, that spurred the front-loading process." For the most part, voters outside of New Hampshire and Iowa do not actually see much of what the candidates are doing there, because the news media instead focus on the horse race of the preprimary process as opposed to the actual campaigning and discussion of issues by the candidates.[15] Often, "media buzz" about a candidate can amplify the effects of raising money, hiring staff, and shaping the message of the candidate early on in the process; by February 2007, for example, several Democratic hopefuls had already withdrawn (former Iowa Governor Tom Vilsack and former Virginia Governor Mark Warner) or decided against entering the race (Senator Russ Feingold of Wisconsin and Senator Evan Bayh of Indiana).[16] Similarly, in 2011, former Minnesota governor Tim Pawlenty became the first in a crowded Republican field to withdraw that August, only three months after announcing his candidacy, due to a poor showing in the Ames, Iowa, straw poll.

Gaining Party Support

In the early stages of a campaign, relationships with party insiders can be just as significant as early attention from the press. Although the changes that occurred during the Progressive Movement in the early twentieth century, and after the McGovern–Fraser Commission reforms in the early 1970s, successfully opened up the nomination process to more influence by rank-and-file voters, party insiders still seek to control who runs for the presidency. Potential nominees then seek to reassure party insiders of their willingness to support and work for the party as a whole. Governors of states, particularly larger and/or swing states (states that are not solidly Democratic or Republican), are of critical importance, not just for an endorsement but for their potential assistance since governors control their party's state organization and its roster of volunteers and supporters who can be turned out to help a campaign effort.

Certain groups can also be critical in the pre-primary period for endorsements and the promise of support—both volunteers and financial. For example, in 1999, George W. Bush was able to capitalize on Republican groups' distaste for John McCain's political stances on issues such as campaign finance reform, taxes, and gay marriage.[17] As a result, interest groups lined up to support Bush over McCain and made the next phase of the invisible primary easy for Bush (the eventual Republican nominee). McCain's trouble with party insiders, during both his 2000 and 2008 presidential campaigns, can be explained in part simply by knowing his political nickname—Maverick. Even during his Senate reelection effort in 2010, while fending off a more conservative Republican rival in the primary, McCain addressed the meaning of the label "maverick" during an appearance on *Fox News Sunday*. Host Chris Wallace pressed McCain on the point, playing a 2008 campaign ad that called him "the original maverick" and showing McCain saying, "If you want real reform and if you want change, send a team of mavericks. And what maverick really means, what this team of maverick really means, is we understand who we work for." McCain then responded to Wallace, "Look, when I was fighting against my own president, whether we needed more troops in Iraq, or … spending was completely out of control, then I was a maverick. Now that I'm fighting against this spending [Obama] administration and this out-of-control and reckless health care plan, then I'm a partisan."[18] Party insiders are uncomfortable with this type of variability, "sometimes I am a maverick, and sometimes I am a loyal party member." After all the point of choosing a representative, is to choose someone who can be counted on to represent party principles.

McCain may have lost the Republican nomination in 2000 due, in part, to a lack of support from party insiders (who tended to favor Bush), and may have won the

Read more about the Iowa Straw Poll.

nomination in 2008 with broader support from his party early in the primary process (even though questions continued to plague him over whether or not he was "conservative enough" to attract the base of the party), but the trend toward a more dominant "candidate-centered" campaign process has allowed for viable candidates to emerge without the support of party insiders or to lose the nomination even with that same party support. Bill and Hillary Clinton, respectively, provide an excellent example for both situations. In 1991, no one considered Bill Clinton a frontrunner for the Democratic nomination, and many party officials were not convinced that he was a strong enough contender to challenge incumbent George H. W. Bush in 1992. Clinton's savvy campaign strategy, which included an aggressive response to negative media stories about the candidate's personal life, coupled with the fact that other big-name Democrats (like Mario Cuomo, Richard Gephardt, and Al Gore) were reluctant to get into the race in 1991 while Bush's approval ratings remained high (after the success of the Gulf War), left the Arkansas governor as the most viable candidate in a weak field of Democratic contenders by early 1992.

In contrast, Hillary Clinton had been hailed as the early frontrunner and presumptive Democratic nominee for the better part of three years starting in 2005. News media coverage beginning in 2005 had all but given the Democratic nomination to Clinton due to her political star power, early fundraising advantage, and support from numerous Democratic Party insiders. Yet, Barack Obama's victory in the Iowa Caucus on January 3, 2008, sent a shock wave through the political establishment that changed what had seemed to be the inevitable—Hillary Clinton as the Democratic presidential nominee in 2008. As Obama continued to raise more funds than Clinton, and continued to win key primary contests throughout the winter and spring of 2008, members of the Democratic Party continued to defect from Team Clinton to Team Obama, proving that early support from party insiders does not always guarantee the nomination.[19]

PRIMARIES AND CAUCUSES

Beginning with the pre-nomination period and continuing throughout the primary and caucus contests, perhaps one thing is more important to a presidential candidate than any other—momentum. Several things work together at various levels to build and create (or for unsuccessful candidates to destroy) momentum, including name recognition, support from national and state party officials, media attention, public opinion (as calculated by various public opinion polls), and fundraising. During the Republican primary contest of 1980, candidate George H. W. Bush famously quipped that his campaign had "Big Mo" following his defeat of Ronald Reagan in the Iowa caucus. However, Reagan's campaign regrouped, came back to win the New Hampshire primary, and stole the momentum back from Bush to win an overwhelming majority of the remaining Republican contests (although Bush did secure the vice-presidential spot on the Republican ticket). While one element of momentum (for example, party support) can help to secure other elements (like media attention and fundraising), momentum during the primary season can be fleeting and difficult to build and maintain. For modern presidential campaigns, all of the elements of momentum must fall into place at just the right time for a candidate to capture his or her party's nomination.

As such, the process of the primary contests themselves, as well as the timing and schedule of the contests, are key to understanding how a candidate moves from announcing a campaign to representing a major party during the general election. Aspirants for the title of presidential nominee must run the gauntlet of the state primaries and caucuses. However, the trek is different depending on whether the candidate seeks the Democratic or Republican nomination. Each national party makes its own rules regarding the criteria needed to achieve the nomination. In addition, the states and state parties also create rules and regulations to follow. Some rules, like New Hampshire's state constitution's requirement to always be the first primary of the season, barely influences candidates; other rules, like the number of delegates needed to achieve the nomination, are quite significant.

Iowa and New Hampshire

Long recognized as the first presidential contests, the Iowa caucus and the New Hampshire Primary are the first stops for presidential candidates to prove themselves in the electoral arena. As smaller geographic states with much smaller populations and media markets than delegate-rich states like California or Texas, candidates engage in what is often referred to as "retail politics" by getting up close and personal with residents for many months leading up to the actual contests. While a win in Iowa and/or New Hampshire does not guarantee that a candidate will have what it takes to win his or her party's nomination (as was the case for Bush in 1980 after his win in Iowa), both contests nonetheless receive tremendous

Former Pennsylvania Senator Rick Santorum won the 2012 Republican Caucus in Iowa by a handful of votes.

attention from candidates during the pre-nomination period and can help to catapult a campaign into the national spotlight in an attempt to capture momentum. For example, Barack Obama's Iowa caucus victory over rivals Hillary Clinton and John Edwards in 2008 showed that he could compete with the so-called Clinton political machine as well as the impressive Edwards campaign organization that had been left nearly intact since Edwards' 2004 presidential run. In addition, Obama's victory helped to quell fears within the Democratic Party that an African-American candidate could not win in a predominantly white state like Iowa. For Republicans, Mike Huckabee's Iowa victory may not have put him on the winning track to his party's nomination, but it did provide necessary momentum to sustain his campaign through two more months of contests before he eventually conceded the race to McCain in March 2008 (and in doing so, Huckabee's presence helped to shape the debate about the Republican agenda).

Some candidates opt out of campaigning in one or even both states in an attempt to wait out the primary calendar for states in which they will have a better chance of picking up a sizable number of delegates. For example, Bill Clinton focused most of his primary resources on New Hampshire in 1992 due to the fact that Senator Tom Harkin of Iowa was also in the race (Harkin, as the state's favorite-son candidate, easily won the caucus with little campaigning necessary). In 2008, Republican hopeful Rudy Giuliani believed he would do better in larger states that were later on the primary calendar (such as Florida, California, and his home state of New York) and virtually ignored Iowa and never gave his full attention to campaigning in New Hampshire. Despite leading many national polls throughout 2007, Giuliani's strategy of waiting out the primary calendar failed badly; he dropped out of the race by the end of January 2008 with his campaign deeply in debt and having won only one delegate (out of 2,380) to the Republican National Convention. Former Speaker of the House Newt Gingrich employed a similar strategy in 2012, and fared slightly better, winning South Carolina and some delegates in states like Nevada, but then lost in every other southern state except his home state of Georgia.

More candidates who have won in New Hampshire have gone on to become president than those who have won in Iowa (See Table 3.1). In addition, New Hampshire can also provide candidates with an opportunity for an early "comeback" on the campaign trail. Bill Clinton earned his nickname "the Comeback Kid" after his strong second-place finish in New Hampshire in 1992 (amid media reports that his campaign was finished due to allegations of womanizing and draft dodging), and Hillary Clinton won an important (albeit close) contest over Barack Obama in New Hampshire in 2008 to stem the increasing tide of momentum for Obama's campaign coming out of Iowa.

In 2012, Iowa and New Hampshire heralded an unexpectedly contentious primary season. Former Massachusetts Governor Mitt Romney initially did not put effort into Iowa, making the political calculation that he could not win there. As uncertainty reigned among the more conservative candidates, Romney changed strategies and attempted to earn a commanding swing of momentum by winning both Iowa and New Hampshire, which treated Romney as a favorite son. However, in a surprise, former Pennsylvania senator Rick Santorum surged and captured Iowa. Initially the media called the race for Romney, by eight votes; later the race was certified for Santorum, capturing the state by thirty-four votes.

Table 3.1 Winners in Iowa and New Hampshire since 1976

	IOWA CAUCUS	NEW HAMPSHIRE PRIMARY
1976	Uncommitted*	Jimmy Carter (D)
	Gerald Ford (R)	Gerald Ford (R)
1980	Jimmy Carter (D)	Jimmy Carter (D)
	George H. W. Bush (R)	Ronald Reagan (R)
1984	Walter Mondale (D)	Gary Hart (D)
	Ronald Reagan (R)	Ronald Reagan (R)
1988	Richard Gephardt (D)	Michael Dukakis (D)
	Bob Dole (R)	George H. W. Bush (R)
1992	Tom Harkin (D)	Paul Tsongas (D)
	George H. W. Bush (R)	George H. W. Bush (R)
1996	Bill Clinton (D)	Bill Clinton (D)
	Bob Dole (R)	Pat Buchanan (R)
2000	Al Gore (D)	Al Gore (D)
	George W. Bush (R)	John McCain (R)
2004	John Kerry (D)	John Kerry (D)
	George W. Bush (R)	George W. Bush (R)
2008	Barack Obama (D)	Hillary Clinton (D)
	Mike Huckabee (R)	John McCain (R)
2012	Barack Obama (D)	Barack Obama (D)
	Rick Santorum (R)	Mitt Romney (R)

* More Democratic voters (37%) chose to remain "uncommitted" than to pledge their support to any candidate; Jimmy Carter received the most of any candidate at 28%.

However, while the influence of both Iowa and New Hampshire in the nominating process has been diminished a bit in recent elections due to the excessive front-loading of primaries, and while the demographics of each state are hardly representative of the nation at large (in terms of race, ethnicity, and socioeconomic factors, among others), both states and the national parties are committed to maintaining their status as the first presidential contests, thereby carrying on the tradition of having Iowa and New Hampshire winnow the field of presidential contenders.

Super Tuesday

The term "Super Tuesday" has been around since the 1980s, and first gained prominence in 1988 when nine southern states decided to hold their Democratic primaries on the same day in early March in an effort to create an unofficial regional primary. Since then, Super Tuesday has picked up many other states and has moved up on the primary calendar. Since more delegates can be won on Super

Tuesday than on any other day of the primary calendar, presidential candidates must do well on this day. While candidates can sometimes wrap up the nomination on Super Tuesday by securing a majority of delegates, candidates must at least provide a strong enough showing to continue the flow of money into campaign coffers and to be labeled by the news media as competitive in order for their campaigns to survive. In 2008, Super Tuesday was held earlier than ever before, on February 5, with twenty-four states holding primaries or caucuses where a total of 52 percent of Democratic Party delegates and 41 percent of Republican Party delegates were at stake.

The 2008 campaign also highlighted another issue that has emerged in recent campaigns, which is the front-loading of presidential primaries and caucuses. Front-loading means that states move up the date of their primary contests so that their state will become more relevant in the selection of presidential nominees. For example, in 1992, Californians did not have the chance to cast a ballot for any political candidate in the presidential primary until the first Tuesday in June. However, the contest for the Republican and Democratic nominations (won by George H. W. Bush and Bill Clinton, respectively) had already been decided by early April. That meant voters in the most populous state in the union did not have a real say in who each party would nominate. Consequently, in 1996, California, along with other states like New York and Texas, decided to move their primaries to March in order to play a more influential role in the selection of presidential nominees. This change, in turn, had an impact on the role of money in the primary process. In order to survive the early contests, candidates needed even more money to spend on these big states even earlier in the process. This put more pressure on candidates and their campaigns to raise larger amounts of money, and left those candidates without strong financial support and broader national appeal at an even greater disadvantage. During the 1996 Republican primaries, for example, the well-funded campaign of Senate Majority Leader (and eventual nominee) Bob Dole had a much easier time surviving the numerous March primary contests than did some of his challengers, like political commentator Pat Buchanan or former Education Secretary and Tennessee Senator Lamar Alexander. So, while money had always been an important determining factor in the selection of presidential nominees, front-loading the primaries placed an even higher fundraising burden on White House hopefuls. In 2008, 71 percent of the primaries and caucuses occurred between January 3rd and February 19th. Moreover, those races included big states like California and New York where it is expensive to run state races due to the cost of running advertising in large media markets. Running out of money during the run for the nomination, and the inability to raise more, is a loud signal of the death of a campaign. The 2012 nomination calendar was less front-loaded, as only forty percent of the primaries occurred between January 3rd and Super Tuesday, March 6. In 2012, several big states, including Texas, Pennsylvania, New York, and California, voted after April 1st, with California's primary pushed back to its historical date of the first Tuesday in June.

The Delegate Count

While the goal for all presidential candidates throughout the primary season is to secure enough delegates to capture their party's nomination, the process differs a bit for each major party. The Republican Party traditionally apportioned its delegates based on constitutional allocations in Congress and the Electoral College. Each state's delegate total was equal to the number of members of Congress in its state delegation, plus their state party representatives, plus the number of presidential electors in the Electoral College (which is the House delegation plus two Senators), plus the number of states with Republican governors and a majority in the legislature.[20] In most of the states, the winning Republican candidate in the state's primary or caucus then received all the state's delegates, in what is known as a winner-take-all system. Consequently, the front-loading of the primary calendar benefited Republican hopefuls with the greatest name recognition, as winning early can put the nomination out of reach for late momentum builders or party outsiders. In 2012, two key features changed. First, the national party punished several states for moving up and front-loading the calendar by reducing their delegate count by half and thus reducing their influence on the outcome (The Democratic National Committee similarly punished the states of Michigan and Florida for moving up their primaries in 2008). The Republican nominee needed to earn 50 fewer delegates in 2012 than was necessary in 2008. Second, 81 percent of states dropped the winner-take-all method of allocating delegates in favor of a proportional, hybrid proportional, direct election, or a non-binding method.

The Democrats adjust their rules much more frequently than do the Republicans. Democrats spend more time on their rules as their rules are more complicated and more focused on increasing ordinary rank-and-file member participation. The Democrats emphasize participation and population in their formulas, counting the state's Electoral College allocation, plus the state's popular vote in the last three presidential elections.[21] In addition, the Democrats rely on proportional allocation of delegates, rather than a winner-take-all system. However, the Democratic allocation system does not account for 100 percent of the delegate total at the National Convention, as Democrats also rely on what are known as "superdelegates." First created in 1982, superdelegates were a response to the nomination reforms put into place in 1972 (and championed by that year's nominee, George McGovern) to turn over the selection process to the rank-and-file party members (the voters). In 1982, following Jimmy Carter's failed bid at reelection in 1980, the Democratic Party decided to take back some of that power from the voters and return it to the party bosses. Superdelegates became important names within the party, like those who held political office in Congress or high-profile state politicians (such as governors), and other notables within the party (like a former president or vice president). Superdelegates played an important role in the 2008 nomination battle between Obama and Clinton. At the start of the primary season, Clinton had a commanding lead among superdelegates who had pledged their support to her candidacy, but after Super Tuesday and the emergence of Obama as the frontrunner, unpledged superdelegates slowly began to pledge their support to Obama, while others who had already pledged their support to Clinton switched to Obama once it seemed likely that he would win the nomination 🖱.

🖱 View the list of pledged Superdelegates.

FINANCING PRESIDENTIAL CAMPAIGNS

Running for president is not cheap. In order to run a successful campaign, major expenses include paying consultants and staff, conducting polls, sending direct mail, gaining media exposure through advertisements, and—let's not forget—fundraising itself. Money allows a politician to get his or her message out to the voters, and money is also essential to run and staff an effective campaign operation. Thus, an aspiring presidential candidate must raise funds long before citizens cast any votes in any primary or caucus in order to reach potential voters. As a result, fund-raising becomes its own contest before and during the campaign because it serves as a signal of viability. The linking of fundraising to attractiveness to voters results from the obvious conclusion that donors give money (large or small amounts) to people they want to see win and not to people they think will lose.

Campaign Finance: A Brief History

The influence of money on the American political process is not new. Consider the fact that in the earliest days of the republic, only those who owned land (i.e., had money and wealth) were allowed to vote. One of the best-known stories about George Washington as a politician is about his campaign for the Virginia House of Burgesses in 1758. To entice voters to give Washington their support, his election managers provided a half-gallon of alcoholic beverages per voter on Election Day. Later, in 1777, when James Madison ran unsuccessfully for the Virginia state legislature, he attributed his loss to his failure to provide similar alcoholic refreshments to the voters.[22] From the time of the first presidential elections, many of the candidates, including Washington, John Adams, and Thomas Jefferson, paid for the expenses related to their own campaigns. These were men of means, after all, and the campaigns themselves were not that costly. But within a few decades, it took more money to run for the presidency than most aspiring politicians could afford to spend.

During the 1830s and the era of Andrew Jackson's presidency—also known for the birth of the modern political party—presidents found an effective way to reward those who had financially supported their campaign. Under what became known as the "spoils system," winning candidates rewarded their political supporters with government jobs and contracts. To this day, Democratic and Republican presidents still rely on the spoils system to reward large financial campaign contributors, often with an ambassadorship to a prime locale like France, Italy, Germany, Austria, or Great Britain. For example, George W. Bush appointed Los Angeles investment banker Ronald P. Spogli as U.S. Ambassador to Italy in June 2005. A former classmate of Bush's at Harvard Business School, Spogli was also a top Republican donor, having donated more than $800,000 to Republican candidates and party committees during the 2000, 2002, and 2004 election cycles.[23]

The development of national party committees was another important step in helping candidates raise funds for political campaigns. The Democratic National Committee (DNC) was first established in 1852 to raise funds for the party's presidential candidate, Franklin Pierce. More than 150 years later, national party committees continue to play a significant role in political fundraising. Today the Democratic and Republican National Committees both serve as the headquarters for coordinating each party organization on the national level and serve as the main fundraising apparatus for their respective parties.[24] In 2008, the DNC raised a total of $961,199,298 for campaign expenses, while the RNC raised a total of $920,479,521. Both amounts were nearly tripled compared to 2004, and in both cases, each party spent nearly all of that money on helping to elect their party members to public office.[25] In 2012, the DNC raised a total of $1.2 billion, while the RNC raised a total of $1.3 billion. Similarly, the influence of corporate money on the political process also dates back to the mid-nineteenth century. After the Civil War, some of America's greatest industrialists and the corporations they built (like Union Pacific, Standard Oil, and New York Life Insurance, to name just a few) became an important source of political financing, particularly to those candidates seeking the White House. For example, members of the wealthiest families in America, including the Vanderbilt, Astor, and Cooke families, heavily financed Republican Ulysses S. Grant's 1868 presidential campaign. These influential Americans represented some of America's earliest fat cat donors, a term later used to describe wealthy individuals who spent vast amounts of their money in an attempt to influence the outcome of an election.[26]

By the end of the nineteenth century, the Gilded Age (known as a time of dramatic industrial growth as well as high levels of political corruption at all levels of government) was replaced by the Progressive Era, during which various reform movements arose in an attempt to clean up the corruption and influence of money in politics. Those supportive of the Progressive movement believed that large corporate contributions to campaigns, particularly at the presidential level, were destroying the American democratic process by giving wealthy business owners too much control over the government. At that time, virtually no laws existed to regulate the flow of money into campaign coffers. Consequently, the influence of corporations in American elections became a major concern among reformers, prompting President Theodore Roosevelt to mention the issue in his Annual Message to Congress in 1905:

> In political campaigns in a country as large and populous as ours it is inevitable that there should be much expense of an entirely legitimate kind. This, of course, means that many contributions, and some of them of large size, must be made, and, as a matter of fact, in any big political contest such contributions are always made to both sides. It is entirely proper both to give and receive them, unless there is an improper motive connected with either gift or reception. If they are extorted by any kind of pressure or promise, express or implied, direct or indirect, in the way of favor or immunity, then the giving or receiving becomes not only improper but criminal. It will undoubtedly be difficult, as a matter of practical detail, to shape an act which shall guard with reasonable certainty against such misconduct; but if it is possible to secure by law the full and verified publication in detail of all the sums contributed to and expended by the candidates or committees of any political parties, the result cannot but be wholesome. All contributions by corporations to any political committee or for any political purpose should be forbidden by law; directors should not be permitted to use stockholders' money for such purposes; and, moreover, a prohibition of this kind would be, as far as it went, an effective method of stopping the evils aimed at in corrupt practices acts.[27]

Two years later, Congress passed the first law to alter the campaign finance landscape, banning corporations and national banks from making contributions to candidates for federal office. Over the next decades, other congressional acts would follow, including passage of the Hatch Act in 1939, which barred federal employees from taking an active role in federal campaigns, with amendments passed in 1940 attempting to limit campaign contributions and expenditures for federal candidates. In 1947, passage of the Taft–Hartley Act banned political contributions by labor unions due to the perceived power and influence of union leaders, like corporate leaders, on election outcomes.[28] However, much to the chagrin of those supporting campaign finance reform during the first half of the twentieth century, Congress had little to no authority to enforce these laws. Even when attempts at enforcement were made, candidates and their campaign managers always seemed to find various loopholes to get around the law and keep the money flowing into presidential (and congressional) campaigns. It would take the resignation of a president in the latter part of the twentieth century to make Congress finally get serious about reforming campaign finance laws.

The Federal Election Campaign Acts of 1971 and 1974

Most serious regulations of campaign finance began in the early 1970s as an attempt to end the influence of fat cat donors. As part of this effort, Congress enacted the Federal Election Campaign Act (FECA) of 1971 to provide a format for campaign finance disclosure, which meant that campaigns would have to provide public information about who gave them money and how the money was subsequently spent. The legislation created a comprehensive set of rules by which to regulate money in federal campaigns (including primaries, runoffs, and general elections) and national party conventions. Not only did the law require a "full and timely" disclosure of contributions, but it also set a ceiling on media advertising expenditures, established limits on contributions from candidates and their families, and permitted labor unions and corporations to ask for voluntary contributions from members and employees. As a result, for the first time in 1972, presidential candidates had to disclose where money was actually being spent. That same year, Congress also passed the Revenue Act, which created a public campaign fund for eligible presidential candidates, which took effect in 1976.

Ironically, it was the FECA with its attempts to regulate presidential campaign contributions that in 1974 helped to bring down President Richard Nixon, the same man who had signed the law three years earlier. During the presidential campaign of 1972, when Nixon was running against Democrat George McGovern, the Republican National Committee acted in violation of the 1971 FECA by using a secret "slush fund" to finance various illegal activities. One of these activities was a break-in by White House operatives at the Democratic National Committee headquarters located at the Watergate Complex in Washington, D.C. (hence the term "Watergate," which eventually was used to describe various political scandals associated with Nixon's presidency). Two *Washington Post* reporters, Carl Bernstein and Bob Woodward, were assigned to cover the Watergate break-in and became convinced that the burglars were connected to the Nixon White House. The reporters were instructed by an anonymous source (known only as "Deep Throat" until revealed in 2005 to be former FBI Deputy Director W. Mark Felt) to "follow the money" in order to link the

---

View the disclosed information for recent campaigns on the Center For Responsive Politics' website, www.opensecrets.org.

break-in to Nixon. They did, and a secret White House tape recording that implicated Nixon in the cover-up of the DNC break-in led to Nixon's resignation from the presidency on August 9, 1974.

In October 1974, just two months after Nixon's resignation, Congress passed several major amendments to the FECA, which were promptly signed into law by President Gerald Ford. The legislation became "the most sweeping change imposed upon the relationship between money and politics since the founding of the American republic."[29] Specifically, the 1974 FECA created the Federal Election Commission (FEC), outlined contribution and spending limits at both the presidential and congressional level and created a system of public financing for presidential campaigns. One of the most important changes to the campaign finance system from these amendments included the establishment of the Federal Election Commission (FEC), a bipartisan panel that oversees campaign finance regulations. The overriding goal of the FEC is voluntary compliance with federal election campaign laws, and the agency has the authority to enforce federal campaign laws involving money. Federal candidates (those running for the presidency or Congress) must report their contributions and expenditures to the FEC, and in return the FEC provides public disclosure of that financial information to interested parties like the news media or other watchdog public interest groups.

Other significant changes came through the use of contribution limits, initially established on campaign contributions at $1,000 per candidate per election for individuals and $5,000 per candidate per election for political action committees (PACs) (known as "hard money" contributions). The goal was to diminish political corruption, allow candidates to spend more time campaigning and discussing issues rather than fundraising, and reduce the reliance on and influence from fat cat donors. In addition, PACs, which are basically the fundraising arm of labor unions, corporations, or other special interest groups, began to emerge more prominently in the early 1970s as a way for unions and corporations to get around the ban on campaign contributions by soliciting voluntary contributions from members and employees to help fund campaign expenditures. Since the use of union dues for campaign contributions was illegal, as was the co-mingling of corporate treasury funds with campaign contributions, the 1974 FECA made PACs the legal way for labor unions and big businesses to spend money on behalf of candidates. By the end of the 1970s, interest-group PACs had also taken hold as a way to keep money flowing into the federal electoral process. Along the same lines, the FECA put into place spending limits on how much candidates could spend during their campaigns (including both primaries and general election campaigns for presidential candidates). The general idea was that if all candidates shared the same spending ceiling on campaign expenditures, then the electoral contest would be more fair and less subject to influence by major monetary contributions to one candidate. However, the Supreme Court in its landmark campaign finance decision *Buckley v. Valeo* (1976) criticized this aspect of the law as curtailing freedom of speech unless a candidate was using public funds to pay for their campaign.

Loopholes to Campaign Finance Laws

Despite implementation of these campaign finance reforms, a major loophole in campaign finance laws emerged with the use of "soft money" contributions, which were unlimited funds given by individuals directly to the political parties. Since 1976, soft money played an increasing role in the funding of presidential elections, and also became a public symbol for those wanting to reform campaign finance. Basically, soft money is money raised by national party committees and spent on local voter education or get-out-the-vote efforts. Since there were no limits on the amount of money that could be given to the Democratic or Republican national committees, either by an individual donor or by a PAC, this was a perfect way to get around the rules set out under the FECA and still donate as much money as possible to influence the outcome of a presidential race. For example, during the 1999–2000 federal campaign cycle, which included the 2000 presidential election, the Democratic Party raised a total of $245.2 million in soft money, while the Republican Party raised a total of $249.9 million.

The only rules regulating the use of soft money stated that the funds could not be used for express advocacy for a candidate, but could be used instead for issue advocacy. The difference between the two is that express advocacy would be a television ad that stated "Vote for Bush/Cheney in 2000," meaning it expressly advocated voters to select a particular candidate. Issue advocacy, on the other hand, would be a similar television ad that touted all of Bush and Cheney's political accomplishments and how they supported the Republican policy agenda, as long as the ad did not state "Vote for Bush/Cheney." Avoiding express advocacy for a candidate, then, meant that the expenditure of the funds on the ad would be considered legal under federal guidelines. So while both the DNC and RNC spent some of their soft money contributions on state and local party efforts to increase voter registration and to educate voters about party issues, a large part of soft money funds actually ended up being spent on the presidential race in the form of television advertising. This turned out to be quite a beneficial loophole for both parties, since it allowed presidential candidates to stay within their spending limits during the general election campaign, yet still have their national party committees spend millions of dollars on television advertising right up until election day. And with the help of Supreme Court rulings during the late 1980s and early 1990s that stated issue advocacy was a protected free speech right under the First Amendment, soft money contributions to both the Democratic and Republican parties increased six-fold from $86 million in 1992 to $500 million in 2000 and 2002.[30]

Another loophole that emerged over the years was the use of independent expenditures. Both individuals and PACs utilize independent expenditures, which are contributions made on behalf of, but not directly to, a candidate. So, for example, if someone had $1 million that they wanted to spend to help get Candidate A elected to the White House, they could buy $1 million in television advertising on behalf of Candidate A as long as there was no advisement or support provided by the candidate's campaign staff. This then became a legal way for wealthy individuals or special interest groups to spend large amounts of money on behalf of a candidate so long as there was no coordination with the candidate's official campaign staff. The use of independent expenditures received the blessing of the Supreme Court in *Buckley*, which said that placing limits on this aspect of campaign spending would be unconstitutional since it would not protect the right of free speech. However, the result of these independent expenditures often were not positive ads being run about Candidate A, but instead negative attack ads being used to dissuade voters from supporting Candidate B—thus still benefiting the campaign of Candidate A.

There can sometimes be a downside to this kind of expenditure, since candidates have no control over who is spending money on their behalf or what those people are saying. However, it can also provide a candidate with deniability if someone runs negative attack ads against an opponent on their behalf. An example is the now infamous "Willie Horton" ads from the 1988 presidential campaign in which Republican George H. W. Bush ran against Democrat Michael Dukakis. Horton was an African-American inmate in a Massachusetts state prison who was temporarily released under a furlough program supported by then-Governor Dukakis. He committed a brutal rape while on his release, and supporters of Bush ran a controversial ad blaming Dukakis for the program and its resulting crime. When the ads, which had heavy racial undertones (by highlighting the rape of a white woman by a black man), came under public scrutiny, the Bush campaign was able to distance itself from the ads (that is, use the deniability factor) while still reaping the intended message—that Dukakis was soft on crime.

Bundling, the practice of gathering campaign contributions from friends and associates, is also now a popular strategy seen in presidential campaigns. An individual or PAC can solicit contributions from individuals on behalf of a candidate and then "bundle" them together to make one large (and legal) contribution to the campaign. Since each of the individual contributions is within the limit for hard money prior to being bundled, this allows an individual or group to give a large contribution to a particular candidate.[31] While some groups have a particular policy objective or other goal they hope to achieve by bundling, there are other incentives to bundle thousands of dollars of campaign contributions. Both national parties reward their top contributors with many perks, including private meetings with top policymakers (and even the president for the party that happens to hold the White House), or perhaps being seated next to a prominent politician at a party event. Top fundraisers for the Bush/Cheney election campaign in 2000 and the reelection campaign in 2004 were dubbed "Bush Rangers" if they solicited $200,000 each, and "Bush Pioneers" if they solicited $100,000 each. Many of these contributors earned an appointment within the Bush administration, either as cabinet members, ambassadors, members of federal advisory boards, or other executive branch positions. In fact, nearly one in five of these elite fundraisers from the 2000 and 2004 campaigns received a presidential appointment. For example, four of Bush's cabinet appointments during his first term earned the title of "pioneers" for their fundraising work during the 2000 campaign, including Secretary of Labor Elaine Chao, Secretary of Commerce Donald Evans, Secretary of Housing and Urban Development Alphonso Jackson, and Secretary of Homeland Security Tom Ridge. Bundling, therefore, provides a unique way for someone willing to do some free fundraising on behalf of a candidate to gain influence and access within political circles, as well as a possible political appointment.

In recent years, self-financing candidates have also emerged, adding a new dynamic to the game of campaign finance. Wealthy candidates have no limits on how much of their own money they can spend as long as they do not accept public funding (either matching funds during the primary season or the money given to party nominees during the general election). However, if they do accept public funding, they are limited to spending $50,000 of their own money in either part of the campaign. Wealthy candidates have advantages over challengers, since they can spend lavishly on their campaigns without wasting precious campaign time on fundraising. This can be particularly important since early money is crucial to keep the campaign momentum going. And personal loans from the candidate to his or her campaign can be repaid through fundraising efforts later on. H. Ross Perot, with his run as an independent candidate for the White House in both 1992 and 1996, may be the most famous millionaire presidential candidate in recent years. Perot believed that his success in the business world would translate into running the federal government more efficiently and bringing down the national debt. He was quoted as saying, "If someone as blessed as I am is not willing to clean out the barn, who will?" Perot spent $63.5 million on his 1992 campaign; in 1996, Perot spent only $8 million of his own money since he accepted public funding during the general election campaign.

However, Perot is not the only wealthy candidate to recently seek the presidency. Steve Forbes ran for the Republican nomination in both 1996 and 2000, as did Mitt Romney in 2008 and 2012. While Forbes never garnered much support among voters, the mere fact that he had endless amounts of money to spend on his own campaign without wasting time on fundraising made him a realistic threat to other candidates (he spent $38 million of his own money in 1996 and $48 million in 2000). Romney, who became McCain's chief rival in 2008, remained competitive for much of the primary season due, in part, to his ability to partially fund his campaign from his personal fortune (he contributed $42.35 million of his own money). Romney spent much less in his successful bid for the 2012 Republican nomination (slightly more than $52,000). Candidates like Perot and Forbes also had an important strategic advantage with voters—a point that any self-financing candidate regularly makes: Paying for your own campaign means that you are not tied to special interests or others who funded your run for office.

Public Funding of Presidential Campaigns

In American presidential politics, being either independently wealthy or knowing lots of people who are is not a prerequisite for becoming a presidential candidate. However, without these advantages the problem then becomes, where does the money come from? In response to this problem, the 1974 FECA provided public funding for presidential elections in the form of matching funds during the primary period, a flat grant to major parties to run their nominating conventions, and larger grants for full public financing for major party candidates during the general election. In theory, public funding of any campaign, whether at the national or local level, is supposed to encourage more candidates to run for office by leveling the financial playing field.

Congress decided to fund presidential campaigns, starting in 1976, through what is known as a tax checkoff. This allows tax payers to designate money for the Presidential Election Campaign Fund (PECF) by checking a box on their federal income tax return. This checkoff instructed the Internal Revenue Service (IRS) to earmark $1 from federal taxes to be placed in the fund (the amount was increased to $3 in 1993). However, while many Americans continue to believe that money corrupts the political process, few choose to participate in the tax checkoff for the

PECF. Participation in the tax checkoff program has declined each year, from a high of 28.7% for 1980 returns, to 7.3% for returns filed with the IRS in 2010.[32] Many Americans incorrectly assume that checking the box on their federal income tax return actually increases their tax burden and adds $3 to the amount they owe to the IRS. In reality, it merely earmarks the funds and does not add to an individual's overall tax bill (and presents the only opportunity that a citizen ever has to actually tell Congress how to spend part of the money they pay in taxes).

Primaries

Since an election is more democratic when voters have a higher number of viable choices, the idea of matching funds in a presidential primary seemed like a good idea to keep as many candidates in the race as possible. Money is essential to fund the early stages of a presidential campaign, and a candidate cannot survive long in the primary process if his or her campaign runs out of money. Candidates must meet eligibility requirements to receive federal matching funds during the presidential primaries. To become eligible for these funds, which are administered through the U.S. Treasury, each candidate must raise $5,000 in contributions of $250 or less in at least twenty states. Matching funds are then given for the first $250 received from an individual (with a maximum of half of the overall spending limit). And, if candidates accept matching funds, they must also adhere to spending limits (in 2008, that limit was just over $42 million per candidate). PAC contributions do not receive matching funds. Amendments passed by Congress in 1976 to the FECA also established a 10 percent rule—if the candidate receives less than 10 percent of the vote in two consecutive primaries, he or she becomes ineligible for funding. Funding will be restored if 20 percent of the vote is achieved in a later primary, but if a candidate withdraws, any remaining funds must be returned to the U.S. Treasury. Receiving those funds is no guarantee that a campaign will survive beyond the first few contests. For example, in 2004, Democratic hopeful Richard Gephardt, who resigned his seat in the House of Representatives and his position as Democratic Minority Leader to run for president, received a total of $4.1 million in federal matching funds. Yet, he dropped out of the race on January 20, 2004, the day after his poor showing in the Iowa Caucus (he finished fourth with only 11 percent of the vote). Similarly, retired Army General Wesley Clark ended his bid for the Democratic nomination on February 11, 2004, after collecting $7.6 million in federal matching funds but only one primary win (in Oklahoma).

In 2000, then-Texas Governor George W. Bush showed the importance of fundraising in making it to the front of the presidential pack. During a primary season in which several Republican presidential hopefuls were jockeying in a wide-open field to become the party's frontrunner, Bush broke records with his fundraising prowess. Raising a total of $95.5 million during the primaries, Bush had so much money that he did not need to accept primary matching funds. Moreover, by not taking the government's money, Bush did not have to abide by a spending limit that would have greatly curtailed his ability to run television ads through the late spring and summer months of 2000. His eventual opponent and Democratic nominee Al Gore, on the other hand, did not have that same luxury. Gore accepted matching funds, which brought his total fundraising receipts to $48.1 million during the Democratic primaries. However, he also had to accept the spending limit, and due to the competition he faced in the primary season from former New Jersey Senator and

NBA Hall of Famer Bill Bradley, Gore ran out of money in late spring and did not have other funds at his disposal until after he accepted the Democratic nomination in September. This turned out to be a clear strategic advantage for Bush, who, with no limit, could spend twice as much as Gore.

In an attempt to learn from Gore's misfortune in 2000, leading Democratic contenders in 2004, including eventual nominee John Kerry, Sen. John Edwards (NC), and former Vermont Governor Howard Dean, refused matching funds during the presidential primaries. Bush, seeking reelection, had no challengers within his party and continued his successful fundraising, also without the help of matching funds. For the 2004 primaries, Bush raised a total of $269.6 million, while Kerry raised a total of $234.6 million. And with soft money coffers closed to the DNC and RNC, fundraisers zeroed in on contributions from small donors, which reached record levels in 2004. Similarly, in 2008, nearly all of the top-tier presidential candidates chose not to accept matching funds and the attached spending limit for the primary season. One of the lone exceptions was John McCain, the first candidate in 2008 to accept matching funds.[33] In 2012, only Former Governor of Louisiana, Buddy Roemer, who won no delegates in a Republican primary or caucus, accepted FDC matching funds. The good news of 2004, 2008, and 2012 is that less money was drained from the federal treasury to pay for the presidential primary campaigns. The bad news, however, is that by not accepting matching funds, candidates were able to bypass all spending limits and broke all sorts of records for raising and spending money in each race to get their party's nomination for president.

National conventions

Following the conclusion of the presidential primaries, the two major parties are eligible to receive public funding in the form of a flat grant to pay for nominating conventions (where a candidate and his or her running mate receive the official nomination of their party), as long as they agree not to raise private funds and stick to the spending limit. Major party candidates are defined by law as representing a party that received at least 25 percent of the vote in the previous general election. Third or minor party candidates are eligible for a pro-rated subsidy, provided that the party's candidate received at least 5 percent of the vote in the previous election. In 2008, each party received $16,820,000 from the PECF to pay for their respective conventions. However, that is not the only money that funded the Democratic convention in Denver and the Republican convention in St. Paul, Minnesota, during the summer of 2008. Since public funding first took effect in 1976, the FEC has allowed political parties to rely on host committees and municipal funds in the cities they select for their conventions to raise additional funds to pick up the tab; in 2008, a combined total of $124.3 million was spent on the two conventions by host committees and municipal funds.[34] In 2012, that figure reached a combined total of $189 million.

General election

During the general election, which officially begins when each major party has concluded its nominating conventions (but which unofficially starts on Labor Day weekend), major party candidates then receive their money from the government. In 2004, George W. Bush and John Kerry each received just under $75 million to pay for their general election campaigns (an increase from the $67 million that Bush and Al

Gore each received in 2000). Third party candidates have also received public funds for the general election in the past. Multi-millionaire H. Ross Perot qualified for $30 million in public funds during the 1996 presidential election based on the 19 percent of the popular vote he received in the 1992 presidential election. His party, the Reform Party, qualified again in 2000, and its nominee, Patrick J. Buchanan, received $12.5 million in public funds for his presidential campaign. By accepting the funds, each major party candidate then agreed to the same amount of money serving as their campaign's spending limit. In 2008, John McCain received $84.1 million in public funds to conduct his general election campaign and raised an additional $46.4 million for legal and accounting expenses. His Democratic rival, Barack Obama, raised the record-breaking total of $745.7 million in private funds for his primary nomination and general election campaign. Obama's refusal to accept the general election funds from the federal government marked the first time in the history of presidential public financing that a major party nominee declined to accept public funds for the general election campaign (and with it, the attached spending limit). And, by the end of the general election campaign, the Obama campaign was outspending McCain on television ads by a four-to-one margin.[35] In 2012, President Obama and Mitt Romney raised staggering sums of money: In 2012, President Obama and Mitt Romney raised staggering sums of money: over $1 billion combined. Neither candidate used government money to finance their campaigns. President Obama raised a staggering $214 million (34%) from small donors. Mitt Romney raised just 18% of his $385 million from small donors.

Recent Campaign Finance Reforms

Despite the major campaign finance reforms enacted by Congress in the 1970s, money continued to be the driving force in presidential campaigns through the 1990s. The loopholes created by the system, along with the political desire among many Americans to enact further reform, is exemplified by Bill Clinton's re-election victory in 1996. Clinton, a prolific fundraiser, along with several savvy advisors, had finally reached parity with Republicans in the area of raising soft money. By 1995, in the crucial months leading up to the 1996 presidential primaries (a time when candidates must organize their campaigns), the Clinton reelection team wanted to air a series of television ads touting the President as a centrist Democrat in the wake of the Republican victory in the 1994 congressional midterm elections (which saw the GOP take control of both houses of Congress for the first time in forty years). The ads had a big price tag, and Clinton's advisors were fearful that the strategy would take a large bite out of the campaign budget. If so, then little money would be left to fend off a Democratic challenge in the presidential primaries or a strong Republican opponent in the general election campaign.

Soft money became the perfect solution to the dilemma. Since the ads were policy oriented and did not expressly advocate Clinton's reelection, they could be bought by DNC soft money contributions that Clinton and his vice president, Al Gore, would help to raise. Team Clinton engaged in a "frantic, no-holds barred, fundraising effort" that was so successful that there was no money to be had from Democratic supporters for anyone inclined to challenge the President for the Democratic nomination.[36] However, Clinton's success with fundraising in 1996 did not come without a political price tag. In the frenzy to raise as much money as possible, the Clinton campaign was not very diligent in screening the sources of some of the contributions. The Republican-controlled Congress launched an investigation in 1996 and 1997 into alleged illegal fundraising practices by the President's reelection team. The charges levied against Clinton and Gore included a long list of transgressions: illegal foreign contributions, including attempts by the Chinese government to influence the outcome of the election; nights in the Lincoln Bedroom at the White House in exchange for large campaign contributions; laundering campaign funds through conduit groups; and large sums of soft money being funneled to both political parties from corporations, labor unions, and wealthy individuals.

Democrats tried to fight back by making their own charges against Republicans, especially with regard to the large sums of soft money from corporations and wealthy individuals, but little attention was paid to either side by the public. The reality of the situation was that both parties had abused the campaign finance laws that were in place at the time. Republicans, whose goal had been to expose the Democrats' improprieties, were—in doing so—highlighting the weaknesses of the campaign finance regulations and leading the way to something they never wanted: campaign finance reform. At the same time, despite their newly found success in raising money, Democrats could not back away from the issue of campaign finance reform, which they had championed for so long and which was so strongly supported by their key constituents. So the Democratic Party and Clinton continued to publicly support the policy reform that they knew would now hurt them financially in the same way that they had hoped it would hurt the Republican Party.

The investigation into alleged campaign finance abuses played strategically into the hands of two senators in particular—John McCain and Russ Feingold. The McCain–Feingold proposal, first introduced in 1995, addressed the continuing problem of soft money, especially the so-called issue advocacy ads that both parties were spending millions of dollars to air. The ads, whose producers took great pains to avoid the magic words *vote for*, *vote against*, *oppose*, or *support*, looked more like regular express advocacy campaign ads, which violated the spirit of the campaign finance laws. As a result, the McCain–Feingold bill sought to prohibit corporations and labor unions from using soft money to pay for any electioneering communications, that is, broadcast ads that mention a federal candidate or officeholder within thirty days of a primary or sixty days of a general election. McCain and Feingold also argued that since contribution limits had never been raised since the initial legislation was passed in 1974, candidates were increasingly beholden to other sources of money. Since the contribution limits had not kept up with the rate of inflation, a $1,000 contribution back in 1976 was worth less than $250 by the year 2000.

Finally, after a seven-year struggle, McCain and Feingold, along with their supporters in both the House and the Senate, succeeded in passing their bill, the Bipartisan Campaign Reform Act (BCRA), which President Bush signed into law on March 27, 2002. Of course, Bush had not been a supporter of changing a system that had worked so well for him in the 2000 presidential election, and there was still resentment on his part toward McCain, who had been his strongest rival in the 2000 Republican primaries. So, in contrast to most bill-signing ceremonies held in the White House Rose Garden with the requisite news media coverage, Bush signed the bill into law in the privacy of the Oval Office with little fanfare. While Bush might have vetoed the bill at any other political moment, the nation has just watched the Enron scandal unfold (along with various other corporate scandals), and the White House had been embarrassed by the large amounts of money that the top executives at Enron had given to Bush as both a gubernatorial candidate in Texas and during his run for the White House in 2000. Given the public's mood on the issue, Bush signed the bill, knowing that plenty of others would continue to oppose its new provisions.[37]

Once signed, the law doubled the hard money contribution limits for individuals in federal elections (which includes congressional campaigns) to $2,000 per candidate per election in a given campaign cycle (primaries, runoffs, and the general election are still viewed as separate elections for each candidate). Since then, the amount has been adjusted every two years; for the 2011–2012 campaign cycle, the limit was set at $2,500. But perhaps more importantly, and certainly more controversially, the new law banned soft money, which had a great impact on campaign fundraising strategies for 2004. Immediately after the law went into effect, several groups, including the AFL-CIO, the American Civil Liberties Union, and the National Rifle Association, along with the Republican National Committee and perhaps the law's most outspoken opponent, Senator Mitch McConnell (R-KY), filed a lawsuit in federal court claiming that various provisions of the BCRA were unconstitutional. The legislation was a clear case of an issue that made strange political bedfellows, with "unions, corporations, right-to-lifers, civil libertarians, gun owners, broadcasters, Christians, fat cats, purists who think it doesn't go far enough, Democrats, Republicans, Congress, the White House, and even the regulators who are supposed to enforce it" opposed to some or all of the provisions of the bill.[38]

Initially, in May 2003, a federal court ruled that the ban on soft money was unconstitutional, but on appeal, the U.S. Supreme Court in a December 2003 decision, *McConnell v. FEC,* upheld the ban on soft money contributions. While divided 5 to 4 in its ruling, the Court was able to save the legislation and uphold its original ruling in *Buckley v. Valeo* by stating that Congress had the right to protect the integrity of the electoral process. McCain, Feingold, and all of the ardent campaign finance supporters (including public interest groups like the Center for Responsive Politics and Public Citizen, long-time advocates of serious campaign finance reform) had achieved a big victory. However, the ban on soft money would not only create new and innovative loopholes, but campaign spending by presidential candidates would hit all-time highs during the next three election cycles.

Always resourceful, it did not take long for the presidential candidates and political parties to find other ways to raise money. According to the FEC, the financial activity of all presidential candidates in 2004, including the national Democratic and Republican conventions, totaled more than $1 billion, a 56 percent increase over the same campaign activities just four years prior in 2000, and by 2008, that figure doubled to nearly $2 billion, and grew to $3 billion in 2012. Following the Supreme Court's decision to do away with soft money, politicians discovered another option—527s—to take its place. As tax-exempt groups organized under section 527 of the Internal Revenue Code to raise money for political activities, these nonparty organizations are not required to register with the FEC since their main purpose is not to influence the outcome of federal elections. Most 527s are run by interest groups to raise unlimited soft money, which is then spent on voter mobilization or certain types of issue advocacy activities, just not for efforts that expressly advocate the election or defeat of a federal candidate. These groups, widely viewed as nothing more than shadow committees of the political parties, provided an alternative to soft money by allowing various wealthy individuals to donate large sums of money without technically breaking the new laws that went into effect in 2002. The most prominent of these groups raised millions of dollars from wealthy individuals who wanted to have an impact on the presidential campaign.

Beginning in 2004, the most influential 527 groups included "America Coming Together" and "The Media Fund" on the Democratic side and "Progress for America" and "Swift Boat Veterans and POWs for Truth" on the Republican side. Some of these 527 groups, most notably the "Swift Boat Veterans" who opposed John Kerry's candidacy, broadcast ads attacking the Democratic nominee. Some groups also ran positive ads in support of their chosen candidate, all while skirting the technicalities governing express advocacy. Other groups, like MoveOn.Org, which supported the Kerry campaign during the general election, focused much of their energy and attention on both television ads (some praising Kerry and some attacking Bush) and get-out-the-vote drives in key states.[39] By 2008, MoveOn.Org had closed down its 527 operation in support of Barack Obama's campaign, citing the hope that Obama's fundraising efforts of relying on numerous small donors would help to change the tone of the campaign by decreasing the use of negative attack ads (even though MoveOn.Org had aired numerous such ads attacking both Bush and McCain). Both Obama and McCain also made public pleas to their supporters in 2008 to send contributions to their campaigns directly and not to 527 groups.[40]

In 2010, the Supreme Court issued another ruling regarding the regulation of money and behavior of groups during presidential campaigns. In *Citizens United vs. The Federal Election Commission*, the Court ruled that corporate spending on political advertising, or in this case a political film, entitled *Hillary: The Movie*, could not be limited and was not subject to BRCA guidelines. The Court did not strike down the ban on direct corporate contributions but did strike down the prohibition of both non-profit and for-profit entities broadcasting "electioneering communications." The Court ruled that so long as disclosure of the sponsors occurred, the communication was constitutional. The ruling enraged participants across the system, including Democrats, Republicans, and even Tea Party activists, who condemned the apparent advantage granted to deep-pocketed institutions to influence the political environment of the campaign. The ruling was so controversial that competing institutional views played out on the highest stage during President Obama's 2010 State of the Union address, when Obama called out the Supreme Court for its ruling: "With all due deference to separation of powers, last week the Supreme Court reversed a century of law that I believe will open the floodgates for special interests—including foreign corporations—to spend without limit in our elections. I don't think American elections should be bankrolled by America's most powerful interests, or worse, by foreign entities. They should be decided by the American people. And I'd urge Democrats and Republicans to pass a bill that helps to correct some of these problems."[41] Several members of the Court were in attendance for the President's State of the Union address, and Associate Justice Samuel Alito visibly frowned and said "not true" in response to Obama's lecture. Six weeks later, Chief Justice John Roberts weighed in during his State of the Judiciary address: "First of all, anybody can criticize the Supreme Court without any qualm... some people, I think, have an obligation to criticize what we do, given their office, if they think we've done something wrong.... On the other hand, there is the issue of the setting, the circumstances and the decorum. The image of having the members of one branch of government standing up, literally surrounding the Supreme Court, cheering and hollering while the court—according to the requirements of protocol—has to sit there expressionless, I think is very troubling."[42] The

Supreme Court's application of its *Citizens United* ruling in another case, *SpeechNow.org v. Federal Election Commission* created the so-called Super PACs during the 2012 presidential election, which are independent-expenditure-only committees that can raise unlimited sums from corporations, unions and other groups, as well as individuals. The Super PACs cannot donate directly to candidates, as regular PACs do. Instead, Super PACs raise money to run a campaign parallel to the candidates' campaign.

By the end of the 2012 primary season, Super PAC spending exceeded $120 million, and their fundraising surpassed $220 million. Restore Our Future, a Romney supporting Super PAC, was the dominant fundraiser, raising more than double its closest rival. By the end of the 2012 primary season, Super PAC spending exceeded $120 million, and their fundraising surpassed $220 million. Restore Our Future, a Romney supporting Super PAC, was the dominant fundraiser, raising more than double its closest rival. By the end of the 2012 general election, Super PAC spending exceeded $253 million. During the last weeks of the campaign, Super PACs spent more than $20 million a week.

NATIONAL PARTY CONVENTIONS

The role of the national party convention has changed dramatically during the past century. In the age where party insiders dominated the nominee selection process, the convention was a hotbed of intrigue and activity where rules were created, deals struck, and favorite candidates promoted. Today's convention lacks all that drama because the primary process predetermines who the party's nominee will be months earlier. The national convention instead serves as the kickoff for the start of the general election season, a gathering for party insiders, and unites party regulars who will then go home and fight for their nominee in their state. The convention also serves as an introduction to the nominee for voters who did not participate or even pay attention to the primary process, and is a signal for those voters that the campaign for the presidency is under way. Consequently, both the Republican and Democratic conventions are made-for-TV events, scripted to showcase the party and the nominee. The nominee's acceptance speech serves as the highlight of the convention, as this is the first (and often only) opportunity for each candidate to speak directly to voters with full media coverage and without the usual interpretive filter provided by news reporters, anchors, and other analysts.

The first national conventions to be televised were those of both major parties, both held in Philadelphia, in 1948. For President Harry Truman, his televised acceptance speech at the Democratic National Convention represented an important moment of the campaign; lagging in public opinion polls and having governed in the shadow of FDR since succeeding to the presidency in 1945, Truman's speech rallied Democrats with its stinging attack on the Republican Congress. White House advisors had recognized the significance of the speech as it was being developed 🖰:

> We would like to make the following recommendations for the President's Acceptance Speech: It should be a fighting talk.... The President should not just exude confidence, but confidence with reasons. He should give our side some good solid substance upon which to hinge the campaign arguments. Platitudes and truisms

🖰 Listen to Truman's speech.

> should be avoided like the pox. The speech should be short—ten to fifteen minutes maximum. It should be read after thorough study. The words and phrases should be short, homely, and in character. This is no place for Churchillian grandiloquence. Here is the outline of the attached draft: Introduction—The President's confidence and the reasons therefore—His programs are what the people want—Issue for issue, we're right and they're wrong. High Prices—The story of inflation—The choice facing the American people: No action with the Republicans or price control with the Democrats. Housing...Do we want Democratic action or Republican promises? Education, health, and other progressive measures—How the 80th Congress killed them all—A brief rundown. Conclusion—What the President expects to do himself—The job of everyone who feels as we do on these great issues is to tell this story.[43]

The national party convention continues to offer the presidential nominee of each party a chance to speak directly to the American public at a time when many voters are just tuning in to the election. The reception of the candidate's speech by the press, pundits, and citizens often determines which side gets the convention "bounce" in the polls. Like Truman, incumbent presidents running for reelection still pay special attention to this momentous speech, as it can help to set the tone for the upcoming general election campaign. In August 1992, White House speechwriter Tony Snow provided the strategy behind the convention address by President George H. W. Bush 🖱:

> The President's acceptance speech, for good or ill, will set the tone for this year's Republican Presidential Campaign. It must be a winner, and should be.... A good speech should do two things. It should tell a story and it should make an argument. In this case, we should tell the story of George Bush's life. The President, despite his long tenure in the public eye, remains an enigma to most Americans. We should strip away layers of mystery in ways that fit the man. The argument we seek flows from the biography. Americans should re-elect George Bush because he alone can lead America at this historic juncture. He also has tried to unleash American greatness through a program of continued reform. As the speech tells a story and makes an argument, it should try to achieve several important goals: It must define the President. It must define the opposition. It must draw clear distinctions between the political parties. It must unite the party and the country. And it must create the kind of enthusiasm that will transform viewers into volunteers.... If they meet these conditions, they can lift the President to a plane far above where Clinton could possibly stand. They also will provide the Vision Thing by describing in clear and concrete terms what four more years would provide: a more vigorous economy, thriving in the new international marketplace (Olympic analogies might work); an education system in which parents can choose schools for their children, and in which the schools provide the best education in the world; safe streets and neighborhoods where cops and citizens works together to take on criminals, and especially drug kingpins; smaller government and lower taxes, so you keep more of your hard-earned pay; and an America brimming with confidence and ambition—the America we

🖱 Watch President Bush's acceptance speech.

George H. W. Bush gives his famous "read my lips, no new taxes" pledge to delegates at the 1988 Republican National Convention.

> all know and love. When the President steps off the stage in Houston, every listener should be able to answer the question: If we re-elect George Bush, what will our lives be like four years from now? If they cannot answer that question, we're in deep trouble.[44]

Today, other than the candidate's acceptance speech, while much of the rest of the convention itself is often anti-climactic, excitement can emerge out of the choice for the vice-presidential running mate. This serves as the first major decision the presidential nominee makes; thus, voters, pundits, and even the opposing campaign scrutinize both the process and the person selected. In the framers' original model, the vice president was a candidate for president who came in second in the balloting. In the modern era, the vice presidential choice is a reflection of the candidate at the top of the ticket, and often serves as a statement about what the presidential nominee is lacking from a strategic perspective. Historically, vice presidential candidates have been chosen to promote geographic balance (for example, John F. Kennedy's selection of Lyndon Johnson in 1960; the popular Texan as the running mate to the Massachusetts native) or party unity (for example, Ronald Reagan's selection of George H. W. Bush in 1980 and John Kerry's selection of John Edwards in 2004 both represented the nominee's selection of a close rival during the primary season). Other selections have attempted to shore up a candidate's perceived lack of experience in a certain area (for example, Obama's selection of Joe Biden in 2008 brought years

Table 3.2 Presidential Running Mates since 1960

	DEMOCRATIC	REPUBLICAN
1960	Sen. Lyndon Johnson (TX)	Henry Cabot Lodge, Jr.
1964	Sen. Hubert Humphrey (MN)	Rep. William Miller (NY)
1968	Sen. Edmund Muskie (ME)	Gov. Spiro Agnew (MD)
1972	Sargent Shriver	VP Spiro Agnew
1976	Sen. Walter Mondale (MN)	Sen. Bob Dole (KS)
1980	VP Walter Mondale	George H. W. Bush
1984	Rep. Geraldine Ferraro (NY)	VP George H. W. Bush
1988	Sen. Lloyd Bentsen (TX)	Sen. Dan Quayle (IN)
1992	Sen. Al Gore (TN)	VP Dan Quayle
1996	VP Al Gore	Jack Kemp
2000	Sen. Joseph Lieberman (CT)	Dick Cheney
2004	Sen. John Edwards (NC)	VP Dick Cheney
2008	Sen. Joe Biden (DE)	Gov. Sarah Palin (AK)
2012	VP Joe Biden	Rep. Paul Ryan (WI)

of foreign policy experience to the Democratic ticket), or can provide balance to the insider/outsider perspective (for example, as state governors, both Bill Clinton's selection of Al Gore in 1992 and George W. Bush's selection of Dick Cheney in 2000 brought Washington insiders to their tickets). Sometimes running mates are chosen with a bit of history in mind, such as Walter Mondale's selection of Geraldine Ferraro as the first women vice-presidential nominee in 1984 and Al Gore's selection of Joe Lieberman as the first Jewish nominee in 2000; even public relations considerations can matter, as George H. W. Bush seemed to like the energy and youth that the forty-one-year-old Dan Quayle brought to the Republican ticket in 1988. (See Table 3.2)

Perhaps no selection of a running mate received more attention in recent years than John McCain's choice of Alaska Governor Sarah Palin in 2008. At first glance, Palin filled in some of the holes in McCain's effort to gain broader appeal both within the Republican Party and across the electorate. As a woman much younger than McCain, as a state executive, and as a social conservative, she appeared on the surface as a brilliantly inspired choice. Palin initially galvanized the Republican convention and attracted voluminous media attention as something new and unexpected. Nicole Wallace, a senior advisor to the McCain campaign, who worked in the Bush White House and on the Bush campaign, recalls the selection of Palin:

> We...faced the strategic imperative of needing to win the support of some of Senator Hillary Clinton's former supporters. We were very eager to win over women voters. We were also running in a party that was deeply unpopular and distrusted. It was a strategic imperative and, I think, personally important to John McCain to remind voters of his record of standing up against entrenched special interests and, probably more important, his own party. He sought a running mate who had done some of the same things that he had done, had stood up to special

> interests, had stood up to her own party, had taken a stand against corruption and was a doer and a player on the national energy scene.[45]

The reaction to Palin by Republican convention attendees, the press, pundits, and Democrats dramatically revealed a bipolar response to McCain's decision, which does not usually occur. As Joe Trippi, a Democratic strategist and media consultant, pointed out right after the announcement, "It could be brilliant."[46] Palin was not a safe choice or an expected choice, resulting in a feeding-frenzied atmosphere as talk of the ticket dominated campaign coverage, just one day after Senator Obama concluded his speech and closed the Democratic convention. Focus on Palin successfully cut short any post-convention Democratic bounce in opinion polls and provided an increase in interest in the Republican convention. In the immediate short term, the choice of Palin was inspired. Over the course of the campaign, however, she proved to be a lightning rod of attention, often overshadowing McCain himself. The attention was often harsh and distracting, focusing on fashion spending sprees, her fitness for the office, her knowledge (or lack thereof) of national and international issues, and her family. As a consequence of the Palin choice, the vetting of Romney's running mate in 2012 was more intensive. Rep. Paul Ryan, a member of the House of Representatives from Wisconsin since 1999, was viewed as a more substantive choice based on his knowledge of domestic policy issues, particularly those dealing with national budget issues.

THE GENERAL ELECTION

Although the framers designed an election process removed from direct democracy, which balanced issues of representation and geography, they also rejected the notion of campaigning for the office. An adage of the time claimed, "The office should seek the man, the man should not seek the office."[47] However, the early behavior of the states in Electoral College voting demonstrates how rule design influenced strategy, long before the intentional behavior of campaigning took place.

The Electoral College

The Constitution required the states to select their Electors for the Electoral College, in a manner of their choosing (e.g., by popular vote, by state legislature, by lottery if they wanted to), so long as it was completed within the thirty-four day period prior to the first Wednesday of December, and voting was completed by that Wednesday. Defining a beginning and ending date naturally introduced strategy into the process. States who voted early could produce a momentum shift toward a candidate; states who voted later could be the deciding vote in a close outcome. In 1845, Congress settled the strategic jockeying and created a uniform date for choosing their Electors, which today translates to presidential elections held on the first Tuesday following a Monday in November. The Electoral College vote still does not officially occur until December, as this was a Congressional law and not a constitutional change.

Watch Governor Palin's acceptance speech.

President Obama addresses his supporters on the night of his reelection in 2012.

As discussed in Chapter 2, the Electoral College is an institution created by the Constitution to describe the membership of the body that votes for the president. There is no grand meeting of all the Electors, so it is a college in name only. The Electoral College is made up of the Electors from all fifty states, which are allocated by each state on the first Tuesday in November. Most states today choose their Electors by allocating all Electors to the plurality winner of the popular vote; victors do not need 50 percent of the vote, just more than all the other candidates receive. Only Maine and Nebraska do not allocate electors based on the winner-take-call calculation. Instead, the candidate who wins each congressional district wins that electoral vote, while the candidate who wins the popular vote in the state wins the two votes represented by the state's two seats in the U.S. Senate. The Electors vote in December at their state capitals, and more than half the states have laws that require the Electors to vote for the party nominee that they have been chosen to represent. Rarely, but not recently, do "faithless electors" cast their vote for someone other than the candidate on their slate. Given the automatic nature of the Electoral College vote, the position of Elector is more of a symbolic reward than an opportunity to influence the presidential outcome. Yet, the Electoral College still influences election strategy and ultimately the outcome of the race.

The Electoral College imposes strategic decision making on candidates based on the allocation of votes. The Electoral College, like so much in the framer's design, is a compromise between population and size. The design combines the population allocation of the House of Representatives with the assignment of two Senate seats, thus granting all states a minimum of three Electoral College votes. The number of votes in the Electoral College expanded over time as the number of seats in the House of Representatives increased (due to increased population) and the number of states in the Union expanded. As such, 538 became the magic number in 1964 based on the 435 seats in the House of Representatives, 100 seats in the Senate, and the three votes given to the District of Columbia by the Twenty-Third Amendment. With 538 available Electoral College votes, a candidate needs 270 votes to become president. The pathway to achieving the magic number introduces strategy and "electoral math" to presidential campaigns.

The first calculation that a candidate needs to consider is the winner-take-all aspects of most states. The disparities in Electoral College vote allocation resulting from population seemingly encourage candidates to allocate time, money, and effort to states with the largest populations. From this perspective, California, Texas, New York, Florida, and Pennsylvania are worth more because time and effort translates into a quick run to 270; for example, California is 8.13 times more "attractive per electoral vote" than Alaska.[48] Not only do populous states have more partisan voters but they also have more undecided voters to sway. Over time, however, population calculations were not as effective for creating a campaign strategy since they did not account for voting behavior, as "most people make up their minds about whom they will vote for in a presidential election well before the onset of the campaign... [but] for the typically 20–40 percent of the electorate who are normally undecided about their choice of candidate... the campaign will not only be decisive for [them but also for changing] the outcome of almost all elections."[49]

Campaign strategists have long been aware that there are both decided and undecided voters and that the battle for victory exists in turning out one's supporters and reaching those who remain uncommitted. As a result, the size of a state's population is no longer the only factor that determines campaign strategy. For example, the three largest states in the nation have consistently voted for one party in recent decades—a Republican candidate has not won California since 1988 or New York since 1984, and a Democratic candidate has not won Texas since 1976. As a result, the opposing party's candidate spends little time campaigning in a state where he or she has little chance of winning the electoral votes (although fundraising still occurs among party faithfuls). In effect, consistency of partisan voting led to irrelevancy for some of the largest states in the union as campaigns refocused to so-called "swing" states where the outcome was in doubt.

Competitive states, also known as "battleground" or "swing" states, receive massive attention from candidates' campaigns, the parties, interest groups, and the media, because the outcome is unknown. Correspondingly, voter participation in these states also increases.[50] The more effort and resources political elites put into campaigns, the more people turn out to vote. In states without massive mobilization efforts, turnout remains stable or can decline, as the uncommitted or inactive citizen is not mobilized. Even among committed partisans turnout can decline when the candidates do not appear in the state, run ads, or otherwise demonstrate that the race matters. The number of competitive states is shockingly small; in 2000, only twelve states were considered competitive by both campaigns. In 2008, sixteen states were considered battlegrounds; Obama won fifteen of them, and as a result, achieved a resounding Electoral College victory over McCain (365 to 173). In 2012, only 10 states were considered "in play." In effect, the Electoral College system encourages the modern presidential candidate to reject the notion of running in all fifty states. Candidates also have to consider the practicality of allocating a large percentage of resources to states with few Electoral College votes, or to states with a large number of Electoral College votes that they have little chance of winning. In the states where the candidates do compete vigorously, appeals to uncommitted voters are critical.

For today's presidential candidates, the Electoral College has become part of a campaign strategy, which is much different from what the framers had in mind. Also, as highlighted by the contentious 2000 presidential election, many flaws exist. First, a candidate can win the popular vote yet still lose the election by not securing the necessary 270 electoral votes. While Al Gore bested George W. Bush in the number of total votes cast by roughly 500,000 (Gore earned 48.4 percent of the vote to Bush's 47.9 percent), Bush won the Electoral College when he was declared the winner in Florida by the Supreme Court in the now famous case, *Bush v. Gore* (2000). A popular-vote winner had not lost the Electoral College, and thus the presidency, since 1876, when Democrat Samuel Tilden won 51 percent of the popular vote but Republican Rutherford B. Hayes, with only 47.9 percent of the popular vote, won the Electoral College.

The contentious legal battle in 2000 over the vote count in Florida also highlighted the deadlines set for casting of electoral votes; the Supreme Court's ruling in effect stopped the recount in Florida in order to meet the statutory deadlines set for casting the Electoral College votes. The controversy stemmed from the different standards Florida counties used to count ballots during the recount to determine which candidate had won the popular vote in the state (and thus the twenty-five electoral votes that would decide the presidential contest in the Electoral College). Whether or not the Supreme Court should have accepted the case on appeal from the Florida State Supreme Court also stirred controversy. Nevertheless, the Supreme Court ruled that the Florida Supreme Court's method of recounting ballots was unconstitutional in that the different standards violated the equal protection clause. However, a 5–4 majority also declared that there was not enough time to conduct a recount of the vote and that no other remedy was available in deciding the election. The decision stopped the recount and allowed Florida Secretary of State Katherine Harris to certify Bush as the winner of the Florida electoral votes, giving Bush 271 total votes. The decision was controversial, in part because the justices in both the majority and the minority relied on unprecedented constitutional arguments mostly out of line with their own judicial philosophies. The more conservative justices in the majority had argued against states' rights to end the recount, which gave Bush the victory, while the more liberal justices in the minority had argued on behalf of states' rights to have Florida continue the recount.

The existence of the Electoral College itself remains controversial. Advocates for eliminating what is considered by many to be an "archaic system" argue that it is no longer necessary since voters now have the information they need to make an informed decision. In addition, opponents of the Electoral College argue that the system is dangerous with the possibility of electing a president who is not the

View the 2000 election night controversies.

choice of the people, which would cause a Constitutional crisis (though the latter did not occur in 2000); that some states benefit unduly from this system; that different states use different methods for selecting electors, and there is no guarantee that electors will abide by the popular vote in all states; and because of the winner-take-all system in most states, some popular votes are nullified. On the other side, the Electoral College also has its defenders, who argue that it recognizes the important role of the states as political units and guarantees that the president will be represented by a geographically broad constituency. In addition, the Electoral College combines the elements of popular democracy with representative democracy; it can expand the sense that the president has the mandate to lead the country (for example, Ronald Reagan won 51 percent of the popular vote in 1980, but 91 percent of the electoral vote); it discourages the influence by extreme minor parties; it enables minority groups to wield power through significant blocs of electoral votes in a state; and it discourages voter fraud.[51] To date, no significant progress has been made to either eliminate or amend the Electoral College, as this would require a constitutional amendment. However, several states are considering altering their selection of electors similar to the process used in Maine and Nebraska, thus eliminating the winner-take-all system.

Appealing to Voters

In the late 1800s and early 1900s, voter turnout was much higher than it is today due to the strength of partisanship and the public nature of voting. The Australian balloting process made voting private and by candidate, rather than the process where individuals place the entire slate of candidates in a ballot box in full view of everyone. The parties knew that victory was a simple matter of mobilizing more supporters than the other side. In the twenty-first century, partisanship and turning out supporters matter, but reaching the uncommitted voter is often what determines the outcome of a presidential contest.

Candidates know how to reach partisans; the nomination period is when candidates demonstrate why they should be their party's standard-bearer. The task of reaching non-partisans is much more complicated and requires multiple tools and strategies. Individuals identify with a party because the party's ideals, platform, and candidates correspond well to their own. Few individuals agree with a party 100 percent of the time, but the majority of the time is often acceptable enough for self-identification. Once individuals self-identify as a member of a party, by either registering or volunteering or any myriad of activities, individuals usually remain partisans. Strength of identification can change over time, but partisan identification usually, though not always, remains consistent over time.[52]

Individuals who do not self-identify with a party do so either out of lack of knowledge of the similarity between their own views and the views of one of the parties, or because not enough of their views match the party's ideology. Sometimes individuals simply prefer to consider themselves "independent" rather than affiliated with a partisan entity. Individuals who do not use the party as a cue for a candidate who meets their ideological criteria need other means to decide. Those criteria can be issue based or candidate based. Potential voters can look for candidates who focus on the particular issue or group of issues that matter to them; individuals who rely on issue positions but who do not affiliate with a party often have issues that crosscut the parties (for example, a pro-life Democrat or a pro-choice Republican). In those cases, individuals often look to other issue positions to help decide. Alternatively, a voter can use the same measures used in ordinary life to judge people: trust, likeability, believability, religion, height, good looks, and so on.

Due to the variability in their decision making (which is in contrast to partisan voters), independents—or what scholars term "floating voters"— can either make or break a presidential campaign. Not only does the campaign need to figure out what independent voters want from a presidential candidate, they must also encourage them to actually vote. Although candidates appear at rallies, town hall meetings, and other meet-and greet-events, most individuals never meet a presidential candidate. The information exchange between voters and candidates takes place through the media and technology.

Campaign Communications

Informed citizens are considered a critical component to a functioning democracy, and the media have long been major players in presidential campaigns. The expansion of technology has also enhanced the role that the press can play in electing a president, particularly the start of the television age in the 1950s. Throughout the remainder of the twentieth century and into the twenty-first, voters have had a growing number of choices in how they receive information about candidates; information during the presidential campaign can come from mediated sources (for example, traditional press outlets like newspapers and television, or newer venues such as Internet blogs), unmediated sources (for example, YouTube, Facebook, websites, and candidate advertising), and presidential debates.

Mediated sources

According to the Pew Research Center for People and the Press, Americans average about seventy minutes a day absorbing news, with fifty-seven of those minutes coming from sources that package the content for the individual—i.e., television, radio and newspapers.[53] In presidential campaigns, television remains the most cited source of all political information.[54] The campaign information in television news broadcasts, newspaper articles, and radio spots come through a reporter and anchor or a host. Therefore, for the candidate the media is a double-edged sword: the exposure in terms of name, issue, and other features helpful for voter decision making is free in terms of money but costly in terms of commentary. When candidates appear on television or in news articles, the information is rarely transmitted without interpretation of the information. For partisans, media coverage is unlikely to affect voter choice, although it could influence the decision to participate. For independent voters, the content and quality of information from news sources can have an enormous impact on decision making.

According to media scholar Doris Graber, "Twenty-first-century election campaigns are structured to garner the most favorable media exposure, reaching the largest number of prospective supporters, with the greatest degree of candidate control over the message. Candidates concentrate on photo opportunities, talk show appearances, or trips to interesting events and locations."[55] Prior to 1992 and Ross Perot's appearance on CNN's *Larry King Live*, candidates did not appear on talk shows; those shows were considered "soft" in contrast to the "hard" news shows like *60 Minutes* on CBS or a nightly news program on any of the networks. Candidates, after Perot opened the door, gravitated to the new-media types of shows as not only did voters watch them in large numbers but traditionally the questions were less confrontational, which allowed the candidate greater potential for controlling his or her performance. By 2008, candidates were routinely appearing on daytime talk shows (such as *The View*, *The Ellen DeGeneres Show*, *Live with Regis and Kelly*, and *Dr. Phil*) as well as evening talk shows (*David Letterman*, *The Tonight Show with Jay Leno*) and even late-night comedy shows or political satires (*Saturday Night Live*, *The Daily Show*, and the *Colbert Report*).

Candidates try to avoid reporters yet remain as part of the coverage because of the power of the press to shape the narrative of the campaign, and in a sense define the candidate for voters. During the nominations phase, the press focuses on viability: Is the candidate a legitimate contender, do they have enough money, have they gotten the "right" endorsements, do they run an effective campaign, what are they "really" like? For the independent voter, the press serves a critical purpose by providing voting cues, as they reject the party as a shortcut mechanism for choice but still need to be able to choose among the candidates. The press provides information that should allow voters to distinguish between the candidates. However, campaigns are often frustrated by having little control over the focus and tone of the coverage that the media provide.

Political scientist Thomas Patterson, in his classic book, *Out of Order*, argued that the type of news coverage provided during the campaign dramatically influences voters' beliefs about the candidates. Patterson argued that the weakening of the party–citizen connection awarded the press a role it was unprepared to assume: that of election mediator.[56] The traditional press role of watchdog does not match well with "the responsibility of providing a channel of communication by which the candidates can reach the voters."[57] Patterson contends that the press routinely moves beyond the appropriate watchdog role to that of adversary, in a sense adding a third focal point to the two-candidate contest. The public continually reaffirms Patterson's contention that the press is ill-equipped to do the job thrust upon them. Between 1985 and 2007, the Pew Center for the People and the Press, a non-partisan organization, found: "The American public continues to fault news organizations for a number of perceived failures, with solid majorities criticizing them for political bias, inaccuracy and failing to acknowledge mistakes. But some of the harshest indictments of the press now come from the growing segment that relies on the internet as its main source for national and international news." The report shows that the Internet news audience (roughly 25 percent of all Americans) is younger and better educated than the public as a whole, rely on the Internet as their main news source, express relatively unfavorable opinions of mainstream news sources, and are among the most critical of press performance. In addition, the Internet news audience is particularly likely to criticize news organizations for their lack of empathy, their failure to "stand up for America," and political bias. By comparison, smaller percentages of the general public are critical of the press in these same areas.[58]

Press coverage of presidential campaigns receives even more critical commentary from scholars than from the public. Are the press "establishment tools of corporate power" or "leftist attack dogs" or "scandal-obsessed morality cops?"[59] Any or all of those charges apply to given networks and/or given situations. However, Stephen Farnsworth and S. Robert Lichter argue that the quality and quantity of network news coverage decline relates instead to "the damaging trend toward horse race coverage of who is winning and losing over coverage relating to matters of substance, the less-than-satisfactory performance with respect to the journalists' cardinal issues of accuracy and fairness, and the declining amount of attention paid to candidates (as opposed to that lavished on the correspondents covering them), as well as the declining volume of coverage of the presidential election overall."[60] Interestingly, the coverage is most problematic on television, which is where most Americans still report getting their news, although the Internet as a primary news source is on the rise.[61]

The press preference for coverage that focuses on the "horse race" of the campaign, as well as a narrative about the "game" of presidential politics (who is ahead, who is behind, who has raised the most money, whose campaign runs smoothly, etc.) challenges a candidate's ability to distinguish himself or herself substantively from opponents. Instead, much like *Baseball Tonight* on ESPN, reporters, pundits, and bloggers analyze "performance" indicators and offer predictions of outcomes based on those measures. In presidential primaries, both opinion poll and primary results work in concert as the press highlights candidates rising in the polls and either focus on the negative aspect of less successful candidates or, worst of all, provide no coverage of second-tier candidates. The press preference for these "inside baseball" results, which do not relate to policy positions or to analysis of future behavior, creates a "bandwagon effect" as voters tend to want to support a winner; positive numbers lead to positive coverage, which produces better primary results, which in turn produces positive poll numbers.[62] During the general election, public opinion polls are the only measurable performance indicator between September and Election Day (although the press will also convene focus groups and town hall meetings to evaluate performance, in particular during the presidential debates).

Unmediated information

Campaigns are about choice; the choice to vote and for which candidate. In order to choose, citizens need information. Partisan-leaning citizens receive information from their party. For partisans, the choice of the nominee is often the more significant decision, as they are unlikely to vote for the other party. During the general election, the choice is to vote or not vote. For non-partisans, or less-strongly partisan individuals, the choice to vote and for whom remains throughout the general election. These individuals need information; consequently, the inability of the press to provide distinguishing information potentially undermines citizens' ability to make a choice. It is impossible to choose between candidates based on the information that one candidate is recording more likely voters in poll results. All that information reveals is the choice of those who have already made up their minds.

Candidates do a far better job of providing distinguishing information, which of course makes sense, as it is their responsibility to articulate why they are the best choice. Moreover, the differences between "campaign messages and the media messages are immense.... [T]he mediated coverage of network news has become so negative and so inaccurate that the unmediated speeches, advertisements, and

Internet web pages of the highly self-interested campaigns actually qualify as the more substantive, more useful, and more accurate forms of campaign discourse."[63] Consequently, campaigns spend millions on outreach via advertising, their websites, email, texting, and a presence on YouTube, iTunes, and the numerous social networking sites.

Television ads and, more recently, Internet ads are the primary mechanisms for candidates to reach voters without the filtering provided by the press 🖱. In a thirty- or sixty-second spot, candidates can provide biographical information, set the campaign's issue agenda, cast blame, and manage charges levied by an opponent or the media.[64] Some of the most powerful and memorable advertisements do what Darrell M. West terms priming and defusing. Candidates prime voters by setting up a focal point for the campaign, which might or might not have been on the minds of voters. When defusing, candidates use ads to respond to critiques by downplaying the charge or by reframing the charge.

One of the most effective priming ads of all time only ran once. In 1964, during the campaign between President Lyndon Johnson and Senator Barry Goldwater, the Johnson campaign ran the now-infamous "Daisy" ad, which shows a young girl in a meadow, picking the petals off of a daisy while counting from one to nine. After she reaches nine, an unseen male voice begins counting down from ten. At zero, a mushroom cloud replaces the picture of the little girl. Johnson then warns, "These are the stakes. To make a world in which all of God's children can love, or go into the dark. We must either love each other or we must die."[65] Although the ad only ran once, all three networks reran the ad in its entirety the next night. Consequently, almost everyone in the country saw the ad during approximately the same time frame. Reaction was massive and relatively negative as the ad essentially asserted that a vote for Goldwater was a vote for the use of nuclear annihilation. The ad dramatically primed voters to view Goldwater as a trigger-happy war hawk who would lead the United States into a nuclear showdown with the Soviet Union.

Effective ads do not have to be negative, nor do they even have to mention the opponent. Perhaps the most effective positive ad came from Ronald Reagan's reelection campaign in 1984. The ad opened with the line, "It's morning again in America" and merged a positive narrative about Reagan's performance along with concerns that his opponent, Walter Mondale, would return the United States to the economic and social upheaval of earlier times. With a picturesque montage of America and her citizens, a narrator intoned:

> It's morning again in America. Today more men and women will go to work than ever before in our country's history. With interest rates at about half the record highs of 1980, nearly 2,000 families today will buy new homes, more than at any time in the past four years. This afternoon 6,500 young men and women will be married, and with inflation at less than half of what it was just four years ago, they can look forward with confidence to the future. It's morning again in America, and under the leadership of President Reagan, our country is prouder and stronger and better. Why would we ever want to return to where we were less than four short years ago?

🖱 Watch memorable television campaign ads.

Campaign ads are rarely as positive as Reagan's, partly because it is hard for most candidates to remain above the fray of the campaign but also because of the power of negative ads, which can effectively define negative attributes of an opponent. Due to the increase in the use of negative ads in the 1980s, media organizations began to run "ad watches" to check the accuracy of the charges leveled by opponents. Ad watches became prominent in 1988, and were relatively effective at distinguishing fact from fiction and dispelling dramatic rhetoric and potentially misleading portrayals.[66] However, the media's interest in and their effectiveness at policing campaign advertising has waned in recent years, due in part to the high volume of ads and the speed with which they are now produced, and thus now provide only a limited check on the unfiltered information put out by each presidential campaign.

Beyond traditional television ads, the Internet has emerged as a critical tool for candidates to reach out to voters; candidates have been online since 1996.[67] However, the value of the online world was not evident until Howard Dean's 2004 campaign for the Democratic nominaiton. Dean's candidacy died in the face of relentless media coverage of "the scream," as a microphone picked up Dean's strange sounding exhultation in the midst of a cheering crowd following his loss in the Iowa caucus. Yet, despite his poor showing at the polls, Dean demonstrated that candidates could raise money, meet and organize volunteers, and connect with voters all online. Even more so, the 2008 campaign demonstrated that candidates who embraced the online world increased opportunities and maximized support. Significantly, the Web enabled candidates (who took advantage of it) to distinguish themselves from their opponents; identify and encourage likely voters; and raise money to support their candidacies without the enormous expense of television advertising.

However, it was the Obama campaign's use of the Internet in 2008 to reach voters during the pre-primary, primary, and general election periods that redefined the unmediated options for candidates during the campaign. The Obama campaign brought to fruition the enormous potential of the online environment for fundraising, mobilizing supporters, and setting the campaign agenda. Although the entire slate of candidates in 2008 in both parties crafted effective web pages, the Obama campaign's web page and web presence set a new standard. All candidate web pages include the basics: pictures of the candidates, their families, and an American Flag from some vantage point. Most sites had video and blogging by the candidate and campaign insiders. Obama's web page, which was much more frequently trafficked, encouraged users to investigate and, more importantly, to come back. Visitors to Obama's website could form their own "My Barack Obama" page and thus bookmark things that were of interest to them. The Obama site also encouraged registration, providing the campaign with an easy mechanism for continued outreach through email and texting. The massive fundraising effort which produced $750 million in campaign dollars took place virtually all online, with a large amount in less-than-$100 donations. The Obama campaign successfully married outreach with fundraising, combining traditional participants in the process with new ones, particularly younger voters.

View the 2012 Obama and Romney campaign websites.

The 2008 campaign also marked a turning point for campaigning online in terms of social networking sites, and new media outlets like YouTube and iTunes. All the candidates placed linking icons on their web pages to sites like Facebook and Twitter, encouraging voters to seek out the candidate in places not normally thought of as political. During the 2008 nominating period, Hillary Clinton had 188,952 individuals identify themselves as "friends" on MySpace; Obama had 312,860.[68] The social networking pages were essentially stripped-down versions of the candidates' web pages, but site users could post comments or links to their own pages.

As valuable as the social sites were, the video-sharing site YouTube created a wholly distinct subset of unmediated candidate outreach. YouTube enabled candidates who were not receiving traditional press coverage to connect with interested voters. There are multiple ways to find content on YouTube. An individual can search for content specifically, or for content generally, or can view suggested videos (i.e., most popular, watched now, promoted or featured). During the 2008 primaries, a general search on YouTube for the campaign or campaign names demonstrated the interest in Ron Paul, as he was the most widely noted general hit with over 100,000, with Obama and Clinton trailing with over 40,000.[69] The traditional press coverage of Paul, in contrast, was miniscule, as the press deemed his candidacy not viable.

The most watched video on YouTube during the 2008 campaign was provided by a YouTube user named "Obama Girl." Over six and a half million viewers watched the video, "I Got a Crush on You."[70] It was so popular it spawned spin-offs and a lot of media attention for "Obama Girl" and the Obama campaign. Similarly, inoffensive videos included "John Edwards Feeling Pretty," where over one million viewers watched Edwards comb his hair. YouTube users also watched plenty of videos that contained substantive content, expanding the non-traditional media opportunities in which legitimate information opportunities abounded. Users could watch the videos over and over, unlike viewers of the Daisy ad who saw the ad, at maximum, twice. Moreover, users could watch candidate exchanges without media commentary. Users were definitely interested in the 2008 campaign, as the top campaign videos were watched over 48 million times.

Presidential debates

There are typically three presidential debates and one vice-presidential debate during the general election phase of the campaign. During the primaries, there are typically more; in 2008, they seemed to be almost weekly occurrences, with a total of twenty-six held for Democratic candidates and twenty-one for Republican candidates. Similar frequency of debates occurred for Republican primary candidates; they held twenty-seven debates in 2011 and early 2012. For the two nominees during the general election campaign, the debates enable direct outreach in a live setting. For partisans, the debates offer an opportunity to see their candidate "win"; for independent voters, the debates are an opportunity for comparison shopping. For all citizens, the debates represent the only time both candidates answer the same questions and also address each other directly. Thus, citizens learn about each candidate's issue positions, but also get a feel for the candidate's "presidential-ness."

For candidates, the debates are potential minefields. Not only are voters paying attention (80 percent watched at least one debate in 2008), but the media coverage is intense as well.[70] Consequently, the campaigns negotiate everything with the

Presidential Debate Commission: how many debates, what style (single moderator, multiple questioners, or town hall), podium vs. table, and even camera angles. Yet, the event is live; there are no do-overs. The media typically anoint a debate winner and loser. Often the title is based on expectations. In 2000, Gore was an experienced debater and a heavyweight on the issues, thus for George W. Bush, success was defined more liberally than the norm.

Occasionally, a debate moment becomes the talk of the campaign or defines a candidate for better or for worse. The 1960 debate between Senator John F. Kennedy and Vice President Richard Nixon defined not only the campaign but also the potential for television in campaigns. Live television allowed Kennedy to demonstrate comparably his fitness for the office in terms of knowledge and policy acumen. Moreover, Kennedy famously "won" the debate on television in contrast to the tie that radio listeners reported. Television was a relatively new medium in 1960; consequently, Nixon did not realize the cost of not wearing makeup and sweating profusely under the hot lights. However, most post-debate winners and losers stem from comments, successful one-liners or horrendous gaffes, which can define the candidate for independent voters as the line becomes the focus of the post-debate coverage. Perhaps the most damaging debate utterance came from Gerald Ford, who in 1976 was running in his first campaign after succeeding to the presidency after Nixon's resignation in 1974:

> MR. FRANKEL (Reporter from the *New York Times*): Mr. President, I'd like to explore a little more deeply our relationship with the Russians.... Our allies in France and Italy are now flirting with communism; we've recognized a permanent Communist regime in East Germany; we virtually signed, in Helsinki, an agreement that the Russians have dominance in Eastern Europe; we bailed out Soviet agriculture with our huge grain sales, we've given them large loans, access to our best technology, and if the Senate hadn't interfered with the Jackson Amendment, maybe you would have given them even larger loans. Is that what you call a two-way street of traffic in Europe?
>
> THE PRESIDENT: I believe that we have negotiated with the Soviet Union since I've been President from a position of strength.... If we turn to Helsinki—I am glad you raised it, Mr. Frankel—in the case of Helsinki, thirty-five nations signed an agreement, including the Secretary of State for the Vatican. I can't under any circumstances believe that His Holiness the Pope would agree, by signing that agreement, that the thirty-five nations have turned over to the Warsaw Pact nations the domination of Eastern Europe. It just isn't true. And if Mr. Carter alleges that His Holiness, by signing that, has done it, he is totally inaccurate. Now, what has been accomplished by the Helsinki agreement? Number one, we have an agreement where they notify us and we notify them of any military maneuvers that are to be undertaken. They have done it in both cases where they've done so. There is no Soviet domination of Eastern Europe, and there never will be under a Ford administration.
>
> MR. FRANKEL: I'm sorry, could I just follow—did I understand you to say, sir, that the Russians are not using Eastern Europe as their own sphere of influence and occupying most of the countries there and making sure with their troops that it's a Communist zone, whereas on our side of the line the Italians and the French are still flirting with the possibility of communism?

> THE PRESIDENT: I don't believe, Mr. Frankel, that the Yugoslavians consider themselves dominated by the Soviet Union. I don't believe that the Romanians consider themselves dominated by the Soviet Union. I don't believe that the Poles consider themselves dominated by the Soviet Union. Each of those countries is independent, autonomous; it has its own territorial integrity. And the United States does not concede that those countries are under the domination of the Soviet Union. As a matter of fact, I visited Poland, Yugoslavia, and Romania, to make certain that the people of those countries understood that the President of the United States and the people of the United States are dedicated to their independence, their autonomy, and their freedom.[72]

Whatever the President meant by his response and his follow up, the press and the Carter campaign pounced on the incredible error. The coverage fundamentally undermined the Ford campaign's ability to define itself as more knowledgeable on foreign policy than Carter, a former governor from Georgia. Consequently it is not surprising that presidential campaigns infinitely prefer to disseminate their messages in controlled settings, without the press to interpret their statements.

THE CONSEQUENCES OF WINNING

The candidate who receives more than 269 Electoral College votes, regardless of the popular vote totals (as Al Gore found out in 2000) becomes the President of the United States. From a functional perspective, the campaign ceases after the first Tuesday after the second Monday in November. Campaign offices close, volunteers celebrate or vow to fight harder next time, and supporters begin jockeying for tickets to the Inaugural Balls. Nevertheless, in significant ways, the campaign continues to affect the winning candidate long after the voting booths are packed away. The campaign for president influences the president's coalition, his mandate for action, and governing itself.

The Coalition

A coalition is "a set of groups. Its set of attitudes is within the intersection of the sets of attitudes for the member groups, and its set of behaviors is comprised of these activities which form an interdependent system."[73] Therefore, coalitions form the basis for electoral support. The winning presidential candidate assembled two overlapping but distinct coalitions—one for the nomination and one for the general election. The coalitions are distinct because they serve separate purposes.[74] The nominating coalition consists of party insiders and elites, relevant interest groups, and voters in the primary, which produces the requisite delegate count to win. The general election coalition consists of the nominating coalition plus the elites, groups, and popular supporters, made up of demographic voting profiles, necessary to win the requisite Electoral College votes.

The candidate assembles his electoral coalition with a distinct goal in mind: winning on Election Day. Once the candidate takes the presidential oath, goals change. Once in office, the president will technically not need an electoral coalition

---

View more memorable debate moments.

for four years, but cannot abandon the promises made to these groups, either, without jeopardizing reelection, as the same groups will form the basis for that coalition. Instead, what the president needs to do is translate his electoral coalition into a governing coalition. The governing coalition consists of Congress, presidential staff and other appointees, interest groups, the bureaucracy, the media, and the public.[75]

The governing coalition is the assemblage of groups and individuals who will support and work toward the president's legislative and administrative goals. As discussed in later chapters, the president is limited in his ability to act unilaterally, particularly in the domestic sphere. Thus, coalitions of support must exist to advance the presidential agenda; the margin of victory as well as a strong coalition of support is also known as a presidential mandate (that is, the perception that a president, through his electoral success, has been given a mandate by the public to pursue his policy objectives).

A president who won election with a large, stable, electoral coalition and was able to translate that support to governing support would be fairly confident in the ability to achieve his agenda. A president who won with a narrow coalition and a narrow victory (e.g., Bush in 2000) would conceivably have a hard time achieving his goals. A narrow electoral coalition or an unstable one, defined by transient support from independents, requires a president to search for groups and individuals to create a governing coalition issue by issue. Not only is this an expensive use of presidential capital, it is also dangerous to the initial electoral coalition. Lacking a large, stable core of support, the president must seek compromises that elicit the necessary group support without damaging the interests of his electoral coalition.

However, it is important to remember that other factors outside of the president's control can also play a role in whether or not agenda priorities are achieved, and can also turn the traditional theory about strong versus weak coalitions on its head. For example, while Bush was elected with a narrow coalition and a narrow margin of victory, and while he was not perceived to have been given a strong mandate from the voters, the terrorist attacks on September 11, 2001, provided a national tragedy that galvanized broad support, even among Democrats, for Bush's actions regarding national security issues. Similarly, while Obama was elected with a strong coalition and a seemingly strong mandate in 2008 to bring political change to Washington, the economy (labeled the worst recession since the Great Depression of the 1930s) severely handcuffed the Obama administration's ability to easily pass domestic legislation in 2009–2010 even with a strong majority of Democrats in both houses of Congress.

The Message and the Mandate

Not only does the campaign provide the president with a coalition, it also shapes the presidential agenda. Candidates form their coalitions based on individual appeals but also issue appeals. During the nominating phase, the issue differences between candidates within a party can often be so minimal as to be irrelevant, or they can matter significantly. For example, the power of social conservatives in the Republican Party's nominating phase in recent years has made it difficult for candidates who are not strongly committed to the social conservative agenda (such as being pro-life, opposed to same-sex marriage, etc.) to be successful. During the general election, however, the issue differences between candidates are typically much more meaningful. Moreover, as noted earlier, the candidates are effective at distinguishing themselves from their opponents. The differentiation can take the form of personal characteristics, but more often than not the differentiation occurs over the policy agenda.

The assertions made by the candidate, such as "I will fight to reform health care," "I will make education a top priority," "No New Taxes," or "Change You Can Believe In," shape the campaign battlefield but also determine the presidential agenda. Studies demonstrate that presidents do seek action on their campaign promises and achieve results most of the time, even if the result is a much compromised version of the president's initial plan (for example, health care reform as signed by Obama in early 2010).[76]

The promises made by the candidate are a blueprint for their focus once taking office. It makes sense that candidates tell voters what they want to do for them and the country and voters evaluate their candidate choices based on the congruence between their personal goals and those of the candidates. Consequently, winning candidates often claim to have a mandate for action. In particular, when there is a large disparity in outcome between candidates, the mandate claim is more likely. In 1932, FDR swept to victory with a 472–59 margin in the electoral college with 22,800,000 votes to President Hoover's 15,750,000. FDR's win was so complete that he carried more counties than a presidential candidate had ever won before, including 282 that had never voted Democratic. No Republican candidate had ever been beaten so badly. The campaign between Hoover and Roosevelt centered on the different views of the role of government for responding to the Great Depression. With the overwhelming victory, FDR could easily claim public support for an activist government.

In 1980, Ronald Reagan beat President Jimmy Carter 489 Electoral College votes to 49 and by a margin of 9 percent in the popular vote. Consequently, Reagan argued he had a mandate for advancing his conservative agenda. Public opinion polls throughout the 1980s challenged the notion of a mandate as well as public support for Reagan's programs; Reagan was always personally popular, but his policies were not always as well regarded. In fact, political scientist Robert Dahl claims that mandates are particularly difficult to claim even with the presence of surveys that reveal why people voted for a particular candidate. Although Reagan won a landslide in the Electoral College, his 9 percent victory in the popular vote represented just under 51 percent of the popular vote. Moreover, those post-election surveys revealed a public voting against Carter as much as it did voting for Reagan.

Campaigning vs. Governing

In running for the office of the presidency, candidates spend at least one year, and sometimes as many as four, campaigning in a single four-year election cycle. Winning candidates are effective or become effective in the skills of campaigning. Candidates need to fundraise from big and small donors, they need to speak before crowds and appear in the media and in advertising to get their message out. Candidates must also exercise management skills over an organization facing multi-state campaigns. Some of these skills directly relate to the task of governing as president. Presidents must define their goals and their message and be able to deliver that message via speeches to crowds large and small. Presidents must also be effective managers of the White House staff and the bureaucracy.

Yet, on a fundamental level, campaigning is quite different from governing.[77] Campaigns have a final decision point, as all effort is geared toward achieving results on a given day. Governing is a continuous stream of decision making and decision points; presidents do not go home after losing a vote in Congress on a key agenda item. Campaigning is also by definition adversarial, one candidate against the other, and a choice for one is a choice against the other. Governing in a system of checks of balances is characterized by compromising. Governing is complicated by a purely adversarial approach. Ultimately, the skills that make someone a great campaigner might not serve the office of the presidency. Moreover, an individual with the skills to be a great president might be stymied by the requirements to be a great campaigner.

CONCLUSION

The campaign and election process has changed significantly since the framers designed the Constitution. The modern process reflects the duality of partisanship for both the candidate and the voter. Candidates must appeal both to diehard partisan supporters during the nominating campaign and then to less partisan and non-partisan voters during the general election. The distinct messages and approaches required by a candidate, who must be partisan enough to win the nomination but not so partisan as to turn off moderate and independent voters, offer a wealth of challenges for the modern presidential candidate. Moreover, the modern candidate must be a master of technology, from television to radio to the Internet, so that the candidate can reach voters through both mediated and unmediated systems. In addition, the role of money in the presidential campaign process means that those candidates best suited to successful fundraising will most always have more success than those who are not. As a result, the "survival of the fittest" process of electing a president can winnow out any number of potentially great leaders who may not be great campaigners.

For the twenty-first-century voter, the campaign and elections system is all about choice. Partisan voters now have more choice, as they have the opportunity to participate meaningfully in the selection of the party nominee. Voters also have choice in terms of how and where they receive information about the candidates for president. Voters can engage the candidates directly via Facebook or candidate web pages or watch candidate speeches and advertising on YouTube. Or, voters can seek out information in traditional mediated sources: newspapers, radio talk shows, and television news programs. It is worth considering whether the constitutional system, unchanged since ratification of the Twelfth Amendment in 1804, still functions effectively in the modern environment. For those who seek the further democratization of the process through a more open nominations process or by abolishing the Electoral College in favor of the popular vote, the process appears flawed. Still others contend that the long process with its emphasis on money and media produces candidates that are ill-suited for the job of *being* president even if they can successfully *run* for president.

As discussed in the opening of the chapter, in spite of the efforts to clean up the corruption in politics and stop the flow of money during campaigns, money still plays a determining role not only in who wins an election but also in who will run in the first place. In addition, thanks to the ever-present and watchful eye of the news media, candidates need a positive image and must perform well out on the campaign trail. So, even if someone seems destined for greatness as a president, without adequate campaign financing, or successful public relations, his or her candidacy for public office does not stand a chance. As a result, a disconnect exists between what the framers had in mind for insulating the presidency, and the selection of the president, from the public, and today's style of presidential campaigning where so many relevant aspects of the presidential selection process are played out on center stage. Not only have the men and women who have run for the presidency shaped the presidential selection process, but the winners of these contests have historically shaped the institution of the presidency as well. But, as we discuss in subsequent chapters, what it takes to successfully run for president does not automatically equate to what it takes to be a successful president once in office.

PRESIDENTIAL NOMINATIONS

THEN . . .

In 1974, Gerald Ford became President of the United States without ever running a national campaign either as a presidential or vice presidential candidate. On December 6th, 1973, then-House Minority Leader Ford took the Vice Presidential oath of office after both chambers of Congress approved President Nixon's appointment of Ford to replace resigning Vice President Spiro Agnew. Ford would become president less than a year later on August 9, 1974, after Nixon resigned in the wake of the Watergate scandal. Thus, Ford became president without a single vote cast, outside of the confirmation votes by Congress. Upon taking the Oath of Office on August 9, 1974, Ford acknowledged his peculiar path to the presidency:

> I am acutely aware that you have not elected me as your President by your ballots, and so I ask you to confirm me as your President with your prayers. And I hope that such prayers will also be the first of many. If you have not chosen me by secret ballot, neither have I gained office by any secret promises. I have not campaigned either for the Presidency or the Vice Presidency. I have not subscribed to any partisan platform. I am indebted to no man, and only to one woman—my dear wife—as I begin this very difficult job.[78]

In deciding to run for the presidency in 1976 after serving out the remainder of Nixon's term, Ford, despite being the incumbent, needed to create an electoral coalition much in the way any other candidate would, by first running for his party's nomination. Traditionally, a sitting president is not challenged for his party's nomination, but under certain circumstances it can happen, as it did in 1976 when former California Governor Ronald Reagan challenged Ford for the Republican nomination. The race for the nomination was close and contentious, and it remains the last nomination battle not settled prior to the start of a national party convention.

Ford, a moderate Republican, did not have the full support of the more conservative members of his party, who were troubled by Ford's inability to counter the liberal policymaking by the Democrats, who controlled Congress. More concerning, however, was the President's foreign policy. Reagan criticized Ford for his Vietnam policy, as well as his negotiation of the Helsinki accords with the Soviet Union. Reagan's challenge initially amounted to nothing, as Ford won the first primaries and caucuses with comfortable margins. However, the momentum shifted once Reagan won North Carolina, and then followed by winning the key state of Texas. After Texas, the primaries were much closer and more contentious, culminating in no declarable winner prior to the start of the Republican Convention. Ford had the lead with 1,130 delegates but needed 1,187 for the win.

The lack of an outright winner created an environment in which votes were traded and outcomes were negotiated. Rumors swirled as the candidate entourages negotiated a Ford/Reagan co-presidency, Reagan as Vice President, or Reagan as Transportation Secretary. The tide seemingly turned on Reagan's announcement of Pennsylvania Senator Richard Schweiker as the other half of a Reagan ticket. Schweiker, a moderate, was enough of an anathema to conservatives that enough votes changed sides to give Ford 1,187 votes, enough to win the nomination. The intraparty challenge to Ford revealed the flaws in his efforts to create an electoral coalition. Ford's base Republican coalition was diminished by the reality that half of the party voted for someone other than the President to run to be President. Many believed that Ford's loss to Jimmy Carter was virtually inevitable due to his pardon of Nixon in 1974 and the dire economy of the 1970s, but also because of this disastrous internal party challenge.

. . . AND NOW

The 2008 presidential campaign was unique for many reasons, beginning with the unusual circumstance of a completely open race for the first time since 1952 (meaning that no sitting president or vice president sought the nomination of either party). In addition, the Democratic Party had a strong chance of nominating either the first person of color or the first woman to run for the presidency. For the Democrats, Hillary Rodham Clinton had secured the status of frontrunner as early as 2005. By the end of 2006, most news organizations had all but given the Democratic nomination to Clinton, regularly labeling her as the only candidate capable of winning the nomination. The news media seemed to love the story of Hillary running for president (she was routinely referred to as simply "Hillary" by the news media), and polls at the time began to show that Americans would overwhelmingly support a woman candidate for president.[79]

However, the political landscape by early 2007 presented a different reality for Clinton's candidacy. Still considered the strongest candidate and probable frontrunner among the Democratic candidates for the upcoming primary season, the door was nonetheless left open for other challengers within the Democratic Party. While Clinton's name recognition and star power had obvious advantages, the downside came in the political baggage that she brought to the campaign. Nonetheless, Clinton maintained her frontrunner status throughout

2007, continually besting her other opponents in public opinion polls, as well as Republican contenders (like John McCain and Rudy Giuliani) in national polling in Democratic/Republican matchups. On January 20, 2007, when Clinton officially declared her candidacy, she told supporters on her web-page announcement that "I'm in, and I'm in to win."[80] Clinton's announcement came just days after Barack Obama officially announced his candidacy, and also set off the furious race for campaign donors among all the Democratic hopefuls.

The general assumption seemed to be that no one could match the fundraising prowess of the Clinton machine; Bill Clinton had been perhaps the most successful fundraiser ever for the Democratic Party, and the Clintons turned to the same donors and fundraising methods to fund Hillary's presidential campaign. Bill Clinton's strategy in 1995 and 1996—raise all of the available Democratic funds early to discourage any challengers in the primary—seemed to be the plan for Hillary's presidential campaign as well. The former president was also still a big draw among Democratic donors, and Clinton's campaign had developed a network of large donors known as "Hillraisers," which were donors who not only contributed the maximum legal contribution directly to the Clinton campaign ($2,300) but also bundled contributions of $100,000 or more from other donors as well (in effect serving as fundraisers on behalf of the Clinton campaign). But during the first and second quarters of 2007, the Obama campaign had actually out-fundraised Clinton; Obama had raised $25 million to Clinton's $20 million for the first quarter of 2007, and $31 million to Clinton's $21 million for the second quarter. Not until the third quarter of 2007 did Clinton finally raise more money than Obama—$22 million to $19 million—although that still left her trailing $75 million to $63 million overall going in to the last few crucial months before the Iowa caucus.[81]

The initial primary results quickly matched the excitement gleaned from the dueling fundraising totals (especially among new donors). Unexpectedly, Obama won the Iowa caucus, which immediately changed the script of the campaign. By beating Clinton in a caucus state he demonstrated superior organization, which challenged the idea that Clinton owned the Democratic machine and insiders. By beating Clinton in a state that is 94 percent white, Obama demonstrated that race alone would not be a determining factor in decision making, at least within the Democratic Party. (Pundits would continue to put forth race as a limiting factor for the Obama campaign throughout the nominating process and into the general election).

While Clinton rebounded in New Hampshire, she did not experience another significant victory until Super Tuesday on February 5th (also called Tsunami Tuesday in 2008 given the increased number of states that held primaries). It was then that Clinton won the big population states it was expected she would carry: California, Massachusetts, New Jersey, New York, as well as a few others. However, she did not sweep the day, as Obama won twelve states and had solid showings in the states that Clinton carried. Thus, due to the proportional allocation of delegates in the Democratic Party, Obama actually accumulated more delegates from February 5th and marginally took the lead in the race for the nomination.

In the aftermath of Super Tuesday, the narrative of the race changed again. The press began describing the Clinton campaign as in disarray. There were numerous negative stories regarding the frivolous spending of campaign money, the tension between her top campaign advisors, the need for the candidate to lend money to the campaign, and the loss of frontrunner status. Conversely, the press began marveling at the Obama campaign's fundraising prowess, error-free caucus and primary strategy, and the candidate's star power. In short, in all arenas momentum shifted to Obama.

Certain miscalculations, involving fundraising and mismanagement of campaign funds, ignoring smaller states (particularly those with caucuses as opposed to primary contests), and the campaign's seeming belief in the inevitability that Clinton would win the nomination, all played an integral role in the primary contests that Clinton lost. Having spent $100 million through only the first contest in Iowa, in which she came in third, the Clinton campaign was broke at a time when it needed money most, forcing Clinton to lend herself $5 million to stay afloat through Super Tuesday. The lack of funds after Obama's win in Iowa meant that the Clinton campaign could not effectively staff ground operations in states where it needed to compete with Obama. In addition, when Clinton revealed after the Super Tuesday contests that she had lent herself $5 million, this worked counter to the image she was trying to project going into the big primary states of Ohio, Texas, and Pennsylvania as being able to relate to average, working-class Americans. When Clinton conceded to Obama and announced the end of her candidacy in June 2008, she had raised a total of $223 million, had lent her campaign a total of $11.4 million, and ended the campaign roughly $22.5 million in debt.

Money issues during the campaign were also closely tied to another problem that the Clinton team experienced—the lack of an effective "ground game" that could compete with that of the Obama campaign. During the primary season, grass roots organizers and local volunteers can make a big difference in voter education, voter registration, and voter turnout. Sufficient campaign funds also help to pay staff members in various field offices across the country. For the Obama campaign, which was also having tremendous success in tapping into the youth vote (particularly on college campuses), the "ground game" helped to solidify the Obama fifty-state strategy—compete in every state and for every delegate. The Clinton campaign, on the other hand, had a large-state strategy that assumed that their candidate would wrap up the nomination by Super Tuesday, and with an empty campaign coffer in the weeks after the Iowa caucus, the Clinton campaign had an impossible task in readjusting its strategy with limited resources. In addition, some of the larger states that Clinton would win later on in the spring of 2008, like Ohio, Texas,[82] and Pennsylvania, came too late to alter the outcome as Obama had already built an insurmountable lead in delegates.

Hillary Clinton finally suspended her campaign on June 7, 2008, as Obama had more than the simple majority delegate total he needed to claim the nomination. In contrast to how Reagan's challenge of Ford had weakened the incumbent president on the campaign trail, the competitive contest between Obama and Clinton ultimately appeared to strengthen the Obama campaign, which allowed the Democratic nominee to continue his record-breaking fundraising and to appear more comfortable and confident going forward into the general election against Senator John McCain.

Rivals for the 2008 Democratic nomination, Hillary Rodham Clinton and Barack Obama campaign together in the general election.

SUGGESTED READINGS

Ansolabehere, Stephen, and Shanto Iyengar. 1997. *Going Negative: How Political Advertisements Shrink and Polarize the Electorate*. New York: Free Press.

Campbell, James E. 2008. *The American Campaign: U.S. Presidential Campaigns and the National Vote*, 2nd ed. College Station: Texas A&M University Press.

Geer, John. 2006. *In Defense of Negativity: Attacks Ads in Presidential Campaigns*. Chicago: University of Chicago Press.

Key, V. O. 1966. *The Responsible Electorate: Rationality in Presidential Voting, 1936–1960*. New York: Belknap Press.

Patterson, Thomas E. 1994. *Out of Order*. New York: Vintage.

Polsby, Nelson W., and Aaron Wildavsky. 2004. *Presidential Elections: Strategies and Structures of American Politics*, 11th ed. Lanham, MD: Rowman & Littlefield.

Popkin, Samuel. 1994. *The Reasoning Voter: Communication and Persuasion in Presidential Campaigns*. Chicago: University of Chicago Press.

Wayne, Stephen J. 2011. *The Road to the White House 2012*, 9th ed. Belmont, CA: Wadsworth.

West, Darrell M. 2009. *Air Wars: Television Advertising in Election Campaigns, 1952–2008*. Washington, DC: CQ Press.

ON THE WEB

http://www.opensecrets.org. The Center for Responsive Politics is an independent nonpartisan organization which tabulates the financial information candidates, campaigns, and organizations are required by law to disclose.

http://www.fec.gov. The Federal Elections Commission is the nonpartisan government entity which administers and enforces federal campaign law, and also serves as a clearinghouse for all campaign finance contributions and expenditures for federal elections.

IN THEIR OWN WORDS

THE ELECTORAL COLLEGE STRATEGY

While George H. W. Bush would lose re-election in 1992, during the summer of 1991 the Bush White House was optimistic about their chances for a second term. White House advisors began discussing strategy based on what they perceived to be the plan of the eventual Democratic nominee for the 1992 campaign based on the Electoral College map. While Bill Clinton would only win 43 percent of the popular vote, compared to 38 percent for Bush and 19 percent for H. Ross Perot, Clinton won 370 of the Electoral College votes to Bush's 178 (and zero for Perot), despite early projections by Bush's political team:

> The June 15 *Washington Post* carries a remarkable story out of Middleburg, VA on the Democrats' latest strategy huddle for 1992. According to the *Post*, the Democrats have adopted a strategy of political triage that divides the country into "baskets" of winnable and unwinnable states. Democratic strategists go on to identify 13 states as unwinnable—"so firmly Republican in their presidential voting patterns that an investment of cash and staff is a waste of resources." The basket strategy is remarkable in many ways: The Democrats are ready now to **write off** more states in '92 than they **won** in '88. Mike Dukakis won 10 states and 111 electoral votes in 1988. The 13 states written off by the Democrats for 1992 total 106 electoral votes. They represent a population of close to **50 million Americans—a full one-fifth of the country**. The basket strategy suggests the Democrats are no longer a national party. 17 months before the election, they are ready to run up the white flag. We should do everything possible to make certain the public hears more about the Democrats' basket strategy: The President should refer to the basket strategy—contrast it with a Republican approach that is active and aggressive in all 50 states. Our message: **the Democrats may be ready to write off 50 million Americans, but the Republican Party is ready to reach out to every American in every state. The President should drive home this message whenever he visits one of the "forgotten states."** The basket strategy cuts the legs out from under State Democratic campaigns, and creates an opening for Republicans to translate support for the President into support for the Party. In these states, our objective should shift from "state to slate": we should aim at a Republican sweep to create the coattails we need to make inroads in Congress.[83]

CHAPTER 4

The Public Presidency: Communication and Mass Media

President Barack Obama made history on Thursday, July 29, 2010. This historic event had nothing to do with signing a major piece of legislation, negotiating a peace treaty, or anything else to do with the day-to-day constitutional responsibilities of the office. Instead, he became the first sitting president to ever appear on a daytime television program with his visit to ABC's *The View* (a roundtable discussion hosted by Barbara Walters, Whoopi Goldberg, Joy Behar, Sherry Shepherd, and Elisabeth Hasselbeck). While this was not Obama's first appearance on the show (he had appeared twice before, including while a presidential candidate in March 2008), he nonetheless broke new ground in the ever-expanding media venues in which presidents now make appearances.[1]

Seeing high-profile politicians appear in more diverse and more casual media venues is not a new trend. One of the most memorable such appearances of all time would be Richard Nixon asking "Sock it to *me*?" on the September 16, 1968, episode of NBC's *Rowan & Martin's Laugh-In* less than two months before Election Day. The 1992 presidential election also had some memorable media moments from the candidates, including H. Ross Perot's announcement that he was running as an independent candidate on CNN's *Larry King Live*, and Bill Clinton's saxophone rendition of "Heartbreak Hotel" on *The Arsenio Hall Show*. By 2004, potential media venues for presidential candidates had expanded even more. For example, John Edwards announced his 2004 presidential candidacy on *The Daily Show with Jon Stewart* on the Comedy Central Network. Also in 2004, presidential candidates increased efforts to reach out to women voters, as media strategies began to include daytime television with several appearances by both major party candidates and their surrogates (their spouses, children, respective running mates and *their* spouses and children) on popular television shows with traditionally high female viewership like *The View*, *Live With Regis and Kelly*, and *Dr. Phil* (George W. and Laura Bush, and John and Teresa Heinz Kerry, each made appearances on the latter show to talk about their respective marriages).[2] In 2008, with domestic issues and the economy dominating the presidential campaign, Barack Obama and John McCain, as well as their spouses, made high-profile appearances on *The View* and *Ellen*. Obama also had the early endorsement of Oprah Winfrey, the first time that she had ever endorsed a presidential candidate.[3]

While most Americans may be getting used to seeing presidential candidates reach out to voters in venues such as these, a sitting president making such an appearance is another story. As a result, Obama's appearance on *The View* raised concern for some political pundits over what is considered to be "dignified" or "appropriate" media activities for a sitting president. For example, Pennsylvania Gov. Ed Rendell (D) compared *The View* to *The Jerry Springer Show*, stating that "I think the president of the United States has to go on serious shows."[4] Older Americans might view Obama's appearance on *The View* as a bit out of place, akin to if Richard Nixon had made an appearance on the *Merv Griffin* or *Mike Douglas* shows of the 1970s, if Ronald Reagan had appeared on the *Phil Donahue Show* during the 1980s, or if Bill Clinton had appeared on the *Rosie O'Donnell Show* during the 1990s. Media advisors to President George H. W. Bush actually rejected the idea of Bush appearing with Soviet President Mikhail Gorbachev on *Phil Donahue* in 1989 for fear of pursuing a media strategy that would be seen as "gimmicky" and "unpresidential."[5] However, younger Americans, who are more technologically savvy and use media very differently than older Americans, may see this type of appearance as normal and expected.[6] Obama's presidential campaign had pushed the limits of using new technology and media sources to reach out to voters through fundraising, volunteering, and get-out-the-vote efforts. The White House defended the appearance on *The View* due to the fact that "the media world is now so diffuse (TV, newspaper, Web, cable Twitter, Facebook) that Obama has to do more than his predecessors ever did. That's the reality."[7]

The strategy behind the appearance was not difficult to decipher. As Obama's approval ratings continued to decline during his second year in office, and leading up to the 2010 midterm elections, he began to shift to more of a campaign mode with his public appearances to shore up support for his programs, his party, and his presidency. The appearance itself went well, and the media coverage surrounding it also kept a mostly positive story line in the news for several days, with most media pundits giving Obama high praise for his discussion of political issues with the hosts of *The View*. When presidential communication advisors can exert any type of control over the news cycle to get positive coverage for their president, it is considered a job well done. In addition, Obama's relaxed demeanor in a more informal setting reminded many viewers of candidate Obama in 2008 (and a time before his presidential approval ratings had dropped below 50 percent). According to *Washington Post* media critic Howard Kurtz:

> Anyone who scoffed at the president's decision to hang with Whoopi and the gang was out to lunch.... The appearance was good for him, good for *The View* and, incidentally, good for the audience.... Obama was especially interesting when Barbara Walters said, "You do not describe yourself as a black president, but that's the way you're described. Your mother was white. Would it be helpful, or why don't you say, 'I'm not a black president, I'm biracial?'" David Gregory or Bob Schieffer wouldn't have asked that question, and that's the value of appearing on a different kind of talk show.... No one asked whether it was dignified for Obama to talk bracketology on ESPN or play hoops with CBS's Clark Kellogg. Whoopi and company acquitted themselves well.[8]

Yet the question remains: Is such an appearance beneath the dignity of the office, or instead, must presidents continue to shift their communication strategies to keep up with changes within the news media industry? A clear definition of a president's effectiveness as a communicator requires bringing together a variety of factors, not the least of which is the state of the news industry itself, which is primarily responsible for bringing presidential messages and images to the public on a daily basis. The office of the presidency is the most high-profile and public of any position within the federal government. As a result, presidents who are skilled communicators have a distinct advantage in the many public aspects of the job. Not only have the public and ceremonial aspects increased in recent decades, but the many acts of presidential communication make up a large part of the symbolism attached to the office. In addition, as presidential advisors in recent years have developed more innovative ways for a president to communicate with both the American public and the news media, public expectations for effective communications have also increased. The office of the presidency now demands strong communication skills, even if the president himself falls short of that expectation. The president serves as the communicator in chief, serving as the point man for direct interaction with the American people and a key source of political rhetoric. This public role of the presidency demands the constant development of White House communication strategies, including the public events that are now part of the day-to-day operation of the presidency, as well as management of the presidential–press relationship, which can help determine news media content and tone of coverage of the president.

THE EVOLVING RHETORICAL PRESIDENCY

While most nineteenth-century presidents operated almost exclusively outside of the public's view, by the start of the twentieth century presidents began to rely on the public aspects of the office to rally support for their policy agendas and to increase their own popularity. The emergence of the rhetorical presidency reflected the president's willingness and ability to engage people directly through substantive dialogue, as opposed to the formal, perfunctory, and strictly limited contact with the public during the nineteenth century. The start of what is referred to by scholars as the "rhetorical presidency" can be traced to William McKinley (1897–1901), Theodore Roosevelt (1901–1909), and Woodrow Wilson (1913–1921), as all three relied on public speaking tours and press coverage to garner support for their respective policy agendas.[9] In particular, it was Roosevelt's use of the bully

Theodore Roosevelt helped launch the era of the rhetorical president with his enthusiastic and fiery public speeches.

pulpit to engage in a public dialogue with American citizens that began to advance the president's role as the national leader of public opinion. Roosevelt used his rhetorical skills to increase the power of the presidency through popular support, which was in alignment with his view of the presidency itself—that he was the steward of the people and that weak presidential leadership during the nineteenth century had left the American system of government open to the harmful influence of special interests. Roosevelt expanded presidential power in many areas by drawing on broad discretionary constitutional powers; Roosevelt's "Stewardship Doctrine" demanded presidential reliance on popular support of the people, and also increased the public's expectation of the man and the office. Referring to his speaking tours around the country as "swings around the circle,"[10] Roosevelt often appealed directly to the American public through his active use of the bully pulpit to gain support of his legislative agenda in an attempt to place public pressure on Congress.[11]

As part of what is referred to as a deliberative democracy, some scholars view presidential rhetoric as a positive institutional and constitutional feature, as well as one imagined by the framers as a necessary element of a properly functioning republic that allows presidents to speak directly to the public. Rhetoric also plays an important role in the institutional setting of the presidency by enabling different presidents to shape the presidency in a stable and constant manner.[12] However, other scholars view the rhetorical presidency as a danger to the U.S. constitutional democracy. The founders were quite suspicious of a popular leader and/or demagogue in the office of the presidency, since such a person might rely on tyrannical means of governing.[13] The presidency experienced a fundamental transformation by becoming a "rhetorical presidency" during the early part of the twentieth century, causing an institutional dilemma. By fulfilling popular functions and serving the nation through mass appeal, the presidency had deviated from the original constitutional intentions of the framers, removing the buffer between citizens and their representatives that the framers established.[14] In addition, it has been argued that the rhetorical presidency is a twentieth century creation and a constitutional aberration. The president is not merely a popular leader vested with unconstitutional powers, but also uses rhetoric as a "tool of barter rather than a means of informing or challenging a citizenry."[15]

Later presidents, though not all, would follow Roosevelt's strategy of relying on the bully pulpit to elevate the power of the presidency as the spokesperson for the American public. Through his public leadership, Woodrow Wilson, especially during World War I, established the presidency as a strong position of leadership at both the national and international level. He contributed to a more dominant view of the presidency through his use of the bully pulpit and used his rhetorical skills to promote many progressive policy initiatives. For example, Wilson relied on an "ambitious" whistle-stop railroad tour in an attempt to gain support for U.S. entry into the League of Nations (though he failed to achieve that goal).[16] The emergence of several new communications technologies would begin to change the rhetorical presidency even more.

The Radio Era

Radio emerged as the first such technology to aid presidents in their public efforts. One of the first known public radio broadcasts came in 1916 with a post-election report on Wilson's reelection campaign delivered from an experimental station in New York. The beginning of commercial radio began with the broadcast of the 1920 presidential election results by KDKA in Pittsburgh. This report of Warren G. Harding's election is the political event "that first brought radio's potential to the attention of politicians."[17] Considered by most media scholars as the first "radio president," due mostly to the availability of the new technology during the 1920s, Harding's inauguration was the first to be broadcast by radio, and his was the first presidential voice heard by most Americans. He delivered a series of messages to the American public by radio during the summer of 1923, including an address in St. Louis that was carried by special wire to New York City.[18] Later that year, following Harding's death, Calvin Coolidge delivered his first message to the Congress as president, which was broadcast to a national audience. Mostly unknown during his tenure as Harding's vice president, Coolidge effectively used radio to introduce himself to the nation. His performance on radio broadcasts to the American public was considered successful, and this discouraged any serious challenge for the Republican Party's presidential nomination in 1924.[19]

Elected in 1928, Herbert Hoover also had a long-term relationship with radio. He served as Secretary of Commerce during the Harding and Coolidge Administrations from 1921 through 1928, and one of his main duties was to develop and regulate the use of radio. Hoover recognized the use of radio by government officials as an interesting dilemma; radio could be both a "powerful educational force" and a tool for political propaganda as well. In his memoirs, written in 1952, Hoover wrote, "There is little adequate answer to a lying microphone...propaganda is seldom the whole truth [and] the officials currently in office have preponderant time at the microphone, and theirs becomes the dominant voice."[20] During his four years in the White House, Hoover delivered a total of twenty-three "Radio Addresses to the Nation" on foreign, domestic, and economic policy issues.[21] In one such address, he stated: "Of the untold values of the radio, one is the great intimacy it has brought among our people. Through its mysterious channels we come to wider acquaintance with surroundings and men."[22]

Franklin D. Roosevelt relied heavily on the bully pulpit, particularly his use of radio, to gradually persuade the American public to support his New Deal policies during the 1930s and America's involvement in World War II during the early 1940s. As a means to establish "direct contact with the people," Roosevelt delivered the first of his thirty fireside chats at the end of his first week in the Oval Office in March 1933 🖱.[23] Considered a success, the speech allowed Roosevelt to reassure the American public that he would guide the Depression economy into recovery. He began the first radio address by saying, "I want to talk for a few minutes with the people of the United States about banking," and continued for twenty minutes explaining in simple language what Americans could do to assist in the recovery. This began an effective trend that FDR would rely on throughout his tenure in office—the use of radio to enter the living rooms of Americans to talk about the problems and challenges facing the country. While Roosevelt was also successful in his mastery of the press, skillfully managing news out of the White House through his frequent press conferences in the Oval Office, radio was his "most important link with the people."[24] While not remembered as a great orator, FDR's successor, Harry Truman, used radio with even more frequency as the medium and its presence around the globe expanded through the late 1940s and early 1950s. After a radio address on July 20, 1950, the Truman White House reported that the address "was heard by more people throughout the world than any other address ever delivered.... Radio representatives say 'everyone with a radio or television set' heard the address. Their figures indicate that nearly 130,000,000 persons in the United States heard the President on radio and television."[25]

The Television Age

The rhetorical aspects of the office, as well as the use of the bully pulpit, took on an even greater importance for presidents with the start of the television age. The rapid expansion of television during the 1950s, often referred to as the "golden age" of television, occurred while Dwight Eisenhower occupied the White House.[26] Eisenhower became the first president to utilize television as a means to more effectively communicate with the American public, and his administration became much more visible than any other before it through the use of filmed press conferences for later use by the networks, televised cabinet meetings, and televised fireside chats. Yet, the true potential of television as a governing tool would not be realized until the presidencies of John F. Kennedy in the early 1960s, and then Ronald Reagan in the 1980s. Both were known for their frequent use of inspiring and eloquent speeches

---

🖱 Listen to President Roosevelt give a fireside chat.

Franklin Roosevelt delivers one of his many "fireside chat" radio addresses to the American public.

about public policy and their visions for the country. Kennedy relied on the bully pulpit, aided by television coverage, to talk of a "New Frontier" and motivated many Americans to become active in public service. Reagan saw the bully pulpit as one of the president's most important tools; relying on his skills as an actor, he provided a strong image of moral leadership that helped to restore many Americans' faith in government institutions.

Following Kennedy's election in 1960, the use of television as a means for presidential communication increased dramatically. Where Eisenhower had been somewhat reluctant about his use of television, Kennedy and his advisors saw the expanding medium as an excellent governing tool for the president to expand his influence and power over national politics. By the mid-1960s, the president had become a central focus of news from Washington and began to have more power over shaping the national agenda by rapidly reaching, through both television and print media sources, his national audience. The ability to help shape public opinion, through televised and highly covered speeches and press conferences, began to provide the president with an important advantage during the legislative process. As the influence of television increased, presidents worked even harder to keep the initiative and control over the policy agenda coming out of the White House. Presidential leadership in the television age required effective communication skills and the ability to positively shape public opinion in ways that matched the needs of the medium; as such, the presidential image became crucial.[27]

Kennedy's skillful use of television has had a lasting impact on the office of the presidency 🖱. His use of live televised press conferences, his eloquent speaking style, and the youthful images of both his family and his administration on American television screens set a standard that his predecessors had difficulty matching. Kennedy

🖱 Watch President Kennedy answer questions at a press conference.

also had the advantage of the uniqueness of the new medium; many presidents that followed him have longed for that golden, innocent era during the early 1960s when personal and political scandal did not dominate political reporting from Washington. In addition, most presidents since the start of the television age could never master their use of television; only Kennedy, Reagan, and Clinton are considered strong communicators who were able to use television to their advantage through public leadership efforts, while Johnson, Nixon, Ford, Carter, and George H. W. Bush were "used by television" due to their ineffective use of the bully pulpit.[28]

To understand the significant changes that television created in the relationship between American citizens and their presidents in the three decades between 1960 and 1990, just think about the many changes that occurred in the television industry alone. In 1960, only three television networks existed—ABC, NBC, and CBS—and the evening newscast on each was a black-and-white fifteen-minute broadcast. By 1990, the three networks were competing with not only several independent television stations in major media markets like New York and Los Angeles but the growth among cable and satellite programming options as well. The nature of news had also been forever changed by CNN, whose success as an all-news cable channel created what is known as the "24-hour news cycle." No longer were Americans limited to news in their daily newspapers and the traditional evening network news broadcasts; breaking news could be accessed at any time during the day through cable television. The expanding technological advancements during this time period would contribute to not only major changes within the news industry but also to major changes in the relationship between American citizens, their president, and the news media who were expected to provide the important link of information between the two. The up-close-and-personal look at our presidents that television began to provide also altered the political environment in which the president must lead. In addition, the immediacy of television coverage accelerated the decision-making process for presidents. These trends would only increase with the rapid expansion of technology beginning in the 1990s.

The Internet Age

While it is now tough to imagine life without e-mail or the Internet, these were still relatively new technologies in the early 1990s. The news media as an industry began to consider the use of both, particularly the Internet, as an effective means to communicate with its customers, as government officials and politicians also began to consider use of the technologies in order to better communicate with citizens and voters. Bill Clinton, the first president raised during the television age, often relied on alternative television opportunities or "new media" talk shows and live town hall meetings to bypass the traditional Washington press corps and speak directly to the American people. And while television events such as those worked well for Clinton by giving him more options in delivering his message unfiltered to the audience, expanding media and technology in a more general sense have also adversely affected the leadership potential for presidents.

Throughout the 1990s, the Internet dramatically changed the nature of political reporting. For example, one of the biggest political stories out of Washington in 1998 was the investigation of Bill Clinton's relationship with White House intern Monica Lewinsky. The first news outlet to break the story about Clinton and Lewinsky was an unlikely one—*The Drudge Report*. A website with both political and entertainment news, *The Drudge Report*, maintained by Matt Drudge, first began in 1994. Drudge was able to break the Clinton–Lewinsky story wide open when he posted a report stating that *Newsweek* had information about an inappropriate relationship between the President and an intern, but that the weekly news magazine was holding the story. Soon after, *Newsweek* ran its story, and this incident became one of the earliest in which the Internet had a major impact on how the traditional news media reported political news.

As the Internet grew dramatically by the end of the 1990s, most if not all major publications in the United States—and even globally—developed online versions of their newspapers and magazines. Both television and cable news outlets also developed online versions. In addition, web pages were developed for government entities at the national, state, and local levels. For example, the official White House web page (www.whitehouse.gov) was developed during the 1990s, as were web pages for Congress and its members, the U.S. Supreme Court, and all federal agencies; state and local governments and agencies quickly followed suit, giving American citizens unlimited information about all aspects of their government at all levels. Political candidates also jumped on the Internet bandwagon. For the first time ever, presidential candidates in 1996 developed official campaign web pages, and in 2000 Senator John McCain (R-AZ) was the first to use his presidential campaign web page to successfully solicit funds from campaign donors online.

Throughout the 2000s and beyond, the American political environment continues to be shaped by the increased competition among more and more news outlets, as well as newer and ever-expanding technological advancements. Not only are new media emerging, but new and old media continue to merge, which has led to a greater fragmentation of news. This means that Americans no longer have a shared experience of political news from one of a handful of sources (like a daily newspaper or the evening network news). This, in addition to the hyper-partisan content of news, particularly on cable news and on the Internet, poses many challenges for a president to maintain control over his public image and policy message. What was once referred to as relying on the bully pulpit to speak to the American public is now often viewed as "spinning" the president's message. Due to the "intense focus on marketing" of their presidencies, both Clinton and George W. Bush generated short-term public relations gains but "suffered from severe longer-term political problems as a result of their public relations strategies."[29] In addition, in such a saturated media environment that includes so much political news, the president can rarely command the attention of the American public through rhetorical means as he is sometimes viewed as just another talking head.

While all presidents have had to contend with changes in both technology and the news media industry while in office, the Obama administration may eventually provide one of the most fascinating case studies to date on its use of new and expanding media technology and how a communication strategy was developed accordingly. During his first term, Obama's communication advisors regularly pushed the boundaries of how a president must communicate in the current media environment. Just to name a few examples, Obama and his administration have a strong presence on social networking sites such as Facebook and Twitter, the White

House web page continues to expand, and the presidential weekly radio address has evolved into a weekly video address that can be easily viewed on the White House web page or on YouTube. As the Obama administration shows, managing the rhetorical aspects of the presidency, as it began at the turn of the twentieth century, continues to be an evolving challenge for presidents and their advisors regarding the public aspects of the office, and even a skilled communicator like Obama is no longer guaranteed success while attempting to govern in the current media environment.

PRESIDENTIAL COMMUNICATION: STRATEGIES AND RESOURCES

Communication strategies have become an important and permanent part of the everyday operation of the White House. A communication strategy consists of various components, including the leadership style of the president, presidential rhetoric and speechwriting, presidential public activities, the presidential policy agenda, and the presidential–press relationship. An effective presidential communication strategy can be a critical factor in developing and implementing the administration's policy goals. To understand how a president communicates is to understand an important base of power for the modern presidency,[30] and in "recognizing the importance of communications to everything that a president does."[31] The president for some time has been considered the "interpreter in chief" and the "nation's chief storyteller." Presidential rhetoric has changed over time as media technologies have continued to expand, providing citizens with more in-depth coverage of the president. Due especially to television coverage, presidential advisors now develop communication strategies that seek more support for the president as a person or leader and less support for specific policy proposals. This has led to an emphasis on symbolic and ceremonial, rather than deliberative, speech.[32]

In addition, the television age of politics also brought with it the "going public" strategy, which assumes that a president can gain public support for his policy agenda by speaking directly to the American people through national addresses and other high-profile media appearances.[33] However, in recent years, evidence suggests that this strategy is not always effective in shaping and/or moving public opinion in a president's favor. Not only can the president's voice be easily drowned out among the cacophony of other political voices in the various news media now available, but Americans are not as attentive to the national news as they once were.[34] As a result, more recent occupants of the White House, like George W. Bush and Barack Obama, often opt for a strategy that instead focuses more on "going local." As political parties have become more polarized and media sources more fragmented, presidents now choose to "go local" as opposed to "going national" in their public strategies to gain support from the base of their parties, select interest groups, and voters in key areas since, for example, an address to the nation does not carry the same significance that it once did.[35] Therefore, presidents now seek to gain support among certain constituencies as opposed to the nation at large.

View President Obama's YouTube channel.

All of this means that presidents must adapt their public strategies to the ever-changing media environment in which they attempt to govern; the frustration for a president often comes from the fact that due to intense media coverage there is hardly a moment when the president is not on center stage, yet he seems to have even less control now over how and where he is covered. Regardless of specific strategy, presidents continue to go public more often and in a growing number of venues than their predecessors. As a result, an effective White House communication strategy is a critical component of governing. With so much attention paid to every presidential public moment each day, the president has virtually no room for rhetorical error. With an ever-increasing number of news outlets, there are even more opportunities for the press to catch a presidential gaffe or misquote on some specific policy, or to get the president to respond to a question best left unanswered (at least from the strategic standpoint of White House advisors). Advisors must maximize news coverage of the president's public events as well.

As such, the president relies on two groups of advisors within the White House in an attempt to control his own public image and that of his administration—the Press Office and the Office of Communications. The press secretary heads the press office, and is responsible for preparing press releases, coordinating news and holding daily press briefings for the White House press corps, and facilitating the needs of reporters who cover the president. The press secretary also serves as an important public spokesperson for the president and as a liaison between reporters and the White House. The Office of Communications develops a long-term public relations strategy, and also coordinates presidential coverage in regional and local media outlets.

The Press Office and Press Secretary

In 1983, the Reagan Press Office compiled an extensive report on the role of the office and the responsibilities of the press secretary. Nearly three decades later, the description still accurately reflects the goal of this important office for the contemporary presidency:

> The Office of the Press Secretary is the window through which the world sees the President. This office sits astride a vast pipeline through which flows virtually every action of the President and his Administration—appointments, proclamations, statements, and most important, the articulation of the President's initiatives and policies. At the end of the pipeline is the ever-watchful, all-too-often cynical White House press corps. Through their eyes—like a telescope in reverse—the world sees the President and the judgments of the press become the public perception. The management and direction of the Office of the Press Secretary becomes an important part of the Administration's success—or its failure. The podium of the White House Press Briefing Room is the pulpit most often used to present the President's viewpoint and the Press Secretary becomes the first voice of the Administration.[36]

As the job has continued to evolve, it is especially important for press secretaries to accurately reflect the views and policy goals of the administration. However, some press secretaries have been handicapped in this regard if the president or other top administration advisors do not provide up-to-date or accurate information to be provided to the White House press corps. To effectively perform the duties of the job, a press secretary must maintain credibility with members of the press in both the quality of information provided and facilitating access to top administration officials. Some press secretaries have had closer working relationships with the presidents they have served than others, and some, but not all, have been considered top advisors to the presidents in setting their strategies in handling the press. George Akerson, appointed by Herbert Hoover in 1929, was the first official White House press secretary. Stephen Early, serving during the administration of Franklin D. Roosevelt, and James Hagerty, press secretary to Dwight Eisenhower, were considered two of the most capable of all press secretaries ever to hold the position. Both were former journalists themselves, and both had close working relationships with their respective bosses, which earned each of them the necessary respect and credibility among members of the White House press corps. Hagerty was particularly a close advisor to Eisenhower, and he played a crucial role in the public relations strategy surrounding the President's heart attack in 1954; his effective crisis management helped to avoid public panic over Eisenhower's condition.

Pierre Salinger, press secretary to John F. Kennedy, was influential in developing the television strategy, including live coverage of press conferences, utilized by Kennedy during the early 1960s as television began to gain more prominence in presidential politics. In early 1961, Salinger declared the live coverage of press conferences "... here to stay. I do not see any drastic change in format. Television has not basically altered the character of the Press Conference. And the admittance of television to the press conference on its present basis is only simple justice. To allow other media to use their tools to the fullest extent and to deny this same right to the radio and television industry is in my opinion the grossest of injustice.... People have been given a new dimension of the Presidency and the President. The President is no longer a mysterious figure operating behind closed doors.... Another great cliché in Washington is the subject of over-exposure. In my opinion you cannot over expose the President."[37]

The difficulties associated with the job of press secretary can become obvious when presidents are not always forthcoming with essential information, as with the growing creditability gap that Lyndon Johnson perpetuated during the Vietnam War or his refusal to provide the press with advance information about his travel plans. Each of Johnson's four press secretaries (Pierre Salinger, George Reedy, Bill Moyers, and George Christian) were, at various times, left at the mercy of the White House press corps over the lack or inaccuracy of information given to them by Johnson or other advisors. Presidential scandals can also provide a difficult situation for press secretaries as the point person for providing information to the press. Notable examples include Ron Ziegler's lack of factual information as Nixon's press secretary during Watergate and Mike McCurry's attempts to positively spin the public scandal surrounding Bill Clinton's impeachment in 1998. Ron Nessen, a former journalist, had a difficult relationship with the press as Gerald Ford's press secretary. Nessen, who was known for his quick temper with members of the press, often exacerbated an already hostile situation between the White House and reporters following the Watergate scandal and Nixon's overall inaccessibility to the press. Despite Ford's attempts to provide a more open relationship between him and reporters, Nessen lost credibility in the eyes of the press in his attempts to over-inflate the actions and accomplishments of Ford. Both Jody Powell, Jimmy Carter's press secretary, and Marlin Fitzwater, who served both Ronald Reagan and George H. W. Bush, were considered effective in the job due to the respect they earned among members of the White House press corps and their attempts to attend to the day-to-day needs of reporters in meeting their deadlines.

Both Bill Clinton and George W. Bush employed four press secretaries each during their respective eight years in office, as this is now considered a position that is highly stressful, demanding, and more likely to cause burnout than some other White House staff positions. Dee Dee Myers, the first of Clinton's press secretaries, had been an advisor during the 1992 campaign and became the first woman to hold the job in 1993 (Dana Perino is the only other woman press secretary to date, holding the job from 2007 to 2009). Tony Snow, Bush's third press secretary (2006–2007), was considered effective due to his extensive experience as a journalist (both print and television) and communications advisor and speechwriter for George H. W. Bush. Snow stepped down from his position in September 2007 due to colon cancer, from which he passed away in July 2008 at the age of 53. Obama's first press secretary, Robert Gibbs, had extensive experience as a communications advisor and spokesperson during Obama's senatorial and presidential campaigns, as well as serving as press secretary for John Kerry's 2004 presidential campaign. Gibbs stepped down in February 2011 and was replaced by Jay Carney, a former journalist with *Time*. As recent presidents have shown, the candidate selection pool for the position of press secretary most often includes former journalists (who understand the needs of reporters; see Table 4.1) and/or former campaign or White House advisors (who understand the communication needs of high-profile politicians).

The Office of Communications

Created by Richard Nixon in 1969, the White House Office of Communications serves as the public relations apparatus for the president.[38] The impetus for the creation of this addition to the White House staff came mostly from Nixon's desire to maintain better control over his media image during the 1968 presidential campaign. Following Nixon's election, the office was created as an agency to supervise all of the information services from the Executive Branch. Since its creation, the role of the Office of Communications has continued to expand in an attempt to control both the public agenda and the image of the president in the news media. And while the exact functions of the office can vary depending on the individual director and the needs of the president, general responsibilities have included coordinating local and regional media coverage when a president travels outside of Washington, coordinating White House luncheons for non-Washington journalists, and providing technical expertise in the use of all forms of media for presidential appearances.

The importance of this type of media coordination has increased since the Nixon administration and Watergate due to the increased adversarial relationship between the president and the White House press corps. The news media have become increasingly obsessed with covering conflict, which often results in serious discussions of policy issues within the White House being depicted as dissent among top presidential advisors. As a result, the goal of the White House is to stop any news reports of internal conflict and push for positive coverage of the president's policy agenda. The Office of Communications handles this through a long-term

Table 4.1 Press Secretaries Who Were Former Journalists

PRESS SECRETARY	ADMINISTRATION	YEARS	NEWS ORGANIZATION
Stephen Early	Roosevelt/Truman	1933–1945; 1950	United Press International Associated Press Stars and Stripes Paramount News
Jonathan W. Daniels	Roosevelt/Truman	1945	News & Observer (Raleigh, North Carolina)
Charles Ross	Truman	1945–1950	St. Louis Post-Dispatch
Roger Tubby	Truman	1952–1953	Bennington (VT) Banner
James Hagerty	Eisenhower	1953–1961	New York Times
Pierre Salinger	Kennedy/Johnson	1961–1964	San Francisco Chronicle Collier's
Bill Moyers	Johnson	1965–1966	Marshall (TX) News Messenger KTBC Radio and Television Stations (Austin, Texas)
George Christian	Johnson	1966–1969	International News Service
Jerald terHorst	Ford	1974	Grand Rapids (MI) Press Detroit News
Ron Nessen	Ford	1974–1977	NBC News
Larry Speakes*	Reagan	1981–1987	Oxford Eagle (University of Mississippi) Bolivar Commercial (Cleveland, Mississippi) Progress Publishers (Leland, Mississippi)
Marlin Fitzwater*	Reagan/Bush	1987–1993	Various newspapers in Kansas
Tony Snow	Bush	2006–2007	Greensboro (NC) Record Virginian-Pilot (Norfolk) Daily Press (Newport News) Detroit News Washington Times USA Today Fox News
Jay Carney	Obama	2011–present	Miami Herald Time Magazine

*Both Speakes and Fitzwater technically served as "press secretary" for Reagan, but James Brady maintained the official title throughout the Reagan years despite his inability to return to the job after being shot in an assassination attempt against Reagan in March 1981.

public relations strategy. Advisors usually spread the "line-of-the-day" throughout the administration, which then takes it to the press; the office also takes the White House message directly to the people when necessary. The ultimate goal is to set the public agenda through the use of focus groups, polls, sound bites, and public appearances by the president. This allows ample opportunities for the president to dodge the hostile White House press corps and to rely on alternative modes of communication. Reagan was the first president to master this strategy; his aides had realized that their greatest PR asset was Reagan himself, and they began using two basic tactics to get their message out to the American people: public appearances would be carefully staged and controlled in order to emphasize Reagan's personality, and he would be promoted as a can-do leader rather than placing any emphasis on a particular political philosophy.[39]

Members of the news media have also come to rely on the information provided through the Office of Communications. Staff members work hard to facilitate the needs of journalists and to make their jobs in covering the president easier in hopes of gaining more favorable coverage for the White House. For example, the Office of Communications provides press releases, fact sheets and other background information on policies, radio actualities, satellite feeds, and a variety of daily photo opportunities that provide a positive spin on the president's activities. This can be especially helpful to smaller news organizations who, in recent years, have had diminished operating budgets and increased competition within the industry.

By the time Reagan took office in 1981, the Office of Communications had become an important and permanent institutional aspect of governing. Various departments within the Office of Communications headed up the efforts to cater to the needs of the local news media, which included telephone interviews with the President and other key administration officials for local television and radio stations, news briefings for out-of-town press representatives, and mailing fact sheets about Reagan's policy initiatives to local news editors and publishers. The use of a radio actuality service, similar to the ones used by the Nixon and Carter administrations, was also continued. Local radio stations around the country could call in to the White House on a toll-free number and receive a ready-to-use news clip from the "White House Broadcasting Service," as it was called during the Reagan years. Throughout Reagan's eight years in office, the strategy to gain coverage for administration policies in the local press had become much more aggressive than with previous administrations. Realizing the impact and influence that the White House would have on small news operations across the country, efforts were made to contact radio stations directly to promote the actuality service, and to contact local newspapers with White House statements for inclusion in their stories. Certain states would also be targeted if news out of Washington was of particular interest to citizens in the area to increase the coverage on the President's policies. This continued during the Bush and Clinton administrations as the Office of Communications maintained its role as a public relations outlet for the White House.[40]

Under Clinton, the Office of Communications devised several new techniques to keep in touch with both the press and the public in the new computer age while attempting to control the message about presidential policies. These included an increased access to information through a White House web page, which provided information available to computer users such as Clinton's public remarks, his daily schedule, transcripts of press briefings, and photos. A White House e-mail address was also set up to respond to questions from citizens about Clinton's policies. While each administration builds on the techniques used by prior administrations within the Office of Communications, each administration also tends to develop a unique overall strategy of how to utilize these resources. For example, the Clinton communications operation was "characterized by its flexibility and adaptability in handling unanticipated events and issues, especially where defending the president was involved. Damage control was their strong suit." For George W. Bush, his communications team did better on planning ahead and developing a long-term strategy that "held presidential information very closely" yet often failed to adapt quickly to changing political circumstances where its message was concerned.[41] As in all areas of presidential communication, the challenge of meeting the needs of all political participants is a difficult one to achieve for a president and his advisors.

Speech Writing

Speeches are an integral part of modern presidential leadership. As the rhetorical presidency evolved and expanded during the twentieth century, so too did the importance of presidential speechwriters. The men and women involved in the research and writing of presidential speeches can play a key role in policymaking as they help to shape the president's policy goals and initiatives. Major public addresses, particularly the State of the Union and major policy addresses, set the president's legislative agenda for both the public and Congress. Major speeches and other public appearances are examples of how a president attempts to sell his agenda or other presidential actions, not only to the public but to the news media and other political actors as well. The technological developments of the mass media in recent years have allowed presidents to go public more often and with much greater ease. As such, presidential speechwriters are now an integral part of the White House staff, and some have been extensively involved in the development of White House communication strategies for presidents during the television age.

When considering the history of presidential speeches, some early presidents relied on the help of others to write their speeches, most notably George Washington, Andrew Jackson, and Andrew Johnson, but most wrote their own. Thomas Jefferson, John Adams, James Madison, and Abraham Lincoln are all known for eloquent and effective speeches that they authored themselves. By the twentieth century, the public leadership strategies and the increased attention placed on public addresses by Theodore Roosevelt and Woodrow Wilson gave rise to the need for permanent speechwriters within the White House. Beginning with Warren Harding, ghostwriters were used, since it was unthinkable that a president would deliver someone else's words during a public address. Harding hired the first official White House speechwriter, journalist Judson Welliver, who maintained a low public profile.

By the time FDR entered the White House, presidential speeches became more of a collaborative effort between the president, his advisors, and his speechwriters. Other presidents, most notably John F. Kennedy, Richard Nixon, Ronald Reagan, Bill Clinton, and Barack Obama were also extensively involved in the writing and phraseology of their major public addresses. For example, Obama's director of speechwriting, Jon Favreau, is known as a "speech arranger" due to the routine that he and

Obama have when writing a speech. Favreau will meet with Obama for roughly 30 minutes and write down everything Obama says. Then, Favreau will write a draft of the speech, get edits from Obama, and this process continues to until the speech is finished.[42]

While the organization of key advisors and other staff throughout the White House can differ for each administration, a general practice for most modern presidents when writing an important speech to outline major policy initiatives involves the circulation of a draft for input from various policy experts as well as the speechwriters. Access to the president by speechwriters does not always occur, but it is essential for those who draft remarks to clearly understand a president's view of a particular policy. However, some presidents have struggled with effective coordination between those setting the policy and those in the speechwriting office drafting the remarks about policy. Not everyone within the administration will agree with the content of a speech. For example, in 1987, Ronald Reagan gave his famous address at the Brandenburg Gate in West Berlin when he told Soviet President Mikhail Gorbachev to "tear down this wall." However, prior to the address, then-member of the National Security Council Colin Powell suggested numerous changes during the circulation of the speech draft:

> We (and the State Department) continue to have serious problems with this speech. Our proposed changes are attached. Important substantive fixes we have proposed earlier in the sections on arms control and the Berlin initiative still need to be made. We still believe that some important thematic passages are wrong. For example, we do not make arms control or other proposals to show our "goodwill." It is against our interest to legitimize the idea that western goodwill is the missing ingredient or that our goodwill is tested by our arms control proposals. A better theme is to show the President's sensitivity to European anxieties about war and division and to stress that the real source of tension is the denial of freedom. In addition, we continue to be uneasy at the negative undertone of the section near the end that questions why Berliners stay in Berlin.[43]

As this memo shows, even one of the most memorable and most quoted speeches of the Reagan years encountered difficulties during the speechwriting process.

Public Events

Presidents now rely heavily on public events as an essential component of governing in a media-saturated political environment. A steady increase has occurred in the number of public events, particularly the use of major public addresses, since the start of the 1980s. This can be attributed to the influence and expansion of television coverage, changes in the political environment that have encouraged presidents to go public more often, and each president's public leadership style. It is not surprising that while expanding technologies allowed an increase in the amount and type of White House coverage, the president's schedule of public events also increased. Major public addresses are defined as rhetorical moments when the president addresses the nation, or when his address to a smaller group can expect a larger (and perhaps national or international) audience through mass media dissemination. While presidents since the start of the television age have relied on various public strategies in an attempt to publicize their policy agendas and to improve their standings with the American public, there are certain major public addresses that are required and expected so as to leave no doubt that the president will deliver them (even if he is not a gifted speaker). These include the inaugural address and the annual State of the Union address.

The inaugural address represents the start of a president's time in office, and presidents look to the inauguration, and in particular the inaugural address, as an opportunity to set the tone for their tenure in office with the public, other political actors, and even the news media; it is also a time to talk about broader political principles and not specific policies. This is one of the many symbolic acts in which a president engages, and it is the first time that he can address the American public—the national constituency that he uniquely represents within the political system—as president. Some of the most memorable and quoted inaugural addresses have occurred during times of great national crisis, such as Abraham Lincoln's address in 1861 (often remembered for the "better nature of our angels" line at the end of the speech) or Franklin D. Roosevelt's first inaugural address in 1933 (when he told Americans "the only thing we have to fear is fear itself"). Other presidents, such as John F. Kennedy in 1961 ("ask not what your country can do for you" and "the torch has been passed to a new generation of Americans") and Ronald Reagan in 1981 ("government is not the solution to our problem; government *is* the problem"), were skilled public speakers and used the inaugural address to present a recurring theme for their presidencies.

The president's annual State of the Union address is perhaps the most anticipated and analyzed of all presidential speeches. Article II, Section 3 of the U.S. Constitution requires that the president "shall from time to time give to the Congress information on the state of the Union and recommend to their consideration such measures as he shall judge necessary and expedient," but there is no requirement that the president give this information in an address to a joint session of Congress. For presidents Thomas Jefferson (1801–1809) through William Howard Taft (1909–1913), this constitutional requirement was met by submitting a written report to the Congress on the state of the union. Woodrow Wilson (1913–1921) revived the practice of delivering an address to Congress, which has continued most every year since.[44] It is important to note that the first "State of the Union" address for George H. W. Bush in 1989, Bill Clinton in 1993, George W. Bush in 2001, and Barack Obama in 2009 are technically *not* State of the Union addresses. Instead, they are addresses to a joint session of Congress to lay out administration goals. However, the attention paid to and impact of these speeches is so similar to an actual State of the Union address that they are considered comparable for research classification purposes.[45]

Traditionally delivered near the start of the calendar year, the State of the Union address is not only a report to Congress on the actual "state" of the union, but also a statement of the president's proposed policy agenda for the upcoming year. This has evolved as a unique opportunity for modern presidents, in upholding their constitutional duty, to remind both the audience in attendance (Congress) and those watching and listening at home (the American public) of the president's role in shaping the national agenda. In recent decades, the State of the Union address has involved an extensive White House communications and media strategy plan for events prior to, on the day of, and after the actual speech. The goal is to try to maximize the president's exposure to the news media and the American public through an event where he looks and sounds presidential, since he is both addressing the Congress and speaking to the nation with all the attendant pomp and circumstance that the event brings with it; this is one of the most ritualistic of presidential public events.

Other major policy addresses are also expected of the president, including televised addresses to the nation in times of crisis or national urgency (usually involving national tragedy, U.S. military action, natural disasters, or economic crises), as well as policy addresses with the expectation of national news coverage, thus having an effect on the public agenda (usually delivered before a large group such as a national convention for a particular interest group or a university graduation). While a major policy address by itself demands much attention from White House staffers in various offices (including speechwriting, press, media affairs, etc.), the ancillary events that go along with a major policy address (press conferences, presidential and surrogate interviews, photo ops, speech distribution and other advance work, etc.) also play a large role in the communications strategy for a specific presidential speech.

Since the early 1980s, presidents also began to rely on weekly radio addresses—short talks lasting approximately five minutes about a specific topic—to supplement their public agenda, target specific policies, most often domestic or economic, and reach citizens who may not be watching television. The tradition began with Reagan in 1982 (whose advisors thought the medium was a good fit for Reagan due to his early days in radio during the 1930s and 1940s) and was continued by both Clinton and George W. Bush. George H. W. Bush chose not to follow this PR strategy of Reagan's and gave only a handful of radio addresses in 1991 and 1992. While most Americans never actually heard the weekly radio address, it served a strategic purpose through additional coverage in the news media of a controlled event, since the presidents' remarks routinely made the weekend television news shows, especially on cable news, as well as the national Sunday newspapers.[46] During the Obama administration, the weekly radio address has evolved into a weekly video address that can be easily viewed on the White House web page or other locations on the Internet such as *YouTube*. While this communication venue had traditionally been used to generate news about presidential policies, Obama's video version is much more accessible to Americans without the filter of press coverage.

THE PRESIDENT AND THE PRESS

The president makes news by virtue of being the ideological symbol of American democracy and leadership to both journalists and the public. As a result, the news media has always been among the most influential political actors with which presidents must contend. The relationship is often an adversarial one, since the president and news media need each other yet have different goals—the president wants positive coverage about the actions and policies of his administration, but "big" stories for the news media (which in turn mean higher ratings and circulations) usually come from negative and scandal-oriented stories about the president and/or his administration. Rarely has a president during the modern era not complained about the news media, the White House press corps, and the coverage he was receiving.

The relationship between the president and the American press has a long and colorful history. American newspapers during the late eighteenth and early ninteenth centuries were highly partisan in both their political loyalties and their coverage of events in Washington. By the mid-nineteenth century, with advanced printing capabilities and a desire to provide more objective news coverage for increasing circulations, newspapers began to cover the White House as a formal beat. News coverage of the presidency dramatically increased during the administration of Theodore Roosevelt, who cultivated positive press coverage in an attempt to maintain strong ties to the American public. During the twentieth century, with the rise of the rhetorical presidency and the continual expansion of media technology, presidents have increasingly relied on the press to communicate their vision to both the American public and other important political actors. However, the White House and the Washington press corps often have struggled to define the political agenda. Each wants to control the content of the news, but, like it or not, one cannot do its job without the other.

The White House Press Corps

The White House press corps first received working space within the White House during the administration of Theodore Roosevelt, who included press quarters within the new West Wing built in 1904. The White House Correspondents' Association was formed in 1914, which contributed to the trend of professionalization of reporters within the newspaper industry during the early part of the twentieth century. The White House press corps experienced tremendous growth during the 1930s and 1940s, particularly during the years of the FDR presidency, as presidential influence over national politics increased under the New Deal programs.[47] Also, FDR's frequent and informal meetings with the White House press corps in the Oval Office were newsworthy events for reporters. His use of press conferences and his effective news management efforts contributed to the need for the White House to be covered in various media outlets, since much of the news in Washington was beginning to be generated from the Executive Branch. During the 1930s, more than 350 reporters covered the Washington beat.

Today, more than approximately 1,700 people hold White House press credentials, and while all are not considered "regulars" on the White House beat, the sheer size of the press corps has necessitated a more formalized daily press briefing than in years past. The emergence of the television age during the 1950s, and its expansive growth during the 1960s and 1970s, greatly contributed to the growth in the size of the White House press corps. Other factors contributing to the increase in number of reporters on the White House beat include the increased importance and size of the federal government and the role it plays in the lives of individuals, which requires reporters from non-Washington media outlets to cover policymaking at the national level. Also, the number of foreign correspondents covering the White House has increased in recent decades as other countries have a greater need to understand the impact of American policies in their own countries.[48]

The prominence of the White House beat has also increased within the journalism industry and is now viewed as one of the premier assignments in most news organizations. The reporters who regularly cover the White House include representatives from a variety of media outlets, including the top daily newspapers (*New York Times, Washington Post, Los Angeles Times, Wall Street Journal, USA Today*); the big three weekly news magazines (*Time, Newsweek, U.S. News and World Report*); the major networks (*ABC, CBS, NBC, Fox, CNN, MSNBC*); and the major wire services (*Associated Press, United Press International, Reuters*). In recent years, with the growth of Internet news sources, reporters from such online sources as *Politico* and the *Huffington Post*, just to name a few, are also regulars within the White House press room. The growth in the size of the White House press corps has also contributed to the expansion of both the White House Press Office and Office of Communications, which must handle the increased demands of Washington reporters.

Press Conferences

One of the formal venues in which a president must contend with the press is during presidential press conferences. These events provide the president with an opportunity to make news by formally interacting with the White House press corps. Press conferences have become an institutionalized tradition in which all presidents are expected to participate. A written transcript is kept of all questions and answers, and most presidents begin the session with a prepared opening statement. Since they were first televised live in the 1960s, press conferences have become less about informing reporters and the public about important issues and more about controlling the president's public image. The number of press conferences held by presidents has varied greatly (see Table 4.2). Theodore Roosevelt held some of the earliest press conferences, which were informal sessions with the press on Sundays to combat the lack of interesting news from Washington in Monday's newspapers. William Howard Taft was the first president to hold regular press conferences, which occurred twice a week, until he stopped the practice after what was considered "an unfortunate session" with reporters. Woodrow Wilson, Warren G. Harding, Calvin Coolidge, and Herbert Hoover (until the onset of the Depression) returned to the practice of regular press conferences, usually twice-weekly and formal events. Each also required reporters to submit their questions in advance.

Franklin D. Roosevelt changed that requirement, as well as the formal setting for press conferences. FDR enjoyed an effective relationship with the press, due in part to his frequent and informal meetings with the White House press corps in the Oval Office. FDR held a total of 881 press conferences while in office, a yearly average of approximately seventy. He was famous for his congenial personality toward the press and his "off the record" remarks. Through press conferences, FDR was a master at news management and was able to capture many headlines throughout the nation's newspapers. Following FDR's twelve years in office, no other president would come close to matching the number of press conferences held. Harry Truman, who averaged thirty-eight per year, returned press conferences to a more formal event and moved the location in 1950 out of the Oval Office and into the Executive Office Building. Truman and his advisors began to exercise more control over the content and structure of press conferences, relying on preconference briefings and an increased use of prepared opening statements. Truman also earned a reputation for his "shoot from the hip" speaking style that would regularly produce unpredictable yet quotable comments. Dwight Eisenhower would be the first president to encounter television cameras during a press conference, and he allowed taping for later television release.

John F. Kennedy was innovative with his groundbreaking use of live televised press conferences, which both the press and public found highly entertaining.

Table 4.2 Presidential Press Conferences: Coolidge to Obama

PRESIDENT	TOTAL	MONTHLY AVERAGE	YEARLY AVERAGE
Calvin Coolidge (1923–1929)	407	6.07	72.90
Herbert Hoover (1929–1933)	268	5.58	67.00
Franklin D. Roosevelt (1933–1945)	881	6.05	72.66
Harry Truman (1945–1953)	324	3.48	41.73
Dwight Eisenhower (1953–1961)	193	2.01	24.13
John F. Kennedy (1961–1963)	65	1.91	22.89
Lyndon Johnson (1963–1969)	135	2.18	26.16
Richard Nixon (1969–1974)	39	0.59	7.03
Gerald Ford (1974–1977)	40	1.36	16.32
Jimmy Carter (1977–1981)	59	1.23	14.75
Ronald Reagan (1981–1989	46	0.48	5.75
George H. W. Bush (1989–1993)	137	2.85	34.25
Bill Clinton (1993–2001)	193	2.01	24.13
George W. Bush (2001–2009)	210	2.18	26.25
Barack Obama (2009–2012)*	71	1.82	21.85

*Through April 20, 2012.

Source: Gerhard Peters, "Presidential News Conferences," The American Presidency Project, ed. John T. Woolley and Gerhard Peters, University of California Santa Barbara, http://www.presidency.ucsb.edu/data/newsconferences.php.

Lyndon Johnson could never match the Kennedy style during press conferences, and would contribute to the growing credibility gap with inaccurate reports on the Vietnam War. The frequency of press conferences would drop during the presidency of Richard Nixon, who believed that the mystique of the presidency must be maintained through limited public appearances. Nixon was also famous for his great disdain of the press, and he averaged only seven press conferences per year.

Gerald Ford, during his brief tenure in office, as well as his successor, Jimmy Carter, both attempted to restore credibility to the White House and its relationship with the press by increasing the number of press conferences after the Nixon years. Both used these opportunities to speak bluntly to the press about the problems facing the nation in the mid- to late 1970s. While neither received high marks for style during press conferences, both Ford and Carter were known for their substantive knowledge of government policies. Despite knowing the facts, Carter's advisors did try to improve the President's performance:

> I think your answers at press conferences are generally too long. Although your command of the facts is impressive, you often lose your audience. Short, punchy answers allow for more questions. The give-and-take becomes more rapid fire. You appear in command, almost combative. Remember, a half-hour after the press conference is over most viewers probably can't remember a single question or answer. They do have an over-all impression though. That impression should be of you, like a baseball batter, hitting whatever is thrown at you—disposing of pitchers. Occasionally, of course, long answers are required, but these should be the exception not the rule.[49]

Although his public skills earned him the nickname the "Great Communicator," Ronald Reagan held fewer press conferences than even Nixon did, averaging just less than six per year. This was due to his unfavorable performances, since Reagan often made misstatements and verbal gaffes during the give-and-take of questions from reporters. In an attempt to better control these events, Reagan's advisors implemented new rules for press conferences, including assigned seats for those in attendance (which provided a seating chart for Reagan to reference when calling on reporters) and insisted that reporters raise their hands before asking a question.

George H. W. Bush would hold more press conferences than Reagan, and he would also begin the practice of holding joint press conferences with foreign leaders. Bush afforded the press extensive access to the entire administration; he hoped to gain favorable coverage by holding many informal discussions with reporters, and he courted the press as members of the political elite. Wanting numerous informal, last-minute press sessions in an attempt to create an open and friendly presidency suggests that Bush's strategy reflected what he considered to be his greatest asset, which was face-to-face, personal contact with reporters.[50] As a result, much of Bush's overall communication strategy focused on his use of press conferences, with the goal of meeting the needs of newspapers, and not the network news, hence the focus on informal question-and-answer sessions as opposed to prime-time press conferences. Press secretary Marlin Fitzwater recognized Bush's strengths and weaknesses in this area, and he advised the President accordingly to not "try to compete with former movie star Reagan at prime-time news conferences in the awesome setting of the east Room." Fitzwater's plan included the following recommendations to Bush:

- Press Conferences: We recommend that you hold informal press conferences during the day in Room 405, much as you have done recently in announcing new Cabinet positions. These can be announced the same day they are held, and last for 20 minutes to a half-hour, to get credit for having held a full-scale press conference. A minimum of preparation is required, and you are the focus of the news, rather than the reporters.

- East Room Press Conferences: We recommend holding these dinosauras–showus–maximus extravaganzas only on special occasions—perhaps two or three times a year. The East Room press conference has developed in a way that gives more of a forum to the press than it does to the President. The cutaway cameras focus on the questions, often which are prosecutorial and inflammatory. In terms of viewer impact, the question is just as important as the answer.... In addition, we want to develop press conferences that you will get credit for. It always galled me that the press would not give President Reagan credit for holding a press conference unless it was prime-time, 30 minutes, East Room. We should reverse this so that all forums in which you openly address questions, whether in the briefing room or Room 450, are considered press conferences. The way to do that is to immediately establish the nature of your press conferences.
- Frequent Appearances in the Briefing Room: These could be held for 10–15 minutes duration, on an impromptu, irregular basis. We would recommend doing them without prior notification, so that they are limited to the regular working White House press, and require a minimum of preparation on your part. Again, these have to be frequent enough so that the press views them as routine accessibility, rather than signaling any special announcement.
- Pool Briefings: A new idea would be to establish a rotation among regular White House press corps to form a pool of 3–5 reporters who would be taken into the Oval Office once or twice a week for a 10-minute session with the President. The pool would do a report on the interview, and a transcript could be provided to all members of the press corps.
- Ad Hoc Access: Perhaps the most effective means of establishing your accessibility to the press is through ad hoc visits to the press working area, hallway discussions, motorcade interviews, etc. You have maintained press relationships of this nature throughout the campaign and the transition. These kinds of events are in stark contrast to President Reagan's style, and make a considerable impression on press attitudes. We recommend you maintain these informal contacts.[51]

Clinton would continue the practice of holding joint press conferences with foreign leaders (a trend that has continued with George W. Bush and Barack Obama), yet he would not hold many formal press conferences, particularly during his second term (due in part to the Monica Lewinsky investigation and subsequent impeachment). Since the Reagan years, presidents have held fewer formal press conferences where they appear alone before the White House press corps, relying more on regional and foreign press conferences as well as joint appearances with foreign dignitaries, since these types of press conferences are easier to control and do not give the press as much of a chance to ask questions that the president may not want to answer 🖱. However, Clinton always performed well in these impromptu sessions, deftly fielding questions from seasoned White House correspondents; while Clinton's formal press conferences were infrequent, they would nonetheless represent an important element of his overall communication strategy. Yet, a presidential press conference has some strategic risk given that the White House cannot control what questions reporters will ask; as such, advisors work hard to prepare the president

---

🖱 Watch President Clinton give a joint press conference with President Leonid Makarovych Kravchuk of Ukraine.

for any and all possible situations. For example, Clinton's plan to hold a prime-time press conference in early August 1994 came at a crucial time; major policy issues on the Clinton agenda, including health-care reform, were pending in Congress, various international issues were dominating headlines, and the congressional midterm elections were just three months away. According to his advisors, the time was right for Clinton to hold a press conference, as it gave him

> ...an opportunity to accomplish three major objectives: To give extended remarks on the need for health care reform and the importance of universal coverage; To take credit—if the vote has taken place—for a successful crime bill and pivot off that success to demonstrate that Washington is working for people, that your agenda is moving forward here and to show that health care reform can get done; To reassure the American people about the humanitarian effort in Rwanda, the situation in Haiti and the conflict in Bosnia. The effect of a prime-time news conference will be to increase your stake in the upcoming congressional votes on health care. Obviously, there are several snares to be aware of during the press conference: being drawn into a web of questions on the Whitewater hearings and answering a line of questions about polls and process. Attached is a book with proposed Q & A on a number of topics that may come up during the press conference. We will supplement it on Tuesday and Wednesday.[52]

As this memo shows, press conferences are not only to keep the press informed on important issues; they also serve as one of the many tools presidents have at their disposal in an attempt to implement their overall communication strategy.

The Media Environment

The current political environment with the news media that presidents must face, which has steadily evolved since Vietnam and Watergate, is one that breeds mistrust, cynicism, and fierce competition among members of the White House press corps and their respective publications and news shows. The president is under constant scrutiny by the press but must be careful in his criticisms of reporters, who can not only give voice to his opponents but can present the news as unflattering to the president's public image. Much of this current environment got its start in the 1960s due to the growing influence of television, as well as the emergence of the "credibility gap," known as the growing sentiment among many American citizens to distrust the statements of government officials. One of the first events that contributed to the credibility gap occurred in 1960 when an American military U-2 spy plane was shot down over the Soviet Union. The Eisenhower administration initially denied that the plane had been spying on the Soviet Union, but when the Soviets produced the captured pilot, Gary Powers, on television, U.S. government officials were forced to change their story. The release of the Warren Commission report in 1964 would also contribute to the growing credibility gap. The commission, chaired by Chief Justice Earl Warren, declared that Lee Harvey Oswald had acted alone in assassinating President Kennedy. However, a majority of Americans at the time did not believe the lone-gunman theory and remained skeptical of the findings.[53]

The news media had also begun to distrust the information they were receiving from the government, especially official military reports coming out of the Vietnam

War. By the latter half of the 1960s, both White House and Pentagon officials often insisted to journalists that Americans were winning the war against the communist North Vietnamese (known as the Viet Cong), yet the pictures being broadcast into Americans' living rooms every night on the evening news told a different story. Daily news briefings by military commanders in Saigon were dubbed "The Five O'Clock Follies" by American reporters due to the lack of accuracy in many of the reports. In the battlefields of Vietnam, the Pentagon put few restrictions on American reporters (a policy that would change drastically in the 1980s and beyond), which allowed them direct access to soldiers who could tell their own stories about what was really happening. Both broadcast and print reporters began filing critical stories about American involvement in Vietnam, which contributed to the growing anti-war movement across the nation. In February 1968, Walter Cronkite gave a rare editorial comment on his nightly newscast on CBS, declaring that the war in Vietnam could not be won by the American military. President Lyndon Johnson reportedly told an aide, "If I've lost Cronkite, I've lost Middle America."[54] Just weeks later, on March 31, 1968, Johnson announced to the nation that he would not seek re-election.

As American involvement in the Vietnam War continued into the 1970s, so too did the growing credibility gap between the public, the news media, and government officials. Elected in 1968, Richard Nixon distrusted the American press, deplored leaks from his administration to Washington reporters, and placed the names of countless top journalists who had been critical of his policies on his famous "enemies list." Nixon's vice president, Spiro Agnew, routinely criticized the news media for unfair and biased reporting, particularly for their critical views about Vietnam, claiming that the press wielded too much power over public opinion. Agnew claimed that top news executives were liberal elites who held an "Eastern Establishment bias" that did not reflect the views of average Americans; he once referred to top news executives as "nattering nabobs of negativism."[55] The Nixon administration also attempted but failed to impose prior restraint (which means to stop publication) on the *New York Times* and *Washington Post* in 1971 when both papers began reporting on the Pentagon Papers, a forty-seven-volume study on the "History of the U.S. Decision Making Process on Vietnam Policy" that had been leaked to the press by a former defense department analyst. The Supreme Court ruled against the government in the case, *New York Times v. United States* (1971), but only after the stories had been kept out of the newspapers for approximately two weeks following a restraining order from a federal court judge.

Perhaps the seminal political event that defined the 1970s, Watergate—which is a series of events that unfolded between July 1972 with a break-in of the Democratic Party office at the Watergate Complex in Washington and August 1974 when Nixon resigned from the presidency—also changed the nature of the presidential–press relationship. Bob Woodward and Carl Bernstein, two *Washington Post* reporters who covered the city beat, would eventually win the Pulitzer Prize for their two years of investigative reporting into the links between the Watergate break-in and the Nixon administration. The five burglars arrested in 1972 were

Watch Walter Cronkite discuss his editorial.

Read the complete Pentagon Papers.

part of a political sabotage unit put together by top Nixon aides as part of a larger operation to discredit Democratic candidates and ensure Nixon's reelection that same year. In the first months after the break-in, Woodward and Bernstein were nearly alone in their coverage of the story and their determination to link the break-in to the White House. With the help of their inside source, known only as "Deep Throat," they reported the existence of a Nixon campaign slush fund that had paid the burglars. ("Deep Throat" finally revealed his own identity in 2005 as W. Mark Felt, Sr., who had been Associate Director of the FBI during the Watergate years). While the *Post* was not the only news outlet investigating the Watergate story, their early reporting of the break-in helped to lay the groundwork for many other news organizations as the story gripped the nation throughout much of 1973 and 1974 until Nixon finally resigned from office on August 8, 1974.

Major changes would continue to occur within the news industry with the start of the 1980s, which meant that presidents would need to continue to update their press strategies. Throughout the decade, the network newscasts remained a staple for American television viewers and continued to have influence as major players within American politics. For example, in November 1979, ABC News began a late-night recap of the continuing story of the American citizens held hostage at the American Embassy in Iran. The show would evolve into *Nightline*, hosted by Ted Koppel (who stayed with the late night news show until 2005). Koppel's show, along with Cronkite on the *CBS Evening News*, provided a daily count to American citizens of the number of days the sixty-six Americans had been held hostage in Tehran, which served as a daily reminder to American voters in 1980 that President Jimmy Carter, running for reelection that year, had been unable to solve the crisis. The hostages were eventually released on January 20, 1981, just moments after Ronald Reagan had taken the oath of office; they had been held for a total of 444 days.

The Reagan administration was especially skilled at controlling the images that came out of the White House to provide a complete media package to sell both the president's image and his agenda. Reagan, nicknamed the "Great Communicator," exhibited a style and ease in front of the television cameras due to his prior experience as an actor that was tailor-made for television in the 1980s. The "stagecraft" of the Reagan years would be a tough act for his successor, George H. W. Bush, to follow. Bush, who wanted his presidency to be more about substance than style, had a difficult time articulating his vision for the country within a rapidly changing media environment.[56] Since then, presidents have focused more attention on keeping up with changes in the news media industry and have altered their strategies accordingly. As media scholar Doris Graber reminds us, "Media do more than depict the political environment; they *are* the political environment."[57]

News Coverage of the President

In the post-Watergate years, press coverage of the president and the White House has become more personal, intrusive, and obsessed with scandal. Television coverage of politics, and in particular the presidency, has not only personalized and politicized the functioning of the national government, but the immediacy of television coverage has also accelerated the decision-making process for presidents. The up-close-and-personal look at our presidents that television now provides through the plethora of public venues has also altered the political environment in which the president must lead. Americans have come to expect that the personal lives of presidents will make news, which has also desensitized the public to the tabloid-style reporting about personal indiscretions. Presidents must now pay close attention to their image as it is portrayed on television, but determining what is good for the president in terms of control over the message may not be the same as substantive information about the political process for the American electorate.[58]

In general, there are three phases to the presidential–press relationship. The first is often referred to as the initial honeymoon period, when the president and his advisors are eager to provide access to the press, and the press can be less critical of the president since, in most cases, no major policy initiatives have yet to be introduced. When the White House embarks on its policy agenda, the second phase begins to occur as criticism appears in the press (from other political actors as well as political commentators). The White House response to critical coverage shapes the third phase, which can include an increase in presidential public relations activities that limit press interaction as advisors attempt to regain control of the president's message and image. Presidential honeymoons with the press have become increasingly shorter; Clinton, Bush, and Obama all had relatively short honeymoon periods in terms of press coverage.[59] In addition, while the president and executive branch may dominate news coverage when compared to the other two branches of government, not all of the coverage is positive. More recent presidents have experienced a growing trend in negative press coverage, even during their first year in office. For example, less than 40 percent of the network news coverage of the first year in office for Reagan, Clinton, and George W. Bush was considered positive. In 2009, Obama fared somewhat better, with 47 percent positive coverage on the network news, yet that still leaves a majority of the news coverage negative about the president.[60]

White House Press Strategies

Throughout the twentieth century, prominent reporters who covered the White House beat often played an important role in shaping the image of presidents in their respective media outlets as well as in the eyes of the American public. Therefore, presidents and their advisors during the modern era have actively developed strategies in an attempt to manage and control the news of their administrations in the national media. The president continues to be the most prominent political figure in news coverage, and his actions can dominate day-to-day news coverage. Most press secretaries, during the presidential transition or at the start of the administration, map out a specific press strategy. The ultimate goal is to have the president portrayed in the most favorable light as possible; highlighting the stature and dignity of the office is also frequently a strategic goal. For example, in December 1988, just weeks prior to George H. W. Bush's inauguration, Marlin Fitzwater declared the need for a new press strategy (in a discussion paper written for the president-elect) that would "[throw] out all the old ways of doing things, and [suggest] an entirely new scheme of press relations." The major premise of this new press "scheme" placed a much greater emphasis on pulling the president back from time on the national stage and replacing the staged events that had dominated the Reagan years with more informal press access (that is, emphasizing substance over style):

> The press takes the irrational position that the President is a public entity, and that reporters must keep watch over every move and utterance on behalf of the American people. To this end they have constructed elaborate schemes, committed millions of dollars and untold walkie-talkies and helicopters to pursue you to the ends of the earth. Thus, our basic task is to introduce them to a new kind of President—the private man. The lessons of history in this regard regale us with stories of Lyndon Johnson careening through the Texas countryside with madcap reporters giving chase; Jimmy Carter sneaking away from Camp David for an afternoon of fishing in the Shenandoahs; and Ronald Reagan having the quietest of dinners at the Jockey Club. The conclusion one reaches from these episodes is that there is no answer to this problem which will satisfy all parties. Thus, our task should be to satisfy you first, and the press as much as possible. We are therefore considering the following: An edict that says: The President of the United States has a right to an uninterrupted and unintruded visit to the ice cream store. It's not news. It's unpredictable. It's personal. And security is enhanced by its very unpredictability.[61]

Presidents have attempted control over the news with the knowledge of the news media's preference to report on politics, but only the subject matter can be controlled, not the tone of the news. The president makes news by virtue of being the ideological symbol of American democracy and leadership to both journalists and the public, but the president's relationship with the press is a combination of both strengths and weaknesses. Presidential power can be undermined both by a failure of the administration to effectively manage the news and by both newsgathering norms within the journalism industry and the skepticism of the press. While presidents can usually enjoy deference from the press in terms of coverage during times of crisis or certain ceremonial occasions, usually reporters place presidential actions within a political context that reduces the symbolic nature of the presidency to just another politician seeking to retain political power.

That does not mean, however, that White House advisors do not continue to work at trying to control both the content and the tone of presidential press coverage. For example, at the end of Bill Clinton's first year in office, his advisors sought to shift the focus of press stories assessing the President's first-year accomplishments:

> The press has completed the run of Congress and the presidency accomplishment stories; we are now entering a phase of coverage that will focus more exclusively on you, your Administration, and the first year in office. Attached is a list of your accomplishments arranged thematically which I think will be helpful for your interviews in December. You also asked for a better sense of what we hope to get out of the interviews. That follows—along with a few other suggestions. The essence, however, is this: **Your tone should be optimistic and presidential; you should stress big themes and the progress we have made on them.** The year should not be judged in a vacuum; it is the first year on a long road. Be optimistic; you should be satisfied with the progress we have made, but aware that millions are still hurting—be determined to push ahead. We need an alternative interpretation to the direction the press is headed in their analysis of the first year. **The press' storyline**. You can use these interviews to blunt the emerging conventional wisdom of the press, which is along these lines: This is a President who gets things done, but he too often stumbles across the finish line with his

> shirt ends hanging out. They have a dangerous propensity to do everything at the last minute—and it is bound to catch up with them.... **Our Storyline**. I came to this office with two great objectives: To change the system and to make it work for middle class families.... That was no small order; we live in a uniquely challenging period of time in our nation's history and the needs of working Americans had been neglected for a long time.[62]

While attempts to control press coverage are not always successful, they are among the several factors that can increase the tensions between the president and the press. Presidents have historically viewed the press as a hindrance in achieving the public's support for policies, due mostly to the content of most news originating from the White House. For example, presidents often attempt to use the press to its advantage through leaks. Top aides or even the president himself will leak information as a trial balloon to test public reaction to a proposed policy. In this instance, the press agrees to serve as a communication tool of the government in order to remain competitive with other news outlets. However, sometimes the press can leak information that the White House does not want made public. Often, this information comes from someone else in the executive branch who leaks information without White House approval. For example, in 1941, Harry L. Hopkins, a close aide to FDR, wrote the following memo to the President about a leak from the Defense Department:

> I am enclosing an article from the New York Times of this morning. This article gives the exact figures of our proposed tank production. As usual they quote a "defense official,"... I realize that under ordinary circumstances it is supposed to be bad form to find out how a newspaper man gets stories but when vital defense information like this is given out to newspaper men I think the person who gave out this information should be fired. It is inconceivable to me that people can be so naïve as to think that information like this is not helpful to the Germans. Would it not be possible for Steve [Early] to set up a unit—or, if not Steve, the F.B.I.—to find out who in the government is giving out this information and make an example of him? The story in this morning's paper is simply one of many that are constantly being leaked out and I think we have got to put a stop to it.[63]

The Carter administration experienced similar frustrations over stories in the *New York Times* and *Washington Post* in July 1978 that included leaked information about the Strategic Arms Limitation Treaty (SALT) talks. Press Secretary Jody Powell, who declared the leak to be an internal attempt to alter Carter's policy in this area, wrote the following to the President:

> From what I know of this issue, this sort of leak should not be allowed to pass. Clearly, it came from those who oppose [your policy]. It was done to influence policy and narrow your options. I recommend that you do one of two things: 1. Call in the principals who attended the SALT meeting where this option was discussed and chew them out good. Let them know that you expect your displeasure to be conveyed to their subordinates. 2. Call [Paul] Warnke (ACDA is the most likely source) and let him know that you are upset and want him and his people to know about it. Only if the bureaucracy begins to feel that there is some penalty for this sort of behavior will we see some restraint on their part. Otherwise, the problem will continue to grow worse. There is no doubt in my mind that this leak

> came from the same people who leaked the "Freeze on SALT" story to the same two reporters—Pincus and Kaiser.[64]

A more recent example shows how leaks have continued to be a frustration for each administration. In July 2010, 92,000 documents related to the war in Afghanistan were posted on the web page *WikiLeaks*. While President Obama responded that the leak raised no fundamentally new issues about the conflict, he nonetheless chastised the move by stating the leak "could potentially jeopardize individuals or operations," and the Pentagon initiated a criminal probe to find out from where the leak occurred.[65]

Beyond leaks from the White House, whether intentional or not, other issues create tension between the president and the press. Many stories on the president tend to have a superficial or trivial quality. Stories focusing on the personal aspects of the president's life often gain more prominent coverage than stories analyzing policies. Again, competition among reporters, as well as a lack of expertise on many national political issues, fuels this type of coverage. Finally, while most studies on media coverage of news show no systematic bias along partisan or ideological lines, distortion still occurs in coverage of the president. The presentation of news contains a structural bias in how stories are selected, since all issues do not receive coverage. Due to deadlines and limited time and/or space for stories, important issues are often oversimplified.[66]

Presidents and their advisors have also long been concerned about, and in some cases obsessed with, how the White House is covered in the press. For example, FDR sent the following memo to his press secretary, Steve Early, about his dismay over a story by United Press International: "This is a UP story. I do not in the least mind the headline but it is interesting to note that the only person quoted (twice) was Senator [Robert] Taft [R-OH]. Loads of other things were said by other Senators and this is therefore a partisan story and not worthy of a press association. It is worthwhile to check up with the UP occasionally in order that they may know they are being watched, if for no other reason."[67] The Truman administration also kept regular track of newspaper columns, editorials, and radio comments about the President and his policies. For example, a January 13, 1947 "Column Summary" compiled by the Executive Office of the President included selected comments from a list of seventy papers "as received" by the White House. The first column summarized came from Walter Winchell of the *New York Mirror*: "Notes statement that Mr. Truman in his radio address had Hooper rating of 20.4 without guest stars, but contends all the President had 'was every front page in the land, every radio column, commentator and White House reporter advertising it and still he couldn't attract as many listeners as other comedians.'"[68]

Monitoring of the press reached an extreme during the Nixon administration. Early in the first term, key White House staffers began work on an extensive system of evaluating the President's coverage. The goal of the "covert" operation was to determine which members of the press were friends of the administration, and more importantly, which were enemies. Television commentators were always of particular interest to the White House, which wanted to know where coverage fell into one of three categories: "Generally For Us, Generally Objective, or Generally Against Us." Not only was the project high priority and top secret within the White House, but the attempts to gain detailed profiles on television commentators were extensive, including scouring through correspondent's Secret Service files, which were necessary to obtain a White House press pass. As Press Secretary Ronald Ziegler reported to Chief of Staff H. R. Haldeman in November 1969, the project was somewhat precarious:

> We have exhaustedly explored ways in which we could obtain this background without the possibility of a leak that we were undertaking such a project.... If we were to pursue information such as where these individuals were previously employed, what their general background is, I am very concerned in the light of the Vice President's recent addresses a serious problem could be caused. As we go along we will attempt to compile such information in personal conversations, etc., but this will take some time.[69]

By mid-1970, White House staffers had compiled an extensive list of more than two hundred journalists from television, radio, and print, and placed each into one of six categories: "Friendly to Administration, Balanced to Favorable, Balanced, Unpredictable, Usually Negative, and Always Hostile." Not surprisingly, those considered to be leaning more in favor of the administration came from traditionally more conservative publications, such as *U.S. News and World Report*, *Business Week*, and the *Chicago Tribune*, while many of those considered negative or hostile were from traditionally more liberal publications, such as the *New York Times*, the *Washington Post*, and the *Boston Globe*.[70] Friendly members of the press, it was often suggested by White House advisors, should be rewarded for their efforts. For example, backgrounders with the President, or special invitations or other perks could be given to those reporters providing favorable coverage. According to Haldeman, a good strategy involved attempts "to do more in-depth discussion between friendly members of the press and the President.... We need to develop a plan for working with friendly or potentially favorable members of the press, and also for dividing the hostile working press."[71] The monitoring system was even suggested, at one point, to include keeping tabs on television talk shows such as the *Smothers Brothers* on CBS, where Nixon was the frequent butt of jokes, and *The Tonight Show with Johnny Carson* on NBC, since Nixon was often the subject during the opening monologue. The theory was to have supporters write letters to the producers to object to the anti-Nixon comments, and to also rely on the FCC's Equal Time rule for reply from the White House.[72] According to advisors in the Attorney General's office: "If we simply develop an efficient monitoring system, we probably will find something every night that entitles us to time to reply. And soon the negative comments will become rarer and rarer.... I would like to see a week's output of anti-administration material—I think it would knock our hats off—and would come from surprising sources, not just from politicians, but entertainment personalities and various kinds of celebrities generally."[73]

In addition, the Nixon administration was the first to institutionalize the use of the daily news summary, which included the "ideas and opinions contained in a cross-section of news reports, editorials, columns, and articles" from more than fifty newspapers, thirty magazines, and the *Associated Press* and *United Press International* wire services.[74] The administration received numerous requests from many sources to receive a copy of the news summary, but all were turned down since the summary was "strictly an internal document prepared for the President and the White House staff."[75] The news summary was described as including a representative sample of columns, editorials, news analyses, and cartoons from newspapers and magazines, all condensed to reflect the "central theme as well as a quote or two to give the flavor of the piece." The goal was to keep Nixon informed of the views and opinions of the nation:

> The President is interested not only in comment and reaction to his programs but he also wants to keep abreast of the daily developments which are going on across the nation and affect every citizen—developments which may well be more important to the country than some piece of legislation. By keeping an eye on stories reported in all the media, the President maintains an excellent feel of the nation's pulse.[76]

Since then, the daily news summary has grown into an important informational tool for presidents in the development of their daily communication strategy. A formalized daily news summary has been used in one form or another ever since the Nixon years, a practice that has been institutionalized within the press and/or communications offices. The news summary circulates among senior staff members so that they can evaluate the president's coverage, both nationally and internationally, and so that the White House can respond accordingly.[77] For example, the George H. W. Bush White House relied on several information sources to keep up with coverage of the president and his policy initiatives, including an extensive daily news summary of major print and broadcast sources, as well as weekly "editorial round-ups" that summarized editorials and op-ed pieces in major newspapers.[78] In addition, coverage of Bush in roughly thirty regional newspapers, including larger regional daily newspapers such as the *Seattle Times*, *Dallas Morning News*, *Minneapolis Star Tribune*, *Phoenix Republic*, *San Diego Union*, and *Denver Post*, were tracked by staffers in the communications office.[79] By 1991, the Office of Media Relations had developed an extensive tracking system/content analysis of news coverage of presidential events, including which news organizations covered the event, the placement of the story about the event, and whether or not the coverage was considered "favorable" or "unfavorable."[80] Similar news tracking systems have continued to be used in the Clinton, Bush, and Obama Administrations 🖱.

CONCLUSION

Although the Obama administration may be the most technologically savvy in recent memory, his relationship with the press has been rocky since he first took office. During the 2008 presidential campaign, a common complaint (especially by Republicans) was that the press was "in the tank" for Obama. Yet, President Obama has had what some call a "surprisingly hostile relationship" with the news media, with little day-to-day interaction with the White House press corps, strong pushback from advisors over certain stories, and Obama himself often making caustic or sarcastic comments about the press.[81] In addition, despite complaints that he is often "over-exposed" in television appearances, he has mostly avoided formal press

---

🖱 Read a full daily news summary.

conferences and provides less access to the press corps than his two immediate predecessors, George W. Bush and Bill Clinton. But, as with some of his predecessors, Obama's communication advisors have sought ways for their president to speak more directly with citizens by going around the more traditional venue of the White House press corps. For example, during the same week as his appearance on *The View*, Obama also debuted a web video on the new government website Healthcare.gov. Often, it is goodwill with voters that is a more important component of the communication strategy than positive press relations, as Obama's appearance on *The View* reminds us: "Mr. Obama got a chance to remind viewers who voted for him why they did so in the first place. A lot of goodwill can be reaped with an appearance on *The View* or ESPN or even *WWE Raw*."[82]

While it is still much too early to assess all the many facets of Obama's public presidency, we do know that presidents have an increasingly difficult task in leading the public. Even presidents who are seen as strong communicators, such as Clinton and Obama, have not been immune from the changing media environment and the competitive nature of presidential news coverage. Finding the right balance of major speeches, media appearances, and other public events, as well as crafting an effective press strategy to go along with such events, all while making the president look like a strong and commanding leader, is no easy task for even the most skilled White House communications advisors. However, whether or not presidents are now over-exposed in the media-saturated environment in which they attempt to govern remains an ongoing debate. As media critic Howard Kurtz of the *Washington Post* wrote about Obama's appearance on *The View*: "This little flap about whether it was sufficiently dignified for a POTUS to appear on daytime television was like something out of a time warp. That debate ended when Bill Clinton played the sax for Arsenio back in 1992 and he and the candidates that year were interviewed not only by Larry King but by MTV. As president, Clinton boasted that King had 'liberated' him 'by giving me to the American people directly.' "[83] Obama proclaimed on *The View* that his job is not to campaign but to govern: "The one thing that does frustrate me sometimes is the sense that, we shouldn't be campaigning all the time. You know, there's a time to campaign, and then there's a time to govern. And what we've tried to do over the last 20 months is to govern."[84] Yet, like Clinton, Obama has taken advantage of new media technologies and other strategic opportunities to reach out directly to the American public in an attempt to govern through public leadership. And like both Kennedy and Reagan did with their innovative uses of television, Obama is setting a high standard in terms of using and managing technology as a means to communicate for future occupants of the Oval Office.

ADDRESSING THE NATION

THEN . . .

When a president decides to deliver an address to a joint session of Congress, he normally does so with the intent to make a major policy announcement or to address a national crisis. Aside from the annual State of the Union address, which is a significant—and expected—event for the president to address both Congress and the American public, other presidential visits to Capitol Hill are

Bill Clinton acknowledges the crowd in the House Gallery prior to delivering his State of the Union address January 23, 1996, on Capitol Hill. House Speaker Newt Gingrich and Vice President Al Gore appear behind him.

reserved for significant policy initiatives or items of national significance such as impending military action. Such an address allows the president to capture the attention of both the news media and the American public to make the case for his chosen policy or course of action. For example, FDR was giving an address to a joint session of Congress when he declared "Yesterday, December 7, 1941—a date which will live in infamy—the United States of America was suddenly and deliberately attacked by naval and air forces of the Empire of Japan."[85] In April 1981, Ronald Reagan gave his second address to a joint session of Congress after just three months in office, stating, "I have come to speak to you tonight about our economic recovery program and why I believe it's essential that the Congress approve this package, which I believe will lift the crushing burden of inflation off of our citizens and restore the vitality to our economy and our industrial machine."[86]

Announcing a major policy initiative was exactly what Bill Clinton planned to do in September 1993 when he delivered an address to a joint session of Congress to promote his health-care reform initiative 🖱. As part of his focus on the economy and other domestic issues during the 1992 presidential campaign, Clinton made reforming health care and expanding availability of health insur-

---

🖱 Watch President Clinton give the joint address to Congress.

ance a top priority during his first year in office. Seen as a major speech and an early test for the Clinton presidency, the initial roll out of the health care policy provided an opportunity for Clinton to convince the American public and members of Congress that the plan should be adopted. The speech itself laid out the specifics of how to expand coverage to more Americans while keeping the quality of medical care up and keeping costs down.

Clinton recalled feeling confident as he walked into the packed House of Representatives chamber following the traditional announcement, "Mr. Speaker, the President of the United States." Greeted by members of Congress and members of his cabinet also in attendance, Clinton was fully prepared to deliver his address to a national audience—that is, until he realized that the wrong speech was in the TelePrompTer: "My confidence slipped.... I was looking at the beginning of the speech to Congress on the economic plan I'd delivered in February. The budget had been enacted more than a month earlier; Congress didn't need to hear that speech again."[87] Clinton would turn to his Vice President, Al Gore, who was sitting behind Clinton and next to the Speaker of the House, to inform him of the problem; Gore would then summon White House communications advisor George Stephanopoulos to go fix the problem. It would take seven long minutes into Clinton's address to insert the correct speech into the TelePrompTer and get it caught up with Clinton's actual words. Despite a flurry of words from an earlier speech passing before his eyes, Clinton—a skilled public speaker who had been working on the draft of the speech right up until the limo ride from the White House to Capitol Hill—relied on his written copy of the speech for those first crucial minutes, and no one in the viewing audience was the wiser. Behind the scenes, Stephanopoulos was "sick with worry" over what effect this would have on the President's performance, yet Clinton's speech was considered a "home run," particularly when he pulled out a mock-up of his proposed "Health Care Security Card" for the cameras, which Clinton promised would guarantee health coverage to all Americans if Congress adopted his plan.[88] While the success of the speech was short lived (health-care reform would not pass during the Clinton presidency), the initial public relations strategy for the plan was a success, as the health-care address would highlight one of Clinton's best skills as president—an excellent communicator capable of delivering a strong performance even under less than desirable circumstances.

. . . AND NOW

Like his most recent Democratic predecessor, Barack Obama would also deliver a prime-time, nationally televised address to a joint session of Congress on the topic of health-care reform on September 9, 2009 🖱. The debate about health-care reform throughout the summer of 2009 had been hyperpartisan and divisive, which had left White House advisors questioning their decision not only to let Congress write the bill, but to not have Obama engage in a more direct public relations campaign to support such a major piece of legislation. As one of his top

---

🖱 Watch President Obama give his address to Congress.

domestic priorities during his first year in office, the president made a strong pitch for health-care reform in his speech, stating that, "I am not the first President to take up this cause, but I am determined to be the last. It has now been nearly a century since Theodore Roosevelt first called for health-care reform, and ever since, nearly every President and Congress, whether Democrat or Republican, has attempted to meet this challenge in some way.... Now is when we must bring the best ideas of both parties together and show the American people that we can still do what we were sent here to do."[89] While Obama had already earned a reputation for being a skilled performer in the venue of such a formal speech, it was actually a little-known Congressman from South Carolina that would dominate the headlines the next day. Representative Joe Wilson, Republican from South Carolina, shouted out, "You lie!" at Obama after the President stated, "Now, there are also those who claim that our reform efforts would insure illegal immigrants. This too is false. The reforms I'm proposing would not apply to those who are here illegally." Amid a somewhat shocked House chamber, Obama responded to Wilson: "It's not true. And one more misunderstanding I want to clear up, under our plan, no Federal dollars will be used to fund abortions, and Federal conscience laws will remain in place," as he continued on with his prepared remarks.

Called "the outburst heard 'round the world" by Brian Williams on the next night's opening coverage on *NBC Nightly News*, Wilson's outburst received much media attention in the following days, which had the effect of highlighting the contentiousness of the issue of health-care reform as opposed to the substance of the Democratic proposal endorsed by Obama. The White House received no bump in approval ratings for the health-care plan after the speech, due not only to the news media's obsession with Wilson's bad behavior but also to the fact that fewer Americans now tune in to watch a presidential address (whether on television or the Internet).[90] While Obama deserved high marks for not letting Wilson rattle him during the speech, the news media coverage that followed seemed to underlie the fact that presidents, no matter how skilled at communicating, have little control over the environment—both political and media—in which they attempt to govern. White House communications advisors will no doubt continue their efforts to control both the president's message and image, yet expanding technology and changes within the news industry, along with increasing public expectations for the president to perform flawlessly while on center stage, will continue to make the public aspects of the presidency a challenge for Obama and his successors in the Oval Office.

SUGGESTED READINGS

Campbell, Karlyn Kohrs, and Kathleen Hall Jamieson. 1990. *Deeds Done in Words: Presidential Rhetoric and the Genres of Governance.* Chicago: University of Chicago Press.

Cohen, Jeffrey E. 2008. *The Presidency in an Era of 24-Hour News.* Princeton, NJ: Princeton University Press.

Cohen, Jeffrey E. 2010. *Going Local: Presidential Leadership in the Post-Broadcast Age.* New York: Cambridge University Press.

Edwards, George C., III. 2003. *On Deaf Ears: The Limits of the Bully Pulpit*. New Haven: Yale University Press.

Emery, Michael, and Edwin Emery. 1996. *The Press and America: An Interpretive History of the Mass Media*, 8th ed. Boston: Allyn and Bacon.

Farnsworth, Stephen J. 2009. *Spinner in Chief: How Presidents Sell Their Policies and Themselves*. Boulder, CO: Paradigm Publishers.

Gelderman, Carol. 1997. *All the President's Words: The Bully Pulpit and the Creation of the Virtual Presidency*. New York: Walker & Company.

Grossman, Michael Baruch, and Martha Joynt Kumar. 1981. *Portraying the President: The White House and the News Media*. Baltimore: The Johns Hopkins University Press.

Han, Lori Cox. 2001. *Governing from the Center Stage: White House Communication Strategies during the Television Age of Politics*. Cresskill, NJ: Hampton Press.

Han, Lori Cox, and Diane J. Heith, eds. 2005. *In the Public Domain: Presidents and the Challenges of Public Leadership*. Albany: SUNY Press.

Hart, Roderick P. 1987. *The Sound of Leadership: Presidential Communication in the Modern Age*. Chicago: University of Chicago Press.

Kernell, Samuel. 2007. *Going Public: New Strategies of Presidential Leadership*, 4th ed. Washington, DC: CQ Press.

Kumar, Martha Joynt. 2007. *Managing the President's Message: The White House Communications Operation*. Baltimore: The Johns Hopkins University Press.

Maltese, John Anthony. 1994. *Spin Control: The White House Office of Communications and Management of Presidential News*, 2nd ed. Rev. Chapel Hill: University of North Carolina Press.

Stuckey, Mary E. *The President as Interpreter-in-Chief*. Chatham, NJ: Chatham House, 1991.

Tulis, Jeffrey K. 1987. *The Rhetorical Presidency*. Princeton: Princeton University Press.

ON THE WEB

http://people-press.org/. The Pew Research Center for the People & the Press is an independent, non-partisan public opinion research organization that studies attitudes toward politics, the press and public policy issues.

http://www.presidency.ucsb.edu/. The American Presidency Project contains the *Public Papers of the Presidents* as well as numerous data sets about presidential public activities.

http://www.gpoaccess.gov/wcomp/index.html. Published each Monday by the Office of the Federal Register and the National Archives and Records Administration, the Weekly Compilation of Presidential Documents is the official publication of presidential statements, messages, remarks, and other materials released by the White House Press Secretary.

IN THEIR OWN WORDS

MEDIA EXPOSURE

Presidential advisors and political pundits alike have long pondered the question, "How much is too much?" when considering a president's public strategy. While no definitive answer has ever emerged, it is safe to say that the number of media appearances in which a president engages often corresponds to how skilled he is in public settings. For example, does the president appear comfortable and relaxed on television (like Reagan); is he adept at impromptu questions (like Clinton)? Or is the president likely to commit a verbal gaffe with an incorrect statement (like Reagan) or garbled syntax and prose (like George W. Bush)? One of the most important skills that a presidential advisor can possess is knowing the president's strengths and weaknesses, especially in regards to public strategies. A telling example comes from Pat Buchanan's concerns over a possible televised speech by Richard Nixon in 1971:

> Understand thought is being given to televising national the RN appearance before the Detroit Economic Club. Don't think we should do that—for the following reasons:
>
> 1. An hour's show with Richard Nixon answering the concerns of some Detroit Fat Cats does not seem to me particularly good television; it will lack the adversary setting of a press conference, and the sharpness of questions, RN can expect from editors and writers.
>
> 2. An hour is simply too long—to sustain the interest of Middle America.
>
> 3. We have nothing really new to say, from my knowledge; the President has already covered the "news" in Thursday's [press] conference.
>
> 4. The President's greatest political asset is the Presidency—part of the power of that asset adheres in the distance between the Presidency and the people. Harry Truman as Harry Truman is a clown—as President, he fills the shoes of Lincoln, Wilson, etc. The more we show of RN the individual in front of a camera, the more in my judgment we diminish some of the mystery, aloofness that surrounds the office. We make the President too "familiar" a figure—and not in the best sense of that word.
>
> 5. What makes China such an interesting, important country and [French President Charles] De Gaulle such an interesting man—is the aloofness, the distance, from the hoi polloi. Every time we put the President on camera in a conventional setting—answering Q and A—we tend, I think, to bring him down closer to the average man—and I don't believe that is to our political advantage—partly for the next reason.
>
> 6. I have never been convinced that Richard Nixon, Good Guy, is our long suit; to me we are simply not going to charm the American people; we are not going to win it on "style" and we ought to forget playing ball in the Kennedy's Court. This new emphasis of running the President on the tube at more and more opportunities is a corollary of the theorem that the more people who see the President, the more who will become enthusiastic about him. We are selling personality; but we know from our experience with television shows, how even the most attractive and energetic and charming personalities don't last very long.
>
> 7. As I wrote the President long ago, in 1967, we watched Rocky rise twenty points in the national polls in a year in which he was probably not once on national television. When Rocky took to the airwaves in 1968, running around the country—he dropped in the polls as he did in 1964. In short, what is said

and written around Nelson Rockefeller's accomplishments—compared with the accomplishments of others—is invariably better received than the presence of Rocky himself in a competitive situation.

8. The President is going to be on with Phase II in October, and with the Vietnam announcements in November. My judgment is that we ought not to put him on the air, without serious thought, and usually only in context with some significant pronouncement.

9. Finally, am not at all against some of the more imaginative ideas for presenting the President—but they should come out of a Media Strategy, which I don't know we have right now—or I don't see how this fits into it.[91]

CHAPTER 5

The Public Presidency: Public Opinion

During the 2000 presidential campaign, Texas Governor George W. Bush and Vice President Al Gore did not agree on much, but according to their respective acceptance speeches at their party's national nominating conventions, they seemed to be in agreement about one topic: the president and public opinion. Bush told those in attendance at the Republican National Convention on August 3, 2000: "I believe great decisions are made with care, made with conviction, not made with polls. I do not need to take your pulse before I know my own mind." And during his address at the Democratic National Convention on August 17, 2000, Gore stated: "But the presidency is more than a popularity contest. It's a day-to-day fight for people. Sometimes you have to choose to do what's difficult or unpopular." Both presidential candidates asserted the need for independent decision making and highlighted the notion of resistance to the push of popularity. For the contemporary presidency, the presence of public opinion polling—both approval ratings of presidents and internal White House polling about potential policies—adds another dimension to public leadership: Can the president lead and watch the polls at the same time? Bush and Gore appear to have said no, that leadership requires independence. A representative system of government, however, appears to say yes, as politicians must be mindful of public attitudes.

Political scientists have known for decades the importance of public support in the equation of presidential success. Since the late 1980s and early 1990s, due in part to the expansion of news coverage and the creation of the

Watch candidates Gore and Bush give their 2000 conventions speeches.

Reagan maintained a strong connection to the American public throughout his eight years in office. Here, he addresses the nation from the oval office on the space shuttle "Challenger" explosion, January 28, 1986.

twenty-four-hour news cycle, presidential approval ratings became more volatile through an increasingly critical public as well as divided partisan support within Congress.[1] While many outside factors, including the economy, international events, and the political environment in general all shape how the president's job performance is evaluated, above-average approval numbers suggest that a president is succeeding in terms of leadership, while below-average approval numbers can suggest that the White House is out of step with American voters. A president's approval rating is also one of the best indicators of whether or not a communication strategy with the American public is working. Presidents can also be victims of circumstances that are beyond their control. However, it is important to note that being liked by many Americans does not always translate into an effective method of governing in the public arena. Several recent presidents, including Ronald Reagan, George H. W. Bush, and even Barack Obama tend to do better when Americans are asked if they like the president personally as opposed to whether or not they like his job performance and/or policy positions. This was especially true for the elder Bush. Routinely, polls would show that Americans viewed him as "an intelligent, industrious, cautious, solid leader" and as someone who was "warm, sincere, relaxed, and secure."[2] Yet, despite the fact that most people liked him, he still lost reelection to Bill Clinton in 1992.

The younger Bush's presidency provides an interesting case study in the highs and lows of presidential approval ratings. Elected by the slimmest of margins in the Electoral College, yet losing the popular vote to Gore in the contested 2000 election, President Bush began his first term with public approval numbers in the mid-50 percent range. Eight months later, following the September 11 terrorist attacks, his public approval reached 90 percent. The only other president to have achieved similar approval ratings had been his father during the 1991 Gulf War. Those types of approval ratings, which usually occur during times of national crisis, are difficult to maintain. By the time of Bush's reelection in 2004, his approval rating was back to just above 50 percent. His second term, however, would eventually see a dramatic decline in those numbers, as Bush hit a low of 25 percent approval in 2008 (due in large part to the flagging economy). According to Gallup, Bush enjoyed a first-term approval rating average of 62 percent, yet endured a 37 percent average during his second term. Interestingly, the average approval rating for Bush's eight years in office was 49 percent, which is almost the exact percentage of the public who voted for Bush in 2000.[3]

Beyond external polling and approval ratings, of which presidents have little control, internal polling has also become an important element of the overall White House governing strategy in an attempt to "lead the public" in support of the president's agenda. Presidents dating back to Richard Nixon have relied on such polls, and have been criticized for developing a "permanent campaign" mentality while attempting to govern, with the inference that presidents are too often checking the pulse of the nation through a poll prior to making a policy decision. The White House polling operation since the Nixon years has become an institutionalized aspect of the presidency by influencing how and to whom presidents can choose to communicate.

All of the attention paid to polling and approval ratings suggests that the president's relationship with the public represents an important element of the contemporary presidency. While the public does not directly elect the president, the president's relationship with the public emerged almost in spite of the constitutional design. Without direct representation to dominate the relationship, the president and the public intersect in two distinct mechanisms, not one. The public appears to be a tool for presidential use as a means to pressure Congress to do what the president and the public want. However, through public opinion polls, the public also provides a nearly continuous evaluation of the president's job performance. As a result, the public and public opinion polls are a double-edged sword; they can help the president achieve his goals of legislation and reelection, but they can also hurt the president's standing, his opportunities to exercise leadership, his opportunities to carry out his agenda, his goals of reelection and, ultimately, his legacy.

A RESTRAINED VIEW OF THE PUBLIC

The institution of the presidency has a strange relationship with the public. In the twenty-first century, public commentary on the president seems omnipresent from public officials in statements or news interviews, from members of the press on air or online, from bloggers and other members of the "pundit-ocracy." Typing "President Obama" into Google generates roughly 58,900,000 results in .22 seconds; typing "President Obama and oil spill" during the Gulf of Mexico oil spill crisis in 2010 netted some 51,000,000 results. Yet, the people do not directly elect the president. The Constitution validates the right and relevance of official public commentary, particularly in the right to a free press and the right to petition government. Yet, the Constitution intentionally provides no outlet for the masses between elections. In fact, the framers cautioned against attention to public opinion. Alexander Hamilton argued in *Federalist* 71, "The republican principle demands that the deliberate sense of the community should govern the conduct of those to whom they entrust the management of their affairs; but it does not require an unqualified complaisance to every sudden breeze of passion or to every transient impulse which the people may receive from the arts of men, who flatter their prejudices to betray their interests."[4]

The framers used the constitutional design to insulate government, in varying degrees, from the public. The House of Representatives was and still is directly elected by the people. The Senate was indirectly elected by the people as citizens voted for their state legislature, and their legislature chose their Senator, but after passage of the Seventeenth Amendment, ratified in 1913, the public now chooses their Senators in the same way they choose their Representatives. In contrast, the constitutional design in which the Electoral College, made up of individuals selected by the states, indirectly elects the president, still exists today. The relationship between the public and government then represents another area in which the framers both granted and checked power. The Constitution grants the public means to demonstrate their views about elected officials and policies but also grants officials the means to ignore the public. While the framers clearly supported democratic principles over autocratic principles, they no more trusted the public than they trusted officials with unlimited power. Hamilton, in a speech in 1787, claimed, "The voice of the people has been said to be the voice of God. And however generally this maxim has been quoted and believed, it is not true in fact. The people are turbulent and changing; they seldom judge or determine right."[5]

Despite rejecting the class structure that dominated England's government and society, the framers did not believe entirely in universal access for participation in politics. After all, in their design, only property owners could vote. Although suffrage eventually was extended to nearly all individuals over time through amendments to the Constitution, the fundamental structure of government remained. The Constitution limits the expression of the public will to the choice of who serves in government, and it limits the timing of that expression to election outcomes every two, six, or in the case of the president, every four years. The Constitution provides no mechanism to influence policy directly, as the public's influence on government outcomes is dependent on the representative relationship. Congress members are attentive to their constituents' desires as expressed through letters, meetings, or demonstrations, particularly as the next election is always looming. Members of Congress are attentive to the will of the people because they want to be reelected; however, members of Congress can choose to ignore their constituents but under implicit threat to their continued service.[6] The president technically lacks a similarly direct reelection imperative. However, the evolution in democratic principles that led to the expansion of suffrage and direct elections of senators encouraged the expression of attitudes about presidential behavior as if a direct representative relationship between the nation and the president existed. The evolution concerning the role of the public followed the development of political parties and also reflected the attitudes of the president in office.

The first two Presidents of the United States—George Washington and John Adams—were Federalists and, like Hamilton, were not champions of popular rule or even party rule. Unlike his predecessors, the third President of the United States, Thomas Jefferson, author of the Declaration of Independence and head of the Democratic-Republican Party, appeared to be a supporter of public participation in government decision making. However, Jefferson's writings suggest he did not intend his party to be permanent but rather it was an ad-hoc creation to beat back the Federalists' expansive and elitist tendencies.[7] He instead claimed to want to see his party wither in a return to nonpartisan politics. In practice as president, Jefferson was the first to use the public's support as a rationale for the exercise of presidential power, but he did it through party politics and not mass politics.

Andrew Jackson was the president who forever linked the mass public with the presidency, and cemented the justification of presidential behavior in "the will of the people." Jackson's approach, termed by political scientists and historians as Jacksonian democracy, rests on the idea that the president is the direct representative of the people, and the people's "tribune," the only office with a true national identity.[8] Jackson first invoked the idea of the presidency as the people's representative in the statement associated with his unprecedented veto of the 1832 renewal of the Second Bank of the United States. Moreover, the number of people Jackson could claim to serve was larger and more representative of the populous, as he was the first president elected under expanded suffrage, which included voting by non-property owners. However, the force of Jackson's popularity and power remained, like Jefferson's, mediated through a political party. It was the party in this era, not the presidency, that gained power and spread democracy.[9] The presidents who followed Jackson—Martin Van Buren, William Henry Harrison, John Tyler, James Polk, Zachary Taylor, Millard Fillmore, Franklin Pierce, and James Buchanan—sustained the president's role as party leader but could not sustain the use of the public as a source of personal presidential power.

While not typically thought of as advancing democratic principles, Abraham Lincoln's expansion of presidential behavior continued the evolution for the role of the public in the presidency. Lincoln's presidency was consumed by the actions of a war-time president. As a result, most of the discussion of Lincoln's presidential behavior centers on the expansion of unfettered power; however, he rooted his power in the "will of the people." For Lincoln, the expansion of power was only out of necessity, as he argues in a letter to A. G. Hodges, editor of the *Frankfort Commonwealth*, dated April 4, 1864: "I felt that measures otherwise unconstitutional might become lawful by becoming indispensable to the preservation of the Constitution through the preservation of the nation."[10] While asserting the extensive and potentially illegal expansion of presidential authority in times of crisis, Lincoln also recognized the power of the people to control government. In the Gettysburg Address (given at a dedication of the cemetery where six thousand soldiers were buried), he asserted "that this nation, under God, shall have a new birth freedom—and that government of the people, by the people, for the people, shall not perish from the earth ☝."

By 1860, presidents, newspaper editors, and the people themselves articulated a new participatory role for the public in presidential decision making. However, most

☝ Read Lincoln's letter to Hodges and his Gettysburg Address.

nineteenth-century presidents were not using the public to justify significant or history-changing decision making like Jefferson, Jackson, and Lincoln. Thus, while the root of the presidency in national representation was growing, few presidents relied on it. By the time expansive-minded presidents returned to the White House, in the twentieth century, the public voice in American politics between elections was commonplace. In fact, by 1900, a British journalist claimed, "in no country is public opinion so powerful as in the United States."[11]

EVALUATING THE PRESIDENT

As mass participation grew, so did the view of mass opinion, as opposed to political opinion, which had been elite based. Opinion by the mass public was difficult to quantify, but newspapers tried to do so as part of their political coverage. Initially, newspapers began tracking public views of political figures and events via straw polls (a show of hands, or a tally with pen and paper), letters to the editor, and op-ed pieces. The *Harrisburg Pennsylvanian* conducted the first straw poll in 1824 and accurately predicted that Andrew Jackson would claim the presidency over John Quincy Adams and Henry Clay. Straw polls became a regular feature in newspaper's political coverage, not just their election coverage. Straw polls also became an effective circulation gimmick; when people wanted to participate in the mail-in ballots, they also received a special subscription.[12]

Straw polls, since they were based on those who participated in the mail-in ballots and were not necessarily representative of voting turnout, were not scientific and as such were doomed as predictive tools. The 1936 presidential election and the infamous, erroneous prediction of Republican Alf Landon over President Franklin D. Roosevelt by the *Literary Digest* ended the use of straw polls in favor of scientific polling, which accurately predicted the 1936 outcome. The straw polls prior to 1936 had also been off by 10, 12, or as many as 17 points. However, in 1936, they were off by a whopping 20 percentage points and also got the outcome wrong. Having staked its reputation on the straw polls' popularity, the *Digest* went bankrupt following the debacle. Consistent evaluation and articulation of the mass public's opinion did not occur until the development of the public opinion poll and evidence of its ability to gather successfully the public's views. Archibald Crossly, Elmo Roper, and George Gallup were the first pollsters to use scientific method and sampling to estimate a population to produce more accurate election prediction. These early polls were not perfect; they used in-person interviewing and quotas to make samples look like the population, which were not always effective. Gallup correctly predicted the 1936, 1940, and 1944 presidential races. In the 1948 race, Gallup and the other pollsters incorrectly forecast that Thomas Dewey would beat Harry Truman, leading to the now-infamous newspaper headline in the *Chicago Tribune* on November 2, 1948: "Dewey Defeats Truman." After changing their methodology from quota sampling to probability sampling, the commercial polling business became more accurate and gradually became a trusted source for mass opinion information. Roper

---

Read the original newspaper articles.

Read the Tribune's version of the mistake.

The famous photo of Harry Truman holding the newspaper that incorrectly declared the winner of the 1948 presidential election.

and Gallup's polling organizations are still in business today, and they are considered leaders within the industry.

Job Approval

Regular tracking of the public's view of the president and his job performance began with the Truman administration and the Gallup poll organization. On April 12, 1945, eighty-eight percent of those polled approved of the job President Truman was doing.[13] Not all polling organizations ask the question the same way; in fact, even Gallup has changed its wording over time. In 1980, the National Election Studies (NES) added degrees of approval—e.g., strongly approve—to increase explanatory power. Over sixty-five years of asking the public variations on a single theme affords presidents, the media, and scholars a wealth of comparative information. For example, on January 20, 2010, Gallup released a poll and analysis asserting that approval typically falls 5 points in a president's second year; out of the last eight presidents, only George H. W. Bush and George W. Bush avoided a second-year slump in approval rating.[14]

The public has not been universally kind to presidents, at least according to their approval ratings, as Harry Truman, and every president since, has discovered. Truman began his tenure as president under less than ideal circumstances; having

---

View the National Election Studies website.

only been vice president for three months prior to FDR's death in April 1945 left him at a distinct disadvantage regarding his relationship with the American public. As the junior senator from Missouri when selected as FDR's third vice-presidential running mate in 1944, Truman had to forge a personal relationship with Americans during the waning months of World War II as they mourned the loss of their longest-serving president. Approval ratings for Truman stayed strong throughout the fall of 1945, as a letter from Frank Stanton, Vice President and General Manager of CBS, to the President shows:

> Our Surveys Division has today completed a confidential analysis of U.S. public opinion in which I believe you will be interested personally. The findings are based on face-to-face interviews with representative cross sections of the adult population of the country, conducted in early August and mid-September. The question asked in both surveys was: "Taking everything into consideration, what sort of job do you feel Truman is doing as President—Excellent, Good, Fair, or Poor?" IN SUMMARY, these two soundings of public opinion indicate: 1. Virtually nine in every ten persons throughout the United States think you are doing an "excellent or good" job as President. 2. Approval of the job you are doing as President has taken a strong upward swing since August. (This continues the trend established by other surveys made in April and August.) 3. What slight criticism exists today seems to be chiefly in terms of anxiety about the future; with the handling of the problems of unemployment and wages constituting the chief worry.[15]

However, by 1946, the political winds had shifted dramatically for the Truman administration, as this memo among White House advisors shows:

> One of my very close friends is the right-hand man of Gallup. I talked to him on the phone this morning because I had heard some disquieting news about Gallup's next report. He checked and called me back to confirm the following: Gallup's report will indicate that never since they have been taking polls has there been such a swing away from the Administration as has been taking place the past six weeks. In their opinion the Senate and House will both go Republican. The questions asked that indicate this trend were regarding housing, Wallace, strikes, government expenses, Russia, and cost of living. I think there is still time to do something dramatic to not only stop the trend but reverse it."[16]

The Truman White House, however, did not have any luck in reversing the trend of public opinion during the fall of 1946, and Republicans won both houses of Congress for the first time since 1928, picking up fifty-five seats in the House of Representatives and twelve in the Senate.

Maintaining high approval ratings for any president is no easy task. As Table 5.1 shows, of the twelve presidents Gallup tracked since 1945, only seven averaged approval ratings above 50 percent. Only Dwight Eisenhower, John F. Kennedy, and George H. W. Bush averaged above 60 percent across their entire time in office. The highest approval rating achieved was the 90 percent George W. Bush received after September 11, 2001. The average high rating was 77.5 percent, although three presidents never made it out of the 60 percent range. Richard Nixon mustered a high

Table 5.1 Trends in Job Approval

	AVERAGE APPROVAL %	APPROVAL HIGH %	APPROVAL LOW %
Truman	45.4	87	22
Eisenhower	65	79	48
Kennedy	70.1	83	56
Johnson	55.1	79	35
Nixon	49	67	24
Ford	47.2	71	37
Carter	45.5	75	28
Reagan	52.8	68	35
G. H. W. Bush	60.9	89	29
Clinton	55.1	73	27
G. W. Bush	49.4	90	25
Obama*	49	69	38
AVERAGE		77.5	33.83

* As of September 17, 2012

The Gallup Polling Organization, Presidential Approval, Key Statistics, http://www.gallup.com/poll/124922/Presidential-Job-Approval-Center.aspx

rating of just 67 percent. Ronald Reagan's approval rating high was only 68 percent, and by the middle of his second year Obama's high rating was only 69 percent.

Across these twelve presidents, the lowest approval rating was 22 percent, with Truman receiving that honor. The average low approval was 34.3 percent. The same three presidents with high approval ratings did not have the highest low scores. Eisenhower's and Kennedy's low approval ratings were not all that low—48 and 46 percent, respectively. However, the third highest low score is not the first Bush but instead it is Obama. Both George H. W. and George W. Bush had very high approval but also very low approval. The first President Bush received an 89 percent approval rating and also a 29 percent; his son received a high of 90 percent and a low of only 25 percent of the nation approving his performance as president.

Where do these fluctuations come from; what produces the approval rating and what changes attitudes toward the same president? As discussed in Chapter 4, the public learns about the president via the mass media. However, individuals filter this information about the president through their own experiences and attitudes. In addition, the environment or the context in which citizens judge a president also matters. Presidents are also judged, albeit at times unfairly, on a wide range of issues over which they rarely have control. For example, advisors to Lyndon Johnson became concerned in 1966 that because the President had become so visible to the American public as being in charge of the federal government, his approval ratings were suffering. According to a memo from advisor Tom Johnson to LBJ:

View Gallup's Presidential Approval Center.

> It is my view that you have become so closely associated with all the major issues which face this country that you are suffering from it. The people do not hold the Secretary of Commerce or the Budget Director responsible when fiscal policies displease them. They hold you responsible. The people do not condemn the Secretary of the Treasury for tight money and high interest rates. They condemn you. When labor negotiations break down in major industries, the people hold the President responsible; not the Secretary of Labor, not management, not the unions. The same is true on the Defense front. When the war appears to be going badly, it is not the Secretary of Defense or the Joint Chiefs who catch the heat. It is again the President. Much of this is because the President has been encouraged to speak and comment publicly on all these problems. When there are civil riots and civil disobedience, the press expects you to become immediately involved and to produce a satisfactory solution. Often I believe a better course would be to have your decisions and feelings on particular matters voiced through the Cabinet and through the agency heads who are most directly concerned with the issue. Let them shoulder more of the burden for the faults of their programs. Rather than the President losing popularity for weaknesses, it seems more appropriate for the department head to receive the criticism.[17]

The willingness of an individual to state that they approve of the job the president is doing results from systemic and personal analyses of the political environment. Political scientist John Mueller found that there are three identifiable patterns of approval change present across presidencies.[18] First, Mueller determined that approval declined over time in each presidential term due to the buildup of what he termed the "coalition of minorities." On each small decision a president makes, and even more so on large decisions, someone wins and someone loses. Overtime, the number of groups and individuals who were on the losing side of a president's decisions grows. Mueller argues that the approval rating reflects the pooling of those individual losers into a coalition of those who lost on issues across a president's tenure. The approval rating reflects at any given time the number of people dissatisfied with the president's choices because they were against their own choice. Therefore, when only 28 percent of the nation approved of the job Jimmy Carter was doing in June 1979, Mueller argues that the 72 percent disapproval reflects people who wanted Carter to make different decisions on their issues. The more significant the choice or the more numerous the choices, the larger the coalition of minorities against the president can become.

Second, Mueller identified the "rally around the flag effect"; approval ratings increase in response to foreign events or crises. In contrast to the economy or other domestic issues, approval ratings rise in response to the fact of foreign events or crises but not necessarily the president's handling of them. George W. Bush received his highest approval rating in the polls taken immediately after the terrorist attacks on September 11, 2001. Mueller termed the effect "rallying around the flag" because of the peculiar oddity of signaling approval when a tragedy occurs. On September 14, 2001, ninety percent of the public was not saying, "Great job handling terrorism, President Bush"; instead, the public signaled its support for the president **to do a great job handling terrorism**. The approval rating then becomes a show of support for the president and the country rather than a true evaluation of prior actions. Not surprisingly, these figures go down rather precipitously; Bush sustained ratings over 80 percent for only six months.[19] Between March 2002 and March 2003, Bush's ratings continued to decline, down to 57 percent approval, in reaction not to crisis but to his crisis response. After the first six months, the approval rating returned to reflect what it normally demonstrates: job performance. Bush's approval rating then predictably jumped from 57 percent at the beginning of March 2003 to 71 percent at the end of March 2003 in response to the beginning of the War in Iraq.

Third, Mueller argued, "an economy in slump harms a president's popularity but an economy that is improving does not seem to help his rating."[20] The economy can be difficult for a president to maneuver vis-à-vis approval ratings. The president's popularity always takes a beating in a down economy, often in keeping with the "buck stops here" mentality started by Harry Truman that requires presidents to take responsibility for all things, even things outside their control. More problematic for the presidential approval rating is the fact that the president has few tools with which to improve a down economy. For example, Barack Obama's approval rating hit an all-time low of 38 percent in 2011 as the economy, and particularly unemployment, showed little signs of improvement.

Personal Approval

Instinctively, individuals form judgments about people based on intuitive opinion formation by simply looking at them, while deeper determinations are made by listening to them initially and over time. Judgments about the president follow similar patterns; citizens form impressions from their first moment of introduction to the president, from their former public roles, or during the campaign or once the oath of office is taken. Those reactions have nothing to do with the president's performance and everything to do with his likability or his personal, rather than job-related, approval.

Job approval refers to the job of being president; personal approval refers to that hard-to-define "it" factor. The question pollsters ask is, "Do you have a favorable view of President Obama as a person?" By asking the personal question, pollsters try to distinguish between views of skill and views of personality. Traditionally, personal views and job performance views were related. If you liked the job the president was doing you probably liked the president personally, and vice versa. Interestingly, Gallup finds that some people can view the president favorably while negatively viewing his performance.

Personal favorability ratings are typically higher than approval ratings, although that trend has shifted somewhat in recent years. Table 5.2 shows that the eight presidents prior to 1992 all averaged favorability ratings above 70 percent while in office. Gallup did not ask the favorability question in 1974 (the year Nixon resigned from office). After his resignation, Nixon's favorability rating dropped to just 27 percent. The favorability ratings of the three presidents serving after 1992 look considerably different from those of their predecessors. Their favorability ratings are much lower, and Clinton's and Obama's ratings are almost equivalent to their job approval ratings.

President Obama and Public Opinion

Obama represents an interesting case, as he entered office with rather high approval ratings, both personal and job approval. The Pew Research Center for the People

Table 5.2 Trends in Personal Ratings

	FAVORABILITY RATING %	HIGHER THAN APPROVAL RATING %
Truman	N/A	N/A
Eisenhower	84	19
Kennedy	88	18
Johnson	77	22
Nixon	80	31
Ford	73	26
Carter	70	25
Reagan	70	17
G. H. W. Bush	73	12
Clinton	56	0.9
G. W. Bush	67	18
Obama	52*	3

The Gallup Polling Organization, http://www.gallup.com/poll/8938/historical-favorability-ratings-presidents.aspx.

*As of June 15, 2012. http://politicalticker.blogs.cnn.com/2012/05/30/poll-romney-favorability-rating-increases/

and the Press found that nearly eight in ten people felt favorable toward Obama right before his inauguration. Those ratings were 20 points higher than George W. Bush's and 10 points higher than Bill Clinton's prior to their inaugurals. Of those favorables, 40 percent were highly favorable. Only 24 percent felt similarly about Bush and Clinton. By the midpoint of his first term, only half the public liked Obama personally and only half approved of the job he was doing. The decline in job approval was a response to the dire economy in 2009–2010 as well as the oil spill in the Gulf of Mexico. But what explains the decline in personal approval? An individual's own attitudes, partisanship in particular, affect views of the president. For scholars, studying approval ratings reveals an interesting puzzle: Are approval ratings influenced by events or by the public's view of events? If the public's view is what drives approval-rating change, then it is important to understand what determines public attitudes.

The public evaluation of the president in office resembles behavior by the voting public during campaigns (not surprisingly, since it is the same group of people). Citizens view the president retrospectively or prospectively: What have you done for me lately and what will you do for me in the future? From this perspective, in contrast to entirely macro-level analyses, an economic downturn can theoretically raise the president's approval rating if the public believes the president is handling it well. If the economic forces alone dominated the rating, then no amount of presidential

View the Pew Research Center's website.

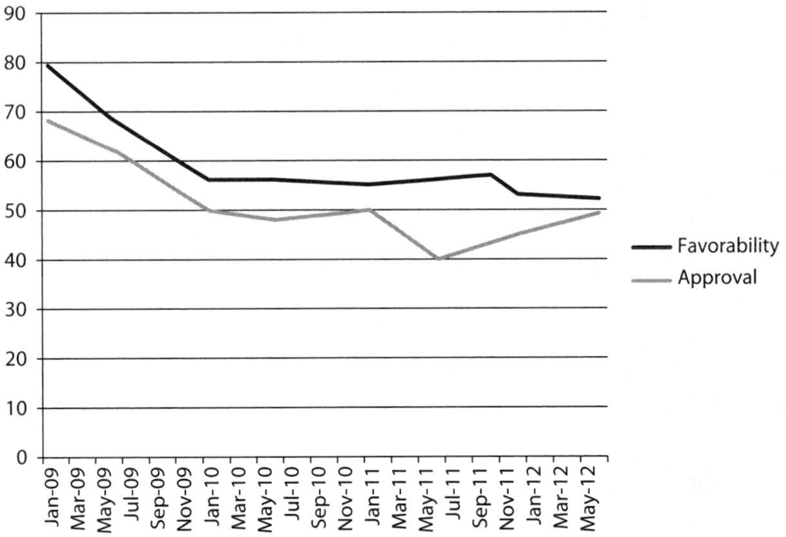

Figure 5.1 President Obama's Approval and Favorability Ratings

effort could shift the reaction, and ratings would rise only when the economic tide lifted. One study showed that "individual level theorizing also highlights significant heterogeneity within the public," raising the possibility that different segments of the population respond differently to individual presidents and events in terms of knowledge and/or the level of support for the president.[21]

Individual factors also influence voting. For example, since 1980, women voted more frequently and differently than men. A gendered vote emerged in response to Ronald Reagan's presidential campaign and the distinction of voting for "guns" (military and defense issues) versus "butter" (domestic programs). Thus, since 1980, both scholars and candidates noted that women were more likely to vote Democratic. Known as the gender gap, this gap traditionally hovers between 4 and 8 percent.[22] It reached a high of 11 percent in 2000, falling to 7 percent in 2004. In 2008, Obama received 8 million more votes from women than from men, a 6 percent difference.[23] Similarly, party identification, gender, and race also influence performance evaluations of the president. Differences in evaluation by groups stem from two different sources: experience and importance of the experience. Blacks and whites may experience a down economy differently, and men and women might weight the importance of having a family leave policy differently. For the president, individual pocketbook considerations influence the level of approval from men, whereas approval from women responds more to perceptions of societal economic well-being.[24]

One of the factors that make public opinion polling so interesting is the ability to aggregate and disaggregate mass opinion. That means that by using polling data it is possible to learn what the entire nation thinks of the president at a given moment in time. It is also possible to determine what different segments of that whole think about the president in that same moment in time. Returning to Obama's ratings, his approval and favorability ratings fell over time, but not uniformly across groups and individuals. According to The Pew Center for the People and the Press, Obama's ratings fell sharply among those outside his core support: Republicans, the elderly, and men. He lost favorability among Independents as well, but not as significantly. However, his support slipped even with Democrats. In the fall of 2009, only 6 percent of Democrats had an unfavorable rating of Obama; by June 2010, 14 percent had an unfavorable view; and by November 2011, 21 percent had an unfavorable view.[25]

The mass public's view of the president's performance is, therefore, the aggregation of individual responses to events (like a recession) filtered through the media and also an individual's own experiences and preferences. Does it have a use within the political process as well? As Gronke and Newman contend, "In a perfect world, if higher approval means greater power, the public would reward the president for meeting realistic and appropriate expectations. Then the president would have an incentive to meet those expectations and would benefit from doing so. However, if the public holds the president accountable for outcomes that he has little control over, or has unrealistically high expectations, then the president's power depends on the whims of the economy or history setting up the president for inevitable failure."[26]

POPULARITY AS A SOURCE OF PRESIDENTIAL POWER

As discussed earlier, the creation of the public opinion tool derived from the media's desire to predict the outcome of elections. However, the utility of the approval rating quickly moved beyond immediate predicting of elections to long-term forecasting. To continue with the weather metaphors, the approval-rating question became a barometer for reelection. The presidential approval rating prior to Election Day is considered to be an excellent predictor of presidential reelection.[27] From this perspective, presidents would work to raise their approval ratings in order to achieve reelection. The ability of the public to evaluate the president between elections would serve as the extraconstitutional means of holding the president accountable in the absence of voting. In addition, the continuous monitoring of presidential job performance injects the public into the political sphere in a manner unintended and unanticipated by the framers' constitutional design. For the framers, the public's opinions mattered only as a single up-or-down vote. In contrast, the modern presidency receives a continuous flow of "votes," producing a tracked measure. The presence of the public's opinions in this constant manner gives power to those opinions in a way that did not previously exist.

Initially, scholars viewed the public as a means to soften up the true avenues to presidential power. In his classic work, *Presidential Power*, Richard Neustadt considered the public an indirect resource providing a generic and limited source of power and authority. Neustadt essentially accepted the constitutional role for the public while simultaneously acknowledging the presence of public opinion polling. Neustadt argued that mass opinion was important because elites pay attention to it; the public's view of the president matters only because elites anticipate public reaction to the president. It is this anticipation that factors into presidential efforts to persuade elites, and for Neustadt persuasion *is* presidential power. In contrast, in *Presidential Leadership of Public Opinion*, Elmer Cornwell argues that the presence of public opinion polls as well as a national media intensely interested in the president offers the president a more significant source of presidential power than articulated by Neustadt.[28] Cornwell argued that with few constitutional tools to influence the course of policy and events, "the President can and does and probably should shape popular attitudes, and not just respond to them passively."[29] Cornwell implicitly rejected the idea that approval of the president is an independent evaluation of the president, tangentially related to the system. Thus, Cornwell began the critical analysis for understanding the relationship between the president and the public that emerges from the technological ability to ask the public what they think. Neustadt and Cornwell are not in opposition to each other, as Neustadt supports the relevance of the public; they differ over the immediacy of the effect. Put another way, do producers and directors make movies for the critics or for the movie-going public, and does that audience influence the critics and/or the moviemakers? Are presidents simply accepting of the public's perception of their behavior, or are they actively courting public support in order to achieve their goals?

Paul Brace and Barbara Hinckley contend that presidents, as strategic actors, do not accept a passive role in public evaluations of their efforts. In fact, they argue that the ability to measure approval ratings produced a dependence on the polls.[30] Brace and Hinckley term this dependence a "follower presidency"—presidents respond with action to the fluctuations in their ratings. The preeminent presidential goal, then, is not reelection, a legacy, or good public policy, but rather to achieve high approval ratings, because the ratings influence everything else.[31] In particular, presidents choose their leadership strategies focused on policies the public already likes.[32]

The approval rating appeared most significant as a source of power for the president to achieve his legislative program, what Samuel Kernell termed "going public." As discussed in earlier chapters, when going public, presidents present their policy desires to the public in order to influence Congress.[33] Neustadt claimed that public opinion influenced the environment for bargaining, since a popular president will have more leverage to bargain with members of Congress. In contrast, Kernell argues that public support preempts bargaining and forces congressional compliance.[34] Kernell contends that the need for members of Congress to be reelected forces acceptance of a popular president's desires. Thus, the popularity rating is not simply a barometer for reelection but is also a source of significant power, or pressure, to achieve legislative success. A popular president, in Kernell's theory, is usually a legislatively successful president.

As a theory, "going public" makes great intuitive sense; people like the president and his performance, they want what the president wants, and so Congress responds. Unfortunately, for the president, the process is not that easy. For the president to *use* his approval rating, and not just be victim to its fluctuations, the president needs to be able to influence the rating. But, in order to influence presidential approval, the president needs to communicate and the public needs to be receptive or at least attentive to the communication. If a tree falls in the forest and no one is around to hear it, does it make a sound? Similarly, if a president speaks and no one listens, does anything happen?

It was easy to determine how many people heard the president say something back when television was in its infancy and there were only three national networks. All researchers had to do was track television usage; if it was on, then people were watching the president. With the introduction of other media outlets, it became hard for the president to capture an audience but also hard for researchers to determine how many people actually heard what the president said.[35] On June 16, 2010, Obama gave a prime-time address to the nation from the Oval Office (his first in this venue). According to the Nielsen Television Ratings, 32 million people watched it live on television. Looking up the speech on YouTube reveals that 165,000 people watched a replay of the speech. On Twitter, there were 83,000 tweets referencing the speech.[36] While 32 million viewers may seem like a large number, Obama's Inaugural Address better demonstrates how many more people can watch the president: 38 million watched on television, and 70 million streamed it live online. So at least 108 million watched Obama's inauguration, but only 32 million watched his address responding to the Gulf of Mexico oil spill.

Watching the president, however, is only part of the equation. The president also needs his approval ratings to improve from the attention. Obama's approval rating did improve after his Oval Office address in June 2010, from 40 percent to 44 percent (although a majority still disapproved of his handling of the crisis).[37] If the president needs to improve his approval rating in order to achieve success, then being unable to improve his rating, either because the nation was not listening or because they do not agree, is problematic.[38] Of course, even when citizens do not hear the president directly, they still might hear about his job performance from the media. However, the media are unlikely to significantly bolster a president's approval rating. As discussed in Chapter 4, the media no longer serve as a neutral transmitter of presidential performance.[39] In the twenty-first century, media organizations are neither friendly nor dependent, nor do they let the White House dominate news about the president. Instead, "talking heads" or pundits set the tone and tenor of debate, and that tone and tenor rarely improve a president's approval rating.[40]

The more significant component of using the approval rating as a source of power is the part furthest outside the president's control: the actions of Congress. For the approval rating to be a source of presidential power, Congress must be responsive to it. Unfortunately for the president, this rarely occurs. For this to work, individual members of Congress must say to themselves, "The president is popular, therefore I should vote for the president's proposed policies." But Congress is only mildly responsive to approval ratings.[41] Research has shown that presidential popularity influences congressional voting only "at the margins," while more traditional congressional explanations for voting behavior dominate (e.g., constituency demands, leadership demands, party demands).[42] In addition, high levels of approval reduce the likelihood of a president achieving a particular policy item.[43] Congress is attentive to the president's agenda as a list of priorities but not as specific calls to action.[44] The president's approval rating does have an effect on congressional elections; low ratings of the president generally signal poor reelection rates for members of his party. However, for voting decisions, the threat from the presidential approval rating appears to dissipate. The approval rating is a national measure and as a result is of lesser meaning to individual members of Congress.[45]

Members of Congress might consider popularity if they knew specifically that their constituents approved of the president. High approval ratings, over 70 percent, make it likely that the majority in most districts approve. Below 70 percent, members of Congress are unlikely to trust that the national measure accurately represents their district and instead will rely on the more traditional measures of constituent opinion. Even presidents who must work with a Congress controlled by their own party can suffer in terms of public opinion as both the executive and legislative branches of government, even under united party control, can pursue different policy priorities. A case in point would be Jimmy Carter's frustration working with a Democratic Congress during his four years in office, which his advisors claimed hurt the President's approval rating with the American public. According to Stu Eizenstat, Carter's chief domestic policy advisor, in a memo to the President:

> After conversations with [White House pollster] Pat Caddell and a number of other people, I am convinced that your rating in the public opinion polls is increasingly a function of your relations with Congress and their capacity to pass legislation. While that is to some extent inevitable, your Presidency risks being measured just by legislative accomplishments. I believe that is dangerous because Congress, in my estimation, has become increasingly unwilling to tackle the tough, substantive issues we have presented and will continue to present throughout your Administration. I think that it is therefore critical that we attempt, to define as much as possible your success as President in non-legislative terms while, of course, continuing to pursue our legislative program with all our resources. (Our legislative record is in fact much better than we have received credit for, and we need to continue to publicize those accomplishments.)[46]

PRESIDENTIAL POLLING AS A SOURCE OF POWER

Up to this point, the public's voice appears to be represented only by the approval rating. Although the approval rating is a virtually continuous measure of the public's opinion of the president, the question itself is a limited picture of what the public thinks. The approval rating question asks the public, "Do you approve of the job the president is doing?" The answer to that question is along a three- or five-point scale: "approve, disapprove, don't know" or "strongly approve, approve, disapprove, strongly disapprove, don't know." The question does not explain for the president or anyone else *why* the respondent approves or disapproves.

When citizens evaluate the job performance of members of Congress, they focus on congressional voting first and foremost. The president does not vote; instead, to quote George W. Bush, the president is the "decider." The approval rating thus evaluates how well citizens think the president decided, managed, and governed, and it is almost entirely retrospective, which means that approval rests on the perception of what has already occurred. For example, the approval rating of how well Obama handled health-care reform will tell the president little about how the public might view his choices when handling job creation in the future. If presidents want to use public opinion strategically and to gain an advantage from public opinion polls, they need to know something about it that no one else knows. They also need to be able to apply that knowledge to future presidential behavior, like supporting policy or making a speech.

Since the days of Franklin Roosevelt's presidency, presidents and their staffs understood that the ability to ask the public questions privately allows presidents to use the answers to their advantage. FDR was the first president to bring public opinion polling into the White House, and he did it for something extremely important—decisions about World War II. FDR recognized that he needed to know how the public felt about potential choices regarding the war if he wanted to change their minds. Polls became FDR's weapon of choice "to defeat the spreading isolationist sentiment."[47] Choices to counter Americans' desire to stay out of the war, like the "lend-lease" program that lent war materials to Britain, appeared to the press and members of Congress divinely inspired as they were widely supported. In August 1940, FDR's press secretary, Steve Early, was keeping the president informed of public opinion on the issue:

> Eugene Meyer of the *Washington Post* just telephoned me from his home in Mt. Kisco, New York, asking that I advise you confidentially. The Gallup Poll to be published next Sunday will show that 62 percent of the voters favor letting Great Britain have American destroyers; that 30 percent are in opposition and 8 percent are indifferent or have no opinion.[48]

In fact, by the time FDR went public with lend-lease, he already knew, due to polling data no one else had, that the public supported it.[49] According to a memo from FDR pollster Hadley Cantril:

> Mrs. Anna Rosenberg [FDR's advisor] thought you might like to have on hand some of the findings of my public opinion research.... I shall be delighted to keep this information up to date for you if you tell Mrs. Rosenberg to whom I should send new material. I shall be glad to make the facilities available to you at any time. We can get confidential information on questions you suggest, follow up any hunch you may care to see tested regarding the determinants of opinion, and provide you with the answers to any questions ever asked by the Gallup or Fortune polls.... The Gallup poll particularly has accumulated a vast amount of information that has never been published.[50]

Roosevelt's White House gathered public opinion in secret for two important reasons. First, to minimize "curiosity and preserve the informality of our relationships;"[51] and second, the Roosevelt White House was afraid of appearing to be unable to lead or dependent on public opinion, particularly in times of crisis.

Roosevelt's immediate successor, Harry Truman, was not as enamored of polls; in fact, he questioned their accuracy. Truman, in his memoirs, claimed that polls

> ...did not represent a true cross section of American opinion.... I did not believe that the major components of our society, such as agriculture, management and labor, were adequately sampled. I also know that the polls did not represent facts but mere speculation, and I have always placed faith in the known facts.... A man who is influenced by the polls or is afraid to make decisions which may make him unpopular is not a man to represent the welfare of the country.[52]

Truman's negative view of polling can be traced to earlier polling debacles, such as the *Literary Digest*'s mistakes in the 1936 presidential race to the inaccurate prediction in Truman's reelection campaign in 1948. Moreover, he was not wrong in his view of sampling problems. In the "Dewey defeats Truman" poll result, the pollsters used the telephone to gather data for the first time. The methodological problem stemmed from the fact that in 1948, few households owned telephones, and those that did were three times more likely to vote Republican than Democrat. Non-telephone owners turned out and voted for Truman but were not represented in the sample.

The Eisenhower administration was not anti-polling, like Truman's, but it is not clear whether Eisenhower himself was interested in or supportive of polling. Like the FDR administration, the Eisenhower White House polled the public about military intervention, particularly on China. The administration polled the public on a variety of issues, for example, whether the public would favor driving the Communists out of all of Korea if it meant: (a) a draft, (b) price and wage controls, (c) fighting alone, (d) an increase in killed and wounded, (e) a full scale war with China on mainland China.[53] Knowing what options the public would and would not tolerate gives the president boundaries for acceptable action. This is not to say that a president would never recommend a draft because 85 percent of the public disapproved, but rather that it would not be his first, second, or even third choice. Polls used this way are sources of representation and accountability. When the majority does not want something in a representative democracy, it does not mean that it never happens, but it does mean that public officials must weigh the political costs of doing something the public does not like. In some ways, this is exactly what the framers intended.

The Kennedy and Johnson administrations polled more frequently than their predecessors did, primarily for elections but also for governing and policy decisions.[54] They also followed the trend of their predecessors by monitoring public opinion on key issues. For example, the Kennedy administration began pushing for tax revision legislation as early as 1961. In October 1962, Kennedy signed into law the Revenue Act of 1962, which included various tax reforms, as well as a tax break for businesses; the President had also been considering a personal income tax cut as well. Mindful of the fact that debt and deficit spending, even with a tax cut, were not popular with the American public, White House advisors kept a close eye on public opinion regarding tax cuts during 1962, as this memo shows:

> We have just learned that the latest Gallup Poll shows heavy popular opposition to tax reduction. The results will appear in tomorrow's newspapers. The question was somewhat loaded, assuming a tax cut meant "the government went further into debt." But the results were lopsided: For tax reduction – 19 percent; Against tax reduction – 72 percent; No opinion – 9 percent. Favoring a tax cut were 15 percent of Republicans, 18 percent of Democrats, and 26 percent of Independents. When asked whether they considered their present income tax payments "about right" or "too high," respondents split about evenly. But only 31 percent of the group that considered their tax burden too large favor tax reduction.[55]

Both the Kennedy and Johnson administrations also had strong relationships with pollsters which emerged out of their presidential campaigns. As discussed in Chapter 3, public opinion polling forms the foundation of any presidential campaign effort. While Chapter 8 will discuss the influence of campaign staffers in the executive branch, here it is important to note that campaign pollsters often make the transition from the campaign to governing. Kennedy began this practice by continuing to request information from Lou Harris, his campaign pollster. Lyndon Johnson had a similar relationship with his pollster, Oliver Quayle. Once in office, Harris and Quayle, who also ran commercial polling operations, would piggy-back specific presidential questions onto commercial polls, saving the administration money and maintaining secrecy.[56]

As presidents and their staffs sought more public opinion data, the effort to gather the public information specifically about presidential issues lost secrecy, cost more, and became a part of the institution of the presidency. The modern use of presidential polling began in the Nixon administration.[57] In the administrations that followed, from Nixon through Obama, all devoted substantial time, money, and attention to building, using, and institutionalizing White House public opinion polling.[58] Because of the consistency of usage, political scientists found patterns in how the White House used polls. These patterns are attributable to the institutional needs of the office and not the individual preferences of the president.

Remember, the usefulness of public opinion polling for the president is knowing something that no one else knows, and using that knowledge strategically. Strategic application of knowledge has nothing to do with political party or even the context in which presidents function. When presidents received public opinion on someone else's schedule, the presidential ability to use public opinion was dependent on whether questions were asked at the right time, and in the right capacity. The Nixon administration, and all subsequent administrations, rejected the variability inherent in not buying the data directly and specifically for the president. There is a problem, however, with making polling part of the White House operation—namely that it is illegal. The Hatch Act of 1939 prohibits all federal employees, except the President and the Vice-President, from engaging in "political activity" while on the job. Public opinion polling is clearly a political activity. There is, however, an exception for members of the Executive Office of the President: "Employees paid from an appropriation for the Executive Office of the President and employees appointed by the President, by and with the advice and consent of the Senate,... may engage in political activity while on duty; in any government room or building; while wearing a uniform or official insignia; and while using a government vehicle, **if the costs associated with the political activity are not paid for by money derived from the Treasury of the United States**."[59] Therefore, for the White House to consistently and continuously ask the public a range of questions in order to apply the answers to the presidential goals of reelection and legislation, presidents turned back to the political party.

Using White House Polls

The purchase of public opinion polls for presidential use exemplifies the tension that exists between the contemporary president and his political party. In the case of polling, the party pays for the public opinion polls that presidents then use to better position themselves in the political sphere, including sometimes against their own party members in Congress. Once presidents began to purchase polls for regular use, fears about discovery concerned the White House, as this diary entry dated Monday, February 3, 1969, by Nixon Chief of Staff H. R. Haldeman shows: "P [Nixon] called tonight very upset by column quoting [Communications Director Herbert] Klein, that we'll be relying heavily on polls. The problem is always with us. P most anxious to avoid any appearance of being like LBJ."[60] Similar concerns emerged within Gerald Ford's White House, with a staffer warning Ford to disavow the White House polling apparatus for fear of appearing too much like Johnson: "I think you should not make any direct reference to a private poll (like LBJ) but simply use these things to strengthen your own personal convictions that the American people support you (when they do) in your policy positions."[61]

The pollsters were also quite cagey when trying to describe their influence on the president without challenging his role as a leader. A pollster for Nixon, Reagan, and Bush, Richard Wirthlin asserted, "The work we do may occasionally focus discussion in the White House on one topic or another. But it wouldn't be fair to typify what I do as getting involved in policy formation."[62] Patrick Caddell, Jimmy Carter's pollster, perhaps summed it up best: "I don't think anybody can run a government, particularly the executive branch, by trying to rely on public opinion. That attempts to substitute followership for leadership."[63] George W. Bush's pollsters were even more cryptic regarding what they did for the president: They never said anything publicly.

The money paid to pollsters by the political parties is public record; examining the amount of money spent reveals a significant change in behavior from the occasional polls utilized in prior administrations. Since 1969, all presidents have spent at least $1 million a year, at a minimum, on public opinion polling. During Nixon's first term he spent over $5 million (in inflation-adjusted dollars) on public opinion polling data.[64] Even the George W. Bush White House, with a president who publicly denied using polls at all, spent at least $1 million a year. However, the amount of money paid to the president's campaign pollster only reveals White House interest in public opinion, not how they used it. Tracking the exchange of polling information in White House documents, like memos and PowerPoint presentations, reveals what information actually informs presidential and staff decision making. Poll usage by the staff and the president peaks in the early years of an administration's tenure.[65] The pattern of high usage followed by a decline in usage matches the pattern of policy activity, which suggests that the president should pursue big policy changes early while they still have political capital from their election victory.

Political science analysis of the presidency is often like building a puzzle. The first piece to the puzzle of understanding how presidents use public opinion and for what end is the amount of money spent; presidents spent a lot of money on polling the public, so it must be significant. The second piece is that all administrations, regardless of party or context, were very attentive to public opinion in the first few years of their terms. The third piece of the puzzle is how presidents use public opinion. Presidents and their staffs, since 1969, use public opinion polls to help the president do his job and keep his job. Presidents paid for private polls in order to design the questions asked of the public. Designing the questions enabled the president to test rhetoric, to test policy proposals, and to monitor and track their electoral coalitions.[66]

Tracking the Constituency

Presidents enter office having spent the previous year (or longer) campaigning. As discussed in Chapter 3, in their campaign for the presidency, candidates spend a great deal of time introducing themselves, disparaging their opponent, and telling the American people what they plan to do once in office. People distinguish between the candidates based on who they like, but also on whose plans for the country they wish to see move forward. Most of the campaign polling operation focused on who is ahead and by how much. However, the campaign polling operation also explores *why* a candidate is ahead. A successful candidate needs to know what drives his supporters, as well as why others are not on board. Even more important are the independents—the fence sitters—those individuals who do not make up their minds to vote for a candidate until the last possible minute. The election vote reveals for the candidates (and the nation) who actually supported the winner, and post-election polls reveal why. These individuals make up the president's electoral coalition. If the public is a source of strength for the president, then the base of his strength comes from his strongest supporters from the campaign. The president needs those people to support his programs, and ultimately he needs those people come reelection time. Therefore, the White House needs a mechanism that will reveal if the president is at a minimum keeping his coalition together or, better still, how to expand it. A president whose coalition abandons him is not a second-term president.

At a basic level, a president's electoral coalition consists of members of the president's party, independents, and those few, if any, members of the opposition party who decided to vote for the president. However, individuals are more than simply their party identification; other classifications can be equally meaningful. Traditional descriptors include party, age, region, race, gender, and labor. The beauty of public opinion polling is that you can inquire into all levels of classification in order to determine who is with you, who is against you, and why. As polling became more sophisticated, so too did the ability to get significant results from micro-level analyses. The liberal–conservative spectrum or the urban/suburban/rural divide became frequent assessments. All of these classifications were legitimate groups of people that if they were all standing in the same place could be sorted, e.g., all people who live in the suburbs over there, urbanites over here.

Polling operations, following the lead of the campaigns, took the classifying of individuals and their support for the president further. Identifying patterns in polling data led pollsters and the White House to create shorthand terminology. For example, the "Silent Majority" was a term coined by the Nixon administration to describe those individuals *not* protesting the Vietnam War. The Nixon White House used the polls to classify people by their attitudes about the war. The White House believed that while the protestors were getting a lot of media coverage, in reality there were more people who supported Nixon and his view of how to handle the war. In 1969, a Nixon White House memo described the "Silent Majority" in detail:

> The vast majority of Americans have deep-rooted and sound moral values. They need reassuring that they are not alone and want leaders who also share such values. Of late the emphasis has been so repeatedly placed on other areas that people are questioning the present strength, if not very existence, of this majority. There are thousands of courageous and thoughtful young men in our Armed Forces who dramatically outnumber the draft card burners and flag desecrators. There are thousands of conscientious and dedicated students serving the communities near their campuses who drastically outnumber members of the SDS and others bent on destroying their universities. There have been thousands of

> young Americans enthusiastically and constructively involved in the mainstream of political life in the past two years who far outnumber the attention-getting and destructive contingent doing so much to provoke present campus turmoil. There are thousands of black Americans working tirelessly and confidently in the private and public sectors throughout the country to accelerate, through legal means, the opportunities black Americans so surely deserve who outnumber the black Americans advocating revolution and destruction. We need to be reminded who, where and how substantial this majority is. Its members constitute the mainstream of American life. Theirs is the spirit and the perspective that continues to attract foreigners to this land. This is the majority that will constructively meet the challenges of today's and tomorrow's problems. It is, as it always has been, the source of our country's greatest hope and pride.[67]

It was not unusual for a White House to consider these individuals' views; however, what was unusual was arguing that these attitudes bound these individuals together into a group. Soccer moms or NASCAR dads have also been popular identifiers of invented descriptions to classify attitudes in recent years. The Reagan White House took constituency monitoring further by classifying group identifiers by strength of commitment to the president. Strong supporters, mixed supporters, and low supporters defined the "core and periphery" of both American society and Reagan's reliable base of support.[68] George H. W. Bush's White House focused on what they termed "base groups" and "target groups," meaning the ones the president had in his corner and the ones that he wanted to add. According to a memo sent between senior staffers, Bush's political base groups were: Republican Conservatives, Republican Office Holders, and Bush supporters, while the target groups were Conservative Democrats.[69] Similar base-versus-target comparisons were made for "ethnic and demographic, geographic, and issue oriented" groups.

The rationale for doing the constituency tracking is to tie current political decisions to reelection. Two recent presidents' problematic electoral constituencies reveal the strategic component of constituency tracking. Nixon appointed Gerald Ford to the vice-presidency after his original vice president, Spiro Agnew, resigned due to scandal. When Nixon resigned due to the Watergate scandal less than a year later on August 8, 1974, Ford became the nation's thirty-eighth president. Ford took office without ever running on a presidential ticket, and therefore he had no independent electoral constituency which was based on support for him and/or his policies. As a result, the Ford White House polled incessantly as staffers tried the unenviable task of constructing a Ford constituency while not losing whatever was left of Nixon's. In order to have something to track, the pollsters created a baseline of what they thought the constituency should be and tracked from there.[70] Without an election, the pollsters found that there was no Ford constituency; there was only a generic Republican president constituency. Because of that, Ford also suffered in the ability to present a vision or philosophy of governing to the American public, as advisors lamented during the 1976 campaign:

> The basic problem with the Ford Administration, the reason I think the President has such a weak base of support, is that people do not perceive him as having a sense of purpose, a vision for the future of the United States. Although we frequently have the pieces right, there is no sense of an overall whole, no umbrella

> under which those pieces fit, no "New Deal," "New Frontier," "Great Society." It is essential that we have such a philosophy. It need not be the overblown rhetoric of a "Great Society," but it ought to be clear and easily understood.[71]

George W. Bush had a different situation that was similarly problematic. Unlike Ford, Bush ran for office in 2000 but lost the popular vote to his opponent, Al Gore. Bush had an electoral constituency but simply maintaining it would not be enough for a reelection bid. Bush's constituency reflected the partisan and group divides in the nation in 2000: "White men and married white women supported Bush, while African Americans, Jews, most Hispanics, Asians, union members, and unmarried women voted for Gore."[72] Immediately upon entering office, the Bush White House recognized the need to "enlarge his fragile electoral base."[73] As a result, the White House developed a program designed to woo independent and minority voters. They realized that if the same percentage of minorities went for the Democratic candidate in 2004, Bush would be a one-term president. The tragic events of September 11, 2001, temporarily muted the constituency problem created by the divisive 2000 election, as the country united in reaction. Bush maintained enough of that unification, which the Iraq war initially buoyed and then challenged, to win reelection.

Rhetorical Design

Like the approval rating, constituency information is something to be monitored, not used. It is useful to know who approves and why, as it is also useful to know who voted for you and would still vote for you and why. Of much greater interest to presidents and their White Houses is using public opinion information to create a beneficial outcome. Presidents used the ability to ask the public their response to anything privately to shape the most frequent thing presidents do: speak about policy. Some presidential rhetoric receives a firestorm of media and public attention, like a State of the Union address, while other speeches are heard by few and remarked upon by even fewer. As discussed in Chapter 4, presidents and their staffs spend a considerable amount of time determining their communication strategies because of the perceived benefit. As mentioned earlier in this chapter, part of the rationale for presidential speech is to influence public opinion, but influence is difficult to achieve. If presidents could improve their odds of getting positive feedback for a speech and for the policy the speech is about, would they? The answer is most likely a resounding yes.

The advent of continuous White House polling allows the president and his staff to use polls the way companies do when selling a product. Ignoring whether the product is good or bad or serves humanity, marketers and public relations firms use product testers and public opinion polls to determine the packaging, the name, the logo and the advertising strategy for any product in order to sell it. If the product does not sell, then it does not matter that it might have, for example, solved the world's energy problem. Presidents and their staffs confront a similar scenario—they clearly believe in their policies, but they recognize that without public support the policy is unlikely to move forward. So, presidents and their staffs turn to polling data to design what they are going to say to the nation. Presidents can test speeches, phrases, and presentation by asking about it in a poll. Political scientists Lawrence Jacobs and Robert Shapiro call efforts to design rhetoric "crafted talk." In crafted talk, presidents are not altering their policies, just the presentation of their policies.[74]

For example, the efforts by Obama's team to use the word "recovery" instead of recession and "investment" instead of infrastructure are strategies determined by presidential polling.[75] The poll data revealed a negative reaction to questions and information with the term "recession" that was absent when using "recovery." The public did not respond to the President's ideas when the negative term was used; "recovery" is more positive and upbeat. Staffers test phrases using both public opinion polls and focus groups. Focus groups are assemblies of ten to twenty citizens who are paid a nominal fee to sit around and discuss politics. Pollsters and political consultants run the sessions and record them. They use the information to determine what resonates with people. Public opinion polls ask respondents to choose answer A, B, C, or D; thus the interviewer determines the range of possible answers. There are some poll questions which allow the public to lead, notably the Most Important Problem (MIP) of the day question: What do you think is the most important problem facing the country? The fill-in-the-blank response generates a top ten list that drives the political agenda. Beyond the MIP, pollsters and presidents use focus groups to flesh out the data obtained from public opinion polls by using a group setting to explore responses. Focus groups allow for following up of unusual responses or clarifying reactions.

As discussed earlier, the public typically rallies around the president in response to military exercises or hostilities. Nevertheless, war is fraught with political danger for the president, in addition to the reality of the danger from placing the nation's troops in harm's way. An episode in the George H. W. Bush administration reveals how polls and politics combine, even in the rhetoric for war. In August of 1990, Saddam Hussein, President of Iraq, invaded Kuwait. The international community responded first by levying sanctions and then with an international coalition of forces led by the United States. Operation Desert Shield sent troops to Saudi Arabia as protection for that country, and Operation Desert Storm was the operational name for the military invasion of Iraq, which lasted just under two months, from January 16 to February 28, 1991.

In preparing the nation for war, Bush did what all presidents do—he spoke to the nation. Bush first gave a radio address on January 5, 1991, and then he gave a televised address to the nation eleven days later. Between August 1990 and January 1991, the Bush White House conducted extensive public opinion polls determining public reaction to Bush's response to the invasion. However, between the President's two speeches in January, the White House also convened focus groups. The White House's political consultants used the focus group sessions to test presidential rhetoric. In a memo to President Bush, his pollster Roger Ailes noted six bulleted points that arose out of the focus group discussions convened *after* the President's January 5th radio address. Consider these points in comparison to what Bush said in his public address before and after the focus group:

- Point One: The focus group did not buy the argument that "we are there for the human rights of smaller nations."[76] (In the January 5th radio address, Bush said: "Saddam already poses a strategic threat to the capital cities of Egypt, Saudi Arabia, Turkey, Israel, and Syria, as well as our own men and women in the Gulf region. In fact, Saddam has used chemical weapons of mass destruction against innocent villagers, his own people."[77] In the January 16th Address to the Nation, that argument is no longer used.)

- Point Two: The focus group supported linking oil to freedom but was vehemently against trading "blood for oil."[78] (In the January 5th radio address, Bush said: "The struggling newborn democracies of Eastern Europe and Latin America already face a staggering challenge in making the transition to a free market. But the added weight of higher oil prices is a crushing burden they cannot afford. And our own economy is suffering, suffering the effects of higher oil prices and lower growth stemming from Saddam's aggression." In the January 16th Address to the Nation, the oil argument is absent with the exception of a quote from Master Sergeant J. P Kendall of the 82nd Airborne, who addresses the issues raised by the focus group, claiming, "We're here for more than just the price of a gallon of gas. What we're doing is going to chart the future of the world for the next 100 years. It's better to deal with the guy now than 5 years from now.")[79]
- Point Three: The American focus group responded positively and supportively when reminded that "Saddam started it."[80] (In the January 5th radio address, Bush does not clearly say, "Saddam started it." In the January 16th Address to the Nation, Bush states: "This conflict started August 2nd when the dictator of Iraq invaded a small and helpless neighbor. Kiuwait—a member of the Arab League and a member of the United Nations—was crushed; its people, brutalized. Five months ago, Saddam Hussein started this cruel war against Kuwait. Tonight, the battle has been joined.")[81]
- Point Four: The focus group really liked hearing "all the steps taken by the President to resolve this peacefully."[82] (In the January 5th radio address, Bush devotes eleven lines to explain the diplomatic steps, including the last effort to have Secretary of State James Baker meet with Iraqi Foreign Minister Tariq Aziz. In the January 16th Address to the Nation, Bush outlines these steps again, more forcefully, in two paragraphs containing eighteen lines.)[83]
- Points Five and Six: The focus group wanted reassurance that "we are showing restraint" and "the U.S. is not the aggressor." (In the January 5th radio address, Bush makes neither point. In the January 16th Address to the Nation, Bush addresses both points. In particular, Bush poses the aggression issue in the form of a question and provides the answer: "Some may ask: Why act now? Why not wait? The answer is clear: The world could wait no longer. Sanctions, though having some effect, showed no signs of accomplishing their objective. Sanctions were tried for well over five months, and we and our allies concluded that sanctions alone would not force Saddam from Kuwait.")[84]

The changes between the two speeches are not simple edits. The response of the focus group, as representative of segments of the population, mattered enough to the White House to induce change in terms of content and approach to this effort to sell going to war. There is a direct link between the focus group responses to the first speech and the language of the second. The focus group reactions did not produce change in policy, or even in any of the facts; instead, the focus group helped the Bush team decide what to emphasize and how to say it. The focus group supported and improved upon the primary usage of the poll apparatus to design "crafted talk."[85] The value of focus groups for designing language is in the feedback mechanism. The discussion format allowed for the evolution of hearing the first speech, and to debating the substance of the first speech. It is in that discussion that the Bush team found commentary about what influenced the respondent attitudes. More importantly, it taught the White House what the nation would want to hear from their president, in order to produce support for the president and his choices 🖱.

CONCLUSION

For the framers, a voting public represented an important check on power, since voting prevents tyranny by creating the ability to remove an autocratic leader. However, voting did not necessarily give the public a role between elections. Instead, technology created a role for the public between elections through the determination of public opinion. Since the time of George Washington's presidency, presidents have given speeches and spoken to the press. However, it is not until the advent of public opinion polls that the public gained a voice and a measure of power between elections. With public opinion polls, the media, pundits, politicians, citizens, and presidents themselves all know where the president stands with the nation-at-large. The continuous nature of the approval rating, over sixty-five years of asking the public if they approve or disapprove, provides an opportunity to assess presidents while in office and to compare them to other presidents. But, public opinion polling on policy issues also allows presidents to design a public relations campaign to support their preferred courses of action.

More significantly, polling the public creates an artificial measure of accountability, as the public pressure revealed by polls would seemingly force presidential compliance. The presence of the polls, then, exists in tension with the distanced relationship between the public and the president envisioned by the framers. The idea of forcing compliance to polls also challenges modern ideas of leadership. The modern presidency must constantly balance whether too much attention to public opinion creates followership and also how little attention amounts to indifference.

POLLING TO SAVE A PRESIDENCY

THEN . . .

> In June 1972, five men broke into the headquarters of the Democratic National Committee at the Watergate Hotel and Office complex in Washington, D.C. They were caught trying to wiretap and photograph sensitive material; they were arrested and then indicted along with two others for conspiracy, burglary, and violation of federal wiretapping laws. While it was considered to be a minor crime, the grand jury Judge John J. Sirica suspected something else: "There were still simply too many unanswered questions in the case. By that time, thinking about the break-in and reading about it, I'd have had to be some kind of moron to believe that no other people were involved. No political campaign committee would turn over so much money to a man like Gordon Liddy without

🖱 Read and watch President Bush's speeches.

someone higher up in the organization approving the transaction. How could I not see that?"[86] It turned out that the leader of the group, James McCord, was security coordinator for the Committee to Re-Elect the President (which produces the unfortunate acronym CREEP). At his trial, McCord implicated top officials, including Attorney General John Mitchell. One by one, President Nixon's top staffers were drawn into covering up the involvement of CREEP in the crime. Instead of distancing themselves immediately, they chose to try to hide it and thus were further entangled.

As history shows, the Watergate scandal had huge implications for the presidency. The scandal also demonstrates how public opinion can be both a check on power and a tool in service to power. President Nixon argued in his memoirs that his fight against impeachment was "a race for public support" and his "last campaign . . . not for political office but for . . . political life."[87] Although the break-in occurred in June of 1972, Nixon was reelected in a landslide in November 1972. Watergate was a maelstrom of intrigue inside the beltway of Washington, D.C., but not outside of it among most of the electorate. As a result, the Nixon White House was not concerned about the mass public response to Watergate until almost a year later. Nixon and his advisors grew more attentive to poll results as the media coverage of the story escalated. According to Chief of Staff H. R. Haldeman, Nixon "went into the Watergate question . . . [and] wanted to know if we had any polls on apparent reaction to whom it affects, analyzed by voter breakdowns and all."[88] Haldeman responded that "Oliver Quayle [the pollster] says nobody gives a damn about the Watergate. Sindlinger [another pollster] says where it used to be during the election only about ten percent was

Richard Nixon gestures toward transcripts of White House tapes after announcing he would turn them over to House impeachment investigators and make them public in April of 1974.

the highest it ever got that said Watergate was a big issue, now it's two or three percent. He said we just can't find anybody who is interested."[89]

By April 1973, Haldeman wrote that, "because of the weight of public opinion, a voluntary departure is necessary" and so he and Assistant to the President for Domestic Affairs John Ehrlichman resigned.[90] In just three months, public opinion had turned against the Nixon White House. The public believed that the President's trusted advisors knew about the break-in and had to go. By May of 1973, Nixon's pollsters were asking questions about the president's behavior. Nixon told his new Chief of Staff, Alexander Haig, "By a vote of 59 to 31, they thought the President should be given the benefit of the doubt on this matter and should be allowed to finish his term. You know, the next three and a half years. But the other interesting thing is by a vote of 77 to 13 they opposed suggestions that the President resign."[91]

Nixon believed that the public was behind him and also believed that public support would protect him from the press feeding frenzy over the congressional investigation into the scandal. On May 8th Nixon told Haig, "I didn't have to see a Harris poll to realize it, I mean apart from anything else the country doesn't want the Presidency to be destroyed."[92] The next day (May 9th), Nixon was so interested in the polling data, he interrupted Press Secretary Ron Zeigler's account of a very tough press briefing:

> President Nixon: Did the Harris poll get any play, the one you mentioned?
> Ziegler: Yes it did. Oh, yes, sir. It got play on TV last night, got good play.
> President Nixon: Of course they had some negative, but did they get across that point that they didn't want the President to resign?
> Ziegler: Yes, sir. Absolutely, yes, sir.
> President Nixon: And that 59 to 31 thought that he ought to continue the work?
> Zeigler: Right.
> President Nixon: Okay.
> Ziegler: We survived, and we're going to continue to.
> President Nixon: Damn right. Okay.[93]

On May 11, 1973, Nixon informed Secretary of State Henry Kissinger, "Hell, I'll stay here till the last Gallup polls. . . . Goddamn it. We're here to do a job and we're doing the right thing. You know it and I know it."[94] Nixon meant it—and that is exactly what happened. Between May of 1973 and August of 1974, a flood of damaging information changed public opinion and challenged Nixon's ability to survive the scandal. The television coverage of the Watergate congressional hearings, where 85 percent of the nation claimed to have watched at least a portion of the coverage, diminished the President's approval rating. But it was the revelation that the President had a recording system in his office, and the release of the tapes after the Supreme Court ruled in *U.S. v Nixon* (1974) that he had to turn them over to the Special Prosecutor, that destroyed any public support Nixon had left. "Until the revelation of the taping system, the polls revealed that the public believed Democrats and Republicans were equally guilty of 'campaign tricks' but that the Nixon campaign 'got caught at it.'"[95] After the release of the tapes, public approval of the president dropped to 20 percent and Nixon resigned, before he could be impeached by the House of Representatives, on August 8, 1974.

. . . AND NOW

For Nixon, the polling apparatus allowed his White House to monitor how important Watergate was to the public. The polls demonstrated what items produced a negative response from the public and thus needed a public relations counter-strategy. The polls for Nixon were a sophisticated communications advance warning system. In contrast, Bill Clinton used his polling apparatus to design the public relations counter-strategy and not just to signal the need for such a strategy. The Clinton–Lewinsky sex scandal became international news on January 21, 1998, when news organizations revealed a sexual relationship between the president and a young White House intern. An inappropriate sexual relationship would create a feeding frenzy under any circumstances, but this was an exceptionally explosive scandal because of the charge that Clinton perjured himself and suborned perjury in the federal grand jury investigating him on another matter, Whitewater, a failed Arkansas land deal, from when Clinton was governor of Arkansas.

Where the Watergate story was a dramatic who-done-it (what did the president know and when did he know it?), revealed piece by tantalizing piece in newspaper accounts and then in the Watergate hearings, the Lewinsky scandal was neither dramatic nor complicated. Yet the media attention dwarfed Watergate. The *New York Times* and the three major television networks (ABC, NBC, and CBS) alone combined to provide more than 1,300 stories in a little more than a year. And the public was paying attention: approximately 60.3 million viewers watched President Clinton's State of the Union speech in January 1998 and his televised apology for the relationship in August 1998. Yet, his approval rating reached its highest point in the month following the revelations, with 69 percent of Americans approving of the job the president was doing after finding out about the scandal. Throughout 1998, Clinton averaged a 65 percent approval rating.

Since scandal usually depresses a president's approval rating, political scientists investigated alternative explanations for Clinton's high rating in the face of scandal. What they found was that the public supported the president professionally, just not personally.[96] The economy was good, so the scandal seemed extraneous. Interestingly, the public opinion apparatus itself turned out to be a component of Clinton's survival. Clinton senior advisor George Stephanopoulos argued in his book, *All Too Human*, that the president received two competing recommendations and he chose to heed the advice that rested on the polling apparatus. Advisors to the president inside and outside the White House, like Erskine Bowles, friend and chief of staff, and Leon Panetta, former chief of staff, recommended coming clean with the country in January 1998. According to Stephanopoulos, "But at his moment of maximum peril, the president chose to follow the pattern of his past. He called [former pollster] Dick Morris. Dick took a poll. The poll said lie."[97]

The polling performed privately for the president tested what knowledge would lead the public to support resignation or impeachment. According to the grand jury investigation led by Independent Counsel Kenneth Starr, "Morris told the grand jury, he did some polling and learned that the public was most concerned about obstruction of justice and subornation of perjury, and not whether Clinton had simply engaged in a sexual affair outside his marriage." The public said, as interpreted by the polls, it would not tolerate a president who committed a crime but would tolerate a president who lied to his wife about an affair. In the polls, a distinction emerged—lying personally and lying legally. The public rightly rejected lying legally.

This seems exactly the same as what Nixon did, polling to find out what the public thought about a presidential scandal. The difference—and it was a significant difference—is that Morris polled the public after the president testified but prior to the scandal becoming public. Clinton insisted throughout the course of the scandal that he never committed perjury or obstructed justice. His efforts seemed laughable as he debated the definition of the word "is." According to footnote 1,128 in the Starr Report, Clinton told the grand jury: "It depends on what the meaning of the word 'is' is. If the—if he—if 'is' means is and never has been, that is not—that is one thing. If it means there is none, that was a completely true statement.... Now, if someone had asked me on that day, are you having any kind of sexual relations with Ms. Lewinsky, that is, asked me a question in the present tense, I would have said no. And it would have been completely true." Yet, in the context of Dick Morris' polling it makes perfect sense. If Clinton wanted to remain President he needed to stick to the public's script—lying personally is tolerable. All along, the president owned lying personally but never, to this day, acknowledged lying legally.

SUGGESTED READINGS

Brace, Paul, and Barbara Hinckley. 1992. *Follow the Leader: Opinion Polls and Modern Presidents.* New York: Basic Books.

Brody, Richard. 1991. *Assessing the President: The Media, Elite Opinion and Public Support.* Palo Alto: Stanford University Press.

Canes-Wrone, Brandice. 2006. *Who Leads Whom? Presidents, Policy, and the Public.* Chicago: University of Chicago Press.

Cornwell, Elmer, Jr. 1965. *Presidential Leadership of Public Opinion.* Bloomington: Indiana University Press.

Edwards, George C., III. 2003. *On Deaf Ears:The Limits of the Bully Pulpit.* New Haven: Yale Univesity Press.

Eisinger, Robert. 2003. *The Evolution of Presidential Polling.* New York: Cambridge University Press.

Heith, Diane J. 2003. *Polling to Govern: Public Opinion and Presidential Leadership.* Palo Alto: Stanford University Press.

Jacobs, Lawrence, and Robert Shapiro. 2000. *Politicians Don't Pander: Political Manipulation and the Loss of Democratic Responsiveness.* Chicago: University of Chicago Press.

Mueller, John. 2009. *War, Presidents and Public Opinion.* Columbus, OH: Educational Publisher.

ON THE WEB

http://www.gallup.com. A comprehensive site with public opinion and analysis, including historical and comparative data from the Gallup Polling organization, dating from the Truman administration.

http://www.pollster.com. Current public opinion and analysis, including blogs about public opinion by practitioners.

http://www.ropercenter.uconn.edu. Housed at the University of Connecticut, a site containing the public opinion datasets of the Roper Center.

http://people-press.org/. The home page for the Pew Research Center for the People & the Press, an independent, non-partisan public opinion research organization, which includes polls and commentaries.

IN THEIR OWN WORDS

PRESIDENTIAL IMAGE AND PUBLIC OPINION

Perhaps no president during the modern era struggled with his public image more than Jimmy Carter. While his image as an outsider who would clean up the mess in Washington following the Watergate scandal helped propel him to victory in 1976, Carter often struggled with projecting a strong image of leadership once in the White House. Five months prior to his now-famous "malaise" speech, where he spoke to the American public about the "crisis of confidence" in the American government, Carter advisors were hard at work analyzing the President's public image, as well as his prospects for governing and reelection in 1980. In a memo to his White House colleagues, advisor Alan Raymond discussed the "state of the presidency":

> Although I am a believer in the cyclical theory of public and media opinion, I also think there's only so far down you can go and still have things swing back your way—or at least swing back far enough. I assume that time and circumstances will lead to a recovery in the second half of this year. My concern is that a large residue of negative feeling and doubt is being built up—around specific issues and around the question of leadership—which may go away temporarily, but which can resurface at the slightest provocation and which is likely, a la Murphy's law, to resurface at the worst possible time.
>
> I don't subscribe to the idea that the President will be judged next year by some vague rating of how well he's done overall. Rather, I think he will be judged in specific areas and on specific issues, and if people think he's not doing *enough*, they'll turn to someone else. People have gotten used to changing Presidents; they have far less respect for the presidency as an institution post-Nixon; and they still see Jimmy Carter as an unknown.
>
> A policy of trying to build support through a general appeal rather than constituency group appeal is risky—because of the lack of excitement in his analytical, rational, structural reform approach to government; and because it guarantees that you'll make some real enemies along the way. We need to be making strong friends—in the media and the electorate—at the same time,

and I don't get the feeling we're doing that. With voter apathy and cynicism as high as it is, we have to counter-act "anti-Carter" sentiment *and* give people a reason to *want* to vote our way.

Carving out the middle of the electorate may sound like a fairly safe course for building support, but I don't think it holds up to close scrutiny. I would argue that there are three major categories of voting blocks. First, all voters—the most important group, but one which can't be easily broken down ideologically when it comes to voting. Next, those who consider themselves in constituency groups—including liberal or conservative—and may vote as such. And third, the growing number of people who have intense feelings about a special interest or issue and will vote on the basis of that issue alone....

In the simplest terms, we need to maximize the appeal to all voters, win over some constituency groups, and neutralize the single issue groups. There are areas of weakness, and there are areas that are largely out of our control. But the overriding message to me is that we have to move quickly and dramatically, to reverse the factors we have working against us. I would much rather have the President seen as "fighting for his political life" (which implies that he is facing up to his problems), than have him seen as assuming he will be judged favorably on his overall performance (which implies that he is willing to be the "lesser of two evils").

The overriding problem with the Carter Presidency at this moment is one of leadership, and it is certainly the issue opponents will focus on in the months ahead. It is a volatile issue, one that can seem to change overnight with a single, dramatic event such as Camp David. But I would argue that the public and media perception of leadership is influenced by a variety of factors....

While there's no question in my mind that the Washington media elite has overreacted to recent events, there's also no question in my mind that there's little enthusiasm for Jimmy Carter among the public. People don't see him as a strong leader and they don't know what he stands for. Unless we reverse that feeling fairly quickly and dramatically, we'll be going into 1980 with a tremendous handicap; vulnerable not only to true public opinion, but to the "political opinion" that the media will spend all its time writing about as they try to make a race out of it.[98]

CHAPTER 6

Presidents and the Legislative Branch

By both constitutional design and political reality, many presidents have had a combative and contentious relationship with Congress. While there have certainly been times when the president and Congress have worked harmoniously in passing legislation, like the support that Franklin Roosevelt received from a Democratic Congress when passing much of the early New Deal legislation beginning in 1933, or passage of Lyndon Johnson's Great Society legislation in 1965, more often than not the White House and its policy agenda is slowed down or even halted by Congress's refusal to support or even compromise with the president. Harry Truman famously campaigned against what he called the "do-nothing" Republican Congress during his 1948 reelection. More recently, Bill Clinton and the Republican Congress faced a showdown over the budget in both 1995 and 1996 that resulted in temporary shutdowns of the federal government. While divided government (when at least one house of Congress is controlled by the opposite party of the president) can contribute to a president's legislative frustration, even presidents working with their own parties in control of Congress, such as John F. Kennedy, who struggled to get a tax cut passed, or Jimmy Carter, who could not achieve the major reform he sought for energy policy, are not guaranteed passage of key policy issues.

In keeping with that tradition, Barack Obama's relationship with Congress has not always gone smoothly. First elected in 2008 with a Democratic majority in both houses of Congress, and facing a severe economic crisis, many assumed that Obama would enjoy the type of deference given to FDR in the face of national adversity in passing his legislative agenda. During his first two years in office, Obama achieved legislative success in the areas of health-care reform, reforms to the financial industry, credit card reform, and a major stimulus package, among other items, but none without a serious political fight (often coming from members of his own party) that, in many cases, resulted in major compromises to the initial legislation Obama had sought. By 2011, Obama's relationship with Congress would only get worse. After Republicans won back the House of Representatives in the 2010 midterm elections, and Democrats held a slimmer majority in the Senate, Obama faced an even more daunting task of passing key pieces of his legislative agenda. With high unemployment, job creation, taxes, the budget deficit, and the national debt dominating the agenda, both parties in Congress sought to stake out their claim of looking out for average Americans in preparation for the 2012 election. Politically, however, that left little room for compromise. While Obama was able to reach an accord with House Speaker John Boehner (R-OH) and Senate Majority Leader Harry Reid (D-NV) on a budget deal to avert a government shutdown in the spring, Obama's relationship with Speaker Boehner deteriorated throughout the summer, and even a round of golf could not salvage it after the two engaged in an "intense message war" over raising the national debt ceiling.[1] In addition, Obama's plan for job creation, despite introducing it in an address to a joint session of Congress in September, went nowhere. By December, with many legislative items like extending payroll tax cuts and plans to create jobs still needing attention, and with no compromise with Congressional Republicans in sight, Obama threatened to keep everyone in Washington working through Christmas, delaying his own family vacation to his home state of Hawaii, until key bills were passed.

The 2011 holiday season in the White House and on Capitol Hill seemed a far cry from what candidate Obama had promised just a few years earlier. During his twenty-one-month campaign for the presidency, Obama had traveled the country describing to potential voters what he would do as president. While on the campaign trail, Obama's stump speech (a term originating in the fact that candidates used to actually stand on tree stumps in the center of town to speak) informed voters about "the change they could believe in," as in this speech in Iowa on November 10, 2007:

> I am in this race to tell the corporate lobbyists that their days of setting the agenda in Washington are over. I have done more than any other candidate in this race to take on lobbyists—and won. They have not funded my campaign; they will not get a job in my White House; and they will not drown out the voices of the American people when I am President. I'm in this race to take those tax breaks away from companies that are moving jobs overseas and put them in the pockets of hard working Americans who deserve it. And I won't raise the minimum wage every ten years—I will raise it to keep pace so that workers don't fall behind. . . . I'm in this race because I want to stop talking about the outrage of 47 million Americans without health care and start actually doing something about it. I expanded health care in Illinois by bringing Democrats and Republicans together. By taking on the insurance industry. And that is how I will make certain that every single American in this country has health care they can count on. And I won't do it twenty years from now. I won't do it ten years from now. I will do it by the end of my first term as President of the United States of America. I run for President to make sure that every American child has the best education that we have to offer—from the day they are born to the day they graduate from college. And I

won't just talk about how great teachers are—as President, I will reward them for their greatness—by raising salaries and giving them more support.[2]

The political evolution from Obama's campaign speeches to the political realities of dealing with Congress in 2011 highlights the tension of modern expectations for presidents: they are expected to advance and achieve a legislative agenda, yet they do not have the unilateral power to do so just because Americans elected them president. As a candidate Obama told audience after audience that he planned to reform health care, improve education, increase the minimum wage, and limit the role for lobbyists. As is typical for most presidents, even one serving during an economic crisis, Obama attempted to honor his extensive list of campaign promises. Obama achieved the centerpiece of his agenda when he signed health-care reform into law in 2010, albeit a much different bill than he had campaigned for, but improvements to education and limits on the role for lobbyists were only partial legislative victories, and on the minimum wage, no legislative action occurred.

All presidents learn relatively quickly once they take office that the gap between expectations, promises, and legislative outcome is enormous. Presidents and their advisors also discover that the skills that helped to win the election, like the ability to raise money, project an attractive image, and put together a successful campaign organization, are much different from the skills it takes to govern, especially when it comes to dealing with Congress. The job of legislating and administering requires talents that can move a cumbersome and complex government to get things done, like persuasion, personal and organizational leadership, and managerial skills. Presidents have made campaign promises, which in turn set expectations, regarding a legislative agenda. Yet, the president has not been granted any additions to the limited set of powers provided for by the Constitution in the domestic legislative arena. Consequently, the president's ability to achieve his agenda is conditional. Individual skill, political context, and system design vary across time and presidents. Legislative success is critical to a president's reelection and legacy, but is difficult to achieve because so much is beyond the president's ability to influence, particularly members of Congress, as well as the political environment in which he attempts to govern.

THE PRESIDENT'S FORMAL ROLE IN THE LEGISLATIVE PROCESS

A recurring theme for the presidency is the lack of specific constitutional direction regarding its function. As discussed in Chapter 2, in comparison to Article I of the Constitution, which is devoted to the legislative branch, Article II is brief and open to interpretation as to the extent of presidential powers. Article I provides Congress specific (enumerated) tasks in the domestic arena (e.g., creating a post office, coining money) as well as generic (implied) grants of power (e.g., the necessary-and-proper clause). Article I, Section 8 gives Congress "all the legislative powers herein granted." The framers expected Congress to have primary responsibility for legislative action while the president's role would be minor. In contrast, Articles I and II grant the president a role in the creation of legislation and public policy, but it is time and precedent that grant power to those assignments. The president's formal legislative powers only include the power to call Congress into special session (which is much less important now, since Congress stays in session most of the year), providing the State of the Union message, along with the budget message and the economic report (all of which serve as a means to announce to the nation the president's goals), recommending legislation to Congress, and the power to sign bills into law or to veto bills. The president's power to sign or veto bills is the first mention of the president in the Constitution in an active capacity in Article I, Section 7, where the formal path to legislation is described:

> Every Bill which shall have passed the House of Representatives and the Senate, shall, before it become a Law, be presented to the President of the United States; If he approve he shall sign it, but if not he shall return it, with his Objections to that House in which it shall have originated, who shall enter the Objections at large on their Journal, and proceed to reconsider it. If after such Reconsideration two thirds of that House shall agree to pass the Bill, it shall be sent, together with the Objections, to the other House, by which it shall likewise be reconsidered, and if approved by two thirds of that House, it shall become a Law.... If any Bill shall not be returned by the President within ten Days (Sundays excepted) after it shall have been presented to him, the Same shall be a Law, in like Manner as if he had signed it, unless the Congress by their Adjournment prevent its Return, in which Case it shall not be a Law.

Thus, every law of the land emerges out of the same process: Each chamber of Congress votes on the same bill, which then goes to the president for his signature. If the president does not sign the bill, it is returned to Congress at which point they can change it and send it back, or override his refusal to sign it. Note that the Constitution does not provide a rationale by which the president determines to approve or object to a bill, just a method.

During the Constitutional Convention, the original Virginia Plan (also known as the large state plan) included the right to return or "veto" acts of Congress. At the time, most governors were able to override the legislature, although some needed the support of a council to do it. Thus, the debate at the time centered on the power of the veto—whether the president could use it alone and whether Congress could override it. However, there was no discussion of why the president would veto legislation. Alexander Hamilton raised the issue of why a president would veto legislation during the ratification process, arguing in *Federalist* 73 the "power to return all bills with objections to the legislature" would grant energy and strength to the presidency. However, he also argued that the "power in question has a further use. It not only serves as a shield to the executive, but it furnishes an additional security against the enaction of improper laws."[3]

Using the Veto

Only bills approved by both the House of Representatives and the Senate go to the president, who can then sign the bill into law or veto the bill. Congress can override a presidential veto by a vote of two-thirds in each house. The president can also pocket a bill for ten days (Sundays excluded), and if the legislature is in session, the bill automatically becomes law. But if the legislature is adjourned, then the bill dies. This is known as a pocket veto, which forces Congress in its next session to start over from the beginning in the legislative process. As a result, the bill must again pass both chambers and is again subject to presidential veto. Beyond these specifics, the lack of constitutional clarity on the use of the veto often elevated presidential choices in this regard to precedent-setting behavior. George Washington established many precedents long adhered to by his successors. In the case of the veto, Washington used it twice in eight years and made his case based only on Constitutional grounds:

> United States [Philadelphia] April 5 1792.
>
> Gentlemen of the House of Representatives
>
> I have maturely considered the Act passed by the two Houses, intitled, "An Act for an apportionment of Representatives among the several States according to the first enumeration," and I return it to your House, wherein it originated, with the following objections.
>
> First—The Constitution has prescribed that representatives shall be apportioned among the several States according to their respective numbers: and there is no one proportion or divisor which, applied to the respective numbers of the States will yield the number and allotment of representatives proposed by the Bill.
>
> Second—The Constitution has also provided that the number of Representatives shall not exceed one for every thirty thousand; which restriction is, by the context, and by fair and obvious construction, to be applied to the separate and respective numbers of the States: and the bill has allotted to eight of the States, more than one for thirty thousand.
>
> George Washington.[4]

The veto rested on constitutional grounds until Andrew Jackson's administration. When Jackson famously vetoed the bill to recharter the national bank in 1832, he too cloaked his veto in constitutionality but also asserted political rationales. Jackson claimed in his veto message, "I sincerely regret that in the act before me I can perceive none of those modifications of the bank charter which are necessary, in my opinion, to make it compatible with justice, with sound policy, or with the Constitution of our country (July 1832)."[5] Jackson contended that the states, and not Congress, retained the power to charter, regulate, and tax corporations. (This was also Jefferson's original position rejected by Chief Justice John Marshall in *McCulloch v. Maryland* in 1819, the case in which the Supreme Court declared the constitutionality of Congress to establish a national bank based on both the supremacy clause and the implied powers of Congress as found in the necessary-and-proper clause). The crux of the political argument Jackson was making was based on "exclusivity and favoritism." By "sounding the loaded words 'monopoly' and 'privilege' over and over... Jackson laid out his core theme: The Bank's charter gave its stockholders a promise of pelf and power not accessible to other citizens. It made them 'a privileged order, clothed both with great political power and enjoying immense pecuniary advantages from their connection with the Government.'"[6] Once Jackson enabled the political nature of the veto, presidents were less circumscribed by constitutionality in rejecting acts of Congress.

However, the use of the veto as a political weapon was probably not envisioned by the framers. Many presidents have used the veto not as a defense against Congress from encroaching on their powers of office, or even against bad legislation, but as a means to implement their own legislative agendas. For example, the first six presidents vetoed a total of nine bills. Presidents Taylor, Fillmore, and Garfield

Bill Clinton vetoing legislation in April 2000 that would have allowed thousands of tons of highly radioactive nuclear waste to be shipped to Yucca Mountain in Nevada.

vetoed no bills. In contrast, Franklin D. Roosevelt vetoed 635 bills (and was overridden only nine times), which reflects his vision of presidential power and his role and influence over the policymaking process. Presidents also use the threat of a veto as a political weapon, like when Reagan told Congress to "make my day" by raising taxes. The use of the veto by the president of one party against a Congress controlled by another is also not what the framers intended. Nonetheless, contemporary presidents and their advisors recognize that a political strategy must be developed in support of a presidential veto, as when George H. W. Bush vetoed civil rights legislation in October 1990:

> It is becoming increasingly clear that within the next two weeks the President will be in the position of having to veto the Civil Rights Act of 1990. On Monday September 24, the conference committee on Civil Rights will hold its first meeting to reconcile the House and Senate versions of the bill. Since the two bills are so similar, the reconciled bill could be reported out of conference early next week and sent back to the President for action.... The President has a strong record on civil rights and it is important that he is viewed as supportive of civil rights at the time of his veto. He must remain on the offensive about his veto of a quota bill. To accomplish this we propose that he deliver his veto statement before an audience of invited guests (tbd) and that he physically present his own major Civil Rights Bill at that time. We recommend that this event be covered by minority press. The picture should be of the President holding his legislation in hand while challenging Congress to pass a true Civil Rights Bill.[7]

Bush would eventually sign into law the Civil Rights Act of 1991, a modified version of the bill that he had vetoed the prior year.

Rarely does Congress actually override a presidential veto; between 1945 and 2008, of the 480 presidential vetoes handed down, Congress only successfully overrode the president's veto forty-eight times. (See Table 6.1) First, it is

Table 6.1 Presidential Vetoes

PRESIDENT	VETOES	POCKET VETOES	VETOES OVERRIDDEN
Washington	2	0	0
J. Adams	0	0	0
Jefferson	0	0	0
Madison	5	2	0
Monroe	1	0	0
J. Q. Adams	0	0	0
Jackson	5	7	0
Van Buren	0	1	0
W. H. Harrison	0	0	0
Tyler	6	4	1
Polk	2	1	0
Taylor	0	0	0
Fillmore	0	0	0
Pierce	9	0	5
Buchanan	4	3	0
Lincoln	2	5	0
A. Johnson	21	8	15
Grant	45	48	4
Hayes	12	1	1
Garfield	0	0	0
Arthur	4	8	1
Cleveland	304	110	2
B. Harrison	19	25	1
Cleveland	42	128	5
McKinley	6	36	0
T. Roosevelt	42	40	1
Taft	30	9	1
Wilson	33	11	6
Harding	5	1	0
Coolidge	20	30	4

(continued)

Table 6.1 ***(continued)***

President	Vetoes	Pocket Vetoes	Vetoes Overridden
Hoover	21	16	3
F. D. Roosevelt	372	263	9
Truman	180	70	12
Eisenhower	73	108	2
Kennedy	12	9	0
L. B. Johnson	16	14	0
Nixon	26	17	7
Ford	48	18	12
Carter	13	18	2
Reagan	39	39	9
G. H. W. Bush	29	15	1
Clinton	36	1	2
G. W. Bush	11	1	4
Barack Obama*	2	0	0
Total	**1,497**	**1,067**	**110**

*As of June 15, 2012

Source: Gerhard Peters. "Presidential Vetoes." The American Presidency Project, ed. John T. Woolley and Gerhard Peters. Santa Barbara, CA: University of California. 1999–2012. Available at: http://www.presidency.ucsb.edu/data/vetoes.php. and http://www.infoplease.com/ipa/A0801767.html.

important to point out that achieving a two-thirds majority in both houses on a particular issue is a difficult task; and second, since the president has become so involved in the legislative process in recent decades, legislation is usually only pursued if members of Congress know that presidential support is likely (since members do not want to waste their time, energy, and resources on legislation that is likely to fail).

The Legislative Veto

As constitutionally mandated, the separated system that requires participation by both Congress and the president in the legislative process has mostly remained unchanged, in part because the Supreme Court has rejected any attempts to alter the process. However, the so-called legislative veto, first used in the 1930s, is a device where one or both houses of Congress passes a resolution to veto certain decisions made in the executive branch. This usually occurs to change a particular policy or spending by an executive agency. A legislative veto, then, is a statutory act that allows a president or an executive branch agency to take certain actions that will be subjected to a later approval or disapproval by one or both houses of Congress. Legislative vetoes are considered an "arrangement of convenience" for both Congress and the executive branch, since "executives gain decision-making authority they might not have otherwise, and Congress retains a second chance to examine the decisions."[8] In 1932, in response to Congress' authorization of the reorganization of the executive departments, Herbert Hoover submitted his proposal subject to the approval or disapproval of one chamber. The logic stemmed from the fact that, like the use of simple or concurrent resolutions for internal housekeeping in Congress, the reorganization was internal to the executive branch and did not really need involvement of the Congress.[9] Between 1932 and 1983, the legislative veto was used for reorganizational purposes hundreds of times.

However, in 1983, in the case *INS v. Chadha*, the Supreme Court invalidated a legislative veto used to alter a decision by Immigration and Naturalization Services (an executive agency created by Congress) partly on the grounds that it violated the presentment requirement of Article I (which simply means that once Congress approves a bill it must be presented to the president for approval) and partly on the grounds of separation of powers (that Congress had no right to interfere by vetoing the action of the agency). However, more than four hundred legislative vetoes have been included in legislation since 1983, often in the form of what are known as "report and wait" provisions that Congress will add to a particular bill to require congressional consultation by an executive agency before specific actions can be taken.

The Line-Item Veto

In 1995, Congress tried again to change a part of the lawmaking process. Following the Republican victory in the 1994 midterm elections, which saw the party take control of both houses of Congress for the first time in forty years, the new majority sought to enact their campaign promises that had been labeled the GOP's "Contract with America ☝." One of those promises, championed by the new Speaker of the House Newt Gingrich, was to create a "line-item veto" to grant the president the ability to eliminate "pork-barrel" spending by Congress line by line, without having to scrap an entire omnibus spending bill. This is a power that nearly all state governors have at their disposal, and a power that many presidents have argued that they needed as well. For example, in 1986, Ronald Reagan urged Congress to give him a line-item veto during his State of the Union address, arguing "we cannot win the race to the future shackled to a system that can't even pass a Federal budget." Reagan's insistence on the line-item veto came from the inability of both Congress and the White House to bring down the budget deficit and the national debt.

Once the line-item veto became law in 1995 (one of the only campaign pledges in the Contract with America to actually become law), Bill Clinton became the first to use this new presidential power; he relied on the line-item veto eighty-two times in just eleven bills. However, in a 7–2 decision, the Supreme Court ruled in *Clinton v. New York* (1998) that the line-item veto, as passed by Congress, was unconstitutional because it interfered with the separation of powers doctrine in the Constitution, and that the only way to change the power balance between the president and Congress was through a constitutional amendment. As Justice John Paul Stevens argued:

> Under the Presentment Clause, after a bill has passed both Houses, but "before it become[s] a Law," it must be presented to the President, who "shall sign it" if he

---

☝ Read the 1994 Contract with America.

> approves it, but "return it," i.e., "veto" it, if he does not. . . . The profound importance of these cases makes it appropriate to emphasize [that] the Court expresses no opinion about the wisdom of the Act's procedures and does not lightly conclude that the actions of the Congress that passed it, and the President who signed it into law, were unconstitutional. If this Act were valid, it would authorize the President to create a law whose text was not voted on by either House or presented to the President for signature. That may or may not be desirable, but it is surely not a document that may "become a law" pursuant to Article I, § 7. If there is to be a new procedure in which the President will play a different role, such change must come through the Article V amendment procedures.[10]

In sum, the legislative process proscribed by the Constitution requires the president to sign or return the bill to both chambers of Congress. The Supreme Court has rejected all attempts to alter the process and grant the president more power over legislative outcomes barring a constitutional amendment.

Recommendations to Congress

With the veto, the framers placed the president at the end of the legislative process, which allowed the president to determine which bills became law. With the recommending provision, the framers placed the president at the beginning of the legislative process. Justice Hugo Black, in *Youngstown Sheet & Tube Co. v. Sawyer* (1952), simplistically summed up the president's engagement as "the recommending of laws he thinks wise and the vetoing of laws he thinks bad."[11] Listing recommending legislation as an enumerated power of the president not only grants the president the power to call attention to issues, but it also requires Congress to pay attention to the president's offering since it is mandated by the Constitution.

The clause in the Constitution focused on recommending also grants the president a third role. In Article II, Section 3, the Constitution asserts that the president "shall from time to time give to the Congress Information of the State of the Union, and recommend to their Consideration such Measures as he shall judge necessary and expedient." In addition to the veto, the president recommends *and also* provides information. As political scientists Donna Hoffman and Alison Howard note, "giving information to Congress and recommending measures to Congress are two different things. Both can, however be accomplished at the same time and routinely are."[12] George Washington and Alexander Hamilton both viewed the provisions as separate, but their views differed; Washington saw them as duties while Hamilton regarded the provisions as powers. Ultimately, Washington's view prevailed, and the president became obligated to provide information on the state of the union and recommendations for the state of the union.

The modern mechanism by which presidents most frequently recommend to Congress is via the State of the Union address. However, the State of the Union address was not always an address (as discussed in Chapter 4), nor was it always viewed as a source of legislative power for the president. George Washington and John Adams delivered their State of the Union messages in a way familiar to modern America: an address before Congress on the floor of the House chamber. However,

---

Read the entire *Clinton v. New York* opinion.

Thomas Jefferson ended that practice and the State of the Union message was no longer an address before Congress but rather was a written document. Until Woodrow Wilson again spoke before Congress in 1913, the clerk of the House read aloud the president's State of the Union document.

Once Wilson returned the obligation to a rhetorical opportunity, the State of the Union address became a significant legislative tool for the modern president as a source of legislative leadership. Where the presidential inaugural addresses focuses on the type of presidency or type of leadership a president wishes to exercise, the State of the Union message is much more specific, functioning as a provider of information, a source for policy prescriptions, and also an opportunity to showcase the president as a player in the legislative process.[13] Of course, the speeches also include relevant foreign policy determined by the current political context. For example, George W. Bush first used the term "axis of evil" to describe the triumvirate of Iran, Iraq, and North Korea in his 2002 State of the Union address.

The State of the Union address serves as an agenda-setting tool by focusing Congress, the media, the public, and the bureaucracy on the issues and policy dilemmas that the president highlights. Moreover, the address represents an opportunity for presidents to single out issues important to him or to key constituents. Consequently, on the domestic side, the modern State of the Union address typically represents competing laundry lists of what the president has done in office, what else he would like to accomplish, and what Congress needs to do to accomplish the latter. However, presidents often use the State of the Union address to emphasize urgency, necessity, and the importance of issues. Thus, the modern State of the Union address serves not only to fulfill the president's constitutional responsibilities but also illuminates the president's leadership strategies and skills.

Interestingly, despite the differences across presidencies in terms of time and political context, presidents universally use the speech as a literal statement of the "state" of the union as well as an opportunity for leadership. Consequently, almost all presidents have uttered a variation on the state of the union being "sound," "strong," "stronger," "never stronger," or "the strongest it has ever been." Gerald Ford, under trying circumstances in 1975 due to tough economic conditions and a lack of public trust in the presidency following Richard Nixon's resignation in August 1974, tried a different tack:

> Mr. Speaker, Mr. Vice President, Members of the 94th Congress, and distinguished guests: Twenty-six years ago, a freshman Congressman, a young fellow with lots of idealism who was out to change the world, stood before Sam Rayburn in the well of the House and solemnly swore to the same oath that all of you took yesterday—an unforgettable experience, and I congratulate you all. Two days later, that same freshman stood at the back of this great Chamber—over there someplace—as President Truman, all charged up by his single-handed election victory, reported as the Constitution requires on the state of the Union.
>
> When the bipartisan applause stopped, President Truman said, "I am happy to report to this 81st Congress that the state of the Union is good. Our Nation is

Read President Jefferson's State of the Union address.

Watch President Bush's 2002 State of the Union address.

> better able than ever before to meet the needs of the American people, and to give them their fair chance in the pursuit of happiness. [It] is foremost among the nations of the world in the search for peace." Today, that freshman Member from Michigan stands where Mr. Truman stood, and I must say to you that the state of the Union is not good.[14]

In contrast, and during a much more severe economic downturn, President Obama took the more familiar path of most of his predecessors by reminding members of Congress about the resilience of the American government:

> Madam Speaker, Vice President Biden, Members of Congress, distinguished guests, and fellow Americans: Our Constitution declares that from time to time, the President shall give to Congress information about the state of our Union. For 220 years, our leaders have fulfilled this duty. They've done so during periods of prosperity and tranquility, and they've done so in the midst of war and depression, at moments of great strife and great struggle. It's tempting to look back on these moments and assume that our progress was inevitable, that America was always destined to succeed. But when the Union was turned back at Bull Run and the Allies first landed at Omaha Beach, victory was very much in doubt. When the market crashed on Black Tuesday and civil rights marchers were beaten on Bloody Sunday, the future was anything but certain. These were the times that tested the courage of our convictions and the strength of our Union. And despite all our divisions and disagreements, our hesitations and our fears, America prevailed because we chose to move forward as one Nation, as one people. Again, we are tested. And again, we must answer history's call. One year ago, I took office amid two wars, an economy rocked by a severe recession, a financial system on the verge of collapse, and a Government deeply in debt. Experts from across the political spectrum warned that if we did not act, we might face a second depression. So we acted, immediately and aggressively. And one year later, the worst of the storm has passed. But the devastation remains.... So we face big and difficult challenges. And what the American people hope, what they deserve, is for all of us, Democrats and Republicans, to work through our differences, to overcome the numbing weight of our politics. For while the people who sent us here have different backgrounds, different stories, different beliefs, the anxieties they face are the same. The aspirations they hold are shared: a job that pays the bills; a chance to get ahead; most of all, the ability to give their children a better life. And you know what else they share? They share a stubborn resilience in the face of adversity. After one of the most difficult years in our history, they remain busy building cars and teaching kids, starting businesses and going back to school. They're coaching Little League and helping their neighbors. One woman wrote to me and said, "We are strained but hopeful, struggling but encouraged." It's because of this spirit, this great decency and great strength, that I have never been more hopeful about America's future than I am tonight. Despite our hardships, our Union is strong.[15]

Senate Confirmations

In stark contrast to the ease with which recommending to Congress passed the Constitutional Convention, designing the appointment power was extremely contentious. When making legislation, and thus domestic policy, Congress was clearly the dominant force, despite carving out a role for the president. In terms of appointments, the assignment of the task would clarify the degree of presidential autonomy with which the delegates were comfortable. The delegates were split over whether the president should have the sole authority to select his subordinates. The cloud hanging over the debate, of course, was King George and his tendencies toward favoritism and patronage. The delegates went back and forth through the hot summer months of 1787 before ending with another grant of shared power. Rather than grant either the Congress or the president the sole ability to fill the executive branch, in Article II, Section 2 of the Constitution, the framers split the decision making between the president and the Senate:

> He shall have Power, by and with the Advice and Consent of the Senate, to make Treaties, provided two thirds of the Senators present concur; and he shall nominate, and by and with the Advice and Consent of the Senate, shall appoint Ambassadors, other public Ministers and Consuls, Judges of the supreme Court, and all other Officers of the United States, whose Appointments are not herein otherwise provided for, and which shall be established by Law: but the Congress may by Law vest the Appointment of such inferior Officers, as they think proper, in the President alone, in the Courts of Law, or in the Heads of Departments.

Congress alone creates departments and agencies, while the President appoints and the Senate confirms or rejects the president's choice, unless the Senate happens to be in recess.

On paper, the appointments process appears simple; however, as with the power of the presidential veto to halt all Congress' efforts, the Senate confirmation process can stymie the staffing of departments and agencies as well as the courts. Barack Obama experienced this firsthand; after taking office in January 2009, several of his nominees for the Treasury Department did not receive confirmation hearings for months, despite the severity of the economic crisis. In addition, the delays on filling judgeships were so acute in 2010 that Chief Justice John Roberts urged, in his 2011 annual report on the state of the judiciary, the President and Congress to put aside differences and work together. One week later, Roberts would applaud Obama's use of the recess appointment process to avoid the "holds" placed on nominees in the Senate for political reasons. A hold is an informal practice by which a Senator can inform the party leadership that he or she does not want a bill to reach the floor of the Senate for consideration, and may filibuster the bill if it does.

SEPARATION OF POWERS

The Constitution provides the president the opportunity to participate in the legislative process, as both the veto and the recommending provision force Congress to pay attention to the president. The president cannot be ignored, unless of course, Congress has the votes to override a presidential veto. Yet, the conflict over the role for the presidency, which emerged during the Constitutional Convention, persisted throughout the nineteenth century. Elites divided over the appropriate role for the president; as a result, nineteenth-century presidents were not universally active in domestic politics. Without granting the presidency any additional formal constitutional tools, precedent-setting behavior expanded the president's power to affect legislation by expanding his informal array of tools and options.

Staking Out a Role

As the first president, George Washington had an incredible task as he fought to establish an independent executive department within the construct of separate institutions sharing powers. Washington defended the executive branch not only from ideology by rejecting the notion of a strong executive but also from a Congress seeking to micromanage. In essence, Washington sought to establish a separate domain for presidential action.

The effort to establish presidential independence was frequently under attack from the first Congress, despite having a congressional ally like James Madison, who at the time was a member of the House of Representatives from Virginia. As Congress formulated the new government by creating departments, it was Washington's job to staff them. Historian Leonard White notes that Washington focused primarily on "fitness," "merit," and "neutral competence" rather than patronage in his hiring choices. However, Washington's sterling choices did not prevent the Senate from exercising its right of refusal of nominees. On August 5, 1789, the Senate rejected one of the 102 Washington nominees to various appointments (e.g., collectors, officers, surveyors). The nominee, Benjamin Fisbourn of Georgia, apparently had offended one of Georgia's Senators at some point in the past. From this first rejection came the precedent that acknowledged the home state senator's ability to reject, without explanation, a presidential nominee.[16] The bigger fight, however, was over removing an individual from office, a power that the Constitution did not clearly designate. Washington achieved greater success here as he again wrangled with Congress over whose authority reigned supreme.

Washington was respectful of the authority of the legislative branch while protective of the rights and prerogatives of the executive. Consequently, Washington did not directly insert himself into the policymaking process. Instead, his Treasury Secretary, Alexander Hamilton, became the administrative figure who urged Congress to adopt the administration's recommendations. It was a fine line, but a significant one. Like Washington, Hamilton was a Federalist, but as his writings in the *Federalist Papers* reveal, he believed in executive power and an active, assertive presidency, perhaps more so than his boss.

Hamilton pushed the first Congress to adopt a comprehensive economic program that included assuming the state's war debts and creating a national bank. The national bank would become one of the more controversial policy recommendations in the early years, as the Jackson veto indicates. The controversy over the administration's program (as well as the activity of the president's subordinate) escalated the divisions between Washington's meritorious cabinet, particularly Hamilton and Jefferson. Even Madison, Hamilton's *Federalist Papers* writing partner, criticized the increased policy role adopted by the executive branch, arguing that it might "strengthen the pretext for an hereditary designation of the magistrate."[17] The fears of the slippery slope toward monarchy solidified the factions, leading to Washington's famous farewell warning, "without looking forward to an extremity of this kind (which nevertheless ought not to be entirely out of sight), the common and continual mischiefs of the spirit of party are sufficient to make it the interest and duty of a wise people to discourage and restrain it."[18]

Washington's retirement and lack of heir easily put to rest fears of monarchy, a hereditary monarchy in particular. However, the path to presidential participation in policymaking did not disappear with the end of the Washington administration. Washington's precedents, asserting executive prerogatives, like the use of the veto, hiring and firing, and offering program recommendations, waxed and waned over the next one hundred years with the strength and ambition of the office holder. Some, like Thomas Jefferson, Andrew Jackson, Abraham Lincoln, Teddy Roosevelt, and Woodrow Wilson, were immensely active and assertive with Congress, while others, like Rutherford B. Hayes, Chester Arthur, and Calvin Coolidge, were not. A continuous presence in the legislative arena for the president did not take shape until Franklin Roosevelt and the Great Depression remade the political landscape.

Creating the Chief Legislator

In 1932, Franklin Roosevelt won a landslide election over incumbent Herbert Hoover. FDR's overwhelming triumph, 472–59 in the Electoral College, stemmed entirely from attitudes regarding Hoover's handling of the Great Depression, which began with the stock market crash of 1929 (just six months after he took office). Hoover, believing in the sanctity of legislative leadership, allowed the Congress to dominate efforts to combat the economic crisis. Despite cries for legislative leadership in the press, Hoover resisted the demands of popular government.[19] Thus, the political environment, made up of ordinary citizens, political elites, and members of government, seemingly were crying out for leadership that met the magnitude of the crisis. Roosevelt approached leadership as a response to crisis, yet fundamentally reshaped the president's legislative role in ordinary times as well. In his Inaugural Address on March 4, 1933, Roosevelt's first exercise of leadership targeted the nation's confidence:

> So, first of all, let me assert my firm belief that the only thing we have to fear is fear itself—nameless, unreasoning, unjustified terror which paralyzes needed efforts to convert retreat into advance. In every dark hour of our national life a leadership of frankness and vigor has met with that understanding and support of the people themselves which is essential to victory. I am convinced that you will again give that support to leadership in these critical days.

Secondly, he offered a way out of the dysfunction that flourished between Hoover and Congress:

> It is to be hoped that the normal balance of executive and legislative authority may be wholly adequate to meet the unprecedented task before us. But it may be that an unprecedented demand and need for undelayed action may call for temporary departure from that normal balance of public procedure. I am prepared under my constitutional duty to recommend the measures that a stricken nation in the midst of a stricken world may require. These measures, or such other measures as the Congress may build out of its experience and wisdom, I shall seek, within my constitutional authority, to bring to speedy adoption. But in the event that the Congress shall fail to take one of these two courses, and in the event that the national emergency is still critical, I shall not evade the clear course of duty that will then confront me. I shall ask the Congress for the one remaining instrument to meet the crisis—broad Executive power to wage a war against the emergency, as great as the power that would be given to me if we were in fact invaded by a foreign foe.[20]

Roosevelt argued that he would pursue the normal presidential role; he would recommend legislation and also would seek to work quickly to produce law with Congress. More significant, however, Roosevelt also contended that if the normal role was not sufficient to the enormity of the crisis, then he would use broad presidential power, as if the country had been invaded by a foreign foe. Roosevelt easily won this ideological shift regarding presidential independence and authority, due to his personal political skills, the devastation of the crisis, and the vivid memory of Hoover's chosen ineptitude. Consequently, FDR authored the largest expansion of the powers of the federal government, and did so under the imprint of executive branch leadership. FDR achieved impressive dominance over Congress, without any additional constitutional powers provided. As a result, he not only created a primer for presidential involvement in the legislative branch, he also increased expectations of the presidency, in particular as "problem solver in chief."

How did Roosevelt do this? He set the agenda, crafted legislation, and got Congress to pass his legislation with little debate. For example, he reshaped the federal–state landscape and the concept of interstate commerce in only one hundred days. He began with the banks; FDR called Congress into special session and declared a national bank holiday. While the banks were closed, FDR offered a bill to Congress which extended government assistance to private bankers to reopen their banks (which actually validated actions the president had already taken, as it gave him complete control over gold movements, penalized hoarding, authorized new Federal Reserve bank notes and arranged for the reopening of liquid banks and reorganized the rest). The House passed the bill sight unseen after thirty-eight minutes of debate. The Senate approved it, slightly amended, 73–7 that same night, and by 8:30 that evening the President had signed the bill into law. Three days later the president gave his first fireside chat to explain to the people that it was now safe to return their savings to the banks. People were then eager to deposit their money rather than withdraw it, as the people trusted FDR's leadership.

Fourteen other pieces of legislation similarly passed, covering not only banking, but putting the unemployed to work, refinancing mortgages, and creating dams as a source of cheap hydro-electric power, to name a few. Industrialists and some members of Congress, who believed the president was going too far, had some impact on the course of the debate, but little on the outcome. When Congress adjourned on June 16, 1933, one hundred days after the special session opened, it had written a series of unprecedented legislation. FDR sent fifteen messages to Capitol Hill and fifteen measures went through to final passage (including two constitutional amendments).[21] The Congress, under the leadership of FDR, committed the country to government and industry cooperation, promised to distribute tremendous sums of money to staple farmers, experimented in regional planning, pledged billions to save homeowners from foreclosure, and provided for huge public works spending.

In the one-hundred-day special session of Congress, Roosevelt achieved extraordinary leadership over Congress and over the crisis. He not only calmed a nation, but also restored a nation's trust in government and trust in core institutions. Roosevelt's success was directly related to his personal persuasive skills (by telling Congress and the nation that "this was the right thing to do"), his party's dominant majority in the House and Senate, as well as his support from the public. In contrast to other presidents and other periods of leadership, Roosevelt successfully bequeathed his approach to leading congress, but also the expectations derived from his success, to his successors.

SHARING POWERS

It can be argued that the most important legacy of the FDR administration was the creation of the modern presidency. FDR designed a pathway out of crisis, and expanded the scope of the presidency by revealing power in the silences created by the Constitution. Even without an epic crisis like the Great Depression, modern presidents have adopted FDR's tactics. The modern president campaigns on an agenda, which requires an active or assertive president. The modern president attempts to lead Congress to produce legislation that advances the presidential agenda. The modern president employs an expanded institutional structure to provide advantage in the exercise of leadership. And, the modern president rests his leadership on support from the public.

The subsequent administrations, which followed FDR's prescriptions for presidential power in the legislative arena, could not hope to achieve FDR's legislative success. Fifteen major bills to fifteen laws in one hundred days is unparalleled. In the absence of a crisis to produce an acquiescent Congress, legislative success for the president is much less certain; it reflects the institutional differences between the branches and also varies with individual skill. One must also consider the institutional effects on the legislative agenda. The Constitution, as many scholars note, separates legislative power. The bulk of the legislative authority goes to the deliberative body, which is Congress. The framers were very careful to delineate both expressed and implied powers to the legislative branch, while leaving the day-to-day structure and design to the current Congress. Consequently, the evolution of the House and Senate occurred in expected and unexpected ways, creating institutional norms that influence presidential–congressional relations greatly. Not only do Congress and the president draw power from diverse constituencies, they have dissimilar decision-making structures and relate differently to political parties and ideology.

Divergent Constituencies

Every four years, on the first Tuesday in November, the entire country chooses a president from the same set of individuals. Consequently, the president's electoral constituency consists of voters from around the country. Yet, this electoral constituency is not evenly distributed across the population. The geographic boundaries of the presidential district may be the nation, but not everyone participates. Moreover, population is not evenly distributed, nor are voting patterns. In 2000, Vice President Al Gore received more popular votes than then-Governor George W. Bush by winning population centers like New York City and Los Angeles. Bush won the presidency, however, by winning Electoral College votes in more states, despite those states having smaller populations and thus fewer voters. A president takes office constitutionally mandated to represent the entire nation, but he achieves that victory through the votes of between 40 and 65 percent of the eligible voting population.[22]

In contrast, the only thing national in congressional elections is the date. Senators represent their states, while House members represent their population-determined districts. Although a percentage of Congress members' districts may vote for the president, the electoral coalitions of Congress members and the president are distinctive. More specifically, the factors that engender voting decisions in congressional races might not produce the same outcome in presidential elections. Moreover, congressional districts are not mini-nations, in terms of geography, ethnicity, race, or class. Thus, by definition, presidents and members of Congress represent different constituencies.

When considering representation actively, the president and members of Congress are different in this regard as well. Political Scientist Richard Fenno argues that a member of Congress views his constituency as a series of concentric circles in which the furthest circle, the geographic district encompassed the broadest view of constituency, those individuals the member is obligated to represent.[23] The smallest circle contains friends, family members, and trusted advisors. As the circles decrease in size, the importance to the member increases. Fenno argues that the relative importance of sectors of the district predictably determine resource allocation, notably the Congress member's time and attention. Congressional constituency behavior creates a chicken-and-egg relationship; members of Congress devote time, attention, and voting choices to constituents who are attentive via time, donations, and activity in the district. Individuals who reside in a district but vote for someone else (or do not vote at all) receive much less targeted attention and representation through congressional behavior.

Unlike the president, Congress reflects the nation and represents the nation through aggregation or accumulation. Each member of Congress represents his or her individual district, yet the institution reflects the totality of all members of Congress representing their districts and states. Thus, the Madisonian design sums individual or district-based representation to produce national outcomes. The two institutions, however, are not entirely dissimilar, despite their different constituencies, as the behavior toward the constituency is more alike than not. Given that in recent elections only slightly more than 50 percent of the voting population has participated, the modern president might claim to be actively representing the entirety of the nation, but his agenda typically represents his electoral constituency. Analysis of presidential rhetoric indicates that presidents "craft their talk" for their supporters and not for the average, or median, American voter. Political Scientist B. Dan Wood argues that presidents ignore mass preferences in favor of strategies designed to persuade "those near the political center to move toward... [the president's] own positions."[24]

Presidents can and often do speak for the nation. However, when pressing their policy agendas in Congress, presidents confront the natural outcome of different institutional designs. From multiple perspectives of constituency, presidents and Congress members represent different voices in the political sphere. Thus, the president's ability to influence legislation must account for the interaction between individuals representing different subsets of the national audience.

THE DECISION-MAKING PROCESS

As President Harry Truman famously said about the decision-making process as president, "The buck stops here." President George W. Bush clarified Truman, noting, "I am the decider." What these two presidents asserted, and all presidents know immediately upon taking office, is that presidents must make choices and they alone bear the responsibility of those choices. The choices and decisions a president must make range from deploying troops, to issuing an executive order, to making an address to the nation regarding a policy preference. As Chapter 8 explores, there is an enormous array of people working to advise the president in the White House and in the Executive Branch. But the final say always remains the president's.

Life functions much differently in Congress. Individual members of Congress do not issue orders, speak to the nation, or deploy troops. Collectively, they do declare war, create legislation, allocate money, and even impeach presidents and members of the judicial branch. Individual members of Congress illustrate their decision making through voting; the final outcome on policy stems from the policy preferences expressed via voting by the majority. For any bill to turn into legislation, the bill must maneuver through the modern congressional system, replete with committees and subcommittees, rules and procedures, some traditional, some unorthodox.[25] From bill introduction, to committee, to subcommittee, back to committee, to the floor of the chamber, to the other chamber, to its committee, to its subcommittee, back to committee, to the floor of the chamber, to conference committee, and finally back to floors of both chambers, there are myriad opportunities for a bill to die. At no point does a single individual control the outcome of anything; even the Speaker of the House, arguably the second most powerful individual in government and second in succession to the presidency, can be stymied by even his or her own majority.

Political Parties

For the president, the political party is an army. These are the troops employed to get out the vote, and to get his message out during campaigns. Once in office, party insiders often assist the president by doing media appearances, where they argue in support of the president's policies. For the president, the party also represents an ideological connection. Voters, donors, volunteers, and other elites affiliate with a particular party for the advancement of ideological goals. The presidency represents the ultimate megaphone for the party's policies, ideologies, and plans for government and for the country.

The party in Congress is more than an identifying ideology and connection with supporters. The political parties also organize the institution; whichever party wins more individual seats determines the rules and assignments within the chamber due to their superior numbers. If all members of the party with the most members in office stick together and vote together, then they determine who is Speaker, who gets committee assignments, who gets committee chairs, and who sits on the Rules Committee in the House. Party discipline and loyalty are especially critical to the functioning of the House of Representatives as they serve to manage the 435 members. These opportunities emerge from majority voting power created by caucusing outside the chamber.

When the president interacts with Congress, the president is in an odd position, as he is both leader of his party and leader of a separate institution with separate institutional demands and goals. This dynamic is most evident when comparing unified and divided government. When one party controls the presidency, the House, and the Senate, a common ideology seemingly unifies policymaking that makes sweeping policy change possible. As political scientists William Lammers and Michael Genovese note, incidents of major or "landmark" legislation occur more frequently than when government is divided between the parties, because the process is more efficient and responsive.[26] Examples of sweeping legislation during a time of unified government include the passage of FDR's New Deal legislation during his first term, and Lyndon Johnson's passage of the Civil Rights Act in 1964, the Voting Rights Act and Medicare in 1965, as well as other Great Society policy changes. Johnson took great pride in his legislative success; the former Senate Majority Leader, known as the Master of the Senate, often kept a legislative scorecard in his coat pocket to readily quote his successes on Capitol Hill. Johnson was perhaps one of the best contemporary presidents in dealing with Congress due to his vast knowledge of the institution; he had served twelve years in the House of Representatives and twelve years in the Senate before being elected Vice President in 1960. The scope of Johnson's legislative agenda, and his strategy in achieving it, is seen in this memo on the administration's legislative program from 1964:

> The following legislative issues should have priority in immediate preparation of materials to be used to support the successful enactment of Administration-sponsored measures pending before the present Congress.
>
> 1. Poverty 2. Foreign Aid 3. Housing 4. Appalachian Bill 5. Mass Transit 6. Transportation Bill 7. ARA 8. Food Stamp 9. Pay Raise 10. Public Debt 11. Medicare 12. Food for Peace 13. Hill-Burton 14. Wilderness Bill 15. Marketing Committee Investigation 16. Civil Rights
>
> On these, we need to establish (a) the need for the legislation, (b) the history of the issue and the legislation, (c) broad context of relationships of each issue to the overall Administration program and National need, (d) the pertinent quotations from the President and from both Democratic and Republican leaders, currently and in some instances historically.[27]

However, not everyone views the ability of unified government to pass major changes to public policy as a positive thing. In fact, the framers, who were generally fearful of factions and the ability for popular support to take over public policies, made gridlock a prominent feature of the American government through separation of powers and checks and balances. As a result, the government created by the framers is one of incrementalism, which tends to avoid the type of sweeping reforms to government policies that can be destabilizing to the government itself. Under this view, divided government can be seen as a stabilizing force, since incremental or transactional change is more likely than transformational change as the disparate sides are forced to compromise to get anything done. In theory, the requirement for compromise between the parties makes episodes of gridlock much more likely during times of divided government. For example, one of the most significant pieces of legislation signed into law by Bill Clinton came in 1996; he achieved his promise to reform "welfare as we know it" with passage of the Personal Responsibility and Work Opportunity Act by working with a Republican Congress. Two years earlier, he had failed to pass several key issues of his domestic agenda, including health-care reform, working with a Democratic Congress. It is important to note, however, that Clinton's political skill played a role in passing welfare reform as well. Relying on the now-famous Clinton strategy of "triangulation," Clinton, a moderate Democrat, put together his version of welfare reform by co-opting some of the most popular aspects of both Republican and Democratic plans. By taking a little from the left and a little from the right, and bringing it together in the middle (to form the triangle), Clinton's strategy provided just enough incentive for support on both sides of the political aisle to pass the legislation.

However, Clinton's legislative success with the Republican Congress serves as more of an exception rather than the rule. The individual political skill of the president, as well as factors that contribute to the political environment (such as the economy, or the public mood on a particular issue), can determine whether or not bipartisanship is possible. Gridlock relates significantly to the intensity of partisanship, high intensity, or hyperpartisanship, which makes compromise and negotiation much less likely as positions and sides harden. This is an important point, since divided government has occurred with regularity since 1832 after reforms to the Electoral College moved the nomination of presidential candidates from congressional caucuses to party conventions. Since then, through the 2010 election, Americans have elected a divided government more than 40 percent of the time. Since 1932, of the forty congressional elections held (which also encompass twenty-one presidential elections), unified government has only occurred nineteen times (see Table 6.2).

Table 6.2 Party Government

YEAR	PRESIDENT	HOUSE	SENATE	U/D
1933–1945	F. Roosevelt (D)	D	D	Unified
		D	D	Unified
		D	D	Unified
		D	D	Unified
		D	D	Unified
		D	D	Unified
1945–1952	Truman (D)	D	D	Unified
		R	R	Divided
		D	D	Unified
		D	D	Unified
1953–1959	Eisenhower (R)	R	R	Unified
		D	D	Divided
		D	D	Divided
		D	D	Divided
1961–1963	Kennedy (D)	D	D	Unified
1963–1967	Johnson (D)	D	D	Unified
		D	D	Unified
		D	D	Unified

(continued)

Table 6.2 ***(continued)***

YEAR	PRESIDENT	HOUSE	SENATE	U/D
1969–1973	Nixon (R)	D	D	Divided
		D	D	Divided
1973–1976	Nixon/Ford (R)	D	D	Divided
		D	D	Divided
1977–1980	Carter (D)	D	D	Unified
		D	D	Unified
1981–1987	Reagan (R)	D	R	Divided—House
		D	R	Divided—House
		D	R	Divided—House
		D	D	Divided
1989–1992	G. H. W. Bush (R)	D	D	Divided
		D	D	Divided
1993–2000	Clinton (D)	D	D	Unified
		R	R	Divided
		R	R	Divided
		R	R	Divided
2001–2008	G. W. Bush (R)	R	D	Divided—Senate
		R	R	Unified
		D	D	Divided
2009–present	Obama (D)	D	D	Unified
		R	D	Divided—House
		R	D	Divided—House

Individual Behavior

The institutional differences between the executive and legislative branches are powerful forces, which enhance the constitutional system of checks and balances. Legislation is easiest to pass when all actors are of the same political persuasion, yet even then the labyrinthine process makes no legislative outcome easy. Moreover, although both branches seek to be representative, the power of their connection to constituents stems from different sources, creating different pressures on office holders. However, the institutional push and pull of the constitutional design does not entirely explain the president's role in the process. Despite lacking constitutional tools, the president has an array of individual options, opportunities, and choices when engaging in the legislative process.

As noted earlier, the Constitution provides the president with a role in the beginning of the legislative process and at the end. Presidents can recommend or even request legislation they want, and they can veto legislation they do not want to see become law. If, as the saying goes, "the devil is in the details," then the Constitution formally keeps the president out of the critical period where Congress actually constructs legislation. Informally, however, the constitutional bookends actually grant the president a role throughout the process. However, the president's ability to influence the specifics of legislation as well as the outcome relates much more to individual skill than to the institutional capacity of the office.

As discussed in Chapter 1, the view of the president as a strategic actor in the legislative process originates with Political Scientist Richard Neustadt, who argued that the "power to persuade is the power to bargain. Status and authority yield bargaining advantages."[28] The president is the preeminent status holder in the corridors of power in Washington, D.C.— and around the world, for that matter. However, the Constitution grants Congress more authority than it grants the president in the legislative arena. Thus, Neustadt argued, "in a government of separate institutions sharing powers," Congress too has power and an array of counter pressures to what the president brings to the table." Consequently, "command has limited utility; persuasion becomes give-and-take." For Neustadt, the essence of presidential leadership is persuasion, and specifically, the convincing of individuals "that what the White House wants of them is what they ought to do for their sake and on their authority."[29]

When creating legislation, presidential persuasion targets members of Congress in multiple ways. First, a member of Congress must be persuaded to sponsor the president's preferred version of the bill on which the president seeks action. Second, the president must persuade individual committee members that the president's preferred language must shape the bill. Here, the president's prestige, to use Neustadt's terms, elevates the president's request, but even so, Congress members routinely receive similar persuasive attempts from constituents as well as from interest groups. The president must then persuade individual committee members to vote for the bill in committee and then persuade a majority of the chamber to vote for the bill as well.

Despite framing presidential power in terms of individual interactions, the president is not speaking individually to 535 members of Congress. Nor does the president have to speak with all members of Congress. From the first day of each congressional term, the president knows the level of difficulty he will face when seeking passage of his agenda. The institutional norms of Congress determine the president's strategic actions, and the majority/minority status of his party enormously shapes his opportunities to exercise a Neustadtian style of influence.

Bargaining within

A president facing unified government will likely be negotiating the details with his own party, primarily. While the president's own party shares the president's larger goals, the details can result in painful intraparty battles. In 2002, President George W. Bush, buoyed by both a Republican Congress and soaring post-9/11 approval ratings, attempted to tackle an entitlement program, often the most legislatively contentious type of program, since programs that offer benefits and services have both vociferous defenders and detractors. Bush wanted to add a prescription drug component to Medicare. Since the 1990s, the rising costs of prescription drugs moved coverage of the drugs for the elderly to the top of the agenda. The issue had supporters on both sides, as liberals desired an expansion of Medicare toward more universal coverage, while conservatives wanted to control costs.

From the initial proposal in the State of the Union, Congress and the President were at odds, despite Republican control of Congress. The Bush plan, which required seniors to abandon the traditional form of Medicare in order to receive the new benefit, "raised a storm of protest...from Republicans and Democrats."[30] The Bush White House designed their plan behind closed doors with little input or sharing with congressional Republicans. Republicans went so far as to call Tommy Thompson, Secretary of Health and Human Services, to testify about the president's plan. However, the White House still refused to release details. Despite lacking any details beyond the President's initial outline in the State of the Union, more and more individuals, groups, and actors in the system, stepped in to pressure Congress to resist the idea of requiring seniors to join a private plan. When the President finally released his plan, the requirement was not a part of it, as Congress had pressured the President to change his plan. However, the Bush White House still set up a two-tiered system where those in a private plan received better benefits than those in traditional Medicare.[31] With the release of the President's proposal, the Republican-led Congress went to work, grumbling about the President's offering, which was likely to cause trouble for Congress members with their politically active, elderly constituents.

Given the close split between the parties in the Senate at the time, the Republicans could not legislate with impunity and were forced to compromise with Senate Democrats. Consequently, they produced a bi-partisan solution, which rejected President Bush's preferred option regarding the different levels of coverage, but they did allow for private coverage. The White House signaled through the media their willingness to accept the compromised Grassley–Baucus bill. In the House, the wrangling in committee between Republicans and Democrats was more contentious, as the Republican plan was more in line with the Bush proposal.

The response to the Bush Prescription Drug proposal in committee and then on the floors of both the House and Senate demonstrates how the president's goals and agenda only go so far, as individual pressure on members of Congress does not necessarily triumph over congressional pressures. In the Senate, the bill passed 76 to 21, in true compromise fashion, as forty Republicans and thirty-five Democrats joined together. However, Bush lost ten members of his own party on a bill that was important to him and his overall agenda.

Aware that the outcome of the bill was in jeopardy, the White House sent Vice President Dick Cheney to lobby those Republican House members on the fence. In the House, the situation was much more complicated, as they must first vote on the rules for debate, generated by the Rules Committee, and then vote on the bill. The Committee, governed by the Republican majority, opted for a modified closed rule that would limit the number and type of amendments that could be offered.[32] The division over the rule would signal the division over the bill; it passed but with four Republican defections. Between the vote on the rule and the vote on the bill, the House leadership (but not the President) leaned on the Republicans who had voted "nay" earlier. The outcome was precarious; the allotted time for the vote had to be extended from 15 minutes to an hour. The result: 216–215, with nineteen Republicans rejecting the House's version of the President's proposal.[33]

The process does not end with the two chamber votes; the bill must be reconciled, as the president can only receive one bill to sign. The House and the Senate passed two different bills, so they must produce a compromise which the chambers must also pass. President Bush met with the entire conference, made up of selected members of the House and Senate, to encourage a swift resolution. However, during July and August, the conference was driven largely by congressional behavior and activity, particularly lobbying by constituents and large groups hoping to influence the outcome. Months went by, and little to no progress was made, primarily in terms of the divisions between Republicans. Finally, they passed a compromise with little White House input, which Democrats and conservative Republicans both despised. Yet, the conference had won the sanction of the American Association of Retired Persons (AARP), a critical ally as it is the largest and one of the most influential interest groups in the nation. However, both chambers still needed to pass the conference bill, five months after the passage of the House and Senate versions.

At this stage, President Bush weighed in heavily, using all the powers Neustadt articulated in terms of bargaining and persuasion. Bush telephoned many members of the Republican caucus personally. The vote in the House, after the pressure from the President and the House leadership, was 220–215. The Senate vote was more contentious this second time, as the compromise moved the bill away from the original Senate bill. Moreover, the President had an enormous critic in Senator Ted Kennedy (D-MA), who went so far as to signal a filibuster (the procedure by which one senator can bring legislative action in the Senate to a halt by talking a bill to death). Here, too, a rules debate took place, and the Republicans had to scramble to come up with enough votes to bring the bill to the floor. The final Senate vote was 54–44; nine Republicans voted against the bill, and only eleven Democrats voted for passage.[34]

The bill signing ceremony reflected the importance the President accorded the passage of the Prescription Drug program. Two thousand invitees watched the President sign the bill alongside mostly Republican members of Congress. The President did not get exactly what he had wanted, namely the private system, but he did ultimately achieve more privatization of the Medicare system than had existed before. Bush, at various points in the process, expended significant presidential capital, relying on his prestige and position to induce voting in support of the bill. However, this bill process also demonstrates that even with unified government, the president is limited in terms of how much alteration to the congressional process a president can generate via individual bargaining and persuasion.

Bargaining across and within party

In divided government, the president faces two chambers of Congress controlled entirely or partially by the other party. As a result, from day one, the president faces considerably more difficulty for the passage of his agenda. Under unified government, the president and the congressional leadership work in tandem to keep a majority together. However, in divided government, the majority party wants something different from the president even if they share the same desire to tackle the issues on the president's agenda. In divided government, the president needs to persuade his party to remain united with him, all the while working to compromise to bring the other party closer to the president's preferred point of view. It is a delicate balancing act fraught with danger, as compromise with one side creates contentiousness with the other side.

Vice President George H. W. Bush took the presidential oath in 1989 with a big victory after a negative campaign over Massachusetts Governor, Democrat Michael Dukakis. One of the central issues that Bush highlighted during the campaign was the environment; one particular negative ad focused on the need to clean up the Boston Harbor (in Dukakis' hometown). The ad showed Bush standing in a boat in the Boston Harbor declaring: "Two hundred years ago, tea was spilled into this harbor in the name of liberty, now it's something else. We've got to do better." In keeping with the legislative role accepted by both Congress and the president, Bush translated his campaign agenda to his presidential agenda and focused immediately on the environment, specifically air pollution.

The Clean Air Act, originally passed in 1963, was significantly strengthened in 1970. However, during the 1980s, the Democratic House and President Ronald Reagan were gridlocked on opposing sides regarding increased regulation. Moreover, through strategic appointments, the Reagan White House actively worked to undermine the existing legislation. With the election of Bush, whom many called the "environmental president," the Democratic Congress faced a potential ally rather than the veto pen of Reagan, even though ideological and institutional differences abounded. Nonetheless, Bush seized the momentum of his inauguration to inform Congress in his first address to them about his plans for the environment:

> If we're to protect our future, we need a new attitude about the environment. We must protect the air we breathe. I will send to you shortly legislation for a new, more effective Clean Air Act. It will include a plan to reduce by date certain the emissions which cause acid rain, because the time for study alone has passed, and the time for action is now. We must make use of clean coal. My budget contains full funding, on schedule, for the clean coal technology agreement that we've made with Canada. We've made that agreement with Canada, and we intend to honor that agreement. We must not neglect our parks. So, I'm asking to fund new acquisitions under the Land and Water Conservation Fund. We must protect our oceans. And I support new penalties against those who would dump medical waste and other trash into our oceans. The age of the needle on the beaches must end. And in some cases, the gulfs and oceans off our shores hold the promise of oil and gas reserves which can make our nation more secure and less dependent on foreign oil. And when those with the most promise can be tapped safely, as with much of the Alaska National Wildlife Refuge, we should proceed. But we must use caution; we must respect the environment. And so, tonight I'm calling for the indefinite postponement of three lease sales which have raised troubling questions, two off the coast of California and one which could threaten the Everglades in Florida. Action on these three lease sales will await the conclusion of a special task force set up to measure the potential for environmental damage. I'm directing the Attorney General and the Administrator of the Environmental Protection Agency to use every tool at their disposal to speed and toughen the enforcement of our laws against toxic-waste dumpers. I want faster cleanups and tougher enforcement of penalties against polluters.[35]

This was a loud signal that there was a new president in office focused on this issue. Moreover, the Bush White House made a strategic decision to work with the career bureaucrats who staffed the Environmental Protection Agency (EPA) rather than stifle them, like the Reagan White House had. As a result, Bush's sincerity and willingness to produce a good faith proposal gained credibility with the Democratic Congress. Bush made a second key strategic decision for dealing with Congress by creating a small policy group of White House staffers and EPA members who worked quickly and in secret. Consequently, "the proposal they finally produced... packed a wallop. Over time, with secrecy, expertise and wide latitude, the [Bush team]... came to write the first draft of the far-reaching and ambitious overhaul of the nation's Clean Air Act."[36]

The new White House spent its first six months on the environment behind closed doors forging a united front between the White House and the EPA. Bush released the details of his proposal with a big announcement before a large audience, signaling the importance of the proposal. Reaction to the proposal was mixed given the battle lines drawn down the center of Bush's own party. Not only would Bush need to negotiate with the Democrats, but many members of Bush's own party patently rejected the increased regulation and enforcement for business, particularly the automakers and energy producers.

Negotiating with Congressional Democrats would prove tough for Bush as he entered office; as the previous Vice President, many in Washington believed they were familiar with him and understood who Bush was politically. Unfortunately for Bush, the image that most Democrats had of him was as a weak leader. Therefore, not only did Bush not have the advantage of being unknown, he also faced an assertive Democratic Congress. If the Democrats could work together, then Bush was less likely to achieve his version of the legislation. Vetoing a proposal which he initiated and campaigned on would be an enormous failure. Moreover, environmental policy was the cornerstone of a limited domestic agenda for the President, who seemed more focused on the international issues such as the collapse of communism in Eastern Europe and the Soviet Union. Interestingly, rivalries and conflicts within the Democratic majority produced a three-way negotiation of equals between the Senate and House Democratic leadership and the White House. Bush had only limited help from the Republicans in the Senate as Minority Leader Robert Dole, fresh from his loss to Bush in the Republican nomination of 1988, was not helping the President achieve his top priority.[37] Bush benefitted by adopting an agenda item that dovetailed with the Democrats, particularly Senate Majority Leader George Mitchell. On other issues, Bush did not fare as well as Mitchell was "singlehandedly preventing enactment of the presidents' chief economic initiative, a cut in the tax rate on capital gains."[38]

The presence of divided government brings into play a negotiating tool not as easily available when negotiating with one's own party—the veto. During the Clean Air vote in the Senate, the veto became a dramatic game of brinkmanship. An important amendment was offered on the floor by Senator Robert Byrd (D-WV), in defense of his coal mining constituency. The White House was leery of Byrd and his ability to kill the Clean Air reforms. One of the senators being pulled in different directions was Joe Biden (D-DE). In the middle of the voice vote, Biden received a call from White House Chief of Staff John Sununu, "who told Biden point blank that passage of Byrd's amendment would guarantee a Bush veto of the clean-air bill."[39] The final bill passed the Senate 50–49, without the Byrd amendment and with Biden's support.

Even when faced with an aggressive, active Congress, there remains opportunity to engage in Neustadtian leadership—personal leadership of persuasion and bargaining. However, the opportunities of success are much more dependent on the power which comes from actual constitutional tools, like agenda setting via the campaign and bill proposal, as well as with veto threats. Moreover, as both united and divided government reveal, when attempting to employ personal leadership presidents must accept and work within the limitations imposed by the institutional design and nature of the first branch of government.

Going public

Since FDR, expectations of the president increased exponentially but without a vast increase in official, constitutional powers. Consequently, presidents are in the awkward position of being judged on outcomes that they are unable to control. FDR altered the dynamic of understanding the presidency by revealing alternate means to influence the outcome via non-constitutional tools. Central to the extra-institutional premise is Neustadt's power of persuasion, which is the power to get someone else to do what you want them to do, *on their authority*. A skillful president will succeed by virtue of the bargained outcome. Neustadt's argument only narrowly includes the institutional realities under which members of Congress receive presidential persuasive efforts, and thus only explains a narrow portion of presidential behavior or the outcomes of the presidential agenda.

The main institutional feature which is left out of Neustadt's argument is the influence of a member of Congress's constituency. As political scientist David Mayhew noted, an electoral connection exists between members of Congress and those they represent. Mayhew, along with Richard Fenno, noted the increased time and energy members of Congress and their staffs devote to serving the needs of their constituents. Mayhew argued that Congress reallocated their time between Washington and their districts and increased staff in their district due to electoral pressures.[40] The need to be reelected in fact drives most members of Congress' decision making; after all, you cannot accomplish anything in Congress if you are not reelected. It is easy to dismiss the attention that members devote to their districts, but this has become a core component of representation. Every decision made by members of Congress must include the electoral reality check—will this help me or hurt me during my next campaign? Senators have the luxury of time; their next campaign could be up to six years away, while House members by contrast are always thinking about reelection as their elections are every two years.

While party affiliation, personal ideology, and what is good for the country matter, the needs of constituents within the congressional district often take precedence for members of Congress, as elections are always looming. This factors significantly into the exercise of Neustadtian leadership. When the president wants something from a member of Congress, which might result in trouble back home, the member is between a rock and a hard place and will often choose the district over the president.

FDR, however, demonstrated that there is another tool in the extraconstitutional tool box which presidents can employ to affect congressional decision making: the public. A new form of leadership emerged when FDR used his fireside chats to calm fears and encourage the public to put their money back into the banks. The president, by virtue of his relationships with the media and the public, has another way to influence members of Congress. The influence stemming from the connection between the president and the public is not individual the way Neustadtian leadership is. Political scientist Samuel Kernell argues that using the relationship with the public is a form of leadership itself. Kernell identified a pattern: The president influences the public through a televised speech, the public responds, and the public then pressures their member of Congress to support the president's preferred option.[41]

The leadership method uses what belongs to the president exclusively (i.e., a national platform) to try to affect congressional decision making by attacking the electoral connection between voters and members of congress. In 1981, Ronald Reagan certified this new style of leadership. Reagan's personal popularity coupled with support for his ideals (i.e., increased defense spending, lower taxes, eliminating waste) created an opportunity and advantage, which the president and his advisors seized. Reagan wanted a budget reflecting his priorities and also wanted tax cuts. He illustrated his plan in several speeches to the nation but initially engaged in traditional Neustadtian bargaining with the opposition party. The Democratic majority hacked away at the president's budget proposals and tax cuts. Reagan resisted these changes, rejecting congressional options time and time again. The Speaker of the House, Tip O'Neill, said in a nationally televised interview, "if the vote were tomorrow we could win it. Right now we have the votes. Can he take them away from us? Let's wait and see."[42]

President Reagan rose to O'Neill's challenge in devastating fashion. In order to change those votes, the president undertook a public strategy. Two days before the crucial floor vote in the House, the president gave a nationally televised speech. In the speech, Reagan again argued for his preferred option. However, in this speech, the president inserted a new leadership approach, a new tactic in the struggle with Congress. The president used his representative relationship as a lever against Congress' relationship with the public:

> I ask you now to put aside any feelings of frustration or helplessness about our political institutions and join me in this dramatic but responsible plan to reduce the enormous burden of Federal taxation on you and your family. During recent months many of you have asked what can you do to help make America strong again. I urge you again to contact your Senators and Congressmen. Tell them of your support for this bipartisan proposal. Tell them you believe this is an unequalled opportunity to help return America to prosperity and make government again the servant of the people.[43]

The reaction from the public and from lawmakers was swift and certain. Citizens' calls in support of the president's plan inundated members of Congress with millions more letters and calls than normal.[44] The president won, not by bargaining and persuasion, but by going over the heads of Congress to force compliance from their own constituents.

The identification of going public as a leadership style highlights multiple changes in presidential behavior since the FDR administration. In particular, Kernell drew attention to the abandonment of insider strategies for outsider strategies. The change in tactics directly relates to the changing demands on the individual president as well as the institution of the presidency. With the increasing expectations of FDR-like achievements, the president needed more leverage over Congress. Simultaneously, the president became the focal point of an increasingly news-hungry media, driven by the growth of television news in the twentieth century. Radio, then television, and then the Internet granted the president the tools to reach a national audience, who could in turn influence Congress.

Presidential behavior appeared to anoint "going public" as the preferred means for achieving legislative success in Congress. Since FDR, the number of speeches given by a president increased exponentially. Whether big speeches, little speeches, interviews, or other public appearances, presidents speak constantly about their issues and their agendas.[45] Yet, the increase of rhetoric in the public sphere did not lead to continuous presidential success in Congress. Several factors influence the power of going public. First, presidents must be able to reach a sizeable enough audience to pressure enough members of Congress to support the president's choice. With the abundance of media outlets, it seems odd that the president might not be able to reach a sizeable audience. In the days of the big three networks, it was easy for a president to be confident that a televised speech would reach a large percentage of Americans. However, once cable multiplied the number of channels available to a viewer, the audience watching major presidential addresses declined.[46] The Internet only intensified the fragmentation of the presidential audience.

Not only is it now more difficult for presidents to find an audience, but presidents are less likely to change a significant portion of the electorate's mind on an issue. The Reagan budget experience, where millions were motivated to contact their Congress member, rarely happens. Interestingly, recent presidents are relatively unlikely even to ask citizens to contact Congress.[47] A recent example, however, is Barack Obama's address to the nation on July 25, 2011, when he spoke to Americans about the need for Congress to raise the debt ceiling and urged citizens to contact their members of Congress about the issue. It is so unlikely that citizens contact government that scholars typically rely on public opinion polls to demonstrate citizen approval and support rather than actual examples of support.

Relying on polls introduces a different dynamic to the "going public" style of leadership. It is easy to measure the effect of a presidential speech (simply measure approval before and after the speech), but it is actually quite difficult to move public opinion significantly.[48] If the president through the force of his message or the skill of his rhetoric actually manages to shift opinion in his favor, there is still the issue of whether that matters to Congress. Opinion polls are national measures of a national figure. Local voters and local influences determine members of Congress' fortunes, thus national polls only matter "at the margins."[49] What truly limits the power of going public is the simple fact that a president cannot use it all of the time, or even some of the time. Congress deals with too many issues for the president to call on the public every single time he wants to affect an outcome. However, when a president does choose to use public leadership for a particular legislative outcome, he is likely to be successful.[50]

Veto Politics

At the heart of both bargaining and going public is the presidential veto. There are two types of public veto threats: the line in the sand and the signal.[51] Ronald Reagan, speaking to the American Business Conference, famously issued the line-in-the-sand type:

> The scene in the Senate Budget Committee this past week was a disappointing one, I think, for the American people. They seem to be in full-scale retreat from spending cuts and are talking about raising people's taxes again. When push comes to shove, I guess it's always easier to let the taxpayer take the fall. Well, let them be forewarned: No matter how well intentioned they might be, no matter what their illusions might be, I have my veto pen drawn and ready for any tax increase that Congress might even think of sending up. And I have only one thing to say to the tax increasers: Go ahead, make my day.[52]

Bill Clinton illustrated the other form of veto threat, signaling a willingness to negotiate and avoid a bad outcome:

> We should not destroy the foreign aid budget. But, furthermore, we should not handcuff the President. That is not the way to conduct the foreign affairs of this country. You cannot micromanage foreign policy.... If this bill passes in its present form, I will veto it.[53]

The line-in-the-sand veto threats do not occur all that often, but when they do, they usually are rather dramatic and often remembered. From Reagan's "make my day" comment, to George H. W. Bush's promise, "read my lips, no new taxes," explicit veto threats are not the norm. Instead, the signaling type of veto—I will veto it *in the present form*—are used more frequently and often with more success for influencing the passage of legislation.[54] However, vetoes do not always have to be public, as private veto threats in the course of bargaining can also be quite effective for achieving concessions in private bargaining with Congress.[55]

CONCLUSION

The president's role in the legislative process is both guaranteed and limited by the Constitution. However, the degree to which the president can influence legislative outcomes rests on circumstances that are typically in flux. Moreover, institutional conditions combine with the personal skill set of the president in unexpected ways. Does the president's party control all or part of the Congress? Unified government often makes it easier for a president to accomplish his goals, but not always. Does the president keep his word when he makes deals or draws lines in the sand? Presidential behavior in public and behind the scenes can have powerful effects during negotiations with Congress.

The president's success in achieving his legislative agenda is also influenced by circumstances, events and individuals outside the legislative process. A large electoral victory can provide the president with momentum and a mandate for his agenda. A popular president has more sway with Congress, because it is likely that a majority of congressional constituents like the president. Ultimately, the president's role in the legislative process is emblematic of the modern presidency. The president remains limited by narrowly proscribed responsibilities (the veto, the state of the union) yet challenged by increased expectations as problem solver in chief. The ability to meet those expectations rest on factors that can be both opportunities as well as obstacles.

BUDGET SHOWDOWNS AND SHUTDOWNS

THEN . . .

The central task of the Congress in the constitutional system is to write laws. Of those laws, the most significant and often contentious are the authorization and appropriation for the budget of the U.S. government. Everything the government does requires money. Congress creates laws to acquire that money via taxes, fees, interest on bonds, etc. In an entirely separate process, which begins with the president's proposed budget, the Congress writes laws to spend federal money. The money the U.S. government collects is spent on everything from its own functioning to esoteric pieces of pork. For example, to run the White House in 2010, Congress authorized "For the care, maintenance, repair and alteration, refurnishing, improvement, heating, and lighting, including electric power and fixtures, of the Executive Residence at the White House and official entertainment expenses of the President, $14,006,000." According to President Obama's budget, they spent $13,838,000.[56]

Since lawmaking and appropriating are separate processes, and are negotiated under entirely different circumstances, setting the budget for a given fiscal year is often a battle. In times of plenty, when the government runs a budget surplus, as it did from 1998 to 2001, lawmakers luxuriate in the ability to increase budgets or at least not cut them. In these rare periods, the arguments between the president and Congress soften as disagreements focus on choices. In times where the government takes in less money than it needs to pay all its bills, the process of creating a fiscal-year budget exposes the different priorities between the president and Congress as well as the differences between the two parties. In down economic years, battles often emerge between those who would run a deficit and those who insist the federal government must balance its books. Running a deficit is a lot like having a credit card, since the bills get paid but cost more as government pays interest on the money it borrows. As with any big purchase for an individual, whether a new computer, car, or house, one chooses to save the money first or use credit and pay it back later. Deficit hawks decry the "pay it off later" approach. Consequently, difficult economic times create budget showdowns over whether to fund the programs authorized. Occasionally these tensions boil over, and Congress and the president come to an impasse. When an impasse occurs between the institutions on a regulatory bill or pork barrel spending, the bill simply dies in Congress. In contrast, without reauthorization, the federal government cannot spend money and noncritical offices close their doors, federal employees do not get paid, and all sorts of government activity ceases. During 1995, the government shut down not once but twice due to the inability of Congress and President Clinton to compromise on spending.

That year had ushered in sweeping change as the Republicans captured both the House and the Senate. During the first two years of his first term, Clinton presided over unified government as the Democrats controlled the House, Senate, and presidency for the first time since Jimmy Carter's presidency (1977–1981). The loss of both chambers of Congress was a devastating blow to the Democrats and to the President personally, particularly in the House, which had been under Democratic control for over 40 years. The Republicans captured the House via a savvy plan designed by Newt Gingrich to aid newcomers vying for the unusually large number of open seats due to retirements. Gingrich unified, in fact, nationalized, the 1994 campaign through his "Contract with America." Among other planks, the Contract specifically called for a balanced budget. As the new Republican Speaker of the House with the support of the new freshman Congress members, Gingrich pressed forward with a vote on a budget resolution in the first one hundred days.

The Contract called for a balanced budget without touching the so-called "third rail" of American politics, Social Security, and without reducing defense spending. The Republicans wanted to balance the budget by cutting numerous programs favored by Democrats, namely Medicare, Medicaid, and other federal welfare programs. The budget process would be the means by which the Republicans would press their agenda forward.[57] However, the Republicans did not have large enough majorities in either chamber to be able to override a presidential veto, thus Clinton and his agenda remained a political force to be reckoned with, despite the devastating midterm losses.

In both the House and the Senate, the new budget proposals, passed on mostly party-line votes, slashed spending and lowered taxes but to different degrees. The Senate Republicans were not tied to the Contract and cared less about adhering to it. However, in Conference Committee the House essentially won the debate as the negotiations between Speaker Gingrich and Majority Leader Bob Dole culminated in a large tax cut, and severe cuts in numerous programs and the limiting of the ability to raise the debt ceiling (the amount that the federal government may borrow). The resolution that Congress passed did

Bill Clinton meets with Republican House Speaker Newt Gingrich of Georgia and Republican Senate Majority Leader Bob Dole of Kansas in an attempt to avert a government shutdown in 1995.

not require a presidential signature, as it was binding only on Congress. The reconciliation bill enacts the necessary policy changes from the resolution into law and does require the president's signature.[58]

The Republicans celebrated what they viewed as the first step in undoing the large, welfare state created by the Democrats. Republican Representative Chris Shays of Connecticut termed it a revolution. Chairman of the House Budget Committee, John Kasich, a Republican from Ohio, set the tone of the upcoming debate with the President, claiming, "we are prepared to shut the government down in order to solve this problem."[59]

While the Republicans were working amongst themselves, shutting out both the President and Congressional Democrats, the President abided by Federal law and submitted a budget in February. He then submitted a revised budget that balanced the federal budget in ten years. The Republicans ignored both proposals, insisting the budget needed to be balanced in just seven years. Clinton employed all the tactics available to him as president. Initially shut out of bargaining and negotiating by the Republicans in the resolution phase, Clinton went public by repeatedly emphasizing his opposition to the deep cuts, particularly those aimed at the poor.

With the government operating under a Continuing Resolution (CR) since the Republicans had missed the October 1 deadline, on November 1, Clinton and the Republican leadership met at the White House but reached no agreements. Just days later, the Republicans passed another CR and increased the debt ceiling but attached provisions the President had signaled he would veto. On November 13, the President vetoed the bill and triggered a government shutdown. The President sent his Chief of Staff Leon Panetta to Capitol Hill seeking to avoid the shutdown, but when they insisted Congressional Democrats be present at the negotiations, Republicans refused.[60] On November 14, the federal government ceased all non-essential operations. On November 15, the Secretary of the Treasury Robert Rubin undertook "extraordinary actions" to avoid a default by the Federal government, which was triggered by the failure to raise the debt ceiling. He used cash on hand at the Federal Reserve to pay without borrowing; he stopped issuing securities to state and local governments, and even raided pension accounts in order to keep the government under the limit that enables it to borrow money.

Once the government shut down, Congress went back to conference committee to fix the bill, and after six days the President and Republican leaders found enough agreement to end the stalemate, but only until December 15. A new round of negotiations would have to ensue in order to pass a veto-proof reconciliation bill. The White House again insisted that Congressional Democrats be included; this time the Republicans relented, likely after seeing public opinion polls that blamed them and not the President for the shutdown.[61]

The second round of negotiations began November 28 and ended November 30 with each side accusing the other of acting in bad faith. On December 6, Clinton vetoed another reconciliation bill and offered his own seven-year balanced budget plan. The Republicans rejected the proposal and the government shut down again until January 2. All non-essential government services were again closed and, more noteworthy, government workers again endured losing their paychecks, this time in the middle of the holiday season.

The government continued to function on CRs until March 28, 1996. In the final set of negotiations, Clinton successfully avoided some of the more draconian cuts proposed by the Republicans, while House Republicans made serious concessions. Clinton fought for money for the environment and education as well as his AmeriCorps program and prevented the abortion riders which the House insisted on attaching to the appropriations bills.

The 1995 government shutdowns reveal how much leverage and strategy the combination of formal and informal tools provides the president. The president repeatedly used the going public strategy to signal displeasure with the Republican budget bill, yet did not alter the trajectory of the majority's plans until he vetoed the reconciliation bill. The Republicans were willing to risk the veto because their large victory in 1994 led them to believe the public wanted what they wanted: smaller government. The Republicans expected the public to blame the President for obstructing the mandate from the midterm election. They also expected the President to cave into that public pressure, but neither scenario happened. Clinton also banked on the support of the public, believing that the public only supported the Republicans in generalities and not when faced with specific cuts; in doing so, he took an enormous risk with the first veto, but not with the second. By portraying his veto as a heroic stand against attacks on the poor, the elderly, education, and the environment, Clinton unexpectedly successfully shifted the balance of power despite the new Republican majority.

. . . AND NOW

In the Fall of 2008, in the midst of the presidential general election, the United States experienced its most severe economic downturn since the Great Depression. Although the housing market began its dramatic decline sometime in 2007, the recognition of a new economic reality occurred abruptly as the investment banking giant Lehman Brothers collapsed under the weight of its debts in September 2008. The economic crisis recalibrated the 2008 presidential campaign and helped propel Barack Obama into office. Once in office, the failing economy dominated the new president's agenda. In two short years, the economy was no longer in freefall but it was not yet recovered. Working with a Democratic Congress in 2009, the Obama administration attempted to stem the economic tide via an enormous stimulus package of government spending. Obama also used the economic downturn to justify seeking Health Care Reform. With the increased spending by the government alongside the bailout of several major banks and the auto industry, the economic free-fall ceased. Wall Street recovered relatively quickly, as did the auto industry. Although not an initial cause of the economic crisis (economists mostly blame irresponsible behavior surrounding mortgages and mortgage debts), the number of unemployed individuals increased significantly. The increase in the unemployment rate, the astronomical government debt and deficit as a result of the spending and falling tax revenue, changed the political dynamic. In the 2010 midterm elections, Republicans made huge gains in the Senate and took control of the House of Representatives. As in 1995, divided government changed the debate regarding budgeting, and the debt ceiling once again became a means to advance a political agenda.

In 2011, there were three issues on the table for the President and the new, divided Congress: the 2011 budget, raising the debt ceiling, and the 2012 budget. In late 2010, the lame duck Congress passed an $858-billion-dollar compromise that extended both tax cuts and unemployment benefits. The compromise in effect punted the ball down the field as the increased borrowing without increased revenue would necessitate an increase in the debt ceiling (the amount which the U.S. government can borrow under law). Despite the unfinished nature of the 2011 budget, federal law required the President to submit his 2012 budget. Obama traveled to Baltimore to "go public" with the core components of his proposal. As is typical of public efforts in smaller locales, Obama reminded the audience of his campaign pledges, explained what he had been doing in the last two years, and then offered his plan for the future:[62]

> ... these investments are an essential part of the budget my administration is sending to Congress, because I'm convinced that if we out-build and out-innovate and out-educate as well as out-hustle the rest of the world, the jobs and industries of our time will take root here in the United States. Our people will prosper, and our country will succeed. But I'm also convinced that the only way we can make these investments in our future is if our Government starts living within its means, if we start taking responsibility for our deficits. And that's why when I was sworn in as President, I pledged to cut the deficit in half by the end of my first term. The budget I'm proposing today meets that pledge and puts us on a path to pay for what we spend by the middle of the decade. We do this in part by eliminating waste and cutting whatever spending we can do without. As I start—as a start, I've called for a freeze on annual domestic spending over the next five years. This freeze would cut the deficit by more than $400 billion over the next decade, bringing this kind of spending—domestic discretionary spending—to its lowest share of our economy since Dwight Eisenhower was President. Let me repeat that: Because of our budget, this share of spending will be at its lowest level since Dwight Eisenhower was President. That level of spending is lower than it was under Ronald Reagan.[63]

Obama called his proposal a "cut and invest" plan; however, Republicans argued that the 2010 election created a mandate for smaller government and a rejection of Obama's "big government" programs. Obama's proposal, combined with the fervor for cuts resulting from the election, spurred House Republicans to offer their own plan for the future. In February 2011, the House passed a budget resolution calling for $60 billion in cuts. Resolving the differences reached critical importance as the lame duck compromise expiration date loomed in early April.

Reminiscent of 1995, the final hours of "Will the government shutdown or won't it?" rested on the tax cuts but also the policy riders the Republicans attempted to attach to the budget reconciliation: specifically, ending the Obama health-care plan and ceasing funding for abortion in Washington, D.C. and funding for Planned Parenthood, an organization that provides health care for

Barack Obama meets with Republican House Speaker John Boehner of Ohio and Democratic Senate Majority Leader Harry Reid of Nevada.

women, including abortions. Interestingly, the president capitulated on the tax cuts, accepting a general number in keeping with House Speaker John Boehner's January numbers (and not the February resolution numbers) but drew a line in the sand over the specific cuts to Planned Parenthood. Senator Harry Reid took to the Senate Floor in support of the President's position and characterized the negotiations as being held hostage to a restrictive social policy agenda.

In the midst of these delicate negotiations focused on the size of tax cuts and abortion, the House Budget Chair, Representative Paul Ryan (R-WI), dropped a bomb into the debate. He authored the Republican response to Obama's 2012 budget, their vision of the future. In stark contrast to the President's cut-and-invest strategy, the Republican plan "would reduce the deficit by $5.8 trillion over the next decade, mainly by making deep cuts in discretionary spending programs and turning Medicare into a 'defined benefit' in which seniors would get vouchers to buy private insurance. Medicaid would shrink as the federal contribution to state programs would be capped. It also proposes reducing the top corporate and individual tax rates to 25 percent."[64]

As in 1996, the effort to curb popular programs created a media firestorm and political consequences for Republicans. Moreover, as in 1996, the Senate was unlikely to pass as restrictive a plan as what the House passed on April 15 along party lines, 235–193. The Ryan proposal changed the tenor of the shutdown debate, giving the President momentum, as the reality of the Republican proposals shrunk its popular support. By the end of April even Republicans were backing away from the plan, although publicly blaming the Democrats.[65] President Obama did not have to veto a Republican reconciliation bill because, unlike President Clinton, Obama did not face a unified Congress. Although the Democrats lost the House in the midterm elections, they did not lose the Senate. The veto threat gave the president the ability to shut down the government when faced with a budget proposal not to his liking, but the compromise was possible due to the Democrats' control of both the executive branch and the Senate to stem the tide of the Republicans.

SUGGESTED READINGS

Bond, Jon, and Richard Fleisher. 1990. *The President in the Legislative Arena.* Chicago: University of Chicago Press.

Edwards, George C., III. 1989 *At the Margins: Presidential Leadership of Congress.* New Haven: Yale University Press.

Eshbaugh-Soha, Matthew. 2006. *The President's Speeches: Beyond "Going Public."* Boulder, CO: Lynne Rienner Publishers.

Fenno, Richard. 1977. "U.S. House Members in Their Constituencies: An Exploration," *American Political Science Review*, 71: 883–917.

Fisher, Louis. 2007. *Constitutional Conflicts between Congress and the President.* Lawrence: University Press of Kansas.

Jones, Charles O. 2000. *Separate But Equal Branches: Congress and the Presidency*, 2nd ed. New York: Seven Bridges Press.

Kernell, Samuel. 2007. *Going Public: New Strategies of Presidential Leadership*, 4th ed. Washington DC: CQ Press.

Mayhew, David. 1974. *Congress: The Electoral Connection.* New Haven: Yale University Press.

Peterson, Mark. 1990. *Legislating Together: The White House and Capitol Hill from Eisenhower to Reagan.* Cambridge: Harvard University Press.

Rudalevige, Andrew. 2002. *Managing the President's Program: Presidential Leadership and Legislative Policy Formation.* Princeton: Princeton University Press.

ON THE WEB

http://www.house.gov/ and http://www.senate.gov/. The official websites of the U.S. Congress, with information about current and past members of Congress, current and past legislation, and the history of the institutions.

http://www.dirksencenter.org/. A nonpartisan, not-for-profit institution that promotes a better understanding of the institution of Congress via archival research.

http://www.c-span.org/. The website of the congressional television channel, C-SPAN. It is a private, non-partisan, not-for-profit company that provides coverage of Congress, the President, and the Supreme Court. The website provides current video and is a repository for videos dating back to its origins in 1979.

IN THEIR OWN WORDS

CAMPAIGNING AGAINST CONGRESS

Harry Truman's campaign against the "do-nothing" Congress in 1948 is perhaps the most famous example of a president attempting to convince the American public that the legislative branch is not doing its job in representing the needs of average Americans. However, other presidents have used similar strategies at election time, since in recent decades, public approval ratings for Congress are often lower than even the most unpopular presidents. In 1992, possible talking points circulated among George H. W. Bush's advisors that would have the President "chastise the Congress for taking so long to complete essential work such as nominations and appropriations." In addition, some of Bush's advisors wanted the president to highlight the fact that despite being in session year-round, the Congress was actually "part time" in the actual work accomplished.[66]

Even more to the point is this memo from the Reagan White House in 1988 on the topic of "Do Awful Congress as a Campaign Theme":

> The performance thus far of the 100th Congress, capped by the acrimony and delay in enacting the FY 1988 budget, affords us an opportunity to make the performance of this Congress a key issue in the 1988 general election. Despite limited historical precedent, this anti-Congress theme might very well become a winning one for the GOP next year.
>
> The polling evidence is overwhelming that Congress is held in low regard by the voting public. However, individual members continue to be popular because of their close attention to the needs of the voters back home. Congressmen are admired less for their legislative acumen than for their casework on behalf of individual constituents. The examples of districts giving Republican presidential candidates hefty majorities while reelecting Democratic incumbents are legion.
>
> The Congress is such an unwieldy institution that it has been difficult to draw a connection between its actions and the overall results of its actions. As such, the Congress is able to take credit for favors targeted to specific audiences without being held politically accountable for the impact on the general population.
>
> Until the advent of C-Span television coverage, the Congress was a mysterious institution that only the most sophisticated of insiders understood. So many procedural and substantive votes were taken on the same issue that a congressman could vote different ways and offer at least some satisfaction to diametrically opposed constituents. It has become more and more difficult to get Congress "on the record" because more often than not the record was not very clear.
>
> Ironically, while TV coverage had the intended effect of raising the visibility of members of Congress (especially the leadership), it has also had the unintended impact of exposing congressional practices to media scrutiny. While real reform will come slowly, the possibility that national politics could be impacted by these practices offers congressional critics an immediate forum for their views. Indeed, to the extent that Congress becomes part of the national debate in 1988, the discussion could very well be a springboard for real reform, thus strengthening the forces for change in the next Congress.
>
> The personal embodiment of abuse of congressional practices is Speaker Wright. He has cultivated a high profile and as such is a very visible target. Observers say he is the most partisan Speaker in a long while. He does not

hesitate to bend the rules when it suits his purposes. Charges of personal corruption have been leveled against him. Any anti-Congress theme would rely heavily upon him for personalization and example.

The only specific example in recent American history where Congress became an issue was the 1948 presidential election. President Harry Truman, trailing badly in the polls and widely unpopular, campaigned against the "do nothing" Republican Congress, blaming it for a wide variety of misdeeds. In this larger electoral context, the President enjoyed a distinct advantage over a body that necessarily speaks with many voices and seems disorganized. The result was a debate on issues framed largely by the incumbent President, resulting in an unexpected, albeit narrow, reelection victory for Truman. (As one example, Truman successfully blamed the Republican Congress for falling farm prices throughout 1948. He carried every farm state in the election).

This "do nothing" Congress campaign was all the more remarkable because, in fact, the President and Congress had cooperated on several important ventures the year before. In 1947, for instance, the Republican Congress overwhelmingly approved key Truman foreign policy initiatives such as the Marshall Plan for reconstruction of Western Europe and military assistance to Greece and Turkey, who were then under communist attack. By the time the political season was underway however, this was forgotten as the President launched his successful attack on the "do nothing" Congress. The moral is that there is a time for cooperation and a time for politics.

I believe the opportunity is there for such a theme against this "do awful" Congress. We can avail ourselves of a number of fruitful themes to highlight the failures of this Congress to address the real needs of the American people.

1) POLICIES

This Congress' priorities and policies are opposite the real beliefs of the American people and are detrimental to the interests of the United States. Specifics include congressional desire for protectionist trade legislation; congressional failure to control spending and budget deficits (Balanced Budget Amendment); Congress' war on small business (mandated benefits legislation); and most importantly, the refusal of Congress to face up to our international obligations by hamstringing the Chief Executive (Persian Gulf, Central America, arms control). The goal is to set our priorities against those of the Congress as a part of the public's choice in 1988.

2) POLITICS

The Congressional art of trading favors, whatever value it once had, has become a drag on the economy and threatens to undermine public support for governmental integrity. Pork barrel pursuit of tax breaks, transition rules, special subsidies for a few communities (note enclosed articles on the recent priority of Senator Inouye), regulatory exemptions, and directed purchase contracts for favored constituents and personal vendettas (enclosures) are doing great harm to the country because the public's confidence in the government is being eroded. The goal is to take the congressman's strong suit of constituent service and turn it into a negative by emphasizing the public interest.

3) PROCESS

The Congressional budget process is in disarray. Rather than offering a serious check in spending, it has become another layer of bureaucracy competing the appropriations and authorization committees. Missed deadlines, special interest pleading, and failure to pass a single appropriations bill have reduced the President's role in the budget process and contributed to the huge annual spending increases since 1974, when the budget act was passed. The goal here is to offer a rational explanation for why the deficit continues to be large despite the President's best efforts and to blame the Congress for the current situation.

4) ETHICS

We now have one dozen incumbent congressmen under investigation or convicted of legal or ethics violations. This is in spite of the fact that the independent counsel law does not apply to Congress. Imagine what the situation would be if Congress were subject to the same scrutiny as the executive branch. The goal here is to launch a preemptive strike against other opponents who will most likely seek to make the sleaze factor an issue this year.

Such a campaign would not lack for themes or new material. The President has credibility to critique an institution he has dealt with for seven years. He would be setting the agenda and defining the differences between the parties, a task that is critical if we are to have any hope of increasing our congressional representation next year. The tone need not be angry, but more in sorrow that things have gone so awry. Finally, of course, the timing is critical. The "do awful" label would appear late, but many of the themes could be developed earlier than that.[67]

CHAPTER 7

Presidents and the Judicial Branch

On May 26, 2009, President Barack Obama exercised one of the most important presidential powers outlined in the U.S. Constitution—he nominated Federal Appellate Judge Sonia Sotomayor to fill the vacancy left by Associate Justice David Souter's retirement on the U.S. Supreme Court. A Supreme Court nomination is an event that all presidents anxiously await—the chance to make a lifelong appointment to not only shape current decisions by the Court but to carry on the president's political legacy long after he has left office. On average, presidents usually get to nominate a new justice every two years. However, there are no guarantees on the timeline. Gerald Ford, who served less than thirty months in office, had one appointment, while his successor, Jimmy Carter, had none during his four years in office. More recently, Bill Clinton and George W. Bush were frustrated by their lack of opportunities to shape the Supreme Court, as each only had two vacancies during their respective eight years in office. The eleven years that passed between Clinton's second nomination in 1994 (of Stephen Breyer) and Bush's first nomination in 2005 (of John Roberts) turned out to be one of the longest droughts of high court vacancies in the nation's history.

For Obama, Souter's retirement presented the new president with his first opportunity to reshape the makeup of the Court within the first few months of his presidency. Many political observers had predicted that Obama could have up to four nominations to the Supreme Court during his first term in office, but Souter's retirement came as a surprise to many. The two most likely contenders for retirement at the end of the 2008–2009 Supreme Court term included John

Paul Stevens and Ruth Bader Ginsberg. Stevens, nominated to the Court in 1975 by Ford and the most senior among the current justices, had just turned eighty-nine that April, while the seventy-six-year-old Ginsberg, nominated by Clinton in 1993, had just undergone surgery that February for pancreatic cancer (after surviving colon cancer in 1999). Yet, it was Souter, the sixty-nine-year-old justice appointed in 1990 by George H. W. Bush, who retired first. (Stevens would announce his retirement on April 9, 2010, and was succeeded on the Court by Elena Kagan, who was confirmed on August 5, 2010). Normally, the retirement of a Republican appointee during a Democratic administration, or vice versa, represents a potential ideological shift on the Court. But Souter's tenure on the Court had not lived up to the expectation of either the president who had nominated him or conservatives within the Republican Party who had been assured in 1990 that Souter would be a reliable conservative vote on key decisions. The Bush White House had promoted Souter as a "believer in judicial restraint, a tough trial court judge with a great legal mind who will interpret the Constitution not legislate from the bench," and due to "his fidelity to the Constitution and the rule of law."[1] Instead, Souter was more often a reliable liberal vote during his nineteen years on the Court, joining his more liberal colleagues in high-profile decisions in areas such as upholding abortion rights, banning school prayer, and limiting the scope of the death penalty. As such, Souter's retirement presented Obama with what would be considered a status-quo pick by keeping the seat in the hands of a moderate-to-liberal justice (as did Kagan's nomination to replace Stevens).

Many assumed that Obama, when faced with his first Supreme Court vacancy, would nominate a woman, or that he would make history by nominating the first Hispanic to the Court. Obama opted for both with his nomination of Sotomayor, whose resume included experience on the U.S. District Court for the Southern District of New York (nominated by Bush in 1991) and the U.S. Court of Appeals for the Second Circuit (nominated by Clinton in 1997). Despite her impressive qualifications for the job, which included eighteen years of experience as a federal judge, a law degree from Yale, and experience both as a prosecutor and in private practice, Sotomayor's nomination received opposition from conservatives. Several conservative Republicans in the Senate, along with conservative interest groups, criticized what they considered Sotomayor's judicial activism (even though assessments of her time on the federal bench suggested she was more of a moderate, as opposed to liberal, judge), as well as her now-famous "wise Latina" remark. In 2001, while giving a talk at Berkeley Law School, Sotomayor remarked: "I would hope that a wise Latina woman with the richness of her experiences would more often than not reach a better conclusion than a white male who hasn't lived that life." While taken somewhat out of context by her critics, Sotomayor answered questions about the remark during her confirmation hearings before the Senate Judiciary Committee, stating that while personal experiences help to shape a judge's perspective, ultimately the law is the only guide for making a decision. Sotomayor was confirmed by the Senate on August 6, 2009, by a vote of 68 to 31 (all opposition votes came from Republicans). The final vote in the Senate to confirm Sotomayor represents how the confirmation process has become more politicized and ideologically contentious in recent years.

The Souter retirement, along with the Sotomayor confirmation, highlight two of the most prominent features of contemporary relations between the president and the judicial branch. First, presidents have no control over a justice once he or

Sonia Sotomayor became Barack Obama's first nomination to the U.S. Supreme Court in 2009.

she is confirmed, and there are no guarantees as to whether or not the justice's decisions will align with the president's political agenda. Also, since justices serve for life terms with no set age for retirement, justices can serve for years, if not decades, well past a president's time in office. Second, the confirmation process for federal judges, and in particular Supreme Court justices, has become highly politicized in recent decades and requires presidents to pay close attention to political considerations in their selections more than ever before. As discussed in the previous chapter about the presidential–congressional relationship, the framers of the U.S. Constitution intended for a system of separated and shared powers among the three branches to prevent the accumulation of too much political power in just one person or one branch of government. As a result, and just as in his relationship with Congress, the president must be mindful of the constitutional balance of political power. While the president may enjoy influence over the federal courts through his power to appoint judges, the president must also adhere to rulings by federal courts regarding the nature and scope of presidential powers as outlined in the Constitution.

NOMINATIONS TO THE U.S. SUPREME COURT

As outlined in Article II, Section 2 of the Constitution, the president "shall nominate, and by and with the advice and consent of the Senate, shall appoint . . . judges of the Supreme Court." In addition, Article III, Section 1 states that "judges, both of the supreme and inferior courts, shall hold their offices during good behavior." Congress holds the power to set the size of the Supreme Court. With passage of the Judiciary Act of 1789, the initial Supreme Court consisted of six justices—a Chief Justice and five associate justices. The number of justices would reach ten in 1863, but was reduced to nine with passage of the Judiciary Act of 1869—a Chief Justice and eight associate justices. The size of the Court has not changed since.

Franklin Roosevelt and the Federal Courts

Roosevelt's attempt to "pack the court" following his reelection in 1936, which would have increased the size from nine to fifteen justices, is the most prominent attempt to alter the size of the Court since 1869. Roosevelt faced intense challenges when he took office in 1933 with the United States mired in the Great Depression. While he had the support of Congress and a majority of the public for his New Deal programs, the Supreme Court did not agree with the president's plan to expand the size and scope of the federal government. The Supreme Court, with seven of its nine members having been appointed by previous Republican presidents, struck down major provisions of New Deal legislation in 1935–36. Frustrated by the lack of vacancies on the Court (none had occurred during Roosevelt's first term), yet determined to capitalize on his huge reelection victory in 1936, Roosevelt crafted his "court packing" plan. In addition, Roosevelt sought advice from his attorney general as to whether or not the jurisdiction of the Supreme Court (that is, their ability to hear cases) could be altered. In a January 14, 1936, memo to Attorney General Homer Cummings, FDR inquired: "What was the McArdle [sic] case (7 Wall 506-year 1869)? I am told that the Congress withdrew some act from the jurisdiction of the Supreme Court."[2] Cummings responded: "The case of ex parte McCardle, 7 Wallace 506, decided in December, 1868, to which you refer in your memorandum, is one of the classic cases to which we refer when considering the possibility of limiting the jurisdiction of Federal Courts. This whole matter has been the subject of considerable study in this Department, and, in view of recent developments, is apt to be increasingly important."[3]

By early 1937, the FDR administration began its attempt to persuade the public, as well as members of Congress, that the "court packing" plan was needed. Six of the nine justices were over the age of seventy, yet none seemed ready to retire. Roosevelt decided that he should receive one new nomination for each of those justices, which would have allowed him to "pack the court" with six new justices of his choice, thereby increasing the size of the Court to fifteen justices. This was part of Roosevelt's proposed reorganization of the judicial branch, which would also add many new judicial posts to lower federal courts to help alleviate the backlog of federal court cases. According to Attorney General Cummings, who was one of Roosevelt's strongest advocates for increasing the number of federal judges, "Delay in the administration of justice is the outstanding defect of our federal judicial system. It has been a cause of concern to practically every one of my predecessors in office. It has exasperated the bench, the bar, the business community and the public.... It is a mockery of justice to say to a person when he files suit, that he may receive a decision years later.... The evil is a growing one."[4] And, as Roosevelt himself argued in a message to Congress:

> Modern complexities call also for a constant infusion of new blood in the court.... A lowered mental or physical vigor leads men to avoid an examination of complicated and changed conditions. Little by little, new facts become blurred through old glasses fitted, as it were, for the needs of another generation; older men, assuming that the scene is the same as it was in the past, cease to explore or inquire into the present or the future. We have recognized this truth in the civil service of the nation and of many states by compelling retirement on pay at the age of seventy.... Life tenure of judges, assured by the Constitution, was designed to place the courts beyond temptations or influences which might impair their judgments: it was not intended to create a static judiciary. A constant

> and systematic addition of younger blood will vitalize the courts and better equip them to recognize and apply the essential concepts of justice in the light of the needs and the facts of an ever-changing world. It is obvious, therefore, from both reason and experience, that some provision must be adopted, which will operate automatically to supplement the work of older judges and accelerate the work of the court.[5]

Roosevelt also made his case about the court-packing plan to the American people through a fireside chat on March 9, 1937, in which he scolded the Supreme Court for thwarting the will of the American citizens by striking down key New Deal legislation:

> The Court in addition to the proper use of its judicial functions has improperly set itself up as a third House of the Congress—a super-legislature, as one of the justices has called it—reading into the Constitution words and implications which are not there, and which were never intended to be there. We have, therefore, reached the point as a Nation where we must take action to save the Constitution from the Court and the Court from itself. We must find a way to take an appeal from the Supreme Court to the Constitution itself. We want a Supreme Court which will do justice under the Constitution—not over it. In our Courts we want a government of laws and not of men.[6]

However, the court-packing plan was not met with as much support, either congressional or public, as Roosevelt's legislative agenda had been. Congress failed to pass the legislation to reorganize the federal judiciary and to allow Roosevelt to pack the Supreme Court; in addition, no legislation passed that would have altered or diminished the Court's jurisdiction ☝. However, just a few weeks after Roosevelt's fireside chat, the Court handed down the first of three 5–4 decisions to uphold New Deal legislation. This move by the Court is known as the famous "switch in time that saved nine." Roosevelt also received his first opportunity to replace a retiring justice in the summer of 1937, the first of a total of nine vacancies on the Court during his twelve-plus years in office.

Tenure and Removal

Roosevelt's frustration with the Supreme Court highlights one of its most important structural features—all Supreme Court justices, along with all other federal judges, are appointed to life terms. While justices and federal judges can be impeached by a majority vote in the House of Representatives and removed by a two-thirds majority vote in the Senate, no Supreme Court justice has ever been removed from office; all have served until retirement or death. The definition of an impeachable offense is not clear, although most would agree that removal should be for a criminal offense or ethical lapse and not purely for partisan and/or political reasons. In 1805 Justice Samuel Chase, who had been appointed by George Washington, was impeached but not removed from the bench due to political opposition to his legal decisions. In the late 1950s and throughout the 1960s, several conservative groups, including the John Birch Society, advocated for the impeachment of Chief Justice Earl Warren, a Dwight

---

☝ View how the Senate Judiciary Committee remembers the plan.

Eisenhower appointee, for what were considered to be the Court's activist and liberal rulings (including the landmark case of *Brown v. Board of Education* in 1954) in the areas of due process rights and civil liberties. Two unsuccessful impeachment attempts were brought against Justice William O. Douglas (an FDR appointee) in the House; the first attempt came in 1953 after Douglas granted a temporary stay of execution to Julius and Ethel Rosenberg, the American couple convicted of selling atomic bomb secrets to the Russians, and the second attempt came in 1970 and was led by House Minority Leader Gerald Ford (R-MI) over alleged ethical concerns stemming from Douglas' publications and involvement with a private foundation. In a speech on the House floor, Ford famously stated that an "impeachable offense is whatever a majority of the House of Representatives considers to be at a given moment in history."[7] Yet, despite Ford's definition, attempts to impeach any federal judge, let alone a Supreme Court justice, have been rare.

Given that Supreme Court justices serve for life, each justice has the potential to serve for several decades. To date, a total of seventeen men have served as Chief Justice, and a total of 112 men and women have served as Associate Justices, with an average tenure on the bench of approximately fifteen years. However, during the twentieth century, two justices attempted to break longevity records for service on the Court. Justice Hugo Black, appointed by FDR in 1937, served for thirty-four years and one month prior to his retirement in 1971. Similarly, Douglas, also appointed by FDR (two years later in 1939), had served a total of thirty-six years and six months when he retired in November 1975. Douglas had surpassed the previous longevity record of Justice Stephen J. Field, who had served for thirty-four years and six months from 1863 to 1897. Ironically, Douglas' replacement on the Court would be named by President Gerald Ford, who had led the impeachment proceedings against Douglas in the House five years earlier. Ford's selection, John Paul Stevens, would also rank high on the list of longest-serving justices, beginning his thirty-fourth year on the Court at the start of the 2009–2010 term, and ending the term with his retirement. The tenure of these justices shows the importance of a presidential nomination to the Court, particularly in regards to a president's legacy.

The Nomination Process

When a vacancy occurs on the Supreme Court, a potential justice is first nominated for the position by the president. Since federal judges are the only public officials to enjoy a lifetime appointment, the nomination and confirmation of a Supreme Court justice represents a significant event during a president's administration. When a president nominates an individual for the Supreme Court, he does so with the intention of influencing the outcome of future decisions to reflect his own political philosophy and policy agenda. However, there is no guarantee that the confirmation process that follows will go smoothly or that the U.S. Senate will automatically approve of the president's choice. The White House must be strategic in its selection of Supreme Court nominees, reflective of the political environment in which the president finds himself, to maximize the nominee's chance for a successful confirmation. In addition, most presidents, with the help of White House staff, have a "short list" of potential nominees ready for when a vacancy should occur. Often, an initial list of judicial nominees takes shape during the transition period after a president wins election in November and prior to the inauguration in January.

Exactly how do presidents choose whom to nominate when a vacancy occurs on the Supreme Court? Presidents rely on many factors in making their decision. According to legal scholar Lawrence Baum, these include objective qualifications, policy preferences, political and personal reward, and building political support.[8] Obviously, a president wants to make a selection that will reflect his policy preferences and that will please his political supporters. The president's "situation" also affects the confirmation process, including his political strength in the Senate (whether or not the confirmation will go smoothly), his level of public approval (there is political pressure on the Senate to confirm the nominee if the president has high public approval ratings), mobilization of interest group activity (whether or not interest groups will support, or more importantly, oppose the nomination), and the importance of the nomination (will it fill the high-profile position of chief justice, or perhaps replace a woman or minority on the Court?).[9] Legal scholar David M. O'Brien argues that a "myth of merit" also exists, since merit (whether or not one is deserving of the position based on experience and skill) plays little if any role in the judicial selection process.[10] Despite attempts to keep the Court an unbiased and independent institution, presidential appointments are nonetheless political. As a result, several highly qualified individuals to both the Supreme Court and to the lower federal courts have been passed over for appointment or have not been confirmed due to political considerations. The political climate often plays a larger role than merit in who is selected, as do race, gender, religion and geography.[11]

Nominees to the Supreme Court are always lawyers, although this is not a constitutional requirement, and many have attended top law schools (the current nine justices attended law school at Harvard, Yale, or Columbia). Previous jobs usually include appellate judgeships (state or federal), jobs within the executive branch, jobs within the Justice Department, or high elected office. Most nominees are older than fifty, and a majority are from upper- or upper-middle-class families. Diversity has not been a prominent feature on the Supreme Court, although race, ethnicity, and gender have played a more apparent role in considering nominees in recent years. Still, only four women have ever served on the Court—Sandra Day O'Connor (a Ronald Reagan appointee who served from 1981 until 2006), Ginsburg, Sotomayor, and Kagan—and only two African-Americans have served on the Court—Thurgood Marshall (a Lyndon Johnson appointee who served from 1967 until 1991) and Clarence Thomas (appointed by George H. W. Bush in 1991). In 1986, Antonin Scalia (a Reagan appointee) became the first justice of Italian descent (Samuel Alito, appointed by George W. Bush in 2006, is of Italian descent as well), and Sotomayor is also the first justice of Hispanic descent. Since eight of the current members of the Supreme Court are former federal appellate court judges (Kagan is the only exception, having never been a judge but holding instead positions such as Associate White House Counsel in the Clinton administration, Dean of Harvard Law School, and Solicitor General in the Obama administration), and since historically this is the most common place for presidents to look for high court nominees, placing more women and minorities on lower federal courts will increase their presence within the eligible pool of candidates for the Court in years to come. (See Table 7.1)

Table 7.1 The United States Supreme Court

JUSTICE	YEAR OF BIRTH	LAW SCHOOL	YEAR OF APPOINT-MENT	APPOINT-ING PRESI-DENT	PRIOR POSITION
Antonin Scalia	1936	Harvard	1986	Reagan	Judge, U.S. Court of Appeals (D.C. Circuit)
Anthony Kennedy	1936	Harvard	1988	Reagan	Judge, U.S. Court of Appeals (Ninth Circuit)
Clarence Thomas	1948	Yale	1991	G. H. W. Bush	Judge, U.S. Court of Appeals (D.C. Circuit)
Ruth Bader Ginsberg	1933	Columbia	1993	Clinton	Judge, U.S. Court of Appeals (D.C. Circuit)
Stephen Breyer	1938	Harvard	1994	Clinton	Judge, U.S. Court of Appeals (First Circuit)
John Roberts	1955	Harvard	2005	G. W. Bush	Judge, U.S. Court of Appeals (D.C. Circuit)
Samuel Alito	1950	Yale	2005	G.W. Bush	Judge, U.S. Court of Appeals (Third Circuit)
Sonia Sotomayor	1954	Yale	2009	Obama	Judge, U.S. Court of Appeals (Second Circuit)
Elena Kagan	1960	Harvard	2010	Obama	U.S. Solicitor General

The Confirmation Process

Once the president makes a nomination, the Senate judiciary committee considers it. If the committee approves, the nomination then goes to the entire Senate with confirmation occurring by a simple majority vote. Since 1790, a total of 160 nominations have been made to the Supreme Court, with only twelve rejected by a vote in the Senate. The three most recent Senate rejections included two of Richard Nixon's nominees (G. Harrold Carswell and Clement Haynsworth) and one Reagan nominee (Robert Bork). One of the closest votes ever to occur in the Senate came in 1991 when Clarence Thomas received a vote of 52–48 following the controversy over sexual harassment allegations during his confirmation process (as we will discuss later). In addition, the Senate has taken no action on five nominations and postponed a vote on three nominations. Seven individuals have declined the nomination (something that has not occurred since 1882), and eight nominations were withdrawn, usually due to impending defeat in the Senate and/or negative public reaction to the nominee.

George W. Bush's nomination of Harriet Miers in 2005 is the most recent example of a nomination to end in withdrawal. Bush nominated Miers, his White House Counsel, to replace Sandra Day O'Connor due to her pending retirement. Initially, John Roberts had been nominated to replace O'Connor, but his nomination was elevated to Chief Justice following the death of William Rehnquist in September 2005. Upon announcing Miers' nomination on October 7, 2005, Bush stated:

> I've given a lot of thought to the kind of people who should serve on the Federal judiciary. I've come to agree with the late Chief Justice William Rehnquist, who wrote about the importance of having judges who are drawn from a wide diversity of professional backgrounds. Justice Rehnquist himself came to the Supreme Court without prior experience on the bench.... And I'm proud to nominate an outstanding woman who brings a similar record of achievement in private practice and public service.... Harriet Miers will strictly interpret our Constitution and laws. She will not legislate from the bench. I ask the Senate to review her qualifications, thoroughly and fairly, and to vote on her nomination promptly.... In selecting a nominee, I've sought to find an American of grace, judgment, and unwavering devotion to the Constitution and laws of our country. Harriet Miers is just such a person. I've known Harriet for more than a decade. I know her heart; I know her character. I'm confident that Harriet Miers will add to the wisdom and character of our judiciary when she is confirmed as the 110th Justice of the Supreme Court.[12]

Despite assurances by Bush that she was the best candidate for the job, Miers' embattled three-week nomination was withdrawn after she had been vilified in the press as being unqualified and lacking sufficient experience in the area of constitutional law. Miers, a corporate attorney from Texas prior to working in the Bush White House, had also been roundly criticized by conservatives who feared that, despite Bush's personal guarantees to the contrary, she would not be committed to their conservative agenda once confirmed to the Court. She had also been sharply criticized by Senate Republicans, including Senate Judiciary Committee Chairman Arlen Specter (R-PA), for lacking an in-depth understanding of constitutional matters. Samuel Alito, a federal appellate court judge with strong conservative credentials, would eventually fill the seat vacated by O'Connor's retirement.

Senators are not the only political actors involved in the confirmation process. Since 1956, Supreme Court nominees have been closely scrutinized by the American Bar Association (ABA). The ABA's fifteen-member Standing Committee on the Federal Judiciary rates nominees as either "well qualified," "qualified" or "not qualified," which can play an influential role in the Senate confirmation hearings. This process has become an important political element for a president in his selection of justices, since having a nominee's professional credentials labeled as "unqualified" would make confirmation difficult in the Senate. Not all presidents have submitted names to the ABA when making a nomination to the Supreme Court, and some ratings by the committee were quite controversial. Nixon's appointees, Clement Haynsworth and G. Harrold Carswell, were both rejected by the Senate (many Senators viewed them as unqualified to serve on the high court) in spite of the ABA's claim that both were qualified. Later nominations by Nixon were not submitted to the ABA, although the ABA continued to provide its own rating.

The ABA has never given a "not qualified" rating, but a less-than-unanimous vote among the committee members for a qualified rating can cause a public stir during the confirmation hearings and weaken the nominee's chances of confirmation. Both Reagan's nomination of Robert Bork in 1987 and Bush's nomination of Thomas in 1991, both federal appellate judges, failed to receive unanimous votes from the ABA committee. Even though the votes against the two nominees constituted a small minority of the committee (four voted against Bork, and two voted against Thomas), the results gave political opponents important ammunition in the confirmation process. Many conservative lawmakers have denounced the ABA in recent years for having a liberal bias in both policy positions (like favoring abortion rights and opposing capital punishment) and its stance on judicial nominees. As a result, many Republicans now give less credence to judicial ratings. In 2001, the George W. Bush administration announced that it would not submit the names of judicial nominees to the ABA, eliminating its official role in the nomination process. However, the ABA continued to assess nominees and send its reports to the Senate Judiciary Committee during the Bush years; both Roberts and Alito in 2005 received "well qualified" ratings. In 2009, the Obama administration reinstated the practice of submitting the names of judicial nominees to the ABA, with both Sotomayor and Kagan also receiving a "well qualified" rating.

Beyond the ABA, legal scholars and prominent attorneys also weigh in on whether or not a nominee is qualified. In addition, interest groups can influence the president's selection process, as groups publicly and privately fight for or against nominations. This is not surprising given that interest groups have a large stake in who sits on the Supreme Court through the decisions that are handed down, since interest groups often litigate public policies and provide financial support for certain cases to be appealed to the Supreme Court. Those interest groups that are important to the president and support his policy agenda can exert influence in the nomination stage. For example, conservative groups lobbied the Bush administration against the potential nomination of Attorney General Alberto Gonzalez in 2005 due to his perceived moderate stance on issues such as abortion. Following the nomination, many interest groups engage in campaign-like activities to either support or defeat the nominee. Estimates suggest that liberal interest groups opposed to the conservative legal views of Robert Bork spent up to $15 million to fight his nomination in 1987. Since then, interest group activity surrounding a Supreme Court nomination has continued to expand, which includes airing television ads and creating web pages to lobby for or against a nominee.[13]

Given the campaign environment once a nomination is announced, it is not surprising that the news media also play a prominent role in the confirmation process. Beyond the use of the mass media by interest groups to wage their public campaigns, news coverage of Supreme Court nominees since the late 1980s, particularly on the cable news outlets, has become "highly acrimonious" with intense scrutiny of the nominee's qualifications and legal views.[14] The tone and content of the coverage during the confirmation process often takes on the feel of horse-race coverage similar to that of presidential campaigns, focusing on whether the nominee is up or down in terms of both Senate and public support, as well as money being spent by interest groups. The infrequency of Supreme Court nominations also contributes to the "big story" approach by news media outlets when one does occur, as does the chance to provide live coverage of a controversial story (as was the case with the Bork and Thomas nominations). From the time of Sotomayor's nomination in April 2009 to her confirmation in August 2009, news media coverage focused on her personal and professional history, her "wise Latina" remark, and whether or not any Republican Senators would vote for her. With a strong Democratic majority in the Senate, and several Republicans already on record to support her confirmation, the amount of news coverage leading up to the confirmation vote seemed to belie the political reality of an almost certain confirmation. According to the Pew Research Center's Project for Excellence in Journalism, the Sotomayor nomination regularly dominated political news coverage throughout the summer months, although "the lack of news, and the empty ritualistic nature of the event, seemed to dominate a weary media storyline."[15]

The Confirmation Hearings

During the confirmation hearings, nominees are expected to answer questions by the Senate Judiciary Committee. This became an accepted practice in 1955 during the confirmation of Dwight Eisenhower's nominee John M. Harlan. Most confirmation hearings are routine and draw little public attention. However, in recent years, a few notable exceptions have turned the process into a full-blown media circus. In 1987, Reagan's nomination of Bork, a conservative appeals court judge, faced strong opposition from liberal interest groups around the country. According to Reagan, in announcing the nomination:

> Judge Bork, widely regarded as the most prominent and intellectually powerful advocate of judicial restraint, shares my view that judges' personal preferences and values should not be part of their constitutional interpretations. The guiding principle of judicial restraint recognizes that under the Constitution it is the exclusive province of the legislatures to enact laws and the role of the courts to interpret them. We're fortunate to be able to draw upon such an impressive legal mind, an experienced judge and a man who already has devoted so much of his life to public service. He'll bring credit to the Court and his colleagues, as well as to his country and the Constitution.[16]

Yet, even though Bork was a well-known and accomplished legal scholar and jurist, his nomination hearings were contentious and highly political, in part because Bork did not shy away from answering questions from Democratic senators about how he would rule on specific cases. He believed in original intent and a strict constructionist view of the Constitution, and he believed that many liberal rulings handed down by the Warren and Burger courts, such as *Roe v. Wade* (1973) and other cases expanding privacy rights, should be overturned.

Sensing that the nomination would not go smoothly, Reagan administration officials developed both public and behind-the-scenes strategies in an effort to ensure Bork's Senate confirmation. Senior administration officials were provided with talking points from Director of Communications Tom Griscom:

> As the confirmation hearings conclude, we enter a new phase of the debate about Judge Bork. During the next several weeks each of you has an important role to play in building support for this nomination. Attached are materials that should be of assistance to you in framing your prepared remarks and answers to press briefings. I ask that in the weeks ahead each of you notify in advance the White House Office of Public Affairs and the White House Office of Media Relations of any domestic travel plans. Those offices will provide you with up-to-date guidance and schedule interviews with local reporters as appropriate. The President has seen statements many of you have made in support of Judge Bork. Your continued participation is essential.

KEY POINTS FOR THE WEEKS AHEAD

- Support for Judge Bork is a test of support for President Reagan.
- The American people have consistently stated they believe the President should appoint judges who will be tough on crime. President Reagan has done this. This in part explains why law enforcement groups favor Judge Bork, and the American Civil Liberties Union opposes him.
- Judge Bork enjoys support from across the political spectrum. His supporters include liberals and conservatives, Democrats and Republicans.
- The same cannot be said about opposition to Judge Bork, which comes primarily from the special interests—individuals and groups who have long demonstrated they are outside the American political mainstream.
- These opponents have grown increasingly shrill in their attacks on Judge Bork. Many have resorted to distortions and misstatements in their attempts to undermine Judge Bork's impressive record. These tactics make the choice between the special interests and the American people's interest.
- Judge Bork is superbly qualified to be the next Supreme Court Justice. He has been forthcoming with the Senate and with the American people. He believes that a judge should interpret the law, not make the law.[17]

Reagan advisors were also keeping a close watch on key senators and how they might vote on the Bork confirmation. A White House memo showed the attention being paid to moderate senators in both parties: Dennis DeConcini (D-AZ) was listed as "Generally satisfied with Bork's answers at hearings despite posturing to the contrary. Feels he may have no political alternative (in light of interest group pressure in Arizona) other than to oppose Bork." Lowell Weicker (R-CT) was listed as "Undecided but definitely leaning against Bork. Believes Bork has shifted views to secure confirmation and cannot be trusted." And Lloyd Bentsen (D-TX) was listed as "Truly undecided.... [Thinks] Bentsen will be okay but won't decide until the last moment. Might be worth a personal visit from [Chief of Staff Howard Baker] down the road."[18]

The strategic efforts by the Reagan White House would end up being for naught, as Bork failed in the Senate confirmation. After twelve days of intense questioning by the Senate Judiciary Committee (as part of a Democratic-controlled Senate), intense lobbying by interest groups, and negative press coverage of Bork, the qualified yet controversial jurist lost his confirmation bid by a 58–42 vote in the Senate. The process also helped the media to create the term "borking," which means raising the political significance of the confirmation process through the news media. Since the failed Bork nomination, nominees have been more circumspect during the confirmation hearings and have mostly avoided answering any direct questions from senators about potential cases in the hopes of avoiding similar controversy 🖰.

However, perhaps no confirmation hearing was as controversial as that of Clarence Thomas in 1991. Thomas was nominated by George H. W. Bush to replace the ailing Thurgood Marshall (appointed by Lyndon Johnson in 1967 as the first African-American to serve on the Supreme Court). Thomas, who would become

---

🖰 Watch the Senate Confirmation Hearings for Judge Bork.

only the second African-American on the high court, brought his conservative legal views as well as controversy to the proceedings. Upon his nomination, Bush had described Thomas as "a fiercely independent thinker with an excellent legal mind who believes passionately in equal opportunity for all Americans," and as a justice who would "approach the cases that come before the Court with a commitment to deciding them fairly, as the facts and the law require."[19] But during the confirmation hearings, accusations of sexual harassment by Thomas were leaked to the press. Oklahoma University Law School Professor Anita Hill claimed that Thomas had sexually harassed her while he was her supervisor at the Equal Employment Opportunity Commission. Both testified before the Senate Judiciary Committee, and Thomas denied the allegations on live television as the nation watched, transfixed by the "he said, she said" dialogue that took over the confirmation hearings. In the end, Thomas was confirmed by a close 52–48 vote. Many credit the intense interest in the Thomas confirmation hearings with elevating the national dialogue about sexual harassment in the workplace, as well as contributing to what would be called the "Year of the Woman" in 1992, in which a record number of women ran for and were elected to public office at the state and federal level (many women were outraged at the all-male Senate Judiciary Committee's questioning of Hill). Thomas, however, called himself a victim of a "high-tech lynching" due to the media scrutiny 🖱.

Politicizing the Process

The nomination and confirmation process of Supreme Court justices has changed greatly in recent years. Supreme Court nominations used to occur mostly behind closed doors. In most cases, even the president's political opponents in the Senate would allow the president his constitutional prerogative to shape the nation's highest court (the idea that to the victor of the presidential election go the spoils). Despite the fact that the judicial branch, whose members are appointed to life terms, is the one branch most removed from the political process, confirmations to the Supreme Court have nonetheless become a highly politicized process. According to political scientist Mark Silverstein, since 1968, gone are the days of presidential deference when, barring a major controversy, the confirmation process in the Senate was a quiet vote among Washington insiders where members of both parties gave the president his choice. Starting with the failure of Lyndon Johnson to elevate Associate Justice Abe Fortas to Chief Justice in 1968, confirmations have made the shift from "the politics of acquiescence to the politics of confrontation."[20] Fortas ended up being the wrong candidate at the wrong time for Johnson, who was just months away from leaving the White House. Fortas' close relationship with Johnson also raised conflict-of-interest and separation-of-powers issues, as did his acceptance of perceived improper speaking fees. Several young Senate Republicans decided to defy the old rules of the game and opposed Fortas' nomination, and, after a filibuster, Johnson was forced to withdraw his nominee. Party discipline in the Senate had begun to decline, allowing members to act more independently and at times against the wishes of the party leadership. As Silverstein noted about Fortas' failure to become Chief Justice, "the whales had fallen victim to the minnows."[21]

🖱 Watch the Senate Confirmation Hearings for Justice Thomas.

Lyndon Johnson laughs with close friend and advisor Associate Justice Abe Fortas. Fortas' nomination for Chief Justice in 1968 was unsuccessful.

Since the late 1960s, the Senate has become a more open and visible institution, thanks in part to television coverage, as well as to the much larger role that interest groups and lobbyists now play in many aspects of the policymaking process. The judicial confirmation process is no exception, as interest groups spend millions of dollars to campaign for or against a particular nominee. This may make the process more democratic, but it brings confrontational politics into a branch of government regarded as being "above politics." The Senate has clearly moved away from its constitutional mandate of providing "advice and consent" on such matters as judicial confirmations. As a result, many appointments throughout the federal judiciary are now based on the nominee holding a more moderate ideological view in order to avoid controversy during the confirmation process. For example, after the media feeding frenzy during Thomas' hearings in 1991, both of President Clinton's Supreme Court nominees—Ruth Bader Ginsburg in 1993 and Stephen Breyer in 1994—were considered moderates who therefore caused no controversy in the Senate.

In addition to interest-group activity and media coverage, several other factors also contribute to the politicization of a nominee's confirmation vote, like whether or not the president is from the same party as the Senate majority. Thomas' nomination in 1991 represents the last time that a president's selection for the Supreme Court faced a Senate controlled by the opposing party. Both of Clinton's nominations came when Democrats controlled the Senate (Ginsberg in 1993 and

Breyer in 1994), and Bush's nominations of Roberts and Alito in 2005 occurred with a Republican-controlled Senate (Alito's confirmation vote occurred in early 2006). Obama also enjoyed a Senate controlled by Democrats during his nomination of Sotomayor in 2009 and Kagan in 2010. Anti-presidential motivations can also exist and influence negative voting, as does the ideological base of a Senator's constituents, since senators must consider their voting records for reelection purposes. The president's popularity can play a role as well, since high or low approval ratings can influence whether some senators might be willing to block the president's choice.

Ideological voting by senators on judicial confirmations is much more common now than in previous years. As discussed at the start of the chapter, the thirty-one senators who voted against confirming Sotomayor did so based not on her professional qualifications but on her rulings and the belief that she would be a liberal justice. Consider the change that has occurred just since the 1980s in this regard. Antonin Scalia is considered perhaps the strongest conservative voice on the Court, and his rulings are greatly disliked by liberal citizens who do not share his strict constructionist view of the Constitution. Yet, he was confirmed by a 98–0 vote in the Senate in 1986 due to his judicial experience and constitutional expertise. While no one doubted Scalia's conservative viewpoint on constitutional matters, the Senate was still operating under the assumption that their constitutional duty was to simply determine the qualifications and fitness of a judicial candidate, granting the president the prerogative of making his choice (the view that elections have consequences, and that the president had earned the right to choose the justice of his liking as long as the nominee was qualified). Twenty years later, in early 2006, that assumption had changed to a political question for many senators, who stood ready to judge whether or not Samuel Alito should be disqualified from serving on the Court because of his legal ideology. After the Miers' withdrawal, Alito's resume looked more favorable in terms of experience and matched that of his soon-to-be brethren with sixteen years as an appellate judge for the 3rd Circuit, and a law degree from Yale. Yet, many Democrats in the Senate spoke out against Alito's conservative voting record, and did so while looking ahead to the 2006 and 2008 election cycles. By early 2006, Bush's approval rating had fallen to just above 40 percent, and congressional Democrats sensed an opportunity to win back control of the Congress in the 2006 midterm elections. Other senators were also looking ahead to the 2008 presidential contest. As a result, a total of forty-two Democratic senators voted against Alito, knowing that he would nonetheless be confirmed yet taking a public stand against Bush and his attempt at placing another conservative jurist in a lifelong position on the Supreme Court. One particular senator—Barack Obama of Illinois—spoke out quite forcefully against Alito, with the following remarks on the Senate floor prior to Alito's confirmation vote:

> As we all know, there's been a lot of discussion in the country about how the Senate should approach this confirmation process. There are some who believe that the President, having won the election, should have the complete authority to appoint his nominee, and the Senate should only examine whether or not the Justice is intellectually capable and an all-around nice guy. That once you get beyond intellect and personal character, there should be no further question whether the judge should be confirmed. I disagree with this view. I believe firmly

> that the Constitution calls for the Senate to advise and consent. I believe that it calls for meaningful advice and consent that includes an examination of a judge's philosophy, ideology, and record. And when I examine the philosophy, ideology, and record of Samuel Alito, I'm deeply troubled. I have no doubt that Judge Alito has the training and qualifications necessary to serve. He's an intelligent man and an accomplished jurist. And there's no indication he's not a man of great character. But when you look at his record—when it comes to his understanding of the Constitution, I have found that in almost every case, he consistently sides on behalf of the powerful against the powerless; on behalf of a strong government or corporation against upholding Americans' individual rights.[22]

Ironically, less than four years later, Obama's own words were mostly forgotten as he argued for a swift confirmation of his nominee—Sonia Sotomayor—based not on partisanship but on the qualifications of the nominee:

> There are, of course, some in Washington who are attempting to draw old battle lines and playing the usual political games. . . . I hope the confirmation process will begin without delay. No nominee should be seated without rigorous evaluation and hearing; I expect nothing less. But what I hope is that we can avoid the political posturing and ideological brinksmanship that has bogged down this process, and Congress, in the past.[23]

Yet Sotomayor's confirmation, like Alito's, was another example of ideological voting, with many Republican senators casting their votes more in tune with their own constituents and less concerned about judicial qualifications. Of the ten Republican senators who voted in favor of Sotomayor, all but one came from states that Obama had either won or lost by a slim margin in the 2008 presidential election. In addition, not one of the ten senators would seek reelection in 2010, an important fact given that conservative interest groups, including the National Rifle Association, lobbied heavily against Sotomayor and would have likely lobbied against these same senators due to their confirmation votes in the next election cycle. It is clear that Supreme Court nominations are no longer behind-the-scenes events; they now play out in full public view on the national political stage.

Presidential Legacies

Historically, presidents have selected a new justice an average of every two years. Since justices serve a life term, this is an important opportunity for presidents to enjoy a lasting political legacy long after they leave office. But the outcome of the nomination, as well as the justice's voting record once confirmed, is ultimately out of the president's hands. Presidents hope to shape the makeup of the Supreme Court not only in the number of appointments, but also in the quality of the decisions from the men and women that will serve on the bench long after the president has left the White House. George Washington holds the record for the most appointments, since he appointed the six original justices plus four additional justices before the end of his second term in 1797. During his twelve-plus years as president, Franklin D. Roosevelt came close to Washington's record with eight appointments to the Court as well as elevating Justice Harlan Fiske Stone to be Chief Justice. Not all presidents, however, are happy with their choices to the Supreme Court once confirmed. In a much-quoted story, prior to leaving office in 1961, Dwight Eisenhower was asked if he had made any mistakes as president. He responded that yes, he had, and that they were both on the Supreme Court—Chief Justice Earl Warren and Associate Justice William Brennan—who were much more liberal than Eisenhower would have liked.[24] George H. W. Bush had a similar regret with his appointment of Associate Justice David Souter, who Bush thought would be a conservative jurist, but who was a solid vote in the liberal wing of the Court.

Ultimately, as history has shown, each president will nominate an individual to satisfy his own agenda. For example, Ronald Reagan promised voters to nominate the first woman to the Court during the 1980 presidential campaign, and he kept that promise by nominating Sandra Day O'Connor in 1981. But even such an historic appointment was not without some controversy. First, with so few women holding judicial appointments at the time, and even fewer with a conservative background, Reagan did not have a long list of potential women candidates to consider. He would have to look outside of the federal court system to find his nominee; O'Connor was a member of the Arizona State Court of Appeals at the time. Second, upon O'Connor's nomination, Reagan was criticized by both liberals and conservatives for his choice. Liberals were happy to see the first woman join the high court, but they feared that O'Connor's positions, particularly on women's issues, would be too conservative. Conservatives, on the other hand, feared that O'Connor lacked adequate federal judicial experience and knowledge of the U.S. Constitution, and would also uphold abortion rights (Reagan had campaigned to make abortion illegal). Nearly twenty-five years later, when she announced her retirement from the Court in 2005, O'Connor had earned a reputation as a pragmatic and often centrist voice as an important swing vote on issues like abortion, affirmative action, and privacy rights.[25] Yet, in her quarter-century on the high court, her positions on key social issues did not live up to the more conservative policy agenda supported by Reagan during his time in office.

Former Chief Justice William Rehnquist is an excellent example of positive legacy building for a president. First nominated as an Associate Justice by Richard Nixon in 1971 and confirmed in early 1972, Rehnquist was a strong advocate for the law-and-order, states' rights approach to the U.S. Constitution that Nixon advocated. Within three years of Rehnquist's confirmation to the Court, Nixon had resigned from office in 1974 because of the Watergate scandal. Nixon died twenty years later in 1994, and Rehnquist, following his elevation to Chief Justice by Ronald Reagan in 1986, still remained on the Court as one of its most influential members. Prior to his death in 2005, more than thirty-three years after his initial nomination to the Court, and thirty-one years following Nixon's resignation, Rehnquist was closing in on the record for longest serving member of the Supreme Court. Nixon, obviously, had chosen well for the purposes of a long-lasting political legacy, as did Reagan with his elevation of Rehnquist to Chief Justice. Given how long a justice can serve, or how powerful the Court can be in setting certain public policies, that is no small accomplishment.

NOMINATIONS TO LOWER FEDERAL COURTS

The U.S. Constitution provides little guidance as to the development of the federal court system. Article III states that a supreme court will exist, and other federal courts would be established by Congress as needed. From the time the Congress passed the Judiciary Act of 1789 establishing the first lower federal courts, Congress has continued to expand the size of the federal judiciary, passing several newer versions of the Judiciary Act as the nation grew both in size (geographically and in terms of population) and complexity (in terms of public policies). Today, more than one hundred courts make up the federal judicial branch. The lowest federal courts are the district courts, which serve as trial courts with juries. If a district court case is appealed, the next step is a federal court of appeals. There are twelve federal judicial circuits (or territories), and each has its own court of appeals. Congress has also created other specialty courts over the years. They include the U.S. Court of Military Appeals, which hears appeals of military courts-martial, the U.S. Court of Federal Claims, where cases in which the U.S. government has been sued for damages are tried, and the U.S. Court of International Trade, which hears cases involving appeals to rulings by the U.S. Customs Office.

Just as with the Supreme Court, district and appeals court judges serve for lifetime terms. When a vacancy occurs, the president nominates individuals who then must be confirmed by a majority vote in the Senate; federal judges can also be removed from the bench through the process of impeachment in the House of Representatives and removal by a trial in the Senate. In the history of the United States, a total of thirteen federal judges (including Supreme Court Justice Samuel Chase) have been impeached, and seven have also been convicted in the Senate and removed from office. The first, U.S. District Court Judge John Pickering, nominated by George Washington, was removed from office in 1804 for mental instability and intoxication on the bench. The two most recent federal judges to be convicted in the Senate and removed from office, both of which occurred within months of each other in 1989, include U.S. District Court Judges Alcee Hastings, a Jimmy Carter appointee who was removed from office for perjury and conspiracy to solicit a bribe (in 1992, Hastings was elected to the House of Representatives from Florida's 23rd Congressional District, where he continues to serve), and Walter L. Nixon, a Lyndon Johnson appointee who was removed from office for committing perjury before a federal grand jury (he is no relation to President Richard Nixon, who escaped impeachment by the full House by resigning from office in 1974).

Nominating and Confirming Federal Judges

Given the number of federal judgeships and the fact that they are lifetime appointments, presidents can have significant influence over the makeup of the judicial branch by nominating judges who are sympathetic to their policy agendas. So, while presidents may not get the opportunity to nominate individuals to the Supreme Court all that often, they do make more frequent selections for lower court judgeships (about two hundred per four-year term). As such, this is an important opportunity for a president to leave his mark on the judicial branch for many years to come. While lower court appointments are not as high profile as those to the Supreme Court, they are still important decisions made by the White House with the potential for a long-lasting effect on the policy agenda. According to political scientist Sheldon Goldman, judicial selection is influenced by a combination of the president's own policy agenda (the substantive policy goals of the administration), his partisan agenda (using the selection process for political gain for himself or other members of his party), and his personal agenda (the use of the president's decision-making authority to favor a personal friend or colleague). Goldman argues that judicial selection by the president is "an exercise of policy-making furthering a presidential agenda." For example, the Reagan administration, which considered the federal courts to be "so activist as to have created an imbalance in the federal system that threatened state powers and expanded federal judicial policymaking beyond the competence and capacity of the courts... saw judicial appointments as intimately linked to the success of the president's domestic-affairs agenda."[26]

As of 2012, there were more than 850 federal judgeships throughout the lower courts of the judicial branch, with the number of district and appellate judges more than doubling since 1950. This number often fluctuates, as Congress either increases or decreases the number of judicial positions (the latter rarely occurs), or as judges retire or die and the vacancy remains pending the confirmation process. Some presidents have greatly benefitted from the addition of several lower court judgeships while in office, since having more vacancies provides a greater opportunity to reshape the federal bench to reflect the president's governing philosophy (see Table 7.2). The Constitution set forth no specific requirements for qualifications for these positions. However, being seen as qualified for the position (in nearly all cases, holding a law degree and having some professional experience in the legal field) and being sympathetic to the president's political views are important factors in the selection process.

Table 7.2 Total Appointments to the Federal Bench, FDR through Obama

PRESIDENT	U.S. DISTRICT COURT	U.S. COURT OF APPEALS	U.S. SUPREME COURT
Roosevelt	134	51	9
Truman	101	27	4
Eisenhower	129	45	5
Kennedy	102	21	2
Johnson	126	40	2
Nixon	181	46	4
Ford	50	11	1
Carter	203	56	0
Reagan	290	83	4
G. H. W. Bush	148	42	2
Clinton	305	66	2
G. W. Bush	261	61	2
Obama*	126	30	2

*Through September 2012

Source: Biographical Directory of Federal Judges, Federal Judicial Center, www.fjc.gov

Due to the volume of appointments, the president does not usually play a direct role in nominating individuals to lower court positions. The Department of Justice, usually through the deputy attorney general, helps to screen potential nominees, along with other White House staff members. For these appointments, members of Congress also typically recommend potential nominees. In particular, members of the U.S. Senate rely on what is known as senatorial courtesy in the selection and nomination process, most notably for district court nominations. A tradition involving federal appointments that dates back to the early days of the republic, senators from the state where a vacancy has occurred are given the opportunity to have a say in the president's nomination. This is done by the so-called blue-slip procedure, where the senators from the home state of the judicial nominee receive notification by letter from the chair of the Senate Judiciary Committee, along with a blue sheet of paper on which the senator can comment on the nominee. If the senator does not return the blue slip, it is understood to mean that the senator does not approve. In addition, if the senator is not consulted, then he or she has the right to request that the confirmation be denied. Due to the traditions and usual collegiality in the Senate, other senators will normally grant this "courtesy" to their colleagues. Often, the failure to return the blue slip equals a one-person veto to block a particular nomination. Knowing this, presidents usually listen to what senators have to say about filling lower court vacancies. Depending on who is chairing the Senate Judiciary Committee, there have been times when only those senators from the president's party have been allowed to use the practice of senatorial courtesy. For example, during the last six years of the Clinton administration and during which time Republicans controlled the Senate, Judiciary Committee Chairman Orrin Hatch (R-UT) allowed Republican senators to veto Clinton nominees through the blue-slip procedure. But, when fellow Republican George W. Bush entered the White House in 2001, Hatch attempted to weaken the blue-slip procedure to deny home-state Democrats the same opportunity.

Normally, presidents have greater control over the selection of appellate court judges than district court judges, since appellate districts encompass several states, which can serve to weaken the influence of individual senators in the selection process. Since the Reagan administration, presidents have also made a greater effort to select appellate court judges who are closely aligned with their own political ideology. The President's Committee on Judicial Selection, which is made up of White House and Justice Department staffers, was created during the Reagan years to help screen potential judicial appointees based on their previous rulings, speeches, writings, and other types of work to determine their judicial philosophy and political ideology. The Reagan administration, as well as both Bush administrations, was committed to appointing conservative judges to the federal bench (meaning that judges would adhere to judicial restraint and use a more narrow—and literal—view to interpret the Constitution). However, Bill Clinton did not use a similar strategy to appoint liberal judges (those that are considered activist and rely on a more fluid interpretation of the Constitution to match the political and social times), as he focused more on qualifications and an emphasis to appoint more women and minorities to the federal bench.

The increased emphasis by presidents in recent years to shape the federal court system to better match their policy agendas and political philosophies has also increased the contentiousness over nominations in the Senate confirmation process. This was a significant issue during the George W. Bush presidency, as Senate Democrats attempted to block several of Bush's judicial appointments (particularly those at the appellate court level). Prior to 2001, senators had rarely relied on the filibuster to derail a judicial nomination. But when Bush first became president, Democrats in the Senate began relying on the filibuster to successfully block several of his judicial nominations to lower federal courts that they believed were too extreme in their conservative views—a clear example of divisive and partisan politics playing a much larger role in the process. A filibuster is often used by the minority party in the Senate to kill legislation; a filibuster represents unlimited Senate debate which can allow a senator to literally talk a bill to death. In order to end a filibuster, a vote of cloture must be taken, which requires sixty votes for success. Democrats successfully blocked several of Bush's nominees during his first four years in office. In response, Senate Republicans threatened to use the "nuclear option" to bypass the opposition by Democrats, a plan proposed to change the Senate rules to allow a vote of cloture with only a simple majority (fifty-one votes) as opposed to sixty, thereby taking away the Democrats' power to block a judicial nominee. In 2005, a bipartisan compromise brokered by fourteen senators from both parties (nicknamed "the Gang of 14") resulted in an agreement by Democrats to stop filibusters of Bush's judicial nominees except in "extraordinary circumstances"—a term that would not be applied by Democrats until Samuel Alito's nomination to the Supreme Court.

The Candidate Pool

Throughout the federal judiciary, white males still dominate the federal bench. As with Supreme Court nominees, those nominated to the lower federal courts are lawyers, although this is not a constitutional requirement. In addition, many federal judges served previously as state or local judges and/or have worked as a prosecutor. Most nominees also share the partisan affiliation of the president, and many have been involved in partisan politics at some level (which is how many nominees come to light for the White House). Historically, few women have been appointed to federal judicial positions. The main reason for the small number of women being appointed stems from the fact that up until the 1970s few women were entering the legal profession, so a limited pool of qualified women existed for presidential consideration for such posts. As a result, the "integration of women into the federal judiciary has been achingly slow."[27] The same has been true of minority candidates for the federal bench.

FDR appointed the first woman to a federal bench; Florence Ellinwood Allen, appointed in 1934, served on the Sixth Circuit Court of Appeals for twenty-five years. No other woman would be appointed to a court of appeals for thirty-four years, when in 1968 Lyndon Johnson nominated Shirley Ann Mount Hufstedler to the Ninth Circuit Court of Appeals (where she served until 1979). Burnita Shelton Matthews became the first woman to serve on a U.S. district court when Harry Truman issued her a recess appointment to the U.S. District Court for the District of Columbia in October 1949. The Senate confirmed her nomination in April 1950. John F. Kennedy appointed one woman to a district court position, and Johnson appointed two women to district courts. Richard Nixon and Gerald Ford would appoint one woman each to a federal judgeship, both to a district court with no appointments to an appeals court.

Jimmy Carter was the first president to seriously increase the number of women and minorities serving in the judiciary, and as president he had "both the interest and the opportunity to diversify the federal courts" in terms of gender, race, and ethnicity.[28] He appointed a total of forty women to the federal judiciary (twenty-nine to district courts, and eleven to courts of appeal), and fifty-seven minorities (forty-five to district courts, and twelve to courts of appeal). Carter's immediate successors, Ronald Reagan and George H. W. Bush, appointed fewer women and minorities to the federal bench. Reagan, who disapproved of using affirmative action policies in judicial appointments, named a total of thirty women to federal judgeships (twenty-four to district courts and six to courts of appeal), and twenty-three minorities (twenty-one to district courts, and two to courts of appeal). During his one term in office, Bush appointed a total of thirty-six women to the federal bench (twenty-nine to district courts and seven to courts of appeal), and twenty minorities (sixteen to district courts, and four to courts of appeal). Since then, Bill Clinton, George W. Bush, and Barack Obama made important progress in nominating more women and minority-group judges to federal district and appellate courts during their administrations. Clinton appointed 108 women who would serve in federal judicial posts (eighty-eight to district courts and twenty to courts of appeal), and ninety-three minorities (seventy-six to district courts, and seventeen to courts of appeal). During his eight years in office, George W. Bush appointed a total of seventy-one women to the federal bench (fifty-four to district courts and seventeen to courts of appeal), and fifty-seven minorities (forty-nine to district courts and eight to courts of appeal). During Barack Obama's first three years and eight months in office, he appointed a total of sixty-eight women to the federal bench (fifty-seven to district courts and eleven to courts of appeal), and fifty-eight minorities (forty-four to district courts and fourteen to courts of appeal).[29]

Nominations to federal district and appellate courts remain one of the most significant ways that a president can shape the makeup of the judicial branch. While these nominations are rarely as high-profile as a nomination to the Supreme Court, the process has nonetheless become more politicized in recent years as presidents and their advisors continue to view the lower courts as an important opportunity to leave an ideological mark on one aspect of the federal government once their term in office has ended. In addition, much progress has been made in recent decades in regards to naming more women and minorities to the federal bench, a trend that has now taken on a bipartisan approach thanks to efforts by both the Clinton and George W. Bush administrations.

THE PRESIDENT'S RELATIONSHIP WITH THE JUDICIAL BRANCH

While the nomination of federal judges is perhaps the most obvious aspect of the presidential/courts relationship, there are many other ways in which the president interacts with the judicial branch, and in particular the Supreme Court. The political give-and-take among the branches comes through the system of checks and balances within the Constitution. In addition to shaping the personnel of the judicial branch through the nomination process, the president also has some influence over proceedings within the Supreme Court through his selection of the solicitor general, who serves as the attorney representing the federal government when cases are brought challenging the constitutionality of federal laws. Also, the Supreme Court is reliant on other political actors at all levels of government to implement the rulings that it hands down when it decides a case. Since the executive branch is responsible for the implementation of federal laws, the president can play a significant role in the adherence by other federal officials to a Supreme Court ruling. When looking at this relationship from the Supreme Court's perspective, it has often made decisions that define the parameters of presidential powers. As we saw in Chapter 2, the Constitution provides few enumerated powers to the office of the presidency, but the expansion of implied and/or inherent powers of the presidency have often come through Supreme Court decisions. According to presidential scholar Larry Berman, the Supreme Court "constrains and sustains presidential power," and "has generally upheld presidents when they exceeded strict constitutional limits."[30] As such, the relationship between the president and the judiciary has been, and continues to be, complex from both a governing and a political perspective.

The Role of the Solicitor General

While the debate over whether or not the Supreme Court should be involved in policymaking can be a rather contentious one, the fact is that at various times in the nation's history, the Court *has* played a role in shaping public policy. One needs to look no further than the landmark decision of *Brown v. Board of Education* (1954) to see a striking example of the judicial branch acting first, with subsequent actions by the president and Congress, to end segregation in public schools and to provide a significant and early political victory for the Civil Rights Movement. In addition, the Supreme Court's agenda has, at particular times in history, been primarily focused on one specific policy area. From the turn of the twentieth century through the late 1930s, economic issues dominated the cases heard by the Court. Then, civil rights issues, as well as issues involving due process, dominated through the late 1960s (as part of what is often referred to as the Warren Revolution from 1954–1969) and into the early 1970s. During the Rehnquist Court era (1986–2005), issues of federalism and states' rights reemerged, while the Court also kept a strong focus on civil rights and due process issues.[31] Clearly, a president's selection for a Supreme Court justice can alter the output from the Court in terms of its decisions, but other actors within the executive branch play a role as well. As political scientist Robert Dahl observed, "By itself, the Court is almost powerless to affect the course of national policy."[32]

Perhaps the most important position within the executive branch regarding the Supreme Court and its agenda is the U.S. Solicitor General. As the third-ranking official in the Department of Justice, behind the Attorney General and the Deputy Attorney General, the Solicitor General holds one of the most important legal positions within the government; it is also the only high-level position within the federal government that requires, through statute, that the person holding the position be "learned in the law." The solicitor general is nominated by the president and confirmed by the Senate. The Office of Solicitor General was created in 1870; the size of the office is rather small, with twenty-five to thirty attorneys and administrative support. The office is responsible for directly arguing cases before the Court when the federal government is a party to a case. In addition, the solicitor general decides which cases among those lost by the federal government should be appealed to a higher federal court, which makes it the gatekeeper for all appellate litigation involving the federal government. As such, the Solicitor General or one of his or her deputies is the legal advocate for all cases where officers or agencies of the federal government are parties before the Supreme Court. To exemplify the significance that the Solicitor General can have in the selection of cases and/or their outcomes, the position is often referred to as the tenth Supreme Court justice.[33]

Since the solicitor general's office usually shares political and legal viewpoints with the president, the president's policy views will be reflected in the overall pattern of positions that the Solicitor General's office takes in litigation.[34] Despite that fact, the Court gives significant deference to the Solicitor General regarding cases, which makes it a unique position working with both branches of government. According to political scientist Richard L. Pacelle, the solicitor general is expected to formulate consistent legal positions despite the views of the president for whom he or she works, and must pursue a changing agenda within the executive branch while assisting the Court in imposing "doctrinal equilibrium." As a result, "Politics and law are at the intersection of the solicitor general's responsibilities.... The solicitor general operates in a dynamic political environment, but is charged with imposing stability upon the law and legal positions."[35]

Implementing Supreme Court Decisions

As Alexander Hamilton explained in *Federalist* 78, the Supreme Court "has neither force nor will, but merely judgment." As a result, the cooperation of many other political actors at the federal, state, and local levels is necessary to successfully implement decisions by the Court. Chief among those actors is the president, who, along with the rest of the executive branch, is responsible for the implementation of federal laws. While decisions by the Court may affect all Americans, those who most immediately respond to actions by the Court include the Solicitor General, the Attorney General, Cabinet heads, and legal counsel for executive branch agencies. Since decisions handed down by the Court are not self-executing, these executive branch officials play an important role by interpreting judicial rulings and advising the president and others within the executive branch on how to implement the ruling through advisory opinions and the creation of agency policies. State attorneys general play a similar role in advising state and local officials on implementation strategies of Supreme Court decisions. Often, the Court is at the mercy of these other political actors to make sure that the ruling goes into effect. The struggle to implement the *Brown* ruling, particularly in southern states, provides an important example. In 1957, Dwight Eisenhower sent National Guard troops into Little Rock, Arkansas, to end racial segregation at the all-white Little Rock Central High and to quell the violence over the enrollment of nine African American students. John F. Kennedy took similar action in 1962 to force integration at the University of Mississippi to allow enrollment by James Meredith, the first-ever African American student to attend "Ole Miss."

However, it is important to note that presidents can also ignore rulings by the Supreme Court, block attempts at implementation, or attempt to strike back at the Court for rulings that the president does not like. Since the earliest days of the republic, presidents have at times found themselves frustrated by the Supreme Court's power of judicial review. Considered the cornerstone of American constitutional law, judicial review denotes the power of a court to review a policy of government and to invalidate that policy if it is contrary to constitutional principles. However, the Constitution remains silent on the issue of judicial review. The Supreme Court assumed the power to review legislation as early as 1796, when it upheld a federal tax on carriages as valid. Judicial review is also implied, according to some interpretations, through the supremacy clause in Article 6, and in Article 3, which establishes the power of the Court to decide cases. However, the framers were never fully committed to the concept of judicial review. Judicial review had not been discussed at the Convention, but many delegates assumed that courts would have the final power of interpretation. Many at the time were critical; Alexander Hamilton attempted to allay the fears in *Federalist* 78 by declaring the judiciary to be "the least dangerous branch."

The main power of judicial review comes from the Court's ability to strike down legislation, which would not happen until 1803 in *Marbury v. Madison* (1803). The origin of the case has a direct link to the presidency; the Federalists and John Adams lost the presidency and both houses of Congress to the Jeffersonian Republicans in 1800, but sought to preserve their influence over the national government through the courts. The lame duck Congress quickly passed the Judiciary Act of 1801, which created a number of additional federal judgeships for Adams to fill. William Marbury was a Federalist politician appointed to fill a newly created position as a justice of the peace for the District of Columbia. The Senate confirmed Marbury's commission on March 3, 1801, Adams' last day in office. John Marshall, who was then Secretary of State, placed the seal of the United States on the letter of commission, which was ready to be delivered. Marshall's brother James was to deliver the commission, but it went undelivered, and was eventually lost. Thomas Jefferson became president the next day, and ordered his new Secretary of State, James Madison, to not deliver copies of the commission to Marbury and other Federalists who failed to get their judgeships. Jefferson then mounted an effort to repeal the Judiciary Act of 1801. Congress, now controlled by Jeffersonian Republicans, obliged, and also abolished the Supreme Court term of 1802.

The following year, Marbury filed suit against Madison in the Supreme Court, asking the Court, under its original jurisdiction, to issue a writ of mandamus, an order directing Madison to deliver the disputed judicial commission. By then, Marshall was the new Chief Justice (appointed by Adams and confirmed in the last weeks of his administration), but despite the conflict of interest, he did not recuse himself. The Court ruled that Marbury had a legal right to his commission, and that the Jefferson administration was wrong to deny him. However, the Court would not issue the writ of mandamus because it had no authority to do so. The Court's presumed authority to issue the writ was based on Section 13 of the Judiciary Act of 1789, which granted the Court authority to issue writs of mandamus "in cases warranted by the principles and usages of law." But in Marshall's opinion, the Court could not do that since the relevant provision of Section 13 was unconstitutional because it expanded the Court's original jurisdiction. Article III, Section 2 expressly provides that Congress has the authority to regulate the appellate jurisdiction of the Court, which also implies that Congress has no such authority to regulate or change original jurisdiction. Therefore, Section 13 was invalid since it permitted the Court to issue a writ of mandamus in a case under the Court's original jurisdiction. This is the first time that the Court held an act of Congress to be null and void.[36]

Beyond the legendary dispute between Jefferson and Marshall, Andrew Jackson also provides an early example of a president's attempt to challenge the authority of the Supreme Court, particularly its power of judicial review. When Congress passed a bill in 1832 to recharter the Second Bank of the United States, Jackson vetoed the bill and declared in his lengthy veto message that the Supreme Court alone did not have the power to determine the constitutionality of laws. Jackson wrote:

> The Congress, the Executive, and the Court must each for itself be guided by its own opinion of the Constitution. Each public officer who takes an oath to support the Constitution swears that he will support it as he understands it, and not as it is understood by others. It is as much the duty of the House of Representatives, of the Senate, and of the President to decide upon the constitutionality of any bill or resolution which may be presented to them for passage or approval as it is of the supreme judges when it may be brought before them for judicial decision. The opinion of the judges has no more authority over Congress than the opinion of Congress has over the judges, and on that point the President is independent of both. The authority of the Supreme Court must not, therefore, be permitted to control the Congress or the Executive when acting in their legislative capacities, but to have only such influence as the force of their reasoning may deserve.[37]

Jackson, the popular war hero considered to be the first "people's president" and a strong states' rights advocate, often challenged the rulings of the renowned Federalist, Chief Justice Marshall. Also in 1832, Jackson famously, and allegedly, declared, "Well, John Marshall has made his decision, now let him enforce it," after the Court ruled to protect Indian tribal sovereignty against encroachment by state laws.[38]

Presidents can take other actions against the Supreme Court as well. For example, a president can initiate a congressional attack on the Court, as Franklin Roosevelt attempted to do with his court-packing plan 1937. Presidents can also initiate changes in policies or even a constitutional amendment. George H. W. Bush sought a constitutional amendment to ban flag burning after the Court ruled in *Texas v. Johnson* (1989) that the burning of an American flag was an act of free speech protected by the First Amendment. In response, Congress passed H.R. 2978, a bill that provided for a prison term of up to one year for anyone who "knowingly mutilates, defaces, physically defiles, burns, maintains on the floor or ground, or tramples upon" any United States flag. Instead of signing the bill, which he believed would not withstand the Court's scrutiny after the *Texas v. Johnson* ruling, Bush instead urged Congress to pass a constitutional amendment to override the Court's decision. As Bush stated in a written message to Congress:

> After a careful study of the Court's opinion, the Department of Justice concluded that the only way to ensure protection of the flag is through a constitutional amendment. Pursuant to that advice, I urged the adoption of such an amendment.... While I commend the intentions of those who voted for this bill, I have serious doubts that it can withstand Supreme Court review. The Supreme Court has held that the Government's interest in preserving the flag as a symbol

> can never be compelling enough to justify prohibiting flag desecration that is intended to express a message. Since that is precisely the target of this bill's prohibition, I suspect that any subsequent court challenge will reach a similar conclusion. Nevertheless, because this bill is intended to achieve our mutual goal of protecting our Nation's greatest symbol, and its constitutionality must ultimately be decided by the courts, I have decided to allow it to become law without my signature. I remain convinced, however, that a constitutional amendment is the only way to ensure that our flag is protected from desecration.[39]

Since 1989, despite the introduction of such a constitutional amendment being introduced year after year in Congress, the amendment has never received the necessary two-thirds vote in both the House of Representatives and the Senate to then be presented to the states for ratification.

Defining Presidential Powers

Through its power of judicial review, the Supreme Court has often found itself in a position to determine the scope and legitimacy of presidential powers. As discussed in Chapter 2, most often, the Supreme Court approves, expands, or legitimizes presidential powers. One of the most often-cited examples of a Supreme Court ruling that expanded presidential power came in *U.S. v. Curtiss-Wright Export Corp.* (1936). Franklin Roosevelt had placed an arms embargo on countries at war in South America, and the Curtiss-Wright Export Corporation was indicted for ignoring the embargo. The Supreme Court ruled that the embargo was constitutional, and that the president could be empowered to act alone involving foreign affairs. This has stood as an important precedent in the expansion of presidential powers, suggesting that the president has more powers in the arena of foreign as opposed to domestic affairs. Other notable expansions of presidential powers include *The Prize Cases* (1863), in which the Court ruled that Abraham Lincoln's blockade of southern ports during the Civil War was indeed constitutional, even though it was considered an act of war against the Confederate army and Congress (which has the sole authority to declare war) had not taken action. Also, in one of the Court's most infamous rulings, in 1944 (*Korematsu v. United States*), it declared constitutional FDR's decision to relocate and place Japanese Americans in internment camps during World War II. These cases illustrate the Court's willingness to support an expansive view of presidential powers.

However, the Supreme Court can also restrict presidential powers, avoid particular issues regarding presidential actions, or give a two-sided opinion in which it rules against a particular president's actions yet expands presidential authority. The latter occurred in two prominent decisions by the Court. In 1952, the Court both restricted and expanded presidential powers in *Youngstown Sheet and Tube Co. v. Sawyer*. Harry Truman wanted to seize the nation's steel mills to prevent a strike, and he issued an executive order to have the Secretary of Commerce seize and operate the steel mills based on the military needs stemming from America's ongoing involvement in the Korean War. Truman argued that as commander in chief, he had constitutional authority to take this action. Congress had deliberated this issue in 1947 when it passed the Tart–Hartley Act (which limited strikes by labor unions), but had voted down the provision to give the president the type of power that Truman was claiming. In its decision, the Court ruled that the president could not take such an action without the approval of Congress. Yet, the Court also recognized that the president does have certain inherent powers to take actions not specified by the Constitution. Similarly, in *U.S. v. Nixon* (1974), Richard Nixon challenged the special prosecutor's subpoena for White House tapes during the Watergate investigation. While the Court ruled against Nixon and made him turn over the tapes (which implicated him in the cover-up of the Watergate scandal and led to his resignation from office), the Court also claimed for the first time that executive privilege does exist (which means that a president can have private conversations with advisors). However, the Court did not support unlimited executive privilege, which Nixon had tried to claim.

CONCLUSION

While Alexander Hamilton may have declared the Supreme Court to be "the least dangerous branch" in *Federalist* 78,[40] the life tenure of federal judges, along with the difficulty in overturning a Supreme Court decision (which can occur only through a constitutional amendment or the Court overturning its own decision), has at times posed a significant challenge to a president's attempts at and ability to govern. Yet, while the president may have no control over the Supreme Court's power to interpret the constitutionality of federal laws and actions by federal officials, the president does play a significant role in the selection of federal judges and can, through the U.S. Solicitor General, help to influence the docket of cases pending in federal courts, including the Supreme Court. There has long been a relationship between the president and the federal judiciary that is based on the give-and-take of shared yet separate powers. Not all presidents have been given carte blanche by the courts in their attempts to expand presidential powers, and not all presidents have been successful in their attempts to reshape the federal judiciary to reflect their ideological perspective and political agenda. Yet, history has shown that certain presidents have, at times, had success in shaping the focus of the Supreme Court through key appointments, and have had their actions (particularly those not explicitly outlined in the Constitution) legitimized by the Court. As this chapter illustrates, the relationship between the president and the federal judiciary represents the challenging task of each trying to balance their constitutional functions against the backdrop of the current political environment. However, the evolution of this relationship has played, and continues to play, a vital role in maintaining the checks and balances as set out by the framers of the Constitution.

SELECTING A CHIEF JUSTICE

THEN . . .

Of the forty-three men who have held the office of the presidency, all but four (William Henry Harrison, Zachary Taylor, Andrew Johnson, and Jimmy Carter) had the opportunity for at least one appointment to the Supreme Court. While the president has an opportunity to shape the ideological leaning of the Court for years to come through his selection of a nominee, it is the opportunity to pick a Chief Justice that is perhaps most significant for the future direction of the Court as well as the evolution of a president's legacy. Throughout the nation's history, only seventeen men have served as Chief Justice, so it is a rare presidential opportunity when such a vacancy occurs. However, not all Chief Justices have been powerful forces on the Supreme Court. Under the first Chief Justice, John Jay (1789–1795), the earliest sessions of the Court were devoted to organizational proceedings; the first cases did not reach the Court until 1790, and the justices would not hand down their first opinion until 1792. Between 1790 and 1799 the Court decided only about fifty cases and made few significant decisions.[41] As a result, the first justices to serve complained that the Court had a limited stature. Jay, concerned that the Court lacked prestige, resigned in 1795 to become envoy to England and later Governor of New York.[42] Jay was followed in the chief justiceship by John Rutledge, who served briefly in a recess appointment (but was never confirmed by the Senate), and then Oliver Ellsworth, who stayed in the position for five years. Like Jay, both men had been appointed by George Washington (the only president to experience more than one vacancy for this position), but all three failed to make a grand mark on the position.

Despite the pleading of President John Adams, Jay could not be persuaded to accept reappointment as Chief Justice when the post again became vacant in 1800. Adams, a Federalist, instead appointed John Marshall in the last weeks of his presidency in January 1801 to save the constitution from the incoming Anti-Federalist Jeffersonian Republicans. Marshall served in this position until his death in 1835, the longest tenure of any chief justice, and he "dominated the Court to a degree that no other justice has matched."[43] With Marshall at the helm, the Supreme Court began to take a much more prominent role in American government. The Marshall Court was aggressive in its assertion of power, granting extensive authority not only to the federal government but to the Court itself. Without a doubt, the most important decision ever handed down by the Court came in 1803, when, in his majority opinion in *Marbury v. Madison*, Marshall established the Supreme Court's power of judicial review. Marshall would later use that power in another important case, *McCulloch v. Maryland* (1819), in which the Court upheld both the "supremacy" and "necessary and proper" clauses of the Constitution in ruling that the State of Maryland could not tax a federal bank. Marshall's greatest legacy is not only in shaping the position of Chief Justice but in advancing policies that he favored to strengthen the national government during its earliest days. His decisions "stand as a comprehensive exposition of the Constitution on a par with the Federalist Papers, on which he drew heavily. Unlike those famous essays, however, Marshall's opinions were the law of the land."[44]

Roger B. Taney, appointed by Andrew Jackson to succeed Marshall as Chief Justice (and who held the position from 1836 until 1864), differed from Marshall in many ways. Whereas Marshall was a supporter of a strong national government, Taney supported states' rights. As a justice, he was also more restrained, and he redefined Marshall's strong nationalist view to allow dual federalism, with states maintaining rights over many social and economic matters. Taney is best remembered for the infamous decision in the 1857 *Dred Scott v. Sandford* case, in which he proclaimed that states were not required to consider blacks as citizens of the United States and that slaves were property, a right protected by the Constitution. The decision enflamed public opinion over the issue of slavery, and played a role in the election of Abraham Lincoln as president in 1860, followed by the start of the Civil War in 1861.

Following the Marshall and Taney courts, where each Chief Justice served for many years and left many legal and political legacies, a Chief Justice of the same significance would not emerge again until the mid-twentieth century. Upon the death of Chief Justice Fred M. Vinson in 1953, Dwight Eisenhower found himself in the position to make a crucial selection for the Supreme Court. After nominating Earl Warren, the former Republican governor of California, Eisenhower explained his selection to reporters:

> From the very beginning, from the moment of the unfortunate death of my great friend, Mr. Vinson, I have been thinking over this whole thing. I certainly wanted a man whose reputation for integrity, honesty, middle-of-the-road philosophy, experience in Government, experience in the law, were all such as to convince the United States that here was a man who had no ends to serve except the United States, and nothing else. Naturally, I wanted a man who was healthy, strong, who had not had any serious illnesses, and who was relatively young—if you can call a man of approximately my age relatively young—relatively young with respect to some

Following his nomination by Dwight Eisenhower, Earl Warren became the fourteenth Chief Justice of the United States in 1953.

> others that I was thinking of. On balance, to my mind he is a man who will make a great Chief Justice; and so I selected him.[45]

In his memoirs, Eisenhower would also write of the Warren nomination: "Among the factors that guided me in the search, partisan politics had no place.... My goal was a United States Supreme Court worthy of the high esteem of the American people."[46] The Warren appointment did indeed become a significant selection to the Supreme Court; the new chief justice barely had time to acclimate himself to his new position before he had to confront one of the most important cases in the Court's history in *Brown v. Board of Education* (1954). But many other significant rulings came from the Warren Court prior to his retirement in 1969, as he greatly expanded civil rights and civil liberties through his leadership on the Court. The Warren Court "revolutionized constitutional law and American society" with important rulings on privacy rights, criminal procedures that protected the rights of the accused, equal voting rights, and many other policy areas.[47] Yet, despite Warren's presence on the list of most influential Chief Justices, Eisenhower was not pleased with the liberal direction in which his nominee took the Court.

Replacing Warren as Chief Justice, however, was not an easy political task. Announcing his retirement in June 1968, the initial nomination to replace Warren fell to Lyndon Johnson at a time when the President was embattled over the ongoing war in Vietnam and had already announced his intentions not to seek the Democratic presidential nomination. Johnson nominated Associate Justice Abe Fortas, whom he had first appointed to the Supreme Court in 1965. A close friend and advisor to Johnson, Fortas's nomination for the Chief Justice job faced considerable opposition in the Senate, particularly from conservatives (including Southern Democrats) who did not like Fortas' liberal rulings. In his confirmation hearings before the Senate Judiciary Committee, Fortas faced tough questions about his close relationship with Johnson as well as speaking fees that he had accepted from private business interests to give a series of talks at American University. Senate Republicans decided to filibuster the Fortas nomination, and after Democrats (who were in the majority) failed 45–43 on a vote of cloture, Fortas withdrew his nomination. Critical news media coverage of the Fortas nomination also played a role, as did Johnson's inability to recognize the difficult political environment in which he was attempting to make a "lame duck" appointment to the Court.[48] As a result, Warren would remain on the Court until after the presidential election of 1968. Richard Nixon would then have the opportunity to fill the vacancy, which he did with Chief Justice Warren Burger, who would serve until his own retirement in 1986.

... AND NOW

The death of William Rehnquist in September 2005 marked the end of yet another era for the Supreme Court. Rehnquist had served more than three decades on the high court, with nearly twenty years as Chief Justice. Naming his replacement would fall to George W. Bush. During the 2000 presidential election, anticipation had run high that the nation's next chief executive would have several vacancies to fill on the Supreme Court. That anticipation helped to galvanize social conservatives within the Republican Party in its support for then-candidate George W. Bush. Throughout his campaign for the White House, Bush had promised to nominate men and women with conservative legal philosophies who were "strict constructionists" (a legal philosophy that limits interpreting the U.S. Constitution to the actual words and phrases used) to federal judicial openings, particularly those on the Supreme Court. Social conservatives had long opposed the judicial activism of earlier Supreme Courts, most notably during the 1960s and 1970s, for expanding privacy rights and due process rights through more liberal interpretations of the U.S. Constitution. Yet, during Bush's first term, he would have no Supreme Court vacancies. In 2004, when Bush was reelected, eight of the nine justices were sixty-five years or older, including two members of the Court—Rehnquist and John Paul Stevens—who were over the age of eighty. In addition, Rehnquist's health had been in decline for some time. Battling thyroid cancer, Rehnquist missed several oral arguments during the 2004–2005 term and was visibly frail in January 2005 when he administered the oath of office to Bush at his second inauguration. Despite that, he had no plans to retire.

Instead, Sandra Day O'Connor announced at the end of the Court's session in June 2005 her intention to retire, finally giving Bush his first opportunity for a Supreme Court appointment. It was also an opportunity for Bush to make good on his promise to the social conservatives within the Republican Party, widely credited with his reelection victory in 2004, who expected a justice that would move the Court in a more conservative direction. While Samuel Alito would eventually replace O'Connor on the Court, John Roberts was the first nominee (followed by Harriet Miers and then Alito). Roberts represented the ideal choice for Bush and his conservative supporters. After graduating from Harvard Law School, Roberts clerked for then-Associate Justice Rehnquist; he also held positions within both the Justice Department and the White House during the Reagan years, and served as a deputy solicitor general from 1989 to 1993 while George H. W. Bush was president. George W. Bush appointed Roberts to the U.S. Court of Appeals for the District of Columbia in 2003. Upon announcing Roberts' nomination to the Supreme Court, Bush stated that Roberts had "the qualities Americans expect in a judge: experience, wisdom, fairness, and civility. He has profound respect for the rule of law and for the liberties guaranteed to every citizen. He will strictly apply the Constitution and laws, not legislate from the bench."[49]

However, Rehnquist died while Roberts' nomination was still pending before the Senate Judiciary Committee, which then prompted Bush to elevate his nomination to Chief Justice. Bush urged the Senate to act quickly on the Roberts nomination with the start of the Supreme Court term near:

> The passing of Chief Justice William Rehnquist leaves the center chair empty just four weeks left before the Supreme Court reconvenes. It is in the interest of the Court and the country to have a Chief Justice on the bench on the first full day of the fall term. The Senate is well along in the

process of considering Judge Roberts' qualifications. They know his record and his fidelity to the law. I'm confident that the Senate can complete hearings and confirm him as Chief Justice within a month."[50]

Roberts would be confirmed by the Senate by a 78–22 vote (with all dissenters from the Democratic Party), and while it was considered a narrow vote for a Chief Justice, the vote margin was wider than that of his predecessor (Rehnquist had been confirmed as Chief Justice by a vote of 65 to 33 in 1986). For many Court observers, Roberts is viewed as similar to Rehnquist in his judicial philosophy—a conservative jurist who more often than not believes in judicial restraint, relying on precedent, and is protective of states' rights. Whether the Roberts Court is viewed as activist or restrained in its rulings, and what impact the Court may have on public policies, will in part be determined by future vacancies on the Court. With his confirmation in 2005 as Chief Justice at the age of fifty, John Roberts is expected to guide the nation's highest court for several years, or even decades, to come.

SUGGESTED READINGS

Abraham, Henry J. 2008. *Justices, Presidents, and Senators: A History of the U.S. Supreme Court Appointments from Washington to Bush II*, 5th ed. Lanham, MD: Rowman & Littlefield.

Baum, Lawrence. 2007. *The Supreme Court*, 9th ed. Washington, DC: CQ Press.

Goldman, Sheldon. 1997. Picking Federal Judges: Lower Court Selection from Roosevelt through Reagan. New Haven: Yale University Press.

McCloskey, Robert G. 1994. *The American Supreme Court*, 2nd ed., rev. by Sanford Levinson. Chicago: University of Chicago Press.

McGuire, Kevin T. 2002. *Understanding the U.S. Supreme Court: Cases and Controversies*. New York: McGraw-Hill.

O'Brien, David M. 2008. *Storm Center: The Supreme Court in American Politics*, 8th ed. New York: W. W. Norton.

Pacelle, Richard L., Jr. 2003. *Between Law and Politics: The Solicitor General and the Structuring of Race, Gender, and Reproductive Rights Litigation*. College Station: Texas A&M University Press.

Rosenberg, Gerald N. 1991. *The Hollow Hope: Can Courts Bring About Social Change?* Chicago: University of Chicago Press.

Salokar, Rebecca Mae.1992. *The Solicitor General: The Politics of Law*. Philadelphia: Temple University Press.

Silverstein, Mark. 1994. *Judicious Choices: The New Politics of Supreme Court Confirmations*. New York: W. W. Norton.

Yalof, David Alistair. 1999. *Pursuit of Justices: Presidential Politics and the Selection of Supreme Court Nominees*. Chicago: University of Chicago Press.

ON THE WEB

http://www.supremecourtus.gov/. The official web page of the U.S. Supreme Court, with information about current cases, biographies of the justices, information about court procedures, and the history of the Court.

http://lp.findlaw.com/. A comprehensive web page providing information on the Supreme Court and its decisions, as well as state courts and relevant decisions.

http://www.uscourts.gov/. The official web page for the federal judicial branch.

http://www.fjc.gov. The Federal Judicial Center, which is the education and research center for the federal courts, including a biographical database of all federal judges, past and present.

IN THEIR OWN WORDS

SEEKING JUSTICE

In 1945, President Harry Truman appointed Supreme Court Associate Justice Robert H. Jackson to serve as U.S. chief of counsel for the prosecution of Nazi war criminals at the Nuremburg Trials, a series of military tribunals held from November 20, 1945, to October 1, 1946. Jackson, a former U.S. Attorney General and a member of the Supreme Court since 1941, would take a leave of absence from his duties on the Court to represent the United States (one of the four allied countries, along with Britain, France, and the Soviet Union conducting the trial). Jackson also helped to draft the London Charter of the International Military Tribunal, which created the legal basis for the Nuremberg Trials. Another former U.S. Attorney General, Francis Biddle, served as a judge at the Nuremburg Trials. Biddle had succeeded Jackson as attorney general after Franklin Roosevelt nominated Jackson to the Supreme Court in 1941. Biddle resigned from the attorney general post after Roosevelt's death in 1945, at Truman's request. According to many historical accounts, this was one of the first resignations of an FDR appointee that Truman sought, and shortly thereafter, Truman appointed Biddle to the Nuremburg post in an attempt to make up for requesting his resignation as attorney general. The following correspondence between Jackson and Truman highlights the political considerations both in the United States and globally surrounding the trials during the spring of 1946.

In a letter dated April 2, 1946, Truman wrote to Jackson:

> I appreciated very much your letter of March twenty-fifth, which I just received along with enclosed correspondence with the Chief Justice. I think you have arrived at the right decision. It is vitally important now particularly that this program, on which you are working, be brought to a successful conclusion, no matter how long it takes and, while I regret exceedingly that it is necessary for you to be away from the Court so long, I don't think it would be in the public interest now to break the continuity of your program. I think you have done a remarkable job and I know you want to see it to a conclusion. The arrangements which you have made with the Chief Justice, I think, are entirely satisfactory to all concerned. Best of luck to you and give them everything that is coming to them. I would appreciate it very much if you would elaborate a little bit in your next letter on Mr. Biddle.[51]

Jackson responded on April 24, 1946:

> Your request that I elaborate concerning Mr. Biddle's attitude toward our case can be answered briefly. Our case has two aspects. One is purely legal—conviction of these particular defendants. The other may be called political. It is the effect of the trial on the future attitude of the German people and other people towards Nazism.

The difficulty is that there seems to be insufficient appreciation on the bench of the international and German aspects of the case. The British judge is an admiralty and equity judge accustomed to handling purely private litigation, but he has seemed unaware of the political implications of this case. I had hoped that Mr. Biddle, in view of his experience in Government, would sense this situation and assert his influence in the direction of a strong control by the Tribunal of such witnesses as Goering and Rosenberg. In this I have been disappointed. Early in my cross-examination, when I tried to get from Goering a "yes" or "no" answer, the Lord Justice, at Biddle's prompting and without any objection by Goering's counsel, informed him that he could make any explanation he desired in connection with his answer. The result was a series of irrelevant speeches full of professions of patriotism and martyrdom which the Allied Control Council fear aroused sympathy for him, and he generally ran over us in a way that gave a bad impression of our own capacity to deal with him. As the *New York Times* said, our appeals for support from the Tribunal were little heeded. I am sure that the ruling proceeded from a zeal to be fair to Goering, coupled with the failure to sense his belligerent determination to revive Nazism and menace to the future peace thereby.

But so far as the strictly legal case is concerned, it has not been harmed. In fact, by their long harangues Goering, Ribbentrop and Rosenberg have been compelled to admit the authenticity of every single document which incriminates them. The defendants themselves have come to a pretty firm conviction that they are licked and have got to the stage of accusing each other and making professions of penitence.

One of the objections to the course the Tribunal has adopted is that it prolongs the case. Five years from now, no doubt, no one will ask whether the case ran a few months more or less. But for today there is a good deal of feeling that it is taking too long. I myself feel that it is, but there are several things to be borne in mind about its duration. In the first place, it is not yet a year from the surrender of Germany and we all know how rare it is that any case in the United States even gets to trial at all within a year after it is commenced. In the second place, we have found much more evidence than we ever expected to get. We now have over 4,000 documents of importance to the case embracing the minutes of secret conferences, speeches, orders, and reports. There never has been a war whose origins have been so carefully documented, and the defense does not impeach them in the least. . . .

The plain fact is there are a good many people (I do not say this includes the judges) who do not want the Nuremburg trail to end in a hurry for they are better billeted and better provided for here than they would be any place else in the world, and at the expense of the United States. This must be borne in mind in deciding whether there should be any future international trials.

I was also disturbed to learn that the British Lord Justice the other night in discussing the delay of the trial remarked that of course I was in a hurry to get the trial over as he understood I desired to get back to the States to run for Governor of New York. Unfortunately, that sort of story has been going around. I have been reluctant to get into the business of answering their rumors, but I shall take pains to let the Lord Justice know and I think you

> should know that under no circumstances would I consider leaving the bench to run for Governor of New York or any other political office. I am sure that you understand that I am not using this task for political purposes, and the rumor that it has that purpose has, or course, tended to stimulate people to make attacks upon it that would not otherwise do so.
>
> I suppose I am unduly sensitive about these delays because I have been away from home nearly a year and my absence from the Court causes criticism of you as well as of me. Now you have additional complications due to the death of the Chief Justice which leaves only a seven-man Court and may disable it from deciding some further cases. As you know, I should have been back for the sitting of the Court if the Chief Justice had not written me as he did. And if the situation becomes embarrassing to you in any way that could be relieved by my returning for an argument session, I will be ready to do it. My impression is, however, that it will be better as Chief Justice Stone thought to let any undecided cases go over to fall when there will doubtless be a full bench to decide them. But I want to make clear that I am ready to do whatever you think best, having in mind both the domestic and foreign situation.[52]

Truman responded on May 1, 1946:

> I appreciated very much your good letter of the twenty-fourth and I am more than happy to have the analysis of the approach of the court in this case. I think you are entirely right that they have overlooked the tremendous political implications of this trial, especially as it will affect future aggressions and psychological attitude of Germany and Japan. As I have said before, I think you have done an outstanding job and I can't tell you how much I appreciate your willingness to undergo the hardship of carrying on the trial. I'll talk with you further about the situation when I see you.[53]

CHAPTER 8

Presidents and the Executive Branch

While the president may serve as the top-ranking official of the executive branch, many presidents have held quite diverse views on the appropriate size of the federal government and role of the executive branch in the day-to-day lives of Americans. For example, on March 4, 1933, facing the Great Depression, Franklin Roosevelt laid out a mandate for a strong federal government to get the country back on track in his first inaugural address: "It is to be hoped that the normal balance of executive and legislative authority may be wholly adequate to meet the unprecedented task before us. But it may be that an unprecedented demand and need for undelayed action may call for temporary departure from that normal balance of public procedure.... I shall ask the Congress for the one remaining instrument to meet the crisis—broad executive power to wage a war against the emergency, as great as the power that would be given to me if we were in fact invaded by a foreign foe."[1] During his twelve-plus years in office, FDR would oversee a tremendous expansion of the federal government in terms of its size and power with the implementation of his New Deal initiatives. Within a few months of taking office, FDR, with Congress' approval, secured a package of measures covering a broad array of social services and expanding the regulatory authority of the executive branch over workers, employers, farmers, utilities, banks, consumer prices, wages, natural resources, and much more.

Ronald Reagan's view of the role of the federal government, as articulated during his first inaugural address in 1981, would stand in stark contrast to FDR's view forty-eight years earlier. A one-time New Deal Democrat turned conservative Republican, Reagan sought to usher in a new era of government with one of the more memorable lines of his presidency: "In this present crisis, government is not the solution to our problem; government *is* the problem."[2] Reagan's belief in the need for smaller government, and his campaign promises to get "Washington" off the backs of average Americans, helped him defeat incumbent Jimmy Carter at a time when Americans were feeling the economic pains from a recession that included high unemployment and inflation. Since the Reagan years, all presidents have felt the public pressure to at least talk about the need to decrease and streamline the size of the federal government. For example, during his State of the Union address in 1996, Bill Clinton proclaimed that "the era of big government is over." Yet achieving the task of shrinking the size of the federal government, whether through the size of the federal budget, the number of federal agencies, or the number of federal employees, has been elusive. Reagan would achieve nominal reductions in a few areas, but he did not achieve consistent results throughout his administration, and he left office in 1989 with a larger executive branch than when he entered office in 1981.[3]

Many ironies can be found in the contrasting views of FDR and Reagan regarding the federal government's role in the day-to-day lives of Americans. Among them is the fact that Reagan talked frequently about how FDR was one of the previous presidents whom he admired most. Yet, political circumstances had changed greatly by the 1980s as the expansion of federal programs from FDR's New Deal in the 1930s, and Lyndon Johnson's Great Society programs in the 1960s (some of which were also expanded by Richard Nixon in the early 1970s) began to take a toll on the federal budget. The growth of the modern conservative movement, of which Reagan served as an early leader, also provided the political rallying call to shrink the size of the federal government and give many powers back to the states. The enduring question over big versus small government continues to highlight the essence of the debate about the role of government in American's lives: Just how active and (in the views of many) intrusive should the federal government be? The question first emerged during the constitutional debates and continues to this day. Reagan's inaugural address sparked the debate anew as he linked the economic woes of the 1970s and early 1980s to big and overly intrusive government. The so-called "Reagan Revolution" refers directly to efforts to dismantle what FDR built—a big government designed to provide a social safety net and regulation of economic behavior. Specifically, the Reagan Revolution objected to the excessive regulation of business, yet Reagan did not explicitly reject FDR's view regarding the active role of the presidency to manage and lead the bureaucracy. Like all modern presidents since FDR, Reagan accepted the role as Chief Executive to "faithfully" execute the laws of the land, to manage the bureaucracy, but also to "encourage" the bureaucracy to execute his political agenda. Yet, managing the bureaucracy is one of the areas where the institutional aspects of the presidency can greatly outweigh the ability of an individual president to leave a lasting political legacy.

THE JOB OF THE CHIEF EXECUTIVE

The president's relationship to the Executive Branch comes from three distinct clauses in Article II of the Constitution:

> The executive Power shall be vested in a President of the United States of America.

> He shall nominate, and by and with the Advice and Consent of the Senate, shall appoint Ambassadors, other public Ministers and Consuls,... and all other Officers of the United States, whose Appointments are not herein otherwise provided for, and which shall be established by Law: but the Congress may by Law vest the Appointment of such inferior Officers, as they think proper, in the President alone, in the Courts of Law, or in the Heads of Departments. He may require the Opinion, in writing, of the principal Officer in each of the executive Departments, upon any subject relating to the Duties of their respective Offices.

As with most aspects of the Constitution, the document is under-defined or silent on critical components of the presidency. For example, what does it mean to "execute?" And, what are the departments? The president receives reports from all departments but beyond the Army, Navy, and Militia, none are specified. The president can hire or "appoint" individuals to serve in the government, but the Constitution makes no mention of firing these individuals. That is the limit to what the Constitution says about the president's preeminent day-to-day job of running the government.

As discussed in Chapter 2, part of the reason for the silence is the desire for a limited presidency. The framers recognized the need for a single individual able to act in a crisis, but they were adamantly opposed to creating an executive with wide-ranging power over a bloated bureaucracy. Moreover, much of the opposition to the Constitution following the Convention in 1787 centered on this new office, which to Anti-Federalists looked suspiciously like a concealed monarchy. Alexander Hamilton, in *Federalist* 69–77, attempted to distance the presidency from the monarchy, specifically by diminishing the powers of the office. In terms of the executive branch, Hamilton noted that a king could appoint and remove whomever he wanted, for whatever position he wanted, whenever he wanted. The president, as defined by the Constitution, could not create offices and could only appoint individuals to them with the consent of the Senate. As a result, Hamilton contended, "Hence it appears that, except as to the concurrent authority of the President in the article of treaties, it would be difficult to determine whether that magistrate would, in the aggregate, possess more or less power than the Governor of New York."[4]

The *Federalist Papers* were, of course, written to be political persuasive propaganda; critics could and did take issue with the powers of the presidency. However, Hamilton was correct in that of all the components of the presidency the executive powers were not controversial. Regarding the powers to "faithfully execute" the office of the presidency, or the requirement of presidential reports, Hamilton argued that "no objection has been made to this class of authorities; nor could they possibly admit of any."[5] Part of the reason for the lack of criticism could simply have been all the other items to which Anti-Federalists took issue; or, the lack of imagination about what the job would entail might have muted some of the criticism.

The Bureaucracy Evolves

For the first one hundred years of the nation, the federal bureaucracy was relatively small. In 1816, the U.S. Census data showed 6,327 paid employees in the Executive Branch, not including military personnel.[6] In contrast, in 2008, there were approximately 2.7 million, non-military, federal employees, who were paid a total of $162,675,000.[7] The first Congress created the first four departments in the Executive

Branch: Treasury, State, and War, plus an Attorney General for legal advice. These same departments existed in the government under the Articles of Confederation. The departments contained few employees beyond the Secretary and minimal staff. For example, the Department of State initially consisted of two diplomats and ten consular posts abroad, and four clerks and a messenger domestically. The total expenditures for the Department were a mere $56,600.[8] Almost immediately, however, like single-celled organisms whose sole purpose is division, the departments enlarged and specialized. In just eleven years, the Treasury Department had enough distinguishable work to add a commissioner of revenue (tax collector), an auditor, and a general land office.[9] The biggest problems with administration for the early presidents were staffing and corruption—after all, the majority of federal employees were not in Washington, D.C. The early federal jobs were collecting duties and taxes and delivering the mail. In order to manage corruption, the Washington administration relied on appointments of "men of good character;" that is, men who were respected in their communities. However, financial incentives existed as well—customs agents received a share of the profits from capturing and selling seized contraband.[10]

George Washington could focus on character because of his nonpartisan approach to the office. Immersed in a partisan atmosphere, Washington's successor, John Adams, tried to use government employment as a political tool. After Adams lost his bid for reelection to Thomas Jefferson in 1800, but before Jefferson took office, Adams appointed numerous loyal Federalists to government positions. In particular, as discussed in Chapter 7, he appointed William Marbury as Justice of the Peace for Washington, D.C. The Senate approved the position but the commission was never delivered, so Marbury sued James Madison (Jefferson's Secretary of State) by writ of mandamus, which was an order to an official to do his duty. John Marshall, Chief Justice of the United States and an ardent Federalist, ruled against Marbury, but in the process he established the power of judicial review. In the aftermath, inter-party battles disappeared as the Federalist Party imploded and Jefferson's Democratic Republican party dominated politics. As a result, appointments to the bureaucracy followed Washington's approach until Andrew Jackson became president.

Attitudes toward the bureaucracy, as well as management of it, changed with Jackson's election in 1828. In keeping with his views of democratizing the federal government, Jackson opened the government job rolls to men outside of the elite, upper classes; instead of relying on "character" to select individuals, Jackson relied on politics. As such, Jackson's approach to making appointments to the executive branch relied on partisanship. After the split in the Jeffersonian Democratic Republicans, which occurred after the 1824 election, Jackson became leader of half of the party and took the name with him. The remaining members, followers of President John Quincy Adams, named themselves the Whigs, beginning the two-party system. With the return of full-scale political party warfare, the rotation of people in office based on political party victory became the "spoils system," named after New York Senator William Marcy's famous quote from 1832, "to the victor belong the spoils of the enemy."[11] However, Jackson's intention was not simply patronage, or rewarding one's supporters, but also shortened service. By 1832, long tenure in office, in the bureaucracy as well as among elected officials, became the norm. Ironically, Jackson's efforts to democratize the administration made it more formal, routinized, and bureaucratic because more procedures and more positions were needed to help novices do their new jobs.[12]

The "spoils system" continued until corruption, incompetence, and the assassination of President James Garfield in 1881 forced civil service reform. Views about the inability to get a government job without being a party insider came to a head as Charles Guiteau stalked several members of Garfield's administration in hope of receiving a consulship to Paris. After failing to secure a position, and being told by Secretary of State William Blaine never to return, Guiteau decided to kill the President. The firestorm after the assassination led to the Pendleton Civil Service Reform Act of 1881. The Act applied only to federal employees (so in effect did not completely challenge the political patronage system still in place at the state level) and made merit the criteria for hiring and firing in all but cabinet-level jobs. By 1933, when FDR took office, 80 percent of federal workers were included in the merit system.[13]

The Bureaucracy Today

The twenty-first century bureaucracy seems enormous, as it is more than four hundred times the size of the U.S. government in the early years. If all military personnel are added to that figure of federal employees, it is 530 times as large. Even more notable, the twenty-first century population is only seventy-seven times as large as that of the late 1780s. If the population grew at the rate of the bureaucracy's growth, the United States' population would be more than 1.5 billion people instead of the current 304 million. Today, the executive branch consists of fifteen separate departments tasked with overseeing the implementation and administration of the laws and programs created by Congress (see Table 8.1). The departments promote, among other things, the farm economy, the business economy, and energy; they protect citizens from illness and provide standards of manufacturing; they provide services to homeowners and renters, senior citizens, veterans, students, and travelers; and they protect citizens at home and abroad. The executive branch of the United States does not make anything, per se, but few aspects of "life, liberty, or the pursuit of happiness" remains untouched by federal government rules and regulations.

For the modern president, the size of government is moot; as Alexander Hamilton noted, the president can neither create nor remove a department, agency, or bureau. The power to reshape the government belongs to Congress and can only be accomplished by legislation. However, contemporary presidents have attempted to shape that legislation by offering proposals to Congress. For example, Jimmy Carter did that in 1979 to help create the Department of Education, which also resulted in the Department of Health, Education, and Welfare being renamed the Department of Health and Human Services with the addition of a stand-alone cabinet agency to handle educational matters. George W. Bush undertook the most recent reshaping of the federal government in 2002 with the addition of a new cabinet-level agency. After the terrorist attacks on September 11, 2001, Congress and the president agreed that poor coordination between federal law enforcement agencies hampered the ability to catch the perpetrators prior to the attacks. Bush charged five White House aides with creating a blueprint for a new department devoted to homeland security to submit to Congress. Although the Senate had its own proposal, the White House's view dominated the outcome. Bush signed a bill into law just five months later, on November 25, 2002, which established the Department of

Table 8.1 The Cabinet

OFFICE	DATE CREATED
Department of State	1789
Department of Treasury	1789
Department of Defense	1949
(Replaced the Department of War, created in 1789, and the Department of Navy, created in 1798.)	
Department of Justice	1870
(The position of Attorney General was originally created by the Judiciary Act of 1789.)	
Department of the Interior	1849
Department of Agriculture	1862
(Not given cabinet status until 1889.)	
Department of Commerce	1903
Department of Labor	1913
Department of Health and Human Services	1980
(Replaced the Department of Health, Education and Welfare, created in 1953.)	
Department of Housing and Urban Development	1965
Department of Transportation	1967
Department of Energy	1977
Department of Education	1979
Department of Veterans Affairs	1989
Department of Homeland Security	2002

(Cabinet offices are listed in order of presidential succession, which by statute is based on the date the agency was originally created.)

Homeland Security (DHS) 🖱. Rather than create new agencies and bureaus redesigned to meet the new goals and eliminate old, obsolete agencies, the new DHS, like the creation of the Department of Education, was a patchwork department created by grabbing assorted agencies out of their old hierarchy and placing them under DHS control. Not only did the swift cobbling together miss important, necessary components to any department, like a "high-level policy planning unit" or a chief intelligence officer, but it also created inevitable turf wars over budget, staffing, and the mission of the agency.[14]

It is also telling to consider the organizational charts for all of the executive branch departments. For example, the DHS (see Figure 8.1) is the third largest of the fifteen cabinet-level departments, behind the departments of Defense and Veterans Affairs,

🖱 View the Department of Homeland Security's website.

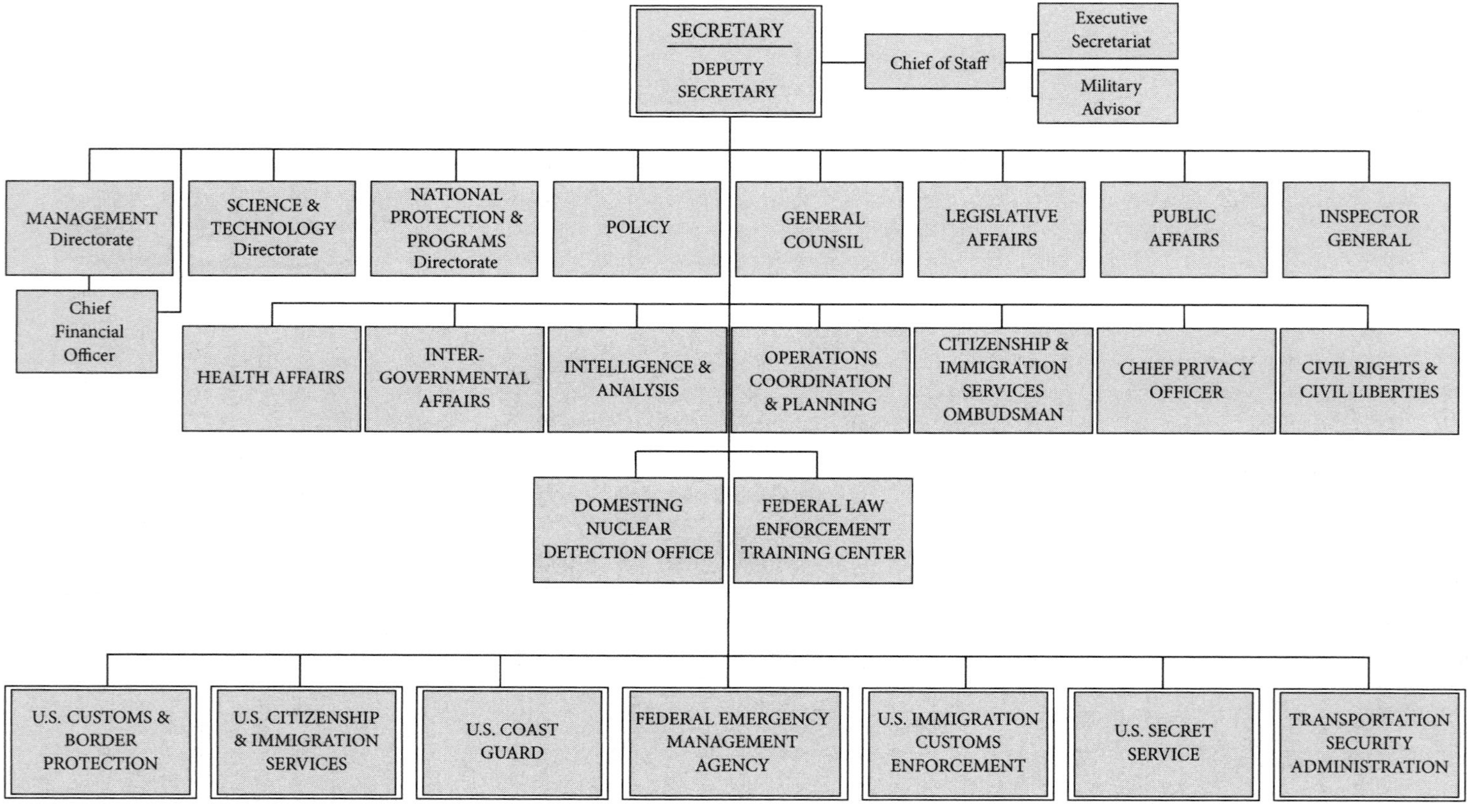

Figure 8.1 Department of Homeland Security

employing more than 200,000 individuals. In contrast, the Department of Education, the smallest department, employs just 4,200 people but has the same number of subunits as the DHS (see Figure 8.2). There are also thirteen other departments with as many or more units, subunits, and employees.

Separation of Power Creates Conflict

Congress is beholden to the people by virtue of voting, which means that voters can hold Congress accountable for their actions at the ballot box when they do not like a member of Congress' voting patterns. Therefore, the individual members of Congress translate their individual accountability into institutional accountability. Congress remains accountable for the implementation and administration of those laws through oversight, which is an evaluation of outcomes, but not the execution. The president's responsibility primarily is to keep the unelected civil servants accountable to elected political authorities. It is the president's task to carry out what Congress designs and hold the bureaucracy accountable to Congress' intentions through execution. Yet, according to political scientist Matthew J. Dickinson, the Constitution "creates a political dynamic in which presidents feel compelled to manage the executive branch, but lack the means to completely do so."[15]

Modern presidents, then, inherit a system separated from electoral politics; the change of party in power in Congress or in the presidency does not remove the majority of civil service employees. Turnover based on partisanship short-circuited the opportunity for employees to develop expertise as the merit system enabled the development of expertise over time. Eliminating partisan turnover purposefully distanced the bureaucracy from politics and the political sphere. The distance produces a beneficial continuity, where not everything changes, in the aftermath of an election. However, when whole-scale electoral change occurs, like in 2008 when the Congress switched from Republican control to Democratic control, then continuity creates a negative distance between the bureaucracy and the nation. Elections reflect changing attitudes or views about issues of the day. With civil service reform, the bureaucracy is immune to these forces, unless the presidency through management and appointments can challenge that immunity and hold the departments accountable.

Part of the problem for the president in controlling the bureaucracy also stems from the designers of the bureaucracy: Congress. In the case of the DHS, President Bush's plan for the department ended up dominating the outcome, but the Senate did initially have a plan as well. Congress' approach to creating departments, agencies, or even programs emerges out of its, and not the president's, institutional perspective. Congress works collectively; individuals act (vote, write legislation, form coalitions), but the institution, without a majority of individuals standing together, accomplishes nothing. Also, members of Congress do not work in a vacuum; they work in a political arena filled with individuals and groups who want to influence them in order to influence political outcomes. Consequently, departments, agencies, and programs reflect the attitudes and behaviors of politicians and interest groups. As political scientists David Lewis and Terry Moe argue, "For both interest groups and legislators, politics is not about the system. It is about the pieces of the system, and about ensuring the flow of benefits to constituents and special interests."[16]

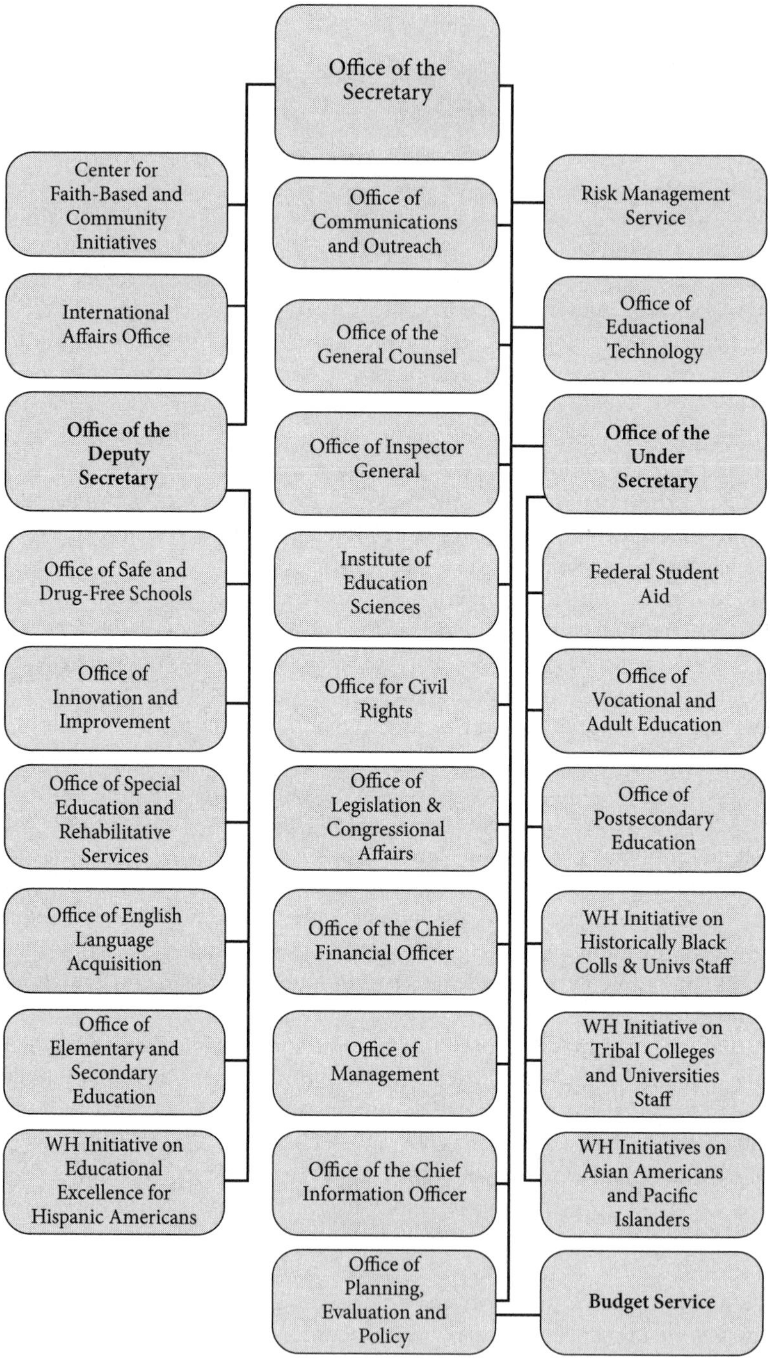

Figure 8.2 Department of Education

To ensure the flow of benefits and maintain the focus that the winning legislative coalition wanted from the department, agency, or program in question, specificity is the weapon. When designing departments, agencies, or programs, winning legislative coalitions seek to specify exactly what the departments, agencies, or programs need to accomplish, "what to do and how to do it."[17] The goal is insulation—to protect the outcome the majority wanted and received from influence from either a new Congressional majority or the president. The winning legislative coalitions are wary of presidents, even of the same party, because the president is institutionally opposed to the way Congress organizes the government. The president is national in focus, whereas legislative coalitions are specialized (either regionally or by being focused on a particular issue or policy). Even when Congress does not intentionally seek to protect their outcomes from presidential interference, they do not design with presidential control and organization in mind. Virtually everything Congress creates is created incrementally—a piece at a time, "agency by agency, program by program, unit by unit, procedure by procedure—with little overarching concern for the whole."[18] With the DHS, the missing key features, like the National Intelligence Officer, were added in 2005 after recognition from all involved that it was necessary. As a result, the bureaucracy is not set up for presidential control.

The Cabinet

The managerial difficulties for the presidency do not arise just from the separation with Congress, but also from the separation within the Executive Branch. The organizational chart certainly implies that everyone in the bureaucracy works for the president. The constitution grants the president the power to hire and (from key Supreme Court cases) fire the political appointees, which also suggests presidential control. However, after the introduction of the merit system, the president can only easily hire and fire approximately 20 percent of the executive branch workforce. These individuals are the top tiers of each department, creating the impression that the president has "his people" in place to execute his agenda.

The organizational chart is ultimately misleading because, while the president does hire and fire, something happens to these individuals once they begin working in an agency, particularly the department secretaries. The department secretaries collectively make up what is referred to as the Cabinet. Initially, George Washington met individually with his secretaries, but he quickly realized the benefit of collective meetings. There is no provision in the Constitution for a "cabinet of advisors"; newspaper reporters actually coined the term during Washington's administration to refer to his four department heads. Today the Cabinet officially encompasses the fifteen executive branch department heads and several other important positions. Cabinet rank is typically accorded to the Vice President and the U.S. Representative to the United Nations so they can attend cabinet meetings. Presidents can accord cabinet rank and the privileges that go with it to whatever agency director they like; as a result, presidents have awarded cabinet status to the Director of the Central Intelligence Agency (CIA) and also the Director of the Office of Management and Budget.

One would expect the Cabinet to be a highly useful body of advisors for the president. However, rarely has that happened. Andrew Jackson hated his Cabinet and instead turned to an informal body of friends and competent individuals who

Barack Obama meets with members of his Cabinet.

newspapers dubbed the "Kitchen Cabinet." Abraham Lincoln, right before he issued his Emancipation Proclamation, convened his Cabinet and said, "I have gathered you together to hear what I have written down. I do not wish your advice about the main matter. That, I have determined by myself."[19] Despite choosing and appointing their cabinet secretaries, presidents rarely trust them. Consider how a president chooses a department secretary. Did the appointee have skill in the policy area of the department? Was the appointee helpful in the campaign, and did the president-elect owe the appointee a favor? Was the president looking for an overall *type* of cabinet, e.g., the "best and the brightest" (like John F. Kennedy) or a Cabinet that "looks like America" (like Bill Clinton)? Whatever the rationale, trustworthiness, loyalty, or good advising are not the only requirements when choosing a Cabinet secretary.

The appointment of Senator Hillary Rodham Clinton as President Obama's Secretary of State highlights the complexities of the relationship between the president and members of his Cabinet. Obama and Clinton had been cordial Senate colleagues, then rivals for the Democratic presidential nomination in one of the most hotly contested nomination races in recent memory. Typically, rivals either join forces during the campaign or the loser drifts away, potentially for another challenge in another race. An example of the former can be found in 1980, when Ronald Reagan chose his opponent, George H. W. Bush, as his vice presidential running mate. Similarly, John Kerry chose his closest primary opponent, John Edwards, as his running mate in 2004. In 1976, when Gerald Ford dropped his Vice President Nelson Rockefeller from the ticket, he could have made his opponent, Ronald Reagan, his running mate. However, after a contentious primary and party convention, Ford chose Senator Bob Dole (KS) for his running mate in what would be his losing bid to be elected in his own right to the presidency (after succeeding to the office after Richard Nixon's resignation in 1974).

For Obama, there was much speculation in the summer of 2008 over whether he would select Clinton as his running mate. Ultimately, Obama chose Senator Joe Biden (DE), another primary participant. Clinton would instead get the nod as Secretary of State once Obama won the general election. The choice of Clinton as Secretary of State was not typical, given the highly charged nature of the campaign, as discussed in Chapter 3. In fact, media organizations focused so excessively on the strained relationship between not only the candidates but also their staffs that their first joint appearance after Clinton's June concession speech was a highly scripted affair, particularly in terms of locale—a battleground state (New Hampshire), whose city was aptly named Unity. After not choosing Clinton as his running mate, media speculation zeroed in on whether Clinton would receive a Cabinet position. Still the junior Senator from New York, Clinton had no need to accept a position in order to continue her political career. Moreover, despite the efforts to make a public show of reconciliation, rumors persisted that the two did not get along. There was also the question about former President Bill Clinton. When Hillary Clinton ran for the White House there was much speculation regarding her husband's role, not only in the campaign but in a potential Hillary Clinton presidency. In an Obama administration, how would the popular ex-President compete with either the new Secretary or the new President? Remarkably, given the all the reasons why the relationship would not work, Obama and Clinton appear, by all accounts, to have created an effective working relationship during Obama's first term. The two are often cited as an example of why a Cabinet of rivals can be a positive challenge for the president, and they have been known to even joke about their "frenemies" status.[20]

Obama's selection of Clinton as Secretary of State was a classic political maneuver, granting her one of the highest ranking positions in his administration as an attempt to mollify and manage her and her supporters after the election. Those rationales, however, do not necessarily lead to a relationship where the president can trust the advice from his advisors. Political scientist Richard Neustadt argued in his seminal work, *Presidential Power*, that a president can never truly trust any advisors as only the president understands what is at stake with any decision.[21] An advisor cannot ultimately share in what is at stake—they might share reflected glory—but do not receive the blame or the victory. While Obama and Clinton seem to have established an effective, trust-based relationship, the unusually adversarial campaign environment that they experienced shaped how others viewed their relationship.

Many institutional reasons exist for the lack of trust between president and Cabinet secretaries. Once approved by the Senate, a cabinet member will run an enormous organization (even the smallest cabinet department has more than four thousand people employed). Although it is not always clear what drove the choice for secretary, once appointed, the secretary works for the president and his agenda. However, with the exception of the Secretary of State, who spends the bulk of his or her time traveling to other countries, most secretaries spend their time within their departments. Remember, 80 percent of that department is made up of career civil servants who are experts in their policy areas. The continued service allows for the development of that expertise but also the development of opinions about the needs and direction of the department. A new president's agenda represents one of two possible paths—in line with the career civil servants or out of line. Even when in line, trade-offs in terms of money, time, and between policies often have to be made by the president who approaches the bureaucracy from a national perspective. Individual civil servants bring their local, narrowed policy views to bear on the political appointees. As a result, top officials and even the department secretary can become captured by special interests, termed by some as "going native." Rather than enforce the president's policies down the organizational chart, the department secretary becomes the voice of his or her people to the president. The focus of the secretary becomes advancing the department goals rather than advancing the president's goals. The worst-case scenario is if the cabinet becomes a political land mine for the president, a table full of separate goals and requests rather than a group united by the president's agenda.

Of course, cabinet members can also become trusted members of the president's inner circle. If the relationship began during the appointment process, then it is much harder, although not impossible. To turn a casual, work relationship into a trusted advisory relationship requires the cabinet member to show the president loyalty, ability, and personality that mesh with the president's needs. Ultimately, the secretary needs to show that he or she is a team player, but this can often be difficult for people who were political stars in their own right. In the executive branch, however, there is only one "star," so to speak, and that title belongs to the president.

THE EXECUTIVE OFFICE OF THE PRESIDENT

The President of the United States is faced with competing interests and the gargantuan task of managing and leading an enormous group of people who may or may not agree with his direction for the nation. How can the president ensure that the bureaucracy is actually executing the will of Congress, let alone try to shape it to support his goals? In short, he needs a lot of help. Initially, the president received little assistance. For the first eighty years, presidents employed a secretary or two. However, both Congress and the president viewed these individuals as personal aides rather than governmental employees. In fact, Congress did not even allocate money ($2,500) for an office worker until 1857.[22] Sixty-seven years passed with the President of the United States employing his son, son-in-law, or nephew and paying him out of his own pocket. After 1857, Congress slowly appropriated more money and the president hired more secretaries, clerks, stenographers, and messengers. Yet, as recently as the Calvin Coolidge administration (1923–1929), the entire budget for the White House staff, including office expenses, was less than $80,000.[23]

Creating the Executive Office of the President

As with most developments in the modern presidency, the size of the White House staff changed dramatically with Franklin Roosevelt. Roosevelt entered office aware that the demands on his Executive Branch from the Great Depression would require greater administration and coordination from the White House. However, the White House did not have the capacity to create the recommendations for Congress and the bureaucracy that the economic crisis required. FDR began his tenure trying to use the cabinet to enforce his agenda on the departments. However, his department secretaries "went native" and worse, leaked information to the media.[24] FDR then tried creating "coordinating bodies" separate from the cabinet, made up of secretaries and the heads of the new agencies he created. He also tried "borrowing" staff from the departments and agencies; individuals were assigned to the White House but their home agencies paid their salaries. None of these techniques was particularly effective. Consequently, Roosevelt pressed ahead with his challenge to Congress in his Inaugural Address: he wanted "broad Executive power to wage a war against the emergency, as great as the power that would be given to me if we were in fact invaded by a foreign foe."[25] He formally requested that power in 1937 and received it in 1939, well into his second term.[26]

In order to determine what the management problems were and how to fix them, Roosevelt created the Committee on Administrative Management, headed by Lewis Brownlow. The Brownlow Committee produced a report with significant, institutional recommendations in 1937. Famously concluding "the President needs help," the Committee produced a five-point plan:

- Modernize the White House business and management organization by giving the President six high-grade executive assistants to aid him in dealing with the regular departments and agencies.
- Strengthen the budget and efficiency research, the planning, and the personnel services of the Government, so that these may be effective managerial arms for the President, with which he may better coordinate, direct and manage all of the work of the Executive Branch for which he is responsible under the Constitution.
- Place the whole governmental administrative service on a career basis and under the merit system by extending the civil service upward, outward and downward to include all non-policy-determining positions and jobs.
- Overhaul the more than 100 separate departments, boards, commissions, administrations, authorities, corporations, committees, agencies and activities which are now parts of the Executive Branch, and theoretically under the President, and consolidate them within twelve regular departments, which would include the existing ten departments and two new departments, a Department of Social Welfare, and a Department of Public Works. Change the name of the Department of Interior to Department of Conservation.
- Make the Executive Branch accountable to the Congress by creating a true postaudit of financial transactions by an independent Auditor General who would report illegal and wasteful expenditures to Congress without himself becoming involved in the management of departmental policy, and transfer the duties of the present Comptroller in part to the Auditor, to the Treasury, and to the Attorney General.[27]

Congress did not universally approve of the reorganization plan and in fact rejected the initial proposal. Congress correctly surmised that granting the president institutional capacity granted the president increased power, potentially at their expense. However, there was no denying the need for assistance; thus, the bill passed and Roosevelt signed the bill into law on April 3, 1939. Reorganization plan number one created the Executive Office of the President and the capacity to pursue the presidential agenda.

The Brownlow report recommended and Congress granted assistance to the President in the form of two offices: the White House Office and the Bureau of the Budget, which already existed, but in the Treasury Department. Over time, the President expanded the office adding offices with increasingly specialized policy expertise and coordination capacity. The President requested units, and Congress did create some by statute. However, once the EOP existed, the President also bypassed Congress and created units by executive order. All the offices provide coordination and advice, but the most important initially were the ones created first—the White House Office, the Bureau of the Budget (today known as the Office of Management and Budget), the Council of Economic Advisers (created in 1946) and the National Security Council, with its Advisor and staff (created in 1947).

As Table 8.2 shows, today the EOP contains numerous offices. The offices created by Congress by statute continue from administration to administration. The offices created by executive order often continue from administration to administration also,

Table 8.2 The Executive Office of the President (2012)

Council of Economic Advisors
Council on Environmental Quality
Executive Residence
National Security Staff
Office of Administration
Office of Management and Budget
Office of National Drug Control Policy
Office of Science and Technology Policy
Office of the United States Trade Representative
Office of the Vice President
White House Office
Domestic Policy Council
Office of National AIDS Policy
Office of Faith-based and Neighborhood Partnerships
Office of Social Innovation and Civic Participation
White House Rural Council
National Security Advisor
National Economic Council
Office of Cabinet Affairs
Office of the Chief of Staff
Office of Communications
Office of the Press Secretary
Media Affairs
Research
Speechwriting
Office of Digital Strategy
Office of the First Lady
Office of the Social Secretary
Office of Legislative Affairs

(continued)

Table 8.2 ***(continued)***

Office of Management and Administration
White House Personnel
White House Operations
Telephone Office
Visitors Office
Oval Office Operations
Office of Presidential Personnel
Office of Public Engagement and Intergovernmental Affairs
Office of Public Engagement
Council on Women and Girls
Office of Intergovernmental Affairs
Office of Urban Affairs
Office of Scheduling and Advance
Office of the Staff Secretary
Presidential Correspondence
Executive Clerk
Records Management
Office of the White House Counsel

Source: www.whitehouse.gov/administration/eop/

as presidents realize that they share the same institutional needs regardless of political point of view. For example, as discussed in Chapter 4, all modern presidents need to deal with the media, so all maintain an Office of Communications. However, the EOP also comes to represent the current president's policy agenda. For example, President Obama's administration has an office of Energy and Climate Change. His predecessor, George W. Bush, did not have that office but did have an Office of Faith-Based and Community Initiatives, which is not part of the Obama EOP.

White House Staff

Technically speaking, the White House staff can range from high-level policy advisors to the White House chef and custodial staff. Politically speaking, the White House staff is connected, according to political scientists Justin Vaughn and Jose Villalobos, to the concept of power: "To be a member of the White House staff is to be a presidential employee directly involved in the business of politics, policy making, or some hybrid of both."[28] For the most part these individuals work in virtual obscurity; few members of the public, generally only the politically attentive, can identify even the president's chief of staff, arguably the most trusted presidential advisor. Yet, they are extremely important to the president. White House staff are not approved by anyone, since they serve at the desire and discretion of the president. Their importance stems from immediate and direct access to the president and presidential decisions, and generally they are long-time associates of the president, often having participated in his election campaign. Beyond the chief of staff (see "Chief of Staff" section later in this chapter), other high-profile White House staff members can include the press secretary (as discussed in Chapter 4), the staff secretary (in charge of handling the communication of messages and the circulation of memos/documents between the president and his senior staff), czars (an assistant chosen to focus on a specific policy area), the White House counsel (the president's top advisor on legal issues), the director of the Office of Personnel Management (who is in charge of seeking out individuals to serve in the administration), and the national security advisor (as discussed in Chapter 10).[29]

The size of Obama's Executive Office, with 487 individuals, is about average, while some presidents have employed more than 550 individuals. Interestingly, working in the White House, the center of power in the United States, is not necessarily lucrative. In 2010, President Obama's 487 staff members earned salaries ranging from a low of $36,000 to twenty-two individuals who made the maximum salary of $172,200. Top-level senior staffers are given the job title of Assistant to the President, second tier staffers are called Deputy Assistant to the President, and third tier staffers are called Special Assistant to the President, while still others are called either counselors or aides. Most of these individuals serve "at the pleasure of the President," meaning only he can hire or fire them. The Director of the Office of Management and Budget, the Chair and Members of the Council of Economic Advisors and the U.S. Trade Representatives, however, are subject to confirmation by the Senate, like the Cabinet Secretaries. The more important members of the EOP are the National Security Advisor, Domestic Policy Advisor, Counsel (the president's lawyer), Director of Legislative Affairs, the Press Secretary, and the Chief of Staff.

Key members of the White House staff often end up doing what the Cabinet could or should do, which is monitor the activities of the various departments and agencies to execute the will of Congress from the president's perspective. Remember, the reason the Cabinet is not always effective in pursuing the president's broad policy agenda is that they do not entirely share the president's national perspective. On the other hand, the EOP and the White House staff are designed specifically to reflect the president's focus. In addition, the White House staff was also created to help manage all the things the president now tries to do in terms of leadership—namely, speaking with and to the media and trying to mobilize public support. If the presidential goal is control of the bureaucracy as well as exercising the modern task of leadership, what are the means to that end? George W. Bush famously articulated the president's central task, and subsequently the media and comics mocked him incessantly for his phrasing. In response to calls for the President to fire his Secretary of Defense, Donald Rumsfeld, Bush said:

> I listen to all voices, but mine is the final decision.... And Don Rumsfeld is doing a fine job. He's not only transforming the military, he's fighting a war on terror. He's helping us fight a war on terror. I have strong confidence in Don Rumsfeld....I hear the voices, and I read the front page, and I know the speculation. But I'm the decider, and I decide what is best. And what's best is for Don Rumsfeld to remain as the secretary of defense.[30]

It is important to remember, however, that "deciders" need information and advice. A president cannot know on his own, or spend the time to find out, all he needs to know about extremely important issues. Instead, the president's staff are the experts on any given subject, or on a policy, or on politics. They provide the president with a never-ending stream of information and advice about solving the nation's problems—whether immediate (such as the Gulf Oil Spill in 2010)—or long-term (such as deficit reduction).

In addition, the White House staff provide coordination between the president and the bureaucracy in an attempt to impose the president's preferred policies on the bureaucracy. While most of the bureaucracy consists of civil servants, several layers of the department's hierarchy are political appointees. By effectively staffing these political positions and also using the White House staff to supervise and put pressure on the civil servants, a president can go a long way toward imposing his views on how policies are implemented. This is only possible because the system requires Congress to legislate through compromise, which provides ambiguity and room to maneuver and which can be used to a president's advantage. For example, with regulation of deep-sea drilling, it makes a difference if an oilman or an environmentalist is in charge at the Minerals and Mining Agency in terms of their policy perspective and how hard they may fight for certain environmental restrictions and standards. In effect, one can tell a lot about a president's goals by his executive branch appointments.

Organizing the White House Staff

If the greatest threat to presidential decision making is isolation, or not receiving the advice necessary, then organizing the White House staff as well as managing the flow of information becomes a critical task. Interestingly, when choosing amongst presidential candidates, his or her management skills rarely enter into voters' selection factors. The media evaluates candidates' management skills obliquely, often using previous job experience as shorthand. For example, a former governor or mayor has executive leadership experience, while a former legislator does not. However, the most important management skill that a president must have is often the ability to choose the right individuals to successfully manage and utilize the institutional structure of the EOP to the president's political advantage. An effective presidential staff system will funnel information to the president and tasks away from the president in a way that enables decision making while allowing for presidential personality quirks. The recognition that there are good ways and bad ways to do this have come through experience.

Since FDR and the creation of the modern White House, there have been only four models of organization: competitive, hierarchical, collegial, and modified. A competitive system is one in which the advisors do not have set roles. Figure 8.3 diagrams how the staff members relate to the president based on assignments. It appears chaotic to the outside world because advisors receive the same task instead of delegating one task to one individual. FDR used to do this in order to avoid presidential isolation so that he could receive information from a variety of sources. It takes a keen intellect to balance the competing egos and ideas, as staff members have unfettered access to the president. To avoid hostility in the White House, FDR juggled the individuals working on assignments so that staff members were not always in opposition with the same individuals. As a management technique, the competitive style is difficult to maintain because it requires excessive presidential

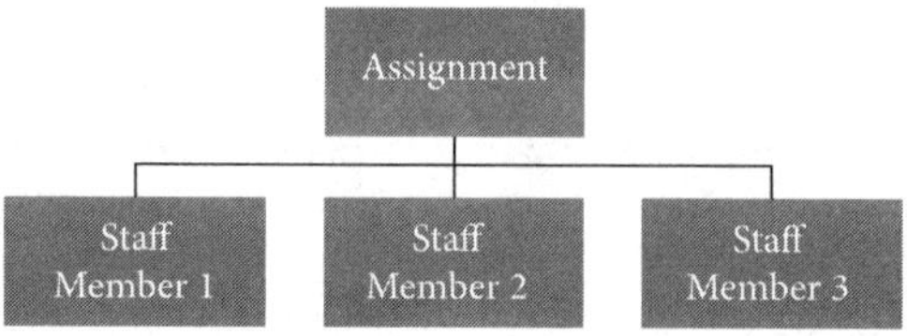

Figure 8.3 Competitive Model—FDR

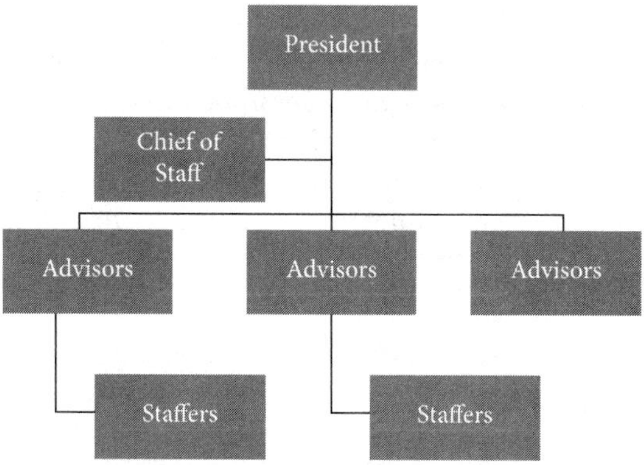

Figure 8.4 Hierarchical Model—Eisenhower and Nixon

participation. As a result, no president other than FDR employed a competitive staffing system.

Both Presidents Eisenhower and Nixon employed hierarchical arrangements. Figure 8.4 demonstrates how strict lines of control and command characterize hierarchical staff arrangements. The chief of staff is the key gatekeeping mechanism, which controls and coordinates the flow of paper as well as access to the president. As a former five-star general in the United States Army, Eisenhower preferred this method due to familiarity with it, as it was similar to the military with strict lines of authority and clear delegations of responsibility. Sherman Adams was his chief of staff and was virtually the second most powerful man in Washington. Adams was so powerful that he was virtually able to run the country while Eisenhower recovered from a mild stroke unbeknownst to the public and most of Washington in 1957.

Nixon and his Chief of Staff, H. R. Haldeman, initially set up a hierarchical system and reduced staff out of familiarity. The inherent isolation from narrow access to the President also served Nixon's personality. He did not deal well with people he did not know very well, and he hated meetings. Instead, he preferred option papers, where staff would detail options and Nixon would pick the one he liked best. Nixon worked well reading volumes of material rather than listening to people talk. Subsequently, Presidents Ford and Carter designed their staffing arrangements in response to Nixon's model and the perceived relationship between the staff organization and Watergate. Watergate is the term used to collectively describe the crimes perpetrated by the Nixon re-election committee and the cover up of that behavior by the White House staff. In the aftermath of the Watergate scandal, critics cited the tendency of Nixon to use his gatekeeper to hide away from staff and issues. Presidents Ford and Carter both pledged openness as a means to wash away the Watergate taint on the presidency.

The collegial system is the epitome of the open door policy; the system is also known as the spokes of the wheel because of how it looks when diagrammed (see Figure 8.5). The collegial model has no hierarchy; all staff members are equal before the president. In contrast to the competitive system, where staffers are equal but tasks are assigned, and the hierarchical system, where access and assignments are rigidly controlled, all ideas and interests funnel to and from the president with no regard to restricting access in the collegial system. Watergate appeared to demonstrate that restricting access to the president led to bad advice and in turn bad decision-making. The collegial system does open up the president to a wider net of ideas and interests, but also provides no mechanism for prioritizing. In the competitive system, staffers fought to have their options chosen. In the collegial system, staffers also fought to have their ideas chosen by the president. The difference between the two is that in the competitive system the president had already decided that the issue was worth the time and competition. In the collegial system, every staffer thinks his or her job is of vital importance, but it might only be second or third tier on the president's list. Unlike the competitive and hierarchical systems, there is no formal institutional arrangement to indicate the relative importance of a person or an issue area.

Instead, rather like *Lord of the Flies*, staffers develop an informal hierarchy based on personality or social status. No official lines of authority exist, but it is still clear who is in charge by virtue of personality and access to the president. The problem is that none of the president's goals or needs, beyond openness, determined this

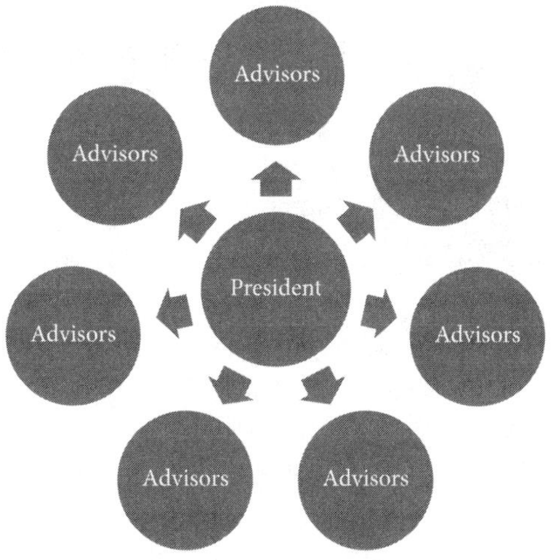

Figure 8.5 Collegial Model—Ford, Carter

informal hierarchy. Thus, the arrangement likely will not serve the president; he will not be isolated, but he might not receive effective advice either. For example, under this arrangement, President Carter was so inundated with detail that neither he nor anyone else made any effort to discriminate and determine which matters could be handled at a level below the president. In early 1978, Press Secretary Jody Powell articulated the problems with the lack of organization among the White House staff in a memo to Carter:

> Although some of the criticism of your staff is overdone, one valid criticism is the lack of coordination among key senior staff. This is generally agreed, but no one is in a position to really do anything on it since we are "all equals." At present there is no effective, daily coordination procedure. This is unprecedented in a White House so far as I have been able to tell. I suggest that you direct [White House Advisor] Hamilton [Jordon] to convene and chair an early morning meeting composed of himself, [National Security Advisor] Zbig [Brzezinski], [Chief Domestic Policy Advisor] Stu [Eizenstat], [congressional liaison] Frank [Moore], [Chief of Staff to Vice President Walter Mondale] Dick Moe and myself to deal ostensibly with legislative matters. (This will justify the smaller group.) It may be that we will want to have [White House Advisor] Tim [Kraft] or [Appointments Secretary] Phil [Wise] sit in regularly or that we will want [DNC Chairman] John White to come in a couple of times each week, but that can be worked out later. The main point is that there is a great need for more coordination and that you must insist that these meetings be held and be religiously attended. (You can enforce your order by requesting minutes of each meeting and list of attendees.) If you will reflect upon my personal distaste for staff meetings, particularly early morning meetings, and my spotty record of attendance at some stretching over the past 6–7 years, you should be convinced that this is an earnest and selfless suggestion on my part.[31]

The management mess created by the collegial system in the Carter White House was highlighted by the media fascination in 1978 and 1979 with the rumor that the President himself kept the schedule of the White House tennis courts. This became a media story partially because it was part of a tell-all article by a former staffer, James Fallows. However, the story gained traction because of the implicit understanding that the President of the United States had better things to do with his time than decide who was using the tennis courts and when. The story represents the clearest example of a president who needed a chief of staff, an individual who was aware of the president's desire to coordinate who played when but prevented the president from devoting his scarcest resource (time) to that desire. Hamilton Jordan became Carter's chief of staff in the summer of 1979, a few months after Carter publicly addressed the tennis court question.

The Reagan White House sought the best of both worlds—the ability to prioritize and control without a loss of access and spontaneity. They created a modified collegial system and set up a hierarchy for prioritizing coupled with collegiality for widespread access to ideas. During his first term, Reagan had three top advisors, Chief of Staff James Baker, Counselor Ed Meese, and Deputy Chief of Staff Michael Deaver (often referred to as the "triumvirate"). Baker ran the operations, Meese was

---

Read James Fallows's article "The Passionless Presidency."

a close, personal friend to Reagan and represented his ideals, and Deaver was Baker's top aide. Only four individuals, those three and National Security Advisor William Clark, had direct access to the president. The top of the Reagan hierarchy was narrow, but the second level was wider, with a lot more access. At the start of the second term, and with the appointment of a new chief of staff, former Treasury Secretary Donald Regan, the Reagan White House sought to refine the organizational system it had in place, as outlined in a memo about meetings to Regan from Director of Policy Development Roger Porter:

> Structuring the various offices within the White House and delineating their responsibilities is important. Also important is how they relate to one another. Perhaps nothing in this respect is more crucial than the pattern of meetings that are held. Anyone who has worked at the White House cannot help but be impressed by the number of meetings that take place. One sometimes looks forward to the regular day ending (no one has adequately defined for me what close of business means, although we all use the phrase), which normally means the stream of meetings finally stops, so that you can get some work done. Of course, meetings are essential. And many meetings are scheduled on short notice to address some urgent problem or to organize the work flowing from an assignment that has just been issued. Typically there is a White House senior staff meeting each morning in the Roosevelt Room at 8:00 a.m. This is a tradition that extends back at least through the last four administrations, and likely before then. There are also cabinet council meetings, legislative strategy group meetings, and issue luncheons that I have discussed elsewhere. The purpose of this memorandum is to suggest three meetings that could prove helpful in building a united White House team if they were held regularly with adequate advance preparation.
>
> 1. <u>Policy Management Group</u>: However many entities comprise the policy development and coordination part of the White House, there will inevitably be a need to do three important things: Clarify who has responsibility for what issues (put less diplomatically, resolving jurisdictional disputes); Inform one another of the current work in progress to avoid duplication and overlap; and Insure that issues are not falling between the cracks because one office believes that another has the lead on addressing the problem. A regular weekly meeting of the responsible officials could help to fulfill these functions as well as build a sense among them that collectively they have responsibility for coordinating policy within the Administration. . . .
>
> 2. <u>Policy Implementation Group</u>: There is also a need to coordinate the activities of the constituency oriented offices in the White House—legislative affairs, public liaison, intergovernmental affairs, communications and press. All these offices are central to the task of building and mobilizing support for the policies the President has approved. All these offices run the danger that they will become captive of their constituency; that is, that they will come to increasingly represent the interests of their constituency to the White House rather than represent the White House to their constituency. A regular meeting, chaired by the Chief of Staff, involving the heads of these four offices dealing with the Congress, the press, public interest groups, and State and local governments, could go a long way to achieving two objectives: Reinforcing their central mission of mobilizing support for the President's programs rather than meeting the needs (if nothing more than keeping calm) of their constituency; and Coordinating their efforts so that they are all pushing on the same issues and rowing in the same direction. . . .

> 3. Overall Strategy Group: There is also a need to consciously devote time and attention to considering overall strategy—what should the Administration try to accomplish over the next six months, or over the next year? The press of day-to-day activities is almost overwhelming, and it is easy to allow the urgent to drive out the important. Many have suggested creating offices within the White House or within the Executive Office of the President to think about the long term and to consider overall strategy. The impulse is correct, but the mechanism misses the mark. One can never expect a group of people who are divorced from the day-to-day flow of activities to dominate or control the agenda. It is crucial that the key figures in any White House form the nucleus of any such effort. But these are busy people and they don't have lots of spare time to sit and think grand thoughts or ponder elaborate long-term strategies. If they get together, however, perhaps once a month or once every other month, to discuss long-term strategy, it could make a contribution.[32]

All of Reagan's successors (Bush, Clinton, Bush, and Obama) chose hierarchical management structures; this style has emerged as the dominant mechanism because most presidents cannot handle the competition or the inevitable power struggle that emerges with the collegial or competitive systems. By default, the chief of staff position has become the most effective mechanism for keeping presidents organized and in control. Unfortunately, the extent to which the Oval Office is open and receptive to advice and information also rests on the chief of staff's relationship with the president.

The Chief of Staff

A president is constantly besieged, both by people who want to see him and by events or crises. There are not enough hours in the day for the president to handle all of them at the presidential level, so it falls to the staff to determine what material and which people are important enough for presidential attention. As the gatekeeper for the president's time and attention, the chief of staff is the most critical component in determining whether the White House staff effectively serves the needs of the president and the country. The chief of staff as an institutional feature determines the quality of information and advice the president sees and also influences the overall management structure of the White House. Of course, the chief of staff is also an individual whose personal skills influence the effectiveness of the office.[33]

An effective chief of staff can positively influence presidential decision making in several ways. Since the chief of staff and his aides determine what flows into the president's in-box, how the president and the chief of staff view information is important: What issues are worthy of presidential attention? How does the president like to receive information? Who has unfettered access to the president? How many individuals attend meetings? When are meetings scheduled? How long are meetings? These are issues critical to a successful presidency, yet are items never debated during a presidential campaign when considering qualifications for the office.

Issue focus and meeting length seem so trivial a factor in organization and decision making, yet the impact can be dramatic. Early into his presidency, President Nixon decided to limit his access not only to individuals but also to issues. He informed his top policy aide, John Ehrlichman, and his chief of staff, Bob Haldeman, that he would see information on only three issues: inflation, busing, and Vietnam.

Granted, in the late 1960s and early 1970s, those were top issues, but it was a fairly blanket directive which probably aided his isolation. President Clinton's administration initially suffered, not from Clinton's choices but from his organizational flaws. President Clinton's chief of staff , childhood friend Thomas "Mack" McLarty, was unable to counter the president's bad organizational habits. Clinton delighted in all things policy and famously wanted to rehash every tiny nugget of information. At meetings, staffers were alternately delighted by the President's focus, depth of knowledge, and attention, and horrified by the inability to disengage and move on to the next meeting or event. As a result, Clinton was notoriously late for everything, keeping everyone from assistants to world leaders waiting. Despite providing trusted advice and being a longtime friend, McLarty was replaced as chief of staff by organizationally minded, bureaucratically skilled Leon Panetta in 1994 (Panetta was a former member of the House of Representatives). The results were significant, as "disorganized" and "unfocused" ceased to be common descriptions of the Clinton administration.

The mechanism for good information and advice is management—same as in the business world. In terms of the White House, how the White House is set up often determines the flow of information and the quality of decision making, and the chief of staff, or even the choice to have one, is critical. The chief of staff, according to political scientists, should be an honest broker for ideas. James Baker, Ronald Reagan's first chief of staff, believed "the worst chief of staff I think would be a yes man who was never willing to tell the president what his views were or what he thought."[34] The chief of staff also ends up being a guardian of the president's time and reputation, both personally and politically, but not all do that well. Ultimately, George H. W. Bush's first chief of staff articulated the truth of the position; John Sununu, a former governor from New Hampshire, understandably said, "the role of the chief of staff is whatever the president wants that role to be."[35]

The need for a chief of staff arises from the task charged to the EOP: manage the bureaucracy from the president's perspective. Thus, there are political tasks for the EOP as well as policy tasks. Reelection looms over everything for a president, even management issues, during his first term in office. Not only does the bureaucracy need to be managed, but the individuals within the EOP and the White House staff also need to be managed. So, in effect, the chief of staff manages the managers. As such, a chief of staff must have political skills as well as management and organizational skills. Unsurprisingly, few chiefs of staff are equally good at both roles, which is why there have often been multiple people doing the "chief" job even when one is appointed, like Reagan's troika of Baker, Deaver, and Meese, or George W. Bush's use of Chief of Staff Andrew Card along with close political advisors Karl Rove and Karen Hughes. The complexity and stress of the job also explain why most presidents have multiple chiefs of staff. Not only is the job extremely demanding with little to no time off, but also, presidents will often realize they need better managers when they have a politico or better politics from a good manager. Typically, management trumps politics as the president can find numerous political advisors but the gatekeeper skill is harder to find.

Presidents naturally seek trusted advisors in the chief of staff role; however, recent presidents learned from Clinton's mistake and reserved the role for those with particular skills, relegating closest advisors to the number two or three roles in the

White House. President Obama's first chief of staff, Rahm Emanuel, was the first to relinquish a seat in Congress for the position. Like Bush, and Clinton after McLarty, Obama hired a skilled outsider to be his chief of staff and kept his close confidants in the non-management roles. Prior to his job as Obama's chief of staff, Emanuel had served as a senior advisor in the Clinton White House, and then served six years in the House of Representatives (including a stint as the Chairman of the Democratic Congressional Campaign Committee in 2006 when his party won back control of the House). Emanuel would leave the chief of staff position to run for Mayor of Chicago, winning the office in November 2010.

CONCERNS WITH AND CONSEQUENCES OF THE EOP

The changes in size and responsibility of the White House staff evoke some serious concerns for people inside and outside government. A staff too large is difficult to supervise; in the worst-case scenario, unsupervised staff members are running around Washington demanding action in the name of the president without the president's knowledge or approval. Watergate and Iran-Contra were both scandals that developed due to a lack of supervision.

The Watergate scandal began June 18, 1972, when five men were caught breaking into the headquarters of the Democratic National Committee trying to wiretap and photograph sensitive material. It turned out that the lead burglar, James McCord, was the security coordinator for the Committee to Reelect the President (CREEP). Even worse, all five were paid by the committee's secret slush fund. All of this came out during the campaign season, but Nixon still won reelection. Between June 1972 and April 1973, the White House attempted to cover up the crimes and the connections between the activities and the president's men. Investigations by the media, particularly Bob Woodward and Carl Bernstein of the *Washington Post*, along with an investigation by Congress, eventually revealed that an even wider net of crimes occurred and were covered up. Seven of Nixon's staffers were eventually indicted 🖱.

The Watergate scandal produced numerous effects on the institution of the presidency. As discussed in Chapter 5, the public lost faith in the president and also in the office, which led in part to Nixon's resignation. In terms of staffing and management, many argue that the scandal occurred because of the "we are not above the law, we are the law" atmosphere from the White House. Well into the scandal, the infamous tape recordings of Oval Office conversations reveal that the president knew of the obstruction of justice and even authorized payment after one of his lower level staffers decided to blackmail the higher-ups. Nixon set that tone with his staff and furthered it by distancing himself from day-to-day operations of most subjects.

The Iran-Contra scandal similarly resulted from a lack of presidential oversight of the Reagan White House staff, and the lack of management seriously influenced American foreign policy. The scandal was nicknamed the arms-for-hostages deal, because Israel would ship weapons to Iran provided by the United States. In turn,

---

🖱 Watch the Watergate Hearings.

the Iranian moderates were supposed to get Hezbollah to release six American hostages. The plan changed as the National Security Council's Lieutenant Colonel Oliver North diverted some of the money received from Israel to fund anti-communist rebels in Nicaragua, known as the Contras.

The actions of Reagan's NSC staff were controversial on multiple fronts. First, the sales violated the Boland Amendment, passed by Congress, which expressly limited assistance to the Contras. Second, the decision to trade the arms for the hostages violated the stated position of Reagan and the United States to not negotiate with terrorists. In terms of staffing and management, like Watergate, Iran-Contra revealed the dangers of setting forth zealous staff members with little oversight. Reagan knew and approved of the original effort to work with the moderate Iranians to attempt to secure the release of the hostages. He also knew and approved of the decision to negotiate not just with Iranians but with the government of Iran. However, he did not know that the NSC changed the plan and diverted money to fund the Contras.

After the scandal became public in 1986, Reagan created the Tower Commission to investigate what went wrong; Reagan himself would testify before the commission. The panel found that Reagan did not know about large aspects of the program. However, the panel asserted that the President should have had better control of his National Security Council, and as such, they recommended putting more authority in the hands of the National Security Advisor. Ultimately, the Tower Commission argued that the illegal, covert activities occurred because established procedures were ignored and senior staff did not review their subordinates frequently enough. In short, bad management can lead to a White House run amok 🖱.

In addition to the dangers of lack of supervision, the sheer existence of a White House staff transfers policymaking and implementation away from the experts in the departments to individuals whose skills and expertise might not be equivalent. Hurricane Katrina starkly revealed this to the nation at the end of August 2005. Hurricane Katrina was one of the costliest and deadliest hurricanes to hit the United States, and parts of Louisiana, Mississippi, and Alabama would never be the same as millions of individuals lost homes and jobs. For the George W. Bush administration, the hurricane revealed layer after layer of poor management and judgment. In terms of staff management, Katrina demonstrated how narrowing the number of individuals who encounter the president can be problematic.

Hurricane Katrina actually took place while the President was on vacation at his Crawford, Texas, ranch. Given the state-of-the-art technology at the President's home, his vacation was not necessarily the issue. However, Vice President Dick Cheney and Chief of Staff Andrew Card and other top staff took advantage of the President's vacation to take their own. As a result, no one informed the President of the seriousness of the catastrophe. The advisors with Bush who had his ear (including Deputy Chief of Staff Joe Hagin and advisors Karl Rove and Dan Bartlett) gave communications and tactical advice but themselves "lacked alternative channels of information and expertise to fill the 'communication void' that debilitated the White House's sense making."[36] Furthermore, the White House staff cannot oversee all programs in the bureaucracy, particularly those which are complex and involve multiple

---

🖱 Watch the Iran-Contra Hearings.

agencies. Ultimately, the most significant issue is one of accountability. Congress does not oversee the Executive Office of the President, so the advisors are not typically called before committees to explain their decision making or their behavior. The rationale for the lack of oversight is that the president requires advice protected by executive privilege. Executive privilege allows for conversations and advice to remain private, as it prevents staffers from subpoena from the legislative or judicial branches. The president could not get unbiased, unvarnished views of events or policies if the staff member had to fear subpoenas and public scrutiny.

The 9/11 commission inadvertently revealed to the public the tension emerging from the tradition of accountability only to the president. There was a bitter behind-closed-doors fight over whether National Security Advisor Condoleezza Rice would testify under oath and in public, about the Bush White House response to terrorism prior to the events of September 11, 2001. Traditionally, White House staff members do not testify because their advice falls under the category of "executive privilege." The Supreme Court defined the limits of executive privilege in *U.S. v. Nixon* (1974) as "...the valid need for protection of communications between high Government officials and those who advise and assist them in the performance of their manifold duties.... Human experience teaches that those who expect public dissemination of their remarks may well temper candor with a concern for appearances and for their own interests to the detriment of the decisionmaking process."[37] The Bush administration eventually caved to public pressure and allowed Rice to testify. Under any other circumstances than a commission about 9/11, it would have probably been easier for the Bush White House to press the tradition of noncompliance. However, the pressure put forth by the 9/11 Widows and the Commission (made up of an even number of Republicans and Democrats) made participation unavoidable. Interestingly, the Bush White House "saved face" by contending that since she was appearing before a unique commission and not a committee of Congress, no undermining of executive privilege actually occurred. As a result, Rice was the first, and as of this date the only, National Security Advisor to testify under oath before Congress or any other body.

The most important problem, beyond accountability and staff management, when considering the president's capacity to make decisions and manage the bureaucracy, is isolation. Is the president getting enough advice to make a decision? Is he surrounded by yes-men or by competing ideas and interpretations? It is impossible to make a good decision if no one will tell you what you do not want to hear. The controversy surrounding the decision by President George W. Bush to go to war in Iraq features the role of staff in presidential decision-making. According to journalist Bob Woodward's account, in the decisive months of late 2002 and early 2003, the President did not ask anybody other than Rice if they should go to war. Bush told Woodward he knew what Cheney thought, "and he decided not to ask Powell or Rumsfeld."[38] In what is often considered one of the most important decisions a president makes—sending troops into combat—George W. Bush chose not to ask the opinions of his Secretaries of Defense and State because he believed he knew what they would say. More significantly, Bush felt that the staff and Cabinet members did not truly understand, remarking, "If you were sitting where I sit, you would be pretty clear."[39] The President chose

Watch the 9/11 hearings.

not to hear divergent opinions. Of course, the president is entitled to make up his mind, and by January of 2003 he had decided to go to war in Iraq. The fact that Colin Powell was not asked was significant, but the fact that the Secretary of State chose not to press his divergent points is more significant in light of what Powell told Woodward regarding events in August of 2002. Powell articulated an "uncertainty that the president fully grasped the potential consequences" of war in Iraq—what became known as the Pottery Barn Doctrine—"you break it, you buy it"—and that the U.S. would be responsible for nation building. If a staff member believes that the president lacks full understanding of the situation but backs down in the face of a certain president and other staffers (like Vice President Cheney), then ultimately the president does not receive the appropriate advice to make a decision. In terms of any issue, but especially war, problematic or just not productive, staff relationships can be costly.

MECHANISMS FOR PRESIDENTIAL CONTROL OF THE BUREAUCRACY

The Executive Office of the President with its White House Staff and Executive Councils gives the president managerial capacity. Since the creation of the EOP in 1939, presidents have expanded techniques that enable some level of control over the political side of the bureaucracy as well as the civil service side. Presidents use, to varying degrees, the appointment process, the budgetary process, executive orders, the regulatory review process, and signing statements.

Appointments

After the Pendleton Act of 1883, the bulk of each department's personnel were career civil servants. The expansion of government under FDR and the New Deal enlarged that civil service, but the bulk of the initial hires were Democrats. Thus, FDR's civil servants in effect became long-term political appointments. When Dwight Eisenhower took office in 1953 as the first Republican president in twenty years, he faced an enormous, largely Democratic bureaucracy. So President Eisenhower issued an executive order that created eight hundred to one thousand appointed positions designed to corral the bureaucracy.[40] Prior to the executive order, top-level jobs, below that of Secretary and Under Secretary, were filled by promotion of career civil servants.[41] After Eisenhower, career civil servants had to compete with the president's appointments. Subsequent presidents followed Eisenhower's approach and filled the top of the hierarchy with political loyalists and also added to the number of political appointments.

Returning to the examples of the Departments of Homeland Security and Education, presidents are able to appoint individuals to positions that require Senate confirmation and to those that do not. In the Department of Homeland Security, there are 575 political appointees, twenty of whom require Senate confirmation, yet there are thirty-six positions that DHS considers "leadership." Due to the large size of the Department, the political appointees represent only 0.2 percent of the total employees. In the Department of Education, there are 150 total political appointees, fifteen of whom require Senate confirmation. However, those 150 represent 3.5 percent of the department.

The relationship with Congress significantly influences the ease of the president's appointment process. As discussed in Chapter 6, whether the Congress and the

President are of the same party (unified government) or not (divided government) greatly affects the relationship between the branches. Not only is it easier for a president to see his appointments confirmed under unified government, but the number of overall appointees expands.[42] Figures 8.2 and 8.3 reveal the strategy behind filling and adding appointed positions to the department hierarchies. The career civil service numbers remain relatively constant, and the department's organization is predetermined, so an increase in the number of appointed managers increases the number of individuals pressing the president's point of view on a group of unchanging size. If the Institute of Education Sciences in the Department of Education had a career staff of ten with two presidential appointees, there is a ratio of one individual pressing the president's view for five civil servants. If the number of appointments increased to four appointees, there are now two individuals on the president's side for every five civil servants. The increase should enable the president's point of view.

Of course, the creation of numerous positions returns the bureaucracy to a facsimile of the patronage era of Andrew Jackson, which can have serious pitfalls for the president. As noted, Hurricane Katrina revealed numerous problems in the management of the Bush Executive Branch. Not only was the president ill served by his closed circle of advisors, but the preference for filling appointments using loyalty over experience also exacerbated the consequences of Katrina. Bush's two appointments to the position of Director of the Federal Emergency Management Agency (FEMA) loudly signaled his approach to appointments in general, and also his view of the agency. In 2001, Bush appointed his former chief of staff from his tenure as Governor of Texas, Joe Allbaugh, Director of FEMA. This appointment suggests loyalty although theoretically also suggests management skills. In his testimony before Congress in 2001, Allbaugh asserted a perspective that reflected the Bush view of the agency: federal disaster assistance had become "an oversized entitlement program." Allbaugh stated his goal and the administration's goal would be to "restore the predominant role of state and local response to most disasters."[43] Thus, the Bush White House's top disaster official's plans for his new agency was for it to do less.

Allbaugh made the other ill-fated hire for FEMA, Michael D. Brown. Brown moved up the ranks quickly. He started as General Counsel and was promoted to Deputy Director in 2002 and Director in 2003, despite no Emergency Management experience. He was, however, Allbaugh's college roommate, and a Republican lawyer who worked as a stewards and judges commission for the International Arabian Horse Association.[44] Brown became the face of mismanagement as President Bush famously claimed "Brownie, you're doing a heck of a job" four days after the hurricane hit. Unfortunately, the complement came a day after Brown told an incredulous CNN anchor that, in contrast to anyone with a television set, he and the government did not know the New Orleans Superdome housed thousands of displaced individuals who lacked food and water. Brown was relieved of his duties on September 9, 2005, by Department of Homeland Security Secretary Michael Chertoff (and officially resigned three days later), just two weeks after Hurricane Katrina made landfall.

Budgeting as Management

Congress created the Bureau of the Budget (BOB), as part of the Treasury Department, in 1921, in order to prevent future fiscal crises, like the one that occurred after World War I. The central task of the BOB was to gather all the department and agency budget estimates into a single federal budget. However, the BOB "soon became a foundation for the expansion of presidential power.... [as] presidents gradually began to use the budget as a policy tool by adjusting budget estimates to promote their own legislative goals."[45] President Nixon expanded the number of political appointees in the agency and renamed it the Office of Management and Budget in 1973. The new name signaled its new focus and responsibilities; the agency would coordinate, prioritize, and not just budget.

Budgeting is a powerful presidential tool, as the size of the budget determines how much an agency can accomplish. Presidents cannot abolish programs, agencies, or departments regardless of what they think of them. Instead, presidents promote programs by adding to their budgets and isolate or downgrade programs by starving them of needed funds. In the scenario of agency starvation, directors become tools of the administration against the agency, a reverse of going native. As noted in the case of FEMA, but also occurred in the Bush Consumer Product Safety Commission (CPSC), the Bush White House's desire to reduce the activism of the federal government often occurred in budgetary fighting with Congress. After a rash of recalls due to the presence of lead paint in children's toys, the Democratic Congress attempted to enable the CPSC to better serve its constituency—consumers. Bush's acting Chairwoman, Nancy Nord, assumed the unusual position of advocating *against* more agency funding. Speaker of the House Nancy Pelosi lambasted Nord, arguing "Any commission chair who (says) ... we don't need any more authority or any more resources to do our job, does not understand the gravity of the situation." Nord argued in response that, "I want to be hiring more safety inspectors and scientists and compliance officers, I don't want to be hiring lawyers.... [the bill] could have the unintended consequence of hampering, rather than furthering, consumer product safety."[46]

Executive Orders

Although Congress tasks the departments and agencies to implement and administer the vague, compromised legislation they produce, as the Chief Executive the president is ultimately responsible for the implementation of legislation. Consequently, the president has considerable leeway to interpret the implementation, as does the bureaucracy. To make sure the civil service interprets the legislation toward the president's agenda, goals, and ideology, presidents issue directives to the bureaucracy. These directives, proclamations, and presidential decision memoranda all seek to mold the output of the Executive Branch in that the "legal authority of an executive order must derive from either the law or the Constitution."[47]

The use of executive orders dates back to George Washington; the Louisiana Purchase (Thomas Jefferson) and the Emancipation Proclamation (Abraham Lincoln) were early examples of how far-ranging and controversial the unilateral behavior could be. However, the orders are not absolute; "they have the force of law, [but] they can be overturned by subsequent administrations,... [and] also by congressional action or court ruling."[48] As Chapter 6 demonstrated, Congress limits the president's ability to enact his agenda by legislation. Executive orders, in contrast, enable the president to do administrative and/or symbolic tasks, but also advance his agenda without encountering the complexities of the legislative process.

The increase in the number of executive orders issued by presidents since FDR directly relates to presidents' desire to maximize their authority and their goals.[49] Executive orders are efficient; presidents simply need a pen rather than a majority in Congress. Moreover, executive orders are direct, as they are not the results of compromise. They tend to receive less public and media scrutiny (although some, like the treatment of detainees at Guantanamo Bay, or the "Don't Ask, Don't Tell" rule about homosexuals serving in the military, can become controversial).[50] As the next tool demonstrates, presidents also like using executive orders to quickly undo their predecessor's work.

Regulatory Review

The regulatory review process is in some ways quite similar to the budgetary process as a presidential tool. In budgeting, departments and agencies submit their budgets to the OMB, which folds each agency budget into the whole federal budget. In regulatory review, the OMB or any other presidential agency that is tasked to review, performs analyses of the rules created to implement congressional legislation. For example, President Reagan created Executive Order 12291, which required not only the submission of proposed rules but also required cost–benefit analyses and evaluations of alternative approaches.[51] Presidents since Reagan have all employed some form of Executive Order to govern regulatory review. President Clinton repealed EO 12291 and replaced it with EO 12866, which altered the review process only by making it more favorable to his agenda. President George W. Bush retained Clinton's EO but targeted it back toward Reagan's EO and a conservative agenda. On January 30, 2009, President Obama revoked Bush's 2007 Executive Order 13422, unentangling the review process from a market-oriented agenda.

Signing Statements

When a president receives a piece of legislation from Congress, which has passed by a majority of both chambers, he has two options: sign it and make it law or veto it. As discussed in Chapter 6, a presidential veto can be overridden by a supermajority of Congress. Since James Monroe was president, presidents have not simply signed or not signed the bill; they have also issued commentary on the legislation with their understanding of how the law should be implemented. These comments are collectively known as "signing statements." Signing statements do not have the force of law which Executive Orders implicitly contain. Instead, signing statements provide symbolic statements as well as guidance for agencies in their rulemaking, and also an opportunity to influence future judicial interpretation.

A signing statement from Andrew Jackson in 1830 illustrates how the early presidents used signing statements:

> *To the Senate and House of Representatives of the United States.*
>
> GENTLEMEN: I have approved and signed the bill entitled "An act making appropriations for examinations and surveys, and also for certain works of internal improvement," but as the phraseology of the section which appropriates the sum of $8,000 for the road from Detroit to Chicago may be construed to authorize the application of the appropriation for the continuance of the road beyond the limits of the Territory of Michigan, I desire to be understood as having approved

this bill with the understanding that the road authorized by this section is not to be extended beyond the limits of the said Territory.

ANDREW JACKSON[52]

Modern presidents, particularly those faced with divided government, used signing statements "as a means for the president to object to congressional incursions across the border between Articles I and II."[53] George W. Bush, in particular, used signing statements to assert the power and prerogatives of the institution of the presidency. Bush asserted in seventy-six distinct signing statements a phrase that encapsulated the president's position: "supervise the unitary executive branch." Here is an example of a Bush signing statement; the phrases in bold type are the ones Bush used to assert presidential authority:

> **Statement on Signing the Palestinian Anti-Terrorism Act of 2006:** Today I have signed into law S. 2370, the "Palestinian Anti-Terrorism Act of 2006." The Act is designed to promote the development of democratic institutions in areas under the administrative control of the Palestinian Authority.
>
> Section 2 of the Act purports to establish U.S. policy with respect to various international affairs matters. **My approval of the Act does not constitute my adoption of the statements of policy as U.S. foreign policy.** Given the Constitution's commitment to the presidency of the authority to conduct the Nation's foreign affairs, **the executive branch shall construe such policy statements as advisory**. The executive branch will give section 2 the due weight that comity between the legislative and executive branches should require, to the extent consistent with U.S. foreign policy.
>
> The executive branch shall construe section 3(b) of the Act, which relates to access to certain information by a legislative agent, and section 11 of the Act, which relates to a report on certain assistance by foreign countries, international organizations, or multilateral development banks, **in a manner consistent with the President's constitutional authority to withhold information that could impair foreign relations, national security, the deliberative processes of the Executive, or the performance of the Executive's constitutional duties**.
>
> Section 620K(e)(2)(A) and 620L(b)(4)(B)(i) of the Foreign Assistance Act of 1961, as enacted by sections 2(b)(2) and 3(a) of the Act, purport to require the President to consult with committees of the Congress prior to exercising certain authority granted to the President by sections 620K and 620L. **Because the constitutional authority of the President to supervise the unitary executive branch and take care that the laws be faithfully executed cannot be made by law subject to a requirement to consult with congressional committees or to involve them in executive decisionmaking, the executive branch shall construe the references in the provisions to consulting to require only notification**.
>
> The executive branch shall construe section 7 of the Act, which relates to establishing or maintaining certain facilities or establishments within the jurisdiction of the United States, in a manner consistent with the President's constitutional authority to conduct the Nation's foreign affairs, including the authority to receive ambassadors and other public ministers.
>
> The executive branch shall construe as **advisory the provisions of the Act,** including section 9, that purport to direct or burden the conduct of negotiations by the executive branch with entities abroad. Such provisions, if construed

> as mandatory rather than advisory, **would impermissibly interfere with the President's constitutional authorities to conduct the Nation's foreign affairs, including protection of American citizens and American military and other Government personnel abroad, and to supervise the unitary executive branch.**
> George W. Bush, The White House, December 21, 2006.[54]

Taken together, budgeting, issuing signing statements, issuing executive orders, and conducting regulatory review offer the modern presidency an array of tools to attempt to manage the seemingly unmanageable. Of course, functionality is not the president's only goal in employing these tactics. Asserting an ideology, accomplishing an agenda, and leaving a legacy are all goals of the modern presidency. Successful management of the executive branch aids in each and every aspect of those goals.

VICE PRESIDENTS

If the framers of the Constitution had anything but minor interest in the vice presidency, the historical record seems to provide no evidence. Of the many pamphlets, essays, and correspondences generated by American writers about the Constitution, not one focuses on the vice presidency itself. Alexander Hamilton devoted two paragraphs to it in *Federalist* 68, but his comments offer no insight about the primary purposes of the office. Although a number of other documents reflect Anti-Federalist concerns over the vice president's role in the Senate, they reveal nothing about the nature of the office, nor do they shed any light on its theoretical foundations. Historically speaking, the vice presidency is unusual. Established to meet the unique demands of a presidential system of government, it was without precedent in the late eighteenth century. Yet, from a modern perspective, despite long periods of inactivity or comparative obscurity, the vice presidency has become one of the more essential political positions.

The History of the Office

The first Vice President, John Adams, claimed, "My country has in its wisdom contrived for me the most insignificant office that ever the invention of man contrived or his imagination conceived."[55] More than a hundred and fifty years later, FDR's first Vice President, John Nance Garner, colorfully informed Lyndon Johnson who was considering becoming John F. Kennedy's running mate in 1960 that the office was "hardly worth a pitcher of spit."[56] The position, as many vice presidents have noted, has two functions, both of which involve lots of waiting. In the event of a tie in the Senate, the vice president casts the deciding vote. In the event of the death, incapacitation, resignation, or impeachment of the president, the vice president assumes the job of president. Thus, on a day-to-day basis, there is no constitutionally defined role. Clearly, the vice presidency lacks both the prestige and the power of the presidency, and it may not be the post to which most politicians aspire. However, it is important to remember that nine vice presidents have succeeded to the office of the presidency (due to four presidential deaths in office, four assassinations, and one resignation), so the office does have more significance than its detractors commonly assert.

The Constitution, as ratified in 1789, mentions the vice presidency four specific times; there are three additional amendments that deal with the position. The four initial references sum up the job description as designed by the Framers:

> The Vice President of the United States shall be President of the Senate, but shall have no Vote, unless they be equally divided. (Article II, Section 3)
>
> The executive Power shall be vested in a President of the United States of America. He shall hold his Office during the Term of four Years, and, together with the Vice-President chosen for the same Term, be elected, as follows... (Article II, Section 1)
>
> In Case of the Removal of the President from Office, or of his Death, Resignation, or Inability to discharge the Powers and Duties of the said Office, the same shall devolve on the Vice President, and the Congress may by Law provide for the Case of Removal, Death, Resignation or Inability, both of the President and Vice President, declaring what Officer shall then act as President, and such Officer shall act accordingly, until the Disability be removed, or a President shall be elected. (Article II, Section I, modified by the 20th and 25th amendments)
>
> The President, Vice President and all civil Officers of the United States, shall be removed from Office on Impeachment for, and Conviction of, Treason, Bribery, or other high Crimes and Misdemeanors. (Article II, Section 4).

In addition, per the framers' intentions, the Constitution required electors to vote for two undifferentiated candidates during presidential elections, which was supposed to produce a president and his presumed successor and, in so doing, preserve stability and the unified and steady progress of the presidency. As such, the framers hoped vice presidents would be among their presidents' closest advisors, supporting presidential policymaking and getting on-the-job training for the nation's highest office. Unfortunately, the framers' plans never materialized, as personal incompatibilities soon undermined original intent, relegating the vice presidency to a back seat in executive politics. The Twelfth Amendment (which required each elector to cast distinct votes for president and vice president, instead of two votes for president) formally acknowledged the inferiority of the vice presidency and subordinated it to the presidency in a way the framers never intended.

Aside from their constitutional role as presiding officers of the Senate, nineteenth-century vice presidents had no real power or authority. John Tyler, Millard Fillmore, Andrew Johnson, and Chester Arthur ascended to the presidency upon the deaths of William Henry Harrison, Zachary Taylor, Abraham Lincoln, and James Garfield, but their contributions as presidents did nothing to enhance the reputation of the vice presidency. None of the four distinguished himself in the White House, at least not in a positive way; Tyler and Johnson each had a special talent for making political enemies (and Johnson became the first president to be impeached in 1868). The assassination of William McKinley and the succession of Vice President Theodore Roosevelt to the presidency in 1901 began a slow but intermittent rehabilitation of the vice presidency. Roosevelt was a vocal and comparatively assertive vice president and became one of America's most admired chief executives, whose effectiveness in the presidency finally alerted Americans to the potential importance of a historically neglected office.

Yet, in the four decades following Roosevelt's presidency, the vice presidency again largely languished. The death of yet another president, Warren Harding, did not prove as fortuitous for his successor, not least because Calvin Coolidge was no Teddy Roosevelt. However, in 1945, the death of Franklin Roosevelt would again catapult a vice president into the political spotlight. At the time, no one could have predicted that Harry Truman, the former junior senator from Missouri and FDR's third vice president (elected to the job in 1944), would become the architect of America's national security state and one of its most formidable commanders in chief. Compared unfavorably to FDR in almost every possible way by the public, Truman was expected to fade into anonymity with the rest of America's vice presidents. FDR's death in April of 1945 shattered those expectations and served as the springboard for an exceptionally effective tenure, especially with respect to foreign policy.

The Contemporary Vice Presidency

In recent years, vice presidents have begun to play a more significant role in the day-to-day operation of the White House. For example, Vice President Joe Biden's job, detailed on the White House web page, is described as follows:

> The Vice President has been tasked with implementing the American Recovery and Reinvestment Act, helping to rebuild our economy and lay the foundation for a sustainable economic future. He is also the chair of the administration's Middle Class Task Force, a major White House initiative targeted at raising the living standards of middle class families in America. In addition, he is providing sustained, high level focus for the administration on Iraq policy and has traveled to the country multiple times since being elected as Vice President. Vice President Biden continues to draw on his vast foreign policy experience, advising the President on a multitude of international issues and representing our country to many regions of the world, including travel to Germany, Belgium, Chile, Costa Rica, Bosnia and Herzegovina, Serbia, Kosovo, Lebanon, Georgia, Ukraine, Iraq, Poland, Romania, the Czech Republic, Israel, the Palestinian Territories, Jordan, Spain, Egypt, Kenya and South Africa.[57]

The growth in the responsibilities of the vice presidency arose from extraconstitutional sources, namely presidential discretion. The vice presidency did not expand in tandem with the growth of the EOP and White House staff. Instead, the vice presidency was slow to evolve as an institutional source of administration and management because, like the cabinet secretaries, vice presidents are chosen for a variety of reasons. As discussed in Chapter 3, candidates choose running mates for geographic balance, for ideological balance, and/or for party unity. Like cabinet secretaries, those reasons do not often support governing and management. However, over time, delegation and management did factor into presidential choice and the expansion of the vice president's role in the executive branch.

An early example would be Dwight Eisenhower allowing his vice president, Richard Nixon, to attend cabinet, NSC and other legislative meetings. When Eisenhower was ill, Nixon presided over the meetings as well. Nixon was also the first vice president to actually have an office inside the White House. Most of Nixon's authority comprised foreign-policy responsibilities, as Eisenhower relied on Nixon's expertise on international matters. Vice President Nixon even represented the administration on several foreign trips (including his famous "kitchen debates" with Soviet Premier Nikita Khrushchev at the American National Exhibition in Moscow in 1959), increasing the visibility of an institution that had been relatively anonymous throughout the previous 150 years. This strongly contrasted with the FDR model; for example, Vice President Harry Truman was not exposed to sensitive information. In fact, Truman did not find out that the country had atomic capabilities until after becoming president in April 1945. Vice President Lyndon Johnson (who took the job despite Garner's opinion of it) participated more frequently in legislative efforts, in keeping with the skill set of a former Senate Majority Leader, yet was still not considered among the inner circle of advisors within the Kennedy administration.

Walter Mondale was the first Vice President to achieve institutional power for the office. As noted in the staffing and cabinet discussions, access to the president is perhaps the most significant sign of power. Staff members who see the president frequently are more able to influence issues as well as the president, versus those who do not. Mondale had a large staff himself; he saw the president frequently and, in Jimmy Carter, he had a willing partner for expanding the role of the office.[58] As a result, he was an active participant in many issues. He took the office well beyond "the job's traditional responsibilities to lobby Congress on the administration's behalf, serve as spokesman to the general public and politically important interest groups, attend ceremonial functions in the president's stead, and assist the party's candidates for office."[59] An active role for the vice president still ultimately depends on the choice of the president to allow it; however, Mondale seems to have permanently expanded the institutional capacity of the office. While not all subsequent presidential–vice presidential relationships were as close (e.g., Reagan–Bush, Bush–Quayle), the trend has been for increased activism, capacity, and management.

The three most recent vice presidents, Al Gore (1993–2001), Dick Cheney (2001–2009), and Joe Biden (2009–present) have all received extensive staff, continuous access to the president, and a president willing to rely on the vice president's skill and expertise in specific areas. Gore was unquestionably the most effective vice president since the creation of the American republic, eclipsing many presidents in terms of his accomplishments. Intimately involved in policymaking, and taking a special interest in environmental issues, bureaucratic reform, and information technology, Gore was a trusted advisor to President Clinton and an integral part of the administration.

During his two terms, Cheney became even more powerful than Gore had been, leading some of his detractors to refer to him mockingly as the real president. Cheney, a seasoned veteran of two previous administrations with a take-no-prisoners mentality, was the president's point man on national-security issues. Viewed as the leading advocate of war in the Middle East, Cheney had unprecedented authority over strategic planning and military operations, as well as substantial responsibility over diplomatic issues. However, many in the press and in academia consider Vice President Cheney's expansive exercise of power a worrisome precedent, as Cheney

Vice President Dick Cheney expanded the powers of his office during the George W. Bush administration.

took the office well beyond the activities of his predecessors. His role, particularly in the early years of the Bush administration, has been described as a "surrogate chief of staff," "co-president," and "deputy president."[60] Not only did Cheney manage the response to terrorism on the morning of 9/11 (Bush was at an education event in Florida), but he and his office were also involved in some of the most controversial decisions and events during the Bush administration. Cheney's vice presidential office has been linked to: creating a domestic surveillance program; creating policies for detained suspected terrorists; outing a CIA agent; and linking Saddam Hussein to Al Qaeda (proven false) and to weapons of mass destruction (also proven false) which led, in part, to the invasion of Iraq in 2003.

Since Cheney's tenure, Vice President Joe Biden has chosen a less confrontational path by reducing the profile of the office during his first term in office. As an experienced legislator with impressive foreign-policy credentials, Biden has, consciously or unconsciously, steered the institution back toward the standard set by Richard Nixon in the 1950s by acknowledging the vice presidency's inherent limitations and attempting to make the most of its capabilities within them by never attempting to outshine his chief executive. Whether the Bush–Cheney co-presidency, as some have labeled it, is unique or sets a precedent, the twenty-first-century vice presidency remains an expanded, influential part of the institution of the presidency.

FIRST LADIES

There is no constitutional role for the president's family, yet there is no avoiding the public role that comes with marriage to the President of the United States. For most of the country's history, the president's wife has served as hostess in chief. In the modern era, the duties of the first lady include some or all of the following: wife and mother, public figure and celebrity, the nation's social hostess, symbol of U.S. womanhood, White House manager and preservationist, campaigner, champion of social causes, presidential spokesperson, presidential and political party booster, diplomat, and political and presidential partner.[61] As with the vice president, the extent to which the first lady adopts any, or all, of these roles depends on private negotiations with the president and to some extent public negotiations with the country. The Office of the First Lady has become, in recent years, part of the official organizational structure of the Executive Office of the President. One of the main responsibilities of the first lady's staff is in the day-to-day dealings with the news media. In addition to a press secretary, most first ladies have also employed a chief of staff, a social secretary, a projects director (for causes that a first lady may adopt), and several other special assistants. Since the 1970s, first ladies have employed anywhere between twelve and twenty-eight full-time employees for their staffs.[62] First ladies also have an office in the White House; to date, only one—Hillary Rodham Clinton—chose to have her office in the West Wing, as opposed to the East Wing, of the White House, which was a clear indication of the advisory role that she planned to play within her husband's administration. Regardless of the role that they play in their husband's administrations, first ladies are, according to political scientist MaryAnne Borrelli, "complicated women" who are "called upon to clarify and calm, or to inspire and motivate, projecting a voicing of confidence, reason, and balance."[63]

First Ladies in Historical Perspective

Given the prevailing attitudes toward women during most of the nation's history, the political assertiveness of its first ladies has been a comparatively recent phenomenon, yet there were two early exceptions to the rule. Abigail Adams, wife of the second president, though observant of contemporary social graces, was opinionated and firm, offering advice and counsel to her husband throughout his political career. Likewise, James Madison considered his wife, Dolley, an invaluable aide while president, relinquishing control over the presidential residence to her and relying on her to coordinate the evacuation of the White House during the War of 1812. The first presidential spouse, however, to truly break the mold was Edith Wilson, who, for all intents and purposes, ran the presidency following Woodrow Wilson's stroke in 1919.

Like Edith Wilson, Franklin Roosevelt's wife, Eleanor, was pushed into service by unusual circumstances. FDR contracted polio in 1921 and depended on Eleanor for his political survival thereafter. Eleanor campaigned vigorously for her husband, managed his schedule, acted as his closest advisor, and did as much as anyone to sustain the myth of a vigorous and healthy president. During FDR's presidency, she spoke out against sexism and discrimination, worked hard for the realization of lifelong progressive political goals, and transformed the purely ceremonial role of first lady into a substantive presence within the White House. From both a political and social perspective, Eleanor Roosevelt's accomplishments were formidable. As first lady, her power rivaled that of FDR's key aides and cabinet secretaries, demonstrating an influence over the president that was rare for anyone, especially a president's wife.

Contemporary First Ladies

The public role for first ladies has mostly been a social one, yet several first ladies since Eleanor Roosevelt's tenure provide distinct examples of the power and influence that can come with being the first spouse. Both Rosalyn Carter and Hillary Rodham Clinton opted for active involvement in policy decisions and publicly acknowledged their political role within the administration. Carter became an advocate for numerous causes, most notably research in the area of mental health issues. At the request of her husband, she also sat in on cabinet and other policy meetings, acted as one of his closest advisors, and even served as an envoy abroad in Latin America and other areas. Clinton, perhaps rivaling only Eleanor Roosevelt in the politically significant role that she would play in her husband's administration, was a successful attorney and long-time advocate for children's issues before moving into the White House. As first lady, she acted as one of Bill Clinton's top policy advisors (hence the office in the West Wing), and most notably headed up the Clinton administration's health-care reform policy initiative (first introduced in 1993, but which failed to achieve congressional

As First Lady, Michelle Obama has promoted healthier eating and exercise habits for children, and has also been active in providing support for military families.

approval in 1994). After the failure with health-care reform, Clinton lowered her political profile and embraced more traditional activities for a first lady, as well as focusing on social issues, particularly those dealing with women and children.[64]

Other first ladies, like Mamie Eisenhower, Ladybird Johnson, Barbara Bush, and Laura Bush, opted for more traditional, nonpublic roles in their husbands' White Houses. Regardless of the public versus private role of the first lady, several have played unique roles in their husbands' administrations. Jackie Kennedy, a former debutante, is remembered for her trend-setting fashions, redecorating the aging White House, bringing art and culture into Washington political circles, and providing glamour to the Kennedy administration at the start of the television age of politics. Betty Ford was an outspoken advocate for women's rights, and is also remembered for raising public consciousness about addiction by publicly acknowledging her own problems with alcohol. While mostly a traditional first lady while in the public eye, Nancy Reagan was a formidable presence in the Reagan White House in protecting her husband's best interests. President Reagan trusted her judgment supremely and even consulted her regarding staffing decisions in the White House and major policy objectives. Michelle Obama, a Princeton- and Harvard-educated attorney who put her career on hold during her husband's presidential campaign in 2008, has chosen the more traditional role of first lady by supporting non-political causes such as support for military families and fighting obesity in America's children. And, like several of her predecessors, Mrs. Obama is also tasked with raising two young daughters while living in the White House.

CONCLUSION

The executive branch of the U.S. government is a complex institution; it has multiple missions and an enormous workforce, and its divisions are not all centrally located. Coordinating and controlling this massive organization falls on the president. The president has an array of tools, with ranging degrees of effectiveness, to ensure that the branch does what the president swears an oath to do, which is to faithfully execute as well as preserve, protect, and defend the Constitution of the United States.

The defining dividing line between the traditional and the modern presidency emerged out of the Brownlow Committee's famous line: "The president needs help." The president needed help because the breadth and depth of the job had increased over time. Hand in hand with the increased responsibility is the president's increased desire to control the output of the bureaucracy—in effect, to make it more presidential. To gain control and to benefit from the increased workload, presidents developed an Executive Office of the President to manage, coordinate, and control the bureaucracy. The degree to which presidents are able to manage, coordinate, and control, however, is considerably influenced by Congress, as well as the bureaucracy itself, the president's own cabinet, and even the federal courts. Presidents must deal with the scrutiny of their decisions, the tensions between the political arms and the civil service arms of the bureaucracy, and the compromised legislation emerging out of Congress, as well as the redefinition of legislation by the Court. It is perhaps the president's most difficult assignment for which he receives the least public payoff.

Watch First Lady Hillary Clinton testify before Congress on health care reform.

CRISIS MANAGEMENT

THEN . . .

In addition to the leadership of the executive branch, a central aspect of the presidency for the framers was crisis management. Shays' Rebellion in 1786 awoke the new nation to the pace of legislative reaction. Despite fears of tyranny, the framers recognized that during a crisis a singular individual often can respond with speed and efficiency where a legislature cannot. For most presidents, crisis is thrust upon them at some point during their tenure in office. However, Franklin Roosevelt ran his triumphant campaign in 1932 in response to crisis. FDR knew that from day one in office he would be dealing with a vast economic crisis, which by that point had stymied both Congress and President Herbert Hoover. As noted in the introduction, FDR asked for broad executive power to wage war against the crisis; however, a president cannot wage war alone. Like any good general going to war, the incoming president had a plan; the plan had been created by a group of advisors chosen specifically to create this plan. The press nicknamed Roosevelt's campaign advisors the "brain trust," but the team that developed and executed his New Deal equally fit that bill.

Roosevelt was elected in November 1932; his inauguration was March 4, 1932, as delineated by the Constitution. During this time frame, two important factors occurred: (1) Roosevelt gathered advisors to assist in formulating what became known as the "New Deal" and (2) the Great Depression worsened significantly. President Hoover, after losing his bid for reelection, served out the remainder of his term while the country spiraled further downward: "By the end of Hoover's reign, more than fifteen million workers had lost their jobs"; across the nation people were hungry and cold.[65] The four months were, in contrast, a boon to Roosevelt.

Roosevelt used his four-month time in waiting to determine a course of action. His choice of advisors was critical to designing and ultimately pursuing his New Deal. Roosevelt chose his advisors from outside the political world, which was not unusual but was certainly not the norm. As governor of New York, Roosevelt often turned to academia for guidance. He continued this practice as president-elect. Raymond Moley, a Barnard College professor, led the campaign brain trust and after Roosevelt's victory continued to serve as he "interviewed experts, assigned men to draft bills, and hammered out the legislation of the Hundred Days."[66]

As the forerunner to Roosevelt's competitive management approach, FDR was not wedded to any one economic doctrine. Most likely, in response to the Republican's rigid adherence to balancing the budget and maintaining sound currency, which was not working, Roosevelt flung ideology out the window. Led by Moley and other academics, this new "brain trust" "attempted to weave together" conflicting policies and ideologies.[67] The New Deal was the combination of populism (suspicion of Wall Street and regulating agriculture), directing the economy (mobilization from World War I), urban social reformers (concern for the elderly and impoverished), and new nationalism (a rejection of natural law, free competition, and the idolization of small business owners).

Throughout the White House, "the New Dealers shared... [the] conviction that organized social intelligence could shape society" toward a form of balance.[68] By bringing together a group of disparate people with different perspectives on how to attack the Great Depression, Roosevelt forged a new approach, and a new ideology. He shaped his government and his government's policies around the information and advice received from his advisors.

... AND NOW

President Obama, like President Roosevelt, entered office knowing his administration faced a crisis of monumental proportions. Whereas Roosevelt's entire campaign centered on the Great Depression, the economy actually collapsed just two months prior to Election Day in 2008. Like FDR, president-elect Obama knew his priority would be the economy. Unlike FDR, due to the Twentieth Amendment, which changed Inauguration Day to January 20th, Obama became President just two months after his election. FDR had time to debate, discuss, consider and design his advisory team; he also had time to plan with them prior to Inauguration Day. The famed Hundred Days in which the Roosevelt administration sent fifteen pieces of legislation to Congress, and all fifteen passed with minimal changes or debate, directly resulted from the four-month time prior to Roosevelt taking office. The speed with which Obama needed to form an advisory circle, however, was not the only difference between his choices of advisors and FDR's.

Typically, presidential candidates begin planning their "transition" from president-elect to president well before they gain the title. The bulk of this planning for the modern presidency is devoted to staffing. As the eventual creator of the modern presidency, at least in terms of the size and scope of the executive branch, FDR's post-election transition not only benefitted from four months but also, as FDR lacked an enormous apparatus to staff, his advisors could focus almost entirely on the crisis in their planning. By virtue of FDR's creation of the EOP, as well as the expansion in the number of cabinet positions, Obama needed to fill White House staff positions, as well as the political positions in the bureaucracy. Obama's "brain trust," in acknowledgment of the crisis, subdivided the transition along two critical tasks: policy and personnel.

Obama and his transition team assembled a White House staff and a roster of cabinet nominees who met the recent criteria used by administrations not facing crises. His predecessors, not functioning in times of great crisis, focused on creating a "Cabinet which looks like America." Presidents Clinton and George W. Bush surrounded themselves with more women and people of color than prior administrations. Obama made no overt discussion of race and gender, although he has employed a significant number who meet those criteria. Not only did he seek the best and the brightest who were representative of America, President-Elect Obama made ending the revolving door between the executive branch and the lobbying industry a key factor in his staffing decisions. The crisis did not shake the president-elect off the path of ethical reform.

The desire to promote distance between those who worked in the executive branch and the lobbying industry resulted in a massive inquiry into nominees and potential staff members' lives via a sixty-three-item questionnaire and FBI background checks. Despite the existence of the most invasive questioning of potential executive branch employees, several of Obama's nominations had ethical problems. Tim Geithner became Secretary of the Treasury despite some unpaid taxes; however, New Mexico Governor Bill Richardson and former Senate Majority Leader Tim Daschle withdrew their nominations to become Secretary of Commerce and Secretary of Health and Human Services, respectively.[69]

While the effort to fill these numerous positions continued, simultaneously another group focused on the president's policy priorities. John Podesta, a former Clinton chief of staff, led the Obama transition during the campaign and after the election. Podesta, who runs a Washington think tank, gave the Obama team an unprecedented policy resource: "no pre-election effort in the past has had a director who could so easily and directly tap into such a policy and planning resource."[70] However, the teams assembling the president's advisors were kept separate from those focused on policy. They created the "virtual firewall," again following Obama's ethical strictures: "departmental and policy team members would not have favored access to executive branch positions."[71]

Although Obama's team did set records in terms of its White House staff appointments, they were not as effective in filling the departments' subcabinet levels. The effect was most notable in the Treasury, where media reports and even former Federal Reserve Chair Paul Volcker noted how alone Tim Geithner was: "The Secretary of the Treasury is sitting there without a deputy, without any undersecretaries, without any, as far as I know, assistant secretaries responsible in substantive areas at a time of very severe crisis. He shouldn't be sitting there alone."[72]

More interesting, in comparison to FDR, was the separation between campaign policy formation and White House policy formation. FDR hit the ground running, literally acting on day one to close the banks and call Congress into session, during which they voted on his first bill, just five days later. The first eleven Obama executive orders were items high on the President's to do list, but were not specifically related to the crisis, except symbolically (he froze pay on the top White House staffers making more than $100,000). Congress had been in session since early January, and it still took the Obama administration nine days to get a stimulus package through Congress. The plans for the banking industry and the auto industry took longer; without help, Secretary Geithner took until March 23 to bail out the banks.

SUGGESTED READINGS

Aberbach, Joel D., and Mark A. Peterson, eds. 2006. *The Executive Branch*. New York: Oxford University Press.

Borrelli, MaryAnne. 2011. *The Politics of the President's Wife*. College Station: Texas A&M University Press.

Burke, John P. 2000. *The Institutional Presidency: Organizing and Managing the White House from FDR to Clinton*. Baltimore: Johns Hopkins University Press.

Dickinson, Matthew J. 1996. *Bitter Harvest: FDR, Presidential Power and the Growth of the Presidential Branch*. Cambridge: Cambridge University Press.

Kumar, Martha Joynt, and Terry Sullivan, eds. 2003. *The White House World: Transitions, Organization, and Office Operations*. College Station: Texas A&M University Press.
Mayer, Kenneth. 2001. *With the Stroke of a Pen: Executive Orders and Presidential Power*. Princeton: Princeton University Press.
Patterson, Bradley H., Jr. 2000. *The White House Staff: Inside the West Wing and Beyond*. Washington, DC: Brookings Institution Press.
Patterson, Bradley H., Jr. 2008. *To Serve the President: Continuity and Innovation in the White House Staff*. Washington, DC: Brookings Institution Press.
Walcott, Charles, and Karen Hult. 1995. *Governing the White House: From Hoover Through LBJ*. Lawrence: University Press of Kansas.
Walcott, Charles, and Karen Hult. 2004. *Empowering the White House: Governance Under Nixon, Ford and Carter*. Lawrence: University Press of Kansas.
Warshaw, Shirley Anne. 2005. *The Keys to Power: Managing the Presidency*, 2nd ed. New York: Longman.
Weko, Thomas. 1995. *The Politicizing Presidency: The White House Personnel Office 1948–1994*. Lawrence: University Press of Kansas.
Wilson, James Q. 1991. *Bureaucracy: What Government Agencies Do and Why They Do It*. New York: Basic Books.

ON THE WEB

http://www.whitehouse.gov/administration. The official web page of the executive branch, which includes the websites of the cabinet, the White House staff, the Executive Office of the President, and other advisory boards.

http://www.gao.gov/. The official website of the Government Accountability Office, the investigative arm of Congress. GAO supports congressional oversight and accountability of the bureaucracy.

IN THEIR OWN WORDS

MANAGING THE WHITE HOUSE

One of the most important functions of the White House staff is not only to keep the president informed of important events and issues, but also to organize the massive flow of information that works its way through various White House and executive branch offices on a daily basis. When Bill Clinton first took office in 1993, many of his young White House staffers earned a reputation for being disorganized and lacking the discipline needed to run the White House, and manage Clinton's schedule, in an efficient manner. However, John Podesta, Assistant to the President and Staff Secretary in January 1993 (he would become Clinton's fourth and final chief of staff in 1998), laid out the elaborate plan for managing "paperflow" in the early days of the Clinton administration:

> This memo sets forth the procedure for all White House staff to follow in sending paper to the President for signature or review. It is an initial cut at establishing a smoothly working paper flow system and I expect that it will require some refinement.
>
> At the outset, it is important to emphasize that all paper going to the President should come through the Staff Secretary (with certain exceptions for

NSC). All paper leaving the President's office should go back to the Staff Secretary to ensure that decisions will be implemented, the appropriate people notified, and good records maintained.

Daily Briefing Book

Marcia Hale will be responsible for putting together the President's schedule and informing the appropriate offices what their responsibilities are for producing background memos, talking points, etc. (Full speeches are discussed below.) Marcia will distribute a draft of the next day's schedule at noon. All offices will be responsible for forwarding briefing book materials to my office not later than 4:30 pm the night before the day in question.

My office will review such materials for quality, completeness, etc. and produce the President's book. Briefing books will be distributed by 8:00 pm.

Decision Memo Clearance

Perhaps the most important function of the Staff Secretary's office is to ensure that decision memoranda are properly staffed before reaching the President. That will require cooperation of all staff. The following procedures should be followed:

Unless a real emergency exists, decision memos must be forwarded to the Staff Secretary at least 48 hours in advance of presenting the document to the President.

I will route the memo to relevant White House staff for comment. The Chief of Staff and Vice President will receive all draft decision documents for comment. I will also route such drafts to Bernie Nussbaum and to Maggie Williams. Other offices will be routed as appropriate.

Routing will be Assistants to the President. It will be up to each Assistant to decide proper routing procedures within his or her own office.

As a general rule, staffing to Cabinet agencies will be done through the Councils. In the event that comment from Cabinet officers is required that cannot be handled through the regular Council process, paper will be routed through the Cabinet Secretary, who will also serve as a collection point for comments coming back from the Cabinet in those circumstances.

My office will serve as a collection point for all comments from the White House Staff and in the circumstances described in the above bullet from the Cabinet (via the Cabinet Secretary) and will attempt to facilitate consensus, prior to presentation of the matter to the President. Where no consensus can be formed, I will ensure that individual views are noted and accurately presented.

BACKGROUND MEMOS

Briefing papers, where no formal action is requested, will be handled in the same general manner as decision memos. My office will be responsible for preparing or editing summaries of all general briefing papers.

SPEECHES

Different administrations have handled the speech clearance process differently, with some vesting principal clearance responsibility in the Staff Secretary, and others in the speech writers themselves. We are going to try out a process under which the Communications staff will have primary responsibility for clearing all speeches and statements of the President released to the press, provided that these procedures are followed:

My office must be on and see the original distribution list of draft speeches to ensure that all offices with a need to review have received a copy.

Comments to speech writers should be cc'd to me, to ensure that those views have been appropriately considered before forwarding a draft to the President.

Drafts of speeches to be presented to the President should flow to and from the President through my office, so that they can be properly handled and archived.

REPORT TO CONGRESS

The Administration prepares over 300 reports to Congress each year, as a result of statutory requirements. Many are submitted under the President's signature. They are frequently thick documents and often come to us with short deadlines. We will try to ensure that agencies submit reports in a timely fashion to give White House staff a meaningful chance to review these reports. We will route them for clearance to the appropriate people.

LEGISLATION

Enrolled legislation (passed by both houses) is received and time stamped by the Executive Clerk. OMB has responsibility for interagency review of the legislation. The Staff Secretary's office will handle clearance of the legislation, signing statements and veto measures amongst the White House staff. The same procedures outlined for clearance of decision memos should be followed.

CORRESPONDENCE

Congressional correspondence as a rule will be reviewed, personally, by the President. Staffing of letters to the Hill will follow the same procedures as outlined for clearance of decision memos. Other correspondence will be routed initially through Marcia Scott, the Acting Director of Messages and Correspondence who is working furiously to bring up our system for answering mail, whether for the President's or First Lady's signature, or for staff signature. A memo laying out the correspondence system will follow shortly.

SEQUENCING AND TIMING

It can be anticipated that staff sending paper to my office will frequently feel that the President must see it in the next 10 minutes. Barring real emergencies, that will generally not be possible. I will be working with Nancy Hernreich to develop a system that will make the President's day work for him.

<u>Morning</u>. With regard to paper, my expectation is that the President will have a short time in the morning to review his briefing book and paperwork, including (i) papers and letters he must review and sign; (ii) decision memos, briefing memos and other matters which he can review that morning or hold

for evening review; (iii) a summary of documents and important correspondence received, which he can review in more detail if he wishes.

Daytime Period. The President wants to limit review of paper during daytime working hours. Only essential items which must be signed or reviewed will be brought to his attention during those hours. I will forward essential items to the President through Nancy Hernreich who will be responsible for fitting review of essential items into the day's schedule.

Evening. After the President's morning work period all non-essential paperwork will be held until the evening. In the evening, we will give the President a manageable amount of time—no more than 45 minutes to an hour's worth. We will include in these materials all important decision memos which will be discussed the next day.

Weekend. Longer policy papers and think pieces will be held for weekend review, where possible. That will give the President more time to reflect and comment.

FOLLOWING WEEK

By the close of business each Friday, senior staff—and especially the councils—should forward to me a list of any important decision memos that they expect to have presented to the President the next week so that we can build adequate time into the schedule for review at the staff level and by the President.

STYLE

Some changes may be made to the current style of documents intended for the President, but, for now, please use current style forms.

In closing, let me say that my office has a straightforward goal—to protect the President and his decision-making process. Paper coming to him must meet the highest standards of excellence. Papers must be well written. Options must be clearly stated. Those who need to see it must have seen it. Views of advisors must be accurately reflected. Summaries must be brief and accurate. We cannot let the pressure of time compromise those standards.

CHAPTER 9

Presidents and Domestic Policymaking

Certain issues, such as health care, are inherently inflammatory and fuel partisan debates of the worst kind, inspiring rhetorical salvos that perpetuate convenient myths about political rivals and their stands on those issues. Health-care reform is a topic particularly susceptible to hyperbole, because it elicits a profoundly visceral response from most Americans, and it seems to offer little compromise. In recent years, advocates of federal regulation or governmental management of health care have experienced exceptional criticism from their political foes, disparagingly labeled as socialists, or even communists. However, that has not stopped many presidents dating back to the days of Theodore Roosevelt's administration from arguing for the need for some type of health-care reform. During the last eighty years or so, the federal government, usually moved through presidential initiative, has intervened to various degrees to address the market deficiencies in health care that leave millions of Americans with either inadequate coverage or no coverage at all, not to mention the spiraling costs of health care and health insurance. Starting with Franklin D. Roosevelt's New Deal, but not acquiring substantial momentum until Lyndon Johnson's Great Society, modern presidents have almost continuously focused on the seemingly insoluble problem of health care. Although market intervention has traditionally been portrayed as a Democratic cause, both Democratic and Republican presidents have endeavored to formulate a viable government-based strategy for the provision of health care in the United States.

Predictably, due to ideological affinities and their electoral constituencies, Democratic presidents have been more eager to confront health-care reform than their Republican counterparts, as have Democratic legislators, who can be crucial allies for reform-minded presidents such as Bill Clinton and Barack Obama. Bill Clinton decided to tackle health-care reform early in his first term, but the effort was ultimately unsuccessful due to his administration's intransigence over key issues and a sustained attack by his political enemies. Fulfilling a principal campaign promise, President Clinton left the management of his health-care reform package to First Lady Hillary Clinton, whose erudition and intelligence were evident but whose lack of political savvy and willingness to accommodate opposing views quickly became a liability. Dogged by an apparent absence of transparency, deliberation, and choice, which are all hallmarks of legitimate presidential policymaking, the Clintons' health-care initiative became mired in controversy and partisan attacks. The administration's Task Force on National Health Care Reform, charged by the president with formulating a viable plan for universal health care, came under a blistering attack by interest groups and others opposed to health-care reform. By late summer 1994, Senate Majority Leader George Mitchell (D-ME), a Clinton supporter, pulled the plug on the embattled reform effort.[1]

Like Clinton, Barack Obama promised voters during his election campaign to address the nation's health-care problems, such as the decreasing affordability of health insurance, employers' reluctance to provide adequate insurance for workers, and the fact that over forty million Americans were either uninsured or underinsured. Also like Clinton, President Obama made health-care reform an immediate priority and introduced a comprehensive plan early in his first term. However, unlike Clinton, due to a combination of factors that included lessons learned from the Clintons' failed attempt to provide universal health care and a definite difference in leadership style, he relinquished management of the reform effort to Congress. Blamed even by many of his supporters for not being sufficiently proactive and simultaneously vilified as a socialist by an insurgent faction of Republicans that eventually became known as the Tea Party, Obama eventually became more engaged in the process and used both the bully pulpit and his negotiating skills to reconcile seemingly insurmountable differences between separate Senate and House versions of the reform package.

On March 23, 2010, Obama signed the omnibus Patient Protection and Affordable Care Act into law, which was joined a week later by the supplemental Health Care and Education Reconciliation Act. This landmark legislation covered governmental funding and oversight of health care, private and public-sector employers as well as insurers themselves, persons with pre-existing conditions, the uninsured through so-called individual mandates, and Medicare spending.[2] Almost immediately, parts of the law were challenged by opponents in federal court, especially the individual-mandate provision, which was held unconstitutional by the Eleventh Circuit Court of Appeals but upheld by appellate courts for the Sixth and DC Circuits, while the appeals court for the Fourth Circuit dismissed its cases on procedural criteria. The individual-mandate provision was declared constitutional by the Supreme Court in June 2012, although many Republicans remained unhappy with the bill even after the Court's ruling. Still, regardless of the advisability of expanding federal management of health care in the United States, this was a major policy accomplishment for the Obama White House and a triumph that had eluded the Clinton administration almost twenty years prior.

Despite the president's lack of stewardship of his health-care policy during crucial stages of its development, this was an apt representation of the domestic policymaking process. Far from perfect, at least according to normative academic parameters, the process exemplified the key determinants of legitimate policy formulation and implementation. As predicted by most theoretical models of decision making, the president's health-care policy was characterized by deliberation, a consideration of viable alternatives, accountability, and comparative transparency. The administration's policymaking process involved not only the president, his top advisors, and relevant policy councils within the White House but also legislators, interest groups, and even the American public, which made it more inclusive and collaborative than many similar reform efforts in the past. As a vehicle for an understanding of the domestic policymaking process writ large, President Obama's health-care initiative offers valuable insights about constitutive practices, people, and institutions. Without a doubt, no single policy can serve as a complete illustration of the overarching process, but this one had most of its distinguishing features.

U.S. DOMESTIC POLICY

The policymaking process connects presidential agendas to an underlying constitutional logic that legitimates not only presidential politics but also the broader political environment in which it is situated. Although most people may not be accustomed to conceptualizing policymaking in terms of an overarching constitutional rationale, the relationship between policymaking and its associated constitutional principles is inextricable. In other words, policymaking is the process of defining relevant constitutional directives through specific contextual acts. The Constitution is a general framework that awaits application to particular circumstances through policymaking in order to be useful as an actionable framework for political problem solving. As such, policymaking is as crucial to the American political system as the Constitution itself; without it, presidential politics would not exist. Every day, the policymaking process determines constitutionally authorized, practically motivated political objectives that reflect the afore-referenced presidential agendas. (See Figure 9.1)

Policy and Presidential Agendas

As a practical application of corresponding constitutional principles, policymaking drives the most critical dynamic in the American political system and, therefore, sustains its viability and legitimacy. By its nature, the Constitution is neither self-executing nor specific enough as a blueprint for day-to-day governance, which was the intention of its framers, so policymaking exists to implement relevant constitutional principles. It contextualizes corresponding constitutional principles by enabling their implementation through the coordinated and targeted efforts of the institutions and public officials they authorize to act on the people's behalf. Policies, especially presidential policies, translate those constitutional principles into practical acts and address the diverse political, economic, and social needs of American citizens. By maintaining a link to overriding constitutional directives, policymaking is a medium for the conversion of constitutional authority into practical political acts and also the legitimate use of political power and the nation's resources. In a way, policymaking is the glue that binds different parts of the political system, especially the theoretical and the practical, and is one of the truly indispensable elements in American politics.[3]

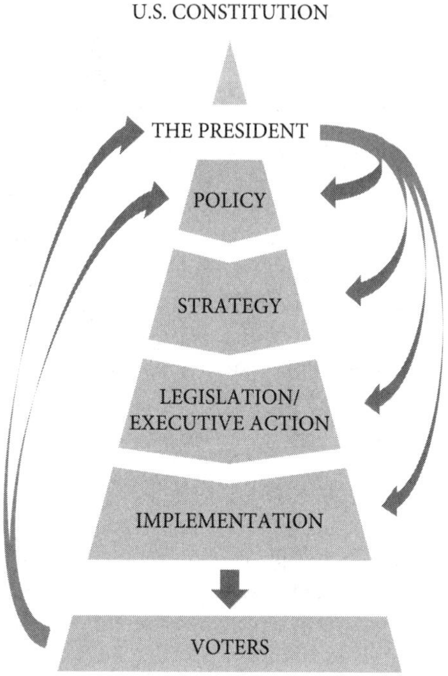

Figure 9.1 The Policymaking Process

Categorized by type and grouped together according to various individual and institutional preferences, policies determine the direction, scope, and effectiveness of presidential tenures. These groups, or sets, of policies, generated by presidents and their administrations, are called policy agendas and they comprise a more or less coherent and comprehensive blueprint for governance, in both the short and long terms. An agenda is a policymaking playbook of sorts, reflecting ideological preferences, partisan loyalties, and personal experiences combined with a corresponding constitutional vision or theory. Unfortunately, because agendas inherently reflect ideology and partisan allegiance, among other factors, political commentators, the public, and even scholars can view them with skepticism and mistrust. This does not mean that agendas, or particular policies within them, cannot become vehicles for political gamesmanship or personal ambition, but that is not a function of agendas themselves but of behavioral and circumstantial inputs. Policy agendas are nothing more than necessary tools for the planning, packaging, and implementation of presidential political priorities and logical, though more contextualized and realistic, extensions of campaign platforms.[4] Although practically oriented and a crucial part of the implementation of relevant constitutional principles, presidential agendas and the individual policies they comprise, like the Constitution, are not self-executing. The identification and definition of policy is, or should be, immediately followed by the formulation of strategy, which refers to an overall plan for the realization of corresponding policy and includes a justification of proposed methods and expected resources. A viable strategy not only demonstrates how political objectives will be realized but also provides a rationale for the subsequent implementation of subordinate initiatives.

The strategy-making stage creates a usable road map for the completion of the policy process and prepares the ground for the next step, which, in military parlance, is known as the operational stage and initiates the implementation of political objectives through enabling executive or legislative action. The operational stage addresses the physical necessities of the policymaking process by providing or creating the programs, materials, personnel, and practical direction demanded or implied by executive strategies for the implementation of presidential agendas. Needless to say, this is a critical part of policymaking, because it transforms presidential agendas into reality by allocating the required resources and political authority for targeted political initiatives. It is concerned with the translation of plans and concepts into operational capabilities that mobilize governmental resources through congressional statutes, executive orders, or regulatory decrees. After the completion of operational tasks, the final phase of policymaking, which marks the actual implementation of presidential policies, involves various tactical activities whose aim is the execution, administration, and management of policy-based initiatives and responsibilities. This encompasses military campaigns; the provision of health, welfare, and educational services; federal law enforcement; improvements in transportation and communication networks; scientific research and exploration; and many other types of services.[5]

Policymaking is divided into two broad categories, domestic and foreign, reflecting internal and external political priorities, respectively. Separate but greatly overlapping, these two policymaking arenas shape each other as part of a recursive process that can make them indistinguishable under certain circumstances. Nonetheless, despite the close and frequently inextricable relationship between domestic and foreign policy, they are separated by fundamental conceptual and practical distinctions. Ironically, though the presidency was created by the framers of the Constitution largely to handle foreign-policy responsibilities that the Confederation government was powerless to fulfill, domestic policy has become the mainstay of the modern presidency. Of course, foreign policy demands a considerable amount of a president's attention, occasionally even consuming most of his administration's energies, but domestic priorities are at the core of presidential agendas. Aside from limited financial concerns involving war debts and periodic, albeit increasing, responsibilities with respect to interstate commerce, the early presidency looked outward, occupying itself with territorial defense, the expansion and consolidation of national borders, and limited international trade.[6] Today, both foreign and domestic duties and capabilities are immeasurably more expansive, yet, whereas the admittedly sizable foreign-policy establishment focuses mainly on strategic diplomacy, national security, and international commerce, the by-now formidable domestic-policy machinery in the executive branch has its hands in almost everything that happens within the country's borders.

Modern presidents frequently become distracted by foreign or international exigencies to the detriment of their domestic-policy agendas, but they nonetheless realize that those domestic agendas get them elected and that their primary and most immediate commitments are to the average citizens within the United States. As commander in chief, the president has greater direct control over foreign-policy resources, and Congress has willingly relinquished much of its war-making authority to the presidency over the last several decades, so presidential management of foreign policy is easier and conspicuous. In addition, foreign policy is frequently viewed as more interesting and compelling by the media and other political observers, and even presidents themselves have found a certain allure, if not glamor, in foreign policy that seems lacking in its domestic counterpart.[7] Yet, as significant as the president's foreign-policy responsibilities are for the country's political and international integrity of the country, and despite the overwhelming importance of a presidential candidate's qualifications as potential commander in chief, his qualifications and credentials as the nation's prospective domestic policymaker in chief matter more.

In the end, his attitudes about pressing domestic dilemmas, his proposed solutions for them, and his broader plans for the development of future domestic-policy objectives are pivotal, because todays' presidents, unlike their eighteenth- and early-nineteenth-century predecessors, spend the bulk of their time dealing with domestic priorities and administering the vast bureaucratic apparatus that fulfills domestic duties and responsibilities. Whether those duties and responsibilities address the economy, sociocultural priorities, social services, natural resources and conservation, or law enforcement, which are the five major categories of domestic policy, they represent the overwhelming majority of the modern presidency's day-to-day business. That business can be quite difficult, especially as far as the eventual acceptance and implementation of the president's domestic agenda is concerned. The risks and uncertainties inherent in the domestic policymaking process can be prohibitive, because domestic policy requires the participation and cooperation of numerous people and institutions not under the president's direct control. Whereas the foreign-policy command structure is more streamlined and unified and can respond quickly to presidential authority when necessary, the domestic-policy establishment is a sprawl that depends on input and agreement from not only the administration but also Congress, the federal bureaucracy, interest groups, and the fifty states—not to mention the various municipal and county governments affected by domestic policy.[8] Nevertheless, the procedural difficulties and the massive scope of the domestic policymaking process only confirm the relative significance of domestic policy to the nation's presidents.

PRESIDENTS AND DOMESTIC POLICYMAKING

As with everything else in political science, no single approach to domestic policymaking is accepted as a universal explanation of how presidential administrations formulate and execute policy. So-called institutionalists believe the policymaking process is definable through recognizable institutional parameters, which means they believe policymaking is animated by a specific institutional logic that gives it meaning and relevance. This approach is one of the most traditional and is based on the broader conviction that institutions are the basic building blocks of politics and, thus, the best vehicles for the examination of political processes. Other approaches, particularly "scientific" ones like behavioralism and rational choice, put the emphasis on individuals, or decision makers, and not on the institutions around them, which are seen as irrelevant, unimportant, or otherwise derivative. Policymaking then becomes an aggregation of motivations, actions, or choices endemic to human behavior and decision making and not an independent or primary process that rises above decision makers and their innate preferences, or attitudes. Still other interpretations of policymaking, adopted by scholars variously known as idealists, liberalists, or even conservatives, stress the centrality of ideas as motive forces in decision making, which transforms policymaking processes into physical manifestations of overarching foundational theories or ideologies.[9]

Except for the Marxist-influenced critical school, which is a methodological outlier in presidential research, these approaches have some important conceptual overlaps, or areas of consensus. Regardless of their methodological emphasis, they all identify, or presume the existence of, certain prerequisites for policymaking, the most prominent of which are constitutionality, rationality, finality, accountability, technical proficiency (subject-matter expertise), and—to a lesser extent—transparency.[10] Of these, constitutionality is considered the cornerstone of legitimate policymaking but is also the least visible and the most poorly understood of the traits that characterize policymaking. On the whole, a constitutionalist culture and an implicit devotion to the rule of law have ensured that most Americans take the constitutionality of policymaking for granted, but that has not manifested itself as active scrutiny of prospective or actual policies.[11] Because constitutional law and theory are comparatively inaccessible and esoteric topics, of interest mainly to legal scholars and a small group of professionals, neither the media nor the public pay much attention to the constitutional ramifications of policymaking.

Be that as it may, the framers of the Constitution established a republic in which all political acts must have a valid constitutional basis, so presidential policies and their downstream products must comply with corresponding constitutional doctrines.[12] More importantly, since policies are instruments for the translation of constitutional principles into practical political activity, the constitutional integrity of the policymaking process must be guaranteed. Unfortunately, despite presidents' obvious dedication to the Constitution and their associated constitutional oaths, a combination of sociopolitical circumstances, partisan pressures, and personal convictions can yield unconstitutional policies. Due to the American public's lack of detailed knowledge about constitutional law and the media's correspondingly poor understanding of the topic, constitutional scrutiny, if it occurs, is left for the courts. Not all relevant transgressions are reviewed by the courts, let alone the Supreme Court, so many questionable policies remain intact. Moreover, due to the high court's customary deference toward the executive branch and particularly its unwillingness to undermine at least three generations of expanding regulatory authority within the presidency, the Supreme Court has been reluctant to challenge the constitutionality of even those policies that reach the bench.[13]

This does not mean that the policymaking process has become illegitimate or that constitutionality is no longer a significant criterion for political decision making, but, for better or worse, political expediency frequently trumps all other concerns. This is an especially pervasive aspect of some social policies, as they resonate on a much more emotional and personal level with both presidents and the public than most other kinds of policy. Issues like religion, abortion, homosexuality, and a few others motivate politicians and their supporters in a visceral rather than intellectual manner, and the pursuit of related policies becomes a cause célèbre that impassions partisan extremes. Under these circumstances, if a president ignores the public mood, the political costs can be unusually high, motivating him to adopt policies that he may not firmly support. Alternatively, an energized electoral base within the president's party unified around a key social policy can also cause him to back initiatives of dubious constitutional validity.[14] In the end, whether it is because of general public pressure or partisan expectations, ordinary politics triumphs over constitutional principle.

Such was the case with the Defense of Marriage Act, passed in 1996 as the culmination of growing public concern and even alarm in southern states about the potential recognition of gay marriage in some northeastern and western states. Worried about the public furor Republicans were fomenting over the issue in an election year and recognizing that many older, rural, and blue-collar Democrats did not support gay marriage either, President Bill Clinton was not willing to cede all of the political momentum to the Republican Party. As a result, he not only signed and endorsed the Republican bill but also made public statements affirming his belief in traditional marriage. Clinton quietly signed the bill into law in the Oval Office, as opposed to a public signing ceremony in the Rose Garden or some other high-profile locale. Instead of making public remarks after the signing, he instead released a written statement:

> Throughout my life I have strenuously opposed discrimination of any kind, including discrimination against gay and lesbian Americans. I am signing into law H.R. 3396, a bill relating to same-gender marriage, but it is important to note what this legislation does and does not do. I have long opposed governmental recognition of same-gender marriages, and this legislation is consistent with that position. The act confirms the right of each State to determine its own policy with respect to same-gender marriage and clarifies for purposes of Federal law the operative meaning of the terms "marriage" and "spouse." This legislation does not reach beyond those two provisions. It has no effect on any current Federal, State, or local antidiscrimination law and does not constrain the right of Congress or any State or locality to enact antidiscrimination laws. . . . I also want to make clear to all that the enactment of this legislation should not, despite the fierce and at times divisive rhetoric surrounding it, be understood to provide an excuse for discrimination, violence, or intimidation against any person on the basis of sexual orientation. Discrimination, violence, and intimidation for that reason, as well as others, violate the principle of equal protection under the law.[15]

The real problem with this legislation was its questionable constitutional rationale, because neither the Congress nor the president had the required constitutional authority to enact such a policy. By all relevant doctrinal standards, the law seemed unconstitutional, but very few people actually opposed it on those grounds. Similarly, the Clinton administration's compromise policy on gays in the military, known as "Don't Ask, Don't Tell," which was also a response to congressional and public pressure, lacked a justifiable constitutional basis and appeared to validate behavior that was clearly unconstitutional. Although it was a tactical retreat from the more stringent policy promulgated in 1982 that sanctioned an outright ban

---

Read the Defense of Marriage Act.

on homosexuals in the military, this version, implemented in 1993, still condoned institutional discrimination based on sexual preference.[16]

In these examples, Clinton reacted to broad public and congressional demands, but his successor, George W. Bush, frequently embraced policies due to profound socio-religious personal convictions and the political influence of the social-conservative base of his party. As arguably the first and only modern president to draw the bulk of his support from voters driven primarily by specific sociocultural priorities, Bush believed his public mandate included the strengthening of ties between faith and governance. Either unconcerned, as his critics have claimed, about the unconstitutional entanglement of church and state or merely convinced of the moral rectitude of his policies, as many others have asserted, Bush pressed ahead with faith-centered programs throughout his time in the White House but was unusually active early in his first term. The creation of the Office of Faith-Based and Community Initiatives, a policy council within the White House, in 2001to facilitate the growth of religious groups and organizations as providers of federally funded social services was just one such instance. Instituted through executive order, this policy council and its proposed activities appeared to lack a valid constitutional basis by running afoul of the establishment clause of the First Amendment.[17] Eventually, President Obama reversed many of his predecessor's religious policies, but the courts never scrutinized them 🖱.

Constitutionality is indeed a critical factor, but scholars have often isolated rationality as the chief determinant of policymaking and decision making generally. This is not rationality in the everyday sense of the word but rationality as a seminal concept in the social sciences, particularly in economics and political science. This kind of rationality does not denote abstract reason, logic, and a lack of emotionalism, all of which may or may not be present in a rational process, but decision making based on deliberation and choice. More to the point, decisions or policies are considered rational if they involve a democratic, or collaborative, consideration of available alternatives for action. If either viable alternatives or informed deliberation are lacking, decision making is irrational.[18] Without a doubt, careful consideration of policy options among qualified individuals presupposes reasonableness, but it does not imply the kind of strict adherence to reason and the strictures of logic demanded by philosophical rationalism.

Needless to say, not all decisions and related policies are defensible or even reasonable, to say nothing of feasibility. The combination of human fallibility, personal psychology, and situational contingency makes presidential policymaking anything but predictable in every circumstance. Like anything else in politics, policymaking deviates from the theoretical norm and, in particular instances, goes completely awry. Sometimes, the choices are often so prolific and the deliberation so prolonged that the process, overwhelmed by procedural inefficiency, comes to a standstill. However, more often than not, the process breaks down because rationality is either in short supply or just absent. Presidential behavior is at its most irrational during crises or when dealing with issues that are very dear to them, since those are the times that presidents act more out of personal conviction than reasoned analysis.

🖱 View the archived Office of Faith-Based and Community Initiatives' website.

Driven either by personal expectations and deeply held beliefs about specific issues or exigent circumstances, or both, in those situations, presidents tend to confine or even prevent deliberation of alternatives in order to steer decision making toward pre-determined policy objectives. Such decision making is largely idiosyncratic and visceral, rather than consistent and logical, thereby undermining the likelihood of success and popular support.[19]

A fitting example of the breakdown of rationality was President Clinton's health-care reform effort early in his first term. Faulted for inhibiting deliberation of his policies and a refusal to compromise about his administration's sweeping health-care agenda, Clinton treated the proposed reform package as a fait accompli, which galvanized his political opponents and ultimately alienated even some of his supporters. Carefully controlled to exclude or marginalize competition, the process was deliberative only to an extent, with policy discussion limited to a like-minded cadre of experts and advisors. To his credit, the president eventually delegated considerable responsibility to others, but, to the dismay of the administration's many detractors, too much authority lay with the First Lady. Hillary Clinton became the public face of a reform agenda in trouble from the start, and the president's health-care policy became one of his major political defeats, stigmatizing even some of the administration's unrelated policies. To be sure, the comparative lack of rationality was not the only reason Clinton's health-care reform effort was unsuccessful, but a more open, deliberative, and competitive process surely would have increased the probability of success.[20]

For example, a more effective strategy in dealing with Congress could have aided passage of the Clinton health-care reform plan. House Majority Leader Dick Gephardt (D-MO) advised Hillary Clinton and Senior Advisor for Policy Development Ira Magaziner as early as March 1993 on the need for adequate consultation with Congress: "The time and effort you have expended in reaching out to Congress on health-care reform have been greatly appreciated. However, to ensure the most positive reception of the health-care reform bill in Congress, and the smoothest most rapid legislative process, it is imperative that you begin consultation in earnest with two critical Congressional groups: the Committee Chairs and CBO [Congressional Budget Office]."[21] Yet most of the advice was unheeded, as White House strategy instead focused more on "a team of Administration lobbyists whose sole task is to pass the President's health care reform bill."[22] Hillary Clinton would testify before congressional committees about the health-care plan in September 1993, just days after her husband gave an address about health-care reform to a joint session of Congress, yet the Clinton strategy remained more focused on "educating" members of Congress through health-care briefings (labeled as "a kind of health care university") as opposed to consulting and collaborating with broader coalitions in Congress, as this memo shows:

> ...if done well, [a health care university] would: (1) Reinvigorate the "need for action" mentality that, until very recently had been effectively fanning the flames of desire for comprehensive health reform in Congress; (2) Ease Congressional concerns about, and raise Member comfort levels with, the President's proposal to address the problems; (3) Better enable perspective Congressional supporters to explain, defend, and sell the President's proposal; and (4) Be utilized to help educate surrogates in home Congressional districts.[23]

Lack of rationality is not always a feature of failed or problematic policies, as both the Great Society and New Deal aptly illustrated. No one would dispute the success and effectiveness of many of FDR's New Deal and LBJ's Great Society policies, and they were also products of comprehensive political-mobilization efforts, pooling the work and contributions of countless advisors, legislators, experts, and others. Still, both programs were pushed through the policymaking machinery and especially through Congress with the kind of tenacity and single-mindedness that made compromise and extensive deliberation difficult, if not impossible. Indeed, LBJ was accused of shoving a done deal down lawmakers' throats, using whatever leverage and political influence was necessary to get the job done. Although many outside the president's core group of advisors looked favorably on LBJ's proposed socioeconomic reforms, which seemed warranted and defensible, the enactment of landmark Great Society policies did not arise out of the kind of collaborative give-and-take that rationality demands. LBJ engaged various participants in the policymaking process, even his critics, but a democratic consideration of major alternatives was never his intent.[24]

Practical deviations from strict rationality notwithstanding, the domestic policymaking process is largely rational. Rationality is not always present in equal measure, but its policymakers do take its existence for granted and rely on deliberation and choice to enhance the legitimacy of the results. It belies the fact, however, that the presidential policymaking process relies on finality, which is achieved through an essentially undemocratic, or non-deliberative, act. President George W. Bush was derided by his critics for declaring "I am the decider," but, he was absolutely correct.[25] In the American political system, the president bears ultimate responsibility for executive decisions, and, regardless of any associated debate or discussion, he makes those decisions because he has the authority and popular mandate to do so. To paraphrase legal scholar Robert Cover's characterization of another aspect of federal governance, presidential authority by its very nature kills deliberation and choice through the finality and supremacy of the president's decisions.[26] Of course, this is neither a deficiency nor a disadvantage, and it does nothing to undermine the legitimacy of the policymaking process itself, since, in any organizational setting, someone must be entrusted and empowered with such finality and supremacy—otherwise nothing would ever get done.

Finality also implies accountability, which is an indispensable part of any liberal-democratic policymaking process, because it promotes political legitimacy and trust both among policymakers and also between policymakers and the public. Accountability means that, from a conceptual standpoint, domestic policymaking begins and ends with the president. Whether the president micromanages practically every aspect of the process like Jimmy Carter or takes a more hands-off approach like Ronald Reagan, as the one with the authority to make final decisions, he is obligated to the public and must answer to them for his policy decisions. That authority manifests itself either explicitly or implicitly, and it does not presuppose that the president always initiates policymaking himself or that he participates fully.[27] However, as a sign displayed on President Harry Truman's desk indicated, "The Buck Stops Here," which implies that the president is the one accountable to the American public and that he will be held responsible for his administration's policy choices.[28]

Aside from obvious ideological and personal distinctions that distinguish individual presidents, differing levels of involvement in the policymaking process lead to corresponding variations in manifestations of presidential authority. Those with a more passive approach, like Reagan, George W. Bush, or Dwight Eisenhower, traditionally delegate key responsibilities to trusted aides and advisors, if not others further downstream, and their authority for many decisions is implicit. On the other hand, presidents like Carter, Clinton, or LBJ usually display their authority explicitly through a close and active oversight of even trivial parts of the policymaking process.[29] Due to deviations in leadership style, presidents will inevitably choose the policymaking approach that suits them, but each carries certain risks that can damage and occasionally derail their administrations. While the latter approach is relatively inefficient and frequently hampers productivity, leading to a bureaucratic paralysis that prevents the simultaneous management of several policies, the former can undermine accountability and credibility by encouraging unauthorized activities.

Bill Clinton was the most recent example of an overinvolved chief executive, though resulting inefficiencies were tempered somewhat by a wide-ranging subject-matter expertise and a genuine enthusiasm for policymaking, which ensured that his leadership never devolved into the kind of sclerotic micromanagement witnessed during the Carter years. Still, had he been more disciplined, Clinton could have addressed more of his policy agenda.[30] Whereas Clinton was clearly hampered by an inability and unwillingness to delegate, neither Ronald Reagan nor George W. Bush had that problem. Bush's credibility was often undermined by the perception that Vice President Dick Cheney and principal advisors Karl Rove and Karen Hughes were making crucial domestic-policy decisions because of his relative lack of interest and participation in policymaking.[31] More seriously, Reagan's hands-off style led to one of the biggest modern-day foreign policy scandals since Watergate, namely the Iran-Contra affair, which was perpetrated by renegade public officials within the executive branch, who used the president's policy objectives regarding the Contra rebels in Nicaragua to justify illegal and unauthorized arms sales to Iran.[32]

In the end, despite variations in leadership style and the finality of presidential decisions, the president heads a deliberative process whose purpose is the selection of the most appropriate, defensible, and feasible policy choices. In that regard, he is part of a team of policymakers acting in concert toward unified goals, and his decisions depend on contributions from those around him, not least the efforts of public officials and *ad hoc* advisors with the requisite subject-matter expertise to address policy issues competently and effectively. Subject-matter expertise, or technical proficiency, is an essential prerequisite for policymaking, but its necessity is so evident that it is often ignored. Without it, deliberation and political choice are also absent, as are realistic opportunities for policy implementation. Along with a related mechanism to manage the flow and exchange of information, technical proficiency maximizes the probability of success and allows the translation of abstract objectives into actionable strategies and operations. As critical as rationality, it helps secure the legitimacy of the policymaking process, and, perhaps most significantly, it maintains relevance through a focus on necessary, achievable goals.[33]

Even a policy wonk like Bill Clinton, or a political veteran like George H. W. Bush, does not have the specific technical proficiency to address the analytical and informational demands of each policy within his administration's agenda, so they rely on others with the required capabilities and credentials. Subject-matter expertise is crucial for every stage of policymaking, whether it involves informed debate about policy alternatives or the creation of actual programs and initiatives. Hence, the presence of qualified experts, or technocrats, throughout the process is a priority for presidents. As a corollary, policymaking also requires an effective, and preferably efficient, means of disseminating information and managing access to it, because a collaborative process substantially dependent on input from various sources cannot survive productively without an appropriate communication infrastructure.[34] In addition, this assumes the comparative transparency of the policymaking process, at least with respect to the key participants, which increases both efficiency and efficacy, to say nothing of trust among policymakers. Obviously, complete transparency is neither desirable nor possible, particularly with classified information, but a lack of transparency can impede policymaking for various reasons, an absence of accountability and trust among them.

Principal Domestic Policymakers

Over the last century, the president has gradually become the most important and visible policymaker in Washington, dominating the planning and execution of domestic policies while engaging both the public and the press to win approval of his political objectives. With few exceptions, such as the Republican-led Contract with America in 1995, presidential domestic agendas are more prominent than those of their congressional counterparts as well as more durable. Because of the fractured and increasingly factionalized character of legislative politics, presidential agendas are usually more cohesive and consistent, and they often receive greater public attention and media coverage. When managed effectively and purposefully, presidential domestic agendas have a substantially higher probability of success than those that originate in Congress, which is something other participants in the policymaking process recognize. In addition, unlike their congressional counterparts, presidential agendas, such as FDR's New Deal or LBJ's Great Society, can profoundly affect the nation's political psyche, thereby exerting a long-term influence over the ongoing development of political ideals and societal goals. For over 120 years, Congress controlled domestic policy, but that is no longer true. During the last one hundred years, the presidency has slowly but steadily increased its hold over the nation's domestic agenda, and the country's presidents have become its chief policymakers.[35]

White House staff

As mentioned in the previous section, the president is at the center of domestic policymaking, but he cannot do everything himself, and he depends on an organizational network that includes thousands of individuals and scores of federal institutions, agencies, and committees. This was not always so, and, as discussed in Chapter 8, because the framers of the Constitution did not envision a president with such expansive policymaking responsibilities, the capabilities and resources of the early presidency were quite restricted. As such, the early presidency was anything but glamorous, elaborate, or resource-intensive, operating on a shoestring budget and without the amenities, personnel, or organizational capabilities modern presidents have taken for granted. The president's domestic-policy advisors, who included only his few cabinet secretaries and his vice-president, could be counted on one hand, and he did without any of the policy aides and assistants, to say nothing of the executive councils, common today.[36]

Congress did not provide the president with a salaried assistant until the late 1850s, but real bureaucratic reforms would have to await the twentieth century. The presidency did benefit from an augmented cabinet during the latter part of the nineteenth century, gaining several new departments between 1849 and 1913.[37] Progressive Era presidents made some important organizational changes, but the most crucial advancement came in 1939 with the creation of the Executive Office of the President (EOP). Finally, the White House was able to address the necessities and demands of an evolving presidency that was increasingly assuming principal responsibility for domestic policymaking. During the ensuing decades, the number of experts, assistants, and advisors increased exponentially, as did the various positions required to manage White House policymaking. Additional organizational reforms between the 1960s and 1990s accounted for the appearance and expansion of a veritable policymaking bureaucracy within the White House that relied on various new councils to facilitate the implementation of presidential agendas.[38]

Next to the president, arguably the most important policymaker is the White House chief of staff, whose principal responsibilities transcend any specific policymaking role he may have. His policymaking duties are more procedural and administrative than substantive, but he is as critical to policymaking as the president. A position initially used by Dwight Eisenhower in the 1950s but not solidified until the Nixon administration, the chief of staff can be the difference between success and failure for a president in terms of his policy agenda.[39] The chief of staff also manages the White House staff, without which domestic policymaking would be impossible. A central administrative network that houses some of the most influential public officials in Washington, it runs the White House and coordinates the procedural elements of presidential policymaking. Comprising everything from clerical help to the presidents' top lieutenants, it is the bureaucratic nerve center of the executive branch. Within it is the president's inner circle of trusted advisors, aides, and assistants, who form a policymaking brain trust of sorts, managing the substantive aspects of policymaking and often acting as negotiators on behalf of the president with Congress, regulatory agencies, and even cabinet heads. Officially known through various innocuous and deceptively unassuming titles that would not be found on a generic EOP organizational chart, its officeholders have included such prominent names as David Axelrod and Rahm Emanuel (Obama), Karl Rove (George W. Bush), George Stephanopolous (Clinton), David Gergen (Clinton, Reagan, Ford, and Nixon), and Jack Valenti (LBJ), and many others.[40]

This inner circle of presidential advisors is customarily more involved in the policymaking process than the president, at least from a step-by-step perspective, overseeing every aspect of presidential policy from planning to implementation. Their strong suit is often the formulation of political strategy, particularly the design of politically marketable policies and associated plans for public, legislative, and special-interest approval of those policies, but they must be equally skilled at managing the procedural aspects of policymaking. Along with the chief of staff, these advisors ensure that policymaking moves on schedule and that all political bases are covered, so the president can concentrate on the big picture. More idea people than experts, they lack the technical proficiency and time to analyze and elaborate the exact practical ramifications of presidential policy, which is frequently left to the various policymaking councils within the EOP and under the nominal control of the chief of staff.

Policy councils

These are the real workhorses behind domestic policy, and their contribution enables the transition from political goals and adoption strategies to actionable programs based on actual circumstances. They compile data, perform analyses, prepare strategy, provide expertise, and fulfill any number of other jobs assigned to them by the president or his staff. The most important of these councils was, until recently, the Office of Policy Development (OPD), which was divided by the Clinton White House into the National Economic Council (NEC) and the Domestic Policy Council (DPC). The OPD was created by the Nixon administration, which significantly expanded the policymaking capabilities of the presidency through numerous organizational innovations, and was heavily used by the Reagan administration, especially for the preparation of their fiscal policies. President Clinton, fulfilling a campaign pledge, split the OPD into the NEC and DPC to address more adequately the country's economic priorities. Both he and President Obama have relied on the DPC considerably, whereas George W. Bush was never as fond of the policy councils.[41] However, within his first ten days in the White House, Bush did establish the Office of Faith-Based and Community Initiatives under the DPC and used it extensively to secure a strategic beachhead for the expansion of federally based religious programs. Later renamed the Office of Faith-Based and Neighborhood Partnerships, President Bush envisioned it as a command center to coordinate certain federally subsidized social services and administer church-based community initiatives.[42] As the name implies, the NEC concentrates on providing the president with economic and financial advice regarding fiscal, business, labor, consumer, and related policy, and it leverages its expertise to outline and explain the technical requirements of specific presidential policies. The DPC, on the other hand, handles most other areas of domestic policy except law enforcement, drug interdiction, and scientific research. Its name is somewhat of a misnomer, because it perpetuates the impression that economic and domestic policy are fundamentally different and separate, but its role in policymaking is crucial, as President Obama's reliance on it can attest.[43]

Other policymaking organs within the EOP include the Office of National Drug Control Policy (ONDGP), created in 1988 with support from President Reagan, and the Office of Science and Technology Policy, established during the Ford administration. Creation of the ONDGP was highly politicized, especially after two terms of emphatic anti-drug rhetoric by the Reagan administration; and its first director, William Bennett, former Education Secretary under Reagan, courted considerable controversy through his outspoken views on drug use. The Drug Czar, as the director was known initially, was an important participant in presidential policymaking during the George H. W. Bush years, but the visibility and influence of the position have declined since the mid-1990s. Another high-profile council, the Office of National AIDS Policy (ONAP), was created by President Clinton in 1993, also within the DPC, but it is funded by the Department of Health and Human Services. ONAP arose from campaign promises made by Clinton to AIDS activists and the gay community and addresses a range of issues, including prevention, treatment, education, and research. Though not as active during the George W. Bush presidency, it has been revived by President Obama, who has made a new national commitment to fighting AIDS both at home and abroad.[44]

Two other organs within EOP have been integral participants in policymaking since their creation, but their primary duties are analytical and administrative rather than political. The Council of Economic Advisors (CEA), created in 1946, provides the president and his key advisors with macroeconomic and financial research and analysis to enable the preparation and development of potential and current economic policies. Whereas the NEC's role is mostly advisory and political, collaborating with the president and his inner circle on the formulation of political objectives and strategies, the CEA, though secondarily used as an advisory body, exists to compile and evaluate necessary data and provide objective subject-matter expertise. In that regard, the CEA is definitely important, but its significance is dwarfed by the Office of Management and Budget (OMB), which has become one of the most essential parts of the executive branch. Prior to the establishment of the OMB's predecessor, the Bureau of the Budget (BOB), in 1921, budgeting was a congressional responsibility over which the president had little control. The BOB became the Trojan horse through which the presidency was able to wrest control of economic policymaking generally, so its emergence marked a turning point in the evolution of domestic policymaking.[45]

Retooled as the OMB to meet the needs of the modern presidency during related EOP reforms by the Nixon administration, the erstwhile BOB provides the technical expertise needed by the president during his annual preparation of the fiscal-year budget. Handling the bulk of the effort required by this mammoth task, the OMB works within the broad political framework set by the president and other policymakers further upstream and provides requisite financial analysis and evaluation. In so doing, it also ensures that budgetary fiscal requirements match revenue and deficit projections and that the various institutional components of the president's budget are reconcilable. In a related capacity, the OMB oversees executive expenditures, guaranteeing that actual expenses align with budgetary stipulations and that executive agencies comply with federal financial laws. Aside from its budgetary and other financial responsibilities, the OMB has supervisory authority over the executive branch's many regulatory agencies, which means that it plays an important role during the operational stage of the policymaking process. In exercising this oversight authority, the OMB scrutinizes regulatory rulemaking to make sure it follows overriding policy objectives, relevant federal laws, and procedural guidelines.[46]

The Federal Reserve

Another pivotal and extremely powerful policymaker that has a substantial impact on the country's economic and financial objectives is the Federal Reserve, which includes the Board of Governors and the Federal Open Market Committee (FOMC). Through the FOMC, its chief target is the monetary policy of the United States; secondarily, it also addresses unemployment and consumer prices. It was created in 1913 to stabilize the banking system and national currency, because the absence of centralized monetary management had contributed to several financial panics and recessions during the preceding several decades. Institutionally and politically independent, neither the Board nor the FOMC is accountable to the president in a political sense, so he has very little influence over its decisions. Not obliged to follow presidential economic or financial directives, both entities nonetheless realize the need to reconcile their monetary goals with the president's fiscal policies. The president does have an indirect ability to shape Federal Reserve policy through appointments to the Board of Governors and the FOMC. He appoints the Chairman, the Vice Chairman, and the remaining governors, who serve on the twelve-member Federal Open Market Committee (FOMC), which controls interest rates and the nation's money supply. Federal Reserve governors serve staggered fourteen-year terms to minimize the effects of turnover, while the chairman, who is selected by the president from among them, serves a renewable four-year term.[47] In short, the president's influence over monetary policy extends no further than his powers of persuasion, his appointment authority, and the manifestations of his economic and financial policies 🖱.

Cabinet departments

Contrary to what is the case with foreign policy, the various department secretaries and their staffs customarily do not serve in an advisory or active policymaking capacity, except for three conspicuous exceptions. Whereas the two foreign-policy departments, State and Defense, have been intimately involved in all stages of the policymaking process and their secretaries have historically been among the president's most trusted advisors, the vast majority of the remaining departments have regulatory, social-service, or informational responsibilities.[48] Only the Justice, Treasury, and Homeland Security departments have significant policymaking roles, especially with respect to the formulation of policy objectives and implementation strategies. Of these, the Justice Department is the most constrained, because the attorney general, who can be a critical influence over the development of law-enforcement policy, must maintain the appearance of impartiality and fairness as the top law enforcement official in the United States. Occasionally, too close of a relationship between the president and his attorney general has been as much a political liability as a personal advantage, as happened with Robert Kennedy, who led the Justice Department during his brother's presidency. On the other hand, some attorneys general, most notably Clinton appointee Janet Reno, have been so fiercely independent in order to preserve the integrity of their department and the legitimacy of their policies that they have frustrated and even alienated their bosses in the Oval Office.[49]

Unlike Justice, the Treasury Department has been a valued member of the president's policymaking team since its creation in the late eighteenth century. One of the original three cabinet departments, along with War and State, Treasury has consistently provided presidents with economic and financial advice, analysis, and forecasting, and Treasury secretaries have often been some of the president's closest policy aides. Initially politicians whose partisan credentials mattered more than their technical expertise, Treasury secretaries have increasingly been economic or financial experts from industry or academia, or both.[50] Timothy Geithner, President

🖱 View the website of the Board of Governors of the Federal Reserve System.

Obama's Treasury chief, studied international economics at Johns Hopkins' well-known School for Advanced International Studies and has spent his career working as a financial expert for the government, most recently with the Federal Reserve. In contrast, but still within the modern norm, George W. Bush's three Treasury heads, Paul O'Neill, John Snow, and Hank Paulson, were all former corporate executives with ample hands-on financial experience. Since the appearance of the NEC, the relative importance of Treasury secretaries as policy advisors has declined somewhat, and their increasingly non-political backgrounds have kept them at arm's length from the Oval Office.[51]

The ostensibly declining significance of Treasury chiefs as policy advisors notwithstanding, the department as a whole is indispensable, even if the overwhelming majority of its responsibilities are not political. It has broad administrative, financial, regulatory, and law-enforcements duties that are as visible and relevant as any within the federal government. As the treasury of the U.S. government, it issues all paper currency, coins, and postage stamps, and it also collects all taxes, tariffs, duties, and other moneys owed to the United States. One of its most prominent agencies is the Internal Revenue Service (IRS), which is in charge of tax collection and revenue-code enforcement but also makes administrative rulings and regulatory decisions. The Treasury Department handles the federal government's financial accounts, managing payables, liabilities, and the public debt, and it oversees the country's banks and savings institutions.[52] Like everything else within the executive branch, its duties and responsibilities far surpass the framers' original intentions, but its expanded authority has been a necessary consequence of macroeconomic and financial management in the industrial age.

Like the Treasury, the Department of Homeland Security (DHS), though a vital advisory body for the president, addresses largely non-advisory priorities and comprises one of the largest bureaucracies in the executive branch. Through the Secretary, the DHS participates in policymaking and provides the president valuable analytical information about emergency-response strategies to internal threats, but homeland-security policy, and thus DHS political objectives themselves, are mostly handled by the Homeland Security Council (HSC) within the White House Office. George W. Bush established the HSC by executive order immediately following the terrorist attacks in September 2001 as a domestic counterpart to the National Security Council, which is the key foreign-policy organ at the EOP. Convinced that the presidency's advisory and command structures did not adequately address domestic security through existing national-security capabilities, Bush charged the HSC with managing the formulation of policy regarding terrorist and other military and paramilitary threats to the homeland. Shortly thereafter, related legislative and executive concerns about the actual management and resolution of both man-made and natural threats prompted the creation of the DHS, which pooled together more than twenty existing agencies under the new department. Unlike the HSC, which concentrates on the prevention of terrorist and similar acts, the DHS has a wider scope that comprises not only attacks on the homeland such as terrorism but also man-made accidents and natural disasters.[53]

Other cabinet departments, like Health and Human Services, Energy, Commerce, and Interior, have limited advisory and policymaking roles, but their primary responsibilities lie elsewhere. Not officially a cabinet-level department, the

Environmental Protections Agency (EPA), whose administrator is considered a cabinet-level appointment, is easily the most visible of these remaining institutions. Created in 1970 at the behest of the Nixon administration, the EPA administers relevant legislation and regulates both public and private entities to insure compliance with environmental protections and standards. Its authority extends to enforcement, oversight, and rulemaking, but, despite the criticisms leveled against it, its actions are restricted to those issues covered by corresponding federal legislation. Because environmental policy has become such an important part of presidential domestic agendas, especially those of Democratic presidents, the advisory role of the EPA administrator in policymaking can be quite substantial, but the responsibilities are nonetheless largely administrative. Probably the most influential EPA administrator as policymaker and advisor was Carol Browner, who served throughout Bill Clinton's two terms at the White House and whose close relationship with Vice President Al Gore ensured access to the President and the policymaking process. However, this has been more the exception than the rule, as most EPA administrators do not enjoy this kind of access.[54]

Interest groups

Lobbyists who represent interest groups seek to influence the policymaking process by asking for a policy to be created, asking for a change to an existing policy, or by seeking to block policy creation or policy change. As Table 9.1 shows, there are multiple ways in which issues and groups are represented. Economist and political scientist Mancur Olson famously reduced the joining of interest groups to the desire for three distinct benefits: material (something tangible, such as a tax break), solidary or social (the desire to associate with like-minded individuals), and expressive or purposive (working toward advancing a particular ideology). Olson argued that small groups with narrow goals are more likely to be successful in achieving those goals than large groups with diverse goals.[55] Interest groups participate in the policymaking process in multiple ways, targeting government actors in all levels and sectors of government. Interest groups used to focus their national lobbying efforts on Congress and the bureaucracy, strategically allocating their resources to the prime decision makers. However, as presidents became more active participants in the policymaking process throughout the twentieth century, they have increasingly become the focus of lobbying by interest groups. In addi-

Table 9.1 Issue Types and Interest Groups

ISSUE TYPE	EXAMPLE
Single Issue	National Rifle Association
Generic Business	Chamber of Commerce
Specific Industry	Air Transport Association
Union	United Auto Workers
Government	National Governors Association
Public Interest	Center for Science in the Public Interest
Professional	American Political Science Association

tion, White House efforts are now directed at strategically working with interest groups.

As early as the FDR administration, White House staff was responsible for maintaining connections with key groups and individuals. However, the Ford White House was the first to create a formal office dedicated to maintaining a relationship with outside organizations within the EOP—the Office of Public Liaison became the contact point for interest groups and also the place where "reverse lobbying" (a White House strategy to gain interest group support of the president's agenda) occurs.[56] Interest groups also lobby other executive offices, like the Office of Intergovernmental Affairs, Office of Legislative Affairs, Office of Political Affairs, and various constituency-based units.[57] The Obama administration centralized and expanded the office that deals with outside groups and renamed the Office of Public Liaison to the Office of Public Engagement and Intergovernmental Affairs (OPE), indicating its wider focus beyond interest groups. Obama considered this office as part of his pursuit of transparent and open government, as he explained on the White House web page: "Our commitment to openness means more than simply informing the American people about how decisions are made. It means recognizing that government does not have all the answers, and that public officials need to draw on what citizens know."[58]

Lobbyists and interest groups do not seek to influence the Executive Branch to the same degree that they lobby Congress. From trade associations to public interest groups, on average, 95 percent of the lobbying contacts are with Congress.[59] Moreover, most of the lobbying efforts remain outside public knowledge, unless media coverage focuses on questionable policy actions by the White House. For example, in 2001 much attention was paid to George W. Bush and Dick Cheney's strong links to the energy industry, and to oil companies in particular. Both Bush and Cheney had worked in the oil industry, as had their Commerce Secretary, Don Evans. In addition, $32 million had been donated to the Bush/Cheney campaign in 2000 by the energy industry. Industry spending in elections is newsworthy; however, what draws greater attention is when the linkage between donations and policy outcomes becomes overt. In the case of the Bush administration, two events emphasized an arguably unfair attentiveness: the policy recommendations of the Vice President's Energy Task Force and the Enron scandal. The report from the Energy Task Force, which was guiding Bush energy policy, was initially secret. Two public interest groups, the Sierra Club and Judicial Watch, filed a lawsuit under the Freedom of Information Act (FOIA) to identify publicly who participated in the formulation of energy policy. The Government Accounting Office initially sought to sue as well but dropped the case, contending it could not determine whether industry executives improperly influenced policy. The focus on energy executives' participation and environmentalists' exclusion intensified when the energy company Enron collapsed in late 2001. Enron CEO Kenneth Lay was a close personal friend of President Bush, to whom he reached out for help amid the crisis. The perception gleaned from these revelations is that money buys access and opportunity to influence policy outcomes significantly, which those without money do not enjoy.

View the Office of Public Engagement and Intergovernmental Affairs' website.

The list of domestic policymakers discussed in this section is certainly not exhaustive, as presidential policymaking involves countless additional people and organizations both in Washington and beyond, but these are the key players and groups that define it. Obviously, congressional input and participation is indispensable, since, aside from unilateral presidential actions such as executive orders, the translation of policy objectives into actual programs cannot be achieved without enabling legislation. This list would not be complete without mentioning the numerous state, county, and local governments and officials affected by federal policies and whose influence can be substantial. Without a doubt, the news media must be included in the discussion, whose effect on the modern public presidency has been indescribable.[60] Still, the actors and institutions covered in detail herein form a critical mass of sorts, without which presidential policymaking would not be what it is; as such, they stand above the rest in terms of significance and contribution.

THE EVOLUTION OF U.S. DOMESTIC POLICY

Over the last several decades, domestic-policy agendas have ballooned, and the presidency has become involved in so many aspects of its citizens' lives that almost nothing is accomplished without its input, contribution, or influence. The public's reliance on the expansive executive machinery that plans and administers essential and non-essential federal programs is so pervasive that it demands continuous attention from the administration and its institutional infrastructure. As a result, people have become dependent on the executive assistance, regulation, and enforcement activities within the executive branch, and they expect their presidents to maintain and ultimately improve these services. By now, after decades of federal provision of services and consistent increases in executive authority and responsibility, this reliance transcends issues of subsistence and basic survival and includes expectations regarding quality of life, professional success, and personal well-being. This clearly deviates from traditional liberal-democratic ideas about the government's role in society, and it cannot be reconciled with framers' intentions regarding legitimate governance, but Americans have accepted the expanded and perhaps extraconstitutional character of the modern presidency as normal and necessary. Consequently, presidential administrations are motivated and compelled to devote considerable attention to the numerous domestic-policy areas that reflect public demand, which include the economy, sociocultural priorities, social services, natural resources and conservation, and law enforcement.

Economic Policy

Some political commentators and scholars have separated domestic from economic policy, largely due to the fact that the Clinton administration often made a similar distinction, but economic policy is manifestly a subset of domestic policy, and conceptual separation of the two poses some insurmountable theoretical and practical obstacles. Of these five general categories, economic policy, if not the most important, is frequently portrayed as the most critical for presidential candidates. Indeed, voters seem most worried about their financial and economic circumstances and, as such, presidential candidates' abilities and willingness to tackle nagging economic questions. Voters may or may not always vote with their pocketbooks, as common wisdom implies, but the economy is undoubtedly a primary concern, so presidential agendas reflect that reality.

Economic policy means different things to different people, but, from an academic perspective, it includes largely macroeconomic concerns, some microeconomic issues, and public finance. Often called economic and financial policy, which is a more inclusive label, it facilitates, oversees, or regulates various aspects of the production, distribution, and consumption of goods and services, focusing especially on income (gross domestic product, or GDP), unemployment, and inflation, while it simultaneously manages governmental expenditures, long-term liabilities, and revenues. Economic and financial policy is further subdivided into smaller policy areas that reflect the major economic components over which the federal government has authority.[61] Easily the most abstruse aspect of domestic policy, economic policy can confuse even veteran politicians, as its constitutive topics often require a technical and academic proficiency that eludes all but a handful of experts. Consequently, much of it is reduced to convenient and catchy sound bites intended for public consumption, which fuels some glaring misconceptions about the nature of economic policy and the presidency's ability to control or influence the economy.[62]

Until the twentieth century, federal economic policy was minimal, and presidential involvement in it was largely absent. Aside from management of the public debt, improvement of transportation networks, some oversight of interstate commerce, and few other regular duties, the federal government did not interfere in the economy, which is what the framers of the Constitution intended.[63] Despite the remarkable physical and economic growth witnessed during the nineteenth century, the presidency did little to address associated factors, because the Constitution did not authorize presidents or the rest of the federal government to manage or regulate socioeconomic activity. By the last third of the nineteenth century, the hands-off approach, though constitutionally warranted, was becoming problematic, as the framers' rural and agrarian republic was being transformed into an industrial and urbanized giant. Initially, the states and then Congress intervened with minor remedial measures to help those dislocated by the processes of industrialization and urbanization, but a combination of oppositional court rulings wedded to the binding yet seemingly outdated notion of governmental noninterference and scant institutional resources undermined those early efforts. In the early twentieth century, and definitely by the Great Depression, the need for an active federal role was obvious to most, and both Congress and presidents committed themselves to providing the necessary federal resources and capabilities for the task at hand.[64]

Mass industrialization posed structural problems and created economically dislocated groups that had not existed, at least not on a permanent basis as was the case with an industrialized society. Unemployment, inflation, and currency control, to say nothing of consumer and labor protection, became concerns for policymakers and economic planners, as did the provision of necessary yet lacking social services. For various reasons, among which were the unique nature of presidential authority and the creation of a federal regulatory bureaucracy within the executive branch, presidents became the chief architects of economic policy by the second third of the twentieth century.[65] During the last eighty years, the perception of the president as an economic arbiter of sorts has taken hold, and they are widely portrayed and viewed as having the ability to manage, if not control, economic conditions ☝. However, this image has become problematic for the presidency and the public at large, as it perpetuates a prevailing myth concerning economic policymaking. Despite the unimaginable gains in presidential domestic authority, resources, and capabilities and the pervasive federal involvement in the nation's economic activities, the president's power over the economy is rather limited.[66]

For a variety of reasons, not least the news media's portrayal of presidents and their power over the economy, voters in the United States have customarily given presidents too much credit for contemporary economic conditions, exaggerating presidential ability to manage the economy. Based on a fundamental misunderstanding of the business cycle and prevailing microeconomic facts, public expectations in this regard have been increasingly unrealistic, so presidents will frequently be blamed for recessions or praised for recoveries, neither of which they can actually prevent, cause, or substantially alter. The truth is that presidential administrations, and particularly individual presidents, have far less ability to manage the economy than the public and the news media believe, for, in the final analysis, they cannot control either the market or the business cycle.[67] Nevertheless, the common perception of a president as economic arbiter persists, so people continue to believe that the presidency can and should successfully address their chief economic concerns. For this reason alone, presidents do whatever they can, and often what they cannot, to guide or shape economic and financial development in the United States. Obviously, the presidency is not powerless in this arena, and its reliance on nominally nonpartisan appointees who head key bureaucratic institutions within the executive branch is crucial, but its limitations must be acknowledged.

The two most prominent aspects of economic policymaking are monetary and fiscal policy. Of all economic policy areas, the president has the least control over monetary policy, which is probably the most obscure economic topic policymakers must address. Handled by the Federal Reserve (a.k.a. the "Fed") through the Board of Governors and the Federal Open Market Committee (FOMC), monetary policy targets the U.S. money supply through the control of key lending rates, the sale of government bonds, and the regulation of banking assets. In this way, the Fed manages inflation, known as the consumer price index, and tries to keep unemployment low and prices stable. The president's influence over monetary policy is limited to his powers of persuasion and his authority to appoint governors and members of FOMC, including the powerful Chairman of the Board of Governors. Since the public and the news media devote relatively little attention to Fed policy beyond its setting of benchmark interest rates, and because monetary policy addresses mostly medium-term and long-term objectives and does not concentrate on the short-term issues that animate presidential politics, presidents are normally content to leave monetary policy to the Fed and are loath to meddle or interfere.[68]

Whereas presidents have little control over monetary policy, they have become the central figures in the development of fiscal policies. Fiscal policy refers to those issues associated with governmental revenues and expenditures, or, in lay terms,

---

☝ View presidential job approval and economic confidence.

taxes and spending. During the last eighty years, presidents have taken control of fiscal policy, not only as a consequence of increasing budgetary responsibilities but also due to greater public awareness of the impact of fiscal policies on their lives. As incredible as it may sound, presidents did not originally play a role in budgeting, which was under congressional management, nor did they appreciably concern themselves with governmental revenues or expenditures. Changing socioeconomic circumstances and an ever-expanding, resource-intensive executive bureaucracy pushed presidents into the fiscal-policy arena to the point that revenue and spending plans have become centerpieces of presidential domestic agendas. Today, with a billowing public debt and regular annual budget deficits, everyone is aware of the need to address the nation's fiscal problems, and presidents are being held accountable by the public. Presidents cannot afford to ignore or minimize the significance of either taxes or spending, and they have been compelled to consider both short-term and long-term solutions to structural and cyclical fiscal deficiencies.

Despite numerous and almost perennial debates about progressive taxation, the validity of taxation generally, or indirect versus direct taxation for generations among industrialists, social scientists, and other experts, tax policy emerged as a veritable public issue only in the 1960s as the Kennedy administration began to tackle what it perceived as prohibitively high marginal tax rates among certain socioeconomic groups. Much to the chagrin of many Republicans, Kennedy was the first presidential proponent of supply-side policies, which were based on the belief that minimizing the tax burden of producers and those with potential investment capital would eventually benefit consumers and cause per-capita income growth at all levels. In October 1962, Kennedy signed into law the Revenue Act of 1962, which included various tax reforms as well as a tax break for businesses intended to promote industrial investment. Kennedy also pursued a personal income tax cut as well that would encompass "permanent and basic reform and reduction."[69]

During the summer of 1962, White House advisors were busy devising a strategy for how and when Kennedy would pursue the tax cut policy. In an address at Yale University in June 1962, Kennedy spoke extensively on fiscal policy in the United States, but declined to offer much specific detail about any forthcoming plans. According to Ted Sorensen, one of Kennedy's closest advisors, the speech was not a trial balloon about an upcoming policy proposal, but "an academic exercise before an academic audience." However, the reaction to the speech by the business community and conservatives showed the administration that "debt and deficit spending were as unpopular as ever."[70] In July, Sorensen warned Kennedy about the crucial political timing involved with the issue: "A tax cut is a massive economic weapon. It can only be used once. It has not been used in any previous recession in my memory. . . . You did not want us to over-react in Berlin with a national emergency—I do not want us to over-react now." Sorensen urged Kennedy to only seek a tax cut if both the economic and political timing were right; that is, if employment and production continued to decline, if the cut would not result in too high of a deficit, and if both Congress and the business community seemed receptive to the move: "Once you are able to go to the Congress and country with positive answers to these items, such a move will be both right and successful. Until then, it is likely to be neither."[71] Kennedy continued to push for tax cut legislation throughout 1963, but congressional support and action were slow in coming. Congress would not pass such a bill until early 1964, just weeks after Kennedy had died; instead, President Lyndon Johnson signed the Revenue Act of 1964 into law on February 26, 1964, an $11.5 billion omnibus tax reduction and reform bill intended to promote economic growth.[72]

Much was made of supply-side economics during the 1980s as Ronald Reagan's economic team concentrated on tax relief for those capable of increasing investment and production, but these policies had a solid historical basis. On the other side, so-called Keynesian, or demand-side, theories, which are still pervasive among today's mainstream Democrats, reject supply-side efforts as inadequate or inequitable. They are based on the assumption that fundamental structural problems prevent lower-income and impoverished groups from competing equitably by denying them opportunities and depressing economic benefits, which can only be addressed through demand-side remedial measures such as stimulus spending, redistributive taxation, and the provision of needed social services.[73]

Interestingly enough, although the gap between supply-siders and demand-siders has closed over the past four decades and recent presidents, most notably George H. W. Bush and Bill Clinton, have been a little of both, the political rhetoric has become more polarized. Recent controversies over the legacy of George W. Bush's tax-relief measures and the Obama administration's efforts to address their expiration have posed a false dichotomy between untrammeled capitalism and naked socialism, with politicians and the public bitterly divided regarding the results. During presidential election seasons, like the most recent in 2012, one side is portrayed by its political opponents as inherently hostile to American business, wealthy citizens, and free enterprise, while the other is painted as callous, disconnected, and the handmaidens of rich and powerful industrialists. Regrettably, the truth is lost in the rhetorical free-for-all, as is a willingness to compromise and cooperate, but, in a strange way, the situation only affirms the importance of tax policy for presidents and ordinary Americans.

The other side of fiscal policy deals with government expenditures, which are divided into discretionary and non-discretionary categories. Federal spending has become a particular concern as the size of government and its financial obligations have increased during the last eighty years but especially over the last three decades or so, during which federal deficits and an expanding federal debt have become unusually problematic. As the total federal debt begins to exceed 100 percent of national income (Gross Domestic Product, or GDP) and entitlement spending spirals out of control, presidents are under mounting pressure to find a solution to the looming financial crisis. Unfortunately, non-discretionary, or mandatory, spending accounts for roughly two-thirds of all federal expenditures, and this is the most intractable category. It includes entitlements, federal pensions, related fixed obligations, and debt service, all of which continue to increase and do not show signs of abating within the foreseeable future. Tackling entitlements, which pose the most acute financial problem in both the short and the long term, is something most presidents do not have either the political capital or will to do. But, with an aging population relative to previous generations and steadily growing financial obligations, only fundamental structural reforms that would be quite painful in the short term, particularly to programs such as Social Security and Medicare, would suffice. The prospects for such reforms seem comparatively dim at this juncture, not least because they would require the kind of bipartisan cooperation that has been lacking during the last couple of decades.[74]

Discretionary spending, on the other hand, is a misnomer of sorts, since it involves such hot-button issues as the defense budget and is based on the assumption that the status quo will be maintained in order to preserve commitments made to key electoral constituencies. Ironically, defense spending, which is the subject of some of the most vitriolic partisan debates in Washington, did not become a veritable campaign issue or public concern until the last thirty years. For the bulk of the Cold War, the necessity of increased military spending and the associated arms build-up was largely unquestioned, as both Democratic and Republican administrations presided over massive increases in military budgets. By the 1980s, however, both the public mood and the overall political culture had begun to change, galvanized by controversy over Ronald Reagan's intensification of the arms race with the Soviets. Mounting federal deficits, expanding defense budgets, and decreasing federal tax rates motivated the President's political opponents to question the prudence of continued military-spending increases. By the end of Reagan's second term, the debate over defense spending had become a permanent feature of latter-day Washington politics, and the defense budget became an integral aspect of both parties' campaign platforms. In practice, contrary to the political rhetoric, Republican as well as Democratic presidents are still committed to sizable defense budgets and are unwilling to do anything that would either weaken U.S. military capabilities or, more importantly, create the impression internationally of military decline and retrenchment.[75]

As for other parts of the discretionary budget, they are replete with sacred cows ostensibly impervious to negotiation and compromise and also essential to the president and the legislators on whom he must depend for approval of his budget. Aside from constituency-based commitments, like industrial or farm subsidies, infrastructure projects and other government contracts, and various state and local programs, to name only a few examples, this includes funding for the various federal departments and agencies whose institutional inertia prevents serious spending cuts. So, in the end, with so much of the federal budget dependent on mandatory or politically sensitive obligations, presidents really have little short-term control over federal spending. As a result, budgetary debates frequently devolve into mutual recriminations over so-called earmarks, which consist of numerous yet financially marginal a priori legislative obligations to specific constituencies, or ideological polemics concerning defense and entitlement spending. This is one reason why tax policy has become so central to presidential agendas. Seemingly unable, yet also unwilling, to control federal expenditures, presidents increasingly concentrate on increasing federal revenues.[76] Ultimately, none of this is insoluble, but it will require serious and sustainable structural changes which carry considerable short-term political costs.

Other aspects of economic policymaking include business, labor, and consumer policies, which target three major market participants and equally important political constituencies. Balancing the needs and priorities of these three groups can be quite tricky, especially since business policies can adversely affect both labor and consumer policies. Theoretically speaking, particularly from a free-market perspective, the three go hand in hand, since an efficient and productive marketplace benefits all simultaneously. Nevertheless, policies intended to aid or support certain industries or corporations are often perceived as anti-labor or anti-consumer. On other occasions, such as the recent bailouts of the auto industry by the Obama administration, business-friendly policy clearly works to the advantage of workers by preserving jobs and perhaps even of consumers by forcing technological and design changes that make products better. Likewise, protectionist policies, such as George W. Bush's steel tariffs, though highly unpopular with much of his party and free-market advocates generally, were designed to help both the steel manufacturers and their workers.[77]

Business, or industrial, policy has both microeconomic and macroeconomic components, which are intended to facilitate the growth and preservation of key U.S. economic sectors. On the macroeconomic side, broad monetary and fiscal policies already discussed seek to manage the business cycle, or at least its effects, by countering recessionary trends and promoting expansion and recovery. In this arena, the president's influence over business policy is mostly a function of the bully pulpit and his related ability to affect investor and consumer confidence as well as his willingness to change relevant fiscal policies. With respect to microeconomic objectives, the president and his advisors seek to influence the supply–demand dynamic through industry-specific measures, such as protective tariffs, subsidies, government contracts, and mediation. Free-market purists oppose all of these as market-distorting mechanisms, but presidents of both parties have viewed them as necessary tools for the preservation of short-term stability and the maintenance of key political relationships. Nonetheless, over the last twenty years, both Democratic and Republican presidents have begun to recognize, albeit reluctantly, the decreasing effectiveness and growing unpopularity of such measures.[78]

Industry-specific aid, despite the benefits to associated workers, has been perceived by a skeptical public as corporate welfare, while its long-term economic effects can be debilitating and inconsistent with the nation's global market objectives. Although industrial assistance of one kind or another has definite advantages in the short term, it tends to compound existing problems of efficiency and productivity by artificially supporting unhealthy companies or ailing industries. As Japan's futile but perennial attempts to resuscitate the banking, construction, and real-estate industries, to name only some, have demonstrated, the long-term consequences can be paralytic from both an economic and a financial standpoint. In addition, as the United States continues to fight for regional and global free trade through the reduction of barriers such as subsidies and tariffs, its protectionist policies become decreasingly defensible.[79] Finally, industrial assistance such as farm subsidies, though they result in lower retail prices on agricultural products according to its proponents, have come under fire from ordinary Americans who believe their taxes are being used to benefit the rich. Moreover, subsidies of this kind and other forms of corporate aid provide a competitive advantage to industrial giants over family-owned farms and small businesses, which does not resonate well with middle-class and lower-income Americans.[80]

Like business policy, labor policy comes with its own set of problems and concerns, but it is a crucial part of presidential agendas, especially during economically challenging times such as the recession that began at the end of George W. Bush's second term and lasted into Barack Obama's first term in the White House. Labor policy is actually one of the oldest areas of domestic policymaking in the modern era, with roots that stretch back to the initial waves of industrial unionization and worker politicization during the late nineteenth and early twentieth centuries. Organizations like Samuel Gomper's American Federation of Labor (AFL) were instrumental in putting labor policy on the political map and legitimizing it as a principal area of presidential policymaking. Unlike radical groups such as the Industrial Workers of the World (IWW), AFL and other mainstream labor unions accepted industrial capitalism as a fact of life and even a medium for socioeconomic progress and agreed to work within it to improve their working conditions. This made them much more acceptable to politicians than far-left unions like IWW, which advocated the abolition of the wage system and capitalism altogether. By 1913, the old Bureau of Labor had become the Department of Labor and a pivotal member of the president's cabinet. The high point for many workers came in 1935 with the passage of the Wagner Act and the creation of the National Labor Relations Board (NLRB) to protect workers, supervise industrial employment and unionization policies, and oversee union elections. Known unofficially as "Labor's Magna Carta," the Wagner Act was an official recognition of the growing power of workers and the nations' increasing reliance on a stable and productive industrial workforce.[81]

By the 1950s, unionization rates had peaked at approximately a third of the national workforce and so had organized labor's influence in Washington. After the passage of the pro-business Taft–Hartley Act in 1947, which undermined certain provisions of the Wagner Act and reduced the authority of the NLRB, Democrat Harry Truman and his Republican successor, Dwight Eisenhower, shifted their focus to the nation's key industries and their corporate leadership in order to secure the economic and military competitiveness of the United States against the Soviet Union. The enlistment of the country's corporate leaders in the drive to contain Soviet aggression and preserve U.S. dominance in the West during the Cold War became a paramount objective for all postwar presidents, as did the involvement and support of ordinary Americans in the consolidation of national-security assets. Therefore, when President Truman seized the country's steel mills in the early 1950s, many Americans supported the extraordinary expression of authority. The Supreme Court invalidated the president's action, but that did not deter future chief executives. Truman also exerted executive control through the Wage Stabilization Board, because both he and Eisenhower dedicated themselves to the optimization of national-security resources.[82]

Over the ensuing decades, as unionization rates fell to roughly 20 percent by 1980 and less than 12 percent by 2011, the decoupling of labor policy from union policy was gradual but slow, as presidents and their administrations searched for a coherent and comprehensive approach to labor-specific issues. The most common responses to labor demands during the last few decades have included stimulus spending in the form of public-works projects and broader infrastructural initiatives, modifications in unemployment and disability benefits, worker-training programs, and industrial mediation on behalf of certain groups of workers. Unionization rates among public-sector workers are still above 35 percent, but public-sector unions have neither the clout nor the mobilization capabilities of their once-prominent private-sector counterparts, so their ability to affect labor policy has also been declining. Nevertheless, under Presidents Clinton and especially Obama, who has been confronted with one of the highest unemployment rates in recent history, both unionized and non-unionized workers have received greater attention from White House policymakers.[83] Still, the effective power of the presidency in this area, as with other components of economic policy, is comparatively limited.

Finally, consumer policy, which is wholly a twentieth-century phenomenon, is largely within the purview of the executive branch's regulatory agencies, which the president can influence through his appointment authority and powers of persuasion. Although presidents customarily devote some attention in their campaign platforms and policy agendas to timely consumer issues, consumer policies are managed through the rulemaking authority of regulators such as the Federal Trade Commission, Consumer Financial Protection Bureau, Consumer Product Safety Commission, and Food and Drug Administration. Their authority and administrative scope are, in turn, delimited by corresponding congressional statutes, which can be products of presidential policies. As the names of these regulatory agencies imply, the focus of consumer policy is the safety and protection of American consumers by establishing and maintaining appropriate quality standards that minimize potential physical harm or danger, curb fraudulent products and services, and expose offenders.[84]

Social Policy

Another area over which the president has little actual control, though he can exert some influence through the use of the bully pulpit, is social policy. This kind of policy is often the centerpiece of campaign platforms and of special importance to presidents personally, but it was not originally considered a legitimate focus of governmental activity. Although sociocultural issues were a significant concern for the framers of the Constitution, they wished to prevent, if not wholly obviate, governmental interference in private and personal matters, which could be regulated through family, church, and community measures. Eventually, the emergence of social movements dedicated to moral and ethical reform, such the early temperance efforts, became amalgamated with contemporary political and economic reform efforts, which provided them political credibility.[85] Culminating in the politicization of a full spectrum of sociocultural issues previously considered off limits to the federal government, the American political system has incorporated sociocultural as well as strictly political ideals within its ideological foundation. This means that the presidency, even more so than other parts of the federal government, is viewed, perhaps wrongly, as a principal sociocultural policymaker and standard-bearer.

Interestingly enough, though the presidency and the federal government more broadly have acquired vast authority and capabilities in most domestic policy areas during the past century or so, and despite the by-now commonplace expectation that presidents should set sociocultural policy, the presidency has developed neither the authority nor the capability to do so. Of course, modern presidents have the power to effect certain changes in sociocultural policy through executive action, such as making decisions about the provision of abortion-related services at federal facilities, but these are merely tactical privileges that affirm rather than contradict the comparative impotence of the presidency in this arena. Be that as it may, Americans expect their presidents to have clear and ostensibly actionable positions on topics like abortion, homosexuality, stem cell research, religion, marriage, and so on. Whether these are legitimate targets of federal governance or issues the federal government is even equipped to address no longer concerns most Americans—that part seems settled. The only thing open to debate is the viability of presidential policies designed to deal with particular sociocultural issues.

Arguably the most enduring and divisive of these sociocultural issues is abortion, which, like the rest of them, is out of the federal government's control. Although presidents have a marginal ability to affect abortion policy through certain executive funding decisions, the real power is with the courts, which are constrained by legal precedent. Even avowedly conservative justices such as John Roberts and Samuel Alito, George W. Bush's appointees, would not and could not summarily overturn a binding precedent like *Roe v. Wade* (1973), particularly without compelling doctrinal reasons. Abortion-rights activists point out that the Rehnquist Court weakened the *Roe* ruling through subsequent abortion-related cases, but the reversal of *Roe* itself is not a guaranteed outcome regardless of the makeup of the Court.[86] In addition to abortion, issues like gay marriage, religion and prayer, sexual promiscuity, parenting, working mothers, and a host of others promote debate about appropriate societal norms, but, as with abortion, presidents are all but powerless to do anything but educate and persuade. Once in a while, a presidential initiative will manifest itself through measures such as the previously mentioned Defense of Marriage Act or the creation of executive faith-based programs, but those efforts are rare and politically costly.

According to the federal design of the republic and related theories of federalism, the states retain authority over the regulation of these social issues, provided their efforts do not violate relevant constitutional doctrine. Social regulatory legislation by the states has been viewed with some skepticism by progressives, and, over the past four decades, the courts have scrutinized state-centered attempts to control sociocultural preferences. Still, aside from the federal judiciary and particularly the Supreme Court, the federal government has minimal authority to intervene, and presidential policies in this area are, therefore, primarily symbolic.[87] That has not stopped either of the major political parties or their presidential nominees from making sweeping promises and declarations concerning pivotal sociocultural issues, which has done nothing to disabuse voters of the misapprehension that presidents have the authority to make sociocultural policy. They can, however, influence the Supreme Court through their appointment power, so presidential candidates make commitments to their constituents about potential nominations to the high bench and also the appellate courts. That, of course, can backfire, since, even if the opportunity to name someone to the Supreme Court arises, judicial voting behavior is highly unpredictable. The two most glaring examples, though many others exist, are Republican President Dwight Eisenhower's appointments of Earl Warren and William Brennan, who turned out to be two of the more liberal justices that have sat on the modern-day Supreme Court.[88]

The situation has not been helped by the political climate in Washington or the high-stakes rhetorical swordplay during the last few decades. The so-called culture wars, which have fueled the political controversies surrounding sociocultural issues, have their origins in the 1960s and some of its radical social movements that often threatened and discomfited traditionalists and most mainstream politicians on both sides of the aisle. These movements and their supporters, though the predecessors of some of today's institutionalized Democratic sociocultural efforts, did not focus on the kinds of issues that characterize today's culture wars, such as abortion and gay marriage, but concentrated on the alleviation of perceived political and socioeconomic inequities.[89] All the same, the politicization of radical efforts provoked a strong reaction from the Nixon administration, which viewed this counterculture, as it was known, as both a cultural and a political threat to the integrity of the American political system and its underlying set of national ideals. Nixon's concern was never with the types of sociocultural priorities valued by today's social conservatives, but he was nonetheless eager to discredit these movements and their leaders.[90]

During the 1970s, residual reformist radicalism inherited from the 1960s did eventually translate into the promotion of by-now familiar sociocultural priorities like gay rights, the availability of safe and legal abortions, and women's equality. Seminal phenomena, such as the *Roe v. Wade* ruling by the Supreme Court and the prolonged but ultimately unsuccessful campaign for the Equal Rights Amendment, to say nothing of the associated emergence of feminism from its academic confines, only alienated and even enraged traditionalists and conservatives still reeling from the countercultural attacks of the 1960s.[91] By Ronald Reagan's election to the White House, sociocultural policy had become a principal focus of electoral politics, while Democratic and Republican platforms incorporated what have become almost obligatory positions on sociocultural issues.[92] So, when Republican Pat Buchanan delivered his famous speech at the 1992 Republican National Convention that has been widely credited with reigniting the culture wars, during which he declared that "there is a religious war going on in our country for the soul of America,"[93] both sides were already so entrenched in their positions and so invested in their defense that productive dialogue between them seemed impossible.[94]

Despite the heightened rhetoric, Bill Clinton's election offered a rare opportunity to bridge the gap between mainstream Republicans and Democrats on some key social issues. Clinton's Southern heritage and his pragmatic political outlook tempered his stand on some of the most controversial social policies and should have provided the necessary momentum for compromise between the two parties and their constituents. Though a supporter of abortion rights, he viewed abortion as a last-resort option to avoid death or debilitating illness in mother or child, which should have made him more palatable to moderate pro-life Republicans. Moreover, he openly professed his support for traditional marriage and against state-sanctioned gay unions, and, perhaps most importantly, he had a profound religious streak that connected him to Southern voters. Moreover, as a member of the centrist Democratic Leadership Council in the 1980s, he advocated a move away from the traditional leftist policies of the party's Keynesian base much in the same way that Tony Blair had refashioned Britain's Labor Party at approximately the same time. Clinton and like-minded politicians, who were often called New Democrats, successfully pushed the Democratic Party toward the political center and made it more competitive after the Reagan-dominated 1980s.[95]

Nevertheless, compromise was not in the cards, as any real chance of attenuating the culture war was destroyed by a combination of Clinton's personal problems and a vitriolic Republican opposition that viewed the president as the embodiment of 1960s-era sociocultural excess. Clinton's dalliances and past affairs with other women were indeed a distraction that diverted his administration's attention and energy from a promising domestic agenda, but his foes' characterization of Clinton as a 1960s radical motivated sustained attacks on the President. The situation was exacerbated by the Republicans' intense dislike of First Lady Hillary Clinton, who did not hide her own animosity toward her husband's political opponents. Her unabashed candor and aggressive posture made her a less-than-favorable spokesperson for the administration, and her 1996 book *It Takes a Village and Other Lessons Children Teach Us* was perceived by Republicans, and especially social conservatives, as a deliberate intensification of the culture wars. By the 2000 presidential election, as Bill Clinton was preparing to leave office after two terms in the White House, the chasm between social conservatives and progressives was unbridgeable.[96]

After eight years of seemingly constant personal scandals, many of them generated by the outgoing president's private transgressions, the stage was set for a conservative backlash. As already mentioned, George W. Bush, Clinton's successor, was one of the only presidents in U.S. history, and certainly the first modern president, whose main electoral base was primarily concerned with a core set of sociocultural priorities. Bush's political strategists, led by long-time Bush advisor Karl Rove, mobilized social conservatives in record numbers and reoriented the Republican Party away from its customary fiscal and law-and-order focus to the sociocultural right. The newly energized social-conservative base of the Republican Party expected its president to institutionalize long-sought social policies that addressed abortion, gay marriage, religion and prayer, scientific research, families, and a bevy of related priorities. Hamstrung by the president's aforementioned lack of real authority over social policy, Bush nonetheless did what he could to satisfy supporters. Through executive order, he increased the involvement of church-centered organizations in governance, limited stem cell research, and curbed federally funded abortion-counseling services, while signing statements, which carried no official statutory authority, became an extension of the presidential bully pulpit.[97]

The Bush presidency may have been free of the kinds of personal scandals that plagued the Clinton White House, but, after eight years of social-conservative revivalism, much of the country appeared to grow weary of the politics of morality. What's more, declining economic conditions and one of the worst recessions since the Great Depression diverted national attention to bread-and-butter issues, which robbed the culture war of its political momentum. This does not imply that sociocultural issues ceased to be important or that the social-conservative surge that elevated George W. Bush to the White House had become irrelevant, but, as has normally been the case throughout U.S. history, urgent economic priorities ultimately trumped competing concerns. Despite reversing some of Bush's executive orders and related conservative social policies, President Obama has largely steered clear of overt sociocultural debates. Admittedly, he has been consumed by more pressing problems, such as high unemployment and a shaky economic recovery that may or may not prove sustainable, but his tenure in office has fostered the conditions that could lead to a cease fire in the culture wars.[98]

Social Services

In terms of influence over the day-to-day aspects of Americans' lives, the most important category within the domestic-policy arena is social services. It is also the most resource-intensive, as it accounts for the bulk of domestic federal spending and the plurality of the domestic federal work force. Covering assistance for the socioeconomically dislocated, social security, health care, education, and many other areas, this part of the president's domestic-policy agenda has grown consistently and almost uncontrollably since its appearance approximately one century ago. It encompasses central programs like Social Security, Medicare, and Medicaid, whose management has become as much a focus of fiscal policy as anything else, along with much-needed services for the disabled, America's veterans, dependent children, and students.[99] Partly because of the looming fiscal concerns over entitlements but also the existence of over forty million uninsured and underinsured Americans coupled with skyrocketing medical costs, health-care policy has become the centerpiece of social-services planning for presidential administrations.[100] Although Democratic presidents have been more emphatic in their push for health-care reform, the financially dubious state of the nation's entitlement programs has made this part of social-services policy an essential concern even for Republican presidents.

Social services constitute the biggest single policy area for presidential administrations, at least from a resource and capabilities perspective, but that has been a historically recent development. Until the so-called Progressive Era, and especially the presidency of Woodrow Wilson from 1913 to 1921, neither presidents nor the federal government generally devoted much attention to what is now the single biggest policy concern for presidential administrations. This state of affairs was not a product of governmental negligence but a pre-industrial mentality rooted in a strict adherence to the framers' intentions to restrict the role of the federal government and its involvement in social and economic matters. Wilson was not the first to realize that a Constitution designed for a largely rural, agrarian society would have to evolve in order to accommodate an urban, industrialized America, but his administration was the first to confront seriously the problems posed by mass industrialization and urbanization. Still, despite Wilson's adaptations and innovations, the requisite executive capability and willingness to remedy some of these problems, particularly the structural socioeconomic deficiencies, did not emerge until the 1930s and Franklin Roosevelt's attempts to ameliorate living conditions during the Great Depression, during which the key macroeconomic indicators were at unprecedented levels.[101]

During the Great Depression, unemployment reached 25 percent, though some estimates are as high as 33 percent, while a steady deflationary trend that made goods and services much cheaper and even worthless raised the international value of the dollar to unsupportable heights. Between 1929, when the stock market crashed, and the beginning of FDR's first term in office, national income (GDP) declined by almost a half, and the Dow Jones Industrials average plunged by more than 85 percent. Banks collapsed, businesses were insolvent, people lost their homes, and farms were abandoned.[102] Faced with a national emergency on a scale previously unimaginable, Roosevelt pushed Congress to enact appropriate remedial legislation. Within a few months, Roosevelt secured a package of social-service and regulatory measures targeting workers, employers, farmers, utilities, banks, consumer prices, wages, natural resources, and much more.

The newly created Federal Emergency Relief Administration (FERA) distributed direct and indirect aid to the poor, while the Civil Works Administration (CWA) provided sorely needed jobs for a few million unemployed. On FDR's prompting, Congress also established the Civilian Conservation Corps (CCC) to handle environmental restoration, particularly reforestation, and put younger Americans to work. Depressed Southern states benefited from the Tennessee Valley Authority (TVA), which built dams, provided electricity along the Tennessee River Valley, and addressed infrastructural degradation and squalor in local communities. The farming crisis was managed by the Agricultural Adjustment Administration, whose authority to control production, set commodity prices, and subsidize farmers set significant precedents for the subsequent eight decades. Its industrial counterpart, the National Recovery Administration (NRA), was given broad authority to fix wages, working hours, and consumer prices, while the Securities and Exchange Commission (SEC) had authority to regulate equity markets and eliminate unfair stock-trading practices. All in all, this First New Deal, as it has been called, concentrated on the supply of goods and commodities through the regulation of production.[103]

The Second New Deal more aggressively confronted the demand-side manifestations of the Depression by increasing consumer purchasing power and capabilities through programs for dislocated minorities, industrial workers, retired persons, and others disproportionately affected by the economic crisis. As such, the presidency and the federal government generally became committed to the redistribution of wealth and income in order to secure not only social and economic equity but also sustainable per-capita income growth. Early in 1935, FDR's administration launched the Works Progress Administration (WPA), one of the nation's largest relief agencies and a lasting symbol of New Deal activism. With over 30 percent of the nation's unemployed among its ranks, it coordinated public-works projects throughout the United States and distributed various kinds of assistance to families hit hardest by the Depression. Having a profound impact on rural America and western states, the WPA built schools, libraries, roads, and bridges, while providing food, clothing, and shelter in resource-starved communities.[104]

As significant as most New Deal programs were, no single initiative has been as closely associated with the New Deal as the Social Security Act, which institutionalized a U.S. welfare state by authorizing the federal government to provide basic social services. All subsequent welfare-state enhancements and reforms were inspired and empowered by the Social Security Act, and most ensuing attempts to increase domestic executive authority used it as a political and legal precedent. The law, enacted in 1935 as the core of the Second New Deal, created a guaranteed federal pension for the elderly, unemployment compensation, aid for dependent children, support for unwed mothers, and related services.[105] Over the next eight decades, the presidency's focus on social services has only become more intense and the social-service capabilities and resources of the executive branch immense. Its ability and authority to dispense various forms of assistance, distribute basic necessities, and administer remedial and redistributive programs have far surpassed anything accomplished during the 1930s and are taken for granted as inherent characteristics of the modern presidency.

Further substantial gains in executive social-services capability came with the Lyndon Johnson administration, whose accomplishments in that regard actually exceeded those of the FDR team. LBJ's Great Society would cover the poor, the elderly, the young, political and social minorities, mothers, the workplace, schools, housing, the nation's cities, and more. One of the most prominent parts of LBJ's Great Society was the War on Poverty, which sought to mitigate poverty by addressing long-term structural deficiencies that depressed the dislocated. As LBJ declared in his 1964 State of the Union address:

> This administration today, here and now, declares unconditional war on poverty in America. I urge this Congress and all Americans to join with me in that effort.

> It will not be a short or easy struggle, no single weapon or strategy will suffice, but we shall not rest until that war is won. The richest Nation on earth can afford to win it. We cannot afford to lose it. One thousand dollars invested in salvaging an unemployable youth today can return $40,000 or more in his lifetime. Poverty is a national problem, requiring improved national organization and support. But this attack, to be effective, must also be organized at the State and the local level and must be supported and directed by State and local efforts. For the war against poverty will not be won here in Washington. It must be won in the field, in every private home, in every public office, from the courthouse to the White House.[106]

LBJ's Office of Economic Opportunity (OEO), modeled on New Deal precedents, was charged with the development of relevant economic and social-services policies. The OEO and its agencies provided job training, housing assistance, educational enrichment, food and clothing subsidies, basic health care, resources for neighborhood improvement, and other services.[107]

The War on Poverty was supplemented by related educational reforms that increased federal funding for states and local communities, which provided billions of dollars for facilities, teachers, supplies, training, and students. In addition, the newly created Department of Housing and Urban Development (HUD) focused on the revitalization of America's cities through building projects, renovations, and improvements in public infrastructure. HUD, OEO, and other Great Society institutions were social-services landmarks, but LBJ's signal achievements with respect to the expansion of welfare-state capabilities were Medicare and Medicaid. Medicare looked to the nation's retired persons, with health-care benefits that included hospital treatment, nursing-home subsidies, and physician care, while Medicaid, which was to be a joint program with the states, would service the poor, disabled, elderly not eligible for Medicare, dependent children and unwed mothers, and others identified as needy by federal or state governments.[108]

Johnson's expansion of the social-services bureaucracy eventually defined the boundaries of legitimate executive authority for many Democrats and Republicans, but the reformist impulse did not last. By the early 1970s, continued antiwar agitation, social unrest in more than 150 cities, and three political assassinations in less than a decade produced public cynicism and apathy. An economic recession compounded by an international energy crisis also limited the government's ability to enact further reforms, and the Watergate scandal diverted valuable political capital and public attention from more pressing issues. In addition, America's biggest cities were riddled with systemic police corruption, drug abuse, and racial violence. When President Richard Nixon resigned in August of 1974, any vestiges of idealism and faith in federal governance had already disappeared.[109] The real tragedy of the Nixon resignation is that it overshadowed significant domestic and international achievements at a time when the country desperately needed presidential leadership. Definitely no LBJ, Nixon was nonetheless an activist domestic-policy chief whose lackluster image and personal foibles prevented the kind of national healing the political system demanded. Still, he secured increased benefits for dependent children, social-security recipients, and even minorities and, unlike most Republicans, defended deficit spending as a way to relieve unemployment, inflation, and a lack of investment.[110]

After Nixon, many politicians and especially an insurgent group of fiscally conservative law-and-order Republicans were ready to reassess the wisdom of decades of ongoing social-services expansions. The short-lived and politically hamstrung administration of Gerald Ford concentrated on inherited policy issues that left little room for political maneuverability and also political reconciliation after the Nixon fiasco, while his successor, Jimmy Carter, was one of the most ineffective modern presidents, whose proclivity for micromanagement and lack of political skill undermined his presidency from the start. This left the nation's political mood particularly susceptible to Ronald Regan's anti-government rhetoric and almost infectious individualism. Capitalizing on the political disillusionment of the preceding years, Reagan blamed big government for the country's social and economic ills. His portrayal of a bloated and meddlesome executive bureaucracy with too much power that sapped American competitiveness and productivity struck a chord with an electorate that increasingly viewed government as the enemy. During its two terms in the White House, the Reagan administration relaxed regulatory control over the private sector by appointing like-minded anti-government technocrats to the FTC, SEC, and NLRB and reduced federal funding for a number of social services that comprised health care, education, poverty prevention, and others.[111]

Aside from its advocacy of the Americans with Disabilities Act, which passed in 1990, the George H. W. Bush administration was happy to maintain the status quo, preferring to avoid the pitched ideological battles of the Reagan years. In many regards the anti-Reagan, devoid of his predecessor's grandfatherly charisma, eloquence, and public stature, Bush became a one-term president who had neither the inclination nor the personal wherewithal for the kind of ideological polemics or political gamesmanship that increasingly characterized the environment in Washington.[112] Bill Clinton, on the other hand, seemed perfectly suited for it, and his natural political skill was only compromised by an absence of personal discipline that caused recurring problems in his private life. Within his first days in the White House, he launched critical social-services reforms and announced his intention to "end welfare as we know it." His commitment drew bipartisan support and signaled a change of direction for the Democratic Party, which had traditionally staked its political credibility on continued support for LBJ-era social programs.

Clinton's domestic policymaking team focused on the much maligned welfare program known as Aid to Families with Dependent Children (AFDC), which had become a favorite target of conservative critics, libertarians, and other opponents of big government. Its assistance to needy children was commonly perceived as an incentive for negligent parents to remain on federal assistance indefinitely and avoid taking responsibility for their own lives. In terms of its share of total federal expenditures on social services, AFDC was hardly the financial problem other parts of the welfare state had become, but it was a symbol of a dysfunctional social-services bureaucracy that contributed to escalating fiscal difficulties. Leveraging the public's rising discontent over the government's inability to balance its books, Clinton's welfare-reform initiative exemplified the political shift in the Democratic Party.[113] Like Britain's Labor Party and Germany's Social Democrats, both of which were left of center, the Democrats in America were adapting their party platform to changing times. Historical support for large welfare states was overtaken by the fiscal realities of the late twentieth century, and pragmatic Democrats such as Clinton reoriented their policies accordingly. Nevertheless, old habits die hard, which meant that bureaucratic momentum and the expectations of the administration's key constituencies, along with Clinton's own ideological inconsistencies, eventually militated against the ambitious reformist rhetoric coming out of the early Clinton White House. In the end, the bureaucracy and its social-services capabilities had expanded by the end of Clinton's second term.[114]

As a domestic policymaker, George W. Bush was an anomaly, because he seemed to abandon the theoretical Republican commitment to small government by presiding over the largest increase in non-discretionary domestic spending since LBJ. Compassionate conservatism, Bush's self-described policy characterization since his days as Texas governor, necessitated greater attention to domestic services than his Republican predecessors had countenanced, but Bush's religious impulses also pushed government further into the provision of social services.[115] Still, Bush and his successor, Barack Obama, have recognized that spending on social services has become unsustainable, though both have been handicapped by a lack of political capital and will to confront a dilemma whose long-term resolution would cause short-term pain. Like its predecessors, the Obama administration has faced a fiscal quagmire that could eventually bring the U.S. government to a standstill. Excessive entitlement spending and looming long-term social-services liabilities intensify the fiscal burdens of an aging population that demands an ever-greater share of the nation's resources.

Law Enforcement

After social services, the most significant domestic-policy concerns for the presidency involve law enforcement, which encompasses federal anti-crime initiatives, border security and immigration, homeland security and domestic counter-terrorism, civil-rights protection, and various associated activities. During much of the antebellum period, presidential law-enforcement policy was conspicuous by its absence, and it did not become a substantial concern until the twentieth century. The early presidency was not equipped to deal with such issues, mostly because the framers of the Constitution did not authorize it to do so, but most of the needs and circumstances for federal law enforcement that exist today were not present at that time. Even when needs and circumstances initially arose, almost all law-enforcement responsibilities were met by state and especially local governments, whereas other areas of law enforcement that are now under federal jurisdiction, such as civil rights and border security, were largely irrelevant or ignored.[116] As the complexities of industrialization and urbanization coupled with continued population growth created a demand for a more active federal law-enforcement role and a burgeoning federal government issued scores of new federal laws that required enforcement, the executive branch acquired increasing duties and responsibilities. Most importantly, evolving public awareness and sociocultural attitudes concerning issues such as civil rights enabled and eventually motivated federal administration of matters that had theretofore been ignored.

These days, presidents and presidential candidates ignore law enforcement at their own peril, since issues like immigration, border security, drug interdiction, and civil-rights protection have become among the most important priorities for Americans. These are hot-button topics sure to spark some of the most spirited, and frequently vitriolic, debates in politics, so a presidential candidate's position on any one of them can make a crucial difference in battleground states. Presidential policies on gun ownership and the death penalty, for example, have become political litmus tests for certain voters, and, while they represent an admittedly narrow portion of a president's overall domestic agenda, they are pivotal issues.[117] For example, the Clinton administration sought and won passage of the Violent Crime Control and Law Enforcement Act in 1994, the largest crime bill in the history of the United States that provided for 100,000 new police officers, billions of dollars in funding for prisons and crime prevention programs, an expanded federal death penalty, and a federal ban on assault weapons. Nearly all aspects of the bill became intense political debating points, particularly the assault weapons ban, as many members of Congress, particularly Republicans, were the targets of intense lobbying by the National Rifle Association to defeat the bill. The Clinton administration's strategy in passing the bill focused on partisan tactics, as explained in this memo from policy advisor Rahm Emanuel to Chief of Staff Leon Panetta:

> We must implement a dual strategy to pass the Crime Bill. This two tiered approach requires that (1) The President set an appropriate tone and tenor; and (2) We organize local officials, cabinet members, and candidates to apply pressure to targeted Republicans.... The message that we must send is simple: members of Congress abandoned their constituents. The President's role in the next four days is to make clear that by voting against the Crime Bill members of Congress championed their own political safety, over the people's safety. He must reiterate that they voted against 100,000 police officers; against three strikes and you're out; against tougher sentencing; against the assault weapons ban; against the death penalty. They abdicated their responsibility to their constituents, showing political cowardice when political courage was needed.[118]

Given the way the presidency has evolved over the last century and the vast powers and capabilities it has acquired especially in the socioeconomic realm, the fact that the executive branch exists to enforce the nation's laws is easily overlooked. Nevertheless, insofar as the generic principles of liberal governance apply to the American political system, law enforcement is a primary function of the presidency, and it is uniquely equipped to fulfill that need. In addition, though some of the presidency's law-enforcement activities are comparatively symbolic or abstract, such as the protection of civil, political, and broader constitutional rights and liberties, all of its law-enforcement duties and responsibilities continuously affirm the rule of law and, by extension, the public's faith in the Constitution and its underlying political ideals. On a more concrete level, personal safety and security are key concerns for all Americans, who expect their presidents to do whatever they can to control crime and supplement local law-enforcement efforts.

The most obvious aspect of law-enforcement policy is crime prevention, which became a high-profile issue during the 1980s and 1990s, particularly among law-and-order Reagan Republicans. Agencies such as the Justice Departments' Federal Bureau of Investigation (FBI) and Drug Enforcement Administration (DEA), the Department of Homeland Security's (DHS) Bureau of Alcohol, Tobacco, Firearms, and Explosives (ATF) and U.S. Secret Service provide essential crime-prevention services, yet the bulk of the nation's crime prevention is handled by state, county, and municipal agencies. Federal crime-prevention policies affect local law-enforcement efforts through various kinds of federal funding for state and community governments, though some measures like federal gun-ownership regulations cannot always be reconciled with local crime-prevention priorities. Still, the primary aim of federal crime-prevention policy is the enforcement of federal laws and the apprehension of those who commit federal crimes. Specialized agencies such as the Secret Service, which investigates counterfeiting of U.S. currency and treasury bonds, fulfill roles that are unique to the federal government or that the states are incapable of handling, like the prevention of interstate criminal activity.[119]

Since 2001, the DHS has become a major part of federal law-enforcement policy, though many of its responsibilities had already been fulfilled by agencies that were incorporated into the DHS upon its creation. The establishment of the DHS involved an intensification and redirection of focus rather than the initiation of new policies, but it did result in some pronounced political changes. A reinvigorated counterterrorism effort through the FBI, the National Security Agency (NSA), and other investigative and intelligence-gathering organizations became a top priority for George W. Bush and his successor, Barack Obama, while a more restrictive immigration policy and border-control regime also emerged. Unfortunately, a greater concentration on the prevention of terrorism also meant a corresponding contraction of civil liberties, as intrusions by agencies like the NSA came under fire from various political circles and eventually the public as well. Nevertheless, especially during the Bush years, federal counterterrorist activities proliferated without serious concerns over countervailing constitutional and political implications.[120]

As indicated previously, law enforcement policy also includes immigration, which is under the supervision of the DHS. One of the most divisive issues of the last thirty years, immigration is not confined to worries about terrorist and criminal infiltration into the United States. The real issue here has been illegal immigration, which many Americans blame for high crime rates and runaway social-services expenditures, to say nothing of the popular impression that it causes higher unemployment among citizens and legal residents. Like abortion or the death penalty, this has become a volatile topic that defies rational debate, and separating fact from fiction has become increasingly difficult. However, regardless of the validity of particular arguments about illegal immigration, as is the case with federal entitlements, this has become a looming problem with associated political risks that most presidential administrations have been reluctant to confront. Still, it requires a long-term solution before it spirals out of control. Unexpectedly, George W. Bush offered a compromise solution that was not very different from what Barack Obama would propose a few years later, but it was neither stringent enough for mainstream Republicans nor sufficiently permissive for Democrats.[121]

Crime prevention, immigration, and border security are top priorities, but federal civil-rights protection has been just as important, if not more so, from a symbolic standpoint. Due to the slow pace of political reform following the Civil War, civil-rights enforcement was not a notable federal concern until the late 1950s, but, even then, federal efforts were clearly deficient. However, by the 1960s, sociopolitical mobilization among black Americans and a critical mass of progressive white

Lyndon Johnson signs the Civil Rights Act of 1964 into law.

activists and politicians began to turn the tide against continued institutionalized discrimination and the deprivation of minority civil rights. Once again, the LBJ administration was a pivotal innovator, and its legacy includes pivotal civil-rights reforms and a considerable expansion of federal authority over civil-rights enforcement. Shepherding the Civil Rights Act of 1964 and the Voting Rights Act of 1965 through Congress, LBJ spearheaded a radical reorientation of executive law-enforcement resources. These crucial pieces of legislation extended civil-rights protections to minorities, women, the elderly, the poor, and other disaffected groups marginalized by political discrimination.[122]

Presidential authority to eradicate discrimination under the Civil Rights Act was nonetheless limited, because the legislation targeted public establishments and federal contracts, but Johnson used his powers liberally. Through the Office of Federal Contract Compliance (OFCC), created to prevent discrimination among government contractors, LBJ instituted affirmative action policies that set a broader political precedent. Convinced that a level playing field for the nation's black community could only be secured through a system of racial preferences, Johnson relied on his authority and political credibility to implement a wide array of affirmative action programs.[123] Despite partisan and ideological differences, his immediate successors did not renounce affirmative action programs, especially after the Supreme Court provided its imprimatur through key rulings in the late 1960s and early 1970s. Until Ronald Reagan's election, Republicans did not seriously challenge the viability of affirmative action, preferring to save their political capital for less contentious issues. By the 1990s, even many Democrats had backed away from affirmative action, but a strong commitment to civil-rights enforcement remained.[124]

The Justice Department under Bill Clinton made civil-rights protection a priority, but its civil-rights policies attracted undue criticism from Clinton's political opponents mostly as a result of a few controversial nominees for top posts at Justice. Perhaps the most problematic of these was Lani Guinier, who was labeled by Republicans as the "Quota Queen" and whose unsuccessful nomination cost Clinton considerable political capital. Aforementioned personal scandals further distracted his administration, but the Civil Rights division at Justice was nevertheless quite vigilant during his eight years in office.[125] Like Clinton's Attorney General, Janet Reno, Obama appointee Eric Holder has made civil-rights enforcement a principal concern, but, unlike Reno, Holder has not been saddled with his president's private transgressions. The Obama years have been scandal free, but Holder has come under fire from Republicans for selective prosecution of civil rights cases and a supposed lack of impartiality. His critics aside, Holder has taken a greater interest in civil-rights protection than many of his predecessors.

Natural Resources and Conservation

Last, but definitely not least in terms of global and ecological significance, comes natural resources and conservation. For many Americans, the relatively abstract and long-term nature of this category of policymaking makes it decidedly less relevant than the ones identified earlier, yet it has also caused some of the most furious political debates among and within politicians, interest groups, the media, scholars, and the public itself. Topics such as the environment and climate change, energy, and federal-land use, for instance, are inherently polarizing and seem to breed controversy instead of compromise, inspiring some of the most impassioned and even fanatical sociopolitical movements in the country. However, compared to their concerns over economic conditions, the provision of needed social services, or crime prevention, natural resources and conservation policy garners little attention from ordinary Americans—unless they are confronted by a concrete and pertinent problem arising therefrom. Higher fuel prices or environmental regulations that impact certain kinds of workers, such as loggers and miners, definitely heighten public awareness, particularly among affected groups, but these are exceptions. On the whole, this is a part of policymaking and executive governance that motivates scholars, activists, and specific politicians much more so than the American people at large.

Perhaps the principal reason for this relative apathy is a fundamental lack of proximity for the overwhelming majority of Americans. The issues that compose natural resources and conservation policy lack both spatial and temporal proximity, which means that the bulk of the public is affected by them neither directly nor immediately. Aside from isolated examples, natural resources and conservation policy has a more direct effect on producers than on consumers, and on employers than on employees, so consumers and employees feel the effects further downstream. Moreover, this kind of policy usually involves long-term costs and benefits, since it aims at the resolution of structural dilemmas often defined by historical, evolutionary, and ecological parameters that cannot change substantially in the short term. As such, it seems less relevant to the public, which tends to focus on immediate problems and short-term solutions. The character of American electoral politics simply reinforces this trend, contributing to a political system with a comparatively short attention span, which makes the formulation and implementation of long-term policies extremely difficult. Modern presidents, who have paid increasing attention to natural resources and conservation policy, have therefore been aware of the need to explain and periodically affirm the relevance and benefits of natural resources and conservation policy before the public.

Until worries over fossil fuels were renewed due to skyrocketing prices during the last several years, environmental issues were the most visible aspect of this policy area. Environmental policy is a comparatively recent phenomenon, since awareness of environmental problems such as pollution and resource contamination did not arise until the 1960s. Even so, mainly experts and academics initially paid attention to emerging environmental questions, while politicians and the public remained largely apathetic until at least the 1970s. Widespread air and water pollution along with pesticide contamination had become so obvious that they could not be ignored any longer, while medical research was exposing the health risks associated with further inaction. The Nixon administration responded with the creation of the Environmental Protection Agency (EPA), while a new generation of environmental activists agitated for appropriate reforms and regulations at all levels.[126]

Despite these gains, environmental protection took a back seat to economic expansion and industrial productivity during the Reagan years, and environmental regulation was increasingly seen as the enemy of economic progress and free enterprise. Gradually, however, both the American public and the broader global community became aware of large-scale problems such as climate change and the degradation of the earth's atmosphere, which ensured that past environmental gains would not be completely lost. Bill Clinton's Vice President, Al Gore, made environmental reform and education a personal mission during his two terms, and Clinton's EPA chief, Carol Browner, was a tireless advocate of stricter environmental controls. Still, environmental reforms were not helped by a few distracting controversies over the protection of comparatively insignificant natural habitats at the expense of jobs in vital resource-rich areas.[127] One such incident involved a debate over the spotted owl in the Pacific Northwest and the impact of logging on its habitat, and eventually it even pitted federal agencies against each other in the process. Although the case was ultimately settled in favor of the logging industry, to critics of federal environmental regulation it was a lasting symbol of governmental intrusion and reformist excess.

During the George W. Bush years, environmental policy was once again surpassed by economic priorities, and many Republicans even began to doubt scientific conclusions about global warming. Accordingly, the Bush administration refused to sign the international Kyoto Protocol concerning climate change, a decision that was widely attacked by environmental activists and the president's Democratic opponents. As with many other policy issues, the Obama administration reversed course and recommitted the United States to international cooperation on climate change and other environmental problems, while it rededicated itself to more progressive environmental standards at home. The president's cap-and-trade proposal in 2009 was a step in that direction, but, after approval in the House of Representatives, it languished in the Senate, where the bill was eventually killed. In the end, however, because of the ongoing war in Afghanistan and the nation's pervasive economic difficulties, President Obama has not been able to devote as much attention to reformulating environmental policy as he had hoped, which is just one reason why the cap-and-trade legislation failed.[128]

In addition to environmental policy, energy policy has been a prominent, albeit intermittent, aspect of domestic agendas for a few decades. During the 1970s, the

Arab oil embargo and by-now discredited calculations that the global supply of fossil fuels could be depleted in as little as one hundred years caused widespread worries, if not outright panic, among policymakers and the public. Jimmy Carter was perhaps the first U.S. president to devote considerable attention to the future development of alternative fuels, and he also decried the country's dependence on foreign oil. Carter made energy reform a cornerstone of his domestic agenda once in office, although it had not been part of his campaign agenda in 1976. No other issue on Carter's domestic agenda received as much attention from the White House as the President's national energy plan. As Carter recalled in his memoirs, "Throughout my entire term, Congress and I struggled with energy legislation. Despite my frustration, there was never a moment when I did not consider the creation of a national energy policy equal in importance to any other goal we had."[129]

Carter's response to the energy crisis was a comprehensive policy proposal that demonstrates the multidimensional and strategic process in which presidents can engage when trying to "solve" a policy problem. Regarding legislative action, an internal White House memo suggested the following: "Just over a year ago, the President sent to the Congress a comprehensive national energy plan. As of last week, four of the five parts of that plan had been approved by the Conference Committee. Those four bills will probably be voted on by the full Congress in late July or early August. . . . The purpose of this plan is to hold Congress' collective feet to the fire. Every member who is up for re-election (and even those who aren't) should have to answer to his constituents for Congress' failure to pass an energy plan. We should make no apology for taking them on. . . . However, we should avoid being unnecessarily antagonistic, strident or personal."[130] Bureaucratic action by the Carter White

Jimmy Carter addresses the nation on the energy crisis in 1977.

House included the following: "Recently the numerous energy programs and agencies scattered throughout the government were organized together by President Carter into a new Department of Energy. Some people say that energy programs and policies will now be run much better in this new department. Others say not much will happen, except one more large bureaucracy will have been created."[131] Carter also spoke publicly about intergovernmental action taken by his administration on energy reform: "My Administration has given energy policy a very high priority during the few months we have been in office. Energy policy is not just a Federal activity. It requires a constructive partnership between the states, local governments and Federal Government. This conference marks the beginning of a continuing relationship and dialogue."[132] Finally, public relations were also an important strategic consideration: "The following is a plan for developing public support for the President's energy program.... [create a] citizen's committee...identify and discuss program with influential columnists, editorial writers, and television types...generate public support and statements among influential interest groups... [create a] speakers bureau."[133]

However, despite the attention devoted to energy reform by the White House, Carter's policy proposal was more failure than success. Carter would eventually sign an energy bill into law in November 1978, but it was a much watered-down and altered version of his original plan, which had intended to increase energy efficiency and to decrease the need for oil through a complex package of regulatory and tax measures aimed mostly at the oil industry and businesses to meet the proposed standards of efficiency. Carter had failed in two regards: convincing the American public of the urgency of the plan, and in his ability to work with Congress in passing a comprehensive energy package.[134]

By the 1980s, an economic recovery, substantial gains in fuel efficiency, and more realistic estimates about the world's energy supplies eased the country's anxiety about fossil fuels. Although the Clinton administration devoted more attention to energy policy than its immediate predecessors and sponsored research on alternative fuels, national awareness of these issues was relatively low. Not until the war in Iraq and the associated rise in oil prices did the American people and its public officials realize that the situation required a change in energy policies and a serious consideration of long-term alternatives. Energy policy had become a matter of economic sustainability and also national security, and the country's dependence on foreign sources of oil was just exacerbating existing economic and strategic vulnerabilities.[135]

CONCLUSION

To an outsider unaccustomed to presidential politics, the domestic policymaking process can look like an unorganized sprawl. Indeed, even to those fully conversant with life in the White House, it can resemble organized chaos, at best. However, the president's domestic policymaking process has an inherent logic that underscores a distinctive set of institutional practices. As such, though particular presidents inevitably put their stamps on domestic policymaking through tactical and even strategic procedural changes, the policymaking process ultimately transcends those individuals by shaping the presidency itself. Whereas domestic policymaking is invariably the product of the ideas, people, and organizations that develop specific policies, the process as a social-scientific and historical phenomenon has a permanence and uniqueness that is trans-historical, because it has become a structural feature of the American system of politics. Therefore, in academic parlance, due to the existence of definable and distinguishing practices whose relevance is not merely circumstantial but evolutionary, the presidential policymaking process is a political institution.

Since this is an institution more in the conceptual than the traditional physical sense, it is analyzed and understood through the principal parameters of legitimate decision making, such as constitutionality, rationality, finality and accountability, technical proficiency, and transparency. Each of these decision-making parameters is part of the domestic policymaking process, and each, in differing proportions and intensities, is reflected in the individual policies that constitute presidential agendas. Those agendas, which are a function of partisan priorities, ideological preferences, and presidents' personal backgrounds and experiences, serve as the blueprints for presidential policymaking while in the White House. Though not static or uniformly consistent during presidential tenures, domestic agendas offer stability and direction, and perhaps, above all, they enable the marketing of presidential policies to the public, which is just one of many participants in the domestic policymaking process.

Without a doubt, the most important domestic policymaker is the president himself, but he is supported by a vast network of individuals and organizations within and outside the White House. From an inner circle of presidential advisors to the various policy councils, agencies, and cabinet departments whose expertise is essential to the formulation of feasible and effective policies, this network eventually involves Congress, interest groups, political contributors, the news media, and countless state, county, and municipal governments. These policymakers may not always work as a team, and the results usually do not match original expectations, but they all contribute in some way to the definition and implementation of presidential domestic policies, which touch most aspects of people's lives.

SAVING THE BIG THREE AUTOMAKERS

THEN . . .

Throughout the 1970s, increasingly stringent emissions and safety regulations forced U.S. automakers to make changes for which they were not prepared. In addition, the ongoing energy crises that produced sharply higher fuel costs and warnings about the depletion of world oil reserves put pressure on the Big Three (Ford, Chrysler, and General Motors) to design smaller, more efficient vehicles to replace the huge gas-guzzlers to which Americans had become accustomed. Because of its size, market share, and product line, Chrysler was at a distinct disadvantage compared to Ford and General Motors (GM), and its efforts to meet shifting consumer demand and also address both regulatory necessities and a restricted supply of oil were largely ineffective. To make matters worse, massive recalls of two of the automaker's leading models only compounded mounting financial difficulties, and a lack of fuel-efficient smaller vehicles to replace its fleet of larger cars depressed sales. Even the appointment of former Ford president Lee Iacocca as chief executive officer (CEO) in 1978 did not immediately change the troubled auto manufacturer's fate.[136]

Faced with bankruptcy and possibly the total collapse of Chrysler Corporation, Iacocca asked Congress in mid-1979 for over $1 billion in loan guarantees to save the company. President Jimmy Carter instructed his Treasury Secretary and former Fed Chairman G. William Miller to formulate a bailout package, provided it came with necessary concessions from unions, dealers, and stockholders. Unlike many Democrats at the time, Carter was no fan of government interventions or increased executive regulatory authority, as his deregulation of the transportation industry demonstrated, yet he also realized that the financial crisis at Chrysler left him with few alternatives. Allowing Chrysler to collapse was not a feasible solution for several reasons, among which were catastrophic job losses at a time of rising unemployment, the broader economic reverberations of Chrysler's prospective demise during a decade of recurring recessions, pressure from automobile dealers, and a prohibitively high political cost. That does not mean that the political or even financial cost of a bailout would be trivial, especially for an embattled presidency and Congress whose public approval had been undermined by several years of political scandals and mismanagement. Nevertheless, Carter felt compelled to act, though he made sure that any bailout package would incorporate clear criteria for accountability and key benchmarks for the automaker's recovery.[137]

Within a few months, under the direction of Secretary Miller and key congressional leaders, the federal legislature produced the Chrysler Corporation Loan Guarantee Act, which Carter signed in January of 1980. The law created the Chrysler Loan Guarantee Board, whose responsibility was to manage the loans and supervise repayment. Under the provisions of the bill, the federal government would not directly lend money to Chrysler but would guarantee $1.5 billion of private financing, and Chrysler's workers, shareholders, and dealers would agree to a further $2 billion of mandated concessions. Widely seen as an ineffective Treasury chief unable to manage critical aspects of economic policy, Miller was praised for what was arguably the only tangible achievement during his tenure. Like Miller, Carter had few domestic-policy successes during his time in office, and his legacy has not improved considerably over the years, but this was ultimately a success. By 1983, Chrysler had repaid all of its loans, and the federal government had profited $350 million from its involvement.[138]

In the short term, the Chrysler bailout was obviously effective and justifiable. Under Iacocca's leadership and aggressive new marketing, design, and production strategies, the company rebounded and met all congressional and presidential expectations, even fulfilling its financial obligations to the federal government ahead of schedule. Nevertheless, all was not well. Neither Chrysler nor the other major U.S. car manufacturers had a sustainable long-term business model that was responsive to global economic, demographic, and regulatory trends, to say nothing of changing energy needs. By the 1990s, all three manufacturers were heavily reliant on the production of Sport Utility Vehicles

(SUVs) and pickup trucks, from which they made most of their profits. Despite improvements in fuel efficiency, trucks and SUVs were relatively fuel-intensive, which made them increasingly expensive to own as oil prices rose. At the same time, because of their dependence on trucks and SUVs, U.S. automakers devoted few research dollars to the development of marketable smaller vehicles or those based on alternative fuels.[139]

Over the same period, competition from abroad intensified, and U.S. consumers increasingly turned to foreign manufacturers for vehicles that were more durable, more efficient, and less expensive than those offered by the Big Three. Growing foreign car sales decreased both market share and profitability for U.S. auto manufacturers, eventually leading to some layoffs and plant closures. But, in the long run, a few layoffs and plant closures could not compensate for ongoing union intransigence, poor planning, and less than competent management, so bloated factories continued to operate at much less than optimum capacity. The Big Three faced escalating production costs because of unsustainable United Auto Worker (UAW) contracts that secured the highest wages in the industry, and they became financially overextended through elaborate pension obligations that far exceeded industry standards. Foreign automakers, on the other hand, were opening plants in the United States, mostly in the non-unionized South, whose labor costs were substantially lower and production processes more efficient. Adding insult to injury, foreign car makers were preparing for the future by building vehicles that reflected a gradually but inexorably changing consumer demand. By the end of the second millennium, the stage was set for another crisis; but the next one would involve not just one but all of the Big Three.[140]

. . . AND NOW

By the beginning of the new millennium, things did not look promising for U.S. auto manufacturers, particularly for GM and Chrysler. Yet, as hobbled as they had become due to a series of management and production blunders and the inability to adapt to evolving market realities, they might have limped into the twenty-first century with some hope of a turnaround had circumstances not intervened and accelerated their decline. The first of these was the terrorist attack on the United States in September 2001, which prompted the wars in Afghanistan and Iraq. The resulting regional political instability coupled with a disruption in oil production led to record fuel prices in the United States and elsewhere. In addition, because the major domestic oil companies had not adequately invested in the expansion of production and refining capabilities, their ability to confront rising oil prices through increased production was limited, which constricted supply and destabilized commodities markets even more. Neither the cost of crude oil nor the price of fuel at the pump declined significantly, compelling consumers to buy less expensive, more efficient foreign cars instead of the big SUVs and trucks that had generated the Big Three's profits. Within a few years, their domestic market share dipped below 50 percent, a significant decline from the almost 80 percent during the troubled 1970s.[141]

Executives from the "Big Three" automakers testify before Congress in 2009.

The second event accelerating the decline of U.S. automakers was the subprime mortgage crisis of 2008, which precipitated a banking collapse that crippled many of the nation's leading investment banks and insurance companies. The lending crisis deepened an economic recession that had begun at the end of 2007, further shrinking consumer confidence and purchasing power and severely restricting the availability of investment capital. Meanwhile, as the health of the U.S. auto industry declined, the Big Three were able to secure minor concessions from auto workers and make some retrenchments through asset divestitures, but it was all too little, too late. In the autumn of 2008, U.S. automakers asked Congress for help, claiming they needed cash immediately to meet benefit costs and pension liabilities and also to avoid financial collapse altogether. In testimony before congressional committees, company representatives warned that failure to act could lead to the loss of as many as three million jobs over the ensuing twelve months. Congress, in turn, requested sustainable restructuring plans from all three automakers, which they submitted, but the legislature was not convinced that auto executives were truly committed to change and viable restructuring.[142]

Having failed to obtain what they needed from Congress, auto executives then turned directly to the George W. Bush administration and Treasury Secretary Henry Paulson, who had been a corporate executive himself. Before the end of the year, the Bush team formulated a plan to save the auto industry with almost $25 billion of government loans for GM and Chrysler and a temporary line of credit for Ford, whose position was not as dire as those of the other two. Contrary to what had been the case with Chrysler in 1979, these were not loan guarantees, whereby the government was just a co-signer for privately obtained financing; they were direct loans from federal coffers. To avoid congressional battles over funding and a prolonged legislative process, the Bush administration decided to use funds from the already created Troubled Asset Relief Program (TARP), which had been established to rescue the banking and insurance industries. Authorized to spend up to $700 billion,

TARP faced a much broader problem than just the failure of U.S. auto manufacturers, so it could more than adequately cover the auto bailout. As a result of the bailout plan, the federal government became a substantial shareholder in GM and Chrysler, which was an equity stake it would relinquish as the companies repaid their loans.[143]

The short-term infusion of cash proved inadequate to the task for both GM and Chrysler, as original congressional skepticism regarding the automakers' plans for restructuring was vindicated. President Obama, who had taken office after the initial bailout agreement had been finalized, refused requests for additional funds unless the two companies were able to provide him and the administration's experts with a viable strategy for long-term sustainability and a restructuring plan that addressed prevailing market realities. In the end, neither company was able to avoid continuing financial problems, declining sales, prohibitive labor costs, and mounting pension obligations, but Chrysler was a particular mess and was faced with the prospect of absolute collapse. Finally, it sought protection under a bankruptcy filing in May 2009, and GM followed only a month later. Since then, all three automakers have implemented significant strategic and operational reforms, while the bankruptcy courts were able to enforce mandated concessions from the unions, shareholders, and member dealers.[144] As Obama reported in his 2012 State of the Union address:

> On the day I took office, our auto industry was on the verge of collapse. Some even said we should let it die. With a million jobs at stake, I refused to let that happen. In exchange for help, we demanded responsibility. We got workers and automakers to settle their differences. We got the industry to retool and restructure. Today, General Motors is back on top as the world's number-one automaker. Chrysler has grown faster in the U.S. than any major car company. Ford is investing billions in U.S. plants and factories. And together, the entire industry added nearly a hundred and sixty thousand jobs. We bet on American workers. We bet on American ingenuity. And tonight, the American auto industry is back.[145]

SUGGESTED READINGS

Axilrod, Stephen H. 2009. *Inside the Fed: Monetary Policy and Its Management, Martin through Greenspan to Bernanke.* Cambridge, MA: MIT Press.

Dolan, Chris J., John Frendreis, and Raymond Tatalovich. 2007. *The Presidency and Economic Policy.* New York: Rowman & Littlefield.

Herrnson, Paul S., Ronald G. Shaiko, and Clyde Wilcox, eds. 2004. *The Interest Group Connection: Electioneering, Lobbying, and Policymaking in Washington,* 2nd ed. Washington, DC: CQ Press.

Kingdon, John W. 2002. *Agendas, Alternatives, and Public Policies.* New York: Longman Press.

Lammers, William W., and Michael A. Genovese. 2000. *The Presidency and Domestic Policy: Comparing Leadership Styles, FDR to Clinton.* Washington, DC: CQ Press.

Levin, Martin A., Daniel DiSalvo, and Martin M. Shapiro, eds. 2012. *Building Coalitions, Making Policy: The Politics of the Clinton, Bush, and Obama Presidencies.* Baltimore:

Johns Hopkins University Press.

Light, Paul. 1998. *The President's Agenda: Domestic Policy Choice from Kennedy to Clinton.* Baltimore: Johns Hopkins University Press.

Nelson, Michael, and Russell L. Riley, eds. 2011. *Governing at Home: The White House and Domestic Policymaking.* Lawrence: University Press of Kansas.

Rudalevige, Andrew. 2002. *Managing the President's Program: Presidential Leadership and Legislative Policy Formation.* Princeton, NJ: Princeton University Press.

Warshaw, Shirley Anne. 1996. *The Domestic Presidency: Policy Making in the White House.* New York: Longman.

ON THE WEB

http://www.cbpp.org/. The Center on Budget and Policy Priorities is a non-profit organization that develops research and analysis on budgeting and tax policy.

http://www.federalreserve.gov/. The web page of the Federal Reserve System, which is the central bank of the United States founded by Congress in 1913 to provide the nation with a safer, more flexible, and more stable monetary and financial system.

http://www.whitehouse.gov/administration/eop/dpc. The Domestic Policy Council (DPC) is the home of the domestic policymaking process in the White House. It offers advice to the president, supervises the execution of domestic policy, and represents the president's priorities to Congress.

IN THEIR OWN WORDS

SIGNING MEDICARE INTO LAW

Passage of Medicare legislation in 1965 is considered one of Lyndon Johnson's greatest domestic policy achievements. As the final vote by Congress to approve the bill neared, discussions began among White House advisors about the public venue in which Johnson would sign the bill into law. Horace Busby, a special assistant to the president and a key domestic policy advisor believed strongly that the bill should be signed at the White House, and not at the Truman Library in Independence, Missouri, with former President Harry Truman in attendance. Despite his objections to his colleagues Special Assistants to the President Jack Valenti and Douglass Cater, Press Secretary Bill Moyers, and Chief of Staff Marvin Watson, Johnson's desire to sign the bill with Truman, one of the first presidents to argue for national health care, won out. Yet, as Busby's memo shows, some of the political concerns that existed in 1965 sound similar to political concerns experienced by later Democratic presidents in their attempts to reform health care:

> I have been working on advance plans for an appropriate ceremony at the time of the President's signing of the Medicare Legislation and want to pass these thoughts on that subject:
>
> 1. The suggested signing at Independence, Missouri, seems inadvisable. [Under Secretary for Legislation of Health, Education, and Welfare] Wilber Cohen shares this view, heatedly. The association of the present legislation with President Truman's 1945 proposal would be grotesque distortion with unhappy and impolitic overtones. President Truman requested medical coverage for all

the population, regardless of age—a close parallel to Great Britain's "socialized medicine." The connotation of a signing at Independence would be not that Truman's work had been completed, but that President Johnson next intended to enlarge Medicare to meet Truman's objectives.

The results of a signing at Independence would—in Wilbur Cohen's judgment and mine—be (1) more unfavorable than favorable reaction, (2) a boycott and denunciation of the ceremony by leaders of the AMA with whom we are now attempting to work and (3) most likely some distasteful remarks by President Truman himself about the medical profession.

2. The Medicare Bill as passed runs 400 pages. Engrossment will be time consuming. If rushed, the Bill could reach the White House in time for signing by the end of this month—on July 30 or 31. Cohen advises that because of certain provisions in the legislation, this would mean a slight speed up in payment of some $30 million to widows and orphans—a speed up of approximately one month.

3. If the processing of the Bill is not accelerated, it would come for signing during the month of August. Cohen points out that August 15 is the anniversary of the original Social Security Act. Since August 15 falls on Sunday, it would be fitting to sign the Bill at Hyde Park on Saturday, August 14—if such a ceremony is desired.

4. My own strong inclination is against dramatizing the Bill by a trip out of Washington. Inevitably, this will turn into a circus. Such a dramatization in a quest for publicity might unhappily coincide with somber decisions or news relative to Viet Nam.

5. Cohen advises that the tentative guest list he will recommend runs up to several hundred—perhaps as many as 700. This assumes a White House ceremony, of course. My opinion is that the Bill Signing needs very little gingerbread to make it newsworthy and historic. I doubt the wisdom of the President "playing FDR" at the particular time in history—it will add credence to the adverse images of vanity, self-centeredness, etc. So, my strong recommendation is that the signing ceremony be held at the White House and that our energies be directed toward making the guest list newsworthy, both in numbers and composition.[146]

CHAPTER 10

Presidents and Foreign Policymaking

On October 9, 2009, the Norwegian Nobel Committee awarded that year's Peace Prize to recently inaugurated President Barack Obama. It was a decision that surprised many, even the recipient himself, not because Obama was undeserving but mostly because he had no tangible foreign-policy accomplishments so early in his tenure. Only two previous sitting presidents, Theodore Roosevelt and Woodrow Wilson, had won the Peace Prize, but they had been recognized for specific contributions to international peace. Roosevelt negotiated an end to the Russo-Japanese War, and Wilson was instrumental in creating the League of Nations following World War I. One former president, Jimmy Carter, also received the Nobel Peace Prize, which reflected his numerous years of work after he left the White House to promote human rights throughout the developing world. Yet, according to analysts and the Nobel Committee itself, President Obama won the prize more for what he and his presidency represented than for any concrete foreign-policy achievements. According to the Committee's statement, Obama was chosen "for his extraordinary efforts to strengthen international diplomacy and cooperation between peoples. The Committee has attached special importance to Obama's vision of and work for a world without nuclear weapons. Obama has as President created a new climate in international politics. Multilateral diplomacy has regained a central position, with emphasis on the role that the United Nations and other international institutions can play. Dialogue and negotiations are preferred as instruments for resolving even the most difficult international conflicts."[1] In the end, this was as much a symbolic gesture of international approbation for a president who ostensibly offered a return to multilateralism and a simultaneous rebuke of George W. Bush as it was a recognition of particular contributions to global peace.

A few months prior to receiving the Nobel Prize, Obama visited Egypt's Cairo University, where he delivered his "New Beginning" speech. Signaling a marked departure in tone, substance, and direction from George W. Bush, if not most of his modern-day predecessors, Obama emphasized comity, compassion, and non-interference as cornerstones of American foreign policy:

> So long as our relationship is defined by our differences, we will empower those who sow hatred rather than peace, those who promote conflict rather than the cooperation that can help all of our people achieve justice and prosperity. And this cycle of suspicion and discord must end. I've come here to Cairo to seek a new beginning between the United States and Muslims around the world, one based on mutual interest and mutual respect, and one based upon the truth that America and Islam are not exclusive and need not be in competition. Instead, they overlap, and share common principles—principles of justice and progress; tolerance and the dignity of all human beings.[2]

Accordingly, tolerance of Islam and Muslim cultures, support for Palestinian statehood, multilateral diplomacy, and respect for self-determination in the Middle East would be just some of the objectives for Obama's foreign-policy team. By its own admission, the Nobel Committee was greatly influenced by this speech in choosing Obama, as it was by the president's ongoing advocacy of nuclear disarmament and climate control, to say nothing of Obama's popularity among nations that had become alienated by Bush's policies. As it had done on other occasions over the years, the committee selected someone with a rising international stature among the disaffected and a reputation as a bridge builder and humanitarian.

In so doing, like various other international actors over the years, the Nobel Committee injected itself into the U.S. policymaking process by providing its imprimatur in key foreign-policy areas. The resulting expectations would inevitably shape the president's goals in those areas and influence the formulation of foreign policies in Obama's administration, as would the associated international pressure to fulfill the promises the prize represented. This does not mean the Nobel Committee's choice was a naked political act devoid of substantive merit, but it does reveal something quite significant about the nature of foreign policy. First, it aptly demonstrates that U.S. foreign policy does not occur in a vacuum, for it cannot be insulated from myriad external inputs. As such, foreign policy reflects both the internal priorities that arise from the domestic political environment and the external influences that emerge from continuing international intercourse. Second, and on a more specific level, this situation illustrates the role of international actors in U.S. foreign policymaking. The policymaking process is complex and multifaceted, and it depends on a diverse and constantly shifting coalition of actors whose contributions, though not always desired, are nonetheless essential.

Within the present context, awarding the Peace Prize to President Obama was noteworthy for another reason. Symbolizing the promise of an Obama presidency and the ideal of post-Soviet multilateralism, which had eluded even Bill Clinton, it ultimately exposed the fundamental difference between hopes and realities. Although Barack Obama came to the White House with hopes of reversing many of his predecessor's policies and establishing a kind of neo-Wilsonian world order based not on a Pax Americana but international comity and global multilateralism, realities have prevailed and have compelled him to compromise that vision. Escalation of the war in Afghanistan and intervention in Libya, albeit as part of a NATO-based coalition, are but two examples of that development, and even the withdrawal of troops from Iraq, which was completed by the end of 2011, did not go according to plan. These provide evidence of the fact that, perhaps above all, foreign policy is about continuity and compromise; compromise between what is desirable and what is achievable and also the invariable continuity, despite occasional transformative changes, among presidencies due to overriding historical factors, geopolitical circumstances, bureaucratic inertia, and public pressure.

A combination of hope and reality, foreign policy invokes many of the seminal foundational principles upon which the republic was created, and it necessitates a proficiency of diplomatic and military skill that only the presidency can provide. Despite variations in leadership style, ideology, and training among presidents and, thus, corresponding disparities regarding strategic and diplomatic priorities, this diversity has not undermined the continuity and evolutionary character of U.S. foreign policy. Moreover, from an institutional perspective, the periodic creation of new agencies, offices, and departments notwithstanding, the policymaking process, though incredibly intricate and frequently sprawling, has developed its own logic that survives individual presidents and helps define the presidency. Governed by a group of actors that includes the president, his staff and advisors, legislators, ad hoc experts, lobbyists, international organizations, foreign governments, and a host of others, and reflecting national strategic priorities and political ideals as well as international concerns, foreign-policy making is an essential part of presidential politics in the United States.

U.S. FOREIGN POLICY

The policymaking process creates a link between political agendas and the foundational principles of government by providing a constitutional basis and practical rationale for institutional action. It applies such principles to targeted political objectives whose realization is critical for effective governance. Complex, intricate, and often confusing, policymaking comprises a number of institutions and scores of individuals, none of which is more important than the President of the United States. Although the president was originally overshadowed by Congress, he has become America's policymaker in chief. Congress, interest groups, the media, and the American people all play central roles and occasionally even pre-empt the president, but only he has the potential to dominate policymaking on an ongoing basis. Of course, this will not happen with a president who lacks required leadership skills and the ability to govern effectively. However, no institution other than the presidency is capable of controlling the policymaking process as thoroughly. Through its public exposure, bureaucratic and political expertise, prospective influence over legislators, and access to other relevant players, the modern presidency is uniquely equipped to set governing agendas.

Every country has both internal and external priorities, which are addressed through their leaders' political agendas. In the United States, these agendas are realized through separate yet overlapping domestic and foreign-policy establishments that intersect at the White House and are unified through executive leadership and an underlying national interest. Domestic policy is often more relevant to the everyday existence of ordinary Americans, and presidential candidates customarily prioritize domestic over international priorities in their campaigns, because bread-and-butter issues resonate more strongly among the electorate. In addition, due to most candidates' comparative lack of foreign-policy experience, all but a few of them unsurprisingly focus on the domestic policy topics with which they are most familiar, which only appears to confirm the greater significance of domestic policy. Still, regardless of their campaign platforms and political leanings, presidents frequently become preoccupied with foreign policy to the exclusion, or detriment, of the domestic agendas that got them elected. Other pertinent factors aside, such as ongoing geopolitical developments and commitments, America's commanders in chief ultimately cannot afford to ignore, minimize, or defer the vital military and diplomatic concerns that define national security and international survival.

Because of the social and political demands of an industrialized economy, domestic priorities have become a predominant focus of federal governance, especially during the past several decades. An overwhelming part of the federal budget is allocated for domestic spending, and the bulk of the government's day-to-day business is devoted to domestic needs. Yet, one of the principal reasons the federal government, and particularly the presidency, exists is to conduct foreign policy. In 1787, the framers of the Constitution created a limited government with comparatively few duties and responsibilities, but foremost among those was foreign policy, which the previous American government was unable to address. So, from a historical perspective, foreign policy is arguably more essential than its domestic counterpart, not least because this was one task the states were incapable of fulfilling individually. The situation may be different today, but the significance of foreign policy cannot be exaggerated.

Foreign policy addresses America's relationship with other countries and its role in the international arena. Viewed another way, it acknowledges the fact that individual countries do not exist in a vacuum and, for better or worse, are shaped by the influences and interactions among them. In the United States, as a manifestation of popular will, foreign policy not only animates core constitutional principles and political ideals but also promotes national interests through resources and capabilities whose aim is the protection of American assets and the advancement of American strategic priorities throughout the world. Although foreign policy invariably focuses outward, its link to an overriding national interest and, thus, the internal integrity of the United States, is undeniable. Whether through the realization of geopolitical objectives that secure the country's international footprint or the pursuit of economic goals that support American growth and prosperity, foreign policy is an outgrowth and function of internal, or domestic, priorities that define national interest. Without this connection, foreign policy would be meaningless and irrelevant, the mere manifestation of naked political will.[3]

Above all, foreign policy is the link between relevant constitutional principles and the political means employed in their pursuit. In other words, foreign policy connects constitutional politics with ordinary politics and, in so doing, transforms ideals into realities. Consequently, viable foreign policies must be constitutionally valid, and connection to an actual constitutional principle or provision is essential. Otherwise, foreign-policy objectives lack legitimacy and could attract debilitating constitutional and statutory scrutiny, to say nothing of public disapproval. History has also shown that viable foreign policies must be achievable, or, as the Vietnam experience proves, they will lose public support and the much-needed consent of the electorate. If American policymaking during the Vietnam War illustrated anything, it was that unachievable foreign policies are politically and constitutionally harmful, because they foster strategic and tactical failures and breed the kind of mistrust that can paralyze the political process. Both Lyndon Johnson and Richard Nixon dealt with extensive protests of their administrations' policies in Vietnam; LBJ often endured chants of "Hey, Hey, LBJ, How many kids did you kill today?" from protesters outside the gates of the White House. Vietnam also played a crucial role in Johnson's decision to withdraw from the Democratic primaries in 1968, as he famously told a stunned nation on March 31, 1968:

> Believing this as I do, I have concluded that I should not permit the Presidency to become involved in the partisan divisions that are developing in this political year. With America's sons in the fields far away, with America's future under challenge right here at home, with our hopes and the world's hopes for peace in the balance every day, I do not believe that I should devote an hour or a day of my time to any personal partisan causes or to any duties other than the awesome duties of this office—the Presidency of your country. Accordingly, I shall not seek, and I will not accept, the nomination of my party for another term as your President. But let men everywhere know, however, that a strong, a confident, and a vigilant America stands ready tonight to seek an honorable peace—and stands ready tonight to defend an honored cause—whatever the price, whatever the burden, whatever the sacrifice that duty may require.[4]

Finally, foreign policy must promote real national interests whose value is not solely determined by partisan priorities. Agenda setting may be intrinsically partisan, but policies whose partisan interest outweighs national interest are patently invalid.[5]

The creation of foreign policy, or non-domestic political objectives, also involves the formulation of strategy, which is an overall plan for the realization of corresponding policy goals and includes a justification of proposed methods and expected resources. Whereas policy is largely determined by the nation's top political leaders and their advisors, such as the president, key Pentagon and State department officials, along with other national-security and intelligence principals, strategic planning primarily involves high-level support personnel who have responsibilities for the implementation of presidential policies. Their work is augmented through the operational and tactical activities of the men and women that execute specific strategies through corresponding military and diplomatic operations. Obviously, this is a crucial step, because, without it, everything else is just talk and conjecture. It turns policy and strategy into reality by allocating required resources and authority for actual programs, whose existence is merely hypothetical until then. Focusing on performance, execution, and service as opposed to mere concepts and ideas, operational activities enhance national-security capabilities and build infrastructural support through military campaigns, diplomatic initiatives, and the enabling congressional legislation that authorizes the mobilization of allocated resources toward the realization of foreign-policy objectives.[6]

However, it is important to remember that the political aspect of foreign policy, and the effect that it may have on public opinion among the American electorate, or other nations around the globe, cannot be ignored. For example, five months into the Korean War in November 1950, the political implications of U.S. involvement were a key element in military strategy for the Truman administration, as shown in this summary of a meeting of the National Security Council, which is a key advisory group for presidents regarding foreign policy:

> Secretary [of State Dean] Acheson said there were three elements involved: (1) political; (2) intelligence; (3) military. Politically we have tried to keep the military conquest of all Korea from being a war aim. In the UN we have never allowed any resolution to require expelling the Communists from all of Korea. We also have not said that we would stay there until that objective has been achieved. Therefore, politically we are not committed to the conquest of all Korea if something short of that can be worked out which is satisfactory.... The Soviets would presumably like to have the U.S. involved in a general war with Communist China, which would mean that our European commitments would have to go by the board. This raises the question as to what point the U.S. will be driven to, to attack the problem at its heart, namely, Moscow, instead of handling it on the periphery as at present. General [Oliver P.] Smith pointed out that the Soviets take no risk, since they are perfectly willing to pull the rug out from under their satellite at any time and start talking peace. General Smith, however, felt that the Soviets could hardly contemplate giving up Korea and suffering a major defeat there. General Smith said that we are at the point of facing the question of either going forward or back. He suggested, however, that the political consequences of either standing pat or drawing back would be tremendous. He saw no real reason to change the previous estimate that the Soviets are not prepared themselves to bring on a general war. They would, however, like us involved in a general war in Asia.[7]

Diplomacy vs. National Security

A president's foreign policy objectives necessarily reflect two complementary but distinct concerns, diplomacy and national security, whose goals and priorities should be unified but are not always reconcilable. Ideally, one is an extension of the other, and they work hand in hand toward underlying political objectives. Whether through failure or success, diplomacy should in some way set the stage for the execution of national-security policies that follow. The negotiation, deliberation, and debate that characterize diplomacy should animate and support the strategic and tactical activities national security demands. However, despite the unification of diplomatic and national-security interests under a common foreign policy, presidents do not always successfully align those interests, and their diplomatic and national-security establishments do not always read from the same script. Indeed, the Departments of State and Defense have frequently been at odds over the resolution of important geopolitical questions and the prioritization of specific national interests. For example, Secretary of State Colin Powell and Secretary of Defense Donald Rumsfeld did not always agree on the foreign policy strategy of the George W. Bush administration following the 9/11 terrorist attacks in 2001, particularly the invasion of Iraq in 2003.[8]

A prominent cause of the institutional, if not inherent, inconsistency between diplomacy and national security is their frequently divergent goals. Theoretically, they promote unified political objectives and, therefore, support complementary policies, but one rejects war while the other depends on it. By definition, diplomacy focuses on the peaceful resolution of strategic questions and the prevention of conflict, whereas national security accepts the possibility, if not probability, of conflict and the use of military force to secure political objectives. America's Cold War containment policy provides a fitting example of this practical inconsistency. While both the diplomatic and defense establishments were committed to containment until at least Ronald Reagan's presidency, they often worked at cross-purposes. For instance, during the 1970s, diplomats promoted détente, or a cooling of tensions between the United States and the Soviet Union, but the military simultaneously pursued its strategy of Mutually Assured Destruction (MAD). MAD, though hardly something defense leaders wanted or anticipated, called for the total deployment of the nation's nuclear arsenal against the Soviets. Despite the fact that MAD was, first and foremost, a deterrent, its implementation was not merely hypothetical.

Another reason for inconsistencies between diplomatic and national-security objectives is much more human, as it arises from institutional territoriality. The Departments of State and Defense may answer to the same commander in chief, but they have developed different cultures and different priorities, which has often led to friction between the two. Partly, this is due to the practical distinction between national security and diplomacy discussed previously, but, in addition, their differences stem from divergent evolutionary paths that have produced two distinct institutions with almost impenetrable boundaries. In the context of international politics, this has manifested itself in some unusual and perhaps unexpected ways, as American presidents' diplomatic and defense teams have developed divergent goals and allegiances.[9]

The differences between diplomacy and national security notwithstanding, foreign policy is a top priority for modern presidents, and its importance is only affirmed through the growth of the so-called national security state over the past several decades. Both the State and Defense Departments have been enthusiastic supporters of the defense buildup during that period, and neither has done much to dispel post–Cold War rumors that foreign policy would take a back seat to domestic political agendas. The creation of vast diplomatic, strategic, and tactical resources during the Cold War was considered necessary by all involved, and, despite recent geopolitical changes, foreign-policy and defense resources are still considerable. The end of the Cold War never brought the peace dividend for which many had hoped, and defense and foreign-policy goals have not become more modest or less significant. The uncertainty of a post-Soviet world seemed to demand better, smarter, and more expensive weapons, and the events of September 11, 2001, merely affirmed America's commitment to state-of-the-art defense and diplomatic capabilities.

Diplomacy and national security may be at odds occasionally, or even inherently, but their overall objective is clear. Foreign policy exists to promote, secure, and maintain national strategic interests in international theaters. Through its foreign policy, the United States manages relationships and treaty obligations with other countries and addresses potential and existing security threats at home and abroad. Although specific policies vary from administration to administration, the overriding goal of U.S. foreign policy has been consistent throughout its history. Some presidents have been unilateralists while others have been internationalists, and still others have been somewhere in between. Some have been dovish while others have been hawkish, and some have been staunchly pro-Israeli while others have been more sympathetic to Palestinian and Arab priorities. Nevertheless, they all have acknowledged that the primary objective of American foreign policy is to optimize national interest and strategic opportunities in a way that conforms with relevant constitutional principles and underlying political ideals. Whether through the neutrality and comparative isolationism of the first several generations or the more interventionist, yet also collaborative, approach of the last several, the main concern of American foreign policy has been its strategic interests at home and abroad.[10]

Economic Interests

Although the essential, if not predominant, focus of foreign policy is the promotion of American strategic interests abroad, it inherently includes economic priorities as well. The media and the public almost invariably concentrate on the political aspects of diplomatic and national-security policies, which is to be expected, but the country's international economic and financial agendas constitute a critical part of its foreign policy. In many ways, economic and political, especially strategic, interests are two sides of the same coin, as the nation's economic and military capabilities are inextricably interdependent, so the advancement of one logically serves the other. However, regardless of this natural interdependence, the country's economic objectives are served through the foreign-policy establishment on their own terms. Continued economic progress depends on the penetration and management of international and foreign markets, and the realization of American economic and financial goals in the global arena is necessary for long-term microeconomic and macroeconomic prosperity.[11]

As indicated, American economic and strategic objectives are often complementary, and, not surprisingly, national-security resources have occasionally been used to secure economic assets abroad. This fact has often provided fodder for conspiracy theorists and other critics of the nation's foreign policies, but the utilization of military resources to protect American economic interests has been necessary at times. Normally, international economic objectives are realized through negotiations, trade agreements, political and economic liberalization initiatives abroad, or similar means, but geopolitical exigencies can and do obviate diplomatic resolutions. The nation's global economic presence obviously supports its political influence abroad, but it also strengthens its domestic viability. America's economic prosperity relies as much on international relationships and global markets as it does on domestic output and consumption, and, because military and political strength is a function of economic strength, continued economic prosperity will always be a primary concern for the nation's foreign-policy establishment.

PRESIDENTS AND FOREIGN POLICYMAKING

Foreign policymaking is complicated, and it involves scores, if not hundreds, of individuals and several institutions. At its best, it is a collaborative process that leverages the combined expertise of its participants toward effective results. At its worst, however, it is a chaotic sprawl captured by petty jealousies and political hypercompetitiveness, promoting nothing more than partisanship and personal ambition. Reality usually lies somewhere between these two extremes. Ideally, of course, policymaking is approximated by the former, not the latter. Envisioned as a collaborative process based on the consideration of viable alternatives, its intentions are best conveyed through the so-called rational-actor model of executive decision making.

The Rational-Actor Model

Pioneered by political scientist Graham Allison after studying the activities of the Kennedy administration during the Cuban Missile Crisis of 1962, the rational-actor model describes how key decisions should be made by political leaders, especially in democratic environments. According to Allison, the key to viable policymaking is rationality, which enhances both the legitimacy and the effectiveness of the process. Decisions without reflection, representative participation, or awareness of valid options are inherently flawed, as are those that arise from coercion, manipulation, or dishonesty. A mock collaboration intended to bias the process toward pre-determined outcomes is irrational and, therefore, lacks merit. The identification of policy and the formulation of strategy must be a function of true collaboration and an earnest consideration of alternatives, and the final decision must optimize the public interest and support the constitutional principles at stake. Above all, the process, though headed by a president who has the ultimate power and authority to make decisions, must be sufficiently democratic to permit free competition among ideas and, thus, enable the survival of the most viable options. The president may have the constitutional right to make decisions without consultation, but the need for rationality contradicts such an approach.[12]

Despite their significance, presidents' contributions to policymaking do not necessarily arise from the kinds of circumstances the rational-actor model predicts. Far from being uniformly rational, presidential policymaking can deviate from the norm considerably. It is not always collaborative, nor is it predominantly deliberative. Presidents frequently steer toward pre-determined political objectives, and their decision making can be more idiosyncratic than logical, all of which precludes free choice and competition. Connection to overriding constitutional principles, though necessary in theory, is often tenuous at best, and national interest habitually takes a back seat to selfish interest. The president's personal ambitions, as well as those of his advisors, his party, influential legislators, and powerful interest groups more than occasionally occupy center stage, while the news media exploit political differences among policymakers to feed consumer demand for sensational stories. The result, though far from disastrous, is also far from the ideal represented by the rational-actor model.

Indeed, Allison's own research ultimately demonstrated that, under extraordinary circumstances, foreign policymaking is anything but rational. In crisis situations, pivotal decisions are usually dominated by the president or a few key advisors, and they customarily produce predetermined outcomes. An apparently collaborative effort is used to steer policymakers toward the president's favored options, while alternative choices are seldom considered seriously. During the Cuban Missile Crisis, for example, John Kennedy crafted a response to Soviet deployment of nuclear weapons in Cuba through the so-called Executive Committee, which he and his brother

Robert Kennedy, the Attorney General, actually utilized to advance their own strategic and tactical priorities. The consensus among Kennedy's top advisors pointed in a direction the president refused to follow until the president persuaded most of his detractors to change their minds. The American response to the Soviet action was ultimately successful and probably averted a nuclear war, but it was hardly rational.[13]

Similarly, George W. Bush's Middle East policy after terrorist incursions against the United States in 2001 was anything but rational. The available evidence indicates that President Bush came to Washington with the desire to reshape geopolitical dynamics in the Middle East and, if possible, to complete the destruction of the Iraqi regime begun by his father ten years earlier. After the terrorist acts of September 2001, President Bush, Vice President Dick Cheney, and Secretary of State Donald Rumsfeld advocated a strategy that called for the democratization of rogue states through the invasion of Iraq and the pursuit of terrorist networks throughout the region. The administration short-circuited serious deliberations and scuttled the consideration of alternatives so it could press for the adoption of its foreign-policy goals, which were eventually accepted by a Congress reluctant to make difficult decisions and more than willing to pass them on to the president. In addition, the public, smarting from the first attacks on American soil since 1941 and eager for revenge, posed few obstacles to the realization of Bush's objectives.[14]

In the end, the preceding examples and others like them say a lot about what policymaking is not, but they also reveal something about what it is. The process is not so much irrational as it is less rational than scholars would like. Presidents and their key aides often dominate the identification of policy, because they wish to fulfill campaign promises and, more importantly, insure the acceptance of those political objectives most dear to them. Rationality may require the identification and deliberation of actual policy alternatives, especially since this leads to more prudent and balanced decision making, but reality does not afford presidents this luxury. The American public expects its political leaders to be resolute, decisive, and clear by offering a recognizable political agenda that sets immediate priorities. Because presidents have distinct and definite policy goals, most of which invariably reflect choices they made prior to assuming office, they are dedicated to the realization of their goals and not someone else's. Thus, to assume that any president would be willing to set his political agenda by committee is foolish. For better or worse, presidential agendas largely reflect the personal preferences and choices of America's chief executives, and, while those agendas are also influenced and shaped by other policymakers and pressure groups, they do not usually emerge through democratic input.

The Political Agenda

Presidents are elected for a number of reasons, not the least of which is the political agendas they promote during campaigns. Whether they ultimately uphold the principles and ideas touted during their campaigns or not, they are nonetheless guided by an overriding and, usually, evolving set of priorities that reflect their beliefs and interests as well as those of their key supporters and advisors. So, foreign policy and the policymaking process generally are inherently influenced by those beliefs and interests, which means that certain alternatives and possibilities are precluded a priori. To be sure, unique geopolitical circumstances or inherited foreign-policy dilemmas can cause presidents, such as Barack Obama in his handling of the so-called War on Terror, to abandon specific parts of their agendas (such as the closing of Guantanamo Bay), at least temporarily, but presidential policy agendas militate against the kind of rationality scholars would like to see. This does not make the policymaking process illegitimate simply because it is structurally skewed toward political and partisan interests that prevent the complete and open consideration of all ideas. It merely confirms that, in the real world, limits to strict rationality of decision making do and must exist.

Yet, history has also demonstrated that, the apparent irrationality that defines crisis situations notwithstanding, even in emergencies, executive policymaking is not unilateral. For many reasons, among them efficiency and efficacy, decision-making processes during crises are abbreviated and confined, but presidents still rely on the advice and input of key advisors. President George W. Bush may have isolated himself from normal decision-making channels during the aftermath of the terrorist attacks on the United States, but he continued to depend on deliberation among his principal foreign-policy officials, whose contributions were essential. Though critics and skeptics often had limited access to the President and the policymaking process, decisions nevertheless reflected a consensus among those closest to Bush, such as Cheney, Rumsfeld, National Security Advisor Condoleezza Rice, and political strategist Karl Rove, to name a few of the most prominent. Admittedly, some presidents have viewed policymaking, even in national-security matters, as a more collaborative process, as was the case with Jimmy Carter and also his successor Ronald Reagan, but ultimately presidents have borne the responsibility for the nation's foreign policies and particularly for decisions made during crisis situations.[15]

While the price for irrationality in foreign policy can be quite high, especially if key policies are driven primarily by ideology without a regard for situational peculiarities and circumstantial demands, foreign-policy making in the United States, whether rational or not, is constrained by standards of accountability that do not exist in authoritarian regimes, or even in many other democratic governments for that matter. American presidents and their foreign-policy teams are accountable to the public, and their decisions must be defensible and at least seemingly rational to maintain public approval. However, foreign policy issues are often complex and not easily summarized by the news media, which is the prime source of information on which American citizens form their opinions on the job the president is doing. The frustration that presidents often experience with news media coverage of foreign-policy matters, as articulated to President Kennedy by a top advisor in 1962, has been a recurring theme in most administrations:

> One of the most critical problems facing this Administration in the field of foreign policy is the great and growing gap between the harsh, complex realities with which Washington policymakers must grapple and the generally limited understanding of these realities by most Americans, including the press and Congress. This gap is already dangerous. Unless it can be narrowed you may find it increasingly difficult to take many actions in the conduct of foreign policy that are essential to our national security. Our media of mass communication carry a large measure of responsibility for this situation. Many reporters and editorial writers fail to do their homework and are therefore unable to place the news in

> perspective or in balance. Many radio and television announcers treat even the most sober world events as "flashes" to be presented in the excited tones of the latest sports bulletin. However, it is not enough for us in government to blame the least responsible of our TV and newsmen or even to point to the failure of our educational system to give even "well educated" Americans an adequate grounding in history and economics. A major share of the responsibility for the information gap lies, in my opinion, in our failure to explain the basis for our policies and to broaden public understanding of the forces with which we must cope. Although more television presentations by you could be helpful, the principal burden rests on our ability to improve and expand our own informational and educational work and to persuade private institutions and foundations to greatly increase their assistance.[16]

Frustration with the news media notwithstanding, first-term presidents always make decisions, even those in crisis situations, with an eye to the electorate, and they cannot afford to pursue policies that will consistently alienate potential voters. Sure, some unpopular decisions can be explained as manifestations of urgent national interest that trumps individual priorities, but first-term presidents are not able to ignore or deemphasize public opinion too often if they wish to be re-elected. Second-term presidents, on the other hand, though ostensibly freed from a direct dependence on voter approval, are customarily too worried about their legacies or the needs of their political parties to depart radically from campaign promises and public expectations, so the likelihood of consistent unilateral action that contravenes public approval is extremely low. In the end, though the public may not always be rational in the casual sense of the word, its input guarantees the ultimate rationality of the policymaking process in the United States.

Furthermore, examples such as JFK's decision making during the Cuban Missile Crisis aside, which did not preclude deliberation but control of it, the formulation and implementation of foreign policy is collaborative—not unilateral. Yes, the president's constitutional roles as commander in chief and chief executive officer confer ultimate responsibility for policymaking on him, and, as such, he has the authority and power to curtail deliberation and make final decisions. Yet, even in the extreme, those decisions reflect the input and influence of numerous advisors and other officials, as well as those outside of government. Unlike heads of state in many other countries, especially authoritarian regimes, presidents are not insular because the presidency is not insular. The presidency functions effectively only if the bureaucracy within which it is embedded works to support it; American presidents are accountable and beholden to too many people, constituents and advisors alike, and their duties are far too complex to be able to make unilateral decisions without a collaborative and cooperative network of key institutions and personnel.[17]

Domestic Actors

In one way or another, foreign policy always begins and ends with the president, even if his ideas do not always initiate the process, but the nuts and bolts of policymaking are in the hands of a small group of trusted aides who act as both advisors and gatekeepers, managing access to key personnel, acting as liaisons between the White House and other participants, and delegating various tasks. Department heads, such as the Secretaries of State and Defense, plus the National Security Advisor, CIA Director, and other key agency leaders, are crucial participants, but they are not always part of the president's inner circle. George W. Bush's administration was unusual in this regard, as Secretary of Defense Rumsfeld, Vice President Cheney, and—to a lesser extent—National Security Advisor Rice had very prominent roles as primary policymakers and also had the ear of the President. Yet most presidents, like Bill Clinton and Ronald Reagan, have relied on a cadre of trusted aides, if not personal friends, for ideas and advice about key foreign-policy objectives. Aside from the obvious players, various groups and individuals within the Executive Office of the President and support staffs from relevant departments and agencies are critical for the formulation of foreign policy. They often serve as the real workhorses, doing the heavy lifting during policymaking by compiling data, performing analyses, preparing strategy, providing expertise, and fulfilling any number of related jobs assigned to them by the president or his staff.[18]

The significance of foreign policy issues, as well as the importance of having staff in place to aid the president in the decision-making process, becomes apparent to every president as soon as he takes office, if not before. For example, in December 1960, President-Elect John F. Kennedy met with President Dwight Eisenhower to discuss the responsibilities of the job, as summarized in a memo by Eisenhower's Press Secretary, James Hagerty:

> The President started the conversation by saying that one of the by-products of the meeting was that he finally could understand why the Senator had won the election.... Once they were alone in the President's office they discussed at length the problems confronting the President now and in the future. These included specifically—Berlin, Cuba and the Communist activities in South America emanating from Cuba; the Far East, particularly the problems created in that area by Communist China and Formosa; African problems, particularly the Congo; the problem [French President Charles] De Gaulle has with Algeria; disarmament and nuclear test negotiations with the USSR; and the balance of payments problem and the need to maintain confidence in the United States dollar. In connection with this last point, the question of redeployment of United States troops in Europe was also raised by the President.... He said that he went over with Senator Kennedy in great detail the workings of the National Security Council and the Operations Coordinating Board. He said that at first Senator Kennedy did not seem to understand the set-up and seemed to think that the National Security Council made final recommendations in the Security field. The President, however, explained that the Council acts only in an advisory position and that while they can present position papers and give suggestions, they are only an advisory group to the President and that the President, and only the President, has to make the ultimate decision. The President explained to Senator Kennedy that many times these National Security Council recommendations did not involve matters where the President had to make an immediate decision and that the President therefore would have some time to mull over the recommendations, study their effects on our allies, the neutral world, and the Communist world before taking the final step.... The President said he had a feeling as he was explaining these matters that the Senator began to realize the magnitude of the responsibility that would rest on his shoulders after January 20th.[19]

Without a doubt, the president is the central figure in the policymaking process, but his involvement will vary according to circumstance and leadership style. Obviously, crisis situations require a more hands-on approach than would otherwise be necessary, as do certain issues that are of particular interest to the president, but leadership style is really the determining factor with respect to his level of participation. Some presidents, such as Dwight Eisenhower, Ronald Reagan, and perhaps George W. Bush, were relatively uninvolved in the policy formulation process itself, concentrating on the broadest strokes by identifying the fundamental ideals of foreign policy but delegating practically all subsequent tasks to others. With Reagan, scholars and other commentators have debated whether his hands-off management style was a result of a growing lack of interest in the nuts and bolts of politics, and, whereas that may have been true, he displayed a consistent approach throughout his political career. Bush, on the other hand, was accused of surrendering too much power to his Vice President, Dick Cheney, and thereby losing rather than actively delegating authority, but the evidence suggests that Bush maintained broad control over foreign policy but remained aloof from its day-to-day management due to a lack of interest in the procedural aspects of policymaking. This type of approach has both advantages and disadvantages, because it increases efficiency and promotes an efficacious division and specialization of labor within bureaucratic environments, but it can also undermine accountability and institutional cohesion, as evidenced by the Iran-Contra Scandal during the late 1980s.

On the other end of the spectrum, presidents as different as Bill Clinton, George H. W. Bush, and Jimmy Carter were intimately involved at almost every level of policymaking, exerting much tighter control and influence over foreign policy, especially from a day-to-day perspective. In Carter's case, this often produced institutional paralysis, as the President's micromanagement of even the most insignificant matters inhibited productivity and efficiency and created bureaucratic gridlock that undermined the resolution of key issues. Bill Clinton frequently suffered from the same problem, but his administration was nonetheless much more effective than Carter's had been. A big part of the reason for this was that, despite Clinton's reluctance to delegate and his unwillingness to distance himself from any aspect of policymaking, he was one of the most gifted and capable politicians ever to occupy the White House and was surrounded by a relatively skilled and informed cadre of advisors. In addition, because Clinton was inherently more interested in domestic policy, he was not nearly as involved in, or preoccupied with, foreign policy, so his participation in the formulation of many foreign policies was limited to that of an architect. Clinton came to the White House with an ambitious domestic-policy agenda, which was ultimately undermined by personal scandals and intense animosity against him and his wife Hillary, and, despite some notable accomplishments in international affairs, he viewed foreign policy as a distraction from his more essential domestic agenda. Still, he was a policy wonk who enjoyed the everyday aspects of politics arguably more than any other president before or since.[20]

Of particular importance in terms of advising the president on foreign policy matters is the National Security Council (NSC), which includes the president's senior national security advisors and cabinet officials. Created during the Truman administration with passage of the National Security Act of 1947 (and placed in the

Executive Office of the President in 1949), the NSC's primary responsibility is to advise and assist the president on national security and foreign policy matters. The NSC is chaired by the president, and meetings are regularly attended by the Vice President, the Secretary of State, the Secretary of the Treasury, the Secretary of Defense, the Assistant to the President for National Security Affairs, the Chairman of the Joint Chiefs of Staff, and the Director of National Intelligence. Other White House officials, such as the Chief of Staff, Counsel to the President, the Assistant to the President for Economic Policy, the Attorney General, the Director of the Office of Management and Budget, or other cabinet secretaries, may also attend. From its inception during the Truman administration, the NSC has served as an important venue for the development of a president's foreign-policy objectives. For example, on June 29, 1950, just four days after North Korea had invaded the Republic of South Korea, the NSC held a meeting at which the following issues were discussed:

- Reviewed the situation in Korea.
- Noted the President's directive that the Council resurvey all policies affecting the entire perimeter of the USSR.
- Agreed that the Council should prepare for consideration by the President recommendations as to the courses of action to be followed in the event that Soviet forces enter Korean hostilities.
- Noted the President's agreement with a suggestion by the Secretary of State that the Department of Defense should prepare for the information of the Council a review of our military capabilities in order to indicate the extent of our freedom of choice.
- Noted Mr. [Averell] Harriman's remarks that the Europeans, though they had grave concern prior to the President's announcement that the United States would not meet the challenge, felt great relief afterwards although they were fully aware of the implications of the statement.
- Noted the President's desire that the British offer of naval assistance, when officially received, be accepted; and that the Vice President, when advised by the Secretary of State of the exact nature of the offer, should inform the appropriate Senators.
- Noted the remarks by the Secretary of the Treasury that a reappraisal of the Treasury situation had been underway since January and was ready, subject to sharpening up, for specific application; and that the Treasury Department had been working closely with the National Security Board in this connection.
- Noted the President's view that the sources of supply in North Korea should be kept under consideration, but that no U.S. attacks should be made across the 38th parallel under current orders.
- Noted that special attention will be devoted to obtaining intelligence concerning clear evidence of Soviet participation in Korean hostilities, and concerning Soviet activities in the vicinity of Yugoslavia and Northern Iran.[21]

After the president and the NSC, the most significant players in the policymaking process are a handful of close aides, or confidants, whose role as advisors and gatekeepers is critical for the successful formulation of foreign policy. The presi-

---

Read the National Security Act of 1947.

dent customarily consults them first regarding relevant issues and relies on them to manage and coordinate the information and organizational dynamics within his foreign-policy team. Obviously, their input is crucial, and their contributions can often exceed their nominal authority, as they are among the most trusted of the president's staff. Frequently, this inner circle of advisors does not actually include top cabinet officers or agency officials but individuals who have developed close personal ties to the president himself. Probably the best recent example of this was Ronald Reagan, whose reliance, particularly with respect to domestic policy, on a core group of informal advisors and political supporters was considerable. In addition, Reagan moved trusted allies such as Caspar Weinberger and William Casey, to name only two, into key high-level positions (Secretary of Defense and CIA Director, respectively) based more on loyalty and service to him and the Republican Party than on specific subject-matter expertise, which ensured that, beyond his inner circle, the President would be surrounded by a dependable and trustworthy foreign-policy team. Unlike Reagan and also Bill Clinton, George W. Bush relied primarily on his principal cabinet officers for primary input regarding foreign policy, and he was unusually close to Dick Cheney, Donald Rumsfeld, and Condoleezza Rice, who eclipsed all but Karl Rove, the President's political strategist, in terms of political clout in the White House.[22]

The president and his inner circle of advisors are crucial to the policymaking process, but the institutional infrastructure beyond them is absolutely essential, and the pursuit of America's foreign policies would be impossible without it. Aside from the presidency itself, the most critical foreign-policy institutions are the Departments of State and Defense, which are primarily responsible for diplomacy and national security, respectively. The State Department is one of the three original cabinet offices created by the founding generation of legislators and, under the authority of the president, plans, coordinates, and mobilizes practically all diplomatic activity within and outside of the United States. Through a vast staff that includes the Secretary of State, a number of undersecretaries, numerous ambassadors, teams of emissaries and other diplomats, and thousands of support personnel, the State Department manages a complex array of international relationships and promotes U.S. strategic, political, and economic interests throughout the globe. Its activities, especially in the economic realm, are occasionally supplemented through related efforts by, for example, the Departments of Commerce and Energy or the Office of the U.S. Trade Representative, but it is the principal organ responsible for American diplomatic initiatives.[23]

The other key foreign-policy institution is the Department of Defense, which, unlike the Department of State, is one of the newer members of the president's cabinet. Created shortly after the end of World War II through the National Security Act of 1947, it is the national-security arm of the U.S. government. Headed by the Secretary of Defense, it comprises civilian leadership such as the Secretaries of the Navy, Army, and Air Force, the military's top brass, including the Joint Chiefs of Staff, intelligence officials, tens of thousands of support personnel, and the nation's armed forces. As the national-security arm of the U.S. government, the Department of Defense is responsible for the planning and execution of operational strategies intended to secure American diplomatic objectives. As such, its role as a policymaker is, at least theoretically, subordinate to that of the State Department, since its task is the realization, and not the formulation, of political objectives; but its influence over certain administrations, especially during the Cold War, has been unusually pervasive. At such junctures, strategic and even ideological priorities have trumped overriding policy goals, particularly those of the State Department, but the trend has been anything but predictable.[24]

In addition to the Departments of State and Defense, the recently created Department of Homeland Security coordinates efforts against internal threats to Americans, whether from domestic or foreign sources. In some ways, it can be envisioned as the domestic counterpart to the Defense Department, but its actual authority and resources are limited, and its ability to implement policy is heavily dependent on other institutions. It was founded in the wake of the 9/11 attacks on the United States, when the country's civilian leadership faced tremendous pressure to indemnify the nation from future terrorist incursions, but its boundaries have never been properly defined, nor have its resources and capabilities. Aside from its primary duties to prevent (if possible), prepare for, and respond to attacks against the United States and its protectorates, the Department of Homeland Security is charged with addressing natural disasters and man-made emergencies, such as oil spills, nuclear contamination, and other domestic accidents. Beyond that, its responsibilities include customs and immigration, air safety through agencies such as the Transportation Security Administration (TSA), maritime security, and the protection of natural resources.[25]

America's national-security and diplomatic capabilities also depend on a network of intelligence resources whose duties include the accumulation and analysis of relevant information and knowledge regarding foreign governments, organizations, and individuals. The most visible, if not most significant, of these is the Central Intelligence Agency (CIA), which is an independent agency that reports directly to the president and his staff through the Director of National Intelligence. Like the Department of Defense, the CIA was established through the National Security Act of 1947 as an acknowledgment of America's changing national-security needs and priorities during the early stages of the Cold War. Envisioned as a clearinghouse of information on American diplomatic targets and concerns throughout the world that would provide actionable analysis of data gathered through a variety of sources, including espionage, the CIA has supported, some would say enabled, the country's diplomatic and military efforts during the past several decades. Like the Departments of State and Defense, it has developed its own priorities and allegiances over the years and has never been a mere conduit of information or unbiased participant. Its tendency to view intelligence as a precursor to enforcement or military activity has often created friction with the State Department and promotes alliances with key Defense personnel, but it has also pushed its own geopolitical agendas.

The CIA exists alongside other intelligence agencies, both within and without specific executive departments, and perhaps the most notable of these is the National Security Agency (NSA), which is part of the Department of Defense. The NSA is a product of the Cold War, created by President Harry Truman upon the recommendation of the CIA in 1951 to improve eavesdropping capabilities and protect the transmission of intelligence among American assets. Leveraging some of the most sophisticated technology on the planet, the NSA coordinates the nation's electronic espionage, decryption, and encryption efforts. Because of its vast resources and capabilities, to say nothing of its potential reach, it has been a more or less constant target of anti-government criticism by both civil libertarians and various reactionary organizations, such as the many independent militias that have arisen throughout the West and South over the last twenty-five years. Nonetheless, its presence has been essential, and presidents have depended on its capabilities to maintain U.S. security.[26]

The aforementioned institutions are all indispensable players in foreign policymaking, and, though they are the most obvious, their input and participation are not sufficient alone, particularly in a liberal democracy such as the U.S. government. At some point, at least by the operational stage but customarily much earlier, legislators become involved in the process. Without them, the implementation of foreign policy is almost impossible, particularly in the long term, so presidents must secure the cooperation of Congress as early as possible. In many, if not most, cases, presidents or their aides consult selected congressional leaders, which can include the Speaker of the House of Representatives, majority or minority leaders of either chamber, heads or ranking members of pertinent committees, and other prominent representatives or senators. Congressional support for presidential policies is indispensable, because lawmakers have the ability to stall, derail, or alter intended legislation and undermine presidential agendas altogether. Of course, the president's duties as commander in chief under the vesting clause in Article II of the Constitution and his emergency powers, to say nothing of his authority to make war under the War Powers Resolution, have offered recent administrations ample opportunities to delay or even prevent Congressional involvement, but Congress does become involved sooner or later.

Beyond the executive and legislative branches, the roles of other participants are more difficult to define, not necessarily because they are not regular but because they are confusing and frequently questionable. The most significant of these are the various interest groups and campaign contributors who have a disproportionate effect on national politics. Not a single policy, even foreign policy, that survives initial discussions among the president and his aides is implemented without early and continuous intervention by lobbyists. Interest groups represent practically every cause and idea and seem to include anyone with a political agenda, which includes the numerous groups that have a stake in the various American diplomatic and military initiatives. Lobbies are a political conduit for everyone with an axe to grind, enabling certain constituencies to exert political pressure that far outweighs their number. Perhaps the most visible and influential among foreign-policy groups is AIPAC (American Israel Public Affairs Committee), whose allegiance should be evident from its name, but countless other interests are represented among foreign-policy lobbyists. In addition to the obvious, such as AIPAC and the like, this comprises practically everything and everyone that relies on the promotion of American diplomatic and strategic priorities, such as oil and gas, mining, weapons manufacturing, agriculture, labor unions, and so on.[27]

International Actors

Although American foreign policy is a function of national priorities identified and pursued by U.S. policymakers, the most important of whom are the president and his principal advisors, it is also a product of various exogenous factors that transcend national interests and domestic political institutions. Prominent among these is the geopolitical development of relevant global theaters and the international political environments in which American diplomatic and military personnel pursue the nation's foreign-policy objectives. Those environments are shaped by a number of influences, not the least of which are the regional and global alliances to which the United States belongs. U.S. foreign policy may be an extension of national ideals and political objectives, but it necessarily reflects the needs and desires of the country's strategic and economic partners as well. Most importantly in that regard, American foreign policy must address the unified international objectives identified through its treaty obligations around the globe.

Without a doubt, the preeminent alliance, military or otherwise, to which the United States belongs is the North Atlantic Treaty Organization (NATO), which has been the core of anti-communist and, more generally, anti-authoritarian defense efforts among the United States and its Western allies for decades. A quintessential product of the Cold War, its original purpose was aptly summarized by a British official who claimed that NATO existed to keep the United States in, the Soviet Union out, and Germany down. Such a characterization may be an anachronism in a post-Soviet world no longer animated by customary east–west polarities, but NATO was indeed established as a bulwark against Soviet expansionism in Europe and a guarantee against German military resurgence. Since the fall of the Soviet Union and its communist satellite states, NATO's mission and direction have been thrown into question, and its role in the geopolitical evolution of twenty-first-century Europe is not clear, nor is its ultimate relevance in a global diplomatic theater that has transcended and redefined traditional relationships and affinities.[28]

After the last round of enlargements in 2009, NATO has comprised twenty-eight states from Europe and North America. Its headquarters is located in Brussels, Belgium, and its membership has grown considerably over the past decade. Contrary to what had been the case for most of its history, NATO now includes members from eastern and central Europe and is, thus, no longer an exclusive club for the United States, Canada, and their Western European allies. Principal political authority lies with the North Atlantic Council, which is a deliberative decision-making body that acts through consensus instead of voting, thereby insuring unity of purpose and strategic coordination for NATO initiatives. NATO is led by the secretary-general, who, as head of the North Atlantic Council, represents NATO in dealings with states and other international organizations. The alliance's political structure is complemented by a unified military command, which is controlled by American military personnel but supported by a staff that represents all member countries.

Despite NATO's obvious political role, it is, first and foremost, a military alliance. NATO exists to protect its members from attack by common enemies and to ensure the physical integrity of its territories. It has maintained its Atlantic focus by preserving a fundamental tie between North America and Europe, but the European part of the alliance has shifted its locus of activity eastward. By admitting former

View NATO's website.

Warsaw Pact countries and erstwhile Soviet republics among its ranks, NATO has undermined some of the cultural and geographic solidarity that characterized the pre-1999 alliance, but that has allowed the alliance to expand beyond the strategic limits imposed on it by the Cold War. Moreover, NATO has become involved in non-European military theaters, such as Afghanistan, but which are nonetheless central to European and American strategic interests, and it has developed a greater appreciation for diplomacy and pre-deployment capabilities. In fact, some scholars believe that NATO's continued viability lies in its readiness, willingness, and ability to morph from a military alliance into a largely diplomatic one.[29]

During the Cold War, NATO policy was driven by U.S. foreign policy, and, aside from occasional resistance from the French government and other left-leaning regimes, NATO's geopolitical agenda was a function of American diplomatic and military objectives. NATO's needs and priorities definitely influenced U.S. foreign policy, yet mostly to the extent that American political and military leaders recognized the alliance's value as an instrument of Cold War anti-communist policies and strategic initiatives. Since 1991, neither the relationship between NATO and the United States nor the geopolitical dominance of the United States has been as clear, so NATO has gradually exerted a more independent influence over American foreign policy. Furthermore, as the political and economic integration of Europe has grown through the European Union (EU), the EU has increasingly served as both a counterweight and an alternative to NATO, which has translated into greater pressure on U.S. policymakers to acknowledge European, as opposed to Atlantic, priorities. Over time, the competition between NATO and the EU will inevitably increase, as will the amount of redundancy between them, and, should the recent continentalist trend continue to prevail over the customary Atlanticist one, the case for NATO's ongoing utility and relevance will be a difficult one to maintain.[30]

Of course, NATO is not the only international organization that plays a role in the formulation of U.S. foreign policy; however, it is by far the most significant. As a member of the United Nations (UN) and, for example, the Organization of American States (OAS), the United States must honor certain commitments that inevitably shape its interaction with participating states, but these other organizations lack NATO's targeted purpose and specific utility, to say nothing of their limited strategic potential in terms of practical capabilities. The OAS is essentially a toothless body that represents a historically recurring, yet continuously failed, attempt to unify the nations of South and North America, and it has never been able to bridge the ideological and constitutional differences within its diverse membership. Latin American countries have frequently viewed the United States not as a partner but as a rival, if not an enemy, and their ability and willingness to cooperate has been undermined by socialist and interventionist policies that contradict U.S. values and political ideals. The United Nations, on the other hand, though broader and more powerful than the OAS, suffers from many of the same problems, and its role as a unified and purposeful policymaker has been limited to no more than a handful of universally acknowledged global crises. Yes, the Security Council, its main policy-setting body, often acts to address major geopolitical problems, but it nonetheless lacks the resolve, enforcement capabilities, and practical resources to make a sustained impact on U.S. foreign policy.[31]

Arguably the most influential international players in U.S. foreign policy, even more so than NATO, are the country's closest allies, such as Great Britain, Canada, Israel, and, to a lesser extent Germany, Japan, and South Korea. The U.S. relationship with Britain stands out, and has historically—the American Revolution and War of 1812 notwithstanding—been the most significant. It has been characterized as "the special relationship," not only due to the obvious cultural and historical ties that bind the two countries but also because of the close alignment between U.S. and British foreign-policy objectives. Within NATO itself, the British have been staunchly Atlantic, resisting the growing continentalist pull and occasional anti-Americanism of its European neighbors across the channel, and have been the most consistent defenders of U.S. priorities among American allies. Therefore, British wishes and needs have always had a strong impact on the formulation of U.S. foreign policy, and British leaders are regularly consulted on key strategic decisions, though President Barack Obama's foreign-policy team has not been as close to its British counterparts as its predecessors.[32]

Like Britain, Israel has been an extremely important ally for the United States, and its significance has at times even eclipsed Great Britain's. Despite the fact that the ideological and cultural affinities between the United States and Great Britain are truly unique and unrivaled, Israel's strategic value, especially during the Cold War, has been unsurpassed. This is why the Department of Defense has been such an avid supporter of Israel and pro-Israeli policy and also why the United States has overlooked a number of Israeli foreign-policy gaffes in the past few decades. Since the late 1940s, Israeli stability and strategic integrity have been key objectives of U.S. foreign policy in the Middle East, though, once again, the Obama administration has departed somewhat from tradition. President Obama's greater accommodation of Palestinian priorities and decreased tolerance of Israel's assertive self-defense posture have produced tension between two allies that have taken each other's support for granted. Admittedly, President Obama is not the first U.S. president to question the wisdom of Israeli defense and negotiating strategies with respect to the Palestinians, as evidenced by Presidents Bill Clinton and, even more so, Jimmy Carter. Nevertheless, because of the unrest and uncertainty in the broader Middle East, particularly after the Arab revolts of the spring and summer of 2011, friction between Israel and the United States could have relatively greater reverberations.[33]

The most frequently forgotten ally, by both the media and the public, is the one directly to the North of the United States. Canada is a founding member of NATO and is part of the North American Aerospace Defense Command (NORAD), which is a joint organization responsible for air defense in Canada and the United States. Its security is closely linked to that of the United States, and the territorial integrity of the North American continent depends on continued cooperation between these two countries. Their mutual affinities are occasionally overshadowed by other issues, such as differences over environmental policy, but the U.S. relationship with Canada is probably its most important strategic asset. With a military strength of only 65,000 troops and a population roughly equal to California's, Canada may not be a geopolitical juggernaut, but, particularly because of the political instability that has plagued Latin America, its support is indispensable to the United States. In addition, the obvious cultural ties and similarities, to say nothing of historical links and geographical proximity, make Canada a more natural strategic partner than any other country.[34]

Whereas the partnerships with Canada, Britain, and Israel arose out of cooperation and mutual interest, those with Germany and Japan were consequences of conquest, which makes them fundamentally different. In both countries, U.S. occupation and temporary military administration evolved into caretaker relationships driven, though not as much today, by American strategic interests. The purpose of initial U.S. involvement was to prevent the re-militarization of Germany and Japan following World War II and thereby promote peace, democratic governance, and geopolitical stability in their respective regions. For the bulk of the postwar period, the United States, supplemented by NATO in Germany's case, provided military defense for both countries and, thus, maintained a substantial troop presence. During the past two decades, both of these relationships have become strained, as domestic politics and nationalist sympathies in Germany and Japan have fueled resentment against the United States. Both countries, especially Germany, have also improved their own self-defense capabilities and reassessed postwar constitutional military restrictions, which has further militated against a continuation of the status quo ante concerning their ties with the United States.[35]

Principal Geopolitical Theaters

Foreign policy focuses on external relations and, as such, invokes specific regional issues and concerns that define differing approaches to various relevant geopolitical theaters. Despite the existence of overarching questions addressed through organizations such as the United Nations or G20 (The Group of Twenty Finance Ministers and Central Bank Governors) and presidential administrations' attention to global priorities, foreign policy focuses on several, mostly disparate, sets of priorities within respective geopolitical regions. Commentators and observers often speak of global policy, and presidents frequently address global issues, but such a concept is really a red herring. Some recurring and widespread problems, such as climate change, famine, genocide, natural disasters, and so on, may seem universal and, therefore, galvanize a global effort to resolve them, but geopolitical global diversity and insuperable regional (and local) differences make a truly global approach to foreign policy impractical, if not impossible. Furthermore, the realities of international politics and foreign policy necessitate the prioritization of certain geopolitical regions over others, because those regions are simply more significant from a strategic perspective, and they require greater care and attention, to say nothing of policies uniquely suited to local conditions and circumstances.

North America

From the standpoint of national security and territorial integrity, the most important geopolitical theater, yet the most frequently overlooked by commentators, is North America, which is why Canada is such a critical ally for the United States. Aside from the recurring political and economic instability coupled with serious drug trafficking in Mexico, North American foreign-policy issues are neither as visible nor as readily identifiable for most Americans and the national media as those in other, higher profile regions, such as the Middle East, Africa, Asia, or even Latin America. Nonetheless, U.S. national security and territorial integrity depend more on regional stability and continued geopolitical progress in North America than on any other single geographic factor. This does not mean that peace, stability, and pro-American policies in other regions are not crucial, because they are, but the realization of U.S. strategic objectives presupposes a favorable geopolitical environment in North America, without which the United States cannot survive. So, it may often be overlooked as the pivotal strategic theater for the achievement of U.S. foreign-policy goals, but North America is a top priority for policymakers.

In North America, economic matters are a principal concern for U.S. policymakers, with respect to both Canada and Mexico. Free trade has been a major issue in this regard, particularly the North American Free Trade Agreement (NAFTA), as have ongoing economic and financial problems in Mexico ☝. A related concern, which also invokes various domestic-policy areas, has been immigration, especially illegal immigration from Mexico and the attendant security ramifications. In addition, North American foreign policy involves the reconciliation of U.S. environmental and labor standards with those of its trading partners, and, through NAFTA and related vehicles, the reduction of governmental subsidies and other market-distorting mechanisms. Still, the central priority for U.S. policymakers is national security, and the integration of defense capabilities with Canada through NORAD is an indispensable aspect of national-security strategy, as is the increasing cooperation between U.S. and Mexican governments in securing the southern border. Latent initiatives between Mexico and the United States to control the cross-border drug trade are also an integral part of national-security efforts, as are those with Canada to prevent potential terrorist threats.[36]

Europe

After North America, the key region for U.S. policymakers is Europe, which has been a principal theater of U.S. diplomatic and military involvement for over a century. In some ways, Europe is as significant for U.S. national security as North America, particularly in terms of the cultural and political affinities between Americans and their European allies. The historical bond between the United States and Europe, especially Britain, is clear and weighs heavily in all national-security calculations, but a traditional U.S. role in European geopolitics since World War II is an overriding factor. During the Cold War (see next section), the United States was the regional caretaker in Western Europe, enabling postwar rebuilding efforts through substantial economic and financial assistance and providing regional security as the physical and political backbone of NATO. As a growing stronghold of liberal democracy, Greece, Spain, Italy, and a few others notwithstanding, Europe is an indispensable part of U.S. economic and political liberalization efforts across the globe, and its NATO members are valued foreign-policy partners for the United States.

Despite the customary overlap between European and U.S. strategic objectives, important differences have begun to surface since the end of the Cold War, and the continued long-term alignment of those objectives is not assured. Growing German and French continentalist influence over the EU and the broader European continent has countered the traditional atlanticist focus of postwar European foreign-

---

☝ Read the legislative timeline for NAFTA.

policy and security strategy, and inconsistencies between U.S. foreign-policy goals and EU priorities have become increasingly apparent. Without the overwhelming Soviet threat of the Cold War years and the necessary U.S. protection from it, some European nations, such as Germany and France, have begun to question the logic of ongoing U.S. dominance in the region, which has created both tension and inconsistencies in trans-Atlantic relations. On the other hand, former communist nations from Eastern and Central Europe, such as Poland, the Czech Republic, Hungary, the Baltic states, and others, have actually favored greater U.S. involvement and leadership, motivated by recent memories of Soviet domination and economic stagnation.[37]

The Middle East

Next to Europe, the Middle East is the most crucial non–North American geopolitical theater for the United States. During the Cold War, the value of this region for both sides was obvious, as the United States and Soviet Union worked diligently to secure key allies. Prized for its natural resources, especially oil, and its strategic position as a gateway to three continents (Europe, Africa, and Asia), the Middle East has been a geopolitical priority for the United States since at least World War II. The main and most consistent American ally in the region has always been Israel, but ongoing relationships with Jordan, occasionally Lebanon, and, until the recent revolution that overturned a friendly regime, Egypt have also helped. As a democratic government, Israel has been stable since its foundation in 1947, and its allegiance to the United States has been the most consistent and abiding in the region. Israeli and American administrations have come and gone, and the relationship between the two countries has waxed and waned during the past sixty-five years or so, but Israel is one of America's top allies, and its strategic significance cannot be overstated. Seen as the linchpin to at least a modicum of stability and predictability in a region with the world's largest oil reserves, Israel's continued friendship is invaluable.

As long as the United States and the rest of the world need oil, the geopolitical prominence of the Middle East will be assured. Critics of U.S. foreign policy have used this fact to impugn U.S. involvement in the Middle East, yet stability and progress in the Middle East along with unimpeded access to its resources are critical for economic survival both here and abroad. Unfortunately, stability has been threatened by two trends over the past two decades, both of which have prompted U.S. intervention in the region. First, state-sponsored terrorism and the transplantation of terrorist networks across the globe from their Middle East sources produced U.S.-led wars in Iraq and Afghanistan, both of which, though eliminating rogue regimes, have ultimately destabilized the region. Second, nascent revolutions and insurrections across North Africa and the Middle East have toppled traditional autocratic regimes and weakened others, and the United States consequently joined an international effort to aid Libyan rebels in their fight against Muammar Qaddafi (who was killed in 2011). Continuing uncertainty in Egypt, Syria, Lebanon, Yemen, and other strategically important states across the Middle East and North Africa will inevitably consume American attention and resources for some time to come, and the ongoing tensions between Israelis and Palestinians will also insure that this region remains a priority for U.S. policymakers.[38]

Israeli Prime Minister Yitzhak Rabin and PLO Leader Yasser Arafat shake hands on the "Declaration of Principles" for peace between the Arabs and Israelis brokered by Bill Clinton in 1993.

Africa

Though not a historically traditional area of concern such as the Middle East, Africa has been of increasing importance to the United States over the past few decades. As should be evident from the preceding discussion, Middle Eastern priorities often overlap with those regarding Africa, particularly North Africa, since these regions have certain political affinities that bind them. Africa was not unimportant to U.S. policymakers prior to the last twenty or thirty years, but European domination of the continent and relatively recent political emancipation (mostly in the 1950s and 1960s) delayed direct U.S. involvement. Like the Middle East, much of the African continent is valued for its natural resources, especially precious metals and diamonds, but latent discoveries of oil and natural gas have also increased its international appeal. Due to the comparatively late political development of most of Africa, especially sub-Saharan Africa (South Africa excepted), the political landscape in many countries is far from settled. Tribal, ethnic, religious, and other divisions throughout the region, to say nothing of the consequences of colonial rule, fuel political friction and conflict throughout the continent. Resource-rich states like Nigeria, Namibia, and Democratic Republic of the Congo are high-profile cases, but numerous others that fly under the radar are just as unstable. Because of its resources and its proximity to the Middle East and Europe, Africa is an integral element of U.S. foreign policy, and stability in the region is a major objective.[39]

Latin America

Closer to home, Latin America, which encompasses Central and South America, is a significant target for U.S. foreign policymakers and has been a relevant geopolitical theater for over a century. As a military and diplomatic power, the United States has been involved in Latin America longer than in any other region outside North America, and its significance to the United States is obvious given the territorial proximity. Starting with its acquisition of Cuba and Puerto Rico at the end of the nineteenth century and the Panama Canal zone shortly thereafter, the United States had consistent strategic and economic interests in the region. Covert action, military assistance, or aid to favored political groups were tools of U.S. foreign policy in Latin America throughout the twentieth century, and even direct military intervention to secure U.S. assets was an option. Foreign policy was used to protect U.S. economic ventures, particularly in agriculture and hospitality, and to counter communist and socialist infiltration during the Cold War. A stronghold of military dictatorships from the 1950s to the 1980s, Latin America was of particular concern to U.S. policymakers because of continued political instability and also repression.

For years, the biggest worry in Latin America for U.S. policymakers was Cuba, which is one of the world's longest surviving communist regimes and was a key Soviet ally. No longer a strategic threat, not least due to a disintegrating economy and enfeebled government, Cuba has become a regional curiosity and a campaign issue in Florida, which has a sizable Cuban population. In Central America and parts of South America, Cold War–era revolutions and civil wars have been replaced by social instability from runaway crime and economic dislocations, whereas other South American countries have witnessed a resurgence of socialist or social-democratic governance. Particularly troubling in this regard have been the Andean nations of Venezuela, Bolivia, and Ecuador, in which socialism and authoritarianism have combined to produce a veritable danger for regional stability, and the narcotics trafficking in neighboring Colombia continues to be a problem for the United States. Relations with Latin American countries have been strained by ongoing political differences, and decreasing U.S. influence has reduced American leverage in the region. Still, given the geographic proximity and the economic importance of South American markets for U.S. products, Latin America will continue to be a principal geopolitical theater of concern to foreign-policy makers in Washington.[40]

Asia

Finally, and by no means insignificant, is Asia, which is frequently subdivided by policymakers into Central Asia, the Indian subcontinent, Southeast Asia, and East Asia. The United States has had economic interests in Asia since the nineteenth century, as well as strong political ties to countries such as the Philippines, which it administered for the first third of the twentieth century. Military intervention in Japan, Korea (later South Korea), and Vietnam cemented U.S. commitments in the region, while geopolitical developments on the Indian subcontinent, and particularly the nuclear aspirations of India and Pakistan, have continued to attract U.S. attention. The post-Soviet states in resource-rich Central Asia have been a concern since their independence from Soviet rule in 1991, as authoritarian governance and occasional instability have created security risks in an area whose oil and natural gas reserves along with its strategic value have secured its status as a pivotal geopolitical hub. From both an economic and political perspective, China has emerged as a regional and global powerhouse, but tensions with the United States over its unwillingness to liberalize government and markets have made for a difficult relationship. China's dogged adherence to statist economic policies, despite important changes since the late 1970s, and communist political ideals that belie prevailing global, and especially Western, trends has unnerved U.S. foreign policymakers and frequently impeded further diplomatic progress on the Chinese front.

Recent military intervention in Afghanistan and a troubled but critical relationship with Pakistan have deepened American involvement in Asia, though current nation-building efforts in Afghanistan have been compromised by an ineffective and corrupt government in Kabul whose instability threatens an already precarious geopolitical theater. An ongoing troop presence in South Korea and Japan along with political uncertainty in North Korea will necessitate continued U.S. commitments in East Asia despite recent South Korean and Japanese reluctance. Recurring Islamist terrorism in the Philippines, Indonesia, and other vulnerable states remains a primary concern for U.S. policymakers, while almost continual political turmoil among Pacific island nations poses ongoing problems. In the end, however, the economic and political well-being of the entire Asian region is paramount for the United States, and continued active involvement is a necessity.[41]

THE EVOLUTION OF U.S. FOREIGN POLICY

The inability to formulate or coordinate foreign policy was one of the main deficiencies of the Confederation government of the 1780s and, thus, a principal reason for the creation of the presidency by the framers of the Constitution. Given the narrow authority of the early presidency, particularly in domestic affairs, foreign policy stood out as one of the key responsibilities of the nation's first several presidents. In addition, though the new nation did not have a large standing army by any means, its defense was a top priority for the founding fathers, and security issues were of paramount importance to everyone. Obviously, no American wanted the recently created republic to perish due to an inability to defend itself, so its presidents were immediately aware of the need to craft effective foreign policies that would preserve and adequately protect the United States. Few people questioned the significance of foreign policy and the president's ability to control it, especially after the ineffectiveness of the Confederation government.

The Early Republic through World War I

The newly created republic had a pressing international agenda. Threats to its very existence were apparent immediately, and the United States was confronted with a slew of international issues that required appropriate attention. One of the biggest problems was a lack of international credibility of an established player, so rivals were eager to test the young nation's resolve. The major European empires resumed their pursuit of key objectives on the North American continent, hoping to secure long-sought territories that surrounded the United States. Britain, France, and Spain, to say nothing of Mexico and the various Indian tribes, all had good reason to provoke the United States, particularly since American gains on the continent had come at their expense. Troubles with France nearly produced a war during John Adams' presidency, while unresolved disputes with Great Britain led to an actual war in 1812, as did border controversies with Mexico in 1846. Indian tribes were handled with special brutality and determination, as American troops drove them beyond the frontier.[42]

Still, during the nineteenth century, U.S. foreign policy looked inward, not outward. For at least the first one hundred years, U.S. presidents followed a policy of strict neutrality and isolation from European geopolitical developments. Determined to steer clear of the debilitating international entanglements that plagued European powers, U.S. policymakers focused on the North American continent. Foreign policy was driven by an insatiable craving for land and the desire to secure the country's borders. Nothing stood in the way of a continuous acquisition of territory and the creation of a continental buffer that would protect the United States from potential adversaries. The promise of vast riches through the exploitation of minerals and the control of other natural resources lured thousands across the frontier and justified any means necessary to tame the wilderness and expand America's boundaries. One of the earliest acquisitions was the Louisiana Purchase of 1803, which more than doubled the total square mileage of the United States and stretched its boundary to the Mississippi River. Despite doubts about President Thomas Jefferson's constitutional authority to negotiate a deal of this sort, the Senate approved the treaty and endorsed the growth of presidential power in this arena. Although the presidency's constitutional role as caretaker of American territorial expansion was questionable, U.S. presidents eagerly accepted this responsibility, and no one ever looked back.[43]

In the 1820s, as executive confidence in its powers as head of state seemed to grow, President James Monroe extended U.S. foreign policy beyond traditional limits by issuing what has become known as the Monroe Doctrine. As much a warning to European empires to stay out of Latin America as a notice to those south of the border that a new international power had arrived, Monroe's declaration drastically increased, at least on paper, the scope of U.S. authority abroad. Monroe's international pretense notwithstanding, the primary focus of American expansionism was not south of the border but west of the Mississippi River, where settlers from all backgrounds looked for opportunity and adventure. Within a few decades, Americans became convinced that the control of all lands as far west as the Pacific Ocean was the country's "manifest destiny," and they pursued this goal with a zest and drive that have rarely been witnessed since. A term coined by a patriotic journalist and appropriated by supporters of President James Polk during the 1840s to justify the annexation of Texas, California, and other parts of the continent west of the Mississippi, "manifest destiny" was the justification for territorial gains at any price. By the 1850s, except for Alaska and Hawaii, the United States had acquired most of the land it now controls.[44]

The Monroe Doctrine aside, for at least the first two-thirds of its existence, the United States was not a global or even regional superpower. In fact, during much of that time, it could not have qualified as even a minor power. Following the Civil War, however, that began to change. The conquest of the North American continent and fulfillment of its "manifest destiny" eventually turned the nation's attention outward. Seeking markets abroad and eager to enhance its strategic leverage, America looked to the world stage for opportunities. Gradually but resolutely, its international stature improved, and its influence over other countries increased, culminating in the kind of foreign adventurism the founding fathers tried to prevent. By the 1940s, its status among other nations had evolved beyond anyone's predictions, and the United States was on its way to becoming an international giant. Historians and political scientists have identified what ensued as the emergence of a "national-security state," a fusion of military, economic, and cultural resources for the maintenance of power at home and abroad.

The last third of the nineteenth century brought with it a gradual but noticeable change in presidential authority. The two most immediate causes, though many others existed, were the Civil War and the closing of the American frontier. With the creation of a formidable administrative machinery to prosecute the war against the South, the federal executive established constitutional precedents during the Civil War that William McKinley, Theodore Roosevelt, and Woodrow Wilson would later use to justify the promotion of American strategic assets abroad. By the end of the nineteenth century, American presidents wielded more authority as heads of state than any of their early predecessors, and they eagerly promoted American military and diplomatic interests outside the North American continent. The closing of the frontier went hand in hand with the nation's new military and diplomatic interests, since America's rapidly industrializing economy needed markets for its products. The conquest of the North American continent meant that domestic markets were finite and that future economic growth would rely on foreign consumption of American goods, so strategic penetration abroad would serve national economic priorities.[45]

In 1898, William McKinley, considered by some to have been the first modern president, manufactured a war with Spain, which resulted in the American acquisition of Cuba, Puerto Rico, and the Philippines. McKinley used the press to promote the administration's international objectives and to popularize an assertive foreign policy that announced America's arrival as an international power. His vice president, Theodore Roosevelt, who became president in 1901 upon McKinley's assassination, was even more enthusiastic about the country's new-found international status. Relying on his new-found clout to act as a power broker in Asia and Latin America, he eagerly pushed America's economic and strategic interests wherever possible. Yet it was one of the country's most unlikely heroes that secured a permanent role for the United States as a world power. Woodrow Wilson, despite an admitted aversion to imperialism and foreign intervention, laid the groundwork for future American global domination. Military incursions into Latin America to protect local populations and U.S. property interests only led to the replacement of foreign rule by American control, and involvement in World War I, though based on Wilson's goal of self-determination for liberated colonies, simply insured American financial and military ascendancy in the West.[46]

World War II and the Cold War

U.S. domination arose from the aftermath of two world wars that obliterated parts of the civilized world and relegated others to political oblivion. After World War I, the United States retreated into isolationism for almost two decades, not abandoning its recently won international status altogether but nevertheless distancing itself from further involvement in European problems. The twin pillars of American foreign policy during the early days of the republic, small standing armies and neutrality, resurfaced as Americans became weary of the consequences of foreign entanglements at a time when their future was far from certain. Through the nation's participation in World War I, they witnessed the carnage that results from increased militarism, and they were not yet prepared to accommodate a sizable military presence at home. In addition, the economic catastrophe of the 1930s made the American public all the more focused on domestic affairs and the necessities of basic survival, so the pursuit of resource-intensive foreign policies became a luxury the country could not afford.[47]

President Franklin D. Roosevelt was initially committed to neutrality and, most of all, aloofness from military developments in Europe and Asia. As it turned out, circumstances forced his hand and pushed America ever closer to war. After the Japanese attack on Pearl Harbor on December 7, 1941, he had no alternative, and Congress declared war on Japan and Germany. Recognizing the implications of a global conflict fueled by enemies devoted to the extermination of whole populations, Roosevelt's dedication to victory was total. Through an unprecedented commitment of American resources, the president's expansion of executive authority was quick, decisive, and irreversible. Over 15 million men and women served in the armed forces in one capacity or another, while tens of millions of others held jobs that supported the war effort. The country's manufacturing potential was channeled into the production of arms, supplies, food, medicine, and anything else required by America's military, while its cultural output was focused on the maintenance of morale. Hollywood, major publishers, and leading radio producers all contributed to the presidency's propaganda machine, churning out movies, books, newspapers, and radio broadcasts that celebrated the superiority of the Allied cause.[48]

Upon the conclusion of the war, the United States emerged as one of two principal global military powers, and, at the risk of overstating things, the fate of the Western world was in its hands. Along with the Soviet Union, it was unchallenged as the arbiter of a new world order. Europe desperately needed international leadership from a country with resources and credentials equal to the task. In 1945, the United States was the only possible choice. Although the desire to avoid another global war was an important aspect of U.S. foreign policy after 1945, the overriding concerns were the rising geopolitical influence of the Soviet Union and the political turmoil in key European states. Teetering on the brink of communism, strategically significant countries such as Italy, Greece, and Turkey could not be allowed to fall under Soviet control and undermine the postwar stability of Europe. Others, like France, Austria, and Germany, were susceptible not only to socialists but also to extremists on the right, which made postwar rebuilding efforts difficult at best. Even Britain, which had been spared the widespread physical devastation that characterized continental Europe, was seriously weakened and confronted by internal problems that created considerable political vulnerabilities. Europe's political situation was precarious, and its susceptibility to Soviet aggression was substantial.[49]

Western policymakers were aware that the military, political, and economic resources to neutralize Soviet aggression could come only from the United States, so the U.S. became the political and economic arbiter in Europe. American economic muscle would provide the strength to rebuild the European continent, and American political knowhow would drive governmental reform, while its military presence would serve as a deterrent against Soviet expansion. Through the Marshall

Plan, President Harry Truman and his foreign-policy team insured the democratic future of Western Europe. The Marshall Plan, named for Secretary of State George Marshall, was a comprehensive aid program that paid for the reconstruction of war-ravaged countries and the resurrection of viable economies. In Germany, Austria, Japan, and other places, the United States remained as an occupying force, dictating the day-to-day governance of their peoples and the political complexion of their regimes, while elsewhere the promise of American defense forces and U.S. dollars encouraged friendly governments to adopt compliant policies. Never before had anyone even contemplated such an exhaustive allocation of U.S. personnel, material, and finances. American presidents oversaw the deployment of millions of American people all over Europe and other parts of the globe and the implementation of liberal-democratic principles of governance throughout its sphere of influence.[50]

At home, burgeoning military and diplomatic needs fueled the growth of an enhanced national-security bureaucracy capable of securing the country's status as a superpower. This effort revolutionized American politics by linking the nation's domestic policies to a more assertive global presence and an ongoing campaign to shape developments abroad. With the overriding goal of maintaining America's strategic leverage and protecting its diplomatic assets, U.S. foreign policy demanded an unprecedented expansion of military and bureaucratic resources during the Cold War. Within a few decades, the United States became a diplomatic and military juggernaut whose ability to take advantage of its economic might was unrivaled. The diplomatic and military resources at its disposal, which included hundreds of thousands of soldiers, a vastly reconditioned State Department, a new Department of Defense with an army of support personnel, an intelligence apparatus comprising the Central Intelligence Agency (CIA), National Security Agency (NSA), and a number of other organizations, and a growing complex of military and industrial contractors, were staggering. The discretion of the president and his foreign-policy team to utilize those resources was largely unchallenged, and the willingness of American commanders in chief to exercise ever-greater authority appeared to be without limits.[51]

The Cold War never produced a physical conflict between the United States and the Soviet Union, but it spawned a number of proxy wars around the globe and a keen political competition that polarized international affairs for over forty years. Each superpower was intent on maximizing its sphere of influence through client states and securing the cooperation of non-aligned countries through political and economic incentives. For the United States, this was the central plank in its policy of containment, so-named because it sought to contain Soviet expansion, aggression, and influence though a countervailing U.S. military, diplomatic, and economic footprint in contested theaters. Support of politically turbulent client states and military insurgencies created head-to-head conflict with Soviet interests, which produced actual wars in almost every part of the world. The bloodiest and arguably the most prominent were on the Korean peninsula, in Indochina and Central Asia, particularly Afghanistan, and throughout Latin America, but plenty of other incidents between Soviet-sponsored and American-backed forces arose in Europe, the Middle East, and Africa. Permanent military deployment was a function of the nation's postwar security needs, and it reflected the international commitments that defined America's role as a superpower, which represented a resounding rejection of the country's traditional rejection of foreign entanglements and its erstwhile devotion to neutrality.[52]

The longest and most debilitating physical conflict of the Cold War, both in terms of casualties and international prestige, was in Vietnam. At a cost of almost sixty thousand American lives during nearly thirty years of involvement of one kind or another, it was an outgrowth of the so-called "Domino Theory" among foreign policymakers in the United States. The Domino Theory was based on the assumption that, because key geopolitical regions were precariously balanced between communism and anti-communism and, by extension, between Soviet and American spheres of influence, a marginal increase in Soviet influence, or communist penetration, in a particular region would lead to the eventual communist takeover of the whole region. In other words, once a strategically significant state in such a region fell to communism, the rest of the states in that region would follow like dominos. American foreign-policy analysts and experts became convinced that Vietnam was the strategic lynchpin in Southeast Asia and that, therefore, the consolidation of communist power in Vietnam had to be prevented at all costs.[53]

Despite clear American military superiority, the commitment of five presidential administrations, and, at least initially, the requisite political will, the Vietnam War was a failure by almost every measure. Most importantly, it was the first war the United States ever lost and, especially to its critics, a conspicuous repudiation of the Domino Theory and much of the rationale for U.S. military intervention during the Cold War. Massively unpopular at home by the late 1960s, it produced unrest and protests in scores of American cities and created mistrust and skepticism regarding federal governance that are still felt today. As a result, distinguished political and military careers were seriously damaged, and—in some cases—ruined, and American politics was irrevocably changed. In terms of foreign policy, Vietnam demonstrated the futility of nation-building, particularly as a military objective, and it ultimately affected American willingness to intervene in foreign conflicts that did not invoke a compelling U.S. interest or present a clear and definite exit strategy. Ironically, the lessons of Vietnam notwithstanding, the United States has once again become involved in nation-building, in both Afghanistan and Iraq.

The Post-Soviet World

Containment, the Cold War policy that dominated U.S. diplomatic and military thinking for much of the postwar period, was actually abandoned prior to the end of the Cold War. The Reagan administration was convinced that the strategic stalemate promoted through containment was a prohibitive obstacle to the eventual resolution of the Cold War, and it adopted a much more assertive, some have said aggressive, posture concerning its dealings with the Soviets. President Reagan and his foreign-policy team committed themselves to reversing Soviet gains in traditionally communist strongholds and exerting pressure on Soviet policymakers through an accelerated build-up of U.S. military capabilities. American diplomatic efforts, not only with the Soviets but also throughout targeted global theaters, complemented Reagan's hard-line military posture by rejecting the existing international balance of power between democratic and communist forces and supporting anti-communist constituencies in various parts of the globe. Whether President Reagan truly was responsible for ending the Cold War due to his comparatively aggressive anti-Soviet initiatives is a matter for debate, but his foreign policies undeniably contributed to the collapse of the Soviet Union and its satellite regimes throughout Eastern and Central Europe.[54]

Unfortunately, the collapse of the Soviet bloc did not inaugurate a new world order characterized by global comity and cooperation, as some had hoped. The peace dividend never materialized, and the predictability of the Cold War was replaced by the unpredictability of post-Soviet opportunism among third-world dictatorships and anti-Western theocracies. Within a decade, rogue regimes, terrorist networks, and religious fundamentalism unleashed a menace that proved more difficult to control than anything encountered during the Cold War. In U.S. foreign policy as well, predictability was replaced by unpredictability, as the George H. W. Bush, Clinton, George W. Bush, and Obama administrations struggled to respond to a quickly evolving geopolitical dynamic that created new relationships, threats, and opportunities (what the first President Bush dubbed a "new world order"). Because of many interrelated factors, not least a growing Anti-Americanism among developing nations and even some of the country's former allies, continued U.S. leadership and ongoing influence in the international arena was no longer guaranteed.

A seasoned statesman and a foreign-policy veteran, the elder Bush endeavored to maintain American dominance in a time of international confusion through American diplomatic and military leadership in key strategic theaters, but that proved increasingly difficult. Heading a multinational coalition, the United States invaded Iraq in January of 1991 to liberate Kuwait, and, though the first Gulf War was actually brief and limited in scope, continued American involvement in the region was not. Through the United Nations, the U.S. and its allies became guarantors of Kuwaiti and, to an extent, Iraqi stability, which required an ongoing commitment of American resources for the next several years. Closer to home, President Bush ordered the invasion of Panama to capture the military dictator Manuel Noriega, a reputed supporter of regional terrorist organizations and narcotics trafficker who posed a security threat to the United States. In other areas, particularly Somalia, the Bush administration intervened for humanitarian reasons, but regional political and military instability eventually undermined the U.S.-led campaign. On the economic front, the Bush foreign-policy team negotiated the North American Free Trade Agreement (NAFTA) and pushed hard for its approval, but misgivings among key senators delayed ratification until Bill Clinton's first term in office.[55]

For better or worse, Bush's successor was not as eager to commit American military resources abroad, and continued American geopolitical dominance was not always a top priority. The Clinton administration, dominated by baby boomers who witnessed the failures of nation-building and interventionism during their formative years, limited U.S. diplomatic and particularly military engagements to situations that invoked a clear national interest or moral imperative. Its reluctance to wield American power as a strategic tool for renewed geopolitical dominance and a willingness to cede U.S. leadership in certain arenas, coupled with an overly cautious, if not unambitious, diplomatic team have drawn criticism from some quarters, but the proper way forward was anything but obvious. The Clinton years were noteworthy for the development of the Powell Doctrine, named after the President's Chairman of the Joint Chiefs of Staff, Colin Powell, and which advocated American military involvement only in those cases with a compelling national interest at stake, a limited engagement, minimal political entanglements, and a recognizable exit strategy. This was a policy, for example, that guided U.S. intervention in the former Yugoslavia and strikes against tactical targets in Iraq.[56]

Within nine months of President Clinton's departure from the White House, the Powell Doctrine became irrelevant and practically meaningless. Whether George W. Bush and his foreign-policy advisors came to the White House with the intent to reverse course and reinvent the country's international posture has been the subject of heated debates for some time. Regardless, the terrorist attacks in the fall of 2001 caused a wholesale reformulation of American foreign policy and a dismissal of the Powell Doctrine (even though Powell was serving as Bush's Secretary of State at the time). The so-called War on Terror, launched shortly after the terrorist attacks, ultimately secured a policy of pre-emptive action against rogue states and organizations, and, according to its neoconservative supporters, also justified foreign intervention for the promotion and protection of liberal-democratic principles. The Bush Doctrine, as some have called it, provided an unabashedly ideological basis, or rationale, for military and diplomatic involvement, and it affirmed pre-emptive military action as a practical, if not moral, necessity. Some have viewed this as an integral part of a neo-conservative agenda embraced by the Bush foreign-policy team, but many of the administration's harshest critics were neo-conservatives themselves, and Bush's own allegiance to neo-conservatism was questionable at best.[57]

In another reversal, President Obama has rejected the Bush Doctrine and has attempted, to the extent possible, to distance himself and his administration from what he perceived as the foreign-policy excesses of his predecessor. Unfortunately, like many before him, Obama learned quickly that reversals of foreign policy, though warranted and defensible in many cases, are not always achievable within inherited geopolitical circumstances. Under President Obama, the United States maintained a significant number of troops in Iraq, though he implemented a gradual reduction of forces until the official end of the war in December 2011, and troop levels in Afghanistan, to say nothing of the U.S. commitment, have actually increased. In other areas, Obama has been cautious and reluctant to commit U.S. resources unless absolutely necessary, but he did approve a U.S.-led military effort to aid Libyan rebels in North Africa. With respect to the nation's key strategic relationship, the President has kept some of the nation's traditional allies, such as Israel and Turkey, at arm's length, nor has he developed the kinds of personal ties with, for instance, British leaders that many of his predecessors had.

Unlike Ronald Reagan and George W. Bush, for example, Barack Obama did not enter the White House with an overriding vision of a new world order, particularly one based on the institutionalization of America political ideals abroad. Bush and Reagan could not have been more different in most regards, but both had an abiding vision of a Pax Americana that promoted liberal-democratic principles throughout the world. Bush's ideas in this regard were not the same as Reagan's, not even similar in fact, but he, like Reagan, believed that American leadership was the prerequisite for geopolitical progress. In foreign policy, President Obama, much like George H. W. Bush, has been more a pragmatist without a specific ideological agenda than a visionary 🖰. Still, as history has demonstrated time and again, existing commitments and geopolitical exigencies may force him to assume a more assertive, if not obtrusive, role in international politics.[58]

🖰 View President Obama's Address to the Middle East from Cairo.

War and U.S. Foreign Policy

Like it or not, war is an extension of politics, and it is also a fundamental part of foreign policy. In liberal-democratic governments, it is customarily viewed as a last resort, but it is nonetheless something whose inevitability, if not necessity, has been clear at particular junctures. The Vietnam War, discussed previously, is just one example of the various military engagements undertaken by the United States since its independence from Great Britain in the late eighteenth century. Overall, the United States has fought ten major wars, including the American Revolution, the latest being the two-front War on Terror, which has been conducted in Iraq and Afghanistan. Following the Revolution, the first conflict was the War of 1812 against Britain, which many have called the Second American Revolution. That war and the following one with Mexico in the late 1840s concerned threats to territorial integrity and the consequent consolidation of U.S. territories on the North American continent.[59]

The next war was the bloodiest in American history and the only one fought against a domestic enemy. Consuming over 600,000 lives and destroying much of the Southern United States, the Civil War was the first modern American war—a total war, which is a concept many attribute to Prussian military theorist Carl von Clausewitz. An unwelcome precedent for twentieth-century wars, it involved the almost total commitment and mobilization of resources and capabilities toward the prosecution of the war. After these early wars, the United States turned its attention outward; war with Spain and the Philippines at the end of the nineteenth century and the turn of the twentieth was a clear sign of U.S. economic and political expansionism and a gradual retreat from traditional isolationism. By the end of the second decade of the new century, the United States was at war again, this time coming to the aid of besieged European allies during the concluding months of World War I, an act that cemented its role as an international power, despite lingering isolationist sentiment at home.[60]

Peace did not last long, and the United States entered the fight against Germany, Japan, and their collaborators at the end of 1941. As already discussed, U.S. participation in World War II made the United States a superpower, catapulting a traditionally neutral and isolationist country into a position of world leadership and military dominance. World War II was also significant because it was a constitutional milestone in U.S. foreign policy. It represented the last U.S. conflict in which Congress actually declared war, as constitutionally mandated. In every war since then, U.S. participation was the result of executive action without a de jure declaration of war by Congress, which marked a considerable increase in presidential war-making authority and a concomitant abdication of Congressional authority. Congressional funding provisions for continued military deployment and resolutions supporting presidential action have frequently been portrayed as de facto declarations of war, but the required constitutional procedures for war making have been ignored and rendered practically irrelevant by presidential usurpation and Congressional inaction.[61]

In 1950, under the auspices of the United Nations, the United States intervened in Korea to repel a communist invasion of the southern peninsula by North Korean forces. Later that year, China, which had fallen to communism just a year prior, joined the North Koreans against the U.S.-led effort to aid South Korea. American

President-elect Dwight Eisenhower visits the troops in Korea in December 1952.

fears of Soviet involvement were confirmed in 1951, when Joseph Stalin decided to provide military assistance to the North Koreans. This was the first major conflict of the Cold War and an important test of Western resolve against the spread of communism. In addition, U.S. policymakers considered stability on the Korean peninsula a key to the preservation of a friendly regime in Japan, so the protection of South Korea became an important part of U.S. foreign-policy objectives in Japan. The Korean War, never officially terminated through a peace treaty but merely ending in a cease-fire that is still effective today, ultimately produced a stalemate that led to the permanent division of the Korean peninsula into North Korea and South Korea. As a result of the hostile geopolitical environment and the lack of a veritable peace treaty, not to mention concerns over the safety of Japan, the United States has maintained a troop presence in South Korea since 1953.[62]

Involvement in Vietnam, which was the next major military campaign for the United States, actually predated the Korean War, but formal U.S. participation in the region did not begin until after the withdrawal of French forces in 1954. Vietnam had been a French colonial possession, so initial postwar anti-communist initiatives were under French control, but those attempts eventually failed. For reasons already discussed, the United States became committed to the preservation of a non-communist South Vietnam and, by the early 1960s, active military support of the South Vietnamese administration. Contrary to rumors among conspiracy theorists and those that have viewed John Kennedy through rose-colored glasses, JFK did not plan to withdraw from Vietnam and had already authorized the deployment of more than 16,000 troops by the time he was assassinated in November of 1963. His successor, Lyndon Johnson, then transformed a limited engagement of several thousand so-called military advisors into a full-scale military endeavor. By July of 1965, armed with the Tonkin Gulf Resolution from the previous summer as a de facto declaration of war, LBJ and the Joint Chiefs of Staff were dedicated to total victory over North Vietnam, not just military and political aid to the South Vietnamese government.[63]

The Tonkin Gulf Resolution, a response to one confirmed and one disputed attack on U.S. naval vessels off the coast of North Vietnam, authorized the President to use whatever means necessary to protect the South Vietnamese from communist aggression. This was not a constitutional declaration of war, but the Johnson and Nixon administrations treated it as such, believing they needed no further congressional sanction to prosecute the war in Vietnam. Just as significantly, Congress, despite growing discontent regarding the war over the ensuing years among certain members, did not limit presidential war-making authority in any manner, nor did it ever try to enact a formal declaration of war. Coming on the heels of the Korean War and its lack of a congressional war declaration, Vietnam affirmed a constitutionally dubious precedent and, despite the military failure, empowered presidents in a way the Constitution had never intended. By the 1970s, although the nation was war-weary and mistrust of government was at an all-time high, U.S. presidents were armed with a war-making authority that no one seemed willing to question seriously.[64]

In 1973, perhaps seeking a way to address this unconstitutional acquisition of presidential authority, Congress overrode President Nixon's veto and passed the War Powers Resolution, which, as it turns out, only exacerbated the problem. Seen by many commentators and scholars as a cynical attempt to codify the status quo and sidestep the congressional responsibility for declaring war, the War Powers Resolution actually recognized a de facto, if not de jure, presidential authority to initiate a war without prior congressional approval. Despite the fact that the resolution attempted to limit the escalation of hostilities following initial military intervention, it nonetheless confirmed that presidents had the unilateral power to authorize military action in the first place. President Ronald Reagan relied on this power to order the invasion of Grenada in 1983 and restore constitutional government to the island nation, as did President George H. W. Bush when he initiated the invasion of Panama at the end of his first year in office in 1989 to capture its military dictator and suspected narcotics trafficker Manuel Noriega.[65]

Backed by a congressional resolution that once again avoided a formal declaration of war, the elder Bush authorized the invasion of Iraq in January of 1991, which produced the First Gulf War and ended in the liberation of Kuwait, the defeat of Iraqi forces, and the imposition of sanctions and UN-administered security controls on the Iraqi government of Saddam Hussein. Unlike its latter-day counterpart, this first Iraqi war was limited in scope and, thus, left the Iraqi government and much of the Iraqi military intact. Also unlike the Second Gulf War, the American-led war in 1991 had broad-based international backing, with more than thirty coalition members supporting the United States in one way or another. Still, Saddam Hussein's regime continued to confront the U.S. and its allies with recurring geopolitical problems, which necessitated a limited military response by the Clinton administration in late 1998. By the beginning of the second millennium, serious questions remained about Iraqi intentions and military capabilities, and many analysts worried that Iraq possessed, or would soon possess, weapons of mass destruction.[66]

Although it now seems doubtful that Iraq ever possessed the kinds of weapons British and American analysts has feared, the terrorist attacks on September 11, 2001, in New York and Washington, D.C., ultimately prevented a reasoned and deliberate consideration of diplomatic alternatives as the United States prepared for war in the Middle East. First, President George W. Bush ordered the invasion of Afghanistan in late 2001, and, backed by congressional resolution, he initiated the Second Gulf War in March of 2003. As had become customary by then, neither military engagement was authorized by a formal congressional declaration of war, and, despite eventual criticism of the war by numerous members of Congress, presidential war-making authority was not circumscribed in any way. These two invasions, part of President Bush's overarching War on Terror, just continued a constitutional precedent established shortly after the end of World War II, by legitimizing a constitutional transfer of authority from Congress to the presidency.[67]

CONCLUSION

Due to the expansion of the modern presidency, as well as the increased role of the United States on the global stage during the past century, the presidential role in foreign policy has expanded tremendously since the founding era. While the presidency may share policymaking responsibilities with Congress, presidents, according to political scientist Meena Bose, bear "the primary responsibility for shaping, negotiating, and conveying U.S. priorities abroad." In addition, the "constitutional preeminence" of the president's role in foreign policy has become "more pronounced" in recent decades as the United States has maintained its status as a superpower since the end of World War II.[68] Since that time, national security has been front-and-center for nearly every president as a rationale for many foreign policy endeavors, whether to deter the spread of communism during the Cold War (including the Korean and Vietnam wars), protecting economic interests, or the War on Terror following 9/11. The irony for the contemporary presidency regarding foreign policy can be found in the fact that rarely does a president come to office with any significant foreign policy experience. Serving as the commander in chief, and being a statesman who represents the United States on the world stage, are not experiences that can be gained in any other job or political position than being President of the United States. Also, as with economic circumstances, presidents must play the hand they are dealt in terms of international situations and crises while they are in office. Often, they must walk a fine line to balance national interests and diplomatic relationships all within the domestic partisan environment in which they must govern. Success in the foreign policy arena is not always guaranteed, but a president who utilizes the institutional resources at his disposal and can articulate clear objectives to the American public can often have a distinct political advantage. However, public expectations can often outweigh political realities for presidents regarding foreign policy, since the process is complex and multifaceted, and successful outcomes depend on a diverse and constantly shifting coalition of actors whose contributions, though not always desired, are nonetheless essential.

NATION-BUILDING

THEN . . .

The 1970s and early 1980s were precarious times for both the United States and the world generally. On May 1, 1975, the last American personnel were ignominiously airlifted out of South Vietnam as Saigon, the capital, fell to the North Vietnamese. It was the first U.S. military defeat in history, and its lessons seemed clear; foremost among them was that the United States would never again engage in nation-building. Unfortunately, political memories are frequently short, and geopolitical contingencies can shatter even the most steadfast of commitments. As the 1980s arrived, political transformations in regions precariously poised between stability and instability threatened the postwar political and economic progress among Western nations and American control of valuable strategic outposts. The recession of European empires, especially the loss of British and French colonial possessions, the pressure on rival regional powers by Soviet and U.S. spheres of influence, and the awakening of third-world nationalism all militated against stability and democratic governance. Coups and countercoups became the norm by the 1960s and 1970s throughout the Middle East, North Africa, Southeast and Central Asia, and Latin America. Military dictatorships of one sort or another were the order of the day, as authoritarianism and anti-democratic forces seemed on the rise. As Ronald Reagan took office in January, 1981, the United States faced not only communist expansion and Soviet aggression but also the proliferation of despotic governments in pivotal strategic theaters. Invariably, communism seemed the greater foe, and, as a result the United States frequently befriended ostensibly unpalatable, anti-democratic regimes or insurgents. Afghanistan and Iraq offer just two such examples.

In early 1978, the communist People's Democratic Party of Afghanistan (PDPA) seized power in Kabul, triggering a long and bloody civil war that eventually involved the Cold War's two superpowers. The Afghan civil war would become for the Soviet Union what Vietnam had been for the United States, a strategic and military miscalculation of the highest order, depleting its resources, morale, and international stature, even contributing to the demise of the Soviet state itself. The presence of Soviet troops to back the communist government against a coalition of Islamist paramilitary factions known collectively as the mujahedeen drew a response from the Carter and Reagan administrations. President Carter authorized covert military aid for the mujahedeen following the Soviet invasion in late 1979, but Ronald Reagan escalated U.S. involvement through a continuing commitment of funds and materiel provided via Pakistan during the 1980s. Abandoning the decades-old policy of containment and initiating the "rollback" of Soviet influence throughout Asia, Africa, and Latin America, Reagan and his foreign-policy team were determined to do whatever they could to undermine the communist regime in Afghanistan and Soviet strategic objectives as well.[69]

By the time the Soviets had withdrawn from Afghanistan in 1989, the United States had provided approximately $20 billion or more to the mujahedeen rebels. The money and military supplies were supplied through proxies in Pakistan, whose government became a significant, though uncertain and often questionable, partner in U.S. efforts against unfriendly authoritarian regimes in the region.[70] As it turned out, the mujahedeen, though not communist and therefore more acceptable than the Marxist PDPA, were no better equipped to rule the country than their communist predecessors. After the fall of the communist government in 1992, the civil war became an internecine conflict among the various ethnic factions that had composed the mujahedeen. Divided by tribal loyalties and complex cultural ties, the only things most of these factions shared was a hatred of the PDPA and a devotion to Islam. However, even an apparently common religion was not sufficient to unify them, as their practices ranged from assimilationist secularism to hard-core fundamentalism. As a result, Afghanistan was a political mess for most of the last decade of the second millennium and a breeding ground for extremism and violence.[71]

During the latter part of the decade, the Taliban, a hard-core fundamentalist political party dedicated to the total Islamification of Afghan society and the rule of a dubious anti-modernist form of Muslim law, consolidated power in the south and established an emirate that lasted until the U.S. invasion in 2001. The Taliban government committed countless atrocities against the Afghan people in the name of Islam and provided safe haven to various anti-Western terrorist organizations, including Al Qaeda. Staunchly anti-American, which is somewhat ironic given the circumstances that enabled its rise, the Taliban devoted itself to the elimination of U.S. influence in the region. More broadly, as a fervently anti-secular purveyor of fundamentalist dogma, it committed itself to the extermination of its seemingly more permissive rivals in the north of the country, yet its grievances against its northern brethren were as much ethnic as religious. Its support for Al Qaeda and similar terrorist groups became a particular threat to Western security, offering a home base for international terrorist initiatives and the spread of global Islamic terrorist networks. Even before the terrorist attacks against the United States in 2001, the Taliban-based regime in Kabul had become an international pariah and the target of Western counter-terrorist efforts.[72]

Afghanistan soon became the first front of George W. Bush's War on Terror, and, from a geopolitical and historical standpoint, it shared some striking similarities with the second front, which was Iraq. In 1980, Iraq invaded Iran to curb the supposed threat of Shia expansionism posed by the recently installed revolutionary regime in Tehran. After the fundamentalist revolution of 1979, the new Iranian theocratic leadership repeatedly displayed a desire to unify regional Shia populations into a greater Persia. The Iraqi government of Saddam Hussein feared that Iranian revolutionary rhetoric would galvanize the oppressed Shia majority in Iraq and destabilize the secularist dictatorship in Baghdad. The resulting Iran–Iraq war, which Iraq initiated on the pretext of an alleged Iranian assassination attempt against its foreign minister, lasted for eight years at a cost of hundreds of thousands of lives, indescribable physical devastation, and irreparable harm to both countries' international reputations. As one of the longest conventional wars of the twentieth century, it accomplished very little, if anything at all, culminating in a status quo ante and the needless depletion of national resources in both Iran and Iraq. It did, however, enable the further consolidation of power by Saddam Hussein and his Ba'athist regime, and it institutionalized a reign of terror that prompted eventual American intervention.[73]

Due to the disdain most Western countries and even the Soviet Union felt for the fundamentalist government in Tehran, the bulk of the international support benefited Iraq, which received various forms of aid, both covert and overt, from several Western nations. The United States was no different in this regard, and although it was forced to choose between the apparent lesser of two evils, it did, however reluctantly provide assistance to Saddam Hussein. The Reagan administration supplied his government with intelligence, technological expertise, and also weapons in an effort to discredit and ultimately defeat the theocracy in Iran, which had become a major geopolitical problem for the United States in the late 1970s. The overthrow of the friendly government led by the Shah of Iran and the subsequent abduction of American hostages by Iranian revolutionaries in Tehran sparked an international feud that lasts to this day. In addition, the theocracy's sponsorship of fundamentalist insurgencies and terrorist organizations throughout the Middle East, as well as its commitment to the destruction of Israel, insured the animosity of the Reagan administration and its own commitment to do whatever it could to undermine the Iranian regime.[74]

Whether Western, and particularly U.S., support of the Iraqi government during the war prevented an Iranian victory is difficult to surmise, but Saddam Hussein emerged emboldened and reassured, despite what was at best a stalemate after eight years of conflict. He either misconstrued Western aid as a validation of his cause or just used it to justify his geopolitical objectives, but the result was the same regardless. Furthermore, U.S. attacks against Iranian positions during the late 1980s, though a response to anti-American Iranian aggression in international waters, created the impression of an active collaboration between the Iraqi and U.S. administrations, which only strengthened the illusory legitimacy of Saddam Hussein's government. Leveraging his seemingly increased credibility among Western governments, he used the excuse of war to subdue the Kurdish and Shia populations within Iraq, resorting to whatever means necessary—even the use of chemical weapons against his own people. The upshot is that, the military stalemate produced by the war notwithstanding, Saddam Hussein's power was secure and unrivaled, as was his control of the Iraqi people.[75]

Saddam Hussein's political control did not translate into improved economic circumstances in Iraq, which had been ravaged by the war with Iran. Unable to repay wartime debts to the Kuwaiti government, which had lent the Iraqi regime considerable sums during its conflict with Iran, and feeling economically threatened by Kuwaiti oil production that exceeded OPEC (Organization of Petroleum Exporting Countries) quotas, Iraq invaded and quickly overran Kuwait in August 1990. The Iraqi regime installed a puppet government in Kuwait, which it annexed as its nineteenth province and refused to bow to international pressure for a complete withdrawal. As the autumn unfolded, the George H. W. Bush administration became increasingly involved in the quagmire, eventually issuing an ultimatum to Saddam Hussein and making preparations for the military liberation of Kuwait. Unwilling to heed U.S. demands, Iraq faced a U.S.-led invasion in early 1991 that swiftly accomplished its objective of liberating Kuwait. This war, too, like the Iran–Iraq War before it, resulted in a status quo ante, though Iraq was confronted with international sanctions and a military inspection and oversight program administered by the victorious powers.[76]

AND NOW . . .

On September 11, 2001, three U.S. commercial jets commandeered by Al Qaeda hijackers deliberately crashed into the World Trade Center in New York and the Pentagon in Washington, D.C., while a fourth, which was reportedly targeting the White House, dove into a field in Pennsylvania after being disarmed by American passengers. The first attack against the United States on its soil since Pearl Harbor, the carefully planned and closely coordinated plot by Afghan-based terrorists stunned the nation and the rest of the world but provoked a relatively quick response from the George W. Bush administration. In early October, predicated on intelligence confirmation of Al Qaeda's responsibility for the attacks and Taliban complicity with Al Qaeda and its leader, Osama bin Laden, the Bush administration launched an invasion of Afghanistan. The immediate purpose was the apprehension of Al Qaeda operatives, the capture of bin Laden, and the dismantling of the rogue Taliban regime that had run the country for almost a decade. Unlike the First Gulf War, which drew support from a widespread multinational alliance against Iraq, this operation was limited to the United States, Great Britain, and a handful of other allies, and it did not have the endorsement of the United Nations.[77]

Unfortunately, despite initial military success and the swift ouster of the Taliban regime, the situation in Afghanistan soon became problematic for the Bush administration and its allies. Due to the dispersed and decentralized nature of the Al Qaeda terrorist network, the capture or elimination of its leadership proved elusive, as did the actual conquest of the Taliban itself, which fled to safe havens in the south of the country and across the border into Pakistan. Moreover, the Northern Alliance, which was the latter-day successor to the mujahedeen remnants that had continued to fight the Taliban government after 1996, was just as fractured, unorganized, and ineffective in terms of national unity and purposeful governance as it had been during the Afghan civil wars of the 1980s and 1990s. It was neither prepared nor qualified to form a government to replace the ousted Taliban regime, yet it was the only option for the United States and its partners. Under UN auspices, the Afghanis created a government under Hamid Karzai, who, as a Pashtun, represented the largest ethnic faction in Afghanistan. His government, though welcomed by most observers initially, has gradually lost credibility within and outside of Afghanistan, which has not promoted long-term stability.[78]

Counter to the reformulated foreign-policy objectives in the aftermath of Vietnam, the United States was once again involved in nation-building, a task for which the military was neither trained nor designed. After initial accomplishments by the Karzai government and the reconstitution of Afghan society following the depredations of the Taliban years, factionalism, ethnic rivalry, and graft began to undermine whatever progress had been made. In addition, newly trained Afghan security forces proved unable to pacify the countryside, and they were also unable to maintain law and order in major urban centers without substantial international assistance. Adding insult to injury, a hobbling economy fell prey to a traditional black-market temptation, opium cultivation, which fueled narcotics trafficking and related criminal activities. Afghanistan is the world's leading producer of opium, and more than a third of its GDP comes from opium production.[79] Making matters worse, a Taliban resurgence starting in 2003 from bases in Pakistan and southern Afghanistan overwhelmed the new government and confronted the U.S.-led forces with a considerable military threat, which is just one of the reasons President Barack Obama authorized a military escalation in late 2009. Although the Obama administration was able to claim a victory of sorts through the capture and execution of Osama bin Laden in 2011, who had eluded President Bush's efforts to apprehend him, it remains mired in a war that has now outlasted every American conflict except Vietnam.[80]

Meanwhile, President Obama has had more success with the second front of the War on Terror, which was initiated by his predecessor in March, 2003. Convinced that Saddam Hussein's government possessed weapons of mass destruction (WMD), such as nuclear, biological, and chemical warheads, and that Iraq was a safe haven for Al Qaeda and other Islamist terrorist groups, Bush declared that, because diplomacy had failed to resolve the growing threat to the West in Iraq, the United States and its allies would seek a military solution. The objectives were similar to those in Afghanistan, so, unlike the First Gulf War in 1991, this Second Gulf War would aim at the conquest of Iraq and the removal of Saddam Hussein from power. The U.S.-led coalition was not as extensive this time, nor was it backed by the UN, which denounced the invasion as premature, provocative, and unnecessary. With wholehearted support from the British and token help from Australia and Poland, combined with various forms of assistance from other countries, the invasion was surprisingly effective in the short term—just as the Afghan campaign had been. Within three weeks, Iraq had been overrun and the government of Saddam Hussein had been toppled after approximately twenty-five years in power.[81]

Nevertheless, like Afghanistan, Iraq soon disintegrated into chaos, and the American military was no better equipped for nation-building in Iraq than it was in the Central Asian nation. After a temporary U.S. military administration, the allies prepared Iraq for democratic governance and a transition to multi-ethnic, multi-party rule, which proved just as elusive as it had in Afghanistan. Rabid competition, jealousy, and fighting among and even within opposing Sunni, Shia, and Kurd factions compromised the government of Prime Minister Nouri al-Maliki, as did the geographic splintering of the country into southern, western, and northern enclaves that frequently left Baghdad isolated. Within a couple of years of the apparent victory against the outgoing Ba'athist regime, Iraq had descended into civil war and widespread sectarian violence. Militant southern-based Shias, led by the fundamentalist cleric Muqtada al-Sadr and some of his Iranian-influenced rivals along with the restive western-based minority Sunni clans, posed ostensibly insurmountable obstacles to the pacification of the country, whereas Kurdish separatism, motivated by years of alienation and repression at the hand of Saddam Hussein, impeded unified governance and the consolidation of natural resources.[82]

As was also the case in Afghanistan, newly established national security forces proved themselves utterly unqualified and unprepared to handle either the military threat or the increasing terrorist incursions in Baghdad and other urban centers. As a result, U.S. and British forces were compelled to shoulder most of the responsibility for safety and security, even policing, though war-weary Americans and Britons on the home front grew tired of the personal and financial costs of the war. The ongoing anti-government political and military campaigns in Iraq along with the new Iraqi government's military impotence forced an escalation of troops by the Bush administration, known as the "Surge," in 2007, which attracted even more criticism of the U.S.-led war at home and abroad. Despite the criticism and the strong anti-war sentiment in many parts of the United States, the Surge was quite effective and ultimately enabled the wounded Iraqi government to make sufficient progress in order to enable U.S. troop reductions and eventual withdrawal.[83] Still, sobered by the loss of lives, materiel, and national credibility, Americans were decreasingly sympathetic, as leading Democrats called for a swift and decisive withdrawal from Iraq. Riding a wave of public discontent regarding the war and other issues, candidate Barack Obama promised to end U.S. involvement in Iraq and bring the troops home in his first year as president.[84] Once in the White House, though his campaign promises had been too ambitious and unrealistic, Obama did fulfill his promise and completed the military withdrawal by the end of 2011.

SUGGESTED READINGS

Adler, David Gray, and Larry N. George, eds. 1996. *The Constitution and the Conduct of American Foreign Policy.* Lawrence: University Press of Kansas.

Berman, Larry. 1983. *Planning a Tragedy: The Americanization of the War in Vietnam.* New York: W. W. Norton.

Berman, Larry. 2002. *No Peace, No Honor: Nixon, Kissinger, and Betrayal in Vietnam.* New York: Touchstone Books.

Ely, John Hart. 1995. *War and Responsibility.* Princeton: Princeton University Press.

Grow, Michael. 2008. *U.S. Presidents and Latin American Interventions: Pursuing Regime Change in the Cold War.* Lawrence: University Press of Kansas.

Herring, George C. 2001. *America's Longest War: The United States and Vietnam, 1950–1975.* New York: McGraw-Hill.

Indyk, Martin S., Kenneth G. Lieberthal, and Michael E. O'Hanlon. 2012. *Bending History: Barack Obama's Foreign Policy.* Washington, DC: Brookings Institution Press.

Jentleson, Bruce W. 2010. *American Foreign Policy: The Dynamics of Choice in the 21st Century.* New York: W. W. Norton.

Karnow, Stanley. 1997. *Vietnam: A History*. New York: Penguin.

LaFeber, Walter. 2002. *America, Russia, and the Cold War, 1945–2002*. Boston: McGraw-Hill.

LaFeber, Walter. 1994. *The American Age: United States Foreign Policy at Home and Abroad, 1750 to the Present*. New York: W. W. Norton.

Lowenthal, Mark M. 2008. *Intelligence: From Secrets to Policy*. Washington, DC: CQ Press.

Mearsheimer, John J., and Stephen M. Walt. 2007. *The Israel Lobby and U.S. Foreign Policy*. New York: Farrar, Straus and Giroux.

Mintz, Alex, and Karl DeRouen, Jr. 2010. *Understanding Foreign Policy Decision Making*. Cambridge: Cambridge University Press.

Rodman, Peter W. 2009. *Presidential Command: Power, Leadership, and the Making of Foreign Policy from Richard Nixon to George W. Bush*. New York: Alfred A. Knopf.

Skidmore, David. 2010. *The Unilateralist Temptation in American Foreign Policy*. New York: Routledge.

Spanier, John, and Steven W. Hook. 2009. *American Foreign Policy Since World War II*. Washington, DC: CQ Press.

ON THE WEB

https://www.cia.gov/library/publications/the-world-factbook/index.html. The World Factbook, located on the Central Intelligence Agency web page, provides information on "the history, people, government, economy, geography, communications, transportation, military, and transnational issues for 267 world entities."

http://www.state.gov/. The home page for the U.S. Department of State.

IN THEIR OWN WORDS

THE AFTERMATH OF THE CUBAN MISSILE CRISIS

The Cuban Missile Crisis in October 1962 is remembered as bringing the United States and the Soviet Union to the brink of nuclear war. President Kennedy's determination to stand firm with Soviet Premiere Nikita Khrushchev about the removal of Soviet missiles from Cuba, accomplished in part through a naval blockade of any additional Soviet ships attempting to arrive in Cuba, is also remembered as a great foreign policy accomplishment. While Kennedy had solidified his reputation, both at home and abroad, as the "cold warrior" who would fight the spread of global communism, the actions during the Cuban Missile Crisis also had reverberating effects on other areas of U.S. foreign policy, as this November 1, 1962, memo to Kennedy from General Lauris Norstad, Supreme Allied Commander in Europe (NATO), shows:

> Dear Mr. President:
>
> The outcome of the Cuban crisis is being hailed with great enthusiasm by almost everyone over here, as you know. It is regarded as a great achievement for the West, particularly for the United States, and is considered a great success for you personally. Regardless of what it may mean in terms of the overall interests and activities of the Soviet Union—and I have Berlin particularly in mind—you have averted an armed clash which could have grown to serious proportions, you have greatly enhanced the authority of the United States in

John F. Kennedy sits at his desk in the White House, on October 23, 1962, shortly after signing a presidential proclamation concerning the Cuban Missile Crisis.

world affairs, and you have established yourself with friend and foe alike as a strong leader at a time when strong leadership is sorely needed.

I am sure that the "tough-line" people, not recognizing that toughness is a means to an end and not an end or a policy in itself, will be saying "I told you so." It is my own firm conviction that your action in Cuba was successful because it was taken against an established background of calm firmness, moderation and restraint. With this background, your words and actions of last week stood out in such bold relief that they were thoroughly convincing.

I share the hope that this success can be exploited to achieve a lessening of tension, and believe that an early initiative along these lines could be most useful. It is on this subject that I would like to send you a few personal observations.

To permit the question of missiles in Turkey to be raised again would seem to deny the soundness of your position on the Soviet missiles in Cuba. Further, any official discussion of this subject would, in my judgment, have a serious morale effect in certain vital areas and would prove to be a most divisive issue at a time when we have achieved great unity within the Alliance. I am confident that there would be the strongest opposition, particularly on the part of the Greeks and the Turks to any consideration of the withdrawal of missiles from Turkey as a return gesture for Soviet action in Cuba.

You must have already been pressed to consider various force reduction, disengagement and denuclearization schemes, most of which have already been studied and have failed to stand up to searching analysis. As seen from here, a numerical reduction in Europe, if meaningful at all, would be disadvantageous to us because of the better geographical position of the USSR. The West would be weakened and tensions would thereby increase. Similarly, the events of the last year have served to emphasize the dangers of disengagement and of denuclearized zones, such as called for in the Rapacki Plan.

Any actions or gestures which do not have a sound military basis, or which are based upon trust rather than control, would cause great concern. Surely there can be no reductions in our military effectiveness without guarantees that at least equivalent security can be achieved by others means. In this connection, you may recall that on 17 November 1961 I addressed a letter to you which outlined broadly a control and inspection plan. This plan has been discussed off and on over the last five years and I believe it has some support among our European allies. Perhaps France would continue to be cool to the proposition, and I have no basis for believing that [West German] Chancellor [Konrad] Adenauer would look more favorably to the idea today than he did in the spring of 1960. However, I believe that a strong position on the part of the United States at that time might well have persuaded the Chancellor. In the present circumstances, the weight of your judgment might be decisive. I realize that this control and inspection plan is not as comprehensive as some of the broad package proposals that have been considered in the past. However, it is simple enough to be workable and clear enough to have an impact on the public. Since there has been a certain amount of NATO support for this idea in the past, perhaps it could be introduced into the North Atlantic Council as a starting point for discussion, or as one of several ideas to be considered by that body.

Faithfully yours,
LAURIS NORSTAD
General USAF[85]

APPENDIX A

Conducting Research at Presidential Libraries

The first step for anyone interested in conducting research at a presidential library is to check out the library's web page for instruction, procedures, and, most importantly, the availability of documents and other materials for the specific research topic. Each library has an extensive web page that details the number and scope of collections, online finding aids, as well as specific instructions on how to arrange for a research visit. In addition, each library has digitized numerous documents in recent years that are now available directly on the library's web page.

Next, it is always recommended to contact an archivist to talk about specific research topics and the availability of documents before arriving at the library. National Archives and Records Administration (NARA) archivists have extensive knowledge of the collections in their respective libraries, and they are a crucial resource in guiding even the most experienced researcher through the many files, documents, photos, videos, and oral histories. Knowing which documents are essential to access ahead of time can maximize the efficiency of the time spent at the library.

While each library sets its own hours and, in some cases, specific procedures for research, general rules apply to all NARA presidential libraries. For example, each researcher must fill out a brief, one-page application that describes the purpose of the research visit. In addition, each researcher is given a brief orientation by one of the archivists prior to the start of research. NARA presidential libraries provide the use of photocopiers at a small fee to researchers, and each library has slightly different, yet specific, rules for how to go about photocopying documents. Digital cameras are also allowed for those who do not wish to make photocopies. Laptop computers are also allowed in the research room, as are any papers needed by the researcher (such as a list of boxes or documents) as long as they are checked and marked in advance by the archivists. The use of pens is not allowed; pencils, paper, and other necessary items are provided by the library.

Most documents at presidential libraries are kept in archival boxes and are numbered and organized by collection. For example, the files of Marlin Fitzwater, Press Secretary to George H. W. Bush, are found in the White House Press Office collection. There are four series, with subseries, included in the Fitzwater files: Subject File (Alpha File, Boxes 1–31, Bush Alpha File, Boxes 23–24); Correspondence File (Alpha/Chron File, Boxes 35–41, Chron File, Boxes 42–44, Alpha File, Boxes 45–53); Guidance File (Boxes 54–128); and Trip Boards (Boxes 129–147). Researchers interested in Bush's press relations, communication strategies, public opinion, or other public relations activities, would also look in the White House Office of Speechwriting collection, or the White House Office of Records Management collection under the subject files of public relations, speechwriting, or other specific policy topics.

Researchers then request to look at certain boxes which are delivered to the research room on a cart (not to exceed eighteen boxes at a time). Only one box can be placed on the researcher's table at a time, only one folder can be removed from a box at a time, and a place holder must be used in the box to mark the location of the folder. All of these rules, as well as others, help to ensure that the collection stays in its proper order for use by future researchers. In addition, video surveillance cameras are used in all presidential libraries to protect against the theft or destruction of any documents. All documents with writings, signatures, or other markings by the president are not open to researchers, but photocopies are available in their place. This is true for many other valuable documents as well that have signatures of certain high-profile officials or dignitaries.

Perhaps the two most important things to remember about conducting research at a presidential library is to prepare for the trip ahead of time by accessing online finding aids and being organized about what documents to access, and to rely on the help and expertise of the archivists. While the archivists may work at specific presidential libraries, they are employees of NARA and their job is to preserve and organize the massive collection of materials and to provide access to those materials to researchers; they do not represent the president, his administration, his family, or any specific political or partisan objective. Beyond the documents themselves, the archivists represent perhaps the most valuable asset to researchers at each presidential library.

National Archives Presidential Libraries Home Page:
http://www.archives.gov/presidential-libraries/

Herbert Hoover Presidential Library and Museum
210 Parkside Drive
West Branch, IA 52358
319–643-5301
http://www.hoover.archives.gov/
E-mail: hoover.library@nara.gov

Franklin D. Roosevelt Presidential Library and Museum
4079 Albany Post Road
Hyde Park, NY 12538
845–486-7770
http://www.fdrlibrary.marist.edu/
E-mail: roosevelt.library@nara.gov

Harry S. Truman Presidential Library and Museum
500 W. US Highway 24
Independence, MO 64050
816–268-8200
http://www.trumanlibrary.org
E-mail: truman.library@nara.gov

Dwight D. Eisenhower Presidential Library and Museum
200 S.E. 4th Street
Abilene, KS 67410
785–263-6700
http://www.eisenhower.archives.gov
E-mail: eisenhower.library@nara.gov

John F. Kennedy Presidential Library and Museum
Columbia Point
Boston MA 02125
617–514-1600
http://www.jfklibrary.org/
E-mail: kennedy.library@nara.gov

Lyndon Baines Johnson Presidential Library and Museum
2313 Red River Street
Austin, TX 78705
512–721-0200
http://www.lbjlibrary.org/
E-mail: johnson.library@nara.gov

Richard Nixon Presidential Library and Museum
18001 Yorba Linda Blvd.
Yorba Linda, CA 92886
714–983-9120
http://www.nixonlibrary.gov
E-mail: nixon@nara.gov

Gerald R. Ford Presidential Library and Museum
Library: 1000 Beal Avenue
Ann Arbor, MI 48109
734–205-0555
Museum: 303 Pearl Street NW
Grand Rapids, MI 49504 616–254-0400
http://www.fordlibrarymuseum.gov/
E-mail: ford.library@nara.gov

Jimmy Carter Presidential Library and Museum
441 Freedom Parkway
Atlanta, GA 30307

404–865-7100
http://www.jimmycarterlibrary.gov/
E-mail: carter.library@nara.gov

Ronald Reagan Presidential Library and Museum
40 Presidential Drive
Simi Valley, CA 93065
805–577-4000
http://www.reagan.utexas.edu
E-mail: reagan.library@nara.gov

George Bush Presidential Library and Museum
1000 George Bush Drive West
College Station, TX 77845
979–691-4000
http://bushlibrary.tamu.edu/
E-mail: bush.library@nara.gov

William J. Clinton Presidential Library and Museum
1200 President Clinton Avenue
Little Rock, AK 72201
501–374-4242
http://www.clintonlibrary.gov
E-mail: clinton.library@nara.gov

George W. Bush Presidential Library
1725 Lakepointe Drive
Lewisville, TX 75057
972–353-0545
http://www.georgewbushlibrary.gov/
E-mail: gwbush.library@nara.gov

APPENDIX B

The United States Constitution

PREAMBLE

We the People of the United States, in Order to form a more perfect Union, establish Justice, insure domestic Tranquility, provide for the common defence, promote the general Welfare, and secure the Blessings of Liberty to ourselves and our Posterity, do ordain and establish this Constitution for the United States of America.

Article I

Section 1.

All legislative Powers herein granted shall be vested in a Congress of the United States, which shall consist of a Senate and House of Representatives.

Section 2.

The House of Representatives shall be composed of Members chosen every second Year by the People of the several States, and the Electors in each State shall have the Qualifications requisite for Electors of the most numerous Branch of the State Legislature.

No Person shall be a Representative who shall not have attained to the age of twenty five Years, and been seven Years a Citizen of the United States, and who shall not, when elected, be an Inhabitant of that State in which he shall be chosen.

Representatives and direct Taxes shall be apportioned among the several States which may be included within this Union, according to their respective Numbers, which shall be determined by adding to the whole Number of free Persons, including those bound to Service for a Term of Years, and excluding Indians not taxed, three fifths of all other Persons. The actual Enumeration shall be made within three Years after the first Meeting of the Congress of the United States, and within every subsequent Term of ten Years, in such Manner as they shall by Law direct. The Number of Representatives shall not exceed one for every thirty Thousand, but each State shall have at Least one Representative; and until such enumeration shall be made, the State of New Hampshire shall be entitled to chuse three, Massachusetts eight,

Rhode-Island and Providence Plantations one, Connecticut five, New-York six, New Jersey four, Pennsylvania eight, Delaware one, Maryland six, Virginia ten, North Carolina five, South Carolina five, and Georgia three.

When vacancies happen in the Representation from any State, the Executive Authority thereof shall issue Writs of Election to fill such Vacancies.

The House of Representatives shall chuse their Speaker and other Officers; and shall have the sole Power of Impeachment.

Section 3.

The Senate of the United States shall be composed of two Senators from each State, chosen by the Legislature thereof, for six Years; and each Senator shall have one Vote.

Immediately after they shall be assembled in Consequence of the first Election, they shall be divided as equally as may be into three Classes. The Seats of the Senators of the first Class shall be vacated at the Expiration of the second Year, of the second Class at the Expiration of the fourth Year, and the third Class at the Expiration of the sixth Year, so that one third may be chosen every second Year; and if Vacancies happen by Resignation, or otherwise, during the Recess of the Legislature of any State, the Executive thereof may make temporary Appointments until the next Meeting of the Legislature, which shall then fill such Vacancies.

No Person shall be a Senator who shall not have attained to the Age of thirty Years, and been nine Years a Citizen of the United States and who shall not, when elected, be an Inhabitant of that State for which he shall be chosen.

The Vice President of the United States shall be President of the Senate, but shall have no Vote, unless they be equally divided.

The Senate shall chuse their other Officers, and also a President pro tempore, in the Absence of the Vice President, or when he shall exercise the Office of President of the United States.

The Senate shall have the sole Power to try all Impeachments. When sitting for that Purpose, they shall be on Oath or Affirmation. When the President of the United States is tried, the Chief Justice shall preside: And no Person shall be convicted without the Concurrence of two thirds of the Members present.

Judgment in Cases of Impeachment shall not extend further than to removal from Office, and disqualification to hold and enjoy any Office of Honor, Trust or Profit under the United States: but the Party convicted shall nevertheless be liable and subject to Indictment, Trial, Judgment and Punishment, according to Law.

Section 4.

The Times, Places and Manner of holding Elections for Senators and Representatives, shall be prescribed in each State by the Legislature thereof; but the Congress may at any time by Law make or alter such Regulations, except as to the Places of chusing Senators.

The Congress shall assemble at least once in every Year, and such Meeting shall be on the first Monday in December, unless they shall by Law appoint a different Day.

Section 5.

Each House shall be the Judge of the Elections, Returns and Qualifications of its own Members, and a Majority of each shall constitute a Quorum to do Business; but a smaller Number may adjourn from day to day, and may be authorized to compel the Attendance of absent Members, in such Manner, and under such Penalties as each House may provide.

Each House may determine the Rules of its Proceedings, punish its Members for disorderly Behaviour, and, with the Concurrence of two thirds, expel a Member.

Each House shall keep a Journal of its Proceedings, and from time to time publish the same, excepting such Parts as may in their Judgment require Secrecy; and the Yeas and Nays of the Members of either House on any question shall, at the Desire of one fifth of those Present, be entered on the Journal.

Neither House, during the Session of Congress, shall, without the Consent of the other, adjourn for more than three days, nor to any other Place than that in which the two Houses shall be sitting.

Section 6.

The Senators and Representatives shall receive a Compensation for their Services, to be ascertained by Law, and paid out of the Treasury of the United States. They shall in all Cases, except Treason, Felony and Breach of the Peace, be privileged from Arrest during their Attendance at the Session of their respective Houses, and in going to and returning from the same; and for any Speech or Debate in either House, they shall not be questioned in any other Place.

No Senator or Representative shall, during the Time for which he was elected, be appointed to any civil Office under the Authority of the United States, which shall have been created, or the Emoluments whereof shall have been encreased during such time: and no Person holding any Office under the United States, shall be a Member of either House during his Continuance in Office.

Section 7.

All Bills for raising Revenue shall originate in the House of Representatives; but the Senate may propose or concur with Amendments as on other Bills.

Every Bill which shall have passed the House of Representatives and the Senate, shall, before it become a Law, be presented to the President of the United States; if he approve he shall sign it, but if not he shall return it, with his Objections to that House in which it shall have originated, who shall enter the Objections at large on their Journal, and proceed to reconsider it. If after such Reconsideration two thirds of that House shall agree to pass the Bill, it shall be sent, together with the Objections, to the other House, by which it shall likewise be reconsidered, and if approved by two thirds of that House, it shall become a Law. But in all such Cases the Votes of both Houses shall be determined by Yeas and Nays, and the Names of the Persons voting for and against the Bill shall be entered on the Journal of each House respectively. If any Bill shall not be returned by the President within ten Days (Sundays excepted) after it shall have been presented to him, the Same shall be a Law, in like Manner as if he had signed it, unless the Congress by their Adjournment prevent its Return, in which Case it shall not be a Law.

Every Order, Resolution, or Vote to which the Concurrence of the Senate and House of Representatives may be necessary (except on a question of Adjournment) shall be presented to the President of the United States; and before the Same shall take Effect, shall be approved by him, or being disapproved by him, shall be repassed by two thirds of the Senate and House of Representatives, according to the Rules and Limitations prescribed in the Case of a Bill.

Section 8.

The Congress shall have Power

To lay and collect Taxes, Duties, Imposts and Excises, to pay the Debts and provide for the common Defence and general Welfare of the United States; but all Duties, Imposts and Excises shall be uniform throughout the United States;

To borrow Money on the credit of the United States;

To regulate Commerce with foreign Nations, and among the several States, and with the Indian Tribes;

To establish an uniform Rule of Naturalization, and uniform Laws on the subject of Bankruptcies throughout the United States;

To coin Money, regulate the Value thereof, and of foreign Coin, and fix the Standard of Weights and Measures;

To provide for the Punishment of counterfeiting the Securities and current Coin of the United States;

To establish Post Offices and post Roads;

To promote the Progress of Science and useful Arts, by securing for limited Times to Authors and Inventors the exclusive Right to their respective Writings and Discoveries;

To constitute Tribunals inferior to the supreme Court;

To define and punish Piracies and Felonies committed on the high Seas, and Offences against the Law of Nations;

To declare War, grant Letters of Marque and Reprisal, and make Rules concerning Captures on Land and Water;

To raise and support Armies, but no Appropriation of Money to that Use shall be for a longer Term than two Years;

To provide and maintain a Navy;

To make Rules for the Government and Regulation of the land and naval Forces;

To provide for calling forth the Militia to execute the Laws of the Union, suppress Insurrections and repel Invasions;

To provide for organizing, arming, and disciplining, the Militia, and for governing such Part of them as may be employed in the Service of the United States, reserving to the States respectively, the Appointment of the Officers, and the Authority of training the Militia according to the discipline prescribed by Congress;

To exercise exclusive Legislation in all Cases whatsoever, over such District (not exceeding ten Miles square) as may, by Cession of particular States, and the Acceptance of Congress, become the Seat of the Government of the United States, and to exercise like Authority over all Places purchased by the Consent of the Legislature of the State in which the Same shall be, for the Erection of Forts, Magazines, Arsenals, dock-Yards, and other needful Buildings;—And

To make all Laws which shall be necessary and proper for carrying into Execution the foregoing Powers, and all other Powers vested by this Constitution in the Government of the United States, or in any Department or Officer thereof.

Section 9.

The Migration or Importation of such Persons as any of the States now existing shall think proper to admit, shall not be prohibited by the Congress prior to the Year one thousand eight hundred and eight, but a Tax or duty may be imposed on such Importation, not exceeding ten dollars for each Person.

The Privilege of the Writ of Habeas Corpus shall not be suspended, unless when in Cases of Rebellion or Invasion the public Safety may require it.

No Bill of Attainder or ex post facto Law shall be passed.

No Capitation, or other direct, Tax shall be laid, unless in Proportion to the Census or Enumeration herein before directed to be taken.

No Tax or Duty shall be laid on Articles exported from any State.

No Preference shall be given by any Regulation of Commerce or Revenue to the Ports of one State over those of another: nor shall Vessels bound to, or from, one State, be obliged to enter, clear or pay Duties in another.

No Money shall be drawn from the Treasury, but in Consequence of Appropriations made by Law; and a regular Statement and Account of Receipts and Expenditures of all public Money shall be published from time to time.

No Title of Nobility shall be granted by the United States: And no Person holding any Office of Profit or Trust under them, shall, without the Consent of the Congress, accept of any present, Emolument, Office, or Title, of any kind whatever, from any King, Prince, or foreign State.

Section 10.

No State shall enter into any Treaty, Alliance, or Confederation; grant Letters of Marque and Reprisal; coin Money; emit Bills of Credit; make any Thing but gold and silver Coin a Tender in Payment of Debts; pass any Bill of Attainder, ex post facto Law, or Law impairing the Obligation of Contracts, or grant any Title of Nobility.

No State shall, without the Consent of the Congress, lay any Imposts or Duties on Imports or Exports, except what may be absolutely necessary for executing it's inspection Laws: and the net Produce of all Duties and Imposts, laid by any State on Imports or Exports, shall be for the Use of the Treasury of the United States; and all such Laws shall be subject to the Revision and Controul of the Congress.

No State shall, without the Consent of Congress, lay any Duty of Tonnage, keep Troops, or Ships of War in time of Peace, enter into any Agreement or Compact with another State, or with a foreign Power, or engage in War, unless actually invaded, or in such imminent Danger as will not admit of delay.

Article II

Section 1.

The executive Power shall be vested in a President of the United States of America. He shall hold his Office during the Term of four Years, and, together with the Vice President, chosen for the same Term, be elected, as follows:

Each State shall appoint, in such Manner as the Legislature thereof may direct, a Number of Electors, equal to the whole Number of Senators and Representatives to which the State may be entitled in the Congress: but no Senator or Representative, or Person holding an Office of Trust or Profit under the United States, shall be appointed an Elector.

The Electors shall meet in their respective States, and vote by Ballot for two Persons, of whom one at least shall not be an Inhabitant of the same State with themselves. And they shall make a List of all the Persons voted for, and of the Number of Votes for each; which List they shall sign and certify, and transmit sealed to the Seat of the Government of the United States, directed to the President of the Senate. The President of the Senate shall, in the Presence of the Senate and House of Representatives, open all the Certificates, and the Votes shall then be counted. The Person having the greatest Number of Votes shall be the President, if such Number be a Majority of the whole Number of Electors appointed; and if there be more than one who have such Majority, and have an equal Number of Votes, then the House of Representatives shall immediately chuse by Ballot one of them for President; and if no Person have a Majority, then from the five highest on the List the said House shall in like Manner chuse the President. But in chusing the President, the Votes shall be taken by States, the Representation from each State having one Vote; A quorum for this Purpose shall consist of a Member or Members from two thirds of the States, and a Majority of all the States shall be necessary to a Choice. In every Case, after the Choice of the President, the Person having the greatest Number of Votes of the Electors shall be the Vice President. But if there should remain two or more who have equal Votes, the Senate shall chuse from them by Ballot the Vice President.

The Congress may determine the Time of chusing the Electors, and the Day on which they shall give their Votes; which Day shall be the same throughout the United States.

No Person except a natural born Citizen, or a Citizen of the United States, at the time of the Adoption of this Constitution, shall be eligible to the Office of President; neither shall any Person be eligible to that Office who shall not have attained to the Age of thirty five Years, and been fourteen Years a Resident within the United States.

In Case of the Removal of the President from Office, or of his Death, Resignation, or Inability to discharge the Powers and Duties of the said Office, the Same shall devolve on the Vice President, and the Congress may by Law provide for the Case of Removal, Death, Resignation or Inability, both of the President and Vice President, declaring what Officer shall then act as President, and such Officer shall act accordingly, until the Disability be removed, or a President shall be elected.

The President shall, at stated Times, receive for his Services, a Compensation, which shall neither be encreased nor diminished during the Period for which he shall have been elected, and he shall not receive within that Period any other Emolument from the United States, or any of them.

Before he enter on the Execution of his Office, he shall take the following Oath or Affirmation:—"I do solemnly swear (or affirm) that I will faithfully execute the Office of President of the United States, and will to the best of my Ability, preserve, protect and defend the Constitution of the United States."

Section 2.

The President shall be Commander in Chief of the Army and Navy of the United States, and of the Militia of the several States, when called into the actual Service of the United States; he may require the Opinion, in writing, of the principal Officer in each of the executive Departments, upon any Subject relating to the Duties of their respective Offices, and he shall have Power to grant Reprieves and Pardons for Offences against the United States, except in Cases of Impeachment.

He shall have Power, by and with the Advice and Consent of the Senate, to make Treaties, provided two thirds of the Senators present concur; and he shall nominate, and by and with the Advice and Consent of the Senate, shall appoint Ambassadors, other public Ministers and Consuls, Judges of the supreme Court, and all other Officers of the United States, whose Appointments are not herein otherwise provided for, and which shall be established by Law: but the Congress may by Law vest the Appointment of such inferior Officers, as they think proper, in the President alone, in the Courts of Law, or in the Heads of Departments.

The President shall have Power to fill up all Vacancies that may happen during the Recess of the Senate, by granting Commissions which shall expire at the End of their next Session.

Section 3.

He shall from time to time give to the Congress Information of the State of the Union, and recommend to their Consideration such Measures as he shall judge necessary and expedient; he may, on extraordinary Occasions, convene both Houses, or either of them, and in Case of Disagreement between them, with Respect to the Time of Adjournment, he may adjourn them to such Time as he shall think proper; he shall receive Ambassadors and other public Ministers; he shall take Care that the Laws be faithfully executed, and shall Commission all the Officers of the United States.

Section 4.

The President, Vice President and all civil Officers of the United States, shall be removed from Office on Impeachment for, and Conviction of, Treason, Bribery, or other high Crimes and Misdemeanors.

Article III

Section 1.

The judicial Power of the United States, shall be vested in one supreme Court, and in such inferior Courts as the Congress may from time to time ordain and establish. The Judges, both of the supreme and inferior Courts, shall hold their Offices during good Behaviour, and shall, at stated Times, receive for their Services, a Compensation, which shall not be diminished during their Continuance in Office.

Section 2.

The judicial Power shall extend to all Cases, in Law and Equity, arising under this Constitution, the Laws of the United States, and Treaties made, or which shall be made, under their Authority;—to all Cases affecting Ambassadors, other public Ministers and Consuls;—to all Cases of admiralty and maritime Jurisdiction; —to Controversies to which the United States shall be a Party; —to Controversies between two or more States; —between a State and Citizens of another State; —between Citizens of different States; —between Citizens of the same State claiming Lands under

Grants of different States, and between a State, or the Citizens thereof, and foreign States, Citizens or Subjects.

In all Cases affecting Ambassadors, other public Ministers and Consuls, and those in which a State shall be Party, the supreme Court shall have original Jurisdiction. In all the other Cases before mentioned, the supreme Court shall have appellate Jurisdiction, both as to Law and Fact, with such Exceptions, and under such Regulations as the Congress shall make.

The Trial of all Crimes, except in Cases of Impeachment, shall be by Jury; and such Trial shall be held in the State where the said Crimes shall have been committed; but when not committed within any State, the Trial shall be at such Place or Places as the Congress may by Law have directed.

Section 3.

Treason against the United States, shall consist only in levying War against them, or in adhering to their Enemies, giving them Aid and Comfort. No Person shall be convicted of Treason unless on the Testimony of two Witnesses to the same overt Act, or on Confession in open Court.

The Congress shall have Power to declare the Punishment of Treason, but no Attainder of Treason shall work Corruption of Blood, or Forfeiture except during the Life of the Person attainted.

Article IV

Section 1.

Full Faith and Credit shall be given in each State to the public Acts, Records, and judicial Proceedings of every other State. And the Congress may by general Laws prescribe the Manner in which such Acts, Records, and Proceedings shall be proved, and the Effect thereof.

Section 2.

The Citizens of each State shall be entitled to all Privileges and Immunities of Citizens in the several States.

A Person charged in any State with Treason, Felony, or other Crime, who shall flee from Justice, and be found in another State, shall on Demand of the executive Authority of the State from which he fled, be delivered up, to be removed to the State having Jurisdiction of the Crime.

No Person held to Service or Labour in one State, under the Laws thereof, escaping into another, shall, in Consequence of any Law or Regulation therein, be discharged from such Service or Labour, but shall be delivered up on Claim of the Party to whom such Service or Labour may be due.

Section 3.

New States may be admitted by the Congress into this Union; but no new States shall be formed or erected within the Jurisdiction of any other State; nor any State be formed by the Junction of two or more States, or Parts of States, without the Consent of the Legislatures of the States concerned as well as of the Congress.

The Congress shall have Power to dispose of and make all needful Rules and Regulations respecting the Territory or other Property belonging to the United States; and nothing in this Constitution shall be so construed as to Prejudice any Claims of the United States, or of any particular State.

Section 4.

The United States shall guarantee to every State in this Union a Republican Form of Government, and shall protect each of them against Invasion; and on Application of the Legislature, or of the Executive (when the Legislature cannot be convened) against domestic Violence.

Article V

The Congress, whenever two thirds of both Houses shall deem it necessary, shall propose Amendments to this Constitution, or, on the Application of the Legislatures of two thirds of the several States, shall call a Convention for proposing Amendments, which, in either Case, shall be valid to all Intents and Purposes, as Part of this Constitution, when ratified by the Legislatures of three fourths of the several States, or by Conventions in three fourths thereof, as the one or the other Mode of Ratification may be proposed by the Congress; Provided that no Amendment which may be made prior to the Year One thousand eight hundred and eight shall in any Manner affect the first and fourth Clauses in the Ninth Section of the first Article; and that no State, without its Consent, shall be deprived of its equal Suffrage in the Senate.

Article VI

All Debts contracted and Engagements entered into, before the Adoption of this Constitution, shall be as valid against the United States under this Constitution, as under the Confederation.

This Constitution, and the Laws of the United States which shall be made in Pursuance thereof; and all Treaties made, or which shall be made, under the Authority of the United States, shall be the supreme Law of the Land; and the Judges in every State shall be bound thereby, any Thing in the Constitution or Laws of any State to the Contrary notwith-standing.

The Senators and Representatives before mentioned, and the Members of the several State Legislatures, and all executive and judicial Officers, both of the United States and of the several States, shall be bound by Oath or Affirmation, to support this Constitution; but no religious Test shall ever be required as a Qualification to any Office or public Trust under the United States.

Article VII

The Ratification of the Conventions of nine States, shall be sufficient for the Establishment of this Constitution between the States so ratifying the Same.

Done in Convention by the Unanimous Consent of the States present the Seventeenth Day of September in the Year of our Lord one thousand seven hundred and Eighty seven and of the Independence of the United States of America the Twelfth

In witness whereof We have hereunto subscribed our Names,

George Washington—President and deputy from Virginia

New Hampshire: John Langdon, Nicholas Gilman
Massachusetts: Nathaniel Gorham, Rufus King
Connecticut: William Samuel Johnson, Roger Sherman
New York: Alexander Hamilton
New Jersey: William Livingston, David Brearly, William Paterson, Jonathan Dayton
Pennsylvania: Benjamin Franklin, Thomas Mifflin, Robert Morris, George Clymer, Thomas FitzSimons, Jared Ingersoll, James Wilson, Gouverneur Morris
Delaware: George Read, Gunning Bedford, Jr., John Dickinson, Richard Bassett, Jacob Broom
Maryland: James McHenry, Daniel of Saint Thomas Jenifer, Daniel Carroll
Virginia: John Blair, James Madison, Jr.
North Carolina: William Blount, Richard Dobbs Spaight, Hugh Williamson
South Carolina: John Rutledge, Charles Cotesworth Pinckney, Charles Pinckney, Pierce Butler
Georgia: William Few, Abraham Baldwin

Amendment I

Congress shall make no law respecting an establishment of religion, or prohibiting the free exercise thereof; or abridging the freedom of speech, or of the press; or the right of the people peaceably to assemble, and to petition the Government for a redress of grievances.

Amendment II

A well regulated Militia, being necessary to the security of a free State, the right of the people to keep and bear Arms, shall not be infringed.

Amendment III

No Soldier shall, in time of peace be quartered in any house, without the consent of the Owner, nor in time of war, but in a manner to be prescribed by law.

Amendment IV

The right of the people to be secure in their persons, houses, papers, and effects, against unreasonable searches and seizures, shall not be violated, and no Warrants shall issue, but upon probable cause, supported by Oath or affirmation, and particularly describing the place to be searched, and the persons or things to be seized.

Amendment V

No person shall be held to answer for a capital, or otherwise infamous crime, unless on a presentment or indictment of a Grand Jury, except in cases arising in the land or naval forces, or in the Militia, when in actual service in time of War or public danger; nor shall any person be subject for the same offence to be twice put in jeopardy of life or limb; nor shall be compelled in any criminal case to be a witness against himself, nor be deprived of life, liberty, or property, without due process of law; nor shall private property be taken for public use, without just compensation.

Amendment VI

In all criminal prosecutions, the accused shall enjoy the right to a speedy and public trial, by an impartial jury of the State and district wherein the crime shall have been committed, which district shall have been previously ascertained by law, and to be informed of the nature and cause of the accusation; to be confronted with the witnesses against him; to have compulsory process for obtaining witnesses in his favor, and to have the Assistance of Counsel for his defence.

Amendment VII

In Suits at common law, where the value in controversy shall exceed twenty dollars, the right of trial by jury shall be preserved, and no fact tried by a jury, shall be otherwise re-examined in any Court of the United States, than according to the rules of the common law.

Amendment VIII

Excessive bail shall not be required, nor excessive fines imposed, nor cruel and unusual punishments inflicted.

Amendment IX

The enumeration in the Constitution, of certain rights, shall not be construed to deny or disparage others retained by the people.

Amendment X

The powers not delegated to the United States by the Constitution, nor prohibited by it to the States, are reserved to the States respectively, or to the people.

Amendment XI

The Judicial power of the United States shall not be construed to extend to any suit in law or equity, commenced or prosecuted against one of the United States by Citizens of another State, or by Citizens or Subjects of any Foreign State.

Amendment XII

The Electors shall meet in their respective states, and vote by ballot for President and Vice-President, one of whom, at least, shall not be an inhabitant of the same state with themselves; they shall name in their ballots the person voted for as President, and in distinct ballots the person voted for as Vice-President, and they shall make distinct lists of all persons voted for as President, and of all persons voted for as Vice-President, and of the number of votes for each, which lists they shall sign and certify, and transmit sealed to the seat of the government of the United States, directed to the President of the Senate;—The President of the Senate shall, in the presence of the Senate and House of Representatives, open all the certificates and the votes shall then be counted;—The person having the greatest number of votes for President, shall be the President, if such number be a majority of the whole number of Electors appointed; and if no person have such majority, then from the persons having the highest numbers not exceeding three on the list of those voted for as President, the House of Representatives shall choose immediately, by ballot, the President. But in choosing the President, the votes shall be taken by states, the representation from each state having one vote; a quorum for this purpose shall consist of a member or members from two-thirds of the states, and a majority of all the states shall be necessary to a choice. And if the House of Representatives shall not choose a President whenever the right of choice shall devolve upon them, before the fourth day of March next following, then the Vice-President shall act as President, as in the case of the death or other constitutional disability of the President. The person having the greatest number of votes as Vice-President, shall be the Vice-President, if such number be a majority of the whole number of Electors appointed, and if no person have a majority, then from the two highest numbers on the list, the Senate shall choose the Vice-President; a quorum for the purpose shall consist of two-thirds of the whole number of Senators, and a majority of the whole number shall be necessary to a choice. But no person constitutionally ineligible to the office of President shall be eligible to that of Vice-President of the United States.

Amendment XIII

Neither slavery nor involuntary servitude, except as a punishment for crime whereof the party shall have been duly convicted, shall exist within the United States, or any place subject to their jurisdiction.

Congress shall have power to enforce this article by appropriate legislation.

Amendment XIV

1: All persons born or naturalized in the United States, and subject to the jurisdiction thereof, are citizens of the United States and of the State wherein they reside. No State shall make or enforce any law which shall abridge the privileges or immunities of citizens of the United States; nor shall any State deprive any person of life, liberty, or property, without due process of law; nor deny to any person within its jurisdiction the equal protection of the laws.

2: Representatives shall be apportioned among the several States according to their respective numbers, counting the whole number of persons in each State, excluding Indians not taxed. But when the right to vote at any election for the choice of electors for President and Vice President of the United States, Representatives in Congress, the Executive and Judicial officers of a State, or the members of the Legislature thereof, is denied to any of the male inhabitants of such State, being twenty-one years of age, and citizens of the United States, or in any way abridged, except for participation in rebellion, or other crime, the basis of representation therein shall be reduced in the proportion which the number of such male citizens shall bear to the whole number of male citizens twenty-one years of age in such State.

3: No person shall be a Senator or Representative in Congress, or elector of President and Vice President, or hold any office, civil or military, under the United States, or under any State, who, having previously taken an oath, as a member of Congress, or as an officer of the United States, or as a member of any State legislature, or as an executive or judicial officer of any State, to support the Constitution of the United States, shall have engaged in insurrection or rebellion against the same, or given aid or comfort to the enemies thereof. But Congress may by a vote of two-thirds of each House, remove such disability.

4: The validity of the public debt of the United States, authorized by law, including debts incurred for payment of pensions and bounties for services in suppressing insurrection or rebellion, shall not be questioned. But neither the United States nor any State shall assume or pay any debt or obligation incurred in aid of insurrection or rebellion against the United States, or any claim for the loss or emancipation of any slave; but all such debts, obligations and claims shall be held illegal and void.

5: The Congress shall have power to enforce, by appropriate legislation, the provisions of this article.

Amendment XV

1: The right of citizens of the United States to vote shall not be denied or abridged by the United States or by any State on account of race, color, or previous condition of servitude.

2: The Congress shall have power to enforce this article by appropriate legislation.

Amendment XVI

The Congress shall have power to lay and collect taxes on incomes, from whatever source derived, without apportionment among the several States, and without regard to any census or enumeration.

Amendment XVII

1: The Senate of the United States shall be composed of two Senators from each State, elected by the people thereof, for six years; and each Senator shall have one vote. The electors in each State shall have the qualifications requisite for electors of the most numerous branch of the State legislatures.

2: When vacancies happen in the representation of any State in the Senate, the executive authority of such State shall issue writs of election to fill such vacancies: Provided, That the legislature of any State may empower the executive thereof to make temporary appointments until the people fill the vacancies by election as the legislature may direct.

3: This amendment shall not be so construed as to affect the election or term of any Senator chosen before it becomes valid as part of the Constitution.

Amendment XVIII

1: After one year from the ratification of this article the manufacture, sale, or transportation of intoxicating liquors within, the importation thereof into, or the exportation thereof from the United States and all territory subject to the jurisdiction thereof for beverage purposes is hereby prohibited.

2: The Congress and the several States shall have concurrent power to enforce this article by appropriate legislation.

3: This article shall be inoperative unless it shall have been ratified as an amendment to the Constitution by the legislatures of the several States, as provided in the Constitution, within seven years from the date of the submission hereof to the States by the Congress.

Amendment XIX

1: The right of citizens of the United States to vote shall not be denied or abridged by the United States or by any State on account of sex.

2: Congress shall have power to enforce this article by appropriate legislation.

Amendment XX

1: The terms of the President and Vice President shall end at noon on the 20th day of January, and the terms of Senators and Representatives at noon on the 3d day of January, of the years in which such terms would have ended if this article had not been ratified; and the terms of their successors shall then begin.

2: The Congress shall assemble at least once in every year, and such meeting shall begin at noon on the 3d day of January, unless they shall by law appoint a different day.

3: If, at the time fixed for the beginning of the term of the President, the President elect shall have died, the Vice President elect shall become President. If a President shall not have been chosen before the time fixed for the beginning of his term, or if the President elect shall have failed to qualify, then the Vice President elect shall act as President until a President shall have qualified; and the Congress may by law provide for the case wherein neither a President elect nor a Vice President elect shall have qualified, declaring who shall then act as President, or the manner in which one who is to act shall be selected, and such person shall act accordingly until a President or Vice President shall have qualified.

4: The Congress may by law provide for the case of the death of any of the persons from whom the House of Representatives may choose a President whenever the right of choice shall have devolved upon them, and for the case of the death of any of the persons from whom the Senate may choose a Vice President whenever the right of choice shall have devolved upon them.

5: Sections 1 and 2 shall take effect on the 15th day of October following the ratification of this article.

6: This article shall be inoperative unless it shall have been ratified as an amendment to the Constitution by the legislatures of three-fourths of the several States within seven years from the date of its submission.

Amendment XXI

1: The eighteenth article of amendment to the Constitution of the United States is hereby repealed.

2: The transportation or importation into any State, Territory, or possession of the United States for delivery or use therein of intoxicating liquors, in violation of the laws thereof, is hereby prohibited.

3: This article shall be inoperative unless it shall have been ratified as an amendment to the Constitution by conventions in the several States, as provided in the Constitution, within seven years from the date of the submission hereof to the States by the Congress.

Amendment XXII

1: No person shall be elected to the office of the President more than twice, and no person who has held the office of President, or acted as President, for more than two years of a term to which some other person was elected President shall be elected to the office of the President more than once. But this article shall not apply to any person holding the office of President when this article was proposed by the Congress, and shall not prevent any person who may be holding the office of President, or acting as President, during the term within which this article becomes operative from holding the office of President or acting as President during the remainder of such term.

2: This article shall be inoperative unless it shall have been ratified as an amendment to the Constitution by the legislatures of three-fourths of the several states within seven years from the date of its submission to the states by the Congress.

Amendment XXIII

1: The District constituting the seat of government of the United States shall appoint in such manner as the Congress may direct: A number of electors of President and Vice President equal to the whole number of Senators and Representatives in Congress to which the District would be entitled if it were a state, but in no event more than the least populous state; they shall be in addition to those appointed by the states, but they shall be considered, for the purposes of the election of President and Vice President, to be electors appointed by a state; and they shall meet in the District and perform such duties as provided by the twelfth article of amendment.

2: The Congress shall have power to enforce this article by appropriate legislation.

Amendment XXIV

1: The right of citizens of the United States to vote in any primary or other election for President or Vice President, for electors for President or Vice President, or for Senator or Representative in Congress, shall not be denied or abridged by the United States or any state by reason of failure to pay any poll tax or other tax.

2: The Congress shall have power to enforce this article by appropriate legislation.

Amendment XXV

1: In case of the removal of the President from office or of his death or resignation, the Vice President shall become President.

2: Whenever there is a vacancy in the office of the Vice President, the President shall nominate a Vice President who shall take office upon confirmation by a majority vote of both Houses of Congress.

3: Whenever the President transmits to the President pro tempore of the Senate and the Speaker of the House of Representatives his written declaration that he is unable to discharge the powers and duties of his office, and until he transmits to them a written declaration to the contrary, such powers and duties shall be discharged by the Vice President as Acting President.

4: Whenever the Vice President and a majority of either the principal officers of the executive departments or of such other body as Congress may by law provide, transmit to the President pro tempore of the Senate and the Speaker of the House of Representatives their written declaration that the President is unable to discharge the powers and duties of his office, the Vice President shall immediately assume the powers and duties of the office as Acting President.

Thereafter, when the President transmits to the President pro tempore of the Senate and the Speaker of the House of Representatives his written declaration that no inability exists, he shall resume the powers and duties of his office unless the Vice President and a majority of either the principal officers of the executive department or of such other body as Congress may by law provide, transmit within four days to the President pro tempore of the Senate and the Speaker of the House of Representatives their written declaration that the President is unable to discharge the powers and duties of his office. Thereupon Congress shall decide the issue, assembling within forty-eight hours for that purpose if not in session. If the Congress, within twenty-one days after receipt of the latter written declaration, or, if Congress is not in session, within twenty-one days after Congress is required to assemble, determines by two-thirds vote of both Houses that the President is unable to discharge the powers and duties of his office, the Vice President shall continue to discharge the same as Acting President; otherwise, the President shall resume the powers and duties of his office.

Amendment XXVI

1: The right of citizens of the United States, who are 18 years of age or older, to vote, shall not be denied or abridged by the United States or any state on account of age.

2: The Congress shall have the power to enforce this article by appropriate legislation.

Amendment XXVII

No law varying the compensation for the services of the Senators and Representatives shall take effect until an election of Representatives shall have intervened.

APPENDIX C

Presidential Election Results, 1789–2012

YEAR	PARTY	PRESIDENTIAL NOMINEE	VP NOMINEE	ELECTORAL VOTE #	ELECTORAL VOTE %	POPULAR VOTE #	POPULAR VOTE %
1789	Federalist (unofficial)	**George Washington**		69	100		
1792	Federalist (unofficial)	**George Washington**		132	100		
1796	Federalist	**John Adams**		71	51.1		
	Democratic-Republican	Thomas Jefferson		68	48.9		
1800	Democratic-Republican	**Thomas Jefferson**		73	52.9		
	Federalist	John Adams		65	47.1		
1804	Democratic-Republican	**Thomas Jefferson**	George Clinton	162	92.0		
	Federalist	Charles Pinckney	Rufus King	14	8.0		
1808	Democratic-Republican	**James Madison**	George Clinton	122	69.7		
	Federalist	Charles Pinckney	Rufus King	47	26.9		
1812	Democratic-Republican	**James Madison**	Elbridge Gerry	128	58.7		
	Federalist	DeWitt Clinton	Jared Ingersoll	89	40.8		
1816	Democratic-Republican	**James Monroe**	Daniel D. Tompkins	183	83.9		
	Federalist	Rufus King	John Howard	34	15.6		

YEAR	PARTY	PRESIDENTIAL NOMINEE	VP NOMINEE	ELEC-TORAL VOTE #	ELECTORAL VOTE %	POPULAR VOTE #	POPULAR VOTE %
1820	Democratic-Republican	**James Monroe**		231	98.3		
	Independent	John Quincy Adams		1	0.4		
1824	Democratic-Republican	**John Quincy Adams**		84	32.2		
	Democratic-Republican	Andrew Jackson		99	37.9		
	Democratic-Republican	William H. Crawford		41	15.7		
	Democratic-Republican	Henry Clay		37	14.2		
1828	Democratic-Republican	**Andrew Jackson**	John C. Calhoun	178	68.2	642,553	56.1
	National Republican	John Quincy Adams	Richard Rush	83	31.8	500,897	43.6
1832	Democratic	**Andrew Jackson**	Martin Van Buren	219	76.0	701,780	54.2
	National Republican	Henry Clay	John Sergeant	49	17.0	484,205	37.4
	Independent	John Floyd	Henry Lee	11	3.8	0	
	Anti-Masonic	William Wirt	Amos Ellmaker	7	2.4	100,715	7.8
1836	Democratic	**Martin Van Buren**	Richard Johnson	170	57.8	764,176	50.8
	Whig	William Henry Harrison	Francis P. Granger	73	24.8	550,816	36.6
	Whig	Hugh Lawson White	John Tyler	26	8.8	146,107	9.7
	Whig	Daniel Webster	Francis P. Granger	14	4.8	41,201	2.7
	Independent	Willie Person Mangum	John Tyler	11	3.7	0	
1840	Democratic	Martin Van Buren	Richard Johnson	60	20.4	1,128,854	46.8
	Whig	**William Henry Harrison**	John Tyler	234	79.6	1,275,390	52.9
1844	Democratic	**James K. Polk**	George M. Dallas	170	61.8	1,339,494	49.5

YEAR	PARTY	PRESIDENTIAL NOMINEE	VP NOMINEE	ELECTORAL VOTE #	ELECTORAL VOTE %	POPULAR VOTE #	POPULAR VOTE %
	Whig	Henry Clay	Theodore Frelinghuy-sen	105	38.2	1,300,004	48.1
1848	Democratic	Lewis Cass	William Butler	127	43.8	1,223.460	42.5
	Whig	**Zachary Taylor**	Millard Fillmore	163	56.2	1,361,393	47.3
	Free Soil	Martin Van Buren	Charles Adams, Sr.	0		291,501	10.1
1852	Democratic	**Franklin Pierce**	William R. King	254	85.8	1,607,510	50.8
	Whig	Winfield Scott	William Graham	42	14.2	1,386,942	43.9
1856	Democratic	**James Buchanan**	John C. Brecken-ridge	174	58.8	1,836,072	45.3
	Republican	John C. Fremont	William L. Dayton	114	38.5	1,342.345	33.1
	Whig-Amer-ican	Millard Fillmore	Andrew Jackson Donelson	8	2.7	873,053	21.6
1860	Democratic	Stephen Doug-las	Herschel Johnson	12	4.0	1,380,202	29.5
	Democratic (Southern)	John Breckenridge	Joseph Lane	72	23.8	848,019	18.1
	Republican	**Abraham Lincoln**	Hannibal Hamlin	180	59.4	1,865,908	39.9
	Constitu-tional Union	John Bell	Edward Everett	39	12.9	590,901	12.6
1864	Democratic	George McClellan	George Pendleton	21	9.0	1,809,445	44.9
	Republican	**Abraham Lincoln**	Andrew Johnson	212	90.6	2,220,846	55.1
1868	Democratic	Horatio Seymour	Francis Blair, Jr.	80	27.2	2,708,744	47.3
	Republican	**Ulysses S. Grant**	Schuyler Colfax	214	72.8	3,013,650	52.7
1872	Democratic	Horace Greeley*	Benjamin Brown	0		2,835,315	43.8
	Republican	**Ulysses S. Grant**	Henry Wilson	286	81.9	3,598,468	55.6
1876	Democratic	Samuel Tilden	Thomas Hendricks	184	49.9	4,288,191	51.0

YEAR	PARTY	PRESIDENTIAL NOMINEE	VP NOMINEE	ELECTORAL VOTE #	ELECTORAL VOTE %	POPULAR VOTE #	POPULAR VOTE %
	Republican	**Rutherford B. Hayes**	William Wheeler	185	50.1	4,033,497	48.0
1880	Democratic	Winfield S. Hancock	William English	155	42.0	4,445,256	48.2
	Republican	**James A. Garfield**	Chester A. Arthur	214	58.0	4,453,611	48.3
1884	Democratic	**Grover Cleveland**	Thomas Hendricks	219	54.6	4,915,586	48.9
	Republican	James G. Blane	John Logan	182	45.4	4,852,916	48.2
1888	Democratic	Grover Cleveland	Allen Thurman	168	41.9	5,539,118	48.6
	Republican	**Benjamin Harrison**	Levi Mor-ton	233	58.1	5,449.825	47.8
1892	Democratic	**Grover Cleveland**	Adlai E. Stevenson	277	62.4	5,554,617	46.0
	Republican	Benjamin Harrison	Whitelaw Reid	145	32.7	5,186,793	43.0
	Populist	James Weaver	James Field	22	5.0	1,029,357	8.5
1896	Democratic	William Jennings Bryan	Arthur Sewall	176	39.0	6,370,897	45.8
	Republican	**William McKinley**	Garret Hobart	271	61.0	7.105,076	51.1
1900	Democratic	William Jennings Bryan	Adlai E. Stevenson	155	34.7	6,357,698	45.5
	Republican	**William McKinley**	Theodore Roosevelt	292	65.3	7,219,193	51.7
1904	Democratic	Alton B. Parker	Henry Davis	140	29.4	5,083,501	37.6
	Republican	**Theodore Roosevelt**	Charles Fairbanks	336	70.6	7,625,599	56.4
1908	Democratic	William Jennings Bryan	John Kern	162	33.5	6,406,874	43.0
	Republican	**William Howard Taft**	James S. Sherman	321	66.5	7,676,598	51.6
1912	Democratic	**Woodrow Wilson**	Thomas R. Marshall	435	81.9	6,294,327	41.8
	Republican	William Howard Taft	Nicholas Butler	8	1.5	3,486,343	23.2

YEAR	PARTY	PRESIDENTIAL NOMINEE	VP NOMINEE	ELECTORAL VOTE #	ELECTORAL VOTE %	POPULAR VOTE #	POPULAR VOTE %
	Progressive	Theodore Roosevelt	Hiram Johnson	88	16.6	4,120,207	27.4
1916	Democratic	**Woodrow Wilson**	Thomas R. Marshall	277	52.2	9.126.063	49.2
	Republican	Charles E. Hughes	Charles W. Fairbanks	254	47.8	8,547,030	46.1
1920	Democratic	James M. Cox	Franklin D. Roosevelt	127	23.9	9,134,074	34.1
	Republican	**Warren G. Harding**	Calvin Coolidge	404	76.1	16,151,916	60.3
1924	Democratic	John W. Davis	Charles W. Bryan	136	25.6	8,386,532	28.8
	Republican	**Calvin Coolidge**	Charles G. Dawes	382	71.9	15,724,310	54.0
	Progressive	Robert LaFollette	Burton K. Wheeler	13	2.4	4,827,184	16.6
1928	Democratic	Alfred E. Smith	Joseph Robinson	87	16.4	15,004,336	40.8
	Republican	**Herbert Hoover**	Charles Curtis	444	83.6	21,432,823	58.2
1932	Democratic	**Franklin D. Roosevelt**	John Nance Garner	472	88.9	22,818,740	57.4
	Republican	Herbert Hoover	Charles Curtis	59	11.1	15,760,425	39.6
1936	Democratic	**Franklin D. Roosevelt**	John Nance Garner	523	98.5	27,750,866	60.8
	Republican	Alfred M. Landon	Frank Knox	8	1.5	16,679,683	36.5
1940	Democratic	**Franklin D. Roosevelt**	Henry A. Wallace	449	84.6	27,243,218	54.7
	Republican	Wendell L. Willkie	Charles L. McNary	82	15.4	22,334,940	44.8
1944	Democratic	**Franklin D. Roosevelt**	Harry S. Truman	432	81.4	25,612,610	53.4
	Republican	Thomas Dewey	John W. Bricker	99	18.6	22,014,160	45.9
1948	Democratic	**Harry S. Truman**	Alben W. Barkley	303	57.1	24,105,810	49.5
	Republican	Thomas Dewey	Earl Warren	189	35.6	21,970,064	45.1
	States' Rights	Strom Thurmond	Fielding Wright	39	7.3	1,169,114	2.4

YEAR	PARTY	PRESIDENTIAL NOMINEE	VP NOMINEE	ELECTORAL VOTE #	ELECTORAL VOTE %	POPULAR VOTE #	POPULAR VOTE %
1952	Democratic	Adlai Stevenson	John Sparkman	89	16.8	27,314,992	44.4
	Republican	**Dwight D. Eisenhower**	Richard M. Nixon	442	83.2	33,777,945	54.9
1956	Democratic	Adlai Stevenson	Estes Kefauver	73	13.7	26,022,752	42.0
	Republican	**Dwight D. Eisenhower**	Richard M. Nixon	457	86.1	35,590,472	57.4
1960	Democratic	**John F. Kennedy**	Lyndon B. Johnson	303	56.4	34,226,731	49.7
	Republican	Richard M. Nixon	Henry Cabot Lodge	219	40.8	34,108,157	49.5
	Democratic	Harry F. Byrd	Strom Thurmond	15	2.8	0	
1964	Democratic	**Lyndon B. Johnson**	Hubert H. Humphrey	486	90.3	43,129,566	61.1
	Republican	Barry Goldwater	William E. Miller	52	9.7	27,178,188	38.5
1968	Democratic	Hubert H. Humphrey	Edmund Muskie	191	35.5	31,275,166	42.7
	Republican	**Richard M. Nixon**	Spiro Agnew	301	55.9	31,785,480	43.4
	American Independent	George Wallace	Curtis LeMay	45	8.4	9,906,473	13.5
1972	Democratic	George McGovern	Sargent Shriver	17	3.2	29,170,383	37.5
	Republican	**Richard M. Nixon**	Spiro Agnew	520	96.7	47,169,911	60.7
1976	Democratic	**Jimmy Carter**	Walter Mondale	297	55.2	40,830,763	50.1
	Republican	Gerald R. Ford	Bob Dole	240	44.6	39,147,793	48.0
1980	Democratic	Jimmy Carter	Walter Mondale	49	9.1	35,483,883	41.0
	Republican	**Ronald Reagan**	George Bush	489	90.9	43,904,153	50.7
	National Union	John Anderson	Patrick Lucey	0		5,720,060	6.6
1984	Democratic	Walter Mondale	Geraldine Ferraro	13	2.4	37,577,185	40.6
	Republican	**Ronald Reagan**	George Bush	525	97.6	54,455,075	58.8

YEAR	PARTY	PRESIDENTIAL NOMINEE	VP NOMINEE	ELECTORAL VOTE #	ELECTORAL VOTE %	POPULAR VOTE #	POPULAR VOTE %
1988	Democratic	Michael Dukakis	Lloyd Bentsen	111	20.6	41,809,074	45.6
	Republican	**George Bush**	Dan Quayle	426	79.2	48,886,097	53.4
1992	Democratic	**William J. Clinton**	Albert Gore, Jr.	370	68.8	44,909,326	43.0
	Republican	George Bush	Dan Quayle	168	31.2	39,103,882	37.4
	Independent	H. Ross Perot	James Stockdale	0		19,741,657	18.9
1996	Democratic	**William J. Clinton**	Albert Gore, Jr.	379	70.4	47,402,357	49.2
	Republican	Bob Dole	Jack Kemp	159	29.6	39,198,755	40.7
	Reform	H. Ross Perot	Pat Choate	0		8,085,402	8.4
2000	Democratic	Albert Gore, Jr.	Joseph Lieberman	266	49.4	50,992,335	48.4
	Republican	**George W. Bush**	Richard Cheney	271	50.4	50,455,156	47.9
	Green	Ralph Nader	Winona LaDuke	0		2,822,738	2.7
2004	Democratic	John F. Kerry	John Edwards	251	46.7	59,028,444	48.3
	Republican	**George W. Bush**	Richard Cheney	286	53.2	62,040,610	50.7
2008	Democratic	**Barack Obama**	Joseph Biden	365	67.8	69,456,897	52.9
	Republican	John McCain	Sarah Palin	173	32.2	59,934,814	45.7
2012	Democratic	**Barack Obama**	Joseph Biden	332	61.5	61,910,594	51.4
	Republican	Mitt Romney	Paul Ryan	206	38.1	58,645,765	48.6

* Horace Greeley died on November 29, 1872, after the popular election but before the Electoral College met. His electoral votes were split among four individuals including eighteen for Benjamin Brown, Greeley's running mate.

Source: The American Presidency Project, "Presidential Elections Data," available at http://www.presidency.ucsb.edu/elections.php.

NOTES

CHAPTER 1

1. "Remarks by the President," April 27, 2011, http://www.whitehouse.gov/the-press-office/2011/04/27/remarks-president.
2. Barack Obama's interview with Steve Croft, *60 Minutes*, CBS, May 8, 2011.
3. For example, see Louis W. Koenig, *The Chief Executive*, 6th ed. (New York: Harcourt Brace, 1996), 2–3.
4. Ibid, 2.
5. Ibid, 3.
6. Jeffrey Cohen and David Nice, *The Presidency* (New York: McGraw-Hill, 2003), 53–59; and Sidney M. Milkis and Michael Nelson, *The American Presidency: Origins and Development, 1776–2007*, 5th ed. (Washington, DC: CQ Press, 2008), 280–85.
7. Milkis and Nelson, 281.
8. The term "imperial president" is most often associated with the classic book of the same title by historian Arthur Schlesinger, Jr., in which he discusses the modern presidency. See Arthur M. Schlesinger, *The Imperial Presidency* (Boston: Houghton Mifflin Company, 1973).
9. Koenig, *The Chief Executive*, 4.
10. For example, see Richard Rose, *The Postmodern President*, 2nd ed. (Chatham, NJ: Chatham House, 1991), 2–6.
11. Joseph A. Pika and John Anthony Maltese, *The Politics of the Presidency*, rev. 7th ed. (Washington, DC: CQ Press, 2010), 1.
12. Hugh Heclo, *Studying the Presidency: A Report to the Ford Foundation* (New York: Ford Foundation Press, 1977), 7–8.
13. See Edward S. Corwin, *The President: Office and Powers 1787–1957* (New York: New York University Press, 1957), 29–30.
14. Clinton Rossiter, *The American Presidency* (New York: Time Incorporated, 1960), 31.
15. See Richard Neustadt, *Presidential Power: The Politics of Leadership* (New York: Wiley, 1960).
16. Heclo, *Studying the Presidency*, 5–6.
17. Ibid, 31–45.
18. Ibid, 30.

19. *Researching the Presidency: Vital Questions, New Approaches*, eds. George C. Edwards, III, John H. Kessel, and Bert A. Rockman (Pittsburgh: University of Pittsburgh Press, 1993), 3–5.
20. Lyn Ragsdale, *Vital Statistics on the Presidency*, 3rd ed. (Washington, DC: CQ Press, 2009), 1–3.
21. Stephen J. Wayne, "An Introduction to Research on the Presidency," in *Studying the Presidency*, eds. George C. Edwards, III, and Stephen J. Wayne (Knoxville: University of Tennessee Press, 1983), 4.
22. Ibid, 5–6.
23. Stephen J. Wayne, "Approaches," in *Studying the Presidency*, eds. George C. Edwards, III, and Stephen J. Wayne (Knoxville: University of Tennessee Press, 1983), 17–49.
24. Early examples include works such as George C. Edwards, III, *At the Margins: Presidential Leadership of Congress* (New Haven, CT: Yale University Press, 1989); Mark A. Peterson, *Legislating Together: The White House and Capitol Hill from Eisenhower to Reagan* (Cambridge: Harvard University Press, 1990); and Samuel Kernell, *Going Public: New Strategies of Presidential Leadership* (Washington, DC: CQ Press, 1986), to name a few.
25. Peter G. Northouse, *Leadership: Theory and Practice* (Thousand Oaks, CA: Sage Publications, 1997), 3.
26. Bert A. Rockman, "The Leadership Style of George Bush," in *The Bush Presidency: First Appraisals*, eds. Colin Campbell and Bert A. Rockman (Chatham, NJ: Chatham House, 1991), 2.
27. James MacGregor Burns, *Leadership* (New York: Harper & Row, 1978).
28. James MacGregor Burns, *Transforming Leadership* (New York: Atlantic Monthly Press, 2003), 29.
29. See Bruce Miroff, *Icons of Democracy: American Leaders as Heroes, Aristocrats, Dissenters, & Democrats* (Lawrence: University Press of Kansas, 2000).
30. Ibid.
31. See Neustadt, *Presidential Power*.
32. See Stephen Skowronek, *The Politics Presidents Make: Leadership from John Adams to George Bush* (Cambridge: Belknap/Harvard Press, 1993); and Rose, *The Postmodern President*.
33. For example, see John H. Kessel, *Presidents, the Presidency, and the Political Environment* (Washington, DC: CQ Press, 2001), and Thomas E. Cronin and Michael A. Genovese, *The Paradoxes of the American Presidency*, 2nd ed. (New York: Oxford University Press, 2004).
34. For example, see John P. Burke, *The Institutional Presidency* (Baltimore: Johns Hopkins University Press, 1992); Thomas J. Weko, *The Politicizing Presidency: The White House Personnel Office, 1948–1994* (Lawrence, KS: University of Kansas Press, 1995), and Shirley Anne Warshaw, *The Keys to Power: Managing the Presidency* (New York: Longman, 2000).
35. For example, see Charles O. Jones, *Separate But Equal Branches: Congress and the Presidency*, 2nd ed. (New York: Chatham House Publishers, 1999); Jeffrey E. Cohen, *Presidential Responsiveness and Public Policy-Making: The Public and the Policies That Presidents Choose* (Ann Arbor, MI: University of Michigan Press, 1997); and William W. Lammers and Michael A. Genovese, *The Presidency and Domestic Policy: Comparing Leadership Styles, FDR to Clinton* (Washington, DC: CQ Press, 2000).
36. For example, see Samuel Kernell, *Going Public: New Strategies of Presidential Leadership*, 4th ed. (Washington, DC: CQ Press, 2007); Jeffrey K. Tulis, *The Rhetorical*

Presidency (Princeton, NJ: Princeton University Press, 1987); Roderick P. Hart, *The Sound of Leadership: Presidential Communication in the Modern Age* (Chicago: University of Chicago Press, 1987); Mary E. Stuckey, *The President as Interpreter-in-Chief* (Chatham, NJ: Chatham House, 1991); John Anthony Maltese, *Spin Control: The White House Office of Communications and the Management of Presidential News*, 2nd ed., rev. (Chapel Hill: University of North Carolina Press, 1994); and Lori Cox Han, *Governing From Center Stage: White House Communication Strategies during the Television Age of Politics* (Cresskill, NJ: Hampton Press, 2001).

37. For example, see Cronin and Genovese, *The Paradoxes of the American Presidency*, 2nd ed., 62–63. See also Robert K. Murray and Tim H. Blessing, *Greatness in the White House: Rating the Presidents from George Washington through Ronald Reagan*, 2nd ed. (University Park, PA: Pennsylvania State University Press, 1994), and Arthur M. Schlesinger Jr., "The Ultimate Approval Rating," *New York Times Magazine*, 15 December 1996: 46–51.
38. See Cronin and Genovese, *The Paradoxes of the American Presidency*, 2nd ed.
39. See Fred I. Greenstein, *The Presidential Difference: Leadership Style from FDR to Barack Obama*, 3rd ed. (Princeton: Princeton University Press, 2009).
40. See James David Barber, *The Presidential Character: Predicting Performance in the White House*, rev. 4th ed. (New York: Prentice Hall, 2008).
41. See Greenstein, *The Presidential Difference,* 296.
42. See Lori Cox Han, "Public Leadership in the Political Arena," in *Leadership and Politics, Vol. 2 of Leadership at the Crossroads*, eds. Michael A. Genovese and Lori Cox Han (Westport, CT: Praeger Publishers, 2008).
43. Tulis, *The Rhetorical Presidency,* 28.
44. Ibid, 4–23.
45. Hart, *The Sound of Leadership,* 212.
46. Kernell, *Going Public,* 10–11.
47. See George C. Edwards, *On Deaf Ears: The Limits of the Bully Pulpit* (New Haven: Yale University Press, 2003).
48. See Jeffrey E. Cohen, *Going Local: Presidential Leadership in the Post-Broadcast Age* (New York: Cambridge University Press, 2010).
49. Examples of this approach include Terry M. Moe, "The Politicized Presidency," in *The New Direction in American Politics*, eds. John E. Chubb and Paul E. Peterson (Washington, DC: The Brookings Institution, 1985); Moe, "Presidents, Institutions, and Theory," in Edwards et al., *Researching the Presidency*; Burke, *The Institutional Presidency*; and Thomas J. Weko, *The Politicizing Presidency.*
50. For an excellent discussion of Terry Moe's work in this area, see Jeffrey Cohen and David Nice, *The Presidency*, 57–59.
51. See Skowronek, *The Politics Presidents Make.*
52. Ibid.
53. See Louis Fisher, *The Politics of Shared Power: Congress and the Executive*, 4th ed. (College Station: Texas A&M University Press, 1998).
54. See Ragsdale, *Vital Statistics on the Presidency,* 7–13.
55. Fred I. Greenstein, *The Hidden-Hand Presidency: Eisenhower as Leader* (Baltimore: Johns Hopkins University Press, 1994), viii–ix.
56. "Presidential Libraries," National Archives and Records Administration, http://www.archives.gov/presidential-libraries/.
57. Letter from Irving Perimeter to Benson Trimble, November 15, 1952, WHCF Permanent File, Subject File, Box 5, Harry S. Truman Presidential Library, Independence, Missouri.

58. Originally dedicated in 1990, the Nixon Library did not become an official NARA presidential library until 2007. After numerous legal battles between the federal government and the Nixon family, Nixon White House documents held in NARA archives in College Park, Maryland, began to be transferred to the Yorba Linda, California, library in 2004; previously, the Nixon Library was run by the privately funded Nixon Foundation and only housed pre- and post-presidential papers.
59. In 2011, the "Presidency Research Group" was renamed "Presidents and Executive Politics."
60. "Call to Action on Executive Order 13233," Society of American Archivists, http://www.archivists.org/news/actnow.asp.
61. John Wertman, "Bush's Obstruction of History," *Washington Post*, February 26, 2006, available at http://www.washingtonpost.com/wp-dyn/content/article/2006/02/24/AR2006022401805.html.
62. At the time, Dr. Leland was Director Emeritus of the American Council of Learned Societies. The other members of the Executive Committee included Dr. Randolph G. Adams, director of the William L. Clements Library for American History, University of Michigan; Judge Charles E. Clark, dean of the Yale Law School; Dr. Robert D. W. Connor, Archivist of the United States; Dr. Helen Taft Manning, dean of Bryn Mawr College; Professor Samuel Eliot Morison of Harvard University; and Dr. Stuart A. Rice, Chairman of the Central Statistical Board, Washington, D.C.
63. Letter from Waldo G. Leland to Franklin D. Roosevelt, December 14, 1938, Files of Waldo G. Leland, Correspondence and Memos, Box 1, Franklin D. Roosevelt Presidential Library, Hyde Park, New York.
64. Statement by Waldo G. Leland at a dinner for advisory and executive committee members of the FDR Library project at the Hotel Carlton, Washington, D.C., February 4, 1939, Files of Waldo G. Leland, Correspondence and Memos, Box 1, Franklin D. Roosevelt Presidential Library, Hyde Park, New York.
65. "The Story of the Franklin D. Roosevelt Library," Address by Waldo Gifford Leland at the Franklin D. Roosevelt Presidential Library, Hyde Park, New York, March 17, 1950, at the opening of the FDR Papers for research, Papers of Waldo G. Leland, Box 1, Franklin D. Roosevelt Presidential Library, Hyde Park, New York.
66. Memorandum for the Director of the Franklin D. Roosevelt Library from Franklin D. Roosevelt, July 16, 1943, Papers of Waldo G. Leland, Box 1, Franklin D. Roosevelt Presidential Library, Hyde Park, New York.
67. Remarks of President Lyndon Johnson at the LBJ Library Dedication, May 22, 1971, http://www.lbjlibrary.org/collections/selected-speeches/post-presidential/05–22-1971.html.
68. Letter from George Bush to Perry Adkisson, February 28, 1989, White House Office of Records and Management, Federal Government, Box 11, George Bush Presidential Library, College Station, Texas.
69. Bush received a letter from Kenneth Lay, Chairman, President and CEO of ENRON Corporation, on March 21, 1989, urging the president to consider placing his library on the University of Houston campus: "More than any other academic institution in your hometown, we believe the University of Houston reflects the values, vision, scope, quality and dedication that characterizes your city and your career in private enterprise and public service.... As our 'education president', it seems proper that your library should be affiliated with a public university in Houston that addresses the broadest current and future educational interests and needs of our country's people, and that reflects in its objectives and interests those areas of study in energy, economics, international affairs

and equality of opportunity that have been the focus of your own life's work." Letter from Kenneth L. Lay to George Bush, March 21, 1989, White House Office of Records and Management, Federal Government, Box 12, George Bush Presidential Library, College Station, Texas.

70. Memorandum for the President from James W. Cicconi, "Presidential Library Correspondence," White House Office of Records and Management, Federal Government, Box 12, George Bush Presidential Library, College Station, Texas.
71. Memorandum for Patty Presock from Jim Cicconi, "Possible Meeting with Presidential Library Architect," White House Office of Records and Management, Federal Government, Box 12, George Bush Presidential Library, College Station, Texas.
72. Letter from George H. W. Bush to Ross D. Margraves, Jr., May 3, 1991, White House Office of Records and Management, Federal Government, Box 12, George Bush Presidential Library, College Station, Texas.
73. Ralph Blumenthal, "S.M.U. Faculty Complains About Bush Library," *New York Times*, January 10, 2007, available at http://www.nytimes.com/2007/01/10/us/politics/10library.html?ex=1326085200&en=3170689537c4434c&ei=5088&partner=rssnyt&emc=rss.
74. Angela K. Brown, "Methodists: No Bush Library at SMU," *Washington Post*, January 18, 2007, available at http://www.washingtonpost.com/wp-dyn/content/article/2007/01/18/AR2007011800796.html?nav=hcmodule.
75. See Tim Taliaferro, "Obama Presidential Library: University of Chicago Already Angling for It?" *Huffington Post*, October 26, 2009, available at http://www.huffingtonpost.com/2009/10/26/obama-presidential-librar_n_333723.html; and "Hawaii Asks Obama for Presidential Library, Setting Up Possible Clash With Illinois," *Huffington Post*, March 23, 2010, available at http://www.huffingtonpost.com/2010/03/23/hawaii-asks-obama-for-pre_n_509283.html.
76. Unsigned memorandum, 7/6/1928, Files of Franklin D. Roosevelt, Family Business and Personal Papers, Writing and Statement File, Box 42, Franklin D. Roosevelt Presidential Library, Hyde Park, New York.

CHAPTER 2

1. Letter from the President regarding the commencement of operations in Libya, March 21, 2001, http://www.whitehouse.gov/the-press-office/2011/03/21/letter-president-regarding-commencement-operations-libya.
2. Barack Obama, "Remarks by the President in Address to the Nation on Libya," National Defense University, Washington, D.C., March 28, 2011, http://www.whitehouse.gov/the-press-office/2011/03/28/remarks-president-address-nation-libya.
3. Charlie Savage and Mark Landler, "White House Defends Continuing U.S. Role in Libya Operation," *New York Times*, June 15, 2011.
4. For classical (ca. 520–380 B.C.) Athenian politics, see Christian Meier, *Athens: A Portrait of the City in Its Golden Age*, trans. Robert and Rita Kimber (New York: Metropolitan Books, 1998); Josiah Ober, *Mass and Elite in Democratic Athens: Rhetoric, Ideology, and the Power of the People* (Princeton: Princeton University Press, 1989); and Martin Ostwald, *From Popular Sovereignty to the Sovereignty of Law: Law, Society, and Politics in Fifth-Century Athens* (Berkeley: University of California Press, 1986).
5. For the Roman republic, see Andrew Lintott, *The Constitution of the Roman Republic* (Oxford: Oxford University Press, 1999), and T. E. J. Wiedemann, *Cicero and the End of the Roman Republic* (London: Oxford University Press, 1991).

6. For Renaissance-era republics, see Paul A. Rahe, *Republics Ancient and Modern: New Modes and Orders in Early Modern Political Thought* (Chapel Hill: University of North Carolina Press, 1994).
7. On the English Civil War, see Christopher Hill, *The Century of Revolution, 1603–1714* (New York: W. W. Norton, 1961), and Derek Hirst, *Authority and Conflict: England, 1603–1658* (Cambridge: Harvard University Press, 1986).
8. For information about the influence of English and British politics on the founding generation, see Bernard Bailyn, *The Ideological Origins of the American Revolution* (Cambridge: Harvard University Press, 1967); Jack P. Greene, *Negotiated Authorities: Essays in Colonial Political and Constitutional History* (Charlottesville: University Press of Virginia, 1994); Forrest McDonald, *Novus Ordo Seclorum: The Intellectual Origins of the Constitution* (Lawrence: University Press of Kansas, 1985); and J. G. A. Pocock, *The Machiavellian Moment: Florentine Political Thought and the Atlantic Republican Tradition* (Princeton: Princeton University Press, 1975).
9. On the classical sources of American political thought, see Thomas Gustafson, *Representative Words: Politics, Literature, and the American Language, 1776–1865* (Cambridge: Cambridge University Press, 1992); Henry F. May, *The Enlightenment in America* (Oxford: Oxford University Press, 1976); Carl J. Richard, *The Founders and the Classics: Greece, Rome, and the American Enlightenment* (Cambridge: Harvard University Press, 1994); and Morton White, *Philosophy, "The Federalist," and the Constitution* (Oxford: Oxford University Press, 1987).
10. On the Enlightenment and its influence on colonial Americans, see May, *Enlightenment.*
11. For information on classical liberalism and its impact on American political history, see John Patrick Diggins, "Comrades and Citizens: New Mythologies in American Historiography," *American Historical Review* 90 (1985): 614–38; Diggins, *The Lost Soul of American Politics: Virtue, Self-Interest, and the Foundations of Liberalism* (Chicago: University of Chicago Press, 1984); David F. Ericson, *The Shaping of American Liberalism: The Debates Over Ratification, Nullification, and Slavery* (Chicago: University of Chicago Press, 1993); David J. Greenstone, *The Lincoln Persuasion: Remaking American Liberalism* (Princeton: Princeton University Press, 1993); and Thomas L. Pangle, *The Spirit of Modern Republicanism: The Moral Vision of the American Founders and the Philosophy of Locke* (Chicago: University of Chicago Press, 1988).
12. On the colonial fear of tyranny, see Bailyn, *Ideological Origins*; McDonald, *Novus Ordo Seclorum*; and Gordon S. Wood, *Creation of the American Republic, 1776–1787* (New York: W. W. Norton, 1969).
13. For more on the irreconcilable interpretations of English constitutional precedents in Britain and America, see John Phillip Reid, *Constitutional History of the American Revolution: The Authority of Law* (Madison: University of Wisconsin Press, 1993); Reid, *Constitutional History of the American Revolution: The Authority to Legislate* (Madison: University of Wisconsin Press, 1991); Reid, *Constitutional History of the American Revolution: The Authority of Rights* (Madison: University of Wisconsin Press, 1986); and Reid, *Constitutional History of the American Revolution: The Authority to Tax* (Madison: University of Wisconsin Press, 1987).
14. On the problems of Confederation governance, see Merrill Jensen, *The New Nation: A History of the United States During the Confederation, 1781–1789* (New York: Alfred A. Knopf, 1950); Richard B. Morris, *The Forging of the Union, 1781–1789* (New York: Harper and Row, 1987); Jack N. Rakove, *The Beginnings of National Politics: An*

Interpretive History of the Continental Congress (Baltimore: Johns Hopkins University Press, 1979); and Wood, *Creation of the American Republic.*

15. For a broader review of the specific deficiencies of the Confederation government, see Morris, *Forging of the Union,* and Wood, *Creation of the American Republic.*
16. For a summary of Hamilton's views and political preferences, see Forrest McDonald, *Alexander Hamilton: A Biography* (New York: W. W. Norton, 1979).
17. The earliest philosophical treatment of sovereignty, focusing on what was at that time called "raison d'etat," was Jean Bodin, *The Six Bookes of a Commonweale*, Trans. by R. Knolles (Cambridge: Harvard University Press, 1962) and originally published in 1576.
18. On the differences between general and limited authority, see Richard Ashcraft, *Revolutionary Politics and Locke's Two Treatises of Government* (Princeton, NJ: Princeton University Press, 1986); Isaac Kramnick, *Republicanism and Bourgeois Radicalism: Political Ideology in Late Eighteenth-Century England and America* (Ithaca: Cornell University Press, 1990); Pocock, *Machiavellian Moment*; Rahe, *Republics Ancient and Modern*; and Reid, *Constitutional History* (4 vols.).
19. To many, the classic defense of unitary sovereignty and the divine right of kings is Sir Robert Filmer's *Patriarcha*, written at some point in the 1630s to 1640s. It can be found in Sir Robert Filmer, *Patriarcha and Other Writings*, ed. Johann P. Sommerville (Cambridge: Cambridge University Press, 1991).
20. For information on the development of popular sovereignty in Anglo-American political thought, see Edmund S. Morgan, *Inventing the People: The Rise of Popular Sovereignty in England and America* (New York: W. W. Norton, 1988).
21. On this point, see McDonald, *Novus Ordo Seclorum*, and Wood, *Creation of the American Republic.*
22. Despite some of the disagreements about the specific scope of presidential powers, both supporters and opponents of an active centralized government strongly endorsed limited authority. See Publius, *The Federalist Papers*, ed. Isaac Kramnick (London: Penguin Books, 1987), and Herbert J. Storing, *The Complete Anti-Federalist* (Chicago: University of Chicago Press, 2007).
23. On this see George W. Carey, *The Federalist: Design for a Constitutional Republic* (Urbana: University of Illinois Press, 1989); Publius [Hamilton], *Federalist* 67–77; and White, *Philosophy, "The Federalist," and the Constitution.*
24. For a discussion of the deficiencies and proposed remedies, see Carey, *The Federalist*; Forrest McDonald, *E Pluribus Unum: The Formation of the American Republic, 1776–1790* (Indianapolis: Liberty Press, 1965); Publius [Hamilton], *Federalist* 15–25; and Wood, *Creation of the American Republic.*
25. On this, see Bailyn, *Ideological Origins*; McDonald, *Novus Ordo Seclorum*; Publius [Hamilton], *Federalist* 8; and Wood, *Creation of the American Republic.*
26. The issue of presidential succession had been somewhat controversial due to the ambiguous language of Article II, Section 1, Clause 6, since it did not expressly state whether the vice president becomes the president, as opposed to simply an "acting" president, if the president dies, resigns, is removed from office, or is otherwise unable to discharge the duties of the office. The problem first arose in 1841, when President William Henry Harrison died after only a month in office. The immediate question was whether Vice President John Tyler would assume the full duties and powers of the office for the remaining forty-seven months of Harrison's term. Tyler assumed the full powers of the office, as did the eight other vice presidents who have succeeded to the office of the presidency.

27. On the importance of Locke and also the Glorious Revolution, see Steven M. Dworetz, *The Unvarnished Doctrine: Locke, Liberalism, and the American Revolution* (Durham, NC: Duke University Press, 1990); David S. Lovejoy, *The Glorious Revolution in America* (New York: Harper Torchbooks, 1972); Edmund S. Morgan, *The Birth of the Republic, 1763–89* (Chicago: University of Chicago Press, 1992); Pangle, *The Spirit of Modern Republicanism*; Garry Wills, *Explaining America: The Federalist* (Garden City, NY: Doubleday, 1981); and Wills, *Inventing America: Jefferson's Declaration of Independence* (Garden City, NY: Doubleday, 1978).
28. Charles de Montesquieu, *The Spirit of the Laws*, ed. Anne M. Cohler et al. (Cambridge: Cambridge University Press, 1989).
29. On the framers' view of separation of powers, see Publius [Madison], *Federalist* 47–51.
30. Hamilton makes numerous references to this in the *Federalist*; see *Federalist* 67–77.
33. See Publius [Madison], *Federalist* 47–51.
32. On the first presidential election, see Stanley Elkins and Eric McKitrick, *The Age of Federalism: The Early American Republic, 1788–1800* (Oxford: Oxford University Press, 1993).
33. On this point, see Publius [Hamilton], *Federalist* 68.
34. For information on presidential politics prior to 1828, see Lance Banning, *The Jeffersonian Persuasion: Evolution of a Party Ideology* (Ithaca, NY: Cornell University Press, 1978); Elkins, *Age of Federalism*; and Charles Sellers, *The Market Revolution: Jacksonian America, 1815–1846* (New York: Oxford University Press, 1991).
35. The framers' world was neither egalitarian nor democratic, and their conceptions of equality differed radically from today's interpretations. See Reid, *Constitutional History*.
36. On the electoral reforms that began in the late 1820s, see Jennifer Nedelsky, *Private Property and the Limits of American Constitutionalism: The Madisonian Framework and Its Legacy* (Chicago: University of Chicago Press, 1990); Karen Orren, *Belated Feudalism: Labor, Law, and Liberal Development in the United States* (Cambridge: Cambridge University Press, 1991); Sellers, *Market Revolution*; and Sean Wilentz, *Chants Democratic: New York City and the Rise of the American Working Class, 1788–1850* (Oxford: Oxford University Press, 1984).
37. On the controversies and interpretive debates regarding the vesting clause, see David G. Adler and Larry N. George, eds., *The Constitution and the Conduct of American Foreign Policy* (Lawrence: University Press of Kansas, 1996); Joseph Bessette and Jeffrey Tulis, *The Presidency in the Constitutional Order* (Baton Rouge: Louisiana University Press, 1981); Edward Corwin, *The President: Office and Powers, 5th ed.* (New York: New York University Press, 1984); and Gordon Silverstein, *Constitutional Interpretation and the Making of American Foreign Policy* (New York: Oxford University Press, 1996).
38. Most experts on the constitution and presidential powers roundly reject the general-authority arguments made by Yoo and others. For an example of this flawed argument about general authority, see John Yoo, *Crisis and Command: A History of Executive Power from George Washington to George W. Bush* (New York: Kaplan Publishing, 2010); Yoo, *The Powers of War and Peace: The Constitution and Foreign Affairs after 9/11* (Chicago: University of Chicago Press. 2005); and John Eastman, "Listening to the Enemy: The President's Power to Conduct Surveillance of Enemy Communications During Time of War," *Journal of International and Comparative Law* 13 (2006): 49.
39. On this point, see Publius [Hamilton], *Federalist* 67–77, and Forrest McDonald, *The American Presidency: An Intellectual History* (Lawrence: University Press of Kansas, 1995).

40. On the presidency relative to other contemporary chief executives, see Samuel H. Beer, *To Make a Nation: The Rediscovery of American Federalism* (Cambridge, MA: Belknap Press, 1993); Stanley Elkins and Eric McKitrick, *The Age of Federalism: The Early American Republic, 1788–1800* (Oxford: Oxford University Press, 1993); McDonald, *American Presidency*; Publius [Hamilton], *Federalist* 67–77; and R. R. Palmer, *Age of the Democratic Revolution: A Political History of Europe and America, 1760–1800*, Vol. 2 (Princeton: Princeton University Press, 1970).
41. On the opposition to standing armies, see Walter LaFeber, *The American Age: United States Foreign Policy at Home and Abroad, 1750 to the Present* (New York: W. W. Norton, 1994), and Russell F. Weigley, *The American Way of War: A History of United States Military Strategy and Policy* (Bloomington: Indiana University Press, 1977). On antimilitarist ideology, see Banning, *Jeffersonian Persuasion*;; Elkins, *Age of Federalism*; Robert Middlekauf, *The Glorious Cause: The American Revolution, 1763–1789* (New York: Oxford University Press, 2007); Wilentz, *Chants Democratic*; and Gordon S. Wood, *The Radicalism of the American Revolution* (New York: Vintage Books, 1991).
42. See Elkins, *Age of Federalism*; Middlekauf, *Glorious Cause*; and Wood, *Radicalism*.
43. For information on budgetary constraints and public frugality, see Elkins, *Age of Federalism*, and Drew R. McCoy, *The Elusive Republic: Political Economy in Jeffersonian America* (New York: W. W. Norton, 1980).
44. On the role of militias, see LaFeber, *The American Age*; Weigley, *American Way of War*; and Wood, *Radicalism*.
45. See Banning, *Jeffersonian Persuasion*; Lawrence S. Kaplan, *Entangling Alliances with None: American Foreign Policy in the Age of Jefferson* (Kent, OH: Kent State University Press, 1987); and LaFeber, *The American Age*.
46. On this point, especially the infancy of American federal law, see Lawrence M. Friedman, *Crime and Punishment in American History* (New York: Basic Books, 1993); Friedman, *A History of American Law* (New York: Simon and Schuster, 1985); Morton J. Horwitz, *The Transformation of American Law, 1780–1860* (Cambridge: Harvard University Press, 1977); Sellers, *Market Revolution*; and Christopher L. Tomlins, *Law, Labor, and Ideology in the Early American Republic* (Cambridge: Cambridge University Press, 1993).
47. See Friedman, *Crime and Punishment*; Horwitz, *Transformation of American Law*; and Tomlins, *Law, Labor, and Ideology*.
48. For information on the late nineteenth century and thereafter, see Friedman, *Crime and Punishment*; Kermit L. Hall, *The Magic Mirror: Law in American History* (Oxford: Oxford University Press, 1989); and Morton J. Horwitz, *The Transformation of American Law, 1870–1960: The Crisis of Legal Orthodoxy* (Oxford: Oxford University Press, 1992).
49. On marshals, see Friedman, *Crime and Punishment*; Hall, *Magic Mirror*; and Horwitz, *Transformation of American Law* (Vol. 1).
50. On fear of treason, see Banning, *Jeffersonian Persuasion*; Carey, *Federalist*; Elkins, *Age of Federalism*; McDonald, *Novus Ordo Seclorum*; Middlekauf, *Glorious Cause*; and Wood, *Creation of the American Republic*.
51. On the Rosenberg case, see Ronald Radosh, *The Rosenberg File* (New Haven, CT: Yale University Press, 1997).
52. See Carey, *Federalist*; Publius [Hamilton], *Federalist* 74; Reid, *Constitutional History*; Tomlins, *Law, Labor, and Ideology*; and Wood, *Creation of the American Republic*.
53. On the Rich pardon, see George Lardner, Jr., "A Pardon to Remember," *The New York Times*, November 22, 2008, A21, and House Committee on Government Reform,

Justice Undone: Clemency Decisions in the Clinton White House (Washington, DC: U.S. Congress, 3/14/02).

54. An article of impeachment needs a majority vote in the House, and then conviction in the Senate needs a two-thirds vote. The Senate trial is presided over by the Chief Justice of the United States.
55. See Carey, *Federalist*; Publius [Hamilton], *Federalist* 73; and Wood, *Creation of the American Republic.*
56. This is evident by implication throughout contemporary documents. For examples, see Publius [Hamilton]; *Federalist* 67–77.
57. On the legislative roles of recent presidents, see Louis Fisher, *Constitutional Conflicts Between Congress and the President* (Lawrence: University Press of Kansas, 2007).
58. See Richard Hofstadter, *The Idea of a Party System: The Rise of Legitimate Opposition in the United States, 1780–1840* (Berkeley: University of California Press, 1970).
59. See Carey, *Federalist*; Publius [Hamilton], *Federalist* 76–77; and Wood, *Creation of the American Republic.*
60. On the emergence of the spoils system, see Arthur M. Schlesinger, Jr., *Age of Jackson* (New York: Back Bay Books, 1988); Sellers, *Market Revolution*; and Wilentz, *Chants Democratic.*
61. Trenchard and Gordon, *Cato's Letters*, contains some pointed contemporary criticisms of the politicization of the crown's appointment powers.
62. For some insight on the pressures exerted by colonial Americans against British officials and the associated political gamesmanship, see Bernard Bailyn, *The Ordeal of Thomas Hutchinson* (Cambridge: Harvard University Press, 1976), and Pauline Maier, *From Resistance to Revolution: Colonial Radicals and the Development of Opposition to Britain, 1765–1776* (New York: W. W. Norton, 1992).
63. See Carey, *Federalist*; Publius [Hamilton], *Federalist* 76–77; and Wood, *Creation of the American Republic.*
64. See Storing, *Complete Anti-Federalist.*
65. On relevant rulings and the evolution of the removal doctrine, see Fisher, *Constitutional Conflicts*; and G. Galvin McKenzie, *The Politics of Presidential Appointments* (New York: Free Press, 1981).
66. Though not about presidential politics, one of the most readable and informative accounts of the corruption and even criminality that ultimately characterized Gilded-Age political patronage is Richard F. Welch, *King of the Bowery: Big Tim Sullivan, Tammany Hall and New York City from the Gilded Age to the Progressive Era* (Albany: State University of New York Press, 2009).
67. On the civil-service reforms, see Stephen Skowronek, *Building a New American State: The Expansion of National Administrative Capacities, 1877–1920* (New York: Cambridge University Press, 1982).
68. See Notes 50–51.
69. For more, see Raoul Berger, *Executive Privilege* (Cambridge: Harvard University Press, 1974); Berger, *Impeachment: The Constitutional Problems* (Cambridge: Harvard University Press, 1973); Louis Fisher, *The Politics of Executive Privilege* (Durham, NC: Carolina Academic Press, 2004); and Mark Rozell, *Executive Privilege: The Dilemma of Secrecy and Democratic Accountability* (Lawrence: University Press of Kansas, 2000).
70. Letter from Abraham Lincoln to A. G. Hodges, 4 April 1864.
71. See Theodore Roosevelt, *The Autobiography of Theodore Roosevelt* (New York: Scribner's, 1913).

72. See William Howard Taft, *Our Chief Magistrate and His Powers* (New York: Columbia University Press, 1916).
73. For an excellent discussion on Taft's presidency, see Sidney M. Milkis and Michael Nelson, *The American Presidency: Origins and Development, 1776–2007,* 5th ed. (Washington, DC: CQ Press, 2008).
74. Milkis and Nelson, 240.
75. See Arthur M. Schlesinger, Jr., *The Imperial Presidency* (Boston: Houghton Mifflin, 1973).
76. See Aaron Wildavsky, "The Two Presidencies," *Trans-Action* 4:7–14 (1966).
77. See David M. O'Brien, *Constitutional Law and Politics: Struggles for Power and Governmental Accountability*, Vol. 1, 7th ed. (New York: W. W. Norton, 2008).
78. Ibid.
79. Ibid.
80. Ibid.
81. "Petition for Pardon," Files of Meredith Cabe, Box 1, William J. Clinton Presidential Library, Little Rock, Arkansas.
82. Memo from C. Boyden Gray to George Bush, "War Powers Issues That May Arise in Your Meeting With Congressional Leaders," August 27, 1990, Formerly Withheld, NLGB Control Number 308, George Bush Presidential Library, College Station, Texas.

CHAPTER 3

1. Sidney Milkis and Michael Nelson, *The American Presidency: Origins and Development 1776–2002*, 4th ed. (Washington, DC: CQ Press, 2003), 52.
2. See Marc Hetherington and Bruce Larson, *Parties, Politics and Public Policy in America,* 11th ed. (Washington, DC: CQ Press, 2010).
3. Melissa Anderson, and Brendan Doherty, "Parties Under Siege or Parties in Control? Gauging Causal Influences on Australian Ballot Reform Laws." Paper presented at the annual meeting of the American Political Science Association, Philadelphia, PA, August 27, 2003.
4. Stephen J. Wayne, *The Road to the White House 2008: The Politics of Presidential Elections* (Belmont, CA: Thompson Wadsworth, 2008), 202–4.
5. For a discussion on this trend in news coverage, see Thomas E. Patterson, *Out of Order* (New York: Vintage Books, 1994), and Larry J. Sabato, *Feeding Frenzy: Attack Journalism and American Politics* (Baltimore: Lanahan Publishers, 2000).
6. One of the earliest studies to consider this trend is Martin J. Wattenberg, *The Rise of Candidate-Centered Politics: Presidential Elections of the 1980s* (Cambridge: Harvard University Press, 1991).
7. Thomas E. Cronin and Michael A. Genovese, *The Paradoxes of the American Presidency* (New York: Oxford University Press, 1998), 32–27.
8. Richard W. Waterman, Robert Wright, and Gilbert St. Clair, *The Image-Is-Everything Presidency: Dilemmas in American Leadership* (Boulder, CO: Westview Press, 1999), 39–42.
9. For a discussion of electing the first woman president, see Lori Cox Han and Caroline Heldman, eds., *Rethinking Madam President: Are We Ready for a Woman in the White House?* (Boulder, CO: Lynne Rienner Publishers, 2007), and Lori Cox Han, *Women and U.S. Politics: The Spectrum of Political Leadership*, 2nd ed. (Boulder, CO: Lynne Rienner Publishers, 2010).
10. See Richard L. Fox and Jennifer L. Lawless, "Entering the Arena? Gender and the Decision to Run for Office," *American Journal of Political Science* 48, no. 2 (2004): 264–80,

and Richard L. Fox, "The Future of Women's Political Leadership: Gender and the Decision to Run for Elective Office," in *Women and Leadership: The State of Play and Strategies for Change*, eds. Barbara Kellerman and Deborah L. Rhode (New York: Wiley, 2007), 251–70.

11. See Arthur T. Hadley, *The Invisible Primary* (Englewood Cliffs, NJ: Prentice-Hall, 1976).
12. Nelson W. Polsby and Aaron Wildavsky, *Presidential Elections: Strategies and Structures of American Politics*, 11th ed. (Lanham, MD: Rowman & Littlefield, 2004), 92–93.
13. For a discussion of media attention during the invisible primary, see Lori Cox Han, "Off to the (Horse) Races: Media Coverage of the 'Not-So-Invisible' Invisible Primary of 2007," in *From Votes to Victory: Winning and Governing the White House in the Twenty-First Century*, ed. Meena Bose (College Station: Texas A&M University Press, 2011).
14. Christopher Hanson, "The Invisible Primary: Now Is the Time for All-Out Coverage," *Columbia Journalism Review*, March/April, 2003.
15. Ibid.
16. See Linda Feldmann, "Before Any Votes, A 'Money Primary,'" *Christian Science Monitor*, February 26, 2007, p. 1, and Craig Gilbert, "'Invisible Primary' Already Begun," *Milwaukee Journal Sentinel*, March 4, 2007, www.jsonline.com/story/index.aspx?id=573038 (accessed February 23, 2008).
17. Marty Cohen, David Karol, Hans Noel, and John Zaller, "The Invisible Primary in Presidential Nominations, 1980–2004," in *The Making of the Presidential Candidates 2008*, ed. William Mayer (Lanham: Rowman and Littlefield, 2008).
18. Bruce Drake, "McCain: I Was a 'Maverick,' Now I'm a 'Partisan,'" *Politics Daily*, available at http://www.politicsdaily.com/2010/04/18/mccain-i-was-a-maverick-now-im-a-partisan/.
19. For a discussion on why Clinton lost the 2008 Democratic nomination, see Lori Cox Han, "Still Waiting for Madam President: Hillary Rodham Clinton's 2008 Presidential Campaign," *Critical Issues of Our Time*, The Centre for American Studies at The University of Western Ontario, London, Ontario, Volume 2, Fall 2009.
20. Stephen J. Wayne, "Why Democracy Works," in *Winning the Presidency: 2009*, ed. William J. Crotty (Boulder: Paradigm Publishers, 2008), 48–69.
21. Ibid., 55.
22. See "Campaign Finance Reform," WorldHistory.com, http://www.worldhistory.com/wiki/C/Campaign-finance-reform.htm.
23. "Embassy Row," The Center for Responsive Politics, www.opensecrets.org, September 27, 2005.
24. Herbert E. Alexander, *Financing Politics: Money, Elections, and Political Reform* (Washington, DC: CQ Press, 1992), 9–10.
25. Figures provided by The Center for Responsive Politics, www.opensecrets.gov.
26. Alexander, *Financing Politics*, 10–11.
27. Theodore Roosevelt, "Fifth Annual Message to the Congress," The American Presidency Project, December 5, 1905, available at, http://www.presidency.ucsb.edu/ws/index.php?pid=29546#axzz1duSNChlK.
28. For a discussion of early campaign finance legislation, see Diana Dwyre and Victoria A. Farrar-Myers, *Legislative Labyrinth: Congress and Campaign Finance Reform* (Washington, DC: CQ Press, 2001), 3–7.
29. Alexander, *Financing Politics*, 32.
30. Richard J. Semiatin, *Campaigns in the 21st Century* (New York: McGraw-Hill, 2005), 157–58.

31. Bundling was first used as a strategy in 1992, pioneered by the group EMILY's List, which stands for Early Money Is Like Yeast (meaning "it makes the dough rise" in providing early seed money for campaigns). EMILY's List played a prominent role in supporting pro-choice Democratic female candidates in 1992, a year that saw a dramatic rise in the number of women elected to Congress and state legislatures.
32. Federal Election Commission, http://www.fec.gov/press/bkgnd/fund.shtml (accessed February 21, 2011).
33. Other than McCain, the candidates who accepted matching funds in the 2008 primary included Democrats Joe Biden, Chris Dodd, John Edwards, Dennis Kucinich, and Mike Gravel; Republicans Duncan Hunter and Tom Tancredo; and Ralph Nader, who filed as a candidate under the Peace and Freedom Party, Delaware Independent Party, Independent Party of Hawaii, Michigan Natural Law Party, New Mexico Independent Party, and the New York Independence Party. See FEC filings, available at http://www.fec.gov/finance/2008matching/2008matching.shtml.
34. "2008 Presidential Campaign Financial Activity Summarized," June 8, 2009, Federal Election Commission, http://www.fec.gov/press/press2009/20090608PresStat.shtml (accessed February 21, 2011).
35. Jim Rutenberg, "Nearing Record, Obama's Ad Effort Swamps McCain," *New York Times*, October 17, 2008.
36. Stephen J. Wayne, *The Road to the White House 2004: The Politics of Presidential Elections* (Belmont: Thomson Wadsworth, 2004), 41.
37. Paul Taylor, "The Short, Unhappy Life of Campaign Finance Reform," *Mother Jones*, March/April 2003, 28–31.
38. Ibid.
39. Thomas E. Mann, "Reform Agenda," in *The New Campaign Finance Sourcebook*, eds. Anthony Corrado, Thomas E. Mann, Daniel R. Ortiz, and Trevor Potter (Washington, DC: Brookings Institution Press, 2005).
40. Jonathan Weisman and Michael D. Shear, "Obama, McCain Aim to Curb '527s,'" *Washington Post*, May 14, 2008.
41. Barack Obama, State of the Union Address, January 27, 2010.
42. Robert Barnes and Anne E. Kornblut, "It's Obama vs. the Supreme Court, Round 2, Over Campaign Finance Ruling," *Washington Post*, March 11, 2010, http://www.washingtonpost.com/wp-dyn/content/article/2010/03/09/AR2010030903040_2.html?sid=ST2010031502480.
43. Memo from William L. Batt, Jr. to Clark M. Clifford, "President's Acceptance Speech," July 9, 1948, Files of Charles S. Murphy, Presidential Speech File, Box 1, Harry S. Truman Presidential Library, Independence, Missouri.
44. Memo from Tony Snow to Ray Price, Bob Teeter, Samuel K. Skinner, and Clayton Yeutter, "Convention Speech," August 12, 1992, Tony Snow Files, Formerly Withheld, NLGB Control Number 6534, George Bush Presidential Library, College Station, Texas.
45. Kathleen Hall Jamieson, ed., *Electing the President 2008: The Insider's View* (Philadelphia: University of Pennsylvania Press, 2009), 13–14.
46. Brian Montipoli, "Early Reaction to McCain's V.P. Pick," CBS News, August 29, 2008, http://www.cbsnews.com/8301-502163_162-4397368-502163.html.
47. See "The Electoral College," *David Leip's Atlas of Presidential Elections*, http://www.uselectionatlas.org/INFORMATION/INFORMATION/electcollege_history.php.
48. Stephen S. Brams and Michael Davis, "The 3/2's Rule in Presidential Campaigning," *American Political Science Review* (1974): 113–34.

49. Ibid.
50. See Steven J. Rosenstone and John Mark, *Mobilization, Participation, and Democracy in America* (New York: Macmillan Press, 1993).
51. See Cronin and Genovese, *The Paradoxes of the American Presidency.* For a full discussion on the Electoral College, see also George C. Edwards, III, *Why the Electoral College Is Bad for America*, 2nd ed. (New Haven: Yale University Press, 2011), and Gary Bugh, ed., *Electoral College Reform: Challenges and Possibilities* (Burlington, VT: Ashgate Publishing, 2010).
52. Donald Philip Green and Bradley Palmquist, "How Stable Is Party Identification?" *Political Behavior*, 16.4 (1994): 437–66.
53. "Americans Spending More Time Following the News," Pew Research Center for People and the Press, September 12, 2010, available at http://people-press.org/report/652/.
54. "Internet Overtakes Newspapers as News Outlet," Pew Research Center for People and the Press, December 23, 2008, http://people-press.org/report/479/internet-overtakes-newspapers-as-news-outlet.
55. Doris A. Graber, *Mass Media and American Politics,* 8th ed. (Washington, DC: CQ Press, 2010), 200.
56. See Patterson, *Out of Order*.
57. Ibid, 26.
58. "Internet News Audience Highly Critical of News Organizations," Pew Research Center for People and the Press, August 9, 2007 http://people-press.org/report/348/internet-news-audience-highly-critical-of-news-organizations.
59. See Stephen Farnsworth and S. Robert Lichter, *The Nightly News Nightmare: Network Television Coverage of U.S. Presidential Elections 1988–2004* (Lanham, MD: Rowman and Littlefield, 2007).
60. Ibid, 3.
61. Ibid.
62. See Larry M. Bartels, *Presidential Primaries and the Dynamics of Public Choice* (Princeton, NJ: Princeton University Press, 1988).
63. Farnsworth and Lichter, *The Nightly News Nightmare,* 6.
64. See Darrell M. West, *Air Wars: 1952–2008* (Washington, DC: CQ Press, 2010).
65. Quoted in West, *Air Wars*, 82.
66. Joseph N. Cappella and Kathleen Hall Jamieson, "Broadcast Ad-Watch Effects: A Field Experiment," *Communication Research* 21 (1994): 341–65.
67. Richard Davis, *The Web of Politics: The Internet's Impact on the American Political System* (New York: Oxford University Press, 1999); and John Tedesco, "Changing the Channel: Use of the Internet for Communication about Politics,"in *Handbook of Political Communication Research,* ed. Lynda Lee Kaid (Mahwah, NJ: Lawrence Erlbaum Associates, 2004), 507–32.
68. As of March 6, 2008.
69. As of March 8, 2008.
70. As of March 6, 2008. On December 18, 2008, 12, 404,334 users had viewed the video.
71. "Most Voters Say News Media Wants Obama to Win," Pew Research Center for People and the Press, October 22, 2008, http://pewresearch.org/pubs/1003/joe-the-plumber
72. http://www.presidency.ucsb.edu/ws/index.php?pid=6414.
73. John Kessel, *Presidential Campaign Politics: Coalitions Strategies and Citizen Response* (Chicago: Dorsey Press 1980), 36.
74. See Lester Seligman and Cary Covington, *The Coalitional Presidency* (Chicago: Dorsey Press, 1989).

75. Ibid.
76. For example, see Jeff Fishel, *Presidents and Promises: From Campaign Pledge to Presidential Performance* (Washington, DC: CQ Press, 1985).
77. Hugh Heclo, "Campaigning and Governing: A Conspectus," in *The Permanent Campaign and Its Future*, eds. Norman Ornstein and Thomas Mann (Washington, DC: Brookings, 2000).
78. Gerald Ford, "Remarks on Taking the Oath of Office," August 9, 1974, http://www.presidency.ucsb.edu/ws/index.php?pid=4409&st=&st1=.
79. For example, see CBS News, "Ready for a Woman President?" *CBS News Polls*, February 5, 2006, www.cbsnews.com; Stewart M. Powell, "Poll Finds Readiness for Female President," *Houston Chronicle*, February 20, 2006, p. A1; and Dan Smith, "Voters Think U.S. Ready for Woman as President," *Sacramento Bee*, March 10, 2006, p. A5. In addition, a February 2005 poll by the Siena College Research Institute found that six out of ten voters were ready for a woman president and that 81 percent of those surveyed would vote for a woman president. Potential candidates for 2008 that topped the survey included Clinton, Rice, and Senator Elizabeth Dole (R-NC).
80. Dan Balz, "Hillary Clinton Opens Presidential Bid: The Former First Lady Enters the Race as Front-Runner for the Democratic Nomination," *Washington Post*, January 21, 2007, p. A1.
81. Patrick Healy, "Clinton Steals Obama's Fundraising Thunder," *New York Times*, October 3, 2007.
82. Texas relied on what became popularly known as a "primacaucus" in which delegates were awarded by both a primary vote and a caucus vote. While the news media declared Clinton the winner in Texas based on her win in the overall popular vote, Obama actually won more delegates from the state after the caucus portion of the state's contest.
83. Memo from Dan McGroarty to David Demarest and Tony Snow, "Basket Case—Democrats New '92 Strategy," June 18, 1991, Formerly Withheld, NLGB Control Number 6512, George Bush Presidential Library, College Station, Texas.

CHAPTER 4

1. Vice President Joe Biden also appeared on *The View* in April 2010. See Frazier Moore, "Obama on 'The View' Thursday," *The Huffington Post*, July 26, 2010, available at http://www.huffingtonpost.com/2010/07/26/obama-on-the-view-thursda_n_659002.html?ref=email_share.
2. Lynn Sweet, "Courting the Ladies," *Chicago Sun-Times*, 13 October 2004, 72.
3. Lori Cox Han, *Women and US Politics: The Spectrum of Political Leadership*, 2nd ed. (Boulder, CO: Lynne Rienner Publishers, 2010), 54.
4. Chris Cillizza, "The Fix," *Washington Post*, 29 July 2010, available at http://voices.washingtonpost.com/thefix/daily-fix-poll/daily-fix-poll-president-obama.html.
5. Memo from Marlin Fitzwater to John Sununu and David Demarest, 10/12/1989, Marlin Fitzwater Files, Press Office, Formerly Withheld, NLGB Control Number 6170, George Bush Presidential Library, College Station, Texas. For a broader discussion of George H. W. Bush's communications strategy, see Lori Cox Han, *A Presidency Upstaged: The Public Leadership of George H. W. Bush* (College Station: Texas A&M University Press, 2011).
6. Martin P. Wattenberg, "The Presidential Media Environment in the Age of Obama," in *Obama: Year One*, eds. Thomas R. Dye, George C. Edwards III, Morris P. Fiorina,

Edward S. Greenberg, Paul C. Light, David B. Magleby, and Martin P. Wattenberg (New York: Longman, 2010), 59.

7. Chuck Todd, Mark Murray, Domenico Montanaro, and Ali Weinberg, "First Read: First Thoughts," *MSNBC First Read News Mail*, July 28, 2010, available at http://firstread.msnbc.msn.com/_news/2010/07/28/4768558-first-thoughts-fundraiser-in-chief?lite.
8. Howard Kurtz, "A Good 'View' for Obama," *Washington Post*, 30 July 2010, available at http://www.washingtonpost.com/wp-dyn/content/linkset/2005/04/11/LI2005041100587.html.
9. See Jeffrey K. Tulis, *The Rhetorical Presidency* (Princeton, NJ: Princeton University Press, 1987), and Mel Laracey, *Presidents and the People: The Partisan Story of Going Public* (College Station: Texas A&M University Press, 2002). The public aspects of McKinley's Administration have only recently been included as part of the "rhetorical presidency" literature; in addition to Laracey, see also Robert P. Saldin, "William McKinley and the Rhetorical Presidency," *Presidential Studies Quarterly*, Vol. 41, Issue I, March 2011, pp. 119–34.
10. For example, a headline in the *New York Times* on December 3, 1904 (p. 8), declared: "Roosevelt's Visit South: Denies That He Plans Swing Around the Circle When He Visits Texas." However, Roosevelt is not the first president to be associated with this phrase. Most notably, the phrase is remembered for what is considered a disastrous speaking tour by President Andrew Johnson in 1866 during which he tried to shore up support for his Reconstruction policies and Democratic candidates prior to the midterm elections. See Eric Foner, *Reconstruction: America's Unfinished Revolution*, 1863–1877 (New York: Harper & Row, 1988).
11. For example, see Sidney M. Milkis and Michael Nelson, *The American Presidency: Origins and Development: 1776–2007*, 5th ed. (Washington, DC: CQ Press, 2008), 215–17.
12. Karlyn Kohrs Campbell and Kathleen Hall Jamieson, *Deeds Done in Words: Presidential Rhetoric and the Genres of Governance* (Chicago: University of Chicago Press, 1990), 1, 213–19.
13. Tulis, *The Rhetorical Presidency*, 28.
14. Ibid, 4–23.
15. Roderick P. Hart, *The Sound of Leadership: Presidential Communication in the Modern Age* (Chicago: University of Chicago Press, 1987), 212.
16. Stephen J. Farnsworth, *Spinner in Chief: How Presidents Sell Their Policies and Themselves* (Boulder, CO: Paradigm Publishers, 2009), 9–10.
17. Newton N. Minow, John Bartlow Martin, and Lee M. Mitchell, *Presidential Television* (New York: Basic Books, 1973), 26.
18. Gleason L. Archer, *History of Radio to 1926* (New York: Arno Press/New York Times, 1971), 317–18.
19. Ibid, 323–24.
20. Herbert Hoover, *The Memoirs of Herbert Hoover: The Cabinet and the Presidency 1920–1933* (New York: Macmillan, 1952), 146–47.
21. See *The Public Papers of the Presidents, Herbert Hoover*, 1929–1933 (Washington, DC: Government Printing Office, 1976–1977).
22. President Herbert Hoover, "Radio Address to the Nation," September 18, 1929.
23. The number of fireside chats given by Roosevelt is somewhat disputed; the total of thirty comes from the FDR Presidential Library and Museum's web page at http://www.fdrlibrary.marist.edu/firesi90.html. Only twenty-one of these radio addresses are listed as "fireside chats" in the Master Speech File in FDR's presidential papers, but the remaining nine, eight of which were delivered between October 1942 and June

1944, were delivered over the radio in the same format as the earlier addresses and are counted as such in most sources.

24. James MacGregor Burns, *Roosevelt: The Lion and the Fox* (New York: Harcourt, Brace and Company, 1956), 167–68.
25. Memo from Eben Ayers to Harry Truman, July 20, 1950, PSF Speech File, Box 42, Harry S. Truman Presidential Library, Independence, Missouri.
26. For example, see Matthew A. Baum and Samuel Kernell, "Has Cable Ended the Golden Age of Presidential Television?" *The American Political Science Review*, Vol. 93, No. 1 (March 1999): 99–114.
27. See Lori Cox Han, *Governing From Center Stage: White House Communication Strategies During the Television Age of Politics* (Cresskill, NJ: Hampton Press, 2001).
28. See the video documentary "Television and the Presidency," The Freedom Forum First Amendment Center at Vanderbilt University, Nashville, TN, 1994.
29. Farnsworth, *Spinner in Chief*, 6.
30. Han, *Governing From Center Stage*, 2.
31. Martha Joynt Kumar, *Managing the President's Message: The White House Communications Operation* (Baltimore: Johns Hopkins University Press, 2007), xiv.
32. Mary E. Stuckey, *The President as Interpreter-in-Chief* (Chatham, NJ: Chatham House, 1991), 1–3.
33. See Samuel Kernell, *Going Public: New Strategies of Presidential Leadership*, 3rd ed.(Washington, DC: CQ Press, 1997).
34. See George C. Edwards, *On Deaf Ears: The Limits of the Bully Pulpit* (New Haven: Yale University Press, 2003).
35. See Jeffrey E. Cohen, *Going Local: Presidential Leadership in the Post-Broadcast Age* (New York: Cambridge University Press, 2010).
36. Report on "The Office of the Press Secretary," February 1983, prepared by the Reagan Press Office, document accessed in the Marlin Fitzwater/Press Office Alpha Files, Box 24, George Bush Presidential Library, College Station, Texas.
37. Memo from Pierre Salinger to Ted Sorensen, "The Relations of the President with the Press," April 17, 1961, Files of Pierre Salinger, John F. Kennedy Presidential Library, Boston, Massachusetts.
38. For in-depth discussions on the Office of Communications, see John Anthony Maltese, *Spin Control: The White House Office of Communications and the Management of Presidential News*, 2nd ed. (Chapel Hill: University of North Carolina Press, 1994), and Kumar, *Managing the President's Message.*
39. Mark Hertsgaard, *On Bended Knee: The Press and the Reagan Presidency* (New York: Farrar Straus Giroux, 1988), 33–37, 105–6.
40. See Maltese, *Spin Control,* Chapter 7.
41. Kumar, *Managing the President's Message,* 71–72.
42. "Jon Favreau: Why He Matters," *Washington Post*, available at http://www.whorunsgov.com/Profiles/Jon_Favreau.
43. Memo from Colin L. Powell to Tom Griscom, "Presidential Address: Brandenburg Gate (Revised)," June 1, 1987, White House Office of Records and Management Files, SP1150, Ronald Reagan Presidential Library, Simi Valley, California.
44. Wilson did not address Congress in 1919 and 1920 due to health reasons. Warren Harding's two messages in 1921 and 1922, along with Calvin Coolidge's first in 1923, were oral addresses to Congress. However, Coolidge's remaining State of the Unions between 1924 and 1928 and all four of Herbert Hoover's (1929–1933) were written messages. Franklin D. Roosevelt delivered an oral State of the Union with his first in 1934.

Exceptions during the modern era include Harry Truman in 1946 and 1953, Dwight Eisenhower in 1961, Richard Nixon in 1973, and Jimmy Carter in 1981. See Gerhard Peters, "State of the Union Messages," The American Presidency Project, http://www.presidency.ucsb.edu/sou.php, accessed 1/26/09.

45. Ibid.
46. See Lori Cox Han, "New Strategies for an Old Medium: The Weekly Radio Addresses of Reagan and Clinton," *Congress and the Presidency*, Volume 33, Number 1, Spring 2006, 25–45.
47. See Michael Emery and Edwin Emery, *The Press and America: An Interpretive History of the Mass Media*, 8th ed. (Boston: Allyn and Bacon, 1996), and Kernell, *Going Public*, 73–81.
48. John H. Kessel, *Presidents, the Presidency, and the Political Environment* (Washington, D.C.: CQ Press, 2001), 58–62.
49. Memo from Jerry Rafshoon to Jimmy Carter, "Press Conferences," September 26, 1978, Files of Jerry Rafshoon, Box 28, Jimmy Carter Presidential Library, Atlanta, Georgia.
50. George C. Edwards III, "George Bush and the Public Presidency: The Politics of Inclusion," in *The Bush Presidency: First Appraisals*, eds. Colin Campbell and Bert A. Rockman (Chatham, NJ: Chatham House Publishers, 1991), 148–9.
51. Memo from Marlin Fitzwater to George Bush, 12/2088, John Sununu Files, Office of the Chief of Staff to the President, Formerly Withheld, NLGB Control Number 11317, George Bush Presidential Library, College Station, Texas.
52. Memo from Mark Gearan to Bill Clinton, "Primetime Press Conference," August 1, 1994, Files of Jonathan Prince, Box 4, William J. Clinton Presidential Library, Little Rock, Arkansas.
53. For a discussion of the credibility gap, see Emery and Emery, *The Press and America*, 443–52.
54. This statement by Johnson to aide Bill Moyers has been widely quoted throughout the years, including in various interviews with Cronkite himself. However, a recent book questions its accuracy; see Joseph W. Campbell, *Getting It Wrong: Ten of the Greatest Misreported Stories in American Journalism* (Berkeley: University of California Press, 2010).
55. Agnew made his famous remarks about the press in an address to the California Republican State Convention in San Diego on September 11, 1970. In the speech, written by Nixon speechwriter and eventual *New York Times* columnist William Safire, Agnew also referred to the press as "pusillanimous pussyfooters" and "vicars of vacillation" who "have formed their own 4-H Club—the hopeless, hysterical hypochondriacs of history." See Lance Morrow, "Naysayer to the Nattering Naybobs," *Time*, September 30, 1996.
56. See Han, *A Presidency Upstaged.*
57. Doris A. Graber, *Mass Media and American Politics*, 8th ed. (Washington, DC: CQ Press, 2010), 229.
58. See Matthew Robert Kerbel, *Remote and Controlled: Media Politics in a Cynical Age*, 2nd ed. (Boulder, CO: Westview Press, 1999); Kernell, *Going Public*; Kessel, *Presidents, the Presidency, and the Political Environment*, and Graber, *Mass Media and American Politics*.
59. Graber, *Mass Media and American Politics*, 8th ed., 234–35.
60. See Stephen J. Farnsworth and S. Robert Lichter, *The Mediated Presidency: Television News and Presidential Governance* (Lanham, MD: Rowman & Littlefield, 2006), 41, and Farnsworth and Lichter, "Network News Coverage of New Presidents, 1981–2009,"

paper presented at the annual meeting of the American Political Science Association, Washington, DC, 2010.

61. Memo from Marlin Fitzwater to George Bush, 12/2088, John Sununu Files, Office of the Chief of Staff to the President, Formerly Withheld, NLGB Control Number 11317, George Bush Presidential Library, College Station, Texas.
62. Memo from Mark Gearan to Bill Clinton, "Interviews," December 1, 1993, Files of Jonathan Prince, Box 1, William J. Clinton Presidential Library, Little Rock, Arkansas.
63. Memo from Harry L. Hopkins to Franklin Roosevelt, November 27, 1941, Memoranda, Box 23, Papers of Steve Early, Franklin D. Roosevelt Presidential Library, Hyde Park, New York.
64. Memo from Jody Powell to Jimmy Carter, July 10, 1978, Files of Jody Powell, Box 40, Jimmy Carter Presidential Library, Atlanta, Georgia.
65. Michael D. Shear and Ellen Nakashima, "Obama says WikiLeaks Disclosure is Reason for Concern but Doesn't Reveal New Issues," *Washington Post*, July 27, 2010.
66. For discussions on the president–press relationship, see Graber, *Mass Media and American Politics*, W. Lance Bennett, *News: The Politics of Illusion*, 8th ed. (New York: Pearson, 2009), and David L. Paletz, *The Media in American Politics: Contents and Consequences*, 2nd ed. (New York: Longman, 2002).
67. Memo from Franklin Roosevelt to Steve Early, April 30, 1942; Memoranda, Box 24, Papers of Steve Early, Franklin D. Roosevelt Presidential Library, Hyde Park, New York.
68. Column Summaries, January 13, 1947, Papers of George M. Elsey, Harry S. Truman Presidential Library, Independence, Missouri.
69. Memo from Ron Ziegler to H. R. Haldeman, 11/25/69, in White House Special Files: Staff Member and Office Files of H. R. Haldeman, Box 124, Richard M. Nixon Presidential Materials Staff, National Archives at College Park, Maryland (now available at the Nixon Presidential Library, Yorba Linda, California).
70. Memo from Mort Allin to H. R. Haldeman, 7/22/70, in White House Special Files: Staff Member and Office Files of H. R. Haldeman, Box 124, Richard M. Nixon Presidential Materials Staff, National Archives at College Park, Maryland (now available at the Nixon Presidential Library, Yorba Linda, California). For a discussion of the ideological leanings of major newspapers, see Emery and Emery, *The Press and America*, 537–70.
71. Memo from H. R. Haldeman to Herb Klein and Ron Ziegler, 11/30/70, in White House Special Files: Staff Member and Office Files of H. R. Haldeman, Box 124, Richard M. Nixon Presidential Materials Staff, National Archives at College Park, Maryland (now available at the Nixon Presidential Library, Yorba Linda, California).
72. Stanley I. Kutler, *The Wars of Watergate: The Last Crisis of Richard Nixon* (New York: Alfred A. Knopf, 1990), 168.
73. Memo from Richard Moore to H. R. Haldeman, 6/24/70, in White House Special Files: Staff Member and Office Files of H. R. Haldeman, Box 124, Richard M. Nixon Presidential Materials Staff, National Archives at College Park, Maryland (now available at the Nixon Presidential Library, Yorba Linda, California).
74. John Tebbel and Sarah Miles Watts, *The Press and the Presidency: From George Washington to Ronald Reagan* (New York: Oxford University Press, 1985), 504.
75. Letter by Mort Allin to Richard Britton, 1/8/71, in White House Special Files: Staff Member and Office Files of Patrick J. Buchanan, Box 3, Richard M. Nixon Presidential Materials Staff, National Archives at College Park, Maryland (now available at the Nixon Presidential Library, Yorba Linda, California). Extensive documentation on the daily news summaries can be found in the Buchanan files, Boxes 1–8.

76. Letter by Mort Allin to Alice Plato, 1/29/71, in White House Special Files: Staff Member and Office Files of Patrick J. Buchanan, Box 3, Richard M. Nixon Presidential Materials Staff, National Archives at College Park, Maryland (now available at the Nixon Presidential Library, Yorba Linda, California).
77. See Han, *Governing from Center Stage*, 82, and Kumar, *Managing the President's Message*, 28.
78. For example, see Memo from Mary Kate Grant to John Sununu, "Weekly Editorial Round-Up," 8/17/89, Mary Kate Grant Files, Speech Office, Box 8, George Bush Presidential Library, College Station, Texas.
79. Memo from Mary Kate Grant to John Sununu, "Regional Newspapers," 3/12/89, Mary Kate Grant Files, Speech Office, Box 8, George Bush Presidential Library, College Station, Texas.
80. Memo from Maria Eitel Sheehan to Dorrance Smith, 5/22/91, Project Files, White House Office of Media Affairs, Freedom of Information Act Request 2003–1478-F, George Bush Presidential Library, College Station, Texas.
81. Josh Gerstein and Patrick Gavin, "Why Reporters Are Down on Obama," *Politico*, April 28, 2010.
82. Alessandra Stanley, "The TV Watch: Daytime Diplomacy," *The New York Times*, 30 July 2010.
83. Kurtz, "A Good 'View' for Obama."
84. Barack Obama, appearance on ABC's *The View*, July 29, 2010.
85. Franklin D. Roosevelt, "Address to Congress Requesting a Declaration of War with Japan," December 8, 1941.
86. Ronald Reagan, "Address Before a Joint Session of the Congress on the Program for Economic Recovery," April 28, 1981.
87. Bill Clinton, *My Life* (New York: Alfred A. Knopf, 2004), 548.
88. George Stephanopoulos, *All Too Human: A Political Education* (Boston: Little, Brown and Company, 1999), 201–3.
89. Barack Obama, "Address Before a Joint Session of the Congress on Health Care Reform," September 9, 2009.
90. See Matthew Eshbaugh-Soha, "The Public Presidency: Communications and Media," in *New Directions in the American Presidency*, ed. Lori Cox Han (New York: Routledge, 2011), 54–55.
91. Memorandum to the President from Patrick J. Buchanan, September 17, 1971, Files of Patrick J. Buchanan, originally accessed in the Richard Nixon Presidential Materials, National Archives, College Park, Maryland (now available at the Nixon Presidential Library, Yorba Linda, California).

CHAPTER 5

1. Henry C. Kenski, "A Man for All Seasons? The Guardian President and His Public," in *Leadership and the Bush Presidency: Prudence or Drift in an Era of Change?* eds. Ryan J. Barilleaux and Mary E. Stuckey (Westport: Praeger, 1992), 95.
2. George C. Edwards, III, "George Bush and the Public Presidency: The Politics of Inclusion," in *The Bush Presidency: First Appraisals*, eds. Colin Campbell and Bert A. Rockman (Chatham, NJ: Chatham House Publishers, 1991), 133–35.
3. George W. Bush Presidential Job Approval, Gallup, http://www.gallup.com/poll/116500/Presidential-Approval-Ratings-George-Bush.aspx.
4. James Madison, Alexander Hamilton, John Jay, "Federalist Number 71: The Same View Continued in Regard to the Duration of the Office," *The Federalist Papers*, ed. Isaac Kramnick (New York: Penguin Books, 1987), 409.

5. Alexander Hamilton, June 18, 1788 speech, in *Selected Writings and Speeches of Alexander Hamilton*, ed. Morton J. Frisch (Washington, DC: American Enterprise Institute, 1985), 108.
6. See David Mayhew, *Congress: The Electoral Connection* (New Haven: Yale University Press, 1974).
7. Thomas Jefferson, "Letter to James Sullivan" February 9, 1797, in *The Writings of Thomas Jefferson*, ed. Paul Leicester Ford (New York: G. P. Putnam's Sons, 1895), 118.
8. Michael Nelson, "Andrew Jackson's Veto of the Bank Bill," in *The Evolving Presidency: Addresses, Cases, Essays, Letters, Reports, Resolutions, Transcripts, and other Landmark Documents, 1787–1998*, ed. Michael Nelson (Washington, DC: CQ Press, 1999), 66.
9. See Richard Rubin, *Press, Party and the President* (New York: W. W. Norton, 1982).
10. Abraham Lincoln, "Letter to Albert G. Hodges" in *The Evolving Presidency: Addresses, Cases, Essays, Letters, Reports, Resolutions, Transcripts, and other Landmark Documents, 1787–1998*, ed. Michael Nelson (Washington, DC: CQ Press, 1999), 73.
11. James Bryce, *The American Commonwealth* (London: MacMillan 1891), 265.
12. Robert Erickson and Kent Tedin, *American Public Opinion: Its Origins, Content and Impact* (New York: Pearson/Longman, 2009).
13. Historical Presidential Approval Rating, available at http://www.usatoday.com/news/washington/presidential-approval-tracker.htm.
14. Jeffrey Jones, "Approval Typically Falls in Second Year" available at http://www.gallup.com/poll/125294/Approval-Typically-Falls-Points-President-Second-Year.aspx.
15. Letter to Harry Truman from Frank Stanton, Vice President and General Manager of the Columbia Broadcasting System, September 29, 1945, PSF Speech File, Box 42, Harry S. Truman Presidential Library, Independence, Missouri.
16. Memo to Matt Connelly from David K. Niles, October 8, 1946, PSF Political File, Box 49, Harry S. Truman Presidential Library, Independence, Missouri.
17. Memo to Lyndon Johnson from Tom Johnson, December 9, 1966, White House Correspondence Files, PR, Box 18, Lyndon Baines Johnson Presidential Library, Austin, Texas.
18. See John Mueller, "Presidential Popularity from Truman to Johnson," *American Political Science Review* (64.1, 1970): 18–34; and John Mueller, *War, Presidents and Public Opinion* (Baltimore: Lanham, 1973).
19. The Gallup Polling Organization, Presidential Approval, Key Statistics, available at http://www.gallup.com/poll/124922/Presidential-Job-Approval-Center.aspx
20. Mueller, *War, Presidents and Public Opinion*, 215.
21. See Paul Gronke and Brian Newman, "From FDR to Clinton, from Mueller to ?? A Field Essay on Presidential Approval," *Political Research Quarterly*, 56 (4):501–12.
22. Lori Cox Han, *Women and American Politics: The Challenges of Political Leadership* (Boston: McGraw Hill, 2007), 48.
23. Obama and the Gender Gap, available at http://us-elections.suite101.com/article.cfm/obama_and_the_gender_gap,
24. Harold Clarke, Marianne Stewart, Mike Ault and Euel Elliott, "Men, Women and the Dynamics of Presidential Approval," *British Journal of Political Science* 35 (2005): 31–51.
25. "Public Remains of Two Minds on Energy Policy," June 14, 2010, Pew Research Center for the People and the Press, available at http://people-press.org/report/622/.
26. Gronke and Newman, 510.
27. Robert S. Erikson, "Economic Conditions and the Presidential Vote," *American Political Science Review*, Vol. 83, No. 2 (June 1989):567–73.

28. See Richard Neustadt, *Presidential Power: The Politics of Leadership* (New York: Wiley, 1960); and Elmer E. Cornwell, Jr., *Presidential Leadership of Public Opinion* (Bloomington: Indiana University Press, 1965), 5.
29. Ibid, 6.
30. See Paul Brace and Barbara Hinckley, *Follow the Leader: Opinion Polls and the Modern Presidents* (New York: Basic Books, 1992).
31. Ibid.
32. See Brandice Canes-Wrone, *Who Leads Whom? Presidents, Policy, and the Public* (Chicago: University of Chicago Press. *2006).*
33. See Samuel Kernell, *Going Public: New Strategies of Presidential Leadership*, 4th ed. (Washington DC: CQ Press, 2007).
34. Ibid.
35. Mathew Baum and Samuel Kernell, "Has Cable Ended the Golden Age of Presidential Television?" *American Political Science Review* 93 (March, 1999): 1–16.
36. Brenna Erlich, "Many Facebook and Twitter Users Unhappy with Obama Speech on BP Oil Spill," available at http://mashable.com/2010/06/16/obama-speech-facebook-twitter-oil-spill/
37. Frank Newport, "Obama Receives 44% Approval on Oil Spill While BP Gets 16%," available at http://www.gallup.com/poll/140957/Obama-Receives-Approval-Oil-Spill-Gets.aspx
38. See George C. Edwards, III, *On Deaf Ears: The Limits of the Bully Pulpit* (New Haven: Yale Univesity Press, 2003).
39. See Jeffrey E. Cohen, *Going Local: Presidential Leadership in the Post-Broadcast Age* (New York: Cambridge University Press, 2010).
40. Ibid.
41. See Jon Bond and Richard Fleisher, *The President in the Legislative Arena* (Chicago: University of Chicago Press, 1990); George C. Edwards, III, *At The Margins: Presidential Leadership of Congress* (New Haven: Yale University Press, 1989); and George C. Edwards, III, "Aligning Tests with Theory: Presidential Influence as a Source of Influence in Congress," *Congress and the Presidency* 24 (1997): 113–30.
42. See Edwards, *At the Margins.*
43. See Mark Peterson, *Legislating Together: The White House and Capitol Hill from Eisenhower to Reagan* (Cambridge: Harvard University Press, 1990).
44. See Jeffrey E. Cohen, *Presidential Responsiveness and Public-Policy Making* (Ann Arbor: University of Michigan Press, 1997); and Jeffrey E. Cohen, "Presidential Rhetoric and the Public Agenda" *American Journal of Political Science,* 39 (1995): 87–107.
45. Stephen A. Borrelli and Grace L. Simmons, "Congressional Responsiveness to Presidential Popularity: The Electoral Context," *Political Behavior*, Vol. 15, No. 2 (June 1993): 93–112.
46. Memo to Jimmy Carter from Stu Eizenstat, February 21, 1978, Files of Jody Powell, Box 39, Jimmy Carter Presidential Library, Atlanta, Georgia.
47. Robert Eisinger, *The Evolution of Presidential Polling* (New York: Cambridge University Press, 2003), 42.
48. Memo to Franklin Roosevelt from Steve Early, August 16, 1940, Files of Steve Early, Box 24, Franklin Delano Roosevelt Presidential Library, Hyde Park, New York.
49. Ibid.
50. Memo to Franklin Roosevelt from Hadley Cantril, March 7, 1941, Gallup Polls, Box 857, Franklin Delano Roosevelt Presidential Library, Hyde Park, New York.
51. Hadley Cantril, *Human Dimension Experiences in Policy Research* (Newark: Rutgers University Press, 1967), 39–40.

52. Harry S. Truman, *Memoirs by Harry Truman, Volume Two: Years of Trial and Hope* (New York: Macmillan 1956), 177, 196.
53. Alfred Politz Research, n.d., Box 105, Dwight D. Eisenhower Presidential Library, Abilene, Kansas.
54. Lawrence Jacobs and Robert Shapiro, "The Rise of Presidential Polling: The Nixon White House in Historical Perspective," *Public Opinion Quarterly* 59 (Summer 1995): 163–95.
55. Memo to John F. Kennedy from Walter W. Heller, July 31, 1962, President's Office Files, John F. Kennedy Presidential Library, Boston, Massachusetts.
56. Jacobs and Shapiro, "The Rise of Presidential Polling," 169.
57. See Diane J. Heith, *Polling to Govern: Public Opinion and Presidential Leadership* (Stanford: Stanford University Press, 2004).
58. See Heith, *Polling to Govern,* and Eisinger, *The Evolution of Presidential Polling,* for a discussion of the evolution of the polling apparatus.
59. Emphasis added, http://www.osc.gov/documents/hatchact/ha_fed.pdf.
60. See H. R. Haldeman, *The Haldeman Diaries: Inside the Nixon White House* (Berkeley: Berkeley Publishing, 1994).
61. Anonymous, Memoranda Re: Polling, February 1975 in Hartmann, Robert, Box 34 Presidential Survey Research Prop 2, Gerald R. Ford Presidential Library, Ann Arbor, Michigan.
62. See Heith, *Polling to Govern.*
63. Ibid.
64. See Jacobs and Shapiro, "The Rise of Presidential Polling."
65. See Heith, *Polling to Govern*; and Katie Dunn Tenpas and Jay McCann, "Testing the Permanence of the Permanent Campaign: An Analysis of Presidential Polling Expenditures, 1977–2002," *Public Opinion Quarterly* 71, No. 3 (2007): 349–366.
66. See Heith, *Polling to Govern.*
67. Memo to Dwight L. Chapin from Gregg Petersmeyer, "A proposal that the President give a series of informal television addresses for the purpose of meeting the country's crisis of the spirit," September 15, 1969, Files of Dwight Chapin, originally accessed in the Richard Nixon Presidential Materials, National Archives, College Park, Maryland (now available at the Nixon Library, Yorba Linda, California).
68. Ibid.
69. Memo to John Sununu from David Demarest, 12/2/90, George Bush Presidential Library, College Station, Texas.
70. See Heith, *Polling to Govern.*
71. Memo to David Gergen from Jim Shuman, "Future Agenda," May 18, 1976, Files of Ron Nessen, Box 135, Gerald Ford Presidential Library, Ann Arbor, Michigan.
72. Diane Heith, "The White House Public Opinion Apparatus Meets the Anti-Polling President," in *In the Public Domain: Presidents and the Challenges of Public Leadership,* ed. Lori Cox Han and Diane Heith (Albany: State University of New York, 2005), 77.
73. Ibid, 81.
74. See Jacobs and Shapiro, "The Rise of Presidential Polling."
75. Mark Blumenthal, "New Flash: Obama Using Polling Data," available at http://www.pollster.com/blogs/news_flash_obama_using_polling.php.
76. Memo to George Bush and John Sununu from Roger Ailes, January 9, 1991, in John Sununu Files, Chief of Staff, Polling (1 of 3) – 1991 [2 of 4] CF04473 2, George Bush Presidential Library, College Station, Texas.
77. George H. W. Bush, "Radio Address to the Nation on the Persian Gulf Crisis," January 5, 1991, *Public Papers of the Presidents.*

78. Memo to George Bush and John Sununu from Roger Ailes, January 9, 1991, in John Sununu Files, Chief of Staff, Polling (1 of 3) - 1991 [2 of 4] CF04473 2, George Bush Presidential Library, College Station, Texas.
79. George H. W. Bush, "Address to the Nation Announcing Allied Military Action in the Persian Gulf," January 16, 1991, *Public Papers of the Presidents.*
80. Memo to George Bush and John Sununu from Roger Ailes, January 9, 1991, in John Sununu Files, Chief of Staff, Polling (1 of 3) - 1991 [2 of 4] CF04473 2, George Bush Presidential Library, College Station, Texas.
81. George H. W. Bush, "Address to the Nation Announcing Allied Military Action in the Persian Gulf," January 16, 1991, *Public Papers of the Presidents.*
82. Memo to Bush and Sununu from Ailes, January 9, 1991.
83. George H. W. Bush, "Address to the Nation," January 16, 1991.
84. Ibid.
85. See Jacobs and Shapiro, "Politicians Don't Pander," for their discussion of "crafted talk."
86. John Sirica, *To Set the Record Straight: The Break-in, the Tapes, the Conspirators, the Pardon* (New York: W. W. Norton, 1979), 56.
87. Richard Nixon, *RN: The Memoirs of Richard Nixon* (New York: Grosset & Dunlap, 1978), 971–72.
88. Ibid., 715–16.
89. Stanley Kutler, ed., *Abuse of Power: The New Nixon Tapes* (New York: Simon & Schuster, 1997), 275–76.
90. Haldeman, *The Haldeman Diaries,* 803.
91. Kutler, *Abuse of Power,* 407.
92. Ibid., 409.
93. Ibid., 425–26.
94. Ibid., 460.
95. Heith, *Polling to Govern,* 126.
96. John Zaller, "Monica Lewinsky's Contribution to Political Science" *PS: Political Science and Politics,* 31.2 (1998): 182–89; Arthur Miller, "Sex, Politics, and Public Opinion: What Political Scientists Really Learned from the Clinton–Lewinsky Scandal," *PS: Political Science and Politics* 32.4 (December, 1999): 721–29; Molly Andolina, and Clyde Wilcox. "Public Opinion: The Paradoxes of Clinton's Popularity," in *The Clinton Scandal and the Future of American Government,* eds. Mark Rozell and Clyde Wilcox (Washington, DC: Georgetown University Press, 2000).
97. George Stephanopoulos, *All Too Human: A Political Education* (Boston: Little, Brown and Company, 1999), 412.
98. Memo to Jerry Rafshoon and Greg Schneiders from Alan Raymond, "State of the Presidency," February 20, 1979, Files of Gerald Rafshoon, Box 27, Jimmy Carter Presidential Library, Atlanta, Georgia.

CHAPTER 6

1. Molly K. Hooper and Bob Cusack, "The Relationship between Obama and Boehner Takes a Nosedive," *The Hill,* 11/25/11, http://thehill.com/homenews/administration/195457-relationship-between-obama-and-boehner-takes-a-nosedive.
2. Barack Obama, Speech at the Iowa Jefferson-Jackson Day Dinner, Des Moines, Iowa, November 10, 2007, http://www.asksam.com/ebooks/releases.asp?file=Obama-Speeches.ask&dn=Iowa%20Jefferson-Jackson%20Dinner.

3. James Madison, Alexander Hamilton, John Jay, "Federalist Number 73: The Same View Continued in Relation to the Provision Concerning Support and the Power of the Negative," in *The Federalist Papers*, ed. Isaac Kramnick (New York: Penguin Books, 1987), 418.
4. Copy, DNA: RG 233, Second Congress, 1791–1793, Records of Legislative Proceedings, Journals; LB, DLC:GW. (From Robert F. Haggard and Mark A. Mastromarino, eds., *The Papers of George Washington, Presidential Series,* ed. Philander Chase, *Vol. 10: March–August 1792* [Charlottesville, VA: University Press of Virginia, 2002], 213–14).
5. President Jackson's Veto Message Regarding the Bank of the United States, July 10, 1832. The Avalon Project, Yale Law School, http://avalon.law.yale.edu/19th_century/ajveto01.asp.
6. Daniel Felle, "King Andrew and the Bank," *Humanities*, January/February 2008, Volume 29, Number 1.
7. Unsigned and undated White House memo, "Civil Rights Communications Plan for Presidential Veto Scenario," Formerly Withheld, NLGB Control Number 4698, George Bush Presidential Library, College Station, Texas.
8. Roger H. Davidson, Walter J. Oleszek, and Frances Lee, *Congress and Its Members*, 13th ed. (Washington, DC: CQ Press, 2012), 337.
9. Louis Fisher, "The Legislative Veto: Invalidated, It Survives," *Law and Contemporary Problems*. Vol. 56, No. 4 (Autumn 1993): 279.
10. *Clinton v. City of New York*, 524 U.S. 417 (1998).
11. *Youngstown Sheet & Tube Co. v. Sawyer* 343 U.S. 579 (1952).
12. Donna Hoffman and Alison Howard, *Addressing the State of the Union: The Evolution and Impact of the President's Big Speech* (Boulder: Lynne Rienner, 2006), 16.
13. Ibid.
14. Gerald R. Ford, State of the Union Address, January 15, 1975, http://www.presidency.ucsb.edu/ws/index.php?pid=4938#axzz1ICCYyQgE
15. Barack Obama, State of the Union Address, January 27, 2010, *The Public Papers of the President: Barack Obama*, http://www.presidency.ucsb.edu/ws.
16. http://www.senate.gov/artandhistory/history/common/briefing/Nominations.htm
17. James Madison, "Consolidation," National Gazette 12/5/1791, *Writings of James Madison* 6:67.
18. George Washington, Farewell Address, 1796, *The Public Papers of the President*, http://www.presidency.ucsb.edu/ws.
19. William Leuchtenburg, *Franklin D. Roosevelt and the New Deal: 1932–1940* (New York: Harper and Row, 1963), 13.
20. Franklin D. Roosevelt, Inaugural Address, March 4, 1933, available at http://www.bartleby.com/124/pres49.html. 21. See Leuchtenburg, *Franklin D. Roosevelt and the New Deal,* for a thorough discussion of FDR's tenure in office.
22. Based on the last eight elections.
23. Richard Fenno, "U.S. House Members in Their Constituencies: An Exploration," *American Political Science Review*, 71 (1977): 887.
24. B. Dan Wood, *The Myth of Presidential Representation* (New York: Cambridge University Press, 2009), 118.
25. See Barbara Sinclair, *Unorthodox Lawmaking: New Legislative Processes in the U.S. Congress* (Washington, DC: CQ Press, 2007).
26. See William W. Lammers and Michael A. Genovese, *The Presidency and Domestic Policy: Comparing Leadership Styles, FDR to Clinton* (Washington DC: CQ Press, 2000).
27. White House Memo, May 19, 1964, "The Administration's Legislative Program," Files of Horace Busby, Box 20, Lyndon Baines Johnson Presidential Library, Austin, Texas.

28. Richard E. Neustadt, *Presidential Power and the Modern Presidents: The Politics of Leadership from Roosevelt to Reagan* (New York: Free Press, 1990), 32.
29. Ibid, 30.
30. Sinclair, *Unorthodox Lawmaking,* 163.
31. Ibid, 163–64.
32. Ibid, 171.
33. Ibid, 173.
34. Ibid, 180.
35. George H. W. Bush, "Address to a Joint Session of the House and Senate," February 9, 1989, http://www.nytimes.com/1989/02/10/us/transcript-of-president-s-address-to-a-joint-session-of-the-house-and-senate.html?pagewanted=all&src=pm.
36. Richard E. Cohen, *Washington at Work: Back Rooms and Clean Air* (New York: Macmillan, 1992), 56.
37. Ibid, 84.
38. Ibid, 85.
39. Ibid, 97.
40. See David Mayhew, *Congress: The Electoral Connection* (New Haven: Yale University Press, 1974).
41. See Samuel Kernell, *Going Public: New Strategies of Presidential Leadership*, 4th ed. (Washington, DC: CQ Press, 2007).
42. Ibid, 157.
43. Ronald Reagan, Address to the Nation, July 27, 1981, www.presidency.ucsb.eduhttp://www.presidency.ucsb.edu/ws/index.php?pid=44120&st=&st1=#ixzz1O2uPgN5b
44. Kernell, *Going Public,* 159.
45. See Lori Cox Han, *Governing from Center Stage: White House Communication Strategies During the Television Age of Politics* (Cresskill, NJ: Hampton Press, 2001), and Lyn Ragsdale, *Vital Statistics on the Presidency,* 3rd ed. (Washington, DC: CQ Press, 2009.
46. Matthew A. Baum and Samuel Kernell, "Has Cable Ended the Golden Age of Presidential Television?" *American Political Science Review* , 93 (1999): 99–114.
47. Diane Heith, *The Presidential Road Show: Public Leadership in an Era of Party Polarization and Media Fragmentation* (Boulder: Paradigm Press, 2013).
48. See Brandon Rottinghaus, *The Provisional Pulpit: Modern Presidential Leadership of Public Opinion* (College Station: Texas A&M Press, 2010).
49. See George C. Edwards, III, *At The Margins: Presidential Leadership of Congress* (New Haven: Yale University Press, 1989).
50. Andrew Barrett, "Gone Public: The Impact of Going Public on Presidential Legislative Success," *American Politics Research,* 32.3 (May 2004): 338–70.
51. Charles Cameron, John Lipinski, and Charles Riemann, "Research Notes: Testing Formal Theories of Political Rhetoric," *Journal of Politics* 62.1 (2000):187–205.
52. President Ronald Reagan, Remarks to the American Business Conference, March 13, 1985, www.presidency.ucsb.edu,http://www.presidency.ucsb.edu/ws/index.php?pid=38318&st=&st1=#ixzz1OctMGKbi
53. President Ronald Reagan, Presidential News Conference, May 23, 1995, www.presidency.ucsb.eduhttp://www.presidency.ucsb.edu/ws/index.php?pid=51404&st=&st1=#ixzz1OcwKtZqd
54. Cameron et al., "Research Notes," 202.
55. Richard Conley, "George Bush and the 102d Congress: The Impact of Public and Private Veto Threats on Policy Outcomes," *Presidential Studies Quarterly,* 33.4 (2003): 730–50.

56. Budget 2011, Appendix, Executive Office of the President, http://www.gpoaccess.gov/usbudget/fy11/pdf/appendix/eop.pdf
57. Sinclair, *Unorthodox Lawmaking,* 216.
58. Ibid, 220.
59. Quoted in Sinclair, *Unorthodox Lawmaking,* 218.
60. Ibid, 223.
61. Ibid, 224.
62. See Heith, *The Presidential Road Show.*
63. Barack Obama, "Remarks on the Federal Budget in Baltimore, Maryland," February 14, 2011, http://www.presidency.ucsb.edu/ws/index.php?pid=88988&st=&st1=#ixzz1QUHT3OGw.
64. "Federal Budget," *New York Times*, available at: http://topics.nytimes.com/top/reference/timestopics/subjects/f/federal_budget_us/index.html?scp=1&sq=government%20shutdown%202011&st=cse
65. Ibid.
66. Memo for Clayton Yeutter to Charles E. M. Kolb, "A Part Time Congress," April 1, 1992, Formerly Withheld, NLGB Control Number 6267, George Bush Presidential Library, College Station, Texas.
67. Memo to Howard Baker from Frank J. Donatelli, "Do Awful Congress as a Campaign Theme," January 7, 1988, Files of Ken Duberstein, Box 3, Ronald Reagan Presidential Library, Simi Valley, California.

CHAPTER 7

1. "White House Discussion Points, Supreme Court Nomination of Judge David Souter," undated, Mary Kate Grant Files, White House Office of Speechwriting, Box 8, George Bush Presidential Library, College Station, Texas.
2. Memo to Homer Cummings from Franklin Roosevelt, January 14, 1936, President's Secretary's Files, Box 165, Franklin D. Roosevelt Presidential Library, Hyde Park, New York.
3. Memo to Franklin D. Roosevelt from Homer Cummings, January 16, 1936, President's Secretary's File, Box 165, Franklin D. Roosevelt Presidential Library, Hyde Park, New York.
4. Memo to Franklin D. Roosevelt from Homer Cummings, February 2, 1937, President's Secretary's File, Box 165, Franklin D. Roosevelt Presidential Library, Hyde Park, New York.
5. Franklin D. Roosevelt, "Message to Congress on the Reorganization of the Judicial Branch of the Government," February 5, 1937. *The American Presidency Project* [online], eds. John T. Woolley and Gerhard Peters, Santa Barbara, CA: University of California (hosted), Gerhard Peters (database). Available at http://www.presidency.ucsb.edu/ws/?pid=15360.
6. Franklin D. Roosevelt, "Fireside Chat," March 9, 1937. *The American Presidency Project* [online], eds. John T. Woolley and Gerhard Peters. Santa Barbara, CA: University of California (hosted), Gerhard Peters (database). Available at http://www.presidency.ucsb.edu/ws/?pid=15381.
7. House Floor Speech: Impeach Justice Douglas, Box D29, Gerald R. Ford Congressional Papers, Gerald R. Ford Presidential Library, Ann Arbor, Michigan.
8. Lawrence Baum, *The Supreme Court*, 9th ed. (Washington, DC: CQ Press, 2007), 35–41.

9. Ibid, 44–45.
10. David M. O'Brien, *Storm Center: The Supreme Court in American Politics*, 8th ed. (New York: W. W. Norton, 2008), 34.
11. Ibid, 47–50.
12. George W. Bush, "Remarks Announcing the Nomination of Harriet E. Miers to Be an Associate Justice of the United States Supreme Court," October 7, 2005, *Weekly Compilation of Presidential Documents* (Washington, DC: Government Printing Office, 2005).
13. Baum, *The Supreme Court*, 30–33.
14. Doris Graber, *Mass Media and American Politics*, 8th ed. (Washington, DC: CQ Press, 2010), 260.
15. Mark Jurkowitz, "Sotomayor Hearings Lead the News Without Making News," Pew Research Center's Project for Excellence in Journalism, July 21, 2009, http://www.journalism.org/index_report/pej_news_coverage_index_july_13_19_2009.
16. Ronald Reagan, "Remarks Announcing the Nomination of Robert H. Bork to Be an Associate Justice of the Supreme Court of the United States," July 1, 1987, *Public Papers of the Presidents,* available at http://www.reagan.utexas.edu/archives/speeches/1987/87jul.htm.
17. Memo to Senior Administration Officials from Thomas C. Griscom, "Judge Robert H. Bork," September 30, 1987, Files of Howard H. Baker, Box 3, Ronald Reagan Presidential Library, Simi Valley, California.
18. Memo to Will Ball from Howard S. Liebengood, "Bork Nomination," September 21, 1987, Files of Howard H. Baker, Box 3, Ronald Reagan Presidential Library, Simi Valley, California.
19. George Bush, "The President's News Conference in Kennebunkport, Maine," July 1, 1991, *Public Papers of the Presidents* (Washington, DC: Government Printing Office, 1992).
20. Mark Silverstein, *Judicious Choices: The New Politics of Supreme Court Confirmations* (New York: W. W. Norton, 1994), 4.
21. Ibid, 29.
22. Barack Obama, "Floor Statement on the Confirmation of Judge Samuel Alito, Jr.," January 26, 2006, available at http://obamaspeeches.com/046-Confirmation-of-Judge-Samuel-Alito-Jr-Obama-Speech.htm.
23. Barack Obama, "Weekly Address," May 30, 2009, http://www.whitehouse.gov/the_press_office/WEEKLY-ADDRESS-President-Obama-Calls-for-Thorough-and-Timely-Confirmation-for-Judge-Sonia-Sotomayor.
24. Henry J. Abraham, *Justices, Presidents, and Senators: A History of U.S. Supreme Court Appointments from Washington to Bush II,* 5th ed. (Lanham, MD: Rowman & Littlefield, 2008), 4.
25. Biography of Sandra Day O'Connor, The Oyez Project, IIT Chicago-Kent College of Law, http://www.oyez.org/oyez/resource/legal_entity/102/biography.
26. Sheldon Goldman, *Picking Federal Judges: Lower Court Selection from Roosevelt through Reagan* (New Haven, CT: Yale University Press, 1997), 1–2.
27. Barbara Palmer, "Women in the American Judiciary: Their Influence and Impact," *Women & Politics*, Vol. 23, No. 3 (2001): 95.
28. Richard L. Pacelle, Jr., "A President's Legacy: Gender and Appointment to the Federal Courts," in *The Other Elites: Women, Politics, and Power in the Executive Branch*, eds. MaryAnne Borrelli and Janet M. Martin (Boulder: Lynne Rienner, 1997), 154.
29. A woman judge who also belongs to a minority group is counted in both categories. Data from the Biographical Directory of Federal Judges, Federal Judicial Center, available at www.fjc.gov.

30. Larry Berman, *The New American Presidency* (Boston: Little, Brown and Company, 1987), 53.
31. See Kevin T. McGuire, *Understanding the U.S. Supreme Court: Cases and Controversies* (Boston: McGraw-Hill, 2002), 171–3.
32. Robert Dahl, "Decision-Making in a Democracy: The Supreme Court as a National Policy-Maker," *Journal of Public Law*, 6 (1957), 279–95.
33. See Stephen R. Routh, "U.S. Solicitor General," in *Encyclopedia of American Government and Civics, Vol. II,* eds. Michael A Genovese and Lori Cox Han (New York: Facts on File, 2009), 645–8.
34. Baum, *The Supreme Court*, 85.
35. Richard L. Pacelle, Jr., *Between Law & Politics: The Solicitor General and the Structuring of Race, Gender, and Reproductive Rights Litigation* (College Station: Texas A&M University Press, 2003), 10.
36. For brief discussions of judicial review and *Marbury v. Madison*, see David M. O'Brien, *Constitutional Law and Politics: Struggles for Power and Governmental Accountability*, Vol. 1, 7th ed. (New York: W. W. Norton, 2008), and Lee Epstein and Thomas G. Walker, *Constitutional Law for a Changing America: Institutional Powers and Constraints,* 7th ed. (Washington, DC: CQ Press, 2010). For a more in-depth discussion of judicial review and its history in the United States, see William E. Nelson, *Marbury v. Madison: The Origins and Legacy of Judicial Review* (Lawrence: University Press of Kansas, 2000).
37. Andrew Jackson, "Veto Message," July 10, 1832, in *A Compilation of the Messages and Papers of the Presidents, Volume II*, ed. James D. Richardson (Washington, DC: Government Printing Office, 1902), 582.
38. As quoted in Abraham, *Justices, Presidents, and Senators,* 77, regarding the case *Worcester v. Georgia,* 31 U.S. 515 (1832).
39. George Bush, "Statement on the Flag Protection Act of 1989," October 26, 1989, *The Public Papers of the Presidents of the United States: George Bush*, 1989 (Washington, DC: Government Printing Office, 1990).
40. Publius [Hamilton], *Federalist* 78, in *The Federalist Papers*, ed. Isaac Kramnick (London: Penguin Books, 1987).
41. Baum, *The Supreme Court*, 9th ed., 20.
42. David O'Brien, *Storm Center: The Supreme Court in American Politics*, 6th ed. (New York: W. W. Norton, 2003), 108–109.
43. Baum, 2007, 20.
44. R. Kent Newmyer, "John Marshall," in *The Oxford Companion to the Supreme Court of the United States*, ed. Kermit L. Hall (New York: Oxford University Press, 1992), 526.
45. Dwight D. Eisenhower, "The President's News Conference," September 30, 1953, *http://www.eisenhowermemorial.org/presidential-papers/index.htm.*
46. Dwight D. Eisenhower, *The White House Years: Mandate For Change 1953–1956* (Garden City, NY: Doubleday, 1963), 26.
47. O'Brien, *Storm Center,* 68.
48. See Parker Hevron, "The LBJ Legacy That Wasn't: The Failed Confirmation of Abe Fortas" (paper presented at the 2005 Annual Meeting of the Western Political Science Association, March, 2005, Oakland, California).
49. George W. Bush, "Address to the Nation Announcing the Nomination of John G. Roberts, Jr., to Be an Associate Justice of the United States Supreme Court," July 19, 2005, *Weekly Compilation of Presidential Documents* (Washington, DC: Government Printing Office, 2005).

50. George W. Bush, "Remarks Announcing the Nomination of John G. Roberts, Jr., to Be Chief Justice of the United States Supreme Court," September 5, 2005, *Weekly Compilation of Presidential Documents* (Washington, DC: Government Printing Office, 2005).
51. Letter to Robert H. Jackson from Harry S. Truman, April 2, 1946, President's Secretary's Files, Box 187, Harry S. Truman Presidential Library, Independence, Missouri.
52. Letter to Harry S. Truman from Robert H. Jackson, April 24, 1946, President's Secretary's Files, Box 187, Harry S. Truman Presidential Library, Independence, Missouri.
53. Letter to Robert H. Jackson from Harry S. Truman, May 1, 1946, President's Secretary's Files, Box 187, Harry S. Truman Presidential Library, Independence, Missouri.

CHAPTER 8

1. Franklin D. Roosevelt, "Inaugural Address," March 4, 1933, available at: http://www.bartleby.com/124/pres49.html.
2. Ronald Reagan, "Inaugural Address," January 20, 1981, available at: http://bartleby.com/124/pres61.html,
3. For a discussion on the current state and size of the executive branch, see Matthew J. Dickinson, "The Presidency and the Executive Branch," in *New Directions in the American Presidency*, ed. Lori Cox Han (New York: Routledge, 2011).
4. James Madison, Alexander Hamilton, John Jay, "Federalist Number 69: The Same View Continued With a Comparison Between the President and the King of Great Britain on the One Hand and the Governor of New York on the Other," *The Federalist Papers*, ed. Isaac Kramnick (New York: Penguin Books, 1987), 401.
5. James Madison, Alexander Hamilton, John Jay, "Federalist Number 77: The View of the Constitution of the President Concluded," *The Federalist Papers*, ed. Isaac Kramnick (New York: Penguin Books, 1987), 435.
6. U.S. Department of Commerce, Bureau of the Census, "Series P 62–68, Government Employment, Federal Government Employment, 1816–1945," Historical Statistics of the United States, 1789–1945, A Supplement to the Historical Abstract of the, United States, 1952.
7. U.S. Department of Treasury, Bureau of Statistics, "Federal Civilian Employment and Annual Payroll by Branch: 1970 to 2008," Statistical Abstract of the United States, Volume 129, Part 2010, Table 484, 2011.
8. U.S. Department of State, "Thomas Jefferson: First Secretary of State," http://future.state.gov/when/timeline/1784_timeline/jefferson_first_secretary.html.
9. Leonard D. White, *The Jeffersonians: A Study in Administrative History 1801–1829* (New York: MacMillan, 1961), 139–40.
10. Ibid, 427–31.
11. Leonard D. White, *The Jacksonians: A Study in Administrative History 1801–1829* (New York: MacMillan 1961), 320.
12. Samuel Kernell and Gary Jacobson, *The Logic of American Politics* (Washington DC: CQ Press, 2010), 369.
13. Ibid, 370.
14. Paul Light, "The Homeland Security Hash," *The Wilson Quarterly* (Spring 2007): 31(2), 36.
15. Dickinson, "The Presidency and the Executive Branch," 139.
16. David Lewis and Terry Moe, "The Presidency and the Bureaucracy," in *The Presidency and the Political System*, 9th ed., ed. Michael Nelson (Washington DC: CQ Press, 2009), 370.

17. Ibid, 371.
18. Ibid, 372.
19. Theodore Sorenson, *Decision Making in the White House: The Olive Branch or the Arrows* (New York: Columbia University Press, 2005), 82.
20. Mark Lander and Helene Cooper, "After a Bitter Campaign, Forging an Alliance," *The New York Times*, March 18, 2010, http://www.nytimes.com/2010/03/19/us/politics/19policy.html.
21. See Richard E. Neustadt, *Presidential Power and the Modern Presidents: The Politics of Leadership from Roosevelt to Reagan* (New York: Free Press, 1990).
22. John Burke "The Institutional Presidency," in *The Presidency and the Political System*, 9th ed., ed. Michael Nelson (Washington, DC: CQ Press, 2009), 42.
23. Ibid, 342.
24. Ibid, 343.
25. Franklin D. Roosevelt, "Inaugural Address," March 4, 1933, available at: http://www.bartleby.com/124/pres49.html.
26. For an excellent discussion of the creation and growth of the Executive Office of the President under FDR, see Matthew J. Dickinson, *Bitter Harvest: FDR, Presidential Power and the Growth of the Presidential Branch* (Cambridge: Cambridge University Press, 1996).
27. Summary of the Report of the Committee on Administrative Management, January 12, 1937, in *The Public Papers of the President: Franklin Roosevelt*, http://www.presidency.ucsb.edu/ws.
28. Justin S. Vaughn and Jose D. Villalobos, "White House Staff," in *New Directions in the American Presidency*, ed. Lori Cox Han (New York: Routledge, 2011), 121.
29. Ibid, 138–31. See also Bradley H. Patterson, Jr., *The White House Staff: Inside the West Wing and Beyond* (Washington, DC: Brookings Institution Press, 2000).
30. Remarks delivered by President George W. Bush in the Rose Garden, April 18, 2006.
31. Memo to Jimmy Carter from Jody Powell, January 16, 1978, Files of Jody Powell, Box 39, Jimmy Carter Presidential Library, Atlanta, Georgia.
32. Memo to Donald T. Regan from Roger B. Porter, "White House Organization VII: Meetings," January 26, 1985, Files of Donald T. Regan, Box 11, Ronald Reagan Presidential Library, Simi Valley, California.
33. See David B. Cohen, Charles E. Walcott, Shirley Anne Warshaw, and Stephen J. Wayne, "The Chief of Staff," *The White House Transition Project*, Report 2009–21, 2008, http://whitehousetransitionproject.org/resources/briefing/WHTP-2009-21-Chief%20of%20Staff.pdf.
34. Terry Sullivan, ed., *The Nerve Center: Lessons in Governing from the White House Chiefs of Staff* (College Station: Texas A&M University Press, 2004), 39.
35. Ibid, 24.
36. Paul 't Hart, Karen Tindall, and Christer Brown, "Crisis Leadership of the Bush Presidency: Advisory Capacity and Presidential Performance in the Acute Stages of the 9/11 and Katrina Crises," *Presidential Studies Quarterly* 39.3 (2009): 473–94.
37. *United States v. Nixon*, 418 U.S. 683 (1974).
38. Bob Woodward, *Plan of Attack* (New York: Simon and Schuster, 2004), 251.
39. Ibid, 252.
40. Lewis and Moe, "The Presidency and the Bureaucracy," 381.
41. Ibid.
42. Ibid, 382.

43. Eric Lipton and Scott Shane, "Leader of Federal Effort Feels the Heat," *New York Times*, September 3, 2005, http://www.nytimes.com/2005/09/03/national/nationalspecial/03fema.html.
44. Charles Perrow, "Using Organizations: The Case of FEMA," *Homeland Security Affairs*, 1.2 (2005).
45. Lewis and Moe, "The Presidency and the Bureaucracy," 386.
46. CBS News, "Consumer Safety Chief Says She Won't Quit," http://www.cbsnews.com/stories/2007/10/31/national/main3434914.shtml
47. Andrew Rudalevige, "The Presidency and Unilateral Power," in *The Presidency and the Political System*, ed. Michael Nelson (Washington, DC: CQ Press, 2009), 473.
48. Ibid, 474.
49. See Adam Warber, *Executive Orders and the Modern Presidency* (Boulder: Lynne Rienner, 2006), and Kenneth Mayer, *With the Stroke of a Pen: Executive Orders and Presidential Power* (Princeton: Princeton University Press, 2001).
50. See Warber, *Executive Orders and the Modern Presidency*.
51. Lewis and Moe, "The Presidency and the Bureaucracy," 390.
52. Andrew Jackson: "Special Message," May 30, 1830. Online by Gerhard Peters and John T. Woolley, *The American Presidency Project*, http://www.presidency.ucsb.edu/ws/?pid=66775.
53. Rudalevige, "The Presidency and Unilateral Power," 471.
54. George W. Bush Statement on Signing the Palestinian Anti-Terrorism Act of 2006, December 21, 2006, *Public Papers of the Presidency, http://www.presidency.ucsb.edu/ws/index.php?pid=24395#axzz1wgqcDTAa.*
55. John Adams, *The Works of John Adams*, vol. 1, ed. C. F. Adams (Boston: Little Brown, 1850), 289.
56. Patrick Cox, "Not Worth a Bucket of Warm Spit," *The History News Network*, August 20, 2008. http://hnn.us/articles/53402.html.
57. See www.whitehouse.gov.
58. Joseph Pika, "The Vice Presidency," in *The Presidency and the Political System*, ed. Michael Nelson (Washington, DC: CQ Press 2009), 512.
59. Ibid, 513.
60. Ibid, 515.
61. Robert P. Watson, *The President's Wives: Reassessing the Office of First Lady* (Boulder: Lynne Rienner, 2000), 72.
62. Ibid, 112–13.
63. MaryAnne Borrelli, *The Politics of the President's Wife* (College Station: Texas A&M University Press, 2011), 1.
64. Lori Cox Han, *Women and US Politics: The Spectrum of Political Leadership*, 2nd ed. (Boulder: Lynne Rienner Publishers, 2010), 132–34.
65. William Leuchtenburg, *Franklin D. Roosevelt and the New Deal: 1932–1940* (New York: Harper & Row, 1963), 19.
66. Ibid, 33.
67. Ibid, 33.
68. Ibid, 33.
69. John P. Burke, "The Obama Presidential Transition: An Early Assessment," *Presidential Studies Quarterly* 39.3 (2009): 591.
70. Ibid, 577.
71. Ibid, 580.

72. Michael D. Shear and Philip Rucker, "Picks for Key Government Posts Play Long Waiting Game," *Washington Post,* March 4, 2009.
73. Memo to Senior Staff from John D. Podesta, "Paperflow," January 22, 1993, Files of Ira Magaziner, Box 1, William J. Clinton Presidential Library, Little Rock, Arkansas.

CHAPTER 9

1. See John F. Harris, *The Survivor: Bill Clinton in the White House* (New York: Random House, 2006); and Bob Woodward, *The Agenda: Inside the Clinton White House* (New York: Simon & Schuster, 2005).
2. See Donald A. Barr, *Introduction to U.S. Health Policy: The Organization, Financing, and Delivery of Healthcare in America* (Baltimore: Johns Hopkins University Press, 2011); and Staff of the *Washington Post, Landmark: The Inside Story of America's New Healthcare Law and What It Means for All of Us* (Washington, DC: Public Affairs, 2010).
3. See Bruce Ackerman, *We the People: Foundations* (Cambridge: Harvard University Press, 1991).
4. See Michael Nelson and Russell L. Riley, eds., *Governing at Home: The White House and Domestic Policymaking* (Lawrence: University Press of Kansas, 2011); Martin A. Levin, Daniel DiSalvo, and Martin M. Shapiro, eds., *Building Coalitions, Making Policy: The Politics of the Clinton, Bush, and Obama Presidencies* (Baltimore: Johns Hopkins University Press, 2012); and John W. Kingdon, *Agendas, Alternatives, and Public Policies* (New York: Longman Press, 2002).
5. See Kingdon, *Agendas.*
6. See Gordon S. Wood, *Empire of Liberty: A History of the Early Republic, 1789–1815* (New York: Oxford University Press, 2011).
7. See Alex Mintz and Karl DeRouen, Jr., *Understanding Foreign Policy Decision Making* (Cambridge: Cambridge University Press, 2010); and Steve Smith, Amelia Hadfield, and Timothy Dunne, *Foreign Policy: Theories, Actors, Cases* (New York: Oxford University Press, 2008).
8. See Nelson and Riley, *Governing at Home*; and Levin et al., *Building Coalitions.*
9. See David Marsh and Gerry Stoker, eds., *Theory and Methods in Political Science* (New York: Palgrave Macmillan, 2010); and Donald Green and Ian Shapiro, *Pathologies of Rational Choice: A Critique of Applications in Political Science* (New Haven: Yale University Press, 1996).
10. See Marsh, *Theory and Methods*; Nelson and Riley, *Governing at Home*; Levin et al., *Building Coalitions*; and Kingdon, *Agendas.*
11. See Ronald Dworkin, *Law's Empire* (Cambridge: Harvard University Press, 1986); Sanford Levinson, *Constitutional Faith* (Princeton: Princeton University Press, 1988); and Ackerman, *We the People.*
12. See Gordon S. Wood, *The Creation of the American Republic, 1776–1787* (New York: W. W. Norton, 1969).
13. See Alexander Bickel, *The Least Dangerous Branch: The Supreme Court at the Bar of Politics* (New Haven: Yale University Press, 1962); and John Hart Ely, *War and Responsibility* (Princeton: Princeton University Press, 1995).
14. See Nelson and Riley, *Governing at Home*; and Levin et al., *Building Coalitions.*
15. Bill Clinton, "Statement on Same-Gender Marriage," September 20, 1996, available at The American Presidency Project, http://www.presidency.ucsb.edu/ws/index.php?pid=51969&st=marriage&st1=#axzz1lLnQcTgf.
16. See Woodward, *The Agenda.*

17. See Julian E. Zelizer, ed., *The Presidency of George W. Bush: A First Historical Assessment* (Princeton: Princeton University Press, 2010); and Robert Draper, *Dead Certain: The Presidency of George W. Bush* (New York: Free Press, 2008).
18. See Marsh and Stoker, *Theory and Methods*; Green and Shapiro, *Pathologies of Rational Choice*; and Kingdon, *Agendas*.
19. See Graham Allison and Philip Zelikow, *Essence of Decision: Explaining the Cuban Missile Crisis* (New York: Longman Press, 1999); Green and Shapiro, *Pathologies of Rational Choice*; and Kingdon, *Agendas*.
20. See Woodward, *The Agenda*.
21. Memo to Hillary Rodham Clinton and Ira Magaziner from Dick Gephardt, "Consultation with Congress," March 3, 1993, Files of Ira Magaziner, Box 3, William J. Clinton Presidential Library, Little Rock, Arkansas.
22. Memo to Hillary Rodham Clinton and Mack McLarty from Howard Paster, "Lobbying on Health Care Reform," May 9, 1993, Files of Ira Magaziner, Box 3, William J. Clinton Presidential Library, Little Rock, Arkansas.
23. Memo to Hillary Rodham Clinton and Jeff Eller from Chris Jennings, "Health Care University," June 28, 1993, Files of Ira Magaziner, Box 3, William J. Clinton Presidential Library, Little Rock, Arkansas.
24. See Robert Dallek, *Lyndon B. Johnson: Portrait of a President* (New York: Oxford University Press, 2005). On his leadership style, see also Larry Berman, *Planning a Tragedy: The Americanization of the War in Vietnam* (New York: W. W. Norton, 1983).
25. George W. Bush, "Remarks on the Nomination of Robert J. Portman to Be Director of the Office of Management and Budget and Susan C. Schwab to Be United States Trade Representative and an Exchange With Reporters," April 18, 2006, available at the American Presidency Project, http://www.presidency.ucsb.edu/ws/index.php?pid=72417&st=decider&st1=#axzz1lLnQcTgf.
26. See Martha Minow, Michael Ryan, and Austin Sarat, eds., *Narrative, Violence, and the Law: The Essays of Robert Cover* (Ann Arbor: University of Michigan Press, 1995).
27. See Nelson and Riley, *Governing at Home*; Levin et al., *Building Coalitions*; and Kingdon, *Agendas*.
28. See David McCullough, *Truman* (New York: Simon & Schuster, 1993).
29. See Richard E. Neustadt, *Presidential Power and the Modern Presidents: The Politics of Leadership from Roosevelt to Reagan* (New York: Free Press, 1991); Nelson and Riley, *Governing at Home*; and Levin et al., *Building Coalitions*.
30. See Woodward, *The Agenda*; Nelson and Riley, *Governing at Home*; and Levin et al., *Building Coalitions*.
31. See John D. Graham, *Bush on the Home Front: Domestic Policy Triumphs and Setbacks* (Bloomington: Indiana University Press, 2010).
32. See Lou Cannon, *President Reagan: The Role of a Lifetime* (New York: Public Affairs Books, 2000); and Richard Reeves, *President Reagan: The Triumph of Imagination* (New York: Simon & Schuster, 2006).
33. See Nelson and Riley, *Governing at Home*; Levin et al., *Building Coalitions*; and Kingdon, *Agendas*.
34. See Green, *Rational Choice*; and Kingdon, *Agendas*.
35. See Nelson and Riley, *Governing at Home*; Levin et al., *Building Coalitions*; and Neustadt, *Presidential Power*.
36. See Stanley Elkins and Eric McKitrick, *The Age of Federalism: The Early American Republic, 1788–1800* (New York: Oxford University Press, 1993); and Wood, *Empire of Liberty*.

37. See Sidney M. Milkis and Michael Nelson, *The American Presidency: Origins and Development, 1776–2011*, 6th ed. (Washington, DC: CQ Press, 2011).
38. See Justin S. Vaughn and Jose D. Villalobos, "White House Staff," in Lori Cox Han, ed., *New Directions in the American Presidency* (New York: Routledge, 2011), 120–35; and Matthew J. Dickinson, "The Presidency and the Executive Branch," in Han, *New Directions*, 136–65.
39. See David Shafie, "The Presidency and Domestic Policy," in Han, *New Directions*, 166–79; Dickinson, "The Presidency and the Executive Branch"; Nelson and Riley, *Governing at Home*; Levin et al., *Building Coalitions*; and Neustadt, *Presidential Power*.
40. See Shafie, "Domestic Policy"; Nelson and Riley, *Governing at Home*; Levin et al., *Building Coalitions*; and Neustadt, *Presidential Power*.
41. See Shafie, "The Presidency and Domestic Policy"; and Nelson and Riley, *Governing at Home*.
42. See Zelizer, *The Presidency of George W. Bush*; and Draper, *Dead Certain*.
43. See Shafie, "The Presidency and Domestic Policy"; and Nelson and Riley, *Governing at Home*.
44. See Chris J. Dolan, John Frendreis, and Raymond Tatalovich, *The Presidency and Economic Policy* (New York: Rowman & Littlefield, 2007); Dickinson, "The Presidency and the Executive Branch"; Nelson and Riley, *Governing at Home*; and Levin et al., *Building Coalitions*.
45. See Dolan et al., *The Presidency and Economic Policy*; Dickinson, "The Presidency and the Executive Branch"; Shafie, "The Presidency and Domestic Policy"; and Nelson and Riley, *Governing at Home*.
46. See George P. Shultz and Kenneth W. Dam, *Economic Policy Beyond the Headlines* (Chicago: University of Chicago Press, 1998); and Dolan et al., *The Presidency and Economic Policy*.
47. See Stephen H. Axilrod, *Inside the Fed: Monetary Policy and Its Management, Martin through Greenspan to Bernanke* (Cambridge: MIT Press, 2009).
48. See Dickinson, "The Presidency and the Executive Branch"; Shafie, "The Presidency and Domestic Policy"; and Nelson and Riley, *Governing at Home*.
49. See Nancy V. Baker, *Conflicting Loyalties: Law and Politics in the Attorney Generals' Office, 1789–1990* (Lawrence: University Press of Kansas, 1992); and Woodward, *The Agenda*.
50. See Milkis and Nelson, *The American Presidency*.
51. See Nelson and Riley, *Governing at Home*; Levin et al., *Building Coalitions*; and Graham, *Bush on the Home Front*.
52. See Shultz, *Economic Policy*; Dolan et al., *The Presidency and Economic Policy*; and Axilrod, *Inside the Fed*.
53. See Graham, *Bush on the Home Front*; Zelizer, *The Presidency of George W. Bush*; and Draper, *Dead Certain*.
54. See Shafie, "The Presidency and Domestic Policy"; and Woodward, *The Agenda*.
55. See Mancur Olson, *The Logic of Collective Action: Public Goods and the Theory of Groups* (Cambridge: Harvard University Press, 1965).
56. See Joseph Pika, "White House Office of Public Liaison" *White House Transition Project Reports, No. 2009-03*; http://whitehousetransitionproject.org/resources/briefing/WHTP-2009-03-Public%20Liaison.pdf
57. Kathryn Dunn Tenpas, "Lobbying the Executive Branch" in *The Interest Group Connection: Electioneering, Lobbying, and Policymaking in Washington*, 2nd ed., eds. Paul S. Herrnson, Ronald G. Shaiko and Clyde Wilcox (Washington, DC: CQ Press, 2004), 251.

58. Barack Obama, "Remarks by the President in Welcoming Senior Staff and Cabinet Secretaries to the White House," January 21, 2009, http://www.whitehouse.gov/the_press_office/RemarksofthePresidentinWelcomingSeniorStaffandCabinetSecretariestothe-WhiteHouse/.
59. Scot Furlong, "Executive Policymaking," in The Interest Group Connection: Electioneering, Lobbying, and Policymaking in Washington, 2nd ed., ed. Paul S. Herrnson, Ronald G. Shaiko, and Clyde Wilcox (Washington, DC: CQ Press, 2004), 292.
60. See Nelson and Riley, *Governing at Home*; and Levin et al., *Building Coalitions.*
61. See Shultz, *Economic Policy*; and Dolan et al., *The Presidency and Economic Policy.*
62. See Nelson and Riley, *Governing at Home*; and Levin et al., *Building Coalitions.*
63. See Elkins, *The Age of Federalism*; and Wood, *Empire of Liberty.*
64. See Howard Gillman, *The Constitution Besieged: The Rise and Demise of Lochner Era Police Powers Jurisprudence* (Durham, NC: Duke University Press, 1993).
65. See Christopher L. Tomlins, *The State and the Unions: Labor Relations, Law, and the Organized Labor Movement in America 1880–1960* (London: Cambridge University Press, 1985); Alan Brinkley, *The End of Reform: New Deal Liberalism in Recession and War* (New York: Vintage, 1996); and William E. Leuchtenburg, *Franklin Roosevelt and the New Deal, 1932–1940* (New York: Harper, 2009).
66. See Nelson and Riley, *Governing at Home*; Levin et al., *Building Coalitions*; and Neustadt, *Presidential Power.*
67. See Nelson and Riley, *Governing at Home*; Levin et al., *Building Coalitions*; Shultz and Dam, *Economic Policy*; and Dolan et al., *The Presidency and Economic Policy.*
68. See Axilrod, *Inside the Fed*; Shultz and Dam, *Economic Policy*; and Dolan et al., *The Presidency and Economic Policy.*
69. *Congressional Quarterly Almanac*, 1964, Vol. XX (Washington, DC: Congressional Quarterly Service, 1965), 525.
70. Theodore Sorensen, recorded interview by Carl Kaysen, May 20, 1964, p. 151, Oral History Program, John F. Kennedy Presidential Library, Boston, Massachusetts.
71. Memorandum from Ted Sorensen to John F. Kennedy, 7/12/62, President's Office Files, John F. Kennedy Presidential Library, Boston, Massachusetts.
72. *Congressional Quarterly Almanac*, 1964, Vol. XX (Washington, DC: Congressional Quarterly Service, 1965), 518.
73. See Nelson and Riley, *Governing at Home*; Levin et al., *Building Coalitions*; Shultz and Dam, *Economic Policy*; Dolan et al., *The Presidency and Economic Policy*; and Neustadt, *Presidential Power.*
74. See Nelson and Riley, *Governing at Home*; Levin et al., *Building Coalitions*; Shultz and Dam, *Economic Policy*; and Dolan et al., *The Presidency and Economic Policy.*
75. See Walter LaFeber, *America, Russia, and the Cold War, 1945–2002* (Boston: McGraw-Hill, 2002); Melvyn Leffler, *A Preponderance of Power: National Security, the Truman Administration, and the Cold War* (Palo Alto: Stanford University Press, 1993); John Spanier and Steven W. Hook, *American Foreign Policy Since World War II* (Washington, DC: CQ Press, 2009); Cannon, *President Reagan*; and Reeves, *President Reagan.*
76. See Nelson and Riley, *Governing at Home*; Levin et al., *Building Coalitions*; Shultz and Dam, *Economic Policy*; Dolan et al., *The Presidency and Economic Policy*; and Neustadt, *Presidential Power.*
77. See Nelson and Riley, *Governing at Home*; and Levin et al., *Building Coalitions.*
78. See Douglas A. Irwin, *Free Trade Under Fire* (Princeton: Princeton University Press, 2009); Nelson and Riley, *Governing at Home*; Levin et al., *Building Coalitions*; Shultz and Dam, *Economic Policy*; Dolan et al., *The Presidency and Economic Policy*; Neustadt,

Presidential Power; Zelizer, *The Presidency of George W. Bush*; and Draper, *Dead Certain*.

79. See Irwin, *Free Trade*; Shultz and Dam, *Economic Policy*; and Dolan et al., *The Presidency and Economic Policy*.
80. See Dolan et al., *The Presidency and Economic Policy*.
81. See Melvyn Dubofsky, *The State and Labor in Modern America* (Chapel Hill: University of North Carolina Press, 1994); William E. Forbath, *Law and the Shaping of the American Labor Movement* (Cambridge: Harvard University Press, 1991); David Montgomery, *The Fall of the House of Labor: The Workplace, the State, and American Labor Activism, 1965–1925* (London: Cambridge University Press, 1989); and Tomlins, *The State and the Unions*.
82. See Philip Dray, *There Is Power in a Union: The Epic Story of Labor in America* (New York: Anchor, 2011); Dubofsky, *The State and Labor*; Tomlins, *The State and the Unions*; and McCullough, *Truman*.
83. Nelson and Riley, *Governing at Home*; Levin et al., *Building Coalitions*; and Dolan et al., *The Presidency and Economic Policy*.
84. See Dickinson, "The Presidency and the Executive Branch"; Shafie, "The Presidency and Domestic Policy"; Nelson and Riley, *Governing at Home*; Levin et al., *Building Coalitions*; and Dolan et al., *The Presidency and Economic Policy*.
85. See Alan Trachtenberg, *The Incorporation of America: Culture and Society in the Gilded Age* (New York: Hill & Wang, 2007).
86. See N. E. H. Hull and Peter Charles Hoffer, *Roe v. Wade: The Abortion Rights Controversy in American History* (Lawrence: University Press of Kansas, 2010); Lawrence H. Tribe, *Abortion: The Clash of Absolutes* (New York: W. W. Norton, 1992); and Levin et al., *Building Coalitions*.
87. See Christopher L. Tomlins, *Law, Labor, and Ideology in the Early American Republic* (London: Cambridge University Press, 1993); William M. Wiecek, *Liberty Under Law: The Supreme Court in American Life* (Baltimore: Johns Hopkins University Press, 1988); and Ronald Kahn, *The Supreme Court and Constitutional Theory, 1953–1993* (Lawrence: University Press of Kansas, 1995).
88. See Henry J. Abraham, *Justices, Presidents, and Senators: A History of the U.S. Supreme Court Appointments from Washington to Bush II, 5th ed.* (New York: Roman & Littlefield, 2008).
89. See Maurice Isserman and Michael Kazin, *America Divided: The Civil War of the 1960s* (New York: Oxford University Press, 2011); and Todd Gitlin, *The Sixties: Years of Hope, Days of Rage* (New York: Bantam, 1993).
90. See Richard Reeves, *President Nixon: Alone in the White House* (New York: Simon & Schuster, 2002).
91. See Dominic Sandbrook, *Mad as Hell: The Crisis of the 1970s and the Rise of the Populist Right* (New York: Anchor, 2012); and Peter N. Carroll, *It Seemed Like Nothing Happened: America in the 1970s* (Piscataway, NJ: Rutgers University Press, 1990).
92. See Sandbrook, *Mad as Hell*.
93. Patrick J. Buchanan, 1992 Republican National Convention Speech, August 17, 1992, available at http://buchanan.org/blog/1992-republican-national-convention-speech-148.
94. See James Davidson Hunter, *Culture Wars: The Struggle to Control the Family, Art, Education, Law, and Politics in America* (New York: Basic Books, 1992).
95. See Woodward, *The Agenda*.
96. See Harris, *The Survivor*; and Woodward, *The Agenda*.

97. See Zelizer, *The Presidency of George W. Bush*; and Draper, *Dead Certain.*
98. See Levin et al., *Building Coalitions.*
99. See Dickinson, "The Presidency and Executive Branch"; Shafie, "The Presidency and Domestic Policy"; Nelson and Riley, *Governing at Home*; Levin et al., *Building Coalitions*; and Dolan et al., *The Presidency and Economic Policy.*
100. See Barr, *Introduction to U.S. Health Policy.*
101. See Stephen Skowronek, *Building a New American State: The Expansion of American Administrative Capacities, 1877–1920* (New York: Cambridge University Press, 1982); Gillman, *The Constitution Besieged*; and Leuchtenburg, *Franklin D. Roosevelt.*
102. See Amity Shlaes, *The Forgotten Man: A New History of the Great Depression* (New York: Harper, 2008); and Leuchtenburg, *Franklin D. Roosevelt.*
103. See Kenneth S. Davis, *FDR: The New Deal Years, 1933–1937* (New York: Random House, 1995); Arthur M. Schlesinger, Jr., *The Coming of the New Deal, 1933–1935* (New York: Mariner Books, 2003); and Leuchtenburg, *Franklin D. Roosevelt.*
104. See Brinkley, *The End of Reform*; Davis, *FDR*; and Leuchtenburg, *Franklin D. Roosevelt.*
105. See Andrew Dobelstein, *Understanding the Social Security Act: The Foundation of Social Welfare in America for the Twenty-First Century* (New York: Oxford University Press, 2009); Daniel Beland, *Social Security: History and Politics from the New Deal to the Privatization Debate* (Lawrence: University Press of Kansas, 2007); Brinkley, *The End of Reform*; Davis, *FDR*; and Leuchtenburg, *Franklin D. Roosevelt.*
106. Lyndon B. Johnson, "Annual Message to the Congress on the State of the Union," January 8, 1964, available at the American Presidency Project, http://www.presidency.ucsb.edu/ws/index.php?pid=26787&st=war+on+poverty&st1=#axzz1lLnQcTgf.
107. See Sidney M. Milkis and Jerome M. Mileur, eds., *The Great Society and the High Tide of Liberalism* (Amherst: University of Massachusetts Press, 2005); Gareth Davies, *From Opportunity to Entitlement: The Transformation and Decline of Great Society Liberalism* (Lawrence: University Press of Kansas, 1999); and Dallek, *Lyndon B. Johnson.*
108. See Milkis and Mileur, *The Great Society*; and Dallek, *Lyndon B. Johnson.*
109. See Sandbrook, *Mad as Hell*; Carroll, *It Seemed Like Nothing Happened*; and Reeves, *President Nixon.*
110. See Reeves, *President Nixon.*
111. See Sandbrook, *Mad as Hell*; Cannon, *President Reagan*; and Reeves, *President Reagan.*
112. See Lori Cox Han, *A Presidency Upstaged: The Public Leadership of George H. W. Bush* (College Station: Texas A&M University Press, 2011).
113. See Harris, *The Survivor*; and Woodward, *The Agenda.*
114. See Woodward, *The Agenda.*
115. See Zelizer, *The Presidency of George W. Bush*; and Draper, *Dead Certain.*
116. See Tomlins, *Law, Labor, and Ideology*; Elkins, *The Age of Federalism*; and Wood, *Empire of Liberty.*
117. See Zelizer, *The Presidency of George W. Bush*; Draper, *Dead Certain*; Nelson and Riley, *Governing at Home*; and Levin et al., *Building Coalitions.*
118. Memo to Leon Panetta from Rahm Emanuel, "Crime Bill Strategy," August 12, 1994, Files of Jonathan Prince, Box 3, William J. Clinton Presidential Library, Little Rock, Arkansas.
119. See Jeffrey B. Bumgarner, *Federal Agents: The Growth of Federal Law Enforcement in America* (New York: Praeger, 2006); Barbara Stolz, *Criminal Justice Policy Making: Federal*

Roles and Processes (New York: Praeger, 2001); and Nancy E. Marion, *Federal Government and Criminal Justice* (New York: Palgrave Macmillan, 2011).

120. See Zelizer, *The Presidency of George W. Bush*; Draper, *Dead Certain*; Bumgarner, *Federal Agents*; and Marion, *Federal Government and Criminal Justice.*
121. See Nicolaus Mills, *Arguing Immigration: The Debate Over the Changing Face of America* (New York: Touchstone, 1994); Carol M. Swain, ed., *Debating Immigration* (London: Cambridge University Press, 2007); and Hugh Davis Graham, *Collision Course: The Strange Convergence of Affirmative Action and Immigration Policy in America* (New York: Oxford University Press, 2003).
122. See Milkis and Mileur, *The Great Society*; and Dallek, *Lyndon B. Johnson.*
123. See Dallek, *Lyndon B. Johnson.*
124. See Steven A. Shull, *American Civil Rights Policy from Truman to Clinton: The Role of Presidential Leadership* (Armonk, NY: M. E. Sharpe, 2000).
125. See Shull, *American Civil Rights Policy*; Harris, *The Survivor*; and Woodward, *The Agenda.*
126. See Daniel J. Fiorino, *Making Environmental Policy* (Berkeley: University of California Press, 1995); Walter A. Rosenbaum, *Environmental Politics and Policy* (Washington, DC: CQ Press, 2010); and Norman J. Vig and Michael E. Kraft, *Environmental Policy: New Directions for the Twenty-First Century* (Washington, DC: CQ Press, 2009).
127. See Rosenbaum, *Environmental Politics*; Vig and Kraft, *Environmental Policy*; Harris, *The Survivor*; and Woodward, *The Agenda.*
128. See Vig and Kraft, *Environmental Policy.*
129. Jimmy Carter, *Keeping Faith: Memoirs of a President* (New York: Bantam Books, 1982), 91.
130. Memo to Jerry Rafshoon from Greg Schneiders, "Developing Public Support for the President's Energy Program," Box 44, Office of Communication, Rafshoon, Jimmy Carter Presidential Library, Atlanta, Georgia.
131. Summary of poll data on Executive Branch Reorganization, Caddell Poll (9/77) CF30 Box 68, Office of Communication, Files of Gerry Rafshoon, Jimmy Carter Presidential Library, Atlanta Georgia.
132. Jimmy Carter, "Remarks to the White House-Governors Conference on Energy," July 9, 1977, available at the American Presidency Project, http://www.presidency.ucsb.edu/ws/index.php?pid=7781&st=energy&st1=#axzz1lLnQcTgf.
133. Memo to Senior Staff from Gerry Rafshoon, "Public Support for the President's Energy Program," Files of Gerry Rafshoon, Office of Communication, Box 44, Jimmy Carter Presidential Library, Atlanta, Georgia.
134. For a discussion on the Carter Administration's strategy in passing energy legislation, see Lori Cox Han, *Governing From Center Stage: White House Communication Strategies During the Television Age of Politics* (Cresskill, NJ: Hampton Press, 2001), 159–163.
135. See John M. Deutch, *The Crisis in Energy Policy* (Cambridge: Harvard University Press, 2011); Brenda Shaffer, *Energy Politics* (Philadelphia: University of Pennsylvania Press, 2011); and Carlos Pasqual and Jonathan Elkind, *Energy Security: Economics, Politics, Strategies, and Implications* (Washington, DC: Brookings Institution Press, 2009).
136. See Doron P. Levin, *Behind the Wheel at Chrysler: Reassessing the Iacocca Legacy* (New York: Mariner Books, 1996); and Charles K. Hyde, *Riding the Rollercoaster: A History of the Chrysler Corporation* (Detroit: Wayne State University Press, 2003).

137. See Levin, *Behind the Wheel*; Hyde, *Riding the Rollercoaster*; and Berton Ira Kaufman and Scott Kaufman, *The Presidency of James Earl Carter, Jr.* (Lawrence: University Press of Kansas, 2006).
138. See Levin, *Behind the Wheel*; and Hyde, *Riding the Rollercoaster.*
139. See Paul Ingrassia, *Crash Course: The American Auto Industry's Road to Bankruptcy and Bailout—and Beyond* (New York: Random House, 2011).
140. Ibid.
141. See Bill Vlasic, *Once Upon a Car: The Fall and Resurrection of America's Big Three Auto Makers—GM, Ford, and Chrysler* (New York: William Morrow, 2011); and Ingrassia, *Crash Course.*
142. Ibid.
143. See Zelizer, *The Presidency of George W. Bush*; Vlasic, *Once Upon a Car*; and Ingrassia, *Crash Course.*
144. See Vlasic, *Once Upon a Car*; and Ingrassia, *Crash Course.*
145. Barack Obama, "Address Before a Joint Session of Congress on the State of the Union," January 24, 2012, available at the American Presidency Project, http://www.presidency.ucsb.edu/ws/index.php?pid=99000#axzz1lLnQcTgf.
146. Memo to Jack Valenti, Douglass Cater, Bill Moyers, and Marvin Watson from Horace Busby, "Signing, Medicare Bill," July 22, 1965, White House Central Files, Aides, Horace Busby, Box 18, Lyndon Baines Johnson Presidential Library, Austin, Texas.

CHAPTER 10

1. Press Release, The Nobel Peace Prize 2009, available at http://www.nobelprize.org/nobel_prizes/peace/laureates/2009/press.html
2. Remarks by the President on a New Beginning, Cairo University, Cairo, Egypt, June 4, 2009, available at http://www.whitehouse.gov/the_press_office/Remarks-by-the-President-at-Cairo-University-6-04-09/.
3. See Alex Mintz and Karl DeRouen, Jr., *Understanding Foreign Policy Decision Making* (Cambridge: Cambridge University Press, 2010); Steve Smith, Amelia Hadfield, and Timothy Dunne, *Foreign Policy: Theories, Actors, Cases* (New York: Oxford University Press, 2008).
4. "President Lyndon B. Johnson's Address to the Nation Announcing Steps to Limit the War in Vietnam and Reporting His Decision Not to Seek Reelection," March 31, 1968, available at http://www.lbjlib.utexas.edu/johnson/archives.hom/speeches.hom/680331.asp.
5. See John Hart Ely, *War and Responsibility* (Princeton: Princeton University Press, 1995).
6. See Mintz and DeRouen, *Understanding Foreign Policy*; Smith et al., *Foreign Policy*; and Bruce W. Jentleson, *American Foreign Policy: The Dynamics of Choice in the 21*st *Century* (New York: W. W. Norton, 2010).
7. Memorandum for the President, November 10, 1950, President's Secretary's File, Subject Files, Box 187, Harry S. Truman Presidential Library, Independence, Missouri.
8. For example, see Bob Woodward, *Plan of Attack* (New York: Simon & Schuster, 2004).
9. On diplomacy and national security, see Melvyn Leffler, *A Preponderance of Power: National Security, the Truman Administration, and the Cold War* (Palo Alto: Stanford University Press, 1993); and John Spanier and Steven W. Hook, *American Foreign Policy Since World War II* (Washington, DC: CQ Press, 2009).

10. See Mintz and DeRouen, *Understanding Foreign Policy*; Smith et al., *Foreign Policy*; and Spanier and Hook, *American Foreign Policy*.
11. See Spanier and Hook, *American Foreign Policy*; Stephen E. Ambrose, *Rise to Globalism: American Foreign Policy Since 1938* (New York: Penguin Press, 2010); Walter LaFeber, *The American Age: United States Foreign Policy at Home and Abroad, 1750 to the Present* (New York: W. W. Norton, 1994); and Walter LaFeber, *America, Russia, and the Cold War, 1945–2002* (Boston: McGraw-Hill, 2002).
12. See Graham Allison and Philip Zelikow, *Essence of Decision: Explaining the Cuban Missile Crisis* (New York: Longman Press, 1999); and Smith et al., *Foreign Policy*.
13. Ibid; see also Ambrose, *Rise to Globalism*; LaFeber, *The American Age*; and LaFeber, *America, Russia, and the Cold War*.
14. See Peter W. Rodman, *Presidential Command: Power, Leadership, and the Making of Foreign Policy from Richard Nixon to George W. Bush* (New York: Alfred A. Knopf, 2009); and Colin Campbell and Bert A. Rockman, eds., *The George W. Bush Presidency: Appraisals and Prospects* (Washington, DC: CQ Press, 2003).
15. See Ambrose, *Rise to Globalism*; LaFeber, *The American Age*; LaFeber, *America, Russia, and the Cold War;* Mintz and DeRouen, *Understanding Foreign Policy*; Smith et al., *Foreign Policy*; and Spanier and Hook, *American Foreign Policy*.
16. Memo to John F. Kennedy from Chester Bowles, "Need for Improving Public Understanding of American Foreign Policy and World Affairs," January 17, 1962, President's Office File, Staff Memos, Chester Bowles, Box 62, John F. Kennedy Presidential Library, Boston, Massachusetts.
17. See Ely, *War and Responsibility*. See also David G. Adler and Larry N. George, eds., *The Constitution and the Conduct of American Foreign Policy* (Lawrence: University Press of Kansas, 1996).
18. See Spanier and Hook, *American Foreign Policy*; Ambrose, *Rise to Globalism*, LaFeber, *The American Age*; LaFeber, *America, Russia, and the Cold War;* Mintz and DeRouen, *Understanding Foreign Policy*; and Smith et al., *Foreign Policy*.
19. Summary of James Hagerty's discussion with Dwight Eisenhower regarding the December 6, 1960, meeting between President Eisenhower and President-Elect John F. Kennedy, Files of James Hagerty, Box 3, Dwight D. Eisenhower Presidential Library, Abilene, Kansas.
20. Ibid; see also Rodman, *Presidential Command*; and Campbell, *George W. Bush*.
21. Memorandum for the President, June 29, 1950, President's Secretary's File, Subject Files, Box 187, Harry S. Truman Presidential Library, Independence, Missouri.
22. See John W. Kingdon, *Agendas, Alternatives, and Public Policies* (New York: Longman Press, 2002; Ambrose, *Rise to Globalism*; LaFeber, *The American Age*; LaFeber, *America, Russia, and the Cold War;* Mintz and DeRouen, *Understanding Foreign Policy*; Smith et al., *Foreign Policy*; and Spanier and Hook, *American Foreign Policy*.
23. See Ambrose, *Rise to Globalism*; LaFeber, *The American Age*; Mintz and DeRouen, *Understanding Foreign Policy*; Smith et al., *Foreign Policy*; Spanier and Hook, *American Foreign Policy*; and Leffler, *Preponderance of Power*.
24. Ibid; see also Amos A. Jordan, William A. Taylor, Michael J. Meese, and Suzanne C. Nielsen, *American National Security*, 6th ed. (Baltimore: John Hopkins University Press, 2009).
25. Ibid; see also Rodman, *Presidential Command*; and Campbell, *George W. Bush*.
26. See Mark M. Lowenthal, *Intelligence: From Secrets to Policy* (Washington, DC: CQ Press, 2008); Ambrose, *Rise to Globalism*; LaFeber, *The American Age*; LaFeber, *America, Russia, and the Cold War;* Mintz and DeRouen, *Understanding Foreign Policy*; Smith et al.,

Foreign Policy; Spanier and Hook, *American Foreign Policy*; and Leffler, *Preponderance of Power*.

27. See Kingdon, *Agendas*; Mintz and DeRouen, *Understanding Foreign Policy*; Smith et al., *Foreign Policy*; and Spanier and Hook, *American Foreign Policy*.
28. See Ambrose, *Rise to Globalism*; LaFeber, *The American Age*; LaFeber, *America, Russia, and the Cold War;* Spanier and Hook, *American Foreign Policy*; and Leffler, *Preponderance of Power*.
29. On NATO, see Lawrence S. Kaplan, *NATO Divided, NATO United* (Greenwood, CT: Praeger Paperbacks, 2004) and Stanley R. Sloan, *NATO, the European Union, and the Atlantic Community* (New York: Roman and Littlefield, 2002).
30. Ibid. See also David P. Calleo, *Rethinking Europe's Future* (Princeton: Princeton University Press, 2003).
31. See Ambrose, *Rise to Globalism*; Calleo, *Rethinking Europe's Future*; LaFeber, *The American Age*; LaFeber, *America, Russia, and the Cold War;* and Spanier and Hook, *American Foreign Policy*.
32. Ibid.
33. See John J. Mearsheimer and Stephen M. Walt, *The Israel Lobby and U.S. Foreign Policy* (New York: Farrar, Straus and Giroux, 2007); Ambrose, *Rise to Globalism*; Calleo, *Rethinking Europe's Future*; LaFeber, *The American Age*; LaFeber, *America, Russia, and the Cold War;* and Spanier and Hook, *American Foreign Policy*.
34. See Ambrose, *Rise to Globalism*; LaFeber, *The American Age*; LaFeber, *America, Russia, and the Cold War;* Spanier and Hook, *American Foreign Policy*; Leffler, *Preponderance of Power*.
35. Ibid.
36. See Tony Payan, *The Three U.S.-Mexico Border Wars: Drugs, Immigration and Homeland Security* (New York: Praeger, 2006); Kaplan, *NATO Divided*; Ambrose, *Rise to Globalism*; LaFeber, *The American Age*; LaFeber, *America, Russia, and the Cold War;* Spanier and Hook, *American Foreign Policy*; and Leffler, *Preponderance of Power*.
37. See Ambrose, *Rise to Globalism*; Calleo, *Rethinking Europe's Future*; Kaplan, *NATO Divided*; LaFeber, *The American Age*; LaFeber, *America, Russia, and the Cold War;* and Spanier and Hook, *American Foreign Policy*.
38. See Mearsheimer and Walt, *The Israel Lobby*; Ambrose, *Rise to Globalism*; Calleo, *Rethinking Europe's Future*; LaFeber, *The American Age*; LaFeber, *America, Russia, and the Cold War;* and Spanier and Hook, *American Foreign Policy*.
39. See Ambrose, *Rise to Globalism*; Calleo, *Rethinking Europe's Future*; LaFeber, *The American Age*; LaFeber, *America, Russia, and the Cold War;* and Spanier and Hook, *American Foreign Policy*.
40. See Lars Schoultz, *Beneath the United States: A History of U.S. Policy Toward Latin America* (Cambridge: Harvard University Press, 1998); and Michael Grow, *U.S. Presidents and Latin American Interventions: Pursuing Regime Change in the Cold War* (Lawrence: University Press of Kansas, 2008).
41. See Ambrose, *Rise to Globalism*; Calleo, *Rethinking Europe's Future*; LaFeber, *The American Age*; LaFeber, *America, Russia, and the Cold War;* and Spanier and Hook, *American Foreign Policy*.
42. See Gordon S. Wood, *Empire of Liberty: A History of the Early Republic, 1789–1815* (New York: Oxford University Press, 2011); Steven E. Woodworth, *Manifest Destinies: America's Westward Expansion and the Road to the Civil War* (New York: Alfred A. Knopf, 2008); and LaFeber, *The American Age*.
43. Ibid. See also Charles Sellers, *The Market Revolution: Jacksonian America, 1815–1846* (New York: Oxford University Press, 1994).

44. See George Dangerfield, *The Awakening of American Nationalism: 1815–1828* (Long Grove, IL: Waveland Press, 1994); LaFeber, *The American Age*; and Woodworth, *Manifest Destinies.*
45. See Steve Fraser and Gary Gerstle, eds., *Ruling America: A History of Wealth and Power in a Democracy* (Cambridge: Harvard University Press, 2005); Lewis L. Gould, *The Spanish-American War and President McKinley* (Lawrence: University Press of Kansas, 1982); and LaFeber, *The American Age.*
46. See Thomas J. Knock, *To End All Wars: Woodrow Wilson and the Quest for a New World Order* (Princeton: Princeton University Press, 1995); Edmund Morris, *Theodore Rex* (New York: Random House, 2002); Fraser and Gerstle, *Ruling America*; and Gould, *The Spanish-American War.*
47. See Robert Dallek, *Franklin D. Roosevelt and America Foreign Policy, 1932–1945* (New York: Oxford University Press, 1995); and Fraser and Gerstle, *Ruling America.*
48. See Dallek, *Franklin D. Roosevelt*; Fraser and Gerstle, *Ruling America*; Ambrose, *Rise to Globalism*; and LaFeber, *The American Age.*
49. See Fraser and Gerstle, *Ruling America*; Ambrose, *Rise to Globalism*; LaFeber, *The American Age*; LaFeber, *America, Russia, and the Cold War*; and Leffler, *Preponderance of Power.*
50. See Fraser and Gerstle, *Ruling America*; Ambrose, *Rise to Globalism*; LaFeber, *America, Russia, and the Cold War*; and Leffler, *Preponderance of Power.*
51. See LaFeber, *America, Russia, and the Cold War*; and Leffler, *Preponderance of Power.*
52. See Fraser and Gerstle, *Ruling America*; Ambrose, *Rise to Globalism*; and LaFeber, *America, Russia, and the Cold War.*
53. See George C. Herring, *America's Longest War: The United States and Vietnam, 1950–1975* (New York: McGraw-Hill, 2001); and Stanley Karnow, *Vietnam: A History* (New York: Penguin, 1997).
54. See Lou Cannon, *President Reagan: The Role of a Lifetime* (New York: Public Affairs Books, 2000); Richard Reeves, *President Reagan: The Triumph of Imagination* (New York: Simon & Schuster, 2006); Fraser and Gerstle, *Ruling America*; Ambrose, *Rise to Globalism*; and LaFeber, *America, Russia, and the Cold War.*
55. See Bob Woodward, *The Commanders* (New York: Simon & Schuster, 2002); Ambrose, *Rise to Globalism*; Fraser and Gerstle, *Ruling America*; and Spanier and Hook, *American Foreign Policy.*
56. See John F. Harris, *The Survivor: Bill Clinton in the White House* (New York: Random House, 2006); Bob Woodward, *The Agenda: Inside the Clinton White House* (New York: Simon & Schuster, 2005); Ambrose, *Rise to Globalism*; Fraser and Gerstle, *Ruling America*; and Spanier and Hook, *American Foreign Policy.*
57. See Rodman, *Presidential Command*; and Campbell, *George W. Bush.*
58. See Martin S. Indyk, Kenneth G. Lieberthal, and Michael E. O'Hanlon et al, *Bending History: Barack Obama's Foreign Policy* (Washington, DC: Brookings Institution Press, 2012); and David Skidmore, *The Unilateralist Temptation in American Foreign Policy* (London: Routledge, 2010).
59. See Wood, *Empire of Liberty*; Woodworth, *Manifest Destinies*; and LaFeber, *The American Age.*
60. See James M. McPherson, *Battle Cry of Freedom: The Civil War Era* (New York: Oxford University Press, 2003); Knock, *To End All Wars*; Morris, *Theodore Rex*; Fraser and Gerstle, *Ruling America*; and Gould, *The Spanish-American War.*
61. See Ely, *War and Responsibility*; and Adler, *The Constitution.*
62. See David Halberstam, *The Coldest Winter: America and the Korean War* (New York: Hyperion Books, 2007); Ambrose, *Rise to Globalism*; and LaFeber, *America, Russia, and the Cold War.*

63. See Larry Berman, *Planning a Tragedy: The Americanization of the War in Vietnam* (New York: W. W. Norton, 1983); Herring, *America's Longest War*; Karnow, *Vietnam*; Ambrose, *Rise to Globalism*; and LaFeber, *America, Russia, and the Cold War*.
64. See Larry Berman, *No Peace, No Honor: Nixon, Kissinger, and Betrayal in Vietnam* (New York: Touchstone Books, 2002); Berman, *Planning a Tragedy*; Herring, *America's Longest War*; Ambrose, *Rise to Globalism*; and LaFeber, *America, Russia, and the Cold War*.
65. See Ely, *War and Responsibility*; and Adler, *The Constitution*.
66. See Harris, *The Survivor*; Ambrose, *Rise to Globalism*; Fraser and Gerstle, *Ruling America*; Spanier and Hook, *American Foreign Policy*; Woodward, *The Agenda*; and Woodward, *The Commanders*.
67. See Rodman, *Presidential Command*; Campbell, *George W. Bush*; Ely, *War and Responsibility*; and Adler and George, *The Constitution*.
68. Meena Bose, "The Presidency and Foreign Policy," in *New Directions in the American Presidency*, ed. Lori Cox Han (New York: Routledge, 2011), 180.
69. See Cannon, *President Reagan*; Reeves, *President Reagan*; Fraser and Gerstle, *Ruling America*; Ambrose, *Rise to Globalism*; and LaFeber, *America, Russia, and the Cold War*.
70. See Fraser and Gerstle, *Ruling America*; Ambrose, *Rise to Globalism*; and LaFeber, *America, Russia, and the Cold War*.
71. See Thomas Barfield, *Afghanistan: A Cultural and Political History* (Princeton: Princeton University Press, 2010); and Seth G. Jones, *In the Graveyard of Empires: America's War in Afghanistan* (New York: W. W. Norton, 2010).
72. See Barfield, *Afghanistan*; Jones, *In the Graveyard of Empires*; and Fraser and Gerstle, *Ruling America*.
73. See Dilip Hiro, *The Longest War; The Iran–Iraq Military Conflict* (New York: Routledge Press, 1990); and Peter Mansfield, *A History of the Middle East* (New York: Penguin Books, 2004).
74. See Cannon, *President Reagan*; Reeves, *President Reagan*; Fraser and Gerstle, *Ruling America*; Ambrose, *Rise to Globalism*; and LaFeber, *America, Russia, and the Cold War*.
75. See Hiro, *Longest War*; Mansfield, *A History of the Middle East*; Woodward, *Commanders*; and Fraser and Gerstle, *Ruling America*.
76. See Woodward, *Commanders*; and Fraser and Gerstle, *Ruling America*.
77. See Bob Woodward, *Bush at War* (New York: Simon and Schuster, 2003); Rodman, *Presidential Command*; and Campbell, *George W. Bush*.
78. See Rodman, *Presidential Command*; and Campbell, *George W. Bush*.
79. See Rodman, *Presidential Command*; Campbell, *George W. Bush*; Barfield, *Afghanistan*; Jones, *In the Graveyard of Empires*; and Fraser and Gerstle, *Ruling America*.
80. See Bob Woodward, *Obama's Wars* (New York: Simon & Schuster, 2010); Indyk, *Bending History*; and Skidmore, *Unilateralist Temptation*.
81. See Woodward, *Plan of Attack*; and Rodman, *Presidential Command*.
82. See Bob Woodward, *State of Denial: Bust at War, Part III* (New York: Simon & Schuster, 2007); and Rodman, *Presidential Command*.
83. See Bob Woodward, *The War Within: A Secret White House History 2006–2008* (New York: Simon & Schuster, 2009); Woodward, *State of Denial*; and Rodman, *Presidential Command*.
84. See Woodward, *Obama's Wars*; Indyk, *Bending History*; and Skidmore, *Unilateralist Temptation*.
85. Letter to John F. Kennedy from Lauris Norstad, November 1, 1962, Presidential Office Files, Subject File, Box 103, John F. Kennedy Presidential Library, Boston, Massachusetts.

BIBLIOGRAPHY

Aberbach, Joel D., and Mark A. Peterson, eds. *The Executive Branch*. New York: Oxford University Press, 2006.

Abraham, Henry J. *Justices, Presidents, and Senators: A History of the U.S. Supreme Court Appointments from Washington to Bush II*, 5th ed. Lanham, MD: Rowman & Littlefield, 2008.

Ackerman, Bruce. *We the People: Foundations*. Cambridge: Harvard University Press, 1991.

Adams, John. *The Works of John Adams*, Vol. 1, ed. C. F. Adams. Boston: Little Brown, 1850.

Adler, David Gray, and Larry N. George, eds. *The Constitution and the Conduct of American Foreign Policy*. Lawrence: University Press of Kansas, 1996.

Adler, David Gray, and Michael A. Genovese, eds. *The Presidency and the Law: The Clinton Legacy*. Lawrence: University Press of Kansas, 2002.

Alexander, Herbert E. *Financing Politics: Money, Elections, and Political Reform*. Washington, DC: CQ Press, 1992.

Allison, Graham, and Philip Zelikow. *Essence of Decision: Explaining the Cuban Missile Crisis*. New York: Longman Press, 1999.

Ambrose, Stephen E. *Rise to Globalism: American Foreign Policy Since 1938*. New York: Penguin Press, 2010.

Anderson, Melissa, and Brendan Doherty. "Parties Under Siege or Parties in Control? Gauging Causal Influences on Australian Ballot Reform Laws." Paper presented at the annual meeting of the American Political Science Association, Philadelphia, PA, August 27, 2003.

Andolina, Molly, and Clyde Wilcox. "Public Opinion: The Paradoxes of Clinton's Popularity," in *The Clinton Scandal and the Future of American Government*, eds. Mark Rozell and Clyde Wilcox, 171–194. Washington, DC: Georgetown University Press, 2000.

Ansolabehere, Stephen, and Shanto Iyengar. *Going Negative: How Political Advertisements Shrink and Polarize the Electorate*. New York: Free Press, 1997.

Archer, Gleason L. *History of Radio to 1926*. New York: Arno Press/New York Times, 1971.

Ashcraft, Richard. *Revolutionary Politics and Locke's Two Treatises of Government*. Princeton, NJ: Princeton University Press, 1986.

Axilrod, Stephen H. *Inside the Fed: Monetary Policy and Its Management, Martin through Greenspan to Bernanke*. Cambridge, MA: MIT Press, 2009.

Bailyn, Bernard. *The Ideological Origins of the American Revolution*. Cambridge, MA: Harvard University Press, 1967.

_____. *The Ordeal of Thomas Hutchinson*. Cambridge, MA: Harvard University Press, 1976.

Baker, Nancy V. *Conflicting Loyalties: Law and Politics in the Attorney Generals' Office, 1789–1990*. Lawrence: University Press of Kansas, 1992.

Banning, Lance. *The Jeffersonian Persuasion: Evolution of a Party Ideology*. Ithaca, NY: Cornell University Press, 1978.

Barber, James David. *The Presidential Character: Predicting Performance in the White House*, rev. 4th ed. New York: Prentice Hall, 2008.

Barfield, Thomas. *Afghanistan: A Cultural and Political History*. Princeton, NJ: Princeton University Press, 2010.

Barr, Donald A. *Introduction to U.S. Health Policy: The Organization, Financing, and Delivery of Health Care in America*. Baltimore: Johns Hopkins University Press, 2011.

Barrett, Andrew. "Gone Public: The Impact of Going Public on Presidential Legislative Success." *American Politics Research*, 32.3 (May 2004): 338–370.

Bartels, Larry M. *Presidential Primaries and the Dynamics of Public Choice*. Princeton, NJ: Princeton University Press, 1988.

Baum, Lawrence. *The Supreme Court*, 9th ed. Washington, DC: CQ Press, 2007.

Baum, Mathew A., and Samuel Kernell. "Has Cable Ended the Golden Age of Presidential Television?" *American Political Science Review* 93 (March, 1999): 99–114.

Beer, Samuel H. *To Make a Nation: The Rediscovery of American Federalism*. Cambridge, MA: Belknap Press, 1993.

Beland, Daniel. *Social Security: History and Politics from the New Deal to the Privatization Debate*. Lawrence: University Press of Kansas, 2007.

Bennett, W. Lance. *News: The Politics of Illusion*, 8th ed. New York: Pearson, 2009.

Berger, Raoul. *Executive Privilege*. Cambridge, MA: Harvard University Press, 1974.

_____. *Impeachment: The Constitutional Problems*. Cambridge, MA: Harvard University Press, 1973.

Berman, Larry. *Planning a Tragedy: The Americanization of the War in Vietnam*. New York: W. W. Norton, 1983.

_____. *The New American Presidency*. Boston: Little, Brown and Company, 1987.

_____. *No Peace, No Honor: Nixon, Kissinger, and Betrayal in Vietnam*. New York: Touchstone Books, 2002.

Bessette, Joseph, and Jeffrey Tulis. *The Presidency in the Constitutional Order*. Baton Rouge: Louisiana University Press, 1981.

Bickel, Alexander. *The Least Dangerous Branch: The Supreme Court at the Bar of Politics*. New Haven, CT: Yale University Press, 1962.

Bodin, Jean. *The Six Bookes of a Commonweale*, Trans. R. Knolles. Cambridge, MA: Harvard University Press, 1962.

Bond, Jon, and Richard Fleisher. *The President in the Legislative Arena*. Chicago: University of Chicago Press, 1990.

Borrelli, MaryAnne. *The Politics of the President's Wife*. College Station: Texas A&M University Press, 2011.

Borrelli, Stephen A., and Grace L. Simmons. "Congressional Responsiveness to Presidential Popularity: The Electoral Context." *Political Behavior*, Vol. 15, No. 2 (June 1993): 93–112.

Bose, Meena. "The Presidency and Foreign Policy," in *New Directions in the American Presidency*, ed. Lori Cox Han, 180–197. New York: Routledge, 2011.

Boumediene v. Bush, 553 U.S. 723 (2008).

Brace, Paul, and Barbara Hinckley. *Follow the Leader: Opinion Polls and the Modern Presidents*. New York: Basic Books, 1992.

Brams, Stephen S., and Michael Davis. "The 3/2's Rule in Presidential Campaigning," *American Political Science Review* (1974): 113–134.

Brinkley, Alan. *The End of Reform: New Deal Liberalism in Recession and War*. New York: Vintage, 1996.

Brody, Richard A. *Assessing the President: The Media, Elite Opinion, and Public Support*. Stanford: Stanford University Press, 1991.

Brown v. Board of Education, 347 U.S. 483 (1954).

Bryce, James. *The American Commonwealth*. London: MacMillan, 1891.

Buckley v. Valeo, 424 U.S. 1 (1976).

Bugh, Gary, ed. *Electoral College Reform: Challenges and Possibilities*. Burlington, VT: Ashgate Publishing, 2010.

Bumgarner, Jeffrey B. *Federal Agents: The Growth of Federal Law Enforcement in America*. New York: Praeger, 2006.

Burke, John P. *The Institutional Presidency*. Baltimore: Johns Hopkins University Press, 1992.

_____. *The Institutional Presidency: Organizing and Managing the White House from FDR to Clinton*. Baltimore: Johns Hopkins University Press, 2000.

_____. "The Institutional Presidency," in *The Presidency and the Political System*, 9th ed., ed. Michael Nelson, 383–409. Washington, DC: CQ Press, 2009.

_____. "The Obama Presidential Transition: An Early Assessment." *Presidential Studies Quarterly*, 39.3 (2009): 574–604.

Burns, James MacGregor. *Leadership*. New York: Harper & Row, 1978.

_____. *Roosevelt: The Lion and the Fox*. New York: Harcourt, Brace and Company, 1956.

_____. *Transforming Leadership*. New York: Atlantic Monthly Press, 2003.

Bush v. Gore, 531 U.S. 98 (2000).

Calleo, David P. *Rethinking Europe's Future*. Princeton: Princeton University Press, 2003.

Cameron, Charles, John Lipinski, and Charles Riemann. "Research Notes: Testing Formal Theories of Political Rhetoric." *Journal of Politics* 62.1 (2000): 187–205.

Campbell, Colin, and Bert A. Rockman, eds. *The Bush Presidency: First Appraisals*. Chatham, NJ: Chatham House, 1991.

_____, eds. *The George W. Bush Presidency: Appraisals and Prospects*. Washington, DC: CQ Press, 2003.

Campbell, James E. *The American Campaign: U.S. Presidential Campaigns and the National Vote*, 2nd ed. College Station: Texas A&M University Press, 2008.

Campbell, Joseph W. *Getting It Wrong: Ten of the Greatest Misreported Stories in American Journalism*. Berkeley: University of California Press, 2010.

Campbell, Karlyn Kohrs, and Kathleen Hall Jamieson. *Deeds Done in Words: Presidential Rhetoric and the Genres of Governance*. Chicago: University of Chicago Press, 1990.

Canes-Wrone, Brandice. *Who Leads Whom? Presidents, Policy, and the Public*. Chicago: University of Chicago Press, *2006*.

Cannon, Lou. *President Reagan: The Role of a Lifetime*. New York: Public Affairs Books, 2000.

Cantril, Hadley. *Human Dimension Experiences in Policy Research*. Newark: Rutgers University Press, 1967.

Cappella, Joseph N., and Kathleen Hall Jamieson. "Broadcast Ad-Watch Effects: A Field Experiment." *Communication Research* 21 (1994): 341–365.

Carey, George W. *The Federalist: Design for a Constitutional Republic*. Urbana: University of Illinois Press, 1989.

Carroll, Peter N. *It Seemed Like Nothing Happened: America in the 1970s*. Piscataway, NJ: Rutgers University Press, 1990.

Carter, Jimmy. *Keeping Faith: Memoirs of a President*. New York: Bantam Books, 1982.

Clarke, Harold, Marianne Stewart, Mike Ault, and Euel Elliott. "Men, Women and the Dynamics of Presidential Approval." *British Journal of Political Science* 35 (2005): 31–51.

Clinton v. Jones, 520 U.S. 681 (1997).

Clinton v. City of New York, 524 U.S. 417 (1998).

Clinton, Bill. *My Life*. New York: Alfred A. Knopf, 2004.

Cohen, David B., Charles E. Walcott, Shirley Anne Warshaw, and Stephen J. Wayne. "The Chief of Staff." *The White House Transition Project*, Report 2009–21. WhiteHouseTransitionProject.org, 2008.

Cohen, Jeffrey E. *The Presidency in the Era of 24-Hour News*. Princeton, NJ: Princeton University Press, 2008.

_____. *Going Local: Presidential Leadership in the Post-Broadcast Age*. New York: Cambridge University Press, 2010.

_____. *Presidential Responsiveness and Public Policy-Making: The Public and the Policies that Presidents Choose*. Ann Arbor, MI: University of Michigan Press, 1997.

_____. "Presidential Rhetoric and the Public Agenda." *American Journal of Political Science*, 39 (1995): 87–107.

Cohen, Jeffrey, and David Nice. *The Presidency*. New York: McGraw-Hill, 2003.

Cohen, Marty, David Karol, Hans Noel, and John Zaller. "The Invisible Primary in Presidential Nominations, 1980–2004," in *The Making of the Presidential Candidates 2008*, ed. William Mayer, 1–38. Lanham, MD: Rowman & Littlefield, 2008.

Cohen, Richard E. *Washington at Work: Back Rooms and Clean Air*. New York: Macmillan, 1992.

Conley, Richard. "George Bush and the 102d Congress: The Impact of Public and Private Veto Threats on Policy Outcomes." *Presidential Studies Quarterly*, 33.4 (2003): 730–750.

Cornwell, Elmer E. Jr. *Presidential Leadership of Public Opinion*. Bloomington: Indiana University Press, 1965.

Corwin, Edward S. *The President: Office and Powers*. New York: New York University Press, 1940.

_____. *The President: Office and Powers*, 5th ed. New York: New York University Press, 1984.

Cox, Patrick. "Not Worth a Bucket of Warm Spit." *The History News Network*, August 20, 2008. http://hnn.us/articles/53402.html.

Cronin, Thomas E., and Michael A. Genovese. *The Paradoxes of the American Presidency*, 2nd ed. New York: Oxford University Press, 2004.

_____. *The Paradoxes of the American Presidency*. New York: Oxford University Press, 1998.

Dahl, Robert. "Decision-Making in a Democracy: The Supreme Court as a National Policy-Maker." *Journal of Public Law*, 6 (1957): 279–295.

Dallek, Robert. *Franklin D. Roosevelt and American Foreign Policy, 1932–1945*. New York: Oxford University Press, 1995.

_____. *Lyndon B. Johnson: Portrait of a President*. New York: Oxford University Press, 2005.

Dangerfield, George. *The Awakening of American Nationalism: 1815–1828*. Long Grove, IL: Waveland Press, 1994.

Davidson, Roger H., Walter J. Oleszek, and Frances Lee. *Congress and Its Members*, 13th ed. Washington, DC: CQ Press, 2012.

Davies, Gareth. *From Opportunity to Entitlement: The Transformation and Decline of Great Society Liberalism*. Lawrence: University Press of Kansas, 1999.

Davis, Kenneth S. *FDR: The New Deal Years, 1933–1937*. New York: Random House, 1995.

Davis, Richard. *The Web of Politics: The Internet's Impact on the American Political System*. New York: Oxford University Press, 1999.

Deutch, John M. *The Crisis in Energy Policy*. Cambridge: Harvard University Press, 2011.

Dickinson, Matthew J. *Bitter Harvest: FDR, Presidential Power and the Growth of the Presidential Branch*. Cambridge: Cambridge University Press, 1996.

_____. "The Presidency and the Executive Branch," in *New Directions in the American Presidency*, ed. Lori Cox Han, 136–165. New York: Routledge, 2011.

Diggins, John Patrick. "Comrades and Citizens: New Mythologies in American Historiography." *American Historical Review* 90 (1985): 614–638.

_____. *The Lost Soul of American Politics: Virtue, Self-Interest, and the Foundations of Liberalism*. Chicago: University of Chicago Press, 1984.

Dobelstein, Andrew. *Understanding the Social Security Act: The Foundation of Social Welfare in America for the Twenty-First Century*. New York: Oxford University Press, 2009.

Dolan, Chris J., John Frendreis, and Raymond Tatalovich. *The Presidency and Economic Policy*. Lanham, MD: Rowman & Littlefield, 2007.

Draper, Robert. *Dead Certain: The Presidency of George W. Bush*. New York: Free Press, 2008.

Dray, Philip. *There Is Power in a Union: The Epic Story of Labor in America*. New York: Anchor, 2011.

Dred Scott v. Sandford, 19 Howard 393 (1857).

Dubofsky, Melvyn. *The State and Labor in Modern America*. Chapel Hill: University of North Carolina Press, 1994.

Dworetz, Steven M. *The Unvarnished Doctrine: Locke, Liberalism, and the American Revolution*. Durham, NC: Duke University Press, 1990.

Dworkin, Ronald. *Law's Empire*. Cambridge: Harvard University Press, 1986.

Dwyre, Diana, and Victoria A. Farrar-Myers. *Legislative Labyrinth: Congress and Campaign Finance Reform*. Washington, DC: CQ Press, 2001.

Edwards, George C., III. "Aligning Tests with Theory: Presidential Influence as a Source of Influence in Congress." *Congress and the Presidency*, 24 (1997): 113–130.

_____. *At the Margins: Presidential Leadership of Congress*. New Haven: Yale University Press, 1989.

_____. "George Bush and the Public Presidency: The Politics of Inclusion," in *The Bush Presidency: First Appraisals*, eds. Colin Campbell and Bert A. Rockman, 129–154. Chatham, NJ: Chatham House Publishers, 1991.

_____. *On Deaf Ears: The Limits of the Bully Pulpit*. New Haven: Yale University Press, 2003.

_____. *Why the Electoral College Is Bad for America*, 2nd ed. New Haven: Yale University Press, 2011.

Edwards, George C., III, John H. Kessel, and Bert A. Rockman, eds. *Researching the Presidency: Vital Questions, New Approaches*. Pittsburgh: University of Pittsburgh Press, 1993.

Edwards, George C., III, and Stephen J. Wayne, eds. *Studying the Presidency*. Knoxville: University of Tennessee Press, 1983.

Eisenhower, Dwight D. *The White House Years: Mandate for Change 1953–1956*. Garden City, NY: Doubleday, 1963.

Eisinger, Robert. *The Evolution of Presidential Polling*. New York: Cambridge University Press, 2003.

Elkins, Stanley, and Eric McKitrick. *The Age of Federalism: The Early American Republic, 1788–1800*. Oxford: Oxford University Press, 1993.

Ely, John Hart. *War and Responsibility*. Princeton: Princeton University Press, 1995.

Emery, Michael, and Edwin Emery. *The Press and America: An Interpretive History of the Mass Media*, 8th ed. Boston: Allyn and Bacon, 1996.

Epstein, Lee, and Thomas G. Walker. *Constitutional Law for a Changing America: Institutional Powers and Constraints*, 7th ed. Washington, DC: CQ Press, 2010

Ericson, David F. *The Shaping of American Liberalism: The Debates Over Ratification, Nullification, and Slavery*. Chicago: University of Chicago Press, 1993.

Erikson, Robert S. "Economic Conditions and the Presidential Vote." *American Political Science Review*, Vol. 83, No. 2 (June 1989): 567–573.

Erikson, Robert, and Kent Tedin. *American Public Opinion: Its Origins, Content and Impact*. New York: Pearson/Longman, 2009.

Eshbaugh-Soha, Matthew. *The President's Speeches: Beyond "Going Public."* Boulder, CO: Lynne Rienner Publishers, 2006.

_____. "The Public Presidency: Communications and Media," in *New Directions in the American Presidency*, ed. Lori Cox Han, 54–70. New York: Routledge, 2011.

Farnsworth, Stephen J. *Spinner in Chief: How Presidents Sell Their Policies and Themselves*. Boulder, CO: Paradigm Publishers, 2009.

Farnsworth, Stephen J., and S. Robert Lichter. *The Mediated Presidency: Television News and Presidential Governance*. Lanham, MD: Rowman & Littlefield, 2006.

_____. "Network News Coverage of New Presidents, 1981–2009." Paper presented at the annual meeting of the American Political Science Association, September 2010, Washington, DC.

_____. *The Nightly News Nightmare: Network Television Coverage of U.S. Presidential Elections 1988–2004*. Lanham, MD: Rowman & Littlefield, 2007.

Feldmann, Linda. "Before Any Votes, a 'Money Primary.'" *Christian Science Monitor*, February 26, 2007.

Fenno, Richard. "U.S. House Members in Their Constituencies: An Exploration." *American Political Science Review*, 71 (1977): 883–917.

Filmer, Sir Robert. *Filmer: Patriarcha and Other Writings*, ed. Johann P. Sommerville. Cambridge: Cambridge University Press, 1991.

Fiorino, Daniel J. *Making Environmental Policy*. Berkeley: University of California Press, 1995.

Fishel, Jeff. *Presidents and Promises: From Campaign Pledge to Presidential Performance*. Washington, DC: CQ Press, 1985.

Fisher, Louis. *Constitutional Conflicts between Congress and the President*. Lawrence: University Press of Kansas, 2007.

_____. "The Legislative Veto: Invalidated, It Survives." *Law and Contemporary Problems*. Vol. 56, No. 4 (Autumn 1993): 273–292.

_____. *The Politics of Executive Privilege*. Durham, NC: Carolina Academic Press, 2004.

_____. *The Politics of Shared Power: Congress and the Executive*, 4th ed. College Station: Texas A&M University Press, 1998.

_____. 2004. *Presidential War Power*, 2nd ed. Lawrence: University Press of Kansas.

Foner, Eric. *Reconstruction: America's Unfinished Revolution, 1863–1877*. New York: Harper & Row, 1988.

Forbath, William E. *Law and the Shaping of the American Labor Movement*. Cambridge, MA: Harvard University Press, 1991.

Ford, Paul Leicester, ed. *The Writings of Thomas Jefferson*. New York: G. P. Putnam's, 1895.

Fox, Richard L. "The Future of Women's Political Leadership: Gender and the Decision to Run for Elective Office," in *Women and Leadership: The State of Play and Strategies for Change*, eds. Barbara Kellerman and Deborah L. Rhode, 251–270. New York: Wiley, 2007.

Fox, Richard L., and Jennifer L. Lawless. "Entering the Arena? Gender and the Decision to Run for Office." *American Journal of Political Science* 48, no. 2 (2004): 264–280.

Fraser, Steve, and Gary Gerstle, eds. *Ruling America: A History of Wealth and Power in a Democracy*. Cambridge: Harvard University Press, 2005.

Friedman, Lawrence M. *Crime and Punishment in American History*. New York: Basic Books, 1993.

_____. *A History of American Law*. New York: Simon and Schuster, 1985.

Frisch, Morton J., ed. *Selected Writings and Speeches of Alexander Hamilton*. Washington, DC: American Enterprise Institute, 1985.

Furlong, Scott. "Executive Policymaking," in *The Interest Group Connection: Electioneering, Lobbying, and Policymaking in Washington*, 2nd ed., eds. Paul S. Herrnson, Ronald G. Shaiko and Clyde Wilcox, 282–297. Washington, DC: CQ Press, 2004.

Geer, John. *In Defense of Negativity: Attacks Ads in Presidential Campaigns*, Chicago: University of Chicago Press, 2006.

Gelderman, Carol. *All the President's Words: The Bully Pulpit and the Creation of the Virtual Presidency*. New York: Walker & Company, 1997.

Genovese, Michael A., and Lori Cox Han, eds. *The Presidency and the Challenge of Democracy*. New York: Palgrave Macmillan, 2006.

Gillman, Howard. *The Constitution Besieged: The Rise and Demise of Lochner Era Police Powers Jurisprudence*. Durham, NC: Duke University Press, 1993.

Gitlin, Todd. *The Sixties: Years of Hope, Days of Rage*. New York: Bantam, 1993.

Goldman, Sheldon. *Picking Federal Judges: Lower Court Selection from Roosevelt through Reagan*. New Haven, CT: Yale University Press, 1997.

Goldwater v. Carter, 444 U.S. 996 (1979).

Gould, Lewis L. *The Spanish-American War and President McKinley*. Lawrence: University Press of Kansas, 1982.

Graber, Doris A. *Mass Media and American Politics*, 8th ed. Washington, DC: CQ Press, 2010.

Graham, Hugh Davis. *Collision Course: The Strange Convergence of Affirmative Action and Immigration Policy in America*. New York: Oxford University Press, 2003.

Graham, John D. *Bush on the Home Front: Domestic Policy Triumphs and Setbacks*. Bloomington: Indiana University Press, 2010.

Green, Donald Philip, and Bradley Palmquist. "How Stable Is Party Identification?" *Political Behavior*, 16.4 (1994): 437–466.

Green, Donald, and Ian Shapiro. *Pathologies of Rational Choice: A Critique of Applications in Political Science*. New Haven: Yale University Press, 1996.

Greene, Jack P. *Negotiated Authorities: Essays in Colonial Political and Constitutional History*. Charlottesville: University Press of Virginia, 1994.

Greenstein, Fred I. *The Hidden-Hand Presidency: Eisenhower as Leader*. Baltimore: Johns Hopkins University Press, 1994.

_____. *The Presidential Difference: Leadership Style from FDR to Barack Obama*, 3rd ed. Princeton: Princeton University Press, 2009.

Greenstone, David J. *The Lincoln Persuasion: Remaking American Liberalism*. Princeton: Princeton University Press, 1993.

Gronke, Paul, and Brian Newman. "From FDR to Clinton, from Mueller to ?? A Field Essay on Presidential Approval." *Political Research Quarterly*, 56 (4): 501–512.

Grossman, Michael Baruch, and Martha Joynt Kumar. *Portraying the President: The White House and the News Media*. Baltimore: Johns Hopkins University Press, 1981.

Grow, Michael. *U.S. Presidents and Latin American Interventions: Pursuing Regime Change in the Cold War*. Lawrence: University Press of Kansas, 2008.

Gustafson, Thomas. *Representative Words: Politics, Literature, and the American Language, 1776–1865*. Cambridge, England: Cambridge University Press, 1992.

Hadley, Arthur T. *The Invisible Primary*. Englewood Cliffs, NJ: Prentice-Hall, 1976.

Haggard, Robert F., and Mark A. Mastromarino, eds., *The Papers of George Washington, Presidential Series*, ed. Philander Chase, *Vol. 10: March–August 1792*. Charlottesville, VA: University Press of Virginia, 2002.

Halberstam, David. *The Coldest Winter: America and the Korean War*. New York: Hyperion Books, 2007.

Haldeman, H. R. *The Haldeman Diaries: Inside the Nixon White House*. Berkeley: Berkeley Publishing, 1994.

Hall, Kermit L. *The Magic Mirror: Law in American History*. Oxford: Oxford University Press, 1989.

Hamdan v. Rumsfeld, 548 U.S. 557 (2006).

Hamdi v. Rumsfeld, 542 U.S. 507 (2004).

Han, Lori Cox. *Governing from Center Stage: White House Communication Strategies during the Television Age of Politics*. Cresskill, NJ: Hampton Press, 2001.

_____. "New Strategies for an Old Medium: The Weekly Radio Addresses of Reagan and Clinton," *Congress and the Presidency*, vol. 33, no. 1, (Spring 2006): 25–45.

_____. "Off to the (Horse) Races: Media Coverage of the 'Not-So-Invisible' Invisible Primary of 2007," in *From Votes to Victory: Winning and Governing the White House in the Twenty-First Century*, ed. Meena Bose, 91–116. College Station: Texas A&M University Press, 2011.

_____. *A Presidency Upstaged: The Public Leadership of George H. W. Bush*. College Station: Texas A&M University Press, 2011.

_____. "The President Over the Public: The Plebiscitary Presidency at Center Stage," in *The Presidency and the Challenge of Democracy*, eds. Michael A. Genovese and Lori Cox Han, 119–37. New York: Palgrave Macmillan, 2006.

_____. "Public Leadership in the Political Arena," in *Leadership and Politics, Vol. 2 of Leadership at the Crossroads*, eds. Michael A. Genovese and Lori Cox Han, 201–25. Westport, CT: Praeger Publishers, 2008.

_____. "Still Waiting for Madam President: Hillary Rodham Clinton's 2008 Presidential Campaign." *Critical Issues of Our Time*, The Centre for American Studies at The University of Western Ontario, London, Ontario, Volume 2, Fall 2009.

_____. *Women and American Politics: The Challenges of Political Leadership*. Boston: McGraw Hill, 2007.

_____. *Women and US Politics: The Spectrum of Political Leadership*, 2nd ed. Boulder, CO: Lynne Rienner Publishers, 2010.

Han, Lori Cox, and Diane J. Heith, eds. *In the Public Domain: Presidents and the Challenges of Public Leadership*. Albany: SUNY Press, 2005.

Han, Lori Cox, and Caroline Heldman, eds. *Rethinking Madam President: Are We Ready for a Woman in the White House?* Boulder, CO: Lynne Rienner Publishers, 2007.

Hanson, Christopher. "The Invisible Primary: Now Is the Time for All-Out Coverage." *Columbia Journalism Review*, March/April, 2003.

Harris, John F. *The Survivor: Bill Clinton in the White House*. New York: Random House, 2006.

Hart, Roderick P. *The Sound of Leadership: Presidential Communication in the Modern Age*. Chicago: University of Chicago Press, 1987.

Heclo, Hugh. "Campaigning and Governing: A Conspectus," in *The Permanent Campaign and Its Future*, eds. Norman Ornstein and Thomas Mann, 1–37. Washington, DC: Brookings Institution Press, 2000.

______. *Studying the Presidency: A Report to the Ford Foundation*. New York: Ford Foundation Press, 1977.

Heith, Diane J. *Polling to Govern: Public Opinion and Presidential Leadership*. Stanford, CA: Stanford University Press, 2003.

______. *The Presidential Road Show: Public Leadership in an Era of Party Polarization and Media Fragmentation*. Boulder, CO: Paradigm Press, 2013.

______. "The White House Public Opinion Apparatus Meets the Anti-Polling President," in *In the Public Domain: Presidents and the Challenges of Public Leadership*, ed. Lori Cox Han and Diane Heith, 75–87. Albany: State University of New York, 2005.

Herring, George C. *America's Longest War: The United States and Vietnam, 1950–1975*. New York: McGraw-Hill, 2001.

Herrnson, Paul S., Ronald G. Shaiko, and Clyde Wilcox, eds. *The Interest Group Connection: Electioneering, Lobbying, and Policymaking in Washington*, 2nd ed. Washington, DC: CQ Press, 2004.

Hertsgaard, Mark. *On Bended Knee: The Press and the Reagan Presidency*. New York: Farrar Straus Giroux, 1988.

Hetherington, Marc, and Bruce Larson. *Parties, Politics and Public Policy in America*, 11th ed. Washington, DC: CQ Press, 2010.

Hevron, Parker. "The LBJ Legacy That Wasn't: The Failed Confirmation of Abe Fortas." Paper presented at the annual meeting of the Western Political Science Association, March, 2005, Oakland, California.

Hill, Christopher. *The Century of Revolution, 1603–1714*. New York: W. W. Norton, 1961.

Hiro, Dilip. *The Longest War; The Iran–Iraq Military Conflict*. New York: Routledge Press, 1990.

Hirst, Derek. *Authority and Conflict: England, 1603–1658*. Cambridge: Harvard University Press, 1986.

Hoffman, Donna, and Alison Howard. *Addressing the State of the Union: The Evolution and Impact of the President's Big Speech*. Boulder, CO: Lynne Rienner, 2006.

Hofstadter, Richard. *The Idea of a Party System: The Rise of Legitimate Opposition in the United States, 1780–1840*. Berkeley: University of California Press, 1970.

Hoover, Herbert. *The Memoirs of Herbert Hoover: The Cabinet and the Presidency 1920–1933*. New York: Macmillan, 1952.

Horwitz, Morton J. *The Transformation of American Law, 1780–1860*. Cambridge, MA: Harvard University Press, 1977.

______. *The Transformation of American Law, 1870–1960: The Crisis of Legal Orthodoxy*. Oxford: Oxford University Press, 1992.

House Committee on Government Reform. *Justice Undone: Clemency Decisions in the Clinton White House*. Washington, DC: U.S. Congress, 3/14/02.

Hull, N. E. H., and Peter Charles Hoffer. *Roe v. Wade: The Abortion Rights Controversy in American History*. Lawrence: University Press of Kansas, 2010.

Hunter, James Davidson. *Culture Wars: The Struggle to Control the Family, Art, Education, Law, and Politics in America*. New York: Basic Books, 1992.

Hyde, Charles K. *Riding the Rollercoaster: A History of the Chrysler Corporation*. Detroit: Wayne State University Press, 2003.

Immigration and Naturalization Service v. Chadha, 462 U.S. 919 (1983).

Indyk, Martin S., Kenneth G. Lieberthal, and Michael E. O'Hanlon. *Bending History: Barack Obama's Foreign Policy*. Washington, DC: Brookings Institution Press, 2012.

Ingrassia, Paul. *Crash Course: The American Auto Industry's Road to Bankruptcy and Bail-out—and Beyond*. New York: Random House, 2011.

Irwin, Douglas A. *Free Trade Under Fire*. Princeton: Princeton University Press, 2009.

Isserman, Maurice, and Michael Kazin. *America Divided: The Civil War of the 1960s*. New York: Oxford University Press, 2011.

Jacobs, Lawrence, and Robert Shapiro. *Politicians Don't Pander: Political Manipulation and the Loss of Democratic Responsiveness*. Chicago: University of Chicago Press, 2000.

_____. "The Rise of Presidential Polling: The Nixon White House in Historical Perspective." *Public Opinion Quarterly* 59 (Summer 1995): 163–195.

Jamieson, Kathleen Hall, ed. *Electing the President 2008: The Insider's View*. Philadelphia: University of Pennsylvania Press, 2009.

Jensen, Merrill. *The New Nation: A History of the United States during the Confederation, 1781–1789*. New York: Alfred A. Knopf, 1950.

Jentleson, Bruce W. *American Foreign Policy: The Dynamics of Choice in the 21st Century*. New York: W. W. Norton, 2010.

Jones, Charles O. *Separate But Equal Branches: Congress and the Presidency*, 2nd ed. New York: Seven Bridges Press, 2000.

Jones, Seth G. *In the Graveyard of Empires: America's War in Afghanistan*. New York: W. W. Norton, 2010.

Jordan, Amos A., William A. Taylor, Jr., Michael J. Meese, and Suzanne C. Nielsen. *American National Security*, 6th ed. Baltimore: John Hopkins University Press, 2009.

Kahn, Ronald. *The Supreme Court and Constitutional Theory, 1953–1993*. Lawrence: University Press of Kansas, 1995.

Kaplan, Lawrence S. *Entangling Alliances with None: American Foreign Policy in the Age of Jefferson*. Kent, OH: Kent State University Press, 1987.

_____. *NATO Divided, NATO United*. Greenwood, CT: Praeger Paperbacks, 2004.

Karnow, Stanley. *Vietnam: A History*. New York: Penguin, 1997.

Kaufman, Berton Ira, and Scott Kaufman. *The Presidency of James Earl Carter, Jr.* Lawrence: University Press of Kansas, 2006.

Kenski, Henry C. "A Man for All Seasons? The Guardian President and His Public," in *Leadership and the Bush Presidency: Prudence or Drift in an Era of Change?* eds. Ryan J. Barilleaux and Mary E. Stuckey, 91–114. Westport: Praeger, 1992.

Kerbel, Matthew Robert. *Remote and Controlled: Media Politics in a Cynical Age*. 2nd ed. Boulder, CO: Westview Press, 1999.

Kernell, Samuel. *Going Public: New Strategies of Presidential Leadership*. Washington, DC: CQ Press, 1986.

_____. *Going Public: New Strategies of Presidential Leadership*, 3rd ed. (Washington, DC: CQ Press, 1997.

_____. *Going Public: New Strategies of Presidential Leadership*, 4th ed. Washington, DC: CQ Press, 2007.

Kernell, Samuel, and Gary Jacobson. *The Logic of American Politics*. Washington DC: CQ Press, 2010.

Kessel, John. *Presidential Campaign Politics: Coalitions Strategies and Citizen Response.* Chicago: Dorsey Press 1980.

_____. *Presidents, the Presidency, and the Political Environment.* Washington, DC: CQ Press, 2001.

Key, V. O. *The Responsible Electorate: Rationality in Presidential Voting, 1936–1960.* New York: Belknap Press, 1966.

Kingdon, John W. *Agendas, Alternatives, and Public Policies.* New York: Longman Press, 2002.

Knock, Thomas J. *To End All Wars: Woodrow Wilson and the Quest for a New World Order.* Princeton: Princeton University Press, 1995.

Koenig, Louis W. *The Chief Executive*, 6th ed. New York: Harcourt Brace, 1996.

Korematsu v. United States, 323 U.S. 214 (1944).

Kramnick, Isaac. *Republicanism and Bourgeois Radicalism: Political Ideology in Late Eighteenth-Century England and America.* Ithaca: Cornell University Press, 1990.

Kumar, Martha Joynt. *Managing the President's Message: The White House Communications Operation.* Baltimore: The Johns Hopkins University Press, 2007.

Kumar, Martha Joynt, and Terry Sullivan, eds. *The White House World: Transitions, Organization, and Office Operations.* College Station: Texas A&M University Press, 2003.

Kutler, Stanley I., ed. *Abuse of Power: The New Nixon Tapes.* New York: Simon & Schuster, 1997.

_____. *The Wars of Watergate: The Last Crisis of Richard Nixon.* New York: Alfred A. Knopf, 1990.

LaFeber, Walter. *America, Russia, and the Cold War, 1945–2002.* Boston: McGraw-Hill, 2002.

_____. *The American Age: United States Foreign Policy at Home and Abroad, 1750 to the Present.* New York: W. W. Norton, 1994.

Lammers, William W., and Michael A. Genovese. *The Presidency and Domestic Policy: Comparing Leadership Styles, FDR to Clinton.* Washington DC: CQ Press, 2000.

Laracey, Mel. *Presidents and the People: The Partisan Story of Going Public.* College Station: Texas A&M University Press, 2002.

Leffler, Melvyn. *A Preponderance of Power: National Security, the Truman Administration, and the Cold War.* Palo Alto: Stanford University Press, 1993.

Leuchtenburg, William E. *Franklin D. Roosevelt and the New Deal: 1932–1940.* New York: Harper & Row, 1963.

Levin, Doron P. *Behind the Wheel at Chrysler: Reassessing the Iacocca Legacy.* New York: Mariner Books, 1996.

Levin, Martin A., Daniel DiSalvo, and Martin M. Shapiro, eds. *Building Coalitions, Making Policy: The Politics of the Clinton, Bush, and Obama Presidencies.* Baltimore: Johns Hopkins University Press, 2012.

Levinson, Sanford. *Constitutional Faith.* Princeton: Princeton University Press, 1988.

Lewis, David, and Terry Moe. "The Presidency and the Bureaucracy," in *The Presidency and the Political System*, 9th ed., ed. Michael Nelson, 410–429. Washington DC: CQ Press, 2009.

Light, Paul. "The Homeland Security Hash." *The Wilson Quarterly* (Spring 2007) 31(2): 36–44.

_____. *The President's Agenda: Domestic Policy Choice from Kennedy to Clinton.* Baltimore: Johns Hopkins University Press, 1998.

Lintott, Andrew. *The Constitution of the Roman Republic.* Oxford: Oxford University Press, 1999.

Lovejoy, David S. *The Glorious Revolution in America.* New York: Harper Torchbooks, 1972.

Lowenthal, Mark M. *Intelligence: From Secrets to Policy.* Washington, DC: CQ Press, 2008.

Madison, James, Alexander Hamilton, and John Jay. *The Federalist Papers*, ed. Isaac Kramnick. New York: Penguin Books, 1987.

Maier, Pauline. *From Resistance to Revolution: Colonial Radicals and the Development of Opposition to Britain, 1765–1776.* New York: W. W. Norton, 1992.

Maltese, John Anthony. *Spin Control: The White House Office of Communications and the Management of Presidential News.* 2nd ed., rev. Chapel Hill: University of North Carolina Press, 1994.

Mann, Thomas E. "Reform Agenda," in *The New Campaign Finance Sourcebook*, eds. Anthony Corrado, Thomas E. Mann, Daniel R. Ortiz, and Trevor Potter, 264–279. Washington, DC: Brookings Institution Press, 2005.

Mansfield, Peter. *A History of the Middle East.* New York: Penguin Books, 2004.

Marbury v. Madison, 1 Cranch 137 (1803).

Marion, Nancy E. *Federal Government and Criminal Justice.* New York: Palgrave Macmillan, 2011.

Marsh, David, and Gerry Stoker, eds. *Theory and Methods in Political Science.* New York: Palgrave Macmillan, 2010.

May, Henry F. *The Enlightenment in America.* Oxford: Oxford University Press, 1976.

Mayer, Kenneth. *With the Stroke of a Pen: Executive Orders and Presidential Power.* Princeton: Princeton University Press, 2001.

Mayhew, David. *Congress: The Electoral Connection.* New Haven: Yale University Press, 1974.

McCloskey, Robert G. *The American Supreme Court*, 2nd ed., rev. by Sanford Levinson. Chicago: University of Chicago Press, 1994.

McConnell v. FEC, 540 U.S. 93 (2003).

McCoy, Drew R. *The Elusive Republic: Political Economy in Jeffersonian America.* New York: W. W. Norton, 1980.

McCulloch v. Maryland, et al., 4 Wheaton 316 (1819).

McCullough, David. *Truman.* New York: Simon & Schuster, 1993.

McDonald, Forrest. *Alexander Hamilton: A Biography.* New York: W. W. Norton, 1979.

______. *The American Presidency: An Intellectual History.* Lawrence: University Press of Kansas, 1995.

______. *E Pluribus Unum: The Formation of the American Republic, 1776–1790.* Indianapolis: Liberty Press, 1965.

______. *Novus Ordo Seclorum: The Intellectual Origins of the Constitution.* Lawrence: University Press of Kansas, 1985.

McGuire, Kevin T. *Understanding the U.S. Supreme Court: Cases and Controversies.* Boston: McGraw-Hill, 2002.

McKenzie, G. Galvin. *The Politics of Presidential Appointments.* New York: Free Press, 1981.

McPherson, James M. *Battle Cry of Freedom: The Civil War Era.* New York: Oxford University Press, 2003.

Mearsheimer, John J., and Stephen M. Walt. *The Israel Lobby and U.S. Foreign Policy.* New York: Farrar, Straus and Giroux, 2007.

Merryman, Ex Parte, 17 F. Cas. 144 (1861).

Meier, Christian. *Athens: A Portrait of the City in Its Golden Age*, trans. Robert and Rita Kimber. New York: Metropolitan Books, 1998.

Middlekauf, Robert. *The Glorious Cause: The American Revolution, 1763–1789.* New York: Oxford University Press, 2007.

Milkis, Sidney M., and Michael Nelson. *The American Presidency: Origins and Development, 1776–2011,* 6th ed. Washington, DC: CQ Press, 2011.

_____. *The American Presidency: Origins and Development, 1776–2007,* 5th ed. Washington, DC: CQ Press, 2008.

_____. *The American Presidency: Origins and Development 1776–2002,* 4th ed. Washington, DC: CQ Press, 2003.

Milkis, Sidney M., and Jerome M. Mileur, eds. *The Great Society and the High Tide of Liberalism.* Amherst: University of Massachusetts Press, 2005.

Miller, Arthur. "Sex, Politics, and Public Opinion: What Political Scientists Really Learned from the Clinton–Lewinsky Scandal." *PS: Political Science and Politics* 32.4 December (1999): 721–729.

Milligan, Ex Parte, 4 Wallace 2 (1866).

Mills, Nicolaus. *Arguing Immigration: The Debate over the Changing Face of America.* New York: Touchstone, 1994.

Minow, Martha, Michael Ryan, and Austin Sarat, eds. *Narrative, Violence, and the Law: The Essays of Robert Cover.* Ann Arbor: University of Michigan Press, 1995.

Minow, Newton N., John Bartlow Martin, and Lee M. Mitchell. *Presidential Television.* New York: Basic Books, 1973.

Mintz, Alex, and Karl DeRouen, Jr. *Understanding Foreign Policy Decision Making.* Cambridge: Cambridge University Press, 2010

Miroff, Bruce. *Icons of Democracy: American Leaders as Heroes, Aristocrats, Dissenters, & Democrats.* Lawrence: University Press of Kansas, 2000.

Missouri v. Holland, 252 U.S. 416 (1920).

Moe, Terry M., "The Politicized Presidency," in *The New Direction in American Politics,* eds. John E. Chubb and Paul E. Peterson, 235–271. Washington, DC: The Brookings Institution, 1985.

_____. "Presidents, Institutions, and Theory," in *Researching the Presidency: Vital Questions, New Approaches,* eds. George Edwards III, John Kessel and Bert Rockman, 337–386. Pittsburgh: University of Pittsburgh Press, 2003.

Montesquieu, Charles de. *The Spirit of the Laws,* eds. Anne M. Cohler, Basia Carolyn Miller, and Harold Samuel Stone. Cambridge: Cambridge University Press, 1989.

Montgomery, David. *The Fall of the House of Labor: The Workplace, the State, and American Labor Activism, 1965–1925.* London: Cambridge University Press, 1989.

Morgan, Edmund S. *The Birth of the Republic, 1763–89.* Chicago: University of Chicago Press, 1992.

_____. *Inventing the People: The Rise of Popular Sovereignty in England and America.* New York: W. W. Norton, 1988.

Morris, Edmund. *Theodore Rex.* New York: Random House, 2002.

Morris, Richard B. *The Forging of the Union, 1781–1789.* New York: Harper and Row, 1987.

Mueller, John. "Presidential Popularity from Truman to Johnson." *American Political Science Review* 64.1 (1970): 18–34.

_____. *War, Presidents and Public Opinion.* New York: Wiley, 1973.

_____. *War, Presidents and Public Opinion.* Columbus, OH: The Educational Publisher, 2009.

Murray, Robert K., and Tim H. Blessing, *Greatness in the White House: Rating the Presidents from George Washington Through Ronald Reagan,* 2nd ed. University Park: Pennsylvania State University Press, 1994.

Myers v. United States, 272 U.S. 52 (1926).

Nedelsky, Jennifer. *Private Property and the Limits of American Constitutionalism: The Madisonian Framework and Its Legacy*. Chicago: University of Chicago Press, 1990.

Nelson, Michael, ed. *The Evolving Presidency: Addresses, Cases, Essays, Letters, Reports, Resolutions, Transcripts, and other Landmark Documents, 1787–1998*. Washington, DC: CQ Press, 1999.

Nelson, Michael, and Russell L. Riley, eds. *Governing at Home: The White House and Domestic Policymaking*. Lawrence: University Press of Kansas, 2011.

Nelson, William E. *Marbury v. Madison: The Origins and Legacy of Judicial Review*. Lawrence: University Press of Kansas, 2000.

Neustadt, Richard E. *Presidential Power: The Politics of Leadership*. New York: Wiley, 1960.

_____. *Presidential Power and the Modern Presidents: The Politics of Leadership from Roosevelt to Reagan*. New York: Free Press, 1990.

Newmyer, R. Kent. "John Marshall," in *The Oxford Companion to the Supreme Court of the United States*, ed. Kermit L. Hall, 523–26. New York: Oxford University Press, 1992.

New York Times v. United States, 403 U.S. 713 (1971).

Nixon v. Fitzgerald, 457 U.S. 731 (1982).

Nixon, Richard. *RN: The Memoirs of Richard Nixon*. New York: Grosset & Dunlap, 1978.

Northouse, Peter G. *Leadership: Theory and Practice*. Thousand Oaks, CA: Sage Publications, 1997.

O'Brien, David M. *Constitutional Law and Politics: Struggles for Power and Governmental Accountability*, Vol. 1, 7th ed. New York: W. W. Norton, 2008.

_____. *Storm Center: The Supreme Court in American Politics*, 8th ed. New York: W. W. Norton, 2008.

_____. *Storm Center: The Supreme Court in American Politics*, 6th ed. New York: W. W. Norton, 2003.

Ober, Josiah. *Mass and Elite in Democratic Athens: Rhetoric, Ideology, and the Power of the People*. Princeton: Princeton University Press, 1989.

Olson, Mancur. *The Logic of Collective Action: Public Goods and the Theory of Groups*. Cambridge: Harvard University Press, 1965.

Orren, Karen. *Belated Feudalism: Labor, Law, and Liberal Development in the United States*. Cambridge: Cambridge University Press, 1991.

Ostwald, Martin. *From Popular Sovereignty to the Sovereignty of Law: Law, Society, and Politics in Fifth-Century Athens*. Berkeley: University of California Press, 1986.

Pacelle, Richard L. Jr. *Between Law & Politics: The Solicitor General and the Structuring of Race, Gender, and Reproductive Rights Litigation*. College Station: Texas A&M University Press, 2003.

_____. "A President's Legacy: Gender and Appointment to the Federal Courts," in *The Other Elites: Women, Politics, and Power in the Executive Branch*, eds. MaryAnne Borrelli and Janet M. Martin, 147–66. Boulder, CO: Lynne Rienner, 1997.

Paletz, David L. *The Media in American Politics: Contents and Consequences*, 2nd ed. New York: Longman, 2002.

Palmer, Barbara. "Women in the American Judiciary: Their Influence and Impact." *Women & Politics*, Vol. 23, No. 3 (2001): 89–99.

Palmer, R. R. *Age of the Democratic Revolution: A Political History of Europe and America, 1760–1800*, Vol. 2. Princeton: Princeton University Press, 1970.

Pangle, Thomas L. *The Spirit of Modern Republicanism: The Moral Vision of the American Founders and the Philosophy of Locke*. Chicago: University of Chicago Press, 1988.

Pasqual, Carlos, and Jonathan Elkind. *Energy Security: Economics, Politics, Strategies, and Implications.* Washington, DC: Brookings Institution Press, 2009.

_____. *The White House Staff: Inside the West Wing and Beyond.* Washington, DC: Brookings Institution Press, 2000.

Patterson, Bradley H. Jr. *To Serve the President: Continuity and Innovation in the White House Staff.* Washington, DC: Brookings Institution Press, 2008.

Patterson, Thomas E. *Out of Order.* New York: Vintage Books, 1994.

Payan, Tony. *The Three U.S.-Mexico Border Wars: Drugs, Immigration and Homeland Security.* New York: Praeger, 2006.

Perrow, Charles. "Using Organizations: The Case of FEMA." *Homeland Security Affairs* 1, No. 2 (Fall 2005): 1–8.

Peterson, Mark A. *Legislating Together: The White House and Capitol Hill from Eisenhower to Reagan.* Cambridge, MA: Harvard University Press, 1990.

Pew Research Center for People and the Press. "Americans Spending More Time Following the News," September 12, 2010.

_____. "Internet News Audience Highly Critical of News Organizations," August 9, 2007.

_____. "Internet Overtakes Newspapers as News Outlet," December 23, 2008.

_____. "Most Voters Say News Media Wants Obama to Win," October 22, 2008.

_____. "Public Remains of Two Minds on Energy Policy," June 14, 2010.

Pfiffner, James P. *The Strategic Presidency: Hitting the Ground Running,* 2nd ed. rev. Lawrence: University of Kansas Press, 1996.

Pika, Joseph. "The Vice Presidency: Dick Cheney, Joe Biden and the New Vice Presidency," in *The Presidency and the Political System,* ed. Michael Nelson, 509–534 Washington, DC: CQ Press 2009.

_____. "White House Office of Public Liaison." *White House Transition Project,* Report 2009–03. WhiteHouseTransitionProject.org, 2008

Pika, Joseph A., and John Anthony Maltese, *The Politics of the Presidency,* rev. 7th ed. Washington, DC: CQ Press, 2010.

Pocock, J. G. A. *The Machiavellian Moment: Florentine Political Thought and the Atlantic Republican Tradition.* Princeton: Princeton University Press, 1975.

Polsby, Nelson W., and Aaron Wildavsky. *Presidential Elections: Strategies and Structures of American Politics,* 11th ed. Lanham, MD: Rowman & Littlefield, 2004.

Popkin, Samuel. *The Reasoning Voter: Communication and Persuasion in Presidential Campaigns.* Chicago: University of Chicago Press, 1994.

Prize Cases, 2 Black 635 (1863).

Publius. *The Federalist Papers,* ed. Isaac Kramnick. London: Penguin Books, 1987.

Radosh, Ronald. *The Rosenberg File.* New Haven, CT: Yale University Press, 1997.

Ragsdale, Lyn. *Vital Statistics on the Presidency: George Washington to George W. Bush,* 3rd ed. Washington, DC: CQ Press, 2009.

Rahe, Paul A. *Republics Ancient and Modern: New Modes and Orders in Early Modern Political Thought.* Chapel Hill: University of North Carolina Press, 1994.

Rakove, Jack N. *The Beginnings of National Politics: An Interpretive History of the Continental Congress.* Baltimore: Johns Hopkins University Press, 1979.

Rasul v. Bush, 542 U.S. 466 (2004).

Reeves, Richard. *President Nixon: Alone in the White House.* New York: Simon & Schuster, 2002.

_____. *President Reagan: The Triumph of Imagination.* New York: Simon & Schuster, 2006.

Reid, John Phillip. *Constitutional History of the American Revolution: The Authority of Law.* Madison: University of Wisconsin Press, 1993.

_____. *Constitutional History of the American Revolution: The Authority to Legislate.* Madison: University of Wisconsin Press, 1991.

_____. *Constitutional History of the American Revolution: The Authority of Rights.* Madison: University of Wisconsin Press, 1986.

_____. *Constitutional History of the American Revolution: The Authority to Tax.* Madison: University of Wisconsin Press, 1987.

Richard, Carl J. *The Founders and the Classics: Greece, Rome, and the American Enlightenment.* Cambridge: Harvard University Press, 1994.

Richardson, James D., ed. *A Compilation of the Messages and Papers of the Presidents, Volumes I–XI.* Washington, DC: Government Printing Office, 1902, 1904.

Rockman, Bert A. "The Leadership Style of George Bush," in *The Bush Presidency: First Appraisals*, eds. Colin Campbell and Bert A. Rockman. Chatham, NJ: Chatham House, 1991.

Rodman, Peter W. *Presidential Command: Power, Leadership, and the Making of Foreign Policy from Richard Nixon to George W. Bush.* New York: Alfred A. Knopf, 2009.

Roe v. Wade, 410 U.S. 113 (1973).

Roosevelt, Theodore. *The Autobiography of Theodore Roosevelt.* New York: Scribner's, 1913.

Rose, Richard. *The Postmodern President*, 2nd ed. Chatham, NJ: Chatham House Publishers, 1991.

Rosenbaum, Walter A. *Environmental Politics and Policy.* Washington, DC: CQ Press, 2010.

Rosenstone, Steven J., and John Mark. *Mobilization, Participation, and Democracy in America.* New York: Macmillan Press, 1993.

Rossiter, Clinton. *The American Presidency.* New York: Time Incorporated, 1960.

_____. *The American Presidency.* New York: Harcourt, Brace, 1956.

Rottinghaus, Brandon. *The Provisional Pulpit: Modern Presidential Leadership of Public Opinion.* College Station: Texas A&M Press, 2010.

Routh, Stephen R. "U.S. Solicitor General," in *Encyclopedia of American Government and Civics, Vol. II*, eds. Michael A. Genovese and Lori Cox Han. New York: Facts on File, 2009.

Rozell, Mark. *Executive Privilege: The Dilemma of Secrecy and Democratic Accountability.* Lawrence: University Press of Kansas, 2000.

Rubin, Richard. *Press, Party and the President.* New York: W. W. Norton, 1982.

Rudalevige, Andrew. *Managing the President's Program: Presidential Leadership and Legislative Policy Formation.* Princeton: Princeton University Press, 2002.

_____. "The Presidency and Unilateral Power," in *The Presidency and the Political System*, ed. Michael Nelson, 463–488. Washington, DC: CQ Press, 2009.

Sabato, Larry J. *Feeding Frenzy: Attack Journalism and American Politics.* Baltimore: Lanahan Publishers, 2000.

Saldin, Robert P. "William McKinley and the Rhetorical Presidency." *Presidential Studies Quarterly*, Vol. 41, Issue I (March 2011): 119–134.

Salokar, Rebecca Mae. *The Solicitor General: The Politics of Law.* Philadelphia: Temple University Press, 1992.

Sandbrook, Dominic. *Mad as Hell: The Crisis of the 1970s and the Rise of the Populist Right.* New York: Anchor, 2012.

Schechter Poultry Corporation v. United States, 295 U.S. 495 (1935).

Schlesinger, Arthur M., Jr. *Age of Jackson.* New York: Back Bay Books, 1988.

_____. *The Coming of the New Deal, 1933–1935.* New York: Mariner Books, 2003.

_____. *The Imperial Presidency*. Boston: Houghton Mifflin, 1973.

_____. "The Ultimate Approval Rating," *New York Times Magazine*, 15 December 1996: 46–51.

Schoultz, Lars. *Beneath the United States: A History of U.S. Policy Toward Latin America*. Cambridge, MA: Harvard University Press, 1998.

Seligman, Lester, and Cary Covington. *The Coalitional Presidency*. Chicago: Dorsey Press, 1989.

Sellers, Charles. *The Market Revolution: Jacksonian America, 1815–1846*. New York: Oxford University Press, 1991.

_____. *The Market Revolution: Jacksonian America, 1815–1846*. New York: Oxford University Press, 1994.

Semiatin, Richard J. *Campaigns in the 21st Century*. New York: McGraw-Hill, 2005.

Shaffer, Brenda. *Energy Politics*. Philadelphia: University of Pennsylvania Press, 2011.

Shafie, David. "The Presidency and Domestic Policy," in *New Directions in the American Presidency*, ed. Lori Cox Han, 166–179. New York: Routledge, 2011.

Shlaes, Amity. *The Forgotten Man: A New History of the Great Depression*. New York: Harper, 2008.

Shull, Steven A. *American Civil Rights Policy from Truman to Clinton: The Role of Presidential Leadership*. Armonk, NY: M. E. Sharpe, 2000.

Shultz, George P., and Kenneth W. Dam. *Economic Policy beyond the Headlines*. Chicago: University of Chicago Press, 1998.

Silverstein, Gordon. *Constitutional Interpretation and the Making of American Foreign Policy*. New York: Oxford University Press, 1996.

Silverstein, Mark. *Judicious Choices: The New Politics of Supreme Court Confirmations*. New York: W. W. Norton, 1994.

Sinclair, Barbara. *Unorthodox Lawmaking: New Legislative Processes in the U.S. Congress*. Washington, DC: CQ Press, 2007.

Sirica, John. *To Set the Record Straight: The Break-in, the Tapes, the Conspirators, the Pardon*. New York: W. W. Norton, 1979.

Skidmore, David. *The Unilateralist Temptation in American Foreign Policy*. London: Routledge, 2010.

Skowronek, Stephen. *Building a New American State: The Expansion of National Administrative Capacities, 1877–1920*. New York: Cambridge University Press, 1982.

_____. *The Politics Presidents Make: Leadership from John Adams to George Bush*. Cambridge: Belknap/Harvard Press, 1993.

Sloan, Stanley R. *NATO, the European Union, and the Atlantic Community*. Lanham, MD: Rowman & Littlefield, 2002.

Smith, Steve, Amelia Hadfield, and Timothy Dunne. *Foreign Policy: Theories, Actors, Cases*. New York: Oxford University Press, 2008.

Sorenson, Theodore. *Decision Making in the White House: The Olive Branch or the Arrows*. New York: Columbia University Press, 2005.

Spanier, John, and Steven W. Hook. *American Foreign Policy since World War II*. Washington, DC: CQ Press, 2009.

Stephanopoulos, George. *All Too Human: A Political Education*. Boston: Little, Brown and Company, 1999.

Storing, Herbert J. *The Complete Anti-Federalist*. Chicago: University of Chicago Press, 2007.

Stolz, Barbara. *Criminal Justice Policy Making: Federal Roles and Processes*. New York: Praeger, 2001.

Stuckey, Mary E. *The President as Interpreter-in-Chief.* Chatham, NJ: Chatham House, 1991.

Sullivan, Terry, ed. *The Nerve Center: Lessons in Governing from the White House Chiefs of Staff.* College Station: Texas A&M University Press, 2004.

Swain, Carol M., ed. *Debating Immigration.* London: Cambridge University Press, 2007.

't Hart, Paul, Karen Tindall, and Christer Brown. "Crisis Leadership of the Bush Presidency: Advisory Capacity and Presidential Performance in the Acute Stages of the 9/11 and Katrina Crises." *Presidential Studies Quarterly* 39.3 (2009): 473–494.

Taft, William Howard. *Our Chief Magistrate and His Powers.* New York: Columbia University Press, 1916.

Tebbel, John, and Watts, Sarah Miles. *The Press and the Presidency: From George Washington to Ronald Reagan.* New York: Oxford University Press, 1985.

Tedesco, John. "Changing the Channel: Use of the Internet for Communication about Politics," in *Handbook of Political Communication Research*, ed. Lynda Lee Kaid, 507–532. Mahwah, NJ: Lawrence Erlbaum, 2004.

Tenpas, Kathryn Dunn. "Lobbying the Executive Branch," in *The Interest Group Connection: Electioneering, Lobbying, and Policymaking in Washington*, 2nd ed., eds. Paul S. Herrnson, Ronald G. Shaiko and Clyde Wilcox, 249–257. Washington, DC: CQ Press, 2004.

Tenpas, Katie Dunn, and Jay McCann. "Testing the Permanence of the Permanent Campaign: An Analysis of Presidential Polling Expenditures, 1977–2002." *Public Opinion Quarterly* (2007) 71 (3): 349–366.

Texas v. Johnson, 491 U.S. 397 (1989).

Tomlins, Christopher L. *Law, Labor, and Ideology in the Early American Republic.* Cambridge: Cambridge University Press, 1993.

_____. *The State and the Unions: Labor Relations, Law, and the Organized Labor Movement in America 1880–1960.* London: Cambridge University Press, 1985.

Trachtenberg, Alan. *The Incorporation of America: Culture and Society in the Gilded Age.* New York: Hill & Wang, 2007.

Tribe, Lawrence H. *Abortion: The Clash of Absolutes.* New York: W. W. Norton, 1992.

Truman, Harry S. *Memoirs by Harry Truman, Volume Two: Years of Trial and Hope.* New York: Macmillan, 1956.

Tulis, Jeffrey K. *The Rhetorical Presidency.* Princeton: Princeton University Press, 1987.

United States v. Curtiss-Wright Export Corp., 299 U.S. 304 (1934).

United States v. Nixon, 418 U.S. 683 (1974).

Vaughn, Justin S., and Jose D. Villalobos. "White House Staff," in *New Directions in the American Presidency*, ed. Lori Cox Han, 120–135. New York: Routledge, 2011.

Vig, Norman J., and Michael E. Kraft. *Environmental Policy: New Directions for the Twenty-First Century.* Washington, DC: CQ Press, 2009.

Vlasic, Bill. *Once Upon a Car: The Fall and Resurrection of America's Big Three Auto Makers—GM, Ford, and Chrysler.* New York: William Morrow, 2011.

Walcott, Charles, and Karen Hult. *Empowering the White House: Governance Under Nixon, Ford and Carter.* Lawrence: University Press of Kansas, 2004.

_____. *Governing the White House: From Hoover Through LBJ.* Lawrence: University Press of Kansas, 1995.

Warber, Adam. *Executive Orders and the Modern Presidency.* Boulder, CO: Lynne Rienner, 2006.

Warshaw, Shirley Anne. *The Domestic Presidency: Policy Making in the White House.* New York: Longman, 1996.

_____. *The Keys to Power: Managing the Presidency*, 2nd ed. New York: Longman, 2005.

_____. *The Keys to Power: Managing the Presidency*. New York: Longman, 2000.

Washington Post. *Landmark: The Inside Story of America's New Healthcare Law and What It Means for All of Us*. Washington, DC: Public Affairs, 2010.

Waterman, Richard W., Robert Wright, and Gilbert St. Clair. *The Image-Is-Everything Presidency: Dilemmas in American Leadership*. Boulder, CO: Westview Press, 1999.

Watson, Robert P. *The President's Wives: Reassessing the Office of First Lady*. Boulder, CO: Lynne Rienner, 2000.

Wattenberg, Martin P. "The Presidential Media Environment in the Age of Obama," in *Obama: Year One*, eds. Thomas R. Dye, George C. Edwards III, Morris P. Fiorina, Edward S. Greenberg, Paul C. Light, David B. Magleby, and Martin P. Wattenberg, 55–72. New York: Longman, 2010.

_____. *The Rise of Candidate-Centered Politics: Presidential Elections of the 1980s*. Cambridge: Harvard University Press, 1991.

Wayne, Stephen J. "An Introduction to Research on the Presidency," in *Studying the Presidency*, eds. George C. Edwards, III, and Stephen J. Wayne. Knoxville: University of Tennessee Press, 1983.

_____. "Approaches," in *Studying the Presidency*, eds. George C. Edwards, III, and Stephen J. Wayne. Knoxville: University of Tennessee Press, 1983.

_____. *The Road to the White House 2004: The Politics of Presidential Elections*. Belmont: Thomson Wadsworth, 2004.

_____. *The Road to the White House 2008: The Politics of Presidential Elections*. Belmont, CA: Thompson Wadsworth, 2008.

_____. *The Road to the White House 2012*, 9th ed. Belmont, CA: Wadsworth, 2011.

_____. "Why Democracy Works," in *Winning the Presidency: 2008*, ed. William J Crotty, 48–69. Boulder, CO: Paradigm Publishers, 2009.

Weigley, Russell F. *The American Way of War: A History of United States Military Strategy and Policy*. Bloomington: Indiana University Press, 1977.

Weko, Thomas J. *The Politicizing Presidency: The White House Personnel Office, 1948–1994*. Lawrence, KS: University of Kansas Press, 1995.

Welch, Richard F. *King of the Bowery: Big Tim Sullivan, Tammany Hall and New York City from the Gilded Age to the Progressive Era*. Albany: State University of New York Press, 2009.

West, Darrell M. *Air Wars: Television Advertising in Election Campaigns, 1952–2008*. Washington, DC: CQ Press, 2010.

White, Leonard D. *The Jacksonians: A Study in Administrative History 1801–1829*. New York: MacMillan 1961.

_____. *The Jeffersonians: A Study in Administrative History 1801–1829*. New York: MacMillan, 1961.

White, Morton. *Philosophy, "The Federalist," and the Constitution*. Oxford: Oxford University Press, 1987.

Wiecek, William M. *Liberty Under Law: The Supreme Court in American Life*. Baltimore: Johns Hopkins University Press, 1988.

Wiedemann, T. E. J. *Cicero and the End of the Roman Republic*. London: Oxford University Press, 1991.

Wildavsky, Aaron. "The Two Presidencies," *Trans-Action* 4 (1966):7–14.

Wilentz, Sean. *Chants Democratic: New York City and the Rise of the American Working Class, 1788–1850*. Oxford: Oxford University Press, 1984.

Wills, Garry. *Explaining America: The Federalist*. Garden City, NY: Doubleday, 1981.

_____. *Inventing America: Jefferson's Declaration of Independence*. Garden City, NY: Doubleday, 1978.

Wilson, James Q. *Bureaucracy: What Government Agencies Do and Why They Do It*. New York: Basic Books, 1991.

Wood, B. Dan. *The Myth of Presidential Representation*. New York: Cambridge University Press, 2009.

Wood, Gordon S. *Creation of the American Republic, 1776–1787*. New York: W. W. Norton, 1969.

_____. *Empire of Liberty: A History of the Early Republic, 1789–1815*. New York: Oxford University Press, 2011.

_____. *The Radicalism of the American Revolution*. New York: Vintage Books, 1991.

Woodward, Bob. *The Agenda: Inside the Clinton White House*. New York: Simon & Schuster, 2005.

_____. *Bush at War*. New York: Simon and Schuster, 2003.

_____. *The Commanders*. New York: Simon & Schuster, 2002.

_____. *Obama's Wars*. New York: Simon & Schuster, 2010.

_____. *Plan of Attack*. New York: Simon & Schuster, 2004.

_____. *State of Denial: Bust at War, Part III*. New York: Simon & Schuster, 2007.

_____. *The War Within: A Secret White House History 2006–2008*. New York: Simon & Schuster, 2009.

Woodworth, Steven E. *Manifest Destinies: America's Westward Expansion and the Road to the Civil War*. New York: Alfred A. Knopf, 2008.

Yalof, David Alistair. *Pursuit of Justices: Presidential Politics and the Selection of Supreme Court Nominees*. Chicago: University of Chicago Press, 1999.

Yoo, John. *Crisis and Command: A History of Executive Power from George Washington to George W. Bush*. New York: Kaplan Publishing, 2010.

_____. *The Powers of War and Peace: The Constitution and Foreign Affairs after 9/11*. Chicago: University of Chicago Press, 2005.

Youngstown Sheet & Tube Co., et al., v. Sawyer, 343 U.S. 579 (1952).

Zaller, John. "Monica Lewinsky's Contribution to Political Science." *PS: Political Science and Politics*, 31.2 (1998): 182–189.

Zelizer, Julian E., ed. *The Presidency of George W. Bush: A First Historical Assessment*. Princeton: Princeton University Press, 2010.

CREDITS

CHAPTER 1

p. 5: Library of Congress Prints and Photographs Division Washington, D.C.; p. 18: Sammie Feeback, Courtesy of Harry S. Truman Library; page 26: George Bush Presidential Library and Museum

CHAPTER 2

p. 38: © Bettmann/CORBIS; p. 65: AP Photo/Ron Edmonds; p. 67: Copyright Bettmann/ Corbis / AP Images

CHAPTER 3

p. 84: AP Photo/Charlie Riedel; p. 104: Time & Life Pictures/Getty Images; p. 107: AP Photo/Jerome Delay; p. 126: AP Photo/John Raoux

CHAPTER 4

p. 131: © Bettmann/CORBIS; p. 134: AP Photo; p. 162: AP Photo/Doug Mills

CHAPTER 5

p. 169: Courtesy Ronald Reagan Library; p. 174: AP Photo/Byron Rollins; p.195: AP Photo

CHAPTER 6

p. 206: AP Photo/J. Scott Applewhite; p. 233: AP Photo/Wilfredo Lee; p. 237: AP Photo/ Charles Dharapak

CHAPTER 7

p. 244: AP Photo/Pablo Martinez Monsivais; p. 255: LBJ Library photo by Yoichi Okamoto; p. 271: AP Photo

CHAPTER 8

p. 288: AP Photo/Susan Walsh; p. 314: AP Photo/Evan Vucci, File; p. 316: Library of Congress Prints and Photographs Division Washington, D.C.

CHAPTER 9

p. 364: LBJ Library photo by Cecil Stoughton; p. 367: © CORBIS; p. 372: AP Photo/Susan Walsh

CHAPTER 10

p. 400: AP Photo/Ron Edmonds; p. 411: The U.S. Army; Dwight D. Eisenhower Presidential Library; p. 421: AP Photo

INDEX